An Economic History of the United States

An Economic History of the United States

Connecting the Present with the Past

Mark V. Siegler

BLOOMSBURY ACADEMIC
LONDON • NEW YORK • OXFORD • NEW DELHI • SYDNEY

BLOOMSBURY ACADEMIC
Bloomsbury Publishing Plc
50 Bedford Square, London, WC1B 3DP, UK
1385 Broadway, New York, NY 10018, USA
29 Earlsfort Terrace, Dublin 2, Ireland

BLOOMSBURY, BLOOMSBURY ACADEMIC and the Diana logo
are trademarks of Bloomsbury Publishing Plc

First published 2017 by PALGRAVE

Reprinted by Bloomsbury Academic

A catalogue record for this book is available from the British Library.

A catalog record for this book is available from the Library of Congress.

ISBN: PB: 978-1-1373-9395-1
ePDF: 978-1-1373-9396-8

To find out more about our authors and books visit
www.bloomsbury.com and sign up for our newsletters.

Brief Contents

Contents

List of Figures

List of Tables

List of "Economic History in Action" Boxes

Preface for Instructors

This book has several innovative features that I hope will make the experience better for both students and instructors:

- A modular approach organized by topic.
- A focus on four main themes.
- The integration of both classic and recent scholarship in a succinct, conversational style.
- Frequent references to both international and comparative elements that link current economic issues in the United States to its longer history.
- The application of the tools of economics throughout the book, not just in occasional footnotes or sidebars, so that U.S. economic history is seen to be more thoroughly integrated with, and complementary to, the rest of the economics curriculum.

I believe this book provides both the economic foundations and the historical background that students need, as well as the flexibility that instructors demand. In particular, instructors can continue to assign many of the same supplementary readings as before, which should make it easier to adopt this text. Instructors can also use this book exclusively to provide a summary of current scholarship in American economic history, along with the tools and background that students will not necessarily have retained from high school history classes or introductory courses in economics.

Each of the main features of the book is described in detail below.

MODULAR APPROACH

Rather than being strictly chronological, the organization of the chapters is by topic. By focusing on the entire history of one major topic in each chapter (a topic that is also tied back to the main themes), the reader gains a better understanding and appreciation of the long-run history of important economic issues.

Although I believe that the advantages of a thematic approach far outweigh those of the standard chronological approach, the book does not ignore the fact that economic history unfolds in real time. Thus, while each chapter stands alone, references to complementary issues and events from other chapters remind the reader of the underlying chronology and show how each topic is part of a larger narrative. In addition, an appendix provides a chronology of important events in American economic history (linked to the relevant chapters), which will be particularly helpful for students who are less familiar with the broad outlines of American history.

The sequencing of chapters is also based on chronology, with early chapters on European settlement, institutional foundations and the American Revolution, followed by chapters on important developments in the nineteenth and twentieth centuries. Throughout the book, current economic issues are connected with the past.

Although I hope that most instructors will be convinced that organization by topic is superior to the standard chronological approach, this book is also amenable to courses that maintain a chronological approach. Several suggested pathways through the book are provided below, including pathways for instructors who prefer to teach the course from a chronological perspective.

Economic history is too often ignored throughout the undergraduate curriculum. While I recognize that stand-alone U.S. economic history courses are not part of the curriculum in all universities, I hope that custom publishing options and e-book formats, together with the modular approach of this text, will allow instructors in other courses—such as survey classes, introductory courses, or upper division electives in economics and history—to use parts of this book to fit their needs. Each chapter can be used as a self-contained resource that provides a long-run perspective on an important economic history topic with current relevance.

FOUR MAIN THEMES

Each chapter relates to at least one of the four larger themes: economic growth, distributional issues, economic fluctuations, and the relationship between markets and government. For example, by comparing and contrasting the changing role of government in the U.S. economy over time, students can gain a better understanding of the benefits and costs of government intervention.

Flowing through all of these themes is an emphasis on path-dependent processes, an important part of economic history scholarship over the past thirty years. Rather than analyzing public policy issues in a historical vacuum, students need to understand that there is a *history* of why the healthcare system is the way it is today, why Social Security can be fixed more easily than Medicare, and why the Great Recession was the worst downturn since the Great Depression.

INTEGRATION OF CLASSIC AND RECENT SCHOLARSHIP

It is not sufficient for a book on economic history to stop in the late 1990s and then tack on some brief remarks about 9/11 and the Great Recession. This book covers material from the dawn of human history and the settlement of indigenous tribes in the Americas to current economic events that are shaping our world today. Second, the scholarship underlying the book is up to date and integrated into the text. Other books add some new scholarship but without integrating it or revising the narrative to come to terms with what new knowledge implies about old debates.

With fewer chapters than the competition, most of this book can be covered in one semester. More generally, I have tried to maintain a narrative thread with a story to tell in each chapter, written in a conversational, organized, and engaging manner.

A picture is often worth a thousand words, and so whenever I can explain something better and more succinctly with a visual aid, I do so. Throughout the text, ample use is made of figures, tables, and photographs. Historical and comparative data are best illustrated using clear and self-contained figures and tables. From the process and grandeur of the Ford assembly line to living in tenement buildings, photographs help bring the narrative to life.

Finally, the emphasis is squarely on the economic history of the United States, not on the history of thought of economic history as a discipline. While I admire and respect the contributions of economic historians, most textbooks in other sub-fields of economics rarely mention scholars by name in the main narrative of the text, and I follow this standard convention. While extensive endnotes provide complete references for the interested reader, the goal of this text is to explain the current state of knowledge as best I can without focusing on the names, debates, and disagreements between individual economic historians.

INTERNATIONAL AND COMPARATIVE

Since the 1980s, numerous scholars have demonstrated that to truly understand the economic history of any area, one must study it in a comparative fashion. In particular, an American economic history textbook must make it clear that globalization is not a recent phenomenon. In fact, the U.S. economy has *always* been globalized. The Columbian Exchange after 1492 was the start of globalization in the Americas.

The ways in which the American economy has been globalized have varied over time. Examples include colonial/mercantilist policies before 1776, the importance of the international cotton market to the antebellum U.S., and the expansion of American agriculture after the Civil War.

Examples of globalization extend throughout American history and beyond patterns of international trade. Technological innovations were often borrowed from abroad, and foreign capital helped finance the railroads and other infrastructure projects. The waves of immigration in the nineteenth century and early twentieth century are similar in many ways to the waves of the late twentieth and early twenty-first centuries.

APPLICATION OF THE TOOLS OF ECONOMICS

A contemporary book on U.S. economic history needs to introduce and use the tools of economics. This is necessary to demonstrate effectively the interaction between economic history and economic theory that is at the heart of modern scholarship. Further, the use of economic tools deepens students' understanding of both economics and history.

This book emphasizes common models and concepts to illuminate historical episodes. Examples include:

- The production possibilities frontier and comparative advantage.
- The supply and demand model in both output and factor markets (including the importance of elasticities).
- Producer surplus, consumer surplus, efficiency, and deadweight losses.
- Production functions and growth accounting.
- Models of discrimination.
- Self-selection immigration models.
- The quantity theory of money.
- Market power and monopoly.
- Game theory and strategic behavior.
- Aggregate demand and aggregate supply.

Growth accounting, for example, provides a useful framework for understanding the contributions of labor, human capital, physical capital (both private and public), natural capital, and technology in economic growth.

In each chapter, basic economic concepts are introduced and applied to the history of the U.S. economy. By emphasizing the tools of economics, this approach allows U.S. economic history to be more thoroughly integrated with, and complementary to, the rest of the economics curriculum, instead of just a course viewed as tangential to the major. In particular, students will build on their introductory skills by applying economic tools to real-world situations.

I assume that most students will have had at least one previous course in economics, but all tools and concepts are explained in such a way that a student completely unfamiliar with economics will be able to benefit and learn from this book as well.

SUGGESTED PATHWAYS

While instructors are free to choose any combination of chapters that fit their needs, I provide several suggested pathways through the book, depending on the length and focus of the particular course. The first suggested pathway includes the core chapters that emphasize the four main themes (economic growth, economic fluctuations, distributional issues, and the relationship between markets and government) in a broad economic and historical context. I have found that these chapters can be effectively covered in a 10-week quarter class. This pathway is also recommended for instructors teaching a 15- or 16-week semester course augmented with journal articles and other supplementary readings.

In these core chapters, I provide both the economic tools and the historical overview so that students can better understand journal articles. If there are relatively few supplementary readings assigned, then instructors may choose to select some of the other chapters in the book as well.

THE CORE

- Chapter 1: Introduction to U.S. Economic History
- Chapter 2: Standards of Living and American Economic Growth
- Chapter 4: Institutional Foundations
- Chapter 5: The Financial System and Capital Accumulation
- Chapter 7: Population and Population Growth
- Chapter 11: Education
- Chapter 12: Labor and Labor Markets
- Chapter 13: The Distribution of Income and Wealth
- Chapter 14: Segregation and Discrimination
- Chapter 16: The Growth of Government
- Chapter 18: Recessions, Depressions, and Stabilization Policies
- Chapter 21: Connecting the Present with the Past and Future

Two suggested pathways for courses that maintain a chronological approach are included below. The first pathway focuses on the period *prior* to the Civil War, while the second pathway emphasizes the economic history of the United States *since* the Civil War. In the pathways below, I assume a 15- or 16-week semester class, but these pathways can be modified for shorter terms.

FOCUS ON THE PRE-CIVIL WAR PERIOD

For courses that focus on the pre-Civil War period, the following chapters are recommended: Chapters 1–7, Chapter 8 (Introduction and Sections 8.1 and 8.2), Chapter 9 (Introduction and Section 9.1), Chapter 10 (Introduction and Section 10.1), and Chapter 21. Parts of Chapters 11, 12, and 13 can also be assigned.

FOCUS ON THE POST-CIVIL WAR PERIOD

For courses that emphasize the period since the Civil War, the following chapters are suggested: Chapter 1, Chapter 2, Chapter 4 (Introduction and Section 4.1), Chapter 5, Chapter 7, Chapter 8 (Sections 8.3 and after), Chapter 9, Chapter 10 (Section 10.2 and thereafter), and any combination of Chapters 11–21.

FOCUS ON ECONOMIC GROWTH AND DEVELOPMENT

Instructors may also want to focus more intensively on one or more of the four main themes. For courses that focus on economic growth and development, the following chapters are recommended: Chapter 1, Chapter 2, Chapter 4 (Introduction and Section 4.1), Chapters 5–11, Chapter 16, Chapter 19, and Chapter 21.

FOCUS ON DISTRIBUTIONAL ISSUES

If the emphasis is on distributional issues, then the following chapters are suggested: Chapter 1, Chapter 2, Chapter 7, Chapters 9–17, and Chapters 20–21.

FOCUS ON PUBLIC POLICY ISSUES

Finally, for courses with a greater emphasis on public policy issues, Chapter 1, Chapter 2, Chapter 4 (Introduction and Section 4.1), Chapter 5, Chapter 6 (Section 6.3), Chapter 9 (Sections 9.3 and 9.5), Chapter 11, Chapter 13, Chapter 14, Chapter 15 (Sections 15.2 and 15.3), and any combination of Chapters 16–21 are recommended.

ONLINE RESOURCES FOR INSTRUCTORS

A number of password-protected resources are available online to instructors using this book, including:

- Sample answers to all of the end-of-chapter questions.
- A test bank containing multiple-choice questions for each chapter.
- An instructor's manual with recommended supplementary readings for each chapter as well as suggestions for lectures and in-class exercises.
- The figures and tables from the text to help instructors who wish to make customized PowerPoint presentations.

CONCLUDING THOUGHTS

Students and instructors in economic history courses need materials that are as up to date as any topics course in economics. In order to provide the best education for their students, instructors teaching microeconomics, macroeconomics, labor economics, public finance, international economics, and other courses demand texts that reflect both current events and relevant scholarship in their fields. Economic history, as a mature sub-field of economics, demands no less, and the intent is that this book will help meet that need.

Author's Acknowledgments

The process of writing this book has been a tremendously rewarding and challenging experience, and I have many people to thank. First, I would like to thank the nearly two thousand students who have taken my U.S. economic history classes over the past twenty years at Bates College, Williams College, UC Davis, and Sacramento State. Their questions convinced me that this was a project worth pursuing. Over the past two years, I have used preliminary chapters in my classes, and my students have helped me improve the book in many ways. I am appreciative of everyone who asked a question, provided a written comment, or discovered a typo. Katie Su, Jamie Marzouk, and Art Stepanov generously volunteered their time to do background research for the book, and I sincerely appreciate their help.

I am indebted to my colleagues at Sacramento State, particularly my colleagues in economic history, Ta-Chen Wang and Michael Dowell, who were always willing to talk and to share their knowledge. Sacramento State also provided me with a sabbatical during the Fall 2014 semester, which allowed me to get this project off the ground.

Special thanks go to my friend and economic historian, Louis Johnston. His input was instrumental in the early stages of the project, and our frequent telephone conversations and e-mail exchanges helped shape the overall structure and content of the book. I would also like to thank Paul Shensa for sharing his wealth of experience and expertise in publishing with me and for his encouragement and enthusiasm. Jon Li carefully read the entire manuscript, and his attention to detail and his thoughtfulness are greatly appreciated.

I have had the privilege of studying and teaching at UC Davis for much of my academic career. In my opinion, there is no better group of economic historians in the world, and I have learned a great deal from Peter Lindert (my dissertation chair), Alan Olmstead, Gregory Clark, Alan Taylor, and Gary Walton. I am also indebted to Kevin Hoover for sharing his expertise with me as my professor, dissertation advisor, and co-author on other publications.

I would also like to thank the reviewers who all provided wonderfully detailed and helpful comments on every aspect of the book. I benefitted tremendously from their knowledge and opinions, and I hope that they will be able to see their contributions in the pages of this book (although any remaining omissions and errors are entirely my own):

Lisa D. Cook, Michigan State University
Gerald Friedman, University of Massachusetts at Amherst
Amanda G. Gregg, Middlebury College
John B. Hall, Portland State University
Jason Lee, University of California, Merced
Clark Ross, Davidson College
Robert M. Whaples, Wake Forest University
Gavin Wright, Stanford University

It was a pleasure working with the great team at Palgrave. Jaime Marshall, Kirsty Reade, Aléta Bezuidenhout, and Amy Wheeler patiently walked me through every step of the publication process, providing valuable help and insights, and their responsiveness to all of my questions is sincerely appreciated. I would also like to thank Andrew Nash for doing a fantastic job copyediting the book.

Most of all, I would like to thank my family. No one writes a book alone, and my family made many sacrifices to allow me to carve out the time to make this happen. Not only was I physically absent for many evenings and weekends, but I was also mentally absent, deep in thought about the book, more times than I care to admit. I am especially grateful to my wife, Lisa, for her unwavering love and support, and for our son, Henry, and our daughter, Ava, each of whom is a joy and an inspiration.

Publisher's Acknowledgments

The author and publisher are grateful to the following for permission to reproduce copyrighted material:

- Nickolay Lamm for Figure 1.1.
- The Maddison Project for the data used to construct Figure 2.1 and Table 2.1.
- MeasuringWorth for the data used to construct Table 2.2.
- Peter H. Lindert and Jeffrey G. Williamson for the data used to construct Figure 3.3.
- The American Lung Association for Figure 7.8.
- Benjamin N. Dennis and Talan B. Iscan for the data used to construct Figure 9.1 and Figure 9.4.
- Peter H. Lindert and Cambridge University Press for the data used to construct Figure 11.2.
- Louis Johnston for the data used to construct Figure 12.7.
- Emmanuel Saez for the data used to construct Table 13.2.
- Facundo Alvaredo, Anthony B. Atkinson, Thomas Piketty, Emmanuel Saez, and Gabriel Zucan, *The World Wealth and Income Database*, for the data used to construct Figure 13.5 and Figure 13.6.
- The Organization of Economic Cooperation and Development (OECD) for the data used to construct Figure 13.7, Figure 16.4, and Figure 20.5.
- The National Bureau of Economic Research (NBER) for Table 18.1.
- Early Elias and Oscar Jorda for the data used to construct Figure 18.2.

Every effort has been made to trace all copyright holders, but if any have been inadvertently overlooked, the publisher will be pleased to make the necessary arrangements at the first opportunity.

1
Introduction to U.S. Economic History

The economic history of the United States is a study in contrasts. It is a story of remarkable successes punctuated with failures and shortcomings.

Perhaps the most notable feature of U.S. economic history is rapid and sustained economic growth. Although average living standards were comparatively high during the colonial period, economic growth accelerated to modern rates in the early nineteenth century. Adjusted for inflation, income per person in 2015 was almost 34 times greater than in 1800 (Table 1.1). Just as important: almost all of the goods and services we take for granted today—think of smartphones, automobiles, airplanes, refrigerators, air conditioners, computers, electric light bulbs, indoor plumbing, and pharmaceuticals, like antibiotics—were not available at *any* price in 1800.

Not only are Americans far better off materially today, they also enjoy longer and healthier lives and have much more leisure time. Life expectancy at birth in 1800 was less than 40 years of age and over 30 percent of children in many American cities did not reach their fifth birthday.[1] Life expectancy in 2015 was almost 79 years of age and infant mortality has fallen by a factor of 20. The typical workweek has fallen from more than 60 hours per week in the early nineteenth century to less than 35 hours a week in recent years. Longer lives and fewer hours of work have led to huge increases in the average lifetime hours of leisure.

Our higher incomes and longer, healthier lives are the result of our capacity to invent, innovate, educate, and build. If the United States continues to grow at the same rate that it has averaged since 1800, Americans can look forward to real incomes that are over twice as high per person by 2050, and almost five times higher by 2100, as compared with 2015.

Life has also changed in many other fundamental ways. Table 1.1 compares several measures of American life in the year 1800 to those measures in the year 2015. In 1800, the vast majority of Americans lived in rural areas and worked on farms. The

U.S. population was only 5.3 million in 1800, compared to 322 million in 2015, and almost everyone lived east of the Appalachian Mountains. Transportation and communication were primitive and painfully slow in 1800.

TABLE 1.1 Changes in American Life from 1800 to 2015		
Measure	1800	2015
Real GDP per capita (2009 dollars)	$1,509	$50,808
Life expectancy at birth	37 years	79 years
Percent of workforce in agriculture	74 percent	1.6 percent
Percent living in urban areas	6 percent	81 percent
Average number of children per woman	7 children	2 children
Population	5.3 million	322 million
Percent living in the Midwest and West	1 percent	45 percent
Travel time coast-to-coast	6 months	5 hours

Sources and Notes: For real GDP per capita, see the sources to Table 2.2. For life expectancy, see Figure 2.3. For percent of workforce in agriculture, see Figure 9.1. For percent living in urban areas, see Figure 7.5. For the average number of children per woman, see Figure 7.7. For population, see the U.S. Census, www.census.gov/population/www/censusdata/files/table-2.pdf (accessed: April 14, 2016). For the percent living in the Midwest and West, see Figure 7.4. Coast-to-coast travel times in 1800 are based on the return time of Lewis and Clark's journey in 1806.

While Table 1.1 shows dramatic improvements in American life since 1800, other evidence, in contrast, suggests that economic well-being and standards of living may not be quite as rosy in recent decades. During the nineteenth century, Americans were the tallest people in the world. Americans, however, have not grown any taller over the last fifty years, while Europeans have grown almost an inch taller each decade. Northern Europeans are now three inches taller, on average, than Americans (Figure 1.1). Some economic historians have argued that height is:

> A kind of biological shorthand: a composite code for all the factors that make up a society's well-being. Height variations within a population are largely genetic, but height variations between populations are mostly environmental. … If
> Joe is taller than Jack, it's probably because his parents are taller. But if the average Norwegian is taller than the average Nigerian it's because Norwegians live healthier lives. That's why the United Nations now uses height to monitor nutrition in developing countries. In our height lies the tale of our birth and upbringing, of our social class, daily diet, and health-care coverage. In our height lies our history.[2]

Using real income per person, the U.S. ranks at the top, yet the height data strongly suggest that the U.S. is not doing as well as the income estimates may indicate. What explains this paradox? Rising inequality may be one of the factors, with income and wealth inequality far greater in the United States than in most other advanced democracies. Although Americans have benefitted from economic growth over the very long run, not all Americans have benefitted equally. Surveys suggest that the vast majority of Americans do not want equality of outcome, but most Americans do want there to be equality of opportunity.

It is clear from an examination of the American past that we have fallen well short of equal opportunity for all Americans. In 2014, almost 150 years after slavery was abolished, median black family income was barely 60 percent of median white family

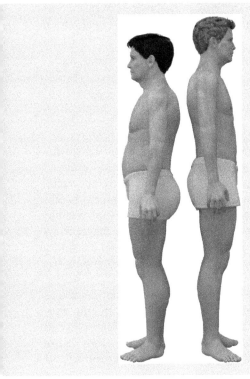

FIGURE 1.1 Differences in Average Heights and Weights of American Men (Left) and Dutch Men (Right), 2015
Source: Image courtesy of Nickolay Lamm, http://nickolaylamm.com/art-for-clients/the-average-man/ (accessed: April 7, 2016).

income.[3] Later chapters will examine the patterns and causes of economic inequality over time, and dig deeper to look at inequality by geographical region, by race, and by gender.

In recent decades, there have also been large and growing disparities in income and wealth among Americans, even among those who are similar in terms of race, gender, and educational attainment. Since the mid-1970s, the gap between rich and poor in the United States has widened substantially. Forty years ago, the chief executive officers (CEOs) of the biggest 100 corporations in the United States earned, on average, 39 times the pay of the typical worker. In recent years, the inequality of income and wealth has approached levels not seen since the 1920s, with CEOs often receiving over 1,000 times the pay of the average worker.[4] While the past few decades have been very good to millions of Americans, in 2015 almost one in six Americans fell below the federal poverty line.

Although America is still often viewed as the "land of opportunity," the likelihood of upward mobility has diminished since the early decades of the twentieth century, and the United States today has lower occupational and income mobility than Germany, Sweden, Finland, or Canada.[5]

The healthcare system in the United States may offer some clues to the paradox of Americans' rising average incomes but largely unchanging heights. The U.S. spends tens of billions of dollars developing new pharmaceuticals and other medical advances that benefit countless Americans. It is common for the rich throughout the world to seek medical treatment here. While some of the very best medical care in the world is available in the United States, however, not everyone receives the highest level of care, and the U.S. has lower life expectancy and higher rates of infant mortality than most other advanced democracies. While this may change as a result of recent healthcare reform, it is too early to make reliable predictions. Americans also have the highest rates of obesity. While much of the rest of the world is getting taller, we are getting wider.[6]

In addition, there are widespread concerns that future growth rates may not be as high as they have been in the past. Past growth was largely based on the "low-hanging fruit" of an abundance of fertile land and natural resources, which attracted millions of ambitious immigrants, on educating smart uneducated kids, on reducing job market discrimination against women and other minorities, and on a tremendous wave of technological innovations from 1870 to 1940 that will be difficult to duplicate.[7]

After the closing of the frontier at the end of the nineteenth century, Americans turned toward massive investments in education. In 1900, only 6.4 percent of Americans graduated from high school. By the 1960s, high school graduation rates had risen to over 80 percent. In 1900, only one in four hundred Americans aged 18–24 were enrolled in college, while over 40 percent are today. Most of this low-hanging fruit has now been picked, so we may be entering a period of "Great Stagnation." While meas-uring the precise sources of past and future growth is difficult (as we will see in Chapter 2), Cowan concludes:

> You can argue about the numbers, but again, just look around. I'm forty-eight years old, and the basic material accoutrements of my life (again the internet aside) haven't changed much since I was a kid. … We still drive cars, use refrigerators, and turn on the light switch … My grandmother, who was born at the beginning of the twentieth century, could not say the same.[8]

Finally, there are fears that continued population and economic growth in the United States and around the world will lead to substantial resource depletion, reduced biodiversity, and global climate change. Although the future is inherently uncertain, there are certainly areas of huge concern, such as large projected government liabili-ties, an underperforming educational system, and record heat and severe weather which look as though they may be the new norm. Scientific advancements, techno-logical innovations, and human ingenuity offer hope that economies around the world, including that of the U.S., will continue to grow and thrive, as the U.S. economy has throughout its history.

While the economy has been characterized by long-run growth from decade to decade, this growth has been far from steady from year to year. Economic fluctua-tions (or business cycles) and shocks, like wars and disease epidemics, have plagued the economy throughout its history. The ups and downs of the economy cause considerable hardships for individuals, particularly for those who lose their jobs or fortunes.

Several periods stand out in terms of poor short-run economic performance. The biggest calamity was the Great Depression of the 1930s. Production fell by a third, thousands of banks failed, and in 1933 the unemployment rate peaked at nearly 25 percent. Not only was the Great Depression severe, it was also persistent, with double-digit unemployment rates throughout the 1930s (Figure 1.2).

The Great Depression, however, was not entirely unique. There were also several severe recessions in the nineteenth century, when banks failed and unemployment increased. The Great Recession, which started in December 2007 after the collapse of the housing bubble, was also a sustained period of poor economic performance.

Like this introduction, the book is organized around four main themes: long-run economic growth, distributional issues, economic fluctuations, and the relationship between markets and government. David Byrne of The Talking Heads asked in a song, "How did I get here?" This book addresses how the United States got to where it is today.[9] What makes the U.S. economy exceptional (both good and bad) along so many different dimensions? To find out how we got here, we have to examine where we have been. Before beginning this journey, however, we must first consider some important concepts in economics and economic history that we will use to help us along the way.

1.1 WHAT IS ECONOMICS?

Economics examines the decisions of economic agents (primarily individuals, house-holds, firms, and governments) about what they produce, exchange, and consume. The discipline is divided into two main branches of study: microeconomics and macroeconomics. Microeconomics examines how individuals and firms make choices, how they interact in markets, and how governments attempt to influence these choices.

FIGURE 1.2 Unemployed Men Outside a Chicago Soup Kitchen, 1931

Source: The U.S. National Archives Catalog, https://catalog.archives.gov/#/id/541927 (accessed: April 10, 2016).

Macroeconomics studies how these choices affect the economy as a whole and examines the causes of unemployment, recessions, inflation, and economic growth.

SCARCITY AND OPPORTUNITY COST

Scarcity implies that choices have to be made, since human wants exceed available resources. Everyone faces scarcity—even Bill Gates and Warren Buffett, since time is the ultimate scarce resource. With only twenty-four hours in the day, each of us must make choices. That is, we are forced to make trade-offs. Your decision to read this book involves a trade-off in that you could be doing something else with your time instead. By doing something or acquiring something, we use up resources that could have been used to do or to acquire something else.

The concept of opportunity cost allows us to measure this trade-off. The opportunity cost of any choice is the value of the best alternative foregone in making that choice. Note that opportunity costs include both monetary and non-monetary costs. For example, if your next best alternative to reading this book is sitting on a blanket in the park enjoying the sunshine, then your opportunity cost is the value you place on that activity. If your next best alternative to reading this book is working for pay, then the opportunity cost of reading this book is the income you did not earn by working.

Scarcity also implies that each economy must address three fundamental questions:

- What goods and services will be produced?
- How will the goods and services be produced?
- Who will receive the goods and services produced?

Broadly speaking, these decisions can be made either by markets or by command, or by some combination of the two. In markets, production and consumption are the result of decentralized decisions by many firms and individuals. Alternatively, in a command system there is a central authority making decisions about production and consumption.

Throughout most of U.S. history, the price system and market incentives were the primary determinants of the production and distribution of goods and services. Today, however, the United States is best described as a mixed economy—that is, in many cases the production and distribution of goods and services are primarily the result of market outcomes, but governments also influence production and distribution.

MARKETS

Markets allow buyers and sellers to exchange goods and services. Markets can take many different forms. In some cases, buyers and sellers meet at a particular place and time, such as in the "pit" at the Chicago Board of Trade or at a local farmers' market. In most cases, however, market exchange takes place at many different places and times. For example, the "market" for gasoline in the United States operates nation-wide, twenty-four hours a day, with buyers and sellers making exchanges at over one-hundred thousand gas stations.

In a market economy, individuals decide which goods and services to buy, where to work, and where to save and invest, based on the signals and incentives provided by market prices. Firms also respond to prices in deciding whom to hire as well as what goods and services to provide. In markets, buyers look at prices to decide how much to demand, while sellers look at prices to decide how much to supply. Market exchange facilitates specialization and gains from trade through better allocation of resources and increased production.

Under certain conditions, markets are "efficient" in the sense that prices cause resources to be used in such a way as to exploit all opportunities to make some individuals better off without making others worse off. That is, the market mechanism through the price system will tend to allocate resources efficiently, as shown in Section 1.3. Adam Smith, in his 1776 book *An Inquiry into the Nature and Causes of the Wealth of Nations*, observed that individuals and firms interacting in markets act as if they are guided by an "invisible hand" that leads to efficient outcomes in which social welfare is maximized.

One important distinction to make is between product markets and factor markets. In product markets, buyers are individuals, while sellers are firms. In most cases, we are consumers (buyers) of products, whether we are buying a hamburger, a haircut, or a new cell phone, and firms are selling us these goods and services. In factor markets, however, individuals are the sellers of the factors of production and firms are the primary buyers. Factors of production (or inputs) are used to produce final products. The most important factor market for most individuals is the labor market, where individuals sell their labor to firms (or to the government, or to the nonprofit sector). The distinction between product markets and factor markets is shown in Table 1.2.

TABLE 1.2 Factor and Product Markets		
Markets	Buyers	Sellers
Product markets	Individuals	Firms
Factor markets	Firms	Individuals

1.2 THE METHOD OF ECONOMICS

What distinguishes economics from other academic disciplines is not the topics that economists study. Historians, for example, also study the economic history of the United States. Sociologists, too, study aspects of the economy. Rather it is the tools and methods that economists use that separate economics from the other social sciences and from other academic disciplines.

ECONOMIC THEORIES AND MODELS

More than any other social science, economics relies on well-specified theories, often represented as mathematical models. A theory consists of a set of assumptions and the conclusions derived from these assumptions. In fact, economics goes far beyond any other social science in its insistence that an explicit, carefully constructed model can be used to represent and explain economic and social phenomena.

A model is nothing more than an abstract representation of reality. Architects build cardboard models of buildings before construction begins. In your high school chemistry class, there was probably a plastic and wire contraption with red, blue, and green balls representing protons, neutrons, and electrons. These are three-dimensional models which you can pick up and hold. Economic models, on the other hand, are not built with cardboard, plastic or metal, but with words, numerical tables, diagrams, and mathematical equations.

John Maynard Keynes defined economics as the "science of thinking in terms of models, joined to the art of choosing models which are relevant to the contemporary world."[10] Any model has to simplify reality. The world is just too complex for any model to mimic every feature of the economy. Part of the art of choosing models is deciding on the appropriate degree of simplification. A "model should be as simple as possible, but not more so."[11] The degree of simplification also depends on the question that is being addressed.

In economics, we use different models for different purposes. This should not be too surprising since we do the same in our everyday lives. A road map is a model since it simplifies and abstracts from reality. A road map of the United States is sufficient to drive from coast to coast, but it is too simple to find your way around San Francisco. Similarly, a map of San Francisco will help you find Golden Gate Park but it is not useful for driving across the United States.

Models are based on deductive reasoning, whereby one or more general principles are used to derive specific predictions. A valid deduction is one in which the conclusion must follow the premises. That is, we are interested in formulating logically consistent "if, then" statements. Each model generally consists of both behavioral assumptions and market structure assumptions. Given these assumptions, deductive conclusions logically follow.

When economists construct models, they are engaging in positive economic analysis. Positive economics predicts the outcomes of alternative actions by answering the question "What is?" or "What will be?" In contrast, normative economics involves value judgments and answers the question "What ought to be?"

There is much greater agreement among economists on positive questions than on normative ones. For example, over 85 percent of economists agree with the positive statement: "Fiscal policy [government spending and/or tax cuts] can have a stimulative impact on a less than fully employed economy."[12] There is, however, far less agreement on the normative decision of whether fiscal policy ought to be undertaken. Fiscal policy has other effects on the economy as well, and the decision to recommend a particular fiscal policy hinges on subjective weighting that will vary from economist to economist. Consider a proposed tax cut to help increase output and reduce unemployment. Two economists may both agree on the positive issue—that the tax cut will increase output and reduce unemployment—yet disagree on the overall desirability of such a policy, since the tax cut will also have distributional implications (i.e., individuals' taxes will not fall equally). Since the distributional implications of tax policy are largely normative, such as who ought to pay more taxes, there are more disagreements among economists on normative issues than on positive issues.

THE "ALL ELSE BEING EQUAL" (CETERIS PARIBUS) ASSUMPTION

Another simplifying device we will often use is the "all else being equal" assumption, also known as the "ceteris paribus" assumption.[13] Instead of letting everything change at once, the ceteris paribus assumption allows us to understand the relationships among variables by examining the impact of a change in one variable on another variable, while holding all of the other variables in the model constant.

Models in economics share the same general structure, which is depicted in Figure 1.3. A variable is a measure of something that can vary (i.e., exhibit a different value) from one observation to the next. Wages, interest rates, prices, and quantities of goods and services are examples of variables.

Models have both inputs and outcomes. Inputs are exogenous variables, which the model builder takes as given or outside the model ("exo-" means "outside"). Based on a set of exogenous variables, the model predicts general outcomes, which are the endogenous variables ("endo-" means "inside").

If one of the exogenous variables is changed while holding all else equal, then the model predicts how the endogenous variables will change. Note that what is exogenous and/or endogenous varies from model to model, based on the economic question being asked.

FIGURE 1.3 Exogenous and Endogenous Variables

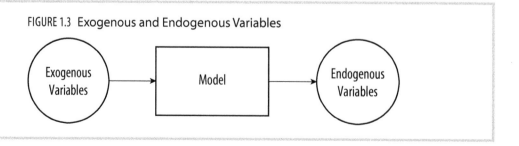

BEHAVIORAL ASSUMPTIONS AND THE MARGINAL PRINCIPLE

Many factors can potentially influence how individuals and firms make choices, but economists believe that choices are not made arbitrarily or randomly. Economists usually assume that individuals and firms are rational maximizers with specific objectives. Individuals are assumed to maximize utility (a fancy name for satisfaction or well-being), subject to their budget constraints. For a firm, profits are the difference between a firm's total revenue (*TR*) and its total cost (*TC*), where total cost includes opportunity costs:

$$Profit = TR - TC$$

Firms are assumed to maximize profits, subject to their resource constraints.

Rationality does not mean that individuals always make the optimal choice, but it does mean that individuals make the best choices on average, based on their preferences and constraints. That is, it is assumed that they learn from their mistakes and do not make systematic errors. The assumption of rationality may not be appropriate in all instances, and the study of behavioral economics examines how individuals are *not* fully rational; nevertheless, rationality is usually a good assumption, particularly for decisions that are not too complex.

Rational maximizing behavior implies that individuals and firms respond to economic incentives. When the costs or benefits of any action change, choices will be affected. That is, incentives matter. In order to make optimal decisions, decisions need to be made "at the margin," where "marginal" means additional. Optimal decisions require that the marginal principle is followed: if the marginal benefit (*MB*) of an action (the additional benefit of that action) exceeds the marginal cost (*MC*) of an action (the additional cost of that action), the marginal principle says *do it*. If the marginal benefit (*MB*) of an action is less than the marginal cost (*MC*) of that action, then *don't do it*. Consider the decision of whether or not to buy a cup of coffee. The marginal cost of the coffee is the price that has to be paid to purchase it. Suppose the coffee costs $2 a cup. If a person decides to buy the coffee, it must be the case that the marginal benefit of that cup of coffee exceeds the marginal cost of $2. If the person does not expect to receive at least $2 in marginal benefit from the coffee, it would not be rational to pay $2 for it.

Economic History in Action 1.1 shows how the marginal principle can be applied in deciding whether or not to have children.

ECONOMIC HISTORY IN ACTION 1.1

Fertility Rates and Opportunity Costs

In 1820, women in the U.S. (if they survived through their childbearing years) had on average nearly seven children each. In 2015, the typical American woman had two children. While the fertility transition is discussed in detail in Chapter 7, we can use the concepts of opportunity cost and the marginal principle to help explain this large decrease in fertility.

Consider the marginal benefit and marginal cost calculation for a woman deciding to have an additional (marginal) child. In 1820, the overwhelming majority of Americans lived on farms, where the marginal benefit of having a child could be quite high since children often worked on the farm at an early age. The marginal cost of an additional child was relatively low, since the marginal monetary costs of having a child did not entail large educational or health expenses.

More importantly, the marginal opportunity cost of a mother's time was relatively low too, since women did not have good alternatives to being on the farm. As a result, women decided to have more children then as compared to today, and continued to have children as long as the expected marginal benefit of having an additional child exceeded the expected marginal cost of having an additional child. Eventually the marginal benefits of having an additional child would fall sufficiently and/or the marginal costs of having an additional child would increase sufficiently so that women would stop having children.

In contrast, the marginal benefit of having a child today is typically lower. Children are no longer economic assets that can milk cows at 6 a.m.; instead they are generally economic liabilities. Of course, parents both then and now receive substantial non-monetary benefits from having children. Most dramatic, however, are the substantial increases in the marginal costs of having children. The opportunity cost of having a child is dramatically higher today. Women have far greater opportunities outside of the home, because increased education and changing social norms provide women with substantial opportunities to work and make money outside of the home. As a result, women have to give up more today (that is, they have higher opportunity costs) when they decide to have children. As the marginal benefits of children have decreased and the marginal costs have increased, many women have decided to have fewer children.

Differences in opportunity costs also help explain why more highly educated women and women with higher earnings typically have fewer children today than less educated and lower-earning women today.[14] Women with more education and more interesting and more lucrative job opportunities face a higher marginal opportunity cost in having children. As a result, many choose to have fewer children (or no children at all).

MARKET STRUCTURE ASSUMPTIONS

Along with behavioral assumptions, we also make assumptions regarding market structure. The discussion above regarding the efficiency of markets and the invisible hand assumes that the market is perfectly competitive, where there are a large number of buyers and sellers; it also makes some other assumptions, which we will explore later in this chapter. At the other extreme is monopoly, the situation where there is only one seller of a good or service.

There are also market structures between perfect competition and monopoly. Many industries in the U.S. economy are oligopolies, in which a few firms dominate the market. In the case of oligopoly, from the firms' perspective it is best to cooperate and to act like a monopolist. Depending on the number of firms in the oligopoly and the degree of cooperation among the firms, oligopolies can end up looking like monopolies (in cases with effective cooperation) or closer to perfectly competitive firms (in cases where the firms can't agree to collude or when collusion is prevented by government policies). In general, the interdependence of firms in an oligopoly leads to strategic behavior on the part of firms. We can use game theory to examine the strategic behavior of firms in an oligopoly setting.

Monopolistically competitive markets consist of many firms, but in such markets each firm has limited price-setting power because each sells a slightly different (heterogeneous) product. Restaurants, for example, are described as monopolistically competitive firms since the menu of each restaurant is distinctive in one way or another.

In perfectly competitive markets, the product is homogeneous, meaning that it is indistinguishable from producer to producer. When you pick up an ear of corn in the supermarket, for instance, it seems like any other ear of corn: you cannot identify the farmer by looking at the corn. In contrast, in monopolistic competition and oligopolies, you can recognize the producer through the characteristics of the product or through branding and logos. In these markets, the product is heterogeneous. The main types of market structures in product markets are summarized in Table 1.3.

TABLE 1.3 Types of Market Structure in Product Markets			
Market Type	Products	Sellers	Buyers
Perfect competition	Homogeneous	Many	Many
Monopolistic competition	Heterogeneous	Many	Many
Oligopoly	Heterogeneous	Few	Many
Monopoly	NA	One	Many

The variables and the predictions from models will differ substantially depending on the assumptions we make regarding the market structure.

1.3   THE SUPPLY AND DEMAND MODEL

Many of the concepts and methods of economics described above can be illustrated using the supply and demand model. This model can be applied to product markets and to factor markets, but the discussion below assumes a product market in which consumers are the demanders (buyers) and firms are the suppliers (sellers).

As with any model, there are both behavioral and market structure assumptions. Consumers are assumed to maximize utility (satisfaction) subject to their income constraints, and firms are assumed to maximize profits subject to their resource constraints. The market structure is assumed to be perfectly competitive, with the key assumption being that there are so many buyers and so many sellers in the market that each consumer and each firm takes the market price as given when they make decisions (i.e., everyone is a price taker).[15] Of course, the combined decisions of all consumers and all firms determine the market price, but no one participant buys or sells enough to make a perceptible difference in the price.

MARKET EQUILIBRIUM

The law of demand states that as the price of a good decreases, the quantity demanded of that good increases, and vice versa, all else being held equal (ceteris paribus). Demand curves slope down for two reasons: the substitution effect and the income effect. As the price of a good decreases, with the prices of all other goods and everything else held constant, the decrease in price makes this good relatively less expensive. In response, consumers will substitute toward this good and buy more: the substitution effect. For example, if the price of apples falls, while the price of oranges remains constant, consumers will substitute away from oranges and toward apples, increasing the quantity demanded for apples because of the fall in the price of apples. The income effect says this: if consumers' money income remains constant, a reduction in the price of a good will increase consumers' real purchasing power, allowing consumers to purchase more of all goods, including the good in question.

Along a demand curve, everything is held constant except the price of the good. However, when one of the variables held constant changes (that is, when one of the exogenous variables changes), there is a change in demand such that the entire demand curve shifts. If demand increases, for example, then the curve shifts to the right (Figure 1.4). This means that the quantity of that good or service demanded by consumers is higher at any given price (or, similarly, that consumers are willing to pay more for any given quantity). As shown in Figure 1.4, the main exogenous variables that lead to an increase in demand, from $Demand_0$ to $Demand_1$, are:

- An increase in consumer incomes for a normal good. Most goods are normal goods in that demand for the good increases as consumer incomes increase.
- A decrease in consumer incomes for an inferior good. Some goods are inferior goods in that a decrease in consumer incomes causes demand to increase. For example, a decrease in consumer incomes may lead to an increase in the demand for inter-city bus travel as consumers can no longer afford more expensive travel by plane or car.
- An increase in the price of a substitute good. Two goods are substitute goods if they largely serve the same purpose (e.g., Coke and Pepsi).
- A decrease in the price of a complementary good. Two goods are complementary goods if they are often used together (e.g., peanut butter and jelly).
- An increase in market size, due to a greater population or lower transportation costs.
- An expected increase in the future price of the good.
- A positive change in tastes or preferences toward the good.
- A reduction in taxes on, or an increase in subsidies for, the good.

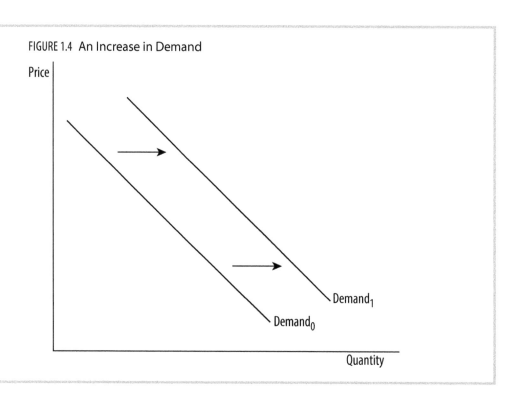

FIGURE 1.4 An Increase in Demand

While demand slopes down, supply curves slope up, illustrating a positive relationship between the price of a good and the quantity supplied of that good. Supply is upward-sloping because marginal costs of production tend to rise as output increases, all else being held equal. There are also exogenous variables that cause the entire supply curve to shift (Figure 1.5). An increase in supply (a shift to the right or down) occurs when the quantity supplied increases at any given price. The main exogenous variables that lead to an increase in supply, from $Supply_0$ to $Supply_1$ as shown in Figure 1.5, are:

- A decrease in the price of a factor of production used to produce the good (e.g., a decrease in wages).
- An increase in technology that reduces the costs of production.
- An expected future price decrease.
- A decrease in the price of a related good in production (e.g., a decrease in the price of corn could cause farmers to substitute away from corn to increase the supply of wheat).
- An increase in the number of firms in the market.
- A decrease in taxes or an increase in subsidies for suppliers.

Suppose that all of the exogenous (shift) variables are held constant. In this case, the market will converge to an equilibrium. Economists use the word "equilibrium" to describe a situation that, once achieved, will not change unless something that has been held constant changes. In equilibrium, the quantity demanded equals the quantity supplied. That is, when a market is in equilibrium there are neither shortages (excess demand) nor surpluses (excess supply).

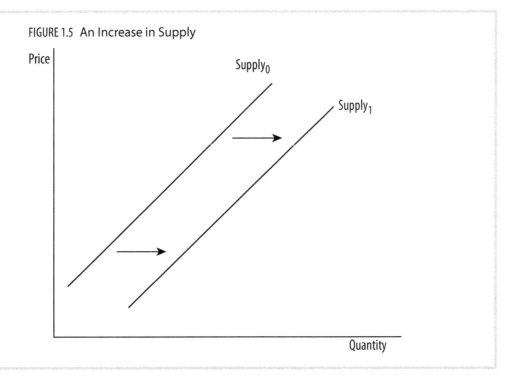

FIGURE 1.5 An Increase in Supply

A perfectly competitive market is self-correcting. If there is a shortage of a good or a service, prices rise, and the quantity supplied increases and the quantity demanded decreases until the quantity supplied equals the quantity demanded. If a surplus occurs, prices fall until the quantity demanded and the quantity supplied equal one another. Equilibrium occurs where the demand and supply curves intersect. If an exogenous variable changes, then either the supply curve or the demand curve shifts, leading to change in the equilibrium price and equilibrium quantity of the good, and a new market equilibrium.

THE EFFICIENCY OF PERFECT COMPETITION

If a market is perfectly competitive, then the outcome is efficient. Efficiency is defined as a market outcome in which the marginal benefit to consumers of the last unit consumed is equal to its marginal cost of production ($MB = MC$), and an outcome in which the sum of the consumer surplus and the producer surplus is maximized. The sum of the consumer surplus and the producer surplus is called the total surplus or the economic surplus. Deviations from perfect competition are market failures since there is a reduction in the economic surplus, which is called a deadweight loss.

Consider a perfectly competitive market in equilibrium. We can illustrate consumer and producer surpluses using demand and supply. There are two ways to interpret a market demand curve. A demand curve shows the quantity that consumers will buy at any given price, ceteris paribus. It also represents the maximum price that consumers are willing (and able) to pay for any given quantity, ceteris paribus. If consumers are willing to pay a given price for a good, then it must be the case that consumers value the good that much. Therefore, a demand curve is both the maximum "willingness to pay" curve and the consumers' marginal benefit curve.

When a competitive market reaches equilibrium, there is one price charged to all buyers. Some buyers, however, are willing (and able) to pay a much higher price than the equilibrium price. Economists say that these buyers are receiving consumer surplus. Consumer surplus is the difference between the price buyers are willing and able to pay and the price actually paid. It is measured by the area below the demand curve and above the price paid, up to the quantity purchased.

Similarly, there are two ways to interpret a supply curve. A supply curve shows the quantity that producers will sell at any given price, ceteris paribus. It also shows the minimum price that producers are willing to accept for any given quantity, ceteris paribus. The minimum price measures the marginal cost of producing that given quantity of the good. Therefore, a supply curve is both the minimum "willingness to sell" curve and the marginal cost curve for the firms in the market.

When a market reaches a perfectly competitive equilibrium, there is one price received by all sellers (which is the same price paid by all buyers). Some sellers, however, are willing to accept a lower price than the equilibrium price. Economists say that these sellers are receiving producer surplus. Producer surplus is the difference between the lowest price a firm would be willing to accept for a good or service and the price it actually receives. It is measured by the area below the market price and above the supply curve, up to the quantity sold.

Figure 1.6 shows consumer surplus and producer surplus in a perfectly competitive market. While demand and supply curves may be nonlinear, the calculation of the dollar values of consumer and producer surplus is easier with linear curves since the area of a triangle is simply one-half base times height ($area = 1/2 \cdot b \cdot h$).

FIGURE 1.6 Consumer and Producer Surplus with Perfect Competition

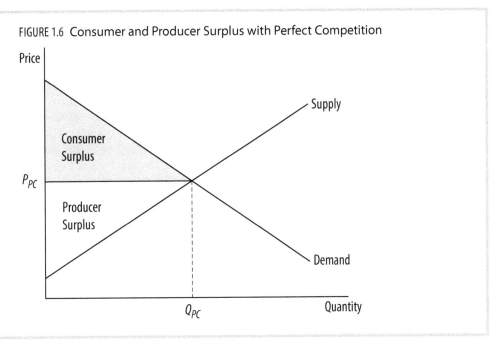

The equilibrium quantity under perfect competition (Q_{PC}) ensures that the aggregate of consumer and producer surplus is at a maximum and that the marginal decision rule ($MB = MC$) is satisfied (Figure 1.7). If the quantity is *less* than Q_{PC}, then the value to buyers exceeds the costs to sellers ($MB > MC$). If the quantity is *greater* than

FIGURE 1.7 Market Efficiency with Perfect Competition

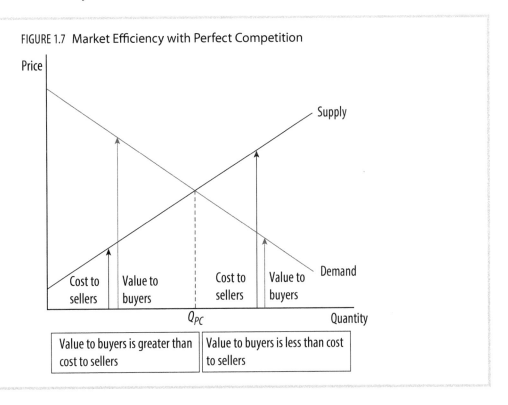

Q_{PC}, then this cannot be the efficient outcome either since the costs to sellers exceed the value to buyers ($MC > MB$).

1.4 MARKETS AND GOVERNMENT

While some market exchanges have existed for thousands of years, governments have many important roles to play in a complex market economy. Governments help to create markets by providing the legal and institutional framework in which markets can thrive. Most importantly, governments help to establish property rights and enforce contracts. If individuals do not have the legal right to own and to exercise control over scarce resources, then the invisible hand cannot operate. A firm will not provide goods and services if those goods and services are stolen. Similarly, individuals will not work for firms if those firms can arbitrarily decide to withhold pay. We rely on social customs, and on the threat from the police and the court system in the background, to enforce our rights over the things we own and produce.

Governments also sometimes override (or attempt to override) markets because of economic, moral, or other concerns. For example, in the U.S. it is illegal to buy or sell kidneys or cocaine, or to engage in prostitution (in all states except parts of Nevada). The Eighteenth Amendment to the U.S. Constitution, which was in effect from 1919 to 1933, outlawed the sale, manufacture, transportation, and consumption of alcohol. Many U.S. states are currently debating whether or not the sale and purchase of marijuana should be legal.

MARKET FAILURES AND GOVERNMENT FAILURES

There are many instances when markets fail to allocate resources efficiently. Economists use the term "market failure" to describe situations in which the market, left to its own devices, leads to an inefficient outcome. While we will be examining many types of market failures throughout this book, let us consider just a few here.

The invisible hand requires that there are enough buyers and sellers in a market such that each individual market participant is a price taker. That is, each participant's impact is so small relative to the size of the market that no one participant has any measurable influence on market price. In many cases, however, firms do have market power in the sense that a few firms have (or in some cases a single firm has) substantial influence on market prices. Consider the case of a monopoly in which a single firm sells a product for which there are no close substitutes. In some cases, the cost structure is such that only one firm can survive in a particular market, as might be the case for an electricity supplier in a city. When this happens, the government may regulate the supplier to ensure that electricity rates are predictable and fair.

Externalities provide another example of a market failure. In this case the actions of an individual (or a firm) can have impacts on others for which they are not compensated. Externalities can be both positive and negative. A classic example is the negative externality of pollution, whereby markets, by themselves, will produce too much. In the case of a negative externality like this, governments can improve outcomes by imposing taxes or regulations, or by creating a market in pollution permits.

Note, however, that while well-designed public policies have the ability to improve market outcomes, not all such policies prove effective. There can also be government failures. There have been many instances throughout U.S. history in which government regulatory agencies, created to act in the public interest, have been "captured" by the industry they were supposed to regulate and have begun to favor that industry instead of acting in the public interest.

One possible example is the Interstate Commerce Commission (ICC), created in 1887 to regulate railroads. The Commission has been blamed for acting in the interests of railroads and trucking companies by setting artificially high transport rates and working to exclude new competitors through a restrictive permit process. In this case, the cure of government intervention may have been worse than the disease of market failure.

Not only are there market failures in individual markets, but there can also be macroeconomic failures (recessions and inflation) that affect the economy as a whole. Here, too, governments can potentially improve (or worsen) market outcomes. For example, most economists believe that rules and policies in the banking sector and adherence to the gold standard lengthened and worsened the Great Depression. In contrast, there is an emerging consensus today that aggressive government action (through the Federal Reserve and U.S. Treasury) prevented the Great Recession from turning into another Great Depression.

Markets also affect the distribution of income and wealth. A market system pays people amounts based on what others are willing to pay for their services. In 2015, the boxer Floyd Mayweather earned more than $300 million in one fight.[16] The high earnings of sports superstars pale in comparison to those at the very top of the income distribution. In 2013, George Soros, a hedge fund manager and founder of Soros Fund Management, earned $4 billion.[17] To put this in perspective, $4 billion is more than the sum of the combined salaries and benefits of the 47,000 faculty members in the California State University System with its twenty-three campuses, which together serve almost 475,000 students.[18]

The invisible hand, even if it achieves an efficient outcome, does not ensure that everyone has sufficient shelter, food, or health care. Governments, through the income tax system, the educational system, the welfare system, and in many other ways, often strive to achieve a more equitable distribution of economic well-being throughout society.

THE GROWTH OF GOVERNMENT

In 1900, federal government spending was only about 3 percent of GDP. In 2015, it was 20.6 percent. Moreover, there are now laws about all sorts of things, from smoking to seat belts. In the late nineteenth century, there were no consumer protection laws, no worker protection laws, no minimum wage laws, no unemployment insurance, no Social Security, no Medicare, no welfare, and no environmental protection laws. The federal government started to regulate railroads and industry only in the decades after the Civil War.

Why did these changes in government occur and what has been the impact on the economy and the daily lives of Americans? The rise of the "welfare state" has insulated Americans from some of the risks associated with advanced age, poor health, a bad economy, or bad luck. Perhaps almost all of these changes were made with good intentions, but many Americans feel that at least some of these changes in the scale and scope of government have caused more harm than good.

Since the 1970s, there has been substantial rhetoric (and some action) to limit government's role in the economy. In the first decade of the twenty-first century, there was some momentum to further reduce the impact of government in the economy.

The Great Recession, however, resulted in increased government spending and reduced tax revenues, which led in turn to large deficit spending and a growing national debt, creating uncertainty regarding the future scale and scope of government in the United States.

1.5 WHAT IS ECONOMIC HISTORY?

Defining "economic history" is more difficult than one might initially suppose. On one level, the answer is obvious: economic history is the study of the history of the economy.[19] On a more fundamental level, however, we need to understand the methodology that economic historians employ to gain insights into the historical development of the economy. Although economic history does use the tools and methods of economics, there are also important differences in how economic historians approach the topic. While it is beyond the scope of this book to discuss all of the methods that economic historians use, we should briefly consider cliometrics, comparative economic history, path dependence, and an emphasis on institutional change, all of which play important roles.

CLIOMETRICS

Cliometrics is the explicit use of economic theory and statistical measurement in the study of economic history. In 1960, Stanley Reiter coined the term "cliometrics" to describe the work of Alfred Conrad and John Meyer (1958).[20] Conrad and Meyer used the capital asset pricing model (CAPM), a common model in finance, to show that slavery was very profitable for slave owners in the decades leading up to the Civil War (1861–1865). Before Conrad and Meyer, many historians had argued that the Civil War was unnecessary because slavery as an institution was becoming less and less profitable and would have died out on its own, without a costly war that killed 752,000 Americans.[21] By using a well-specified economic model, and gathering and analyzing economic data, Conrad and Meyer effectively refuted the notion that slavery would have vanished quickly on its own.

Cliometrics has had a substantial influence on economics in the past half century. In 1993, Douglass North and Robert Fogel, pioneering cliometricians, were awarded the Nobel Prize in Economics. Today, "Many garden-variety economists have become economic historians. Economists no longer question whether to extend an economic series into the past; rather, the issue today is how far and at what cost."[22] One of the great achievements of the cliometric school is the understanding that historical data need not be viewed simply as "one damned thing after another," but instead are often the outcomes of an enduring economic mechanism that conforms reasonably well to economic theory.

While there are certainly some quantitative economic data available all the way back to the founding of the American colonies, it was during the mid-nineteenth century that governments and private companies began collecting extensive data in earnest. However, even during the Great Depression of the 1930s, data were extremely limited. Modern macroeconomic aggregates like gross domestic product, labor productivity, the unemployment rate, and the inflation rate did not exist until after the Great Depression.[23] In recent decades, economic historians have extended many modern data series well into the past.

Although the relative paucity of data can be a limitation to the economic historian, historical data also have some substantial advantages over more recent data. In many instances, we do not have to worry as much about privacy concerns. For example, it is likely that we will know far more about the inner workings of Apple or Google one hundred years from now than we do today, because data, although currently kept secret, will almost certainly become available to researchers at some time in the future.

COMPARATIVE ECONOMIC HISTORY

The pioneering work in cliometrics usually emphasized nation-specific questions in order to shed light on questions from historians' research agendas. Over time, however, a "New Comparative History" developed, which was built on the application of economic methods to questions of history, but "reflects a belief that economic processes can be best understood by systematically comparing experiences across time, regions, and, above all, countries."[24] This work is less nation-specific and focuses on questions from economists' research agendas, such as the causes of long-run economic growth, the development of institutions, and the growth and impacts of globalization.

"Give me your tired, your poor. Your huddled masses yearning to breathe free. The wretched refuse of your teeming shore. Send these, the homeless, tempest-tost to me. I lift my lamp beside the golden door!" You have probably heard this phrase from the famous poem Emma Lazarus inscribed on the Statue of Liberty.[25] This is one way to think about the waves of immigration that washed against America's shores through the 1920s, but it misses the fact that this "wretched refuse" not only traveled to the U.S. but also migrated throughout the world to new homes in places such as Canada, Australia, and Argentina. This view also ignores an insight of economic theory: that flows of people across countries are usually accompanied by flows of physical and financial capital as well.

Thus, to understand the causes of migration and its effects on the U.S. economy, we need to think about how the American experience both parallels and differs from that of other countries, both in terms of human migration and also in terms of capital flows. Economic historians have done exactly this to gain new insights to questions such as the reasons for late-nineteenth-century migration, the factors determining relative wages in the U.S. compared with those in other countries, and insights into how financial markets have evolved both within the U.S. and across the international economy.[26]

PATH DEPENDENCE

Economic history, however, goes beyond using the models and statistical techniques of economics to address the importance of history. Economic history also emphasizes the importance of path dependence, which is defined as "the dependence of economic outcomes on the path of previous outcomes, rather than simply on current conditions. In a path-dependent process, 'history matters'—it has an enduring influence."[27]

Path dependence does not replace the standard assumption of maximizing behavior, but emphasizes that past choices sometimes put additional constraints on later choices, causing the sequence of economic outcomes to follow one possible path rather than another. Path-dependent outcomes often arise when there are increasing returns to the adoption of some technique or other practice (see Economic History in Action 1.2).

ECONOMIC HISTORY IN ACTION 1.2

Path Dependence and the Economics of QWERTY

The economics of QWERTY is one of the first recognized and most debated empirical case studies of path dependence. The familiar keyboard on computers (and typewriters) is called the QWERTY keyboard because the top row of keys (from left to right), typed with the left hand, spells QWERTY. The QWERTY keyboard was introduced in 1873, but why do almost all of us use this keyboard design today, given that we now know there are other, more efficient layouts?[28]

The answer largely stems from the fact that the first typing schools and manuals offered instructions for using a QWERTY keyboard, which was one of many initial keyboard designs. The availability of trained typists in QWERTY encouraged firms to buy QWERTY typewriters, which gave further encouragement for future typists to learn QWERTY too. This positive feedback effect or "lock in" increased QWERTY's market share until it became the standard among all typewriters. When the personal computer was invented, path dependence resulted in QWERTY to remain the standard design, and subsequently this has carried over to iPhones and most other handheld devices.

The QWERTY design is particularly inefficient on handheld devices. Studies show that most of us text between 14 and 31 words per minute, mostly using our thumbs. With the alternative KALQ design, for example, vowels are clustered on the right-hand side to minimize thumb travel distance; and the left hand, which researchers determined is quicker at finding the next key, includes most of the consonants. The KALQ keyboard, after training and practice, has yielded an average of 37 words per minute.[29]

Perhaps the superiority of other designs will eventually displace QWERTY, but, if history is any guide, the positive feedback effects of path dependence may be quite persistent.

Path dependence, however, goes well beyond the adoption of technical standards like keyboard designs. Path dependence also appears to influence the geographic concentration of economic activity, including the emergence of Silicon Valley. These geographical patterns of economic activity help to determine the sources of comparative advantage and the patterns of international trade. Path-dependent processes appear frequently throughout this book. Everything from agricultural subsidies to antitrust laws, government pensions, employer-provided health insurance, and the welfare system are influenced by the course of history.

EMPHASIS ON INSTITUTIONAL CHANGE

A growing body of empirical evidence stresses the impact of historical events on long-run economic development, including institutional changes.[30] The institution of slavery and the impact of the Great Depression each had influences on the U.S. economy that endured for decades (if not centuries). Institutions embody the rules of the game that structure human and economic interactions. They consist of the entire regulatory and legal framework, social norms, and the formal and informal enforcement mechanisms that structure how the economy functions. These include rules regarding property rights and the enforcement of contracts, and a myriad of other rules that help structure exchanges between firms and workers, borrowers and lenders, and producers and consumers. Institutions also govern key aspects of public policy, including taxes, public spending, and monetary policy. Finally, and regrettably, the institutional framework encompasses the written and unwritten rules that provide the basis for discrimination that can exclude broad segments of the population from social and economic opportunities.[31]

Institutional change is often incremental, with changes taking place slowly and sporadically over many decades or centuries. It can also occur abruptly during crises, as with the dramatic changes that occurred as part of the New Deal legislation during the Great Depression of the 1930s.

In many economics courses the period under consideration is often quite brief, so that it is common to assume that the institutional framework is given and fixed. Economic history emphasizes that economics is broader than just the shifting demand and supply curves in models that assume that the rules of the game are always fixed. By examining the economy over long periods of time, economic historians can help identify and document the causes and consequences of long-run institutional changes.

1.6   CONCLUSIONS

This chapter has introduced economics and economic history, and explained the methods and assumptions used by economists and economic historians in seeking to understand the economy. As we examine the economic history of the United States in subsequent chapters, we will be evaluating economic outcomes based on four main criteria: growth, stability, efficiency, and equity. In many ways, the economic history of the United States is a story of triumph and success, but there have also been many instances where economic performance has faltered.

QUESTIONS

1. Briefly list and describe the four main themes of U.S. economic history described in this chapter.

2. Categorize each of the following statements as examples of either positive or normative economics, and as examples of either macroeconomics or microeconomics.

   A. Monetary policymakers should do everything they can to reduce the unemployment rate.

   B. If there is an increase in the price of gasoline, the quantity purchased will decrease.

   C. Budget deficits typically lead to higher rates of inflation.

   D. It is important to invest in preschool programs to improve labor-market outcomes for individuals when they reach adulthood.

3. In the late eighteenth and early nineteenth centuries, birth rates in the United States were generally higher than in Europe. Using the concepts of opportunity cost and the marginal principle, explain why U.S. birth rates were higher.

4. Consider the market in the seventeenth century for tobacco produced in the American colonies.

   A. Graphically illustrate an initial equilibrium on a supply and demand diagram. Label the initial equilibrium price P_0 and the equilibrium quantity Q_0.

   B. Now suppose that colonists have developed a new strain of tobacco that increases yields per acre, but is otherwise indistinguishable from the previous strain, and that smoking tobacco is becoming more popular in Europe. How do these two changes affect the equilibrium price and the quantity of tobacco? Illustrate this graphically on the supply and demand diagram from Part A, and provide a written explanation.

Hint: When two exogenous variables change, the effect on either the price or the quantity is sometimes indeterminate.

5. What distinguishes economic history from the typical course in economics?

6. What is path dependence? Provide and explain two examples of path-dependent processes different from those used in this chapter.

7. What roles do governments play in the modern economy?

NOTES

[1] Michael Hanes, "The Urban Mortality Transition in the United States, 1800–1940," *Historical Working Paper* 134 (Cambridge, MA: National Bureau of Economic Research, July 2001).

[2] Burkhard Bilger, "The Height Gap: Why Europeans are Getting Taller and Taller and Americans Aren't," *New Yorker Magazine* (April 5, 2004), www.newyorker.com/archive/2004/04/05/040405fa_fact?currentPage=all (accessed: June 18, 2014). Anthropometric history is the study of human size as an indicator of well-being. While anthropometric measures are used to complement (and sometimes contradict) other measures of well-being, such as real GDP per capita, the primary advantage of anthropometric measures is that skeletal remains can be studied for time periods for which estimates of real GDP per capita do not exist.

[3] U.S. Census Bureau, *Historical Income Tables*, Table F-5, www.census.gov/hhes/www/income/data/historical/families/index.html (accessed: April 12, 2016). In 2014, the median family income for black families was $43,151 compared to $70,609 for white families.

[4] Thomas Piketty and Emmanuel Saez, "Income Inequality in the United States, 1913–1998." *Quarterly Journal of Economics* 118, no. 1 (February 2003), 1–39. Tables and figures updated to 2014 at Emmanuel Saez's homepage, http://elsa.berkeley.edu/~saez/ (accessed: April 13, 2016). CEO data are from Table B4. In 2006 (the most recent year available), the top 100 CEOs earned $52.4 million on average, compared to about $48,000 for the average American worker.

[5] Joseph P. Ferrie, "History Lessons: The End of American Exceptionalism? Mobility in the United States since 1850," *Journal of Economic Perspectives* 19, no. 3 (Summer 2005), 199–215.

[6] According to the Centers for Disease Control and Prevention, 35.7 percent of Americans were obese in 2012, compared to 13 percent in 1962 www.cdc.gov/obesity/data/adult.html (accessed: January 2, 2014).

[7] Tyler Cowen, *The Great Stagnation: How America Ate All the Low-Hanging Fruit of Modern History, Got Sick, and Will (Eventually) Feel Better* (New York: Dutton, 2001).

[8] Cowen, 9, 22.

[9] These lyrics come from the song "Once in a Lifetime" by The Talking Heads on their 1984 album *Remain in Light*.

[10] John Maynard Keynes, in a letter to Roy Harrod, July 4, 1938, http://economia.unipv.it/harrod/edition/editionstuff/rfh.346.htm (accessed: January 4, 2014).

[11] This quote is attributed to Albert Einstein.

[12] Dan Fuller and Doris Geide-Stevenson, "Consensus on Economic Issues: A Survey of Republicans, Democrats, and Economists," *Eastern Economic Journal* 33, no. 1 (Winter 2007), Table 1, 85.

13 "Ceteris paribus" is a Latin phrase, literally translated as "with other things the same." It is commonly translated in English as "all other things being equal."

14 In 2010, women aged 40–44 had 1.76 children, on average, if they had a B.A. degree, compared with 2.56 children, on average, if they had not completed high school. See *Current Population Survey*, "Fertility of American Women," June 2010, Table 7, www.census.gov/hhes/fertility/data/cps/2010.html (accessed: June 9, 2014).

15 Along with price-taking, the other assumptions of perfect competition include a homogeneous product, perfect information concerning prices and quantities exchanged in the market, no externalities in production and consumption, and freedom of entry and exit, implying that the factors of production are perfectly mobile in the long run. These assumptions are discussed in detail in Section 1.4 and later chapters.

16 Kurt Badenhausen, "With $300 Million Haul, Floyd Mayweather Tops Forbes' 2015 List of the World's Highest-Paid Athletes," *Forbes Magazine* (June 10, 2015), www.forbes.com/sites/kurtbadenhausen/2015/06/10/with-300-million-haul-floyd-mayweather-tops-forbes-2015-list-of-the-worlds-highest-paid-athletes/ (accessed: March 30, 2016).

17 "The 25 Highest-Earning Hedge Fund Managers and Traders," *Forbes Magazine*, www.forbes.com/sites/nathanvardi/2014/02/26/the-highest-earning-hedge-fund-managers-and-traders/ (accessed: August 13, 2014).

18 In 2014–2015, the California State University spent a little more than $3 billion on faculty salaries, retirement, and Social Security, www.calstate.edu/budget/fybudget/2014-2015/executive-summary/uses.shtml (accessed: March 3, 2016).

19 This is not to be confused with the history of economic thought. Economic history studies the development of the *economy*, while the history of economic thought examines the intellectual development of the discipline of *economics*. The history of economic thought focuses on the development of economic theories and insights by individuals throughout history, such as Adam Smith, David Ricardo, Karl Marx, John Stuart Mill, Alfred Marshall, Leon Walras, Frederick Hayek, John Maynard Keynes, and Milton Friedman.

20 "Clio" is the Greek muse of history, while "metrics" means measurement.

21 J. David Hacker, "A Census-Based Count of the Civil War Dead," *Civil War History* 57, no. 4 (December 2011), 307–348.

22 Claudia Goldin, "Exploring the 'Present through the Past': Career and Family across the Last Century," *The American Economic Review* 87, no. 2 (May 1997), 397.

23 Simon Kuznets and Richard Stone were awarded the Nobel Prize in 1971 for their pioneering work in constructing macroeconomic aggregates like GDP.

24 Timothy Hatton, Kevin H. O'Rourke, and Alan M. Taylor, *The New Comparative Economic History: Essays in Honor of Jeffrey G. Williamson* (Cambridge, MA: MIT Press, 2007), 1.

25 The full poem can be found at www.libertystatepark.com/emma.htm (accessed: January 7, 2014).

26 Kevin H. O'Rourke and Jeffrey G. Williamson, "After Columbus: Explaining the Global Trade Boom 1500–1800," *National Bureau of Economic Research Working Paper 8186* (March 2001).

27 Douglas Puffert, "Path Dependence", in Robert Whaples (ed.), *EH.Net Encyclopedia*, February 10, 2008, http://eh.net/encyclopedia/path-dependence/ (accessed: March 14, 2016).

28 For an in-depth discussion of QWERTY, see Paul A. David, "Clio and the Economics of QWERTY," *American Economic Review* 75, no. 2 (May 1985), 332–337; Paul A. David, "Path-Dependence and the Quest for Historical Economics: One More Chorus of the Ballad of QWERTY," *Oxford University Discussion Papers in Economic and Social History*, no. 20 (1997), www.nuff.ox.ac.uk/economics/history/paper20/david3.pdf (accessed: March 14, 2016); and Peter Lewin (ed.), *The Economics of QWERTY: History, Theory, Policy: Essays by Stan J. Liebowitz and Stephen E. Margolis* (New York, NY: New York University Press, 2002). Puffert (2008) provides a concise summary of many of these issues and debates.

[29] Eleanor Smith, "Life after QWERTY," *The Atlantic* (November 2013), 24, www.theatlantic.com/magazine/archive/2013/11/life-after-qwerty/309531/ (accessed: March 15, 2016).

[30] Nathan Nunn, "The Importance of History for Economic Development," *The Annual Review of Economics* 1, no. 1 (2009), 65–92.

[31] Joseph E. Stiglitz, *Rewriting the Rules of the American Economy: An Agenda for Growth and Shared Prosperity* (New York, NY: W.W. Norton & Company, 2016), 4.

2
Standards of Living and American Economic Growth

Economic growth refers to the increase in average standards of living in a country over a sustained period. It is commonly measured as the growth rate of real GDP per capita, which is the amount of production per person. Economic growth, however, is not just more of the same goods and services, but fundamentally new and different ones as well. To appreciate the benefits of economic growth, try to live for just one day by using only the goods and services that were available to Americans in 1776 (or even 1876).

This would be a day without electric lights, flush toilets, indoor plumbing, air conditioning, central heating, refrigeration, automobiles, airplanes, televisions, computers, the Internet, smartphones, vaccinations, antibiotics, or modern medical care. In fact, such a day would be nearly impossible to live because nearly everything we use now relies on inventions and innovations since 1776. For starters, you would not be able to brush your teeth or zip up your pants in the morning![1] Economic growth has also led to longer, healthier, and more educated lives, with far less drudgery and much more leisure time.

What makes the American experience unique is that the United States was able to maintain rapid growth for so long. Because of past economic growth, Americans today are able to consume a vast amount and variety of goods and services that would have been difficult to imagine in 1776. Economic growth, however, is a very recent development in human history. Before the Industrial Revolution, beginning in 1760 or so, average standards of living across the globe did not change perceptibly over the long run.[2] While wars, plagues, and other catastrophes led to transitory changes in living standards, the long-run pace of progress was extremely slow. Between the years 1 A.D. and 1700 A.D., output per person worldwide is estimated to have increased only 0.016

percent per year, less than one-hundredth the rate of economic growth that the United States has experienced over the past two hundred years.[3] At that rate, it takes over 4,300 years for output per person to double; at modern growth rates of 2 percent per year, in contrast, output per person doubles every 35 years.

Figure 2.1 illustrates the dramatic increase in the amount of goods and services produced per person worldwide, most of which has occurred in the past two hundred years.

To gain some perspective on how recent the phenomenon of economic growth is, compress all of human history into one 24-hour period. While it is difficult to determine precisely when modern humans first emerged, the fossil evidence suggests that *Homo sapiens* developed in Africa about 200,000 years ago, yet sustained economic growth did not begin until around 1800.[4] Viewing history as a single 24-hour day, the period of economic growth takes place during the last two minutes!

World averages, however, mask the dramatic differences between countries and over time. A few centuries ago, living standards in Europe differed little from those in the rest of the world. By the early nineteenth century, however, economic growth in England, in much of Western Europe, and in parts of North America, including the United States, led to ever-widening gaps in average living standards across countries. Economic historians refer to this as the "Great Divergence."[5] While economic growth eventually spread to much of the rest of the world, some countries, particularly in sub-Saharan Africa, have witnessed little increase in average living standards over the past 200 years.

Table 2.1 compares several countries to the United States in both 1870 and 2010. The main lesson from the table is that, across countries over the long run, the pace of economic growth has varied tremendously.

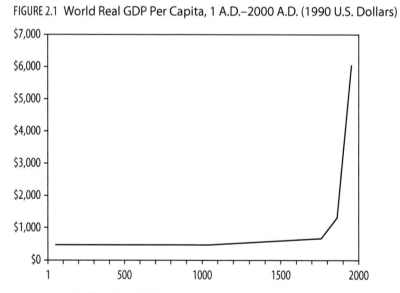

FIGURE 2.1 World Real GDP Per Capita, 1 A.D.–2000 A.D. (1990 U.S. Dollars)

Sources: Angus Maddison, *The World Economy: A Millennial Perspective* (Paris: OECD) and the Maddison Project, 2013 version, www.ggdc.net/maddison/maddison-project/home.htm (accessed: June 4, 2014).

TABLE 2.1 Relative Levels of Real GDP Per Capita, 1870 and 2010		
Country	Real GDP per Capita, relative to the United States (U.S. = 100)	
Rich countries that converged . . .	1870	2010
Canada	69	82
Norway	56	92
Rich countries that experienced "reversal of fortune" . . .		
Australia	134	84
Netherlands	113	80
Poor countries that converged . . .		
Japan	30	72
South Korea	14	71
Poor countries that diverged . . .		
Cuba	38	12
Ghana	18	6

Sources: Angus Maddison, *The World Economy: A Millennial Perspective* (Paris: OECD) and the Maddison Project, 2013 version, www.ggdc.net/maddison/maddison-project/home.htm (accessed: June 4, 2014).

Some countries, such as Australia and the Netherlands, had higher levels of real GDP per capita in 1870 than the United States (a ratio greater than 100), yet had fallen behind the U.S. by 2010 and experienced a "reversal of fortune." Some countries, such as Cuba and Ghana, were already relatively poor in 1870, and had lost further ground and diverged farther away from the U.S. by 2010.

Other countries have converged between 1870 and 2010 to U.S. levels of real GDP per capita. Countries such as Japan and South Korea have converged to U.S. levels, mostly in the post-World War II period, while the convergence of Canada and Norway, for example, has been more gradual.

The vast differences in growth experiences across countries over time, and the large consequences of economic growth for human welfare, make the study of the causes of economic growth perhaps the most important issue in economics and economic history. The purpose of this chapter is to provide a conceptual framework, and an overview of economic growth in the United States in comparative perspective, on which to build from in subsequent chapters.

2.1 MEASURING STANDARDS OF LIVING

While the phrase "standard of living" is commonly used, defining precisely what encompasses living standards is substantially more problematic. In fact, standards of living at any given time and place are so multidimensional that summarizing them with one or more aggregate measures will undoubtedly leave much out. Nevertheless, aggregate measures of average living standards provide a great deal of information. In this section, we use several common measures to examine long-run trends in average U.S. living standards.

REAL GDP PER CAPITA

There is a long history of attempts to measure national product and income in the United States. Samuel Blodgett, writing in 1806, was the first to try to estimate national income.[6] While there were several other attempts at computing aggregate product and income in the nineteenth century, it was Simon Kuznets who developed the modern U.S. system of national income and product accounts. Because of the Great Depression during the 1930s, there was much interest in determining how much production and income had fallen. The U.S. Department of Commerce commissioned Kuznets to report to Congress in 1934 regarding annual estimates of production and income for the 1929–1932 period. By 1946, Kuznets had developed estimates from 1869 to 1943.[7]

Today, the U.S. Bureau of Economic Analysis in the Department of Commerce publishes quarterly and annual estimates of gross domestic product (GDP). Official government estimates extend back to 1929, but the work of numerous economic historians, using other techniques and data, has extended annual estimates of real GDP and real GDP per capita back to 1790, with conjectural estimates available for select years beginning in 1650. The estimates before 1840, in particular, are less accurate than later estimates, and the pre-1840 period has been called a "statistical dark age."[8] Starting with the U.S. Census in 1840, there have been relatively comprehensive surveys of manufacturing and agriculture to build upon.

Nominal GDP is a measure of the value of all final goods and services newly produced in a country during a given time period. There are three equivalent ways to measure nominal GDP: the production approach, the expenditure approach, and the income approach. The *production* (or value-added) approach adds up the value added at each stage of the production process, excluding the value of intermediate goods purchased from other firms to avoid double counting the same production. The *expenditure* approach computes the amount of spending by the ultimate purchasers of output; while the *income* approach computes the incomes received by the producers of output—that is, the income received by the factors of production.

Nominal GDP increases if the prices of goods and services increase or if the quantities of goods and services produced increase. If all that happens is that goods and services get more expensive, while the quantities produced do not change, then it would be hard to argue that we are better off. In contrast, real GDP measures changes in the quantities of goods and services produced, holding prices constant. Real GDP increases if we are producing more stuff, so it is a better measure of living standards than nominal GDP.

The question, however, is which prices should be held constant when measuring the changes in quantities from one period to the next. How to combine into a single measure the relative changes in the prices and quantities of various products over time is called the index number problem, because there is simply no unique way to do this. Whichever year you used to provide the "base year" prices, you would get a different answer if you used any *other* base year, because the relative prices of goods and services change from one period to the next. One way to reduce the importance of which year you use as the base year is to use "chain-weighting." The Bureau of Economic Analysis calculates the changes in quantities produced from one period to the next, valued first in initial-year prices and then in the subsequent year's prices. Chain-weighted real GDP from one period to the next is simply the change in production using an average of the prices in the two periods.[9] Each successive pair of years is linked together, like links in a chain, to measure changes in real GDP over much longer periods.

While real GDP measures the quantities of goods and services produced in an economy, an index of living standards needs to reflect how much is available to each person in the population. One index is real GDP per capita: that is, real GDP divided by the population. This tells us how much each person's share of GDP would be if we divided the total into equal portions. To compute real GDP per capita, we take the value of all goods and services produced within a country's borders, adjust for changes in prices, and then divide by the total population.

Real GDP per capita is a commonly used measure of living standards. However, real GDP per capita does not encompass everything that determines standards of living. It has several well-known limitations. The value of most goods and services in a market economy is determined by market prices. When a slice of pizza is produced in a restaurant, its *value* is determined by the price someone is willing to pay for it. As discussed in Chapter 1, if someone is willing to pay $3 for a slice of pizza, it must be the case that the marginal benefit derived by that person from purchasing a slice of pizza must be at least $3.

There are many goods and services, however, that are not purchased and sold in markets, and that therefore do not have a market price. GDP excludes the value of almost all non-market activities, such as work that occurs in the household, leisure, and goods and services produced in the "underground economy." For example, if you stay at home to take care of your child, your care is omitted from GDP since no market exchange has taken place. If, however, you pay someone else to take care of your child, a market exchange has now occurred and there is a market price for that service. As long as that income is reported to the government (i.e., it is not part of the underground economy), it is included in GDP.

The problem of non-market production is particularly important when we try to compare real GDP per capita over long periods. Two hundred years ago, most production occurred outside the market, while a much larger fraction of production today is market production. The move from non-market to market production over time will cause real GDP growth to overestimate true changes in total production.

Another criticism of GDP is that any final good or service counts, even if it does not make us better off. For example, the costs of housing two million prisoners, crime prevention, medical expenses related to obesity, cancer treatments related to smoking, expenditures on divorce, hurricane cleanup, and commuting expenses all raise GDP, even though many of these things do not necessarily improve aggregate standards of living. Instead of spending billions to fight crime, living standards would be higher if, instead, the crime never took place. While GDP would be lower without having to produce prisons and police services, living standards would almost certainly be higher in the absence of criminal activity.

While the shift from non-market to market production and the inclusion of some goods and services that do not necessarily make us better off causes real GDP to *overestimate* changes in our living standards, the fact that GDP largely ignores quality improvement causes GDP to *underestimate* our living standards. For example, suppose that 100 million smartphones are produced one year and 100 million smartphones are produced the next year. Since the same number of phones is produced in each year, real GDP would not increase. Suppose, however, that the most recent smartphones have more memory, an improved operating system, a better camera, and a brighter screen than the smartphones produced last year. In a quality-adjusted sense, there are "more" smartphones being produced, but these quality improvements are ignored in the computation of GDP. Better smartphones may improve consumer welfare as much as, if not more than, an increase in the production of smartphones that have not improved in quality, but GDP does not reflect this.

The omission of quality differences becomes magnified over longer periods. An automobile from 2016 bears little resemblance to an automobile from 1916. The continual introduction of new and improved goods and services leads many scholars to believe that the growth of real GDP per capita underestimates the rate of change in our true living standards. Overall, arguments can be made that real GDP both overestimates and underestimates changes in production and living standards over time.

Finally, issues of poverty and economic inequality are ignored, since real GDP per capita looks at production per person. It measures the *average* slice of the economic pie, without looking at the actual size of the slice received by each person in the economy. Even given these limitations, however, it is still the most comprehensive measure of what an economy produces per person, and it is closely correlated with other available measures of living standards.

Table 2.2 provides estimates of U.S. real GDP per capita (in 2009 dollars) from 1700 to 2015. Several striking patterns emerge from this table. First, there was almost no growth in real GDP per capita during the colonial and early national periods (1700–1800). Although there was tremendous population growth, from about 235,000 in 1700 to 5.31 million in 1800, total production increased at roughly the same rate, implying that production per person (real GDP per capita) was roughly constant throughout the eighteenth century.

TABLE 2.2 Estimates of U.S. Real GDP Per Capita, 1700–2015		
Year	Real GDP per Capita (2009 dollars)	Average Annual Growth Rate Between Benchmark Years
1700	$1,441	
1800	$1,509	0.05 percent per year
1850	$2,303	0.85 percent per year
1900	$6,004	1.93 percent per year
1950	$14,398	1.76 percent per year
2000	$44,475	2.28 percent per year
2015	$50,808	0.89 percent per year
	1850–2015 average	1.89 percent per year

Sources: Estimates for 1700 from Peter C. Mancall and Thomas Weiss, "Was Economic Growth Likely in Colonial British North America?" *Journal of Economic History* 59, no. 1 (March 1999), Table 2, 26. Estimates for 1800 and after from Louis Johnston and Samuel H. Williamson, "What Was the U.S. GDP Then?" *MeasuringWorth*, www.measuringworth.org/usgdp/ (accessed: April 9, 2016).

That is, there was tremendous growth in total output (called extensive growth) during the eighteenth century, but almost no growth in output per person (called intensive growth). The complete absence of intensive economic growth, however, is somewhat of an artifact of the shock and aftermath of the Revolutionary War. Recent evidence suggests that real incomes per capita were higher in the colonies in 1774 than in England and Wales, but that the United States lost its lead by 1800.[10] That is, real GDP per capita likely increased somewhat from 1700 to 1774, but decreased so much as a result of the War that real GDP per capita in 1800 was no higher than it had been a hundred years before. However, even without the negative shock of the Revolutionary War, per capita growth in the eighteenth century was very slow.

The growth rate of real GDP per capita started to accelerate in the nineteenth century, at a rate of almost 1 percent per year between 1800 and 1850. However, between 1850 and 2015 the growth rate of real GDP per capita averaged almost 2 percent per year, leading to a doubling roughly every 35 years (see Economic History in Action 2.1).

ECONOMIC HISTORY IN ACTION 2.1

Computing Growth Rates

To compute growth rates of real GDP per capita, labor productivity, or any variable, first consider how your money might grow over time. Suppose that you deposit $100 into an investment account that has a 10 percent annual rate of return. Note that the 10 percent rate of return is the annual growth rate of your initial deposit. How much will you have in one year?

$$\$100 \cdot (1 + 0.10) = \$110$$

How much will you have in two years?

$$\$110 \cdot (1 + 0.10) = \$100 \cdot (1 + 0.10) \cdot (1 + 0.10) = \$100 \cdot (1 + 0.10)^2 = \$121$$

Note that in two years you will have $121, since in Year 2 you will be receiving interest on your original principal of $100 plus interest on the interest you received in Year 1. That is, you will receive compound interest.

We can generalize this formula to any number of time periods:

Initial level $\cdot (1 + g)^t =$ Level in t periods

This formula works for any period of time as long as g and t refer to the same units of time (i.e., if g is a yearly growth rate, then t must be the number of years; and if g is a monthly growth rate, then t must be the number of months). The growth rate, g, must also be measured in decimal form such that $g = 0.02$, for example, denotes a growth rate of 2 percent per period.

We can also write this formula using mathematical notation. Let's denote the initial level of a variable as X_0 and the level of the variable in t periods as X_t:

$$X_0 \cdot (1 + g_X)^t = X_t$$

In the example above, the growth rate was given and we solved the level of the variable in t periods. In many cases, you only know the levels of variables in two periods and need to solve for the average annual growth rates between the two points in time. We can easily rewrite the formula above to solve for the average annual growth rate, denoted g_X:

$$g_X = \left(\frac{X_t}{X_0} \right)^{1/t} - 1$$

Let us return to our initial example, and suppose that all the information we have is that your initial deposit of $100 will grow to $121 in two years' time. What will be the average annual growth rate of your investment?

$$g_X = \left(\frac{\$121}{\$100} \right)^{1/2} - 1 = 0.10 \text{ or } 10 \text{ percent per year}$$

Now consider three hypothetical economies, all of which have real GDP per capita of $3,000 in the year 1876. Suppose that between 1876 and 2016 (140 years), Country A grows at 1 percent per year, Country B grows at 2 percent per year, and Country C grows at 3 percent per year. What will be the level of real GDP per capita in each country in the year 2016?

Year	Country A (1 percent growth)	Country B (2 percent growth)	Country C (3 percent growth)
1876	$3,000	$3,000	$3,000
2016 (exact)	$3,000 \cdot (1 + 0.01)^{140}$ $= $12,081.30	$3,000 \cdot (1 + 0.02)^{140}$ $= $47,989.40	$3,000 \cdot (1 + 0.03)^{140}$ $= $188,075.71
2016 ("Rule of 70" approximation)	$12,000	$48,000	$192,000

As is evident from the table above, small differences in growth rates, compounded over a period of more than a century, can have dramatic differences in average standards of living. Country A, which roughly corresponds to the growth experience of Uruguay, quadrupled the level of real GDP in 140 years. In contrast, Country B's real GDP per capita, which resembles the growth experience of the United States, increased almost 16-fold from 1876 to 2016. Country C, an imaginary economy that has never existed in reality, had an average growth rate of 3 percent per year, roughly just 1 percentage point higher than the United States, yet it witnessed a nearly 64-fold increase in real GDP per capita!

One easy way to estimate the miracle of compounding is to use the "Rule of 70." This rule tells you approximately how long it takes something to double. If you take 70 and divide it by the growth rate (in percent), this gives you the years to doubling. For example, if real GDP per capita grows at 2 percent per year, then the level of real GDP per capita doubles every 35 years (70/2). If real GDP per capita grows at only 1 percent per year, then it doubles every 70 years (70/1). For Country A, which grows at 1 percent per year, it doubles every 70 years, so that there are two doublings in 140 years (from 1876 to 2016). One doubling is from $3,000 to $6,000, and the second doubling is from $6,000 to $12,000, as shown in the table.

BIOLOGICAL MEASURES OF LIVING STANDARDS

While real GDP per capita in the United States has increased spectacularly since 1800, biological measures of living standards did not increase for several decades or more after real GDP per capita started to grow.

Anthropometric history focuses on human heights as a measure of average standards of living.[11] Average heights within a population largely reflect average nutrition and the disease environment. A closely related measure is average life expectancy at birth. Increases in heights and life expectancy reflect better nutrition and a reduced prevalence of diseases in the population. Poor diets and diseases during childhood mean that individuals will not be as tall in adulthood, and also that fewer children will survive to adulthood, which lowers average life expectancy.

As is evident from Figures 2.2 and 2.3, for many decades in the early stages of economic growth in the United States, heights and life expectancies both *fell*. Rapid industrialization, urbanization, and transportation improvements led to increased inequality, deprivation, disease, and mortality, even as average incomes were rising. Evidence suggests that the average American's diet deteriorated in the decades after 1830 as transportation improvements led to the nationalization (and internationalization) of the disease environment. Cities in the mid-nineteenth century were far less healthy places than the rural farms of the colonial period. Diseases spread

FIGURE 2.2 Average Height of Native-Born American Males by Year of Birth, 1710–1990

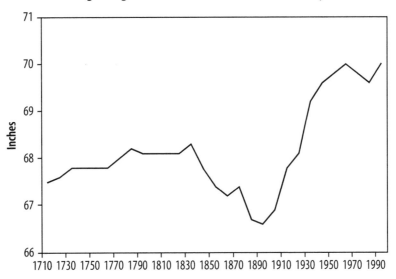

Sources: 1710–1970: Richard H. Steckel, "Selected Anthropometric Measurements—Height, Weight, and Body Mass Index, 1710–1989," in Susan B. Carter, Scott Sigmund Gartner, Michael R. Haines, Alan L. Olmstead, Richard Sutch, and Gavin Wright (eds.), *Historical Statistics of the United States, Earliest Times to the Present: Millennial Edition* (New York, NY: Cambridge University Press, 2006), Table Bd653-687. 1980 and 1990: U.S. Department of Health and Human Services, Centers for Disease Control and Prevention, "Anthropometric Reference Data for Children and Adults, 2007–2010: United States," *Vital and Health Statistics* 11, no. 252 (October 2012), Tables 8 and 9.

FIGURE 2.3 Life Expectancy at Birth, 1850–2010

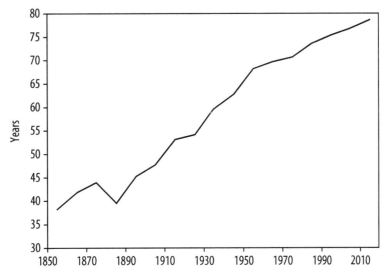

Sources: 1850–1930 from Michael R. Haines, "Expectation of Life at Birth, by Sex and Race, 1850–1998," in Susan B. Carter et al. (eds.), *Historical Statistics of the United States, Earliest Times to the Present: Millennial Edition*, (New York, NY: Cambridge University Press, 2006), Table Ab644-655. 1940–2010 from Sherry L. Murphy, Jiaquan Xu, and Kenneth D. Kochanek, "Deaths: Final Data for 2010," *National Vital Statistics Reports* 61, no. 4 (2013), Table 8, 31, www.cdc.gov/nchs/data/nvsr/nvsr61/nvsr61_04.pdf (accessed: June 8, 2014).

far more easily in cities, which did not have sewage systems and clean water, and where fresh and healthy food was much harder to find.

By the end of the nineteenth century, the introduction of refrigeration led to better nutrition. With the spread of public sanitation, municipal water and sewage systems, indoor plumbing, and the discovery that germs caused diseases, life expectancies and heights started a long upward increase.

During the first half of the twentieth century, there were dramatic increases in real GDP per capita and in health. Life expectancies increased from 49.6 years of age in 1900 to 69.1 years of age by 1950. This was not primarily due to advances in medical technology, but rather to the continuing improvements in urban sanitation, municipal water supplies, indoor plumbing, and a better understanding of germ theory and the causes of communicative diseases.[12] Since 1950, life expectancies have continued to increase, but at a slower rate. Improved medical care has played a larger role in the postwar period. By 2015, life expectancy at birth was almost 79 years of age.

WORK AND LEISURE

Along with dramatic increases in real GDP per capita over the long run, there have also been huge increases in the amount of leisure time and vast improvements in the nature of work. In mid-nineteenth-century America, the typical person started work at the age of 13 and "retirement" as a lifestyle was extremely rare. Estimated lifetime leisure hours have increased from 43,800 in 1880 to 176,100 by 1995, an increase of over 300 percent.[13] In 1830, the typical worker was on the job for almost 70 hours a week. By 1950, the 40-hour workweek had become the norm.

Work was not only longer in the past, but also more physically demanding and more dangerous. Workplace accidents decreased tremendously across the twentieth century, and the rise of white-collar jobs has meant that the physical demands of work have decreased substantially. In 1800, 75 percent of working Americans endured hard work and long hours as farm workers. In 2015, barely more than 1 percent of the workforce was employed in agriculture.

HAPPINESS AND SUBJECTIVE WELL-BEING

Recent research also shows that subjective well-being rises with real GDP per capita, whether looking across countries at a given point in time, or within a given country over time. The United States since 1972, however, has been "a paradoxical counter-example" to this general pattern.[14] Even though real GDP per capita in the United States has more than doubled since 1972, subjective well-being, as measured by the General Social Survey, has *decreased* slightly. While there is no definitive agreement as to why Americans have become less satisfied with their lives over the past 40 years, many scholars have pointed to the dramatic rise in income inequality in the United States, an increase that has been much more pronounced than in Europe or in other parts of the world.[15]

2.2   THE IMPORTANCE OF LABOR PRODUCTIVITY

What factors can account for differences in the growth rate of real GDP per capita over time? In the long run, the growth of real GDP per capita depends crucially on the growth of labor productivity. Labor productivity is defined as the amount of real GDP produced per hour of work. To understand the relationship between real GDP per capita and labor productivity, it is useful to express real GDP per capita as the product of three terms: the level of labor productivity, the average number of hours worked per worker, and the share of the population working. The relationship between these variables is shown below:

$$\underbrace{\left(\frac{\text{real GDP}}{\text{population}} \right)}_{\substack{\text{real GDP} \\ \text{per capita}}} = \underbrace{\left(\frac{\text{real GDP}}{\text{worker hours}} \right)}_{\substack{\text{labor} \\ \text{productivity}}} \cdot \underbrace{\left(\frac{\text{worker hours}}{\#\,\text{of workers}} \right)}_{\substack{\text{worker hours} \\ \text{per worker}}} \cdot \underbrace{\left(\frac{\#\,\text{of workers}}{\text{population}} \right)}_{\substack{\text{employment-to-} \\ \text{population ratio}}}$$

This expression tells us that real GDP per capita can grow only to the extent that there is growth in labor productivity, growth in the number of hours worked per worker, and/or growth in the fraction of the population working. Average hours of work per worker have decreased substantially during the past 180 years, which by itself would have caused real GDP per capita to fall. In the post-World War II period, the employment-to-population ratio did increase for a few decades as women entered the labor force in large numbers, but this was a one-time phenomenon: now that labor-force participation rates of women have almost converged to those of men, we cannot expect the employment-to-population ratio to increase again.

In the long run, then, increases in real GDP per capita arise largely from increases in labor productivity. Throughout American history, the primary source of increases in real GDP per capita has been labor productivity growth.

2.3 GROWTH ACCOUNTING AND THE PROXIMATE CAUSES OF GROWTH

To help determine the reasons for labor productivity growth, in 1957 Robert Solow developed a method called growth accounting.[16] Before Solow, the predominant view was that the accumulation of physical capital was the primary cause of economic growth. The work of Solow and others changed this view and showed that technological change was the engine of growth. In order to understand Solow's contributions, first we need to examine how goods and services are produced.

PRODUCTION FUNCTIONS AND THE FACTORS OF PRODUCTION

Economists often envision the economy as a machine that transforms inputs (the factors of production) into output (real GDP) and they use an aggregate production function to show this. One factor of production is workers or labor hours. To make things more concrete, let labor (L) represent the aggregate number of hours worked per year by all workers in producing final goods and services (real GDP denoted by Y).

In any economy, however, more goes into the production of goods and services than just labor. Workers use other factors of production as well. One such factor is physical capital (K), which is the objects or tools that we use to produce final goods and services. K includes the machines that workers use, such as hammers and computers, as well as the buildings where people work, and also the infrastructure, such as roads and the vehicles used to transport goods and services.

While L is "raw" unskilled labor, workers also differ in terms of their health, knowledge, skills, and training. Human capital (H) is the term economists use to describe the aggregate level of health, knowledge, skills, and experience that workers acquire through nutrition, education, and on-the-job training.

The final factor of production is natural capital or natural resources (N). Natural capital is what nature has provided: it includes land, climate, rivers, soil, and subsurface mineral deposits. A country's natural capital can increase through conquest or purchase. The available amount of natural capital can also increase as more of it is discovered, and as inventors and entrepreneurs discover new ways to use it. Like the supply of other things, the supply curve for natural capital is upward sloping. As the price of natural capital increases, producers have incentives to find more of it and to develop new ways to harness what nature has provided. For example, while the Sun has existed far longer than there has been life on Earth, the ability to effectively harness solar power is a relatively recent phenomenon.

An aggregate production function provides a quantitative link between the factors of production (the inputs) and the final output (real GDP). We will rely on one particular form of a production function, called the Cobb-Douglas production function, which was developed and tested by Charles Cobb and Paul Douglas prior to World War II.[17] Robert Solow used this function because it has several properties that fit the U.S. experience. At any time t, the function links the levels of the factors of production to the amount of real GDP:

$$Y_t = A_t K_t^a H_t^b N_t^c L_t^d$$

In the equation above, Y_t stands for real GDP, while K_t, H_t, N_t, and L_t represent the four factors of production: physical capital, human capital, natural capital, and labor, respectively. A_t, called total factor productivity (TFP), measures the productivity of the factors of production in creating real GDP.

The exponents, a, b, c, and d, represent elasticities. An elasticity is a coefficient that measures the percentage change in one variable that will occur if there is a 1 percentage change in another variable, ceteris paribus. For example, if $a = 1/3$, then a 1 percentage point change in physical capital, all else being equal, leads to a one-third of 1 percentage point change in real GDP. If markets are perfectly competitive, then the exponents also represent the share of GDP paid to each factor of production. If $a = 1/3$, this means that owners of physical capital are paid 1/3 of GDP.[18]

This Cobb-Douglas production function has the property of constant returns to scale (CRTS), since the coefficients on physical capital, human capital, natural capital, and labor hours sum to one. The exponent on labor hours can therefore be written as $1 - a - b - c$. With CRTS, if the quantities of physical capital, human capital, natural capital, and labor all double, while holding total factor productivity constant, then real GDP will double as well. This is based on the notion of replication. That is, suppose that we created an exact replica of the United States, with the same physical, human, and natural capital, along with the same population. We would now have twice the factors of production. It is reasonable to conclude that we would be able to produce twice the goods and services as well.

The A_t in the production function is an index of productive efficiency called total factor productivity (TFP). If we rewrite the production function to solve for A_t, we see that it is simply the ratio of real GDP to a weighted geometric average of the factors of production:[19]

$$A_t = \frac{Y_t}{K_t^a H_t^b N_t^c L_t^{1-a-b-c}}$$

TFP increases whenever real GDP (Y_t) increases more than the weighted average of the inputs, which implies that all of the inputs (the total inputs) are more productive.

ECONOMIC HISTORY IN ACTION 2.2

Growth Rate Rules and Growth Accounting

Any function, such as a Cobb-Douglas production function, can be transformed from levels to growth rates by using three useful rules for computing the growth rates of products, ratios, and exponents. Consider the levels of three variables, denoted as X_t, Y_t, and Z_t. The three rules are:

1. If $X_t = Y_t \cdot Z_t$, then $g_X \approx g_Y + g_Z$
2. If $X_t = Y_t \div Z_t$, then $g_X \approx g_Y - g_Z$
3. If $X_t = Y_t^a$, then $g_X \approx a g_Y$

Although these rules are approximations, we will assume that they hold exactly. For small growth rates, these three approximations are almost exact.[20]

In Section 2.3, the Cobb-Douglas production function with constant returns to scale was introduced:

$$Y_t = A_t K_t^a H_t^b N_t^c L_t^{1-a-b-c}$$

Applying growth rate rules (1) and (3) from above, we can write the Cobb-Douglas production function in terms of growth rates, where g_Y is the growth rate of real GDP, etc.

$$g_Y = g_A + a g_K + b g_H + c g_N + (1 - a - b - c) g_L$$

By distributing and rearranging, this can be written as:

$$g_Y - g_L = g_A + a(g_K - g_L) + b(g_H - g_L) + c(g_N - g_L)$$

The equation above is the growth accounting formula used in Table 2.3. The left-hand side of the equation is the growth rate of labor productivity. The equation says that labor productivity growth depends on the growth of total factor productivity, the growth rate of physical capital per hour of work multiplied by physical capital's share of income, the growth rate of human capital per hour of work multiplied by human capital's share of income, and the growth rate of natural capital per hour of work multiplied by natural capital's share of income.

GROWTH ACCOUNTING

The Cobb-Douglas production function above represents the relationship between the levels of the factors of production and the level of total factor productivity to the level of real GDP at a given point in time. When studying economic growth, however, we are interested in the growth rates of these variables over time. Using the growth rate rules described in Economic History in Action 2.2, the Cobb-Douglas production function can be written in terms of growth rates. The growth rate of labor productivity (the left-hand side of the equation below) is explained by the growth rate of total factor productivity and the weighted shares of the growth rates of the factors of production per hour of work:

$$g_Y - g_L = g_A + a(g_K - g_L) + b(g_H - g_L) + c(g_N - g_L)$$

The growth rate of total factor productivity cannot be estimated directly, but it is the residual or unexplained part after everything else has been accounted for. The growth rate of total factor productivity (g_A) captures anything that causes labor productivity to increase, except increases in the factors of production. It generally measures the growth rate of technological progress and productivity-enhancing institutional and organizational changes.

Since Solow, scholars have extended growth accounting farther back into American history. Table 2.3 estimates the relative determinants of labor productivity growth in the United States since 1800. There are several notable features illustrated in Table 2.3. First, as Solow first discovered, more than half of the increase in labor productivity growth throughout American history is the result of increased total factor productivity growth. From 1800 to 2011, labor productivity grew at an average annual rate of 1.44 percent per year, with total factor productivity growth accounting for almost 60 percent of this increase (0.85 percent / 1.44 percent = 0.59).

TABLE 2.3 Growth Accounting in the United States, 1800–2011 (Average Annual Percentage Changes)

Period	Labor Productivity Growth $g_Y - g_L$	Total Factor Productivity Growth g_A	Physical Capital Growth $a(g_K - g_L)$	Human Capital Growth $b(g_H - g_L)$	Natural Capital Growth $c(g_N - g_L)$
1800–1855	0.4	0.3	0.2	0.0	−0.1
1855–1890	1.1	0.5	0.7	0.0	−0.1
1890–1905	1.9	1.3	0.5	0.1	−0.0
1905–1927	2.0	1.3	0.5	0.2	−0.0
1929–1948	2.0	1.5	0.1	0.4	−0.0
1948–1966	3.1	1.9	0.8	0.4	−0.0
1966–1989	1.2	0.3	0.6	0.3	−0.0
1989–2011	1.8	1.1	0.6	0.1	−0.0
1800–2011	1.44	0.85	0.49	0.14	−0.04

Sources: 1800–1989 figures from Nicholas Crafts, "Solow and Growth Accounting: A Perspective from Quantitative Economic History," Annual Supplement to History of Political Economy (2009), Table 3. These figures are augmented with natural capital growth rates and factor shares from Abramowitz and David (1973 and 2001), to include the relative importance of natural capital. 1989–2011 figures computed from Robert C. Feenstra, Robert Inklaar, and Marcel P. Timmer, "The Next Generation of the Penn World Table" (2013), www.ggdc.net/pwt (accessed: January 16, 2014). For the period 1989–2011, the factor shares used are: $a = 0.35$, and $b = 0.315$, and $c = 0.02$.

It is also evident from Table 2.3 that the growth rates of labor productivity and total factor productivity have varied considerably over time. The period from 1890 to 1966 stands out as the "Golden Age" of labor productivity and total factor productivity growth, with labor productivity growth averaging more than 2 percent per year, and with nearly 70 percent of this growth the result of increases in total factor productivity. A wave of inventions beginning in the 1870s, which included electricity, the internal combustion engine and the automobile, and advances in chemicals and telecommunications, fueled higher rates of total factor productivity growth, which powered the American economy through the 1960s.[21]

The impact of both technological and organizational changes during this period is illustrated in Figure 2.4, which shows the introduction of the assembly line (an organizational change) to produce automobiles (a relatively new invention) at the Ford Motor Company.

Physical capital accumulation per hour of work (or capital deepening) is the second most important determinant of labor productivity growth, contributing about one-third

FIGURE 2.4 The Assembly Line at the Ford Motor Company, 1913

Source: Library of Congress, www.loc.gov/pictures/item/2011661021/ (accessed: April 23, 2016).

of labor productivity growth over the very long run (0.49 percent / 1.44 percent = 0.34). Be careful, however, not to necessarily assume that growth accounting must be causal. For example, some scholars argue that capital accumulation, as an independent source of growth, is less important than growth accounting suggests. For example, in the neoclassical or Solow growth model, which is covered in many intermediate macroeconomics classes, total factor productivity growth causes real GDP to increase. As real GDP rises, so too does the amount of saving in an economy, if individuals save a constant fraction of their incomes. The higher saving leads to higher investment and more physical capital. That is, technological change impacts real GDP directly, but may also impact it indirectly by encouraging capital accumulation. Therefore, technological change, measured as total factor productivity growth, may be the true cause of physical capital accumulation. While we will examine the possibility of these complex interrelationships in later chapters, growth accounting provides an initial starting point and a conceptual framework to help examine these more complex interrelationships.

Another notable feature of Table 2.3 is that the increase in human capital per worker hour did not substantially affect labor productivity growth prior to the dawn of the twentieth century. In 1910, only 9 percent of eighteen-year-olds graduated from high school, but by 1940, the majority of students graduated from high school. Education continued to expand after World War II with the rapid increase of higher education, although the rate of expansion has slowed in recent decades.

Finally, the direct impact of natural capital per hour of work on labor productivity has been relatively unimportant. Consider, for example, the period from 1800 to 1855. Natural capital's share of GDP was approximately 10 percent ($c = 0.10$) during this period.[22] Although the land mass of the United States increased rapidly, population growth was even more rapid, resulting in natural capital per worker hour decreasing by approximately 1 percent per year. Therefore, $c(g_N - g_L) \approx 0.10(0.02 - 0.03) = -0.001$ or -0.1 percent. While the direct impact of natural capital is unlikely to have been large, geography and climate may have indirectly influenced U.S. economic growth in many ways not captured by these simple growth accounting exercises (see Section 2.4 and Chapter 6).

2.4 FUNDAMENTAL SOURCES OF GROWTH

Growth accounting helps us to determine the immediate or proximate sources of economic growth. The growth of labor productivity (and real GDP per capita) will be faster if there is faster growth in the factors of production per hour of work and/or if total factor productivity growth increases due to technological, organizational, or institutional changes.

Factor accumulation, through savings and investment, and total factor productivity growth, through technological and organizational changes, do not occur by accident, however: they take place because of deliberate decisions by individuals through markets and governments. The fundamental causes of growth are the underlying reasons that determine what causes growth in the factors of production and total factor productivity growth. There are several theories regarding the potential fundamental sources of growth. In this section, the main theories are briefly introduced. In later chapters, these theories will be discussed in detail by carefully examining the historical experience of the United States.

Figure 2.5 provides a schematic diagram to help conceptualize the proximate and fundamental sources of growth. Section 2.2 showed that the primary reason for growth in real GDP per capita is growth in labor productivity. Section 2.3 introduced growth accounting to determine the relative importance of factor accumulation and total factor productivity, due primarily to technology, in influencing labor productivity growth. This section introduces the possible fundamental causes for factor accumulation and total factor productivity growth.

The four main theories of fundamental causes emphasize: (1) institutions, (2) science and culture, (3) geography, and (4) market growth.[23] These theories are not mutually exclusive and all have insights into the growth process. Scholars are often at odds, however, in assessing the relative importance of each of these fundamental causes of growth.

INSTITUTIONS

The institutional environment of a country is "the set of fundamental political, social, and legal ground rules that establish the basis for production, exchange, and distribution. Rules governing elections, property rights, and the right of contract are examples of the type of ground rules that make up the economic environment."[24] These rules, together with their enforcement characteristics, constrain human behavior and structure incentives within an economy. The U.S. Constitution, along with the Bill of Rights and later Amendments, defines the rights and obligations of both individuals and

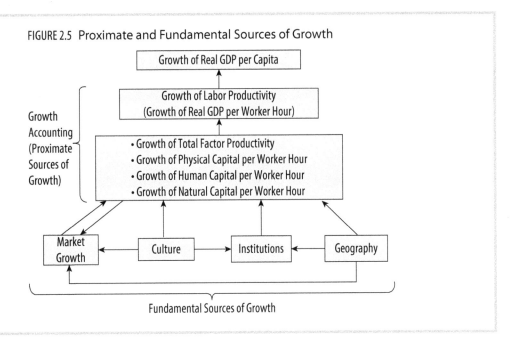

FIGURE 2.5 Proximate and Fundamental Sources of Growth

governments. This document and countless other rules interact to provide incentives that have generally been conducive to economic growth.

SCIENCE AND CULTURE

Institutions are influenced by both cultural and geographical factors. Culture refers to the behaviors, attitudes, and beliefs that are pervasive in a particular society. The Enlightenment or Age of Reason in late-seventeenth-century and eighteenth-century Europe emphasized the importance of reason, individualism, and the advance of knowledge through the scientific method, and its influence is apparent in the U.S. Constitution and the Bill of Rights. Culture can also influence economic growth directly. For example, a widespread belief in individualism and hard work can lead to factor accumulation and new inventions.

GEOGRAPHY

Geography, broadly interpreted to include the climate, navigable rivers and harbors, minerals and fuels, soil types, and the disease environment can also have important direct and indirect implications for growth. It has long been noted that economic growth is faster in temperate climate zones than in the tropics. High heat and humidity both sap human energy and provide the conditions for diseases like malaria, which can directly affect growth.

Geographical factors have likely influenced economic growth indirectly by affecting the institutional development of the United States. Because of the ease of growing crops like corn and wheat on small family farms in the northern U.S., there was widespread land ownership, and this in turn led to institutions that protected private property, and led to widespread voting and early public investment in education. During early settlement, the disease environment influenced where Europeans settled in large numbers and also where slavery developed. In temperate climates with better health conditions, Europeans settled in larger numbers and established institutions that protected individual rights, including property rights, and that limited the power of government.[25]

MARKET GROWTH

As transportation costs fell and communication became more rapid and more widespread, the scope of markets expanded, lowering the costs of goods to consumers and leading to greater division of labor, specialization, and exchange. An abundance of fertile land, as well as gold and silver deposits, contributed to westward expansion and fast population growth both through high rates of natural increase and through immigration. Population growth, along with improvements in transportation and communication, from the railroad and the telegraph to the computer and the Internet, have increased the scale and scope of the market economy and accelerated the rate of technological progress and economic growth.

2.5 CONCLUSIONS

Although money does not buy happiness, economic growth has provided Americans with virtually unlimited food at prices most can afford, an average thirty-year increase in life expectancy since 1900, instantaneous global communication, same-day travel throughout the country, home ownership for the majority, and a vast array of goods and services that our ancestors would have had difficulty comprehending.

Future growth, however, is not guaranteed. In addition, growth can have harmful side effects such as global climate change, so future growth could also lead to further harm. This chapter is the first of several that will examine the history, likely causes, and the future prospects for economic growth in the United States.

QUESTIONS

1. Since the end of the Civil War, real GDP per capita in the United States has grown at roughly 2 percent per year. Some scholars argue that the true standard of living for Americans has increased faster than 2 percent per year, while others believe that standards of living have increased more slowly than 2 percent per year. What types of arguments are used to justify a higher or lower rate in the increase in the standard of living than that indicated by real GDP per capita? Where do you stand on this issue, and why?

2. For simplicity, consider the following production functions, which only include labor hours (L_t) and the quantity of physical capital (K_t) as the factors of production. In each case, determine and explain whether each of the production functions shows decreasing returns to scale, constant returns to scale, or increasing returns to scale. Also, determine and explain whether there is diminishing marginal product, constant marginal product, or increasing marginal product in each factor of production.

   A. $Y_t = K_t + L_t$

   B. $Y_t = K_t L_t$

   C. $Y_t = K_t^{1/3} L_t^{1/2}$

3. Suppose that you deposit $20,000 into a mutual fund on your 20th birthday. Assume that this mutual fund grows at an average annual rate of 7 percent per year. If you never make any additional deposits, approximately how much money will be in the mutual fund on your 70th birthday?

4. Suppose that an economy is described by the following production function:

$$Y_t = A_t K_t^a H_t^b N_t^c L_t^{1-a-b-c}$$

Y_t is real GDP, K_t is the physical capital stock, H_t measures the stock of human capital (the quantity of worker skills, experience, and health), N_t is the stock of natural capital (which consists of land and natural resources), and L_t is the number of worker hours, all at time t. The exponents a, b, c, and $1-a-b-c$ measure both elasticities and factor shares.

Suppose that the stock of land and natural resources is constant. Also, suppose that real GDP and the capital stock are both growing at 4 percent per year and that worker hours and population are growing at 1 percent per year. Also assume that human capital grows at 1 percent per year. Suppose further that the production function exhibits constant returns to scale with $a = b = c = 1/4$.

A. What is the annual growth rate of labor productivity?

B. What *proportion* of labor productivity growth is due to the growth of efficiency (the growth of total factor productivity)?

C. [Challenging] Suppose that in Year 0 the production function above has the following values of capital, human capital, natural capital, and labor:

$K_0 = 625$

$H_0 = 16$

$N_0 = 256$

$L_0 = 16$

Also, assume that the level of total factor productivity in Year 0 is 1 ($A_0 = 1$). What is the real interest rate (r) in this economy in Year 0, where $r = 0.04$, for example, is an interest rate of 4 percent? *Hint:* Use the constant factor share property of a Cobb-Douglas production function.

5. This chapter makes a distinction between proximate and fundamental sources of economic growth. Explain in intuitive terms, as if to someone who is unfamiliar with these concepts, what is meant by "proximate sources" and "fundamental sources".

NOTES

[1] For a history of the modern toothbrush, see the Library of Congress, www.loc.gov/rr/scitech/mysteries/tooth.html (accessed: May 28, 2014). Mass production of toothbrushes in America started in 1885, and Dupont de Nemours did not introduce the modern nylon toothbrush until 1938, calling it "Doctor West's Miracle Toothbrush". For a history of the zipper, see Robert D. Friedel, *Zipper: An Exploration in Novelty* (New York, NY: W.W. Norton & Co., 1994). A clasp locker, a precursor to the modern zipper, made its debut at the 1893 Chicago World's Fair, but it was not until 1917 that Gideon Sundback patented the zipper with which we are familiar today.

[2] Gregory Clark, *A Farewell to Alms: A Brief Economic History of the World* (Princeton, NJ: Princeton University Press, 2007). Although Clark notes that 1760 is commonly given as the start of the Industrial Revolution, he writes that "the conventional picture of the Industrial Revolution as a sudden fissure in economic life is not sustainable. … Arguments can be made for 1600, for 1800, or even for 1860 as the true break between the Malthusian and modern economies," 9.

[3] Angus Maddison, "Historical Statistics on the World Economy, 1–2008 A.D.," www.ggdc.net/maddison/oriindex.htm (accessed: June 4, 2014). World real GDP per capita was $615 in 1700 compared to $467 in 1 A.D. The average annual growth rate is

$$g = \left(\frac{\$615}{\$467} \right)^{1/1,699} - 1 \approx 0.000162 \text{ or } 0.016 \text{ percent per year.}$$

[4] Ian McDougall, Francis H. Brown, and John G. Fleagle, "Stratigraphic Placement and Age of Modern Humans from Kibish, Ethiopia," *Nature* 433 (February 2005), 733–736.

[5] Kenneth Pomeranz, *The Great Divergence: China, Europe, and the Making of the Modern World Economy* (Princeton, NJ: Princeton University Press, 2000).

[6] Samuel Blodget, *Economica: A Statistical Manual for the United States of America* (reprinted Augustus M. Kelley, 1964).

[7] Simon Kuznets, *National Product since 1869* (National Bureau of Economic Research, 1946).

[8] Paul David, "New Light on a Statistical Dark Age: U.S. Real Product Growth before 1840," *American Economic Review* 57, no. 2 (May 1967), 294–306.

[9] See Charles I. Jones, "Using Chain-Weighted NIPA Data," *Economic Letter* 2002–22, Federal Reserve Bank of San Francisco, www.frbsf.org/economic-research/publications/economic-letter/2002/august/using-chain-weighted-nipa-data/ (accessed: June 8, 2014).

[10] Peter H. Lindert and Jeffrey G. Williamson, "American Incomes Before and After the Revolution," *Journal of Economic History* 73, no. 3 (September 2013), 725–765.

[11] John Komlos, *Nutrition and Economic Development in the Eighteenth-Century Habsburg Monarchy: An Anthropometric History* (Princeton, NJ: Princeton University Press, 1989).

[12] Richard H. Steckel, "Biological Measures of the Standard of Living," *Journal of Economic Perspectives* 22, no. 1 (March 2008), 129–152.

[13] Robert Fogel, *The Fourth Great Awakening and the Future of Egalitarianism* (Chicago, IL: University of Chicago Press, 2000).

[14] Richard Easterlin, "Does Economic Growth Improve the Human Lot? Some Empirical Evidence," in Paul A. David and Melvin W. Reder (eds.), *Nations and Households in Economic Growth: Essays in Honor of Moses Abramowitz* (New York, NY: Academic Press, 1974), suggested that there was no relationship between the level of real GDP per capita in a country and the average level of happiness, a suggestion that was subsequently termed the "Easterlin Paradox." Daniel W. Sacks, Betsey Stevenson, and Justin Wolfers, "The New Stylized Facts about Income and Subjective Well-Being," *IZA Discussion Paper No. 7105* (December 2012), showed that as better data for more countries over longer time periods have become available, there no longer appears to be an "Easterlin Paradox."

[15] Sacks, Stevenson, and Wolfers, 10.

[16] Robert M. Solow, "Technical Change and the Aggregate Production Function," *Review of Economics and Statistics* 39, no. 3 (August 1957), 312–320.

[17] Paul H. Douglas, "The Cobb-Douglas Production Function Once Again: Its History, Its Testing, and Some New Empirical Values," *Journal of Political Economy* 84, no. 5 (October 1976), 903–916.

[18] With perfectly competitive factor markets, each factor is paid its marginal product. To continue with the example of physical capital, the marginal product of capital (*MPK*) is equal to the real rental price of capital or real interest rate (*r*). Capital's share of GDP is equal to *a*. Mathematically:

$$\frac{rK_t}{Y_t} = a = \frac{MPK \cdot K_t}{Y_t}$$

To prove this, take the partial derivative of the production function with respect to capital, and put it into the equation above. You will notice that everything cancels out except a.

[19] Everyone is familiar with arithmetic averages. For example, suppose that a student has scores of 80, 90, and 100 on three exams. The (arithmetic) average exam score for this student is:

$$\text{arithmetic average} = \frac{80 + 90 + 100}{3} = 90$$

The denominator in the TFP equation is also an average, but it is a *geometric* average. In most instances, an arithmetic average and a geometric average have very similar answers. Consider the three exam scores again. The geometric average is:

$$\text{geometric average} = \sqrt[3]{80 \cdot 90 \cdot 100} = 80^{1/3} \cdot 90^{1/3} \cdot 100^{1/3} \approx 89.628$$

Therefore, total factor productivity is total output (real GDP) divided by a weighted geometric average of the inputs or factors of production.

[20] Consider, for example, Rule 1 for products: If $X_t = Y_t \cdot Z_t$, then $g_X = g_Y + g_Z$. Note that if this relationship holds in levels in time t, it also holds in levels in time $t+1$, therefore:

$$\frac{X_{t+1}}{X_t} = \frac{Y_{t+1}}{Y_t} \cdot \frac{Z_{t+1}}{Z_t}$$

Note that the one-period percentage change in X or one-period growth rate is:

$$g_X = \frac{X_{t+1} - X_t}{X_t} = \frac{X_{t+1}}{X_t} - \frac{X_t}{X_t} = \frac{X_{t+1}}{X_t} - 1$$

If we add 1 to both sides of the expression above, we get:

$$1 + g_X = \frac{X_{t+1}}{X_t}$$

There are, of course, analogous expressions for Y and Z. If we replace these in the top equation above, we get:

$$1 + g_X = (1 + g_Y)(1 + g_Z)$$

Multiplying out the right-hand side yields:

$$1 + g_X = 1 + g_Z + g_Y + g_Y g_Z$$

Subtracting 1 from both sides and rearranging:

$$g_X = g_Y + g_Z + g_Y g_Z$$

This is the exact relationship. However, for small growth rates, the last term in the expression above is very close to zero, and we can ignore it. Suppose that the growth rate of Y is 2 percent per year and the growth rate of Z is 1 percent per year, then:

$$g_X = 0.02 + 0.01 + (0.02 \cdot 0.01) = 0.0302 \approx 0.03$$

[21] Robert J. Gordon, *The Rise and Fall of American Growth: The U.S. Standard of Living since the Civil War* (Princeton, NJ: Princeton University Press, 2016).

[22] Moses Abramovitz and Paul A. David, "Reinterpreting Economic Growth: Parables and Realities," *American Economic Review* 63, no. 2 (May 1973), Table 2, 431.

[23] Daron Acemoglu, *Introduction to Modern Economic Growth* (Princeton, NJ: Princeton University Press, 2009). Along with the geography, culture, and institutions hypothesis, Acemoglu (in Chapter 4) also discusses "luck" and multiple equilibrium as another

potential fundamental cause. Although fortuitous circumstances undoubtedly influenced economic growth in the United States, the multiple-equilibria models that Acemoglu emphasizes are difficult to interpret in a historical context. The fourth fundamental cause, market growth, is mentioned, but quickly dismissed, by Acemoglu. Charles I. Jones and Paul Romer, for example, stress the importance of growth in population, and thus growth in the size of the market, as an important fundamental cause. See Charles I. Jones and Paul Romer, "The New Kaldor Facts: Ideas, Institutions, Population, and Human Capital," *American Economic Journal: Macroeconomics* 2, no. 1 (January 2010), 224–245.

[24] Lance C. Davis and Douglas C. North, *Institutional Change and American Economic Growth* (New York, NY: Cambridge University Press, 1971), 6.

[25] Ross Levine, "Law, Endowments and Property Rights," *Journal of Economic Perspectives* 19, no. 3 (Fall 2005), 61–88.

3

European Settlement and the Columbian Exchange

The "Columbian Exchange" refers to the widespread exchange of diseases, plants, food crops, animals, ideas, culture, and human populations between the Old World (Eurasia and Africa) and the New World (Americas) following the voyage to the Americas by Christopher Columbus in 1492.[1] This was an unprecedented event in human history, which had profound ramifications throughout the world. This chapter examines how this exchange helped create the foundations for the United States' economy and sowed the seeds for future economic growth and development.

In economics, "exchange" usually refers to voluntary and mutually beneficial exchange, so the Columbian Exchange is somewhat of a misnomer since it was decidedly one-sided. European populations in the Americas and Europe expanded dramatically due to new crops, while indigenous populations and societies in the Americas collapsed because of the onslaught of devastating European diseases and weapons. In 1500, the European share of the world population was 11 percent, while the indigenous populations in the Americas represented 7 percent of the world total. By 1800, however, the European share of the world population had almost doubled to 20 percent, while the indigenous populations in the Americas had plummeted to less than 1 percent.[2] Populations in Africa grew as well, but millions of Africans were enslaved and forcefully transported to the New World, in part to fill the void created by the collapse in Native American populations.

Four main questions are addressed in this chapter:

- What were the consequences of the Columbian Exchange?

- Why did European, African, and indigenous American societies collide when they did? That is, why didn't this happen earlier or later in human history?
- Who were the major European players in the scramble for colonies in North America, and why did England eventually take control of North America?
- How did the American colonial economy develop and grow?

3.1 THE COLUMBIAN EXCHANGE

The immediate impact of the Columbian Exchange in the Americas was the rapid spread of diseases and the collapse of indigenous populations, but the transfer of domesticated animals, food crops, plants, ideas, and human populations also had positive and long-lasting impacts on both sides of the Atlantic.

DOMESTICATED ANIMALS

Domesticated animals are kept by humans as pets, food sources, and work animals, and usually, through selective breeding, are notably different from and tamer than their wild ancestors. Only fourteen kinds of large animals have been domesticated throughout human history, and only one, the llama, is native to the Americas. The five major domesticated animals (with their origins) are sheep (western and central Asia), goats (west Asia), cows (Eurasia and North Africa), pigs (Eurasia and North Africa), and horses (Russia).[3]

The introduction of domesticated animals had three major impacts on the Americas. First, these animals increased the productivity of agriculture and provided new sources of food—horses and oxen pulled ploughs, cows provided milk, and so on. Second, the horse, in particular, allowed dramatic improvements in transportation. Third, domesticated animals helped spread deadly diseases to Native Americans.

DISEASES

Many lethal diseases in humans originated in domesticated animals and mutated in some way to infect humans. Strains of influenza come from pigs and chickens, while cattle are the source of measles. While the origin of smallpox is unknown, it likely came from domesticated animals as well. Ten thousand years of contact with domesticated farm animals in Eurasia had led to repeated epidemics of diseases among humans, but over time Eurasian populations developed some resistance.

In contrast, the geographic isolation of the Americas and the lack of exposure to domesticated animals made indigenous populations far more vulnerable targets. Native Americans caught these diseases at greater rates, and the death tolls were vastly higher as well.

Smallpox was the single biggest killer, but measles, influenza, whooping cough, bubonic plague, typhus, scarlet fever, malaria, and chicken pox, among others, were also often fatal. There is substantial evidence that diseases often reached Native American populations prior to permanent European settlement. For example, there was a major epidemic in present-day Massachusetts from 1616 to 1619, which was likely spread by visiting European fishermen, just before the Pilgrims settled the region in 1620.[4]

It is estimated that between 80 and 95 percent of indigenous populations were wiped out within a century of European contact.[5] While many lives were lost in armed conflicts between European settlers and Native Americans, with war sometimes leading to the near extinction of certain tribes, deaths from violence were relatively small compared to deaths from diseases.[6]

The only major disease that is likely to have had a New World origin and that then spread to the Old World is syphilis.[7] Within fifteen years after 1492, sailors had carried it to Europe, Africa, the Middle East, India, and China. While today syphilis can be cured with antibiotics, in the fifteenth and sixteenth centuries it often proved fatal, after first producing very severe symptoms including genital ulcers, large tumors, severe pain, and dementia.

PLANTS AND CROPS

Europe, Asia, and Africa gained many new staple crops from the Americas, crops that are generally better sources of calories than their Old World counterparts. Average yields in calories per acre are higher for the New World crops of cassava, corn, and potatoes, than for the Old World grains of wheat, barley, and oats.[8] The New World crops are also more versatile: corn can be grown in hotter and drier climates than wheat, while potatoes thrive in cold and damp soils unsuitable for Old World grains.

While we typically associate the potato with Ireland and Russia, the potato is a New World crop. In Europe, the introduction of potatoes and corn greatly expanded available calories, thereby improving diets and leading to population growth and urbanization. Other New World crops also improved diets elsewhere. Cassava (also known as manioc and, in its dried form, as tapioca) is an important source of calories in Africa and in much of the developing world, since it is drought-resistant and can be grown in marginal soils. Peanuts (groundnuts) are another important New World crop, now widely grown throughout the tropical and subtropical regions of the world.

The New World crops of tobacco and cotton have also had profound influences throughout the world.[9] Tobacco use spread across Europe in the seventeenth century, and the cotton varieties native to the Americas fueled the textile boom during the Industrial Revolution, which in turn led to the expansion of slavery.

Many Old World crops also thrived in the New World. Old World grain crops, such as wheat and rice, and other crops, including sugar cane, coffee, soybeans, oranges, and bananas, produced high yields in the various climates of the Americas.

While diseases and war ravaged the indigenous populations of the Americas, the worldwide spread of food crops and people caused Eurasian and African populations throughout the world to increase dramatically. In 1491, 100 percent of the population in what was to become the United States was Native American, yet by 1890 the Native American share of the U.S. population had plummeted to only 0.39 percent, although by 2010 it had rebounded somewhat to 1.7 percent.[10]

3.2   NORTH AMERICA BEFORE EUROPEAN SETTLEMENT

Reconstructing the economic history of Native Americans is challenging, since there are generally no written records.[11] However, extensive evidence from skeletal remains and artifacts from dozens of archaeological sites together provide important clues about how Native Americans lived.[12]

Prior to European contact, millions of Native Americans lived in what is now the United States.[13] There were urban areas with as many as 40,000 people by the year

1100, on a par with the size of London at the time, and Native American economies included agriculture, specialization, division of labor, and trade over long distances.

While it was once common to view Native Americans as a homogeneous group of "Indians," this is inaccurate. A tremendous diversity of languages and cultures existed, with more than 375 separate languages in North America by 1492.[14] Economic organizations also differed substantially across tribes. Some tribes remained hunter-gatherers, while others adopted agriculture. Some tribes engaged in a mix of hunting, gathering, and agriculture, while other tribes changed from one to the other and back again as economic circumstances changed.

Research suggests that Native Americans were often active and sophisticated trading partners with Europeans, and that the traditional story of exploitation and continuous decline is incomplete.[15] Economic tools and concepts can help us understand the choices and behaviors of indigenous populations in North America prior to European contact, as well as Native Americans' abilities to adapt to changing circumstances both prior to and after European contact.

POPULATING THE AMERICAS

Archaeological evidence suggests that modern humans, or *Homo sapiens*, emerged in Africa about 200,000 years ago.[16] Some anthropologists maintain that important, additional changes occurred around 50,000 years ago that led to modern human behaviors, like tool making and greater social cooperation, which were possibly the result of decreasing testosterone levels in humans.[17]

The "out of Africa" hypothesis postulates that all humans originated in East Africa, from where *Homo sapiens* began migrating about 150,000 years ago.[18] Between 45,000 and 40,000 years ago, humans migrated to Siberia in northeast Asia.[19] However, there is considerable controversy regarding when and how humans first migrated to the Americas. The most widely accepted explanation is that about 16,500 years ago, during the last Ice Age, a land bridge between Siberia and Alaska allowed humans to migrate to the Americas in pursuit of large mammals like the woolly mammoth, the mastodon, the ground sloth, the giant beaver, the bison, and the saber-toothed cat.[20]

There were probably later periods of migration to the Americas, with a second wave about 9,000 years ago, and a third wave about 5,000 years ago, but this debate is far from settled.[21] Some scholars, for example, believe that migration to the Americas occurred 30,000 years ago or earlier, while others contend that there was only one wave of migrants to the Americas.[22]

A protein-rich diet of large mammals caused human populations to grow quickly in the Americas, and as populations expanded beyond the carrying capacity of local areas, groups subdivided and moved south and east. As populations grew and multiplied, they became "tribes" with different languages, cultures, and economic organizations. To judge from linguistic research, about 10,000 years ago a movement of tribes occurred along the Rocky Mountain foothills and eastward across the Great Plains to the Atlantic.

A corollary to the "out of Africa" hypothesis is the so-called "serial founder effect." As subgroups left to establish new settlements farther away, these subgroups carried only a fraction of the overall genetic diversity of the original parent groups. Because of the long distance traveled from Africa, probably via Siberia and Alaska, the Native American populations have relatively low levels of genetic diversity, which likely contributed to the vulnerability and decline of indigenous populations in the Americas as environmental and disease conditions changed.[23] Darwin's theory of evolution posits that a greater diversity of traits increases the adaptability and survivability of populations through the process of natural selection.[24] Without this diversity, there is a greater likelihood of population collapse if conditions change.

THE NEOLITHIC REVOLUTION

The Neolithic Revolution, or Agricultural Revolution, started about 12,000 years ago in the Middle East and North Africa.[25] Although farming eventually spread across almost the entire world, Eurasia may have gotten a head start in farming due to its advantageous geographic location and its particular endowments of natural capital.[26]

Parts of Europe and Asia have similar climates, which allowed crops like wheat and barley to spread both east and west from the "Fertile Crescent" in the Middle East. While in Eurasia the distance from east to west is greater than the distance north to south, a so-called east–west continental axis, in Africa and in the Americas there is a greater distance from north to south than from east to west, a north–south continental axis. With a north–south axis, the huge differences in latitude are associated with large differences in climate, rainfall, and soil conditions, and as a result agriculture did not develop as early or spread as easily on these continents.

Humans became highly skilled hunters. Around 9,000 years ago, some combination of climate change and growth in human populations resulted in the rapid extinction of two-thirds of all large mammals in the New World, including the mammoth, the mastodon, the giant beaver, the giant ground sloth, and the horse. Giant bison also vanished, leaving only the smaller bison on the Great Plains. The demise of these large mammals led to dramatic changes in human diets. To kill mammals like deer, antelope, caribou, moose, and elk, hunters had to exhibit greater skill and patience. Native Americans also often incorporated fish, shellfish, birds, nuts, seeds, and berries into their diets.[27]

Some Native American tribes slowly moved toward agriculture. Corn was probably first grown in central Mexico around 7,000 years ago. About 3,500 years ago, tribes in the American Southwest began to cultivate some corn, beans, and squash. By 2,500 years ago, new strains of corn had been developed that were better suited to cooler climates and shorter growing seasons. As a result, by 2,000 years ago agriculture had spread to the Southeast and Midwest of what was to become the United States, and about 1,000 years ago it reached the Northeast. Native Americans in the coastal areas of California and the Pacific Northwest, however, never adopted agriculture, probably because of a tremendous abundance of fish, nuts, and other natural sources of food.[28]

The transition to agriculture across the world appears to have been influenced by the prevalence of livestock, such as cows, horses, and sheep. Evidence shows that the greater the number of livestock in an area, the earlier the transition to agriculture. Places that transitioned to agriculture earlier also had greater population densities by 1500.[29] The relatively late and incomplete transition to agriculture in the Americas was likely influenced by the lack of livestock.

POPULATION AND AGRICULTURE

Consistent with cross-country evidence, the presence of agriculture in Native American tribes was generally associated with greater population densities. For example, in

Maine, where agriculture was not widespread, the average density was about 40 persons per 100 square miles. In contrast, in southern New England, where Native Americans grew corn and other crops, population density averaged 287 per 100 square miles: a density more than seven times greater.[30] It is not clear, however, whether agriculture caused the greater population densities or whether areas with greater population densities were forced to adopt agriculture. Over time, however, Native American "societies became more densely settled and more complex for reasons not fully understood."[31]

In the American Southwest, two large and complex societies emerged between 300 A.D. and 1,000 A.D.: the Hohokam and Anasazi. Both groups relied on extensive and elaborate irrigation systems to grow corn, beans, squash, and other crops. Complex irrigation and abundant crops allowed larger populations and greater population densities. The largest Anasazi pueblo, Pueblo Bonita at Chaco Canyon, contained 800 rooms, including dozens of circular kivas (ceremonial centers).[32]

In the twelfth century, the Hohokam and Anasazi experienced long periods of extreme drought. Because of local overpopulation and an excessive reliance on corn, which depleted the soil of nutrients, there was a "chain reaction of crop failure, malnutrition, and violent feuds."[33] The Anasazi responded to the growing violence by fortifying their pueblos in nearly inaccessible cliffs, like Mesa Verde in modern-day

FIGURE 3.1 Anasazi Cliff Palace, Mesa Verde National Park, Colorado

Source: U.S. National Park System, www.nps.gov/common/uploads/photogallery/imr/park/meve/FF508E56-155D-451F-67D4ADFD1ED318DB/FF508E56-155D-451F-67D4ADFD1ED318DB.jpg (accessed: April 21, 2016).

Colorado (Figure 3.1). In the thirteenth century, the Hohokam and Anasazi pueblos were abandoned and the groups dispersed, becoming what the Spanish called the Pueblo Indians.

The largest and wealthiest Native American settlement was Cahokia, located on the eastern side of the Mississippi River, only seven miles from present-day St. Louis. It flourished from the years 900 to 1100. At its peak, perhaps as many as 40,000 people lived around the massive temple mounds. The Cahokia engaged in a mix of both agriculture and hunting and gathering, and traded with other tribes as far away as western New York and Montana.[34]

Cahokia too was abandoned during the thirteenth century, probably as a result of the depletion of wood and game animals in the area, and smaller villages were established throughout the Mississippi Valley and as far south as the Gulf of Mexico.

LIVING STANDARDS AND THE HEALTH OF INDIGENOUS POPULATIONS

Surprisingly, the emergence of agriculture did not typically improve the human condition in the Americas or elsewhere in the world.[35] In fact, it is likely that the healthiest Native Americans lived several thousand years ago as hunter-gatherers, and that the health of Native Americans was on a "downward trajectory long before Columbus arrived."[36]

Hunter-gatherer societies were healthier than agricultural societies for several possible reasons.[37] First, hunter-gatherers did a lot of brisk walking in pursuit of food, perhaps ten miles a day, in contrast to the more sedentary agricultural societies. In eating wild game instead of domesticated animals, hunter-gatherers also had better sources of protein, and with less fat. Their diets were also more varied, with ample consumption of nuts, fruits, and fish.

Lower population densities of hunter-gatherer groups further contributed to better health. The contamination of food and water by human excrement, the so-called fecal-oral transmission route for disease, was much lower in hunter-gatherer societies since typically they did not stay in one place long enough for human waste to become a serious problem. Life expectancies in hunter-gatherer groups remained low by modern standards, however, because deaths from violence were often quite high. Because there were no formal systems of law and order in hunter-gatherer societies, conflicts and violence were common.

Studies also indicate that hunter-gatherer societies enjoyed far more leisure time than societies in which agriculture had become the norm. Time-allocation studies of modern hunter-gatherer societies indicate very little work and large amounts of leisure.[38]

If agriculture was associated with poorer health and longer work hours, then why did some Native American tribes decide to engage in agriculture? One possible explanation is that the shift to agriculture could have been a second-best choice forced on hunter-gatherers because of resource depletion. Another possible explanation is that the choice may have been voluntary, with native populations willing to trade off poorer health for the benefits of settled agriculture, including a greater availability of consumer goods and more social interaction. By the eighteenth century, cities in the United States and Europe also suffered from poorer health than their rural counterparts, yet cities like London and New York continued to attract residents. It is not unreasonable to think that the same mechanisms may have been at work during the pre-Columbian period as well.[39]

54 Chapter 3

3.3 REVERSAL OF FORTUNE AND MODERN ECONOMIC GROWTH

Perhaps the most controversial aspect of the "Guns, Germs, and Steel" hypothesis is the link from agriculture and domesticated animals to technological superiority. Jared Diamond asserts that the early and more extensive development of agriculture in Eurasia led to larger populations and food surpluses that allowed for greater specialization. Human specialization led to the development of written languages, complex political organizations, ocean-going ships, and weaponry such as guns and steel swords, which in turn resulted in Europeans colonizing the world.

The "Guns, Germs, and Steel" hypothesis provides many important insights, but it falls short as an all-encompassing theory of modern economic growth and development. First, the advantages Diamond describes were present in all of Europe, but the growth experiences across Europe vary substantially. Second, Acemoglu, Johnson, and Robinson document a "reversal of fortune" in relative incomes across former European colonies. They write:

> The Mughals in India and the Aztecs and Incas in the Americas were among the richest civilizations in 1500, while the civilizations in North America, New Zealand, and Australia were less developed. Today the United States, Canada, New Zealand, and Australia are an order of magnitude richer than the countries now occupying the territories of the Mughal, Aztec, and Inca Empires.[40]

This reversal of fortune is problematic for a direct impact of geography on economic development, of the kind that Diamond contends, since the same factors that made countries rich in 1500 should also make them rich today.

Geographic factors, however, can still affect economic growth and development through several indirect channels. Geographic factors helped to determine comparative advantages and specialization by region in the American colonies (see Section 3.5). Differential settlement patterns of Europeans across colonies after 1500 were partly the result of initial geographic factors, and these in turn influenced the distribution of different institutions and other potentially relevant factors and traits brought by Europeans, such as human capital or culture.[41]

3.4 THE VOYAGES OF DISCOVERY AND EUROPEAN SETTLEMENT

From the Native American perspective, settlers were not only the English coming from the east, but also the Spaniards from the south and the French from the north. Other settlers were Dutch, German, or Swedish. Indeed, the first Europeans to reach North America were the Vikings, around year 1000. However, the short-lived settlements in present-day Newfoundland and Labrador, Canada, had very little long-run impact on North America. Europeans probably did not return to the Americas until Christopher Columbus' voyages almost 500 years later.

In 1400, it would have been difficult to predict the relative success of Europe in the centuries to come. Europe's population grew rapidly as it rebounded from the devastation of the Black Death pandemic (1346–1353), which killed at least one-third of Europe's population.[42] There was also the emergence of strong nation-states in Europe: Spain, Portugal, Holland, France, and England. During the fifteenth century, only the king or queen of a unified nation had sufficient power to raise revenues through taxation to finance overseas explorations.

European explorers were also influenced by the Renaissance. In the Middle Ages, humans were seen as inherently sinful and subject to the will of God. During the Renaissance, however, concepts of individualism and human rights reemerged and developed, causing individuals to believe that they could understand and shape the world.

IMPORTANT INVENTIONS

The voyages of discovery were made possible by several important inventions and innovations. Financial innovations, like joint-stock companies (France around 1250) and double-entry bookkeeping (Italy around 1300), were later used to raise funds and to keep track of profits (and losses) during the voyages of discovery. The fifteenth century also brought many important changes to Europe that helped European powers settle and colonize much of the world.[43] The printing press with moveable type, invented by Johannes Gutenberg in 1455, had enormous and widespread implications. Books became easier and cheaper to produce, leading to a rapid expansion and sharing of knowledge.

European interest in overseas exploration probably began in the 1200s when Marco Polo, an Italian merchant from Venice, traveled overland to China. Although he was not the first European to visit Asia, the mass-produced publication in 1477 of an exaggerated account of his journey, and his vivid descriptions of the precious stones, pearls, silks, objects of gold and silver, and spices in Asia, is credited with inspiring Christopher Columbus and many others to seek glory through exploration.[44] Due to the advent of the printing press, news of Columbus' voyage in 1492 also spread quickly. Columbus' published report was widely read throughout Europe, and by 1500 twenty editions had been published.[45]

Innovations in ship design greatly improved the speed and maneuverability of ocean vessels. The caravel, the ship used by most early Portuguese and Spanish explorers, had two, three, or four masts with triangular lateen sails, and was an innovation borrowed from Muslim sailors. Lateen sails meant that ships could tack (i.e., sail on a zigzag course) more directly into the strong winds of the Atlantic than could a square-rigged ship. A hinged sternpost rudder also replaced the earlier rear steering oar. These changes, along with a large hold capable of carrying the considerable cargo needed for long voyages and the ship's narrow, elliptical frame, made the voyages of discovery possible.

Navigation proved to be a formidable challenge, and it took centuries for sailors to learn how to navigate accurately on the open seas. While the magnetic compass was borrowed from the Chinese, the true mariner's compass, in a dry box with a pivoting needle, was invented in Europe by 1300.[46] Although the compass determined direction, accurate navigation required the measurement of both latitude and longitude. To establish latitude was relatively easy: by the early 1500s, sailors were using sextants and astrolabes to determine latitude by calculating the sun's angle at noon or, in the Northern Hemisphere, the angle of Polaris (the North Star) at night.

The accurate determination of longitude, however, was a more difficult problem that depended on the development of a non-pendulum clock (since pendulum clocks are inaccurate on a tilting ship or any moving object). In the eighteenth century, John Harrison invented the marine chronometer to calculate longitude precisely.[47] A chronometer accurately measures time at a fixed location, for example, relative to Greenwich Mean Time (GMT). Because the Earth rotates at a regular rate, longitude can be determined by the time difference between the chronometer and the ship's local time.

In the 1400s, European merchants and explorers began to reexamine the maps drawn by ancient geographers and to revive the art of cartography, or mapmaking. Although far from perfect, their printed maps helped Europeans to start exploring alternative water routes to Asia. The invention of the magnetic compass, the sextant, and the chronometer greatly allowed them to increase the accuracy of maps.

Developments in weaponry also aided European powers. The Chinese were the first to discover gunpowder, and increasing trade between Europe, Asia, and the Middle East brought gunpowder and firearms to Europe. Hundreds of years of conflict in Spain between Muslims and Christians led to many advances in weaponry. By the voyages of discovery, Spanish conquistadors had muskets, cannons, crossbows, helmets, armor, swords, and horses, and were easily able to overwhelm indigenous populations in the Americas.

MERCANTILISM

The intellectual underpinning of the exploration and colonization of the Americas was based on mercantilism. Mercantilism is a national economic policy aimed at accumulating monetary wealth through a positive balance of trade (exports greater than imports). All nation-states in Europe, to varying degrees, followed mercantilist principles, and colonization was pursued with the aim of strengthening the parent nation-states.

It was believed that nation-states achieved greater political and military power through the accumulation of gold and silver. While the Spanish directly accumulated vast amounts of gold and silver from Mexico, the British in the Americas had to rely on positive trade balances to accumulate gold and silver. By exporting more goods than it imports, a country is able to generate an inflow of gold and silver.

Mercantilism led the English and other colonial powers to colonize areas that could provide resources and raw materials that would otherwise need to be imported from other nation-states. Thus, the American colonies were expected to provide England with resources and commodities not available in England, while also serving as a captive market for finished goods produced in England, thereby allowing England to run trade surpluses with other nation-states.

SPANISH EXPLORATION AND SETTLEMENT

On the Atlantic Ocean and close to North Africa, Spain and Portugal were positioned to lead Europe in maritime exploration. In the fifteenth century, Prince Henry the Navigator of Portugal explored the west coast of Africa, and the Portuguese eventually reached India by traveling south and east around Africa.

To avoid hostilities with Portugal, the Spanish instead traveled westward across the Atlantic in search of a direct route to Asia.[48] The voyages of Christopher Columbus, a Genovese sailor from Italy, were financed by Spain. On his first voyage in 1492, three ships and about ninety men sailed across the Atlantic to the Bahamas, less than 100 miles southeast of Florida, and then onto Cuba and Haiti. In 1493, Columbus returned with 17 ships and over 1,200 men, as well as numerous plants, crops, and livestock. Throughout his life, Columbus believed that he had found the East Indies, near the coast of Asia, and he mistakenly called the native peoples he encountered "Indians."

Over the next century, the Spanish dominated the exploration and colonization of the Americas. In 1519, Hernán Cortés conquered the Aztecs at Tenochtitlan, renaming it Mexico City; while in 1532 Francisco Pizarro defeated the Incas of Peru. In search of gold, Spanish conquistadors also began to explore North America. Beginning in 1539, Hernando de Soto led a journey throughout the American Southeast to the Mississippi River, traveling through present-day Florida, Georgia, South Carolina, North Carolina, Tennessee, Alabama, and Mississippi. In 1540, Francisco Vásquez de Coronado led an expedition throughout the American Southwest into present-day Arizona, New Mexico, Texas, Oklahoma, and Kansas.[49] Although these expeditions were marked by brutality toward the indigenous populations they encountered, the introduction of the pig to North America may have been even worse, as it resulted in widespread disease and depopulation of Native Americans after the Spanish had left these areas and prior to French and English settlement.[50]

In 1565, the Spanish established the first permanent settlement in what was to become the United States at St. Augustine, Florida. The Spanish influence continued over the next few centuries. The Spanish founded Santa Fe, New Mexico (1598); San Antonio, Texas (1718); and twenty-one missions throughout California, beginning with the mission in San Diego (1769).

FRENCH EXPLORATION AND SETTLEMENT

The French were the first to challenge the Spanish, when Jacques Cartier made three voyages into present-day Canada in the 1530s. Religious civil wars in France stalled further attempts to explore and colonize North America until 1608, when Samuel de Champlain founded "New France," a territory that included much of eastern Canada. The French colonial efforts were based on trade alliances with Native Americans in which they acquired furs and other products for export to Europe; however, relatively few French settled in New France.

The French also traveled down the Mississippi River, claiming vast amounts of land on both sides of the river from Canada to New Orleans (land that encompasses 15 current U.S. states) and naming it all Louisiana. In 1803, the United States purchased Louisiana from France, thereby nearly doubling the size of the U.S.

DUTCH AND SWEDISH EXPLORATION AND SETTLEMENT

As early as 1609, Henry Hudson, an Englishman employed by the Dutch, sailed up the river that now bears his name. The Dutch established a fur trade with the Iroquois and built trading posts on the Hudson River at Fort Orange and at New Amsterdam on Manhattan Island. In 1621, the Dutch government gave permission to the West India Company to colonize New Netherland and to expand the fur trade.

In 1637, the Swedish founded a new colony along the Delaware River, to the south of New Netherland, in what is now part of Delaware, New Jersey, and Pennsylvania. New Sweden, however, did not last for long as an independent colony: in 1655, the Dutch conquered the area and it became part of New Netherland.

ENGLISH EXPLORATION AND SETTLEMENT

There were three types of colonies in British North America: corporate colonies, proprietary colonies, and Crown colonies. In corporate colonies, decisions were made by a joint-stock company in which investors purchased shares of stock. The purpose of corporate colonies was to earn a profit for the stockholders. Proprietary colonies were given by the monarch to an individual or group to do with as he or they wished, provided that what was done was not in conflict with English law and customs. In contrast, Crown colonies belonged to the monarch and were governed by an appointed governor or council. All of the American colonies started as private ventures, either joint-stock or proprietary. By the time of the Revolution, however, most had become Crown colonies, with the exception of Connecticut, Delaware, Maryland, Pennsylvania, and Rhode Island.

During the 1500s, the Spanish and French explored the Atlantic coast, but thought that the region was of little value for colonization. The British decided to colonize the Atlantic coast, not because it was particularly desirable, but because it was available. The first British attempts to colonize the Atlantic coast ended in disaster. During the 1580s, half-brothers Sir Humphrey Gilbert and Sir Walter Raleigh failed to establish permanent colonies either in Newfoundland or in the Carolinas (the Roanoke Colony).

In 1607, there were two new attempts. The Plymouth Company landed a group of the settlers in Maine on the Kennebec River, but those who survived the harsh winter returned to England the following spring. The London Company, however, succeeded in establishing the first permanent British settlement in North America, at Jamestown in the Chesapeake Bay of Virginia. The mortality rates in the first years of settlement were extreme, with widespread disease and starvation. Of the 6,000 English settlers who arrived in Virginia between 1607 and 1623, at least 4,500 perished.[51] The location of Jamestown was selected as it was judged to be safe from attack, but it was a poor location for human habitation, situated as it was in low-lying swamps filled with mosquitoes carrying malaria and with brackish water that was often unfit to drink. Nevertheless, after the initial "starving time," the introduction of tobacco in 1619, and the move from communal to private property (see Chapter 4), helped Virginia to thrive throughout the colonial period.

Bordering Virginia, Maryland (1632) began as a proprietary colony of Lord Baltimore, who hoped to create a safe haven for English Catholics. In 1663, King Charles II granted the Carolina charter, for land south of Virginia and north of Spanish Florida, to eight proprietors in return for their financial and political support in restoring him to the throne in 1660. In 1712, this colony was divided into North Carolina and South Carolina. Georgia (1733) was another proprietory colony and the last of the original thirteen colonies.

The colonization of New England followed a different path. Wishing to flee religious persecution, the Pilgrims—Puritan Separatists who had challenged the Anglican Church's authority—secured a land patent from the Virginia Company and created their own joint-stock company (the Plymouth Company). In 1620, they set sail for Virginia; but they were blown off course, landing instead at Cape Cod, where they decided to stay. In 1630, the Massachusetts Bay Company, made up of less radical Puritan Reformists, founded a larger colony in Boston and Salem. Other New England colonies were established in Rhode Island (1636), Connecticut (1636), and New Hampshire (1680).

Between New England and the Southern colonies were the Middle colonies. In 1664, King Charles II granted his brother, the Duke of York, permission to drive out the Dutch. When the English fleet arrived, the outmanned Dutch surrendered without firing a shot. The colony became known as New York, with New Amsterdam renamed New York City and Fort Orange renamed Albany. King Charles II also granted the land between the Hudson River and Delaware River to two loyal friends, and this became the colony of New Jersey.

Another proprietary colony was Pennsylvania (1681), given to William Penn, a Quaker, to settle a debt the king owed to Penn's father. Penn was an early advocate of religious freedom, and the settlers of Pennsylvania came from many different countries and religious backgrounds, including many from Germany, Scotland, and Ireland.

Delaware was also part of the Penn proprietorship. Although it gained a separate Assembly in 1701, throughout the colonial period Delaware continued to have the same governor as the rest of Pennsylvania.

The eventual success of the British in North America was due to two main factors: the strength of the British navy in battle and the relatively large population in the British colonies. By the 1730s, the population in the British American colonies was over twenty times larger than the population of New France.[52]

NATIVE AMERICAN ECONOMIES AFTER EUROPEAN CONTACT

As Native American tribes encountered Europeans, they exchanged food, furs, and crafts for blankets, iron and steel implements, horses, firearms, trinkets, combs, and alcohol (Figure 3.2). Trade, however, was not only an economic activity for Native Americans: it also involved principles of reciprocity in mutual gift giving.[53]

Prior to 1600, Native Americans often valued European goods not only for their intended purposes, but also as ornamental objects that they could wear to signal higher social status.[54] Indigenous tribes recognized that trade was mutually beneficial, however. In the 1630s, a Native American remarked to a French missionary, "The beaver does everything perfectly well, it makes kettles, hatchets, swords, knives, bread; and, in short, it makes everything"[55] (see Economic History in Action 3.1).

FIGURE 3.2 European Depiction of Trade with Native Americans

Source: Theodore de Bry or Matthaus Merian, 1627 or 1628, in Matthaus Merian (ed.), *Historia Americae sive Novi Orbis* (Frankfurt: Caspar Rotel, 1628, 1634), 7, Plate XIII.

ECONOMIC HISTORY IN ACTION 3.1

Comparative Advantage, Specialization, and the Gains from Trade

In *Principles of Political Economy and Taxation* (1817), David Ricardo showed that trade improves the welfare of two groups, whether those groups are individuals, regions, tribes, or countries, even in the case where one group is more efficient at producing every good. While productivity determines absolute advantage, the gains from trade depend on comparative advantage. That is, to maximize their gains from trade, groups should specialize and trade in goods that they can produce at a lower opportunity cost. Although the example below is a simple one, the benefits of specializing according to comparative advantage and trade also hold for complex economies.

Suppose there is a shipwreck on an island that leaves two survivors, Gilbert and Raleigh, who wash ashore on opposite sides of the island. Unaware of each other, each must become completely self-sufficient, using the 12 hours of daylight to perform the two tasks necessary for survival: picking berries and catching fish. Assume that Gilbert and Raleigh both derive utility (satisfaction) from consuming goods, and that more goods are preferred to fewer goods. The time requirements for each person and task are shown in the table.

	Time Requirements	
	Picking a Quart of Berries	Catching a Fish
Gilbert	1 hour	1 hour
Raleigh	1.5 hours	3 hours

On one side of the island, Gilbert maximizes his utility by spending 5 hours picking berries and 7 hours fishing, which allows him to produce and consume 5 quarts of berries and 7 fish. On the other side of the island, Raleigh decides to spend 3 hours picking berries and 9 hours fishing, which allows him to produce and consume 2 quarts of berries and 3 fish.

One day, they find each other. Note that Gilbert has an *absolute* advantage in the production of both goods—he can both pick a quart of berries and catch a fish in less time than Raleigh. That is, his labor productivity is higher in both goods. However, if absolute advantage is the criterion for assigning work, then Gilbert should do both tasks. This, however, would leave Raleigh idle, which is certainly not in the pair's best interest. To determine who has comparative advantage in which good, they need to find out who has the lower opportunity cost of producing each good.

For Gilbert, the opportunity cost of 1 fish is 1 quart of berries (1F = 1B). That is: to catch one fish, Gilbert has to give up the opportunity to pick one quart of berries. For Raleigh, the opportunity cost of one fish is two quarts of berries (1F = 2B). That is: if Raleigh spends three hours catching a fish, he foregoes the opportunity to spend those three hours picking two quarts of berries. Therefore, Gilbert has a *comparative* advantage in fishing, since he has a lower opportunity cost. For Raleigh, the opportunity cost of 1 quart of berries is 0.5 fish (1B = 0.5F). For Gilbert, the opportunity cost of 1 quart of berries is 1 fish (1B = 1F). Therefore, Raleigh has a *comparative* advantage in picking berries, since he has a lower opportunity cost.

Therefore, Gilbert should specialize in fishing, catching 12 fish in 12 hours, and Raleigh should specialize in picking berries, picking 8 quarts of berries in 12 hours. Total island production would then increase through specialization, and trade would allow each to be made better off in comparison with the self-sufficient (autarky) outcome.

For both parties to gain from trade, the price at which the goods trade (the terms of trade) must lie between their two opportunity costs. Consider the price of fish. For Gilbert, the producer of fish, the opportunity cost of 1 fish is 1 quart of berries (1F=1B). For Raleigh, the buyer of fish, the opportunity cost of 1 fish is 2 quarts of berries (1F=2B). Any price of a fish between 1 quart of berries and 2 quarts of berries is mutually beneficial.

Suppose that they agree on a price, deciding that 1 fish is equal to 1.5 quarts of berries (1F=1.5B). Suppose further that Gilbert then sells 4 fish to Raleigh, and receives 6 quarts of berries in exchange. The table below summarizes just one of many possible outcomes that makes *both* parties better off.

	Gilbert		Raleigh	
	Fish	Berries	Fish	Berries
Production and consumption without trade (autarky)	7	5	3	2
Production with specialization	12	0	0	8
Consumption with trade	8	6	4	2
Gains from trade (increase in consumption)	**1**	**1**	**1**	**0**

In this example, in comparison to self-sufficiency, specialization according to comparative advantage and exchange has increased Gilbert's consumption of fish by one fish (from 7 fish to 8 fish) and increased his consumption of berries by one quart (from 5 to 6). Since Gilbert's consumption of both goods has increased, he is clearly better off. Similarly, Raleigh has increased his consumption by one fish (from 3 to 4) and maintained his consumption of berries (2 quarts). Therefore, he too is better off.

This can also be shown graphically. The solid lines represent each person's production possibilities frontier (PPF). For example, if Gilbert spends all of his time catching fish, he can catch 12 fish. If he spends all of his time picking berries, he can pick 12 quarts of berries. The trade-off (the opportunity cost) of picking one quart of berries is foregoing catching one fish. The slope of the PPF represents his opportunity cost. Note that with specialization according to their comparative advantages, and then trade, Gilbert's and Raleigh's consumption possibilities (the dashed lines) exceed their individual production possibilities.

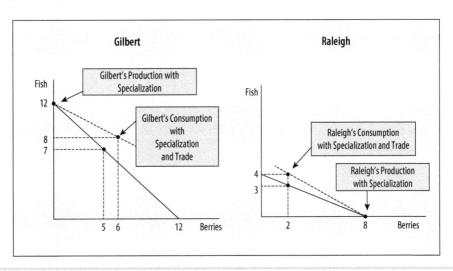

3.5 THE AMERICAN COLONIAL ECONOMIES

Three distinct regional economies developed in the American colonies, based on each region's comparative advantages: in the Southern colonies, cash crops, often grown on plantations; in the Middle colonies, family farms specializing in the production of grains; and in New England, an economy built on natural capital (fishing, lumber, and shipbuilding) and mercantile trade. Throughout the colonial period, the population was overwhelmingly agricultural and rural, with nearly 90 percent working in agriculture and well over 90 percent living in communities with populations of less than 2,500.

Estimates of living standards, economic growth, and economic inequality during the colonial period rely on incomplete and fragmentary data, and any conclusions, therefore, are somewhat speculative. Nevertheless, recent scholarship suggests several key findings about the American colonial experience (Figure 3.3).[56]

- During the colonial period, the level of real income per capita in the 13 colonies was higher than in Great Britain, even when slaves are included in the total.
- The Southern colonies had the highest incomes per capita in the colonies from 1675 to 1770, but that lead declined in relative and absolute terms over the colonial period as the Middle colonies and New England converged.
- The growth rate of real income per capita was close to zero across all 13 colonies during the colonial era.
- Colonial American incomes were relatively equally distributed in 1774; and they were probably the most equal in the Western world, even when slaves are included in the calculations.
- Among all Americans (slave plus free), inequality probably increased over the colonial period, but it was subject to two countervailing trends. Inequality among

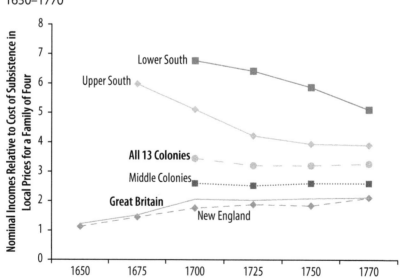

FIGURE 3.3 Real Incomes Per Capita in the American Colonies and Great Britain, 1650–1770

Source: Computed from Peter H. Lindert and Jeffrey G. Williamson, "American Colonial Incomes, 1650–1774," *Economic History Review* 69, no. 1 (February 2016), Table 6, 68. The data are also available at the Global Price and Income History Group, http://gpih.ucdavis.edu/tables.htm (accessed: March 7, 2016).

whites may have decreased over time as more farmers moved to the egalitarian frontier, but the large increase in the slave population—from about 4 percent of the overall population in 1650 to around 21 percent of the population in 1774—more than offset this downward trend and probably caused overall inequality to rise over time.

THE ECONOMY OF THE SOUTHERN COLONIES

The Southern colonies included Virginia and Maryland (the Upper South), and North Carolina, South Carolina, and Georgia (the Lower South). Tobacco thrived in Maryland, Virginia, and North Carolina, while South Carolina and Georgia were well suited for growing rice and indigo, a blue dye used to dye textiles blue and to paint houses. The Southern colonies also produced their share of lumber, tar, pitch, and turpentine.

These cash crops were largely produced on plantations, first staffed by English indentured servants, but later replaced by African slaves (see Chapter 4). By 1770, slaves constituted at least 30 percent of the population in each of the Southern colonies, whereas slaves were 7 percent or less of the population in all of the other colonies, with the exception of New York (11.7 percent).[57] The South was the region with the largest population, with over 700,000 people by 1760 (including more than 300,000 slaves), but it was also the most rural, with only three towns that had populations greater than 4,000 in 1775 (Charleston, Norfolk, and Baltimore).[58] Throughout the colonial period, real incomes per capita were highest in the South, particularly the Lower South, but they declined in absolute and relative terms between 1675 and 1770.

THE ECONOMY OF THE MIDDLE COLONIES

The land between the Potomac and the Hudson (Delaware, New Jersey, New York, and Pennsylvania) had a comparative advantage in the production of grains, including wheat, oats, rye, and barley. The Middle colonies were also important producers of cattle, pigs, and sheep; but international trade was less important in the Middle colonies than in either the South or New England, with only 9.4 percent of income in the Middle colonies from 1768 to 1772 coming from the export of goods and services.[59] In 1775, the Middle colonies had only three cities with a population greater than 4,000, but was home to the two largest cities in colonial America: Philadelphia (40,000) and New York City (25,000).

THE ECONOMY OF NEW ENGLAND

In New England (Connecticut, Massachusetts, New Hampshire, and Rhode Island), cold weather, a short growing season, and rocky soils meant that agriculture did not usually produce enough for all local consumption. New England, however, was the most economically diverse and the most urban (though still overwhelmingly rural). In colonial America in 1775, 11 of the 18 towns with a population of 4,000 or more were located in New England.[60] The region specialized in fishing, shipbuilding, shipping services, whale products (lamp oil and ivory), livestock, wood products, and many other commodities.[61]

Although New England remained the poorest colonial region prior to 1770 (Figure 3.3), living standards were relatively high, and close to those in Great Britain. New England also exhibited the highest growth rates, averaging 0.52 percent per year between 1650 and 1770.[62] The region's economic diversity laid the groundwork for its later commercial and industrial success; and its early commitment to education, with the founding of Harvard University (1636) and the first public high school in America (Boston Latin School, in 1635), put New England on a path to higher growth in the nineteenth century (see Chapter 11).

3.6 CONCLUSIONS

The broad outline of how human populations grew in North America, from prehistoric times to the end of the colonial period, provides the background in understanding the historical path of the United States' economy. During the colonial period, living standards were comparatively high and incomes were distributed comparatively equally. The growth rate of real income per capita was close to zero overall, although prior to the Revolutionary War there was substantial variation across the colonies in per capita incomes, growth rates, and inequality, although aggregate inequality remained quite low.

QUESTIONS

1. What are the Columbian Exchange and the serial founder effect? How might these two concepts be related? Explain.

2. Consider the production of two goods (wine and cloth) in two countries (England and Portugal). The time requirements to produce one bottle of wine and one yard of cloth by workers in each country are given in the table.

	England	Portugal
Time required to produce one bottle of wine	4 hours	1 hour
Time required to produce one yard of cloth	2 hours	1 hour

   A. Which country has the absolute advantage in the production of wine? Which country has the absolute advantage in the production of cloth? Illustrate and explain.

   B. Which country has the comparative advantage in the production of wine? Which country has the comparative advantage in the production of cloth? Illustrate and explain.

   C. Which good or goods should England export to Portugal? Which good or goods should Portugal export to England? Explain.

   D. In terms of the price of wine relative to the price of cloth, what range of prices will make *both* countries better off with specialization and trade? Illustrate and explain.

3. Compare and contrast the theory of mercantilism and the theory of comparative advantage. What are the fundamental differences in the purpose and benefits of international trade?

4. What factors are likely to have caused the health of Native Americans to decline for many centuries prior to European contact?

5. Describe the main trends in living standards, economic growth, and economic inequality across the American colonies between 1650 and 1770.

NOTES

[1] The term "Columbian Exchange" was coined by Alfred W. Crosby, Jr., in *The Columbian Exchange: Biological and Cultural Consequences of 1492* (Westport, CT: Greenwood Press, 1972). See also Nathan Nunn and Nancy Qian, "The Columbian Exchange: A History of Food, Disease, and Ideas," *Journal of Economic Perspectives* 24, no. 2 (Spring 2010), 163–188.

[2] Alan Taylor, *American Colonies* (New York, NY: Penguin Group, 2001), 44.

[3] Jared Diamond, *Guns, Germs, and Steel: The Fates of Human Societies* (New York, NY: W.W. Norton & Co., 1997), Table 9.1, 160.

[4] John S. Marr and John T. Cathey, "New Hypotheses for the Cause of an Epidemic Among Native Americans, New England, 1616–1619," *Emerging Infectious Diseases* 16, no. 2 (February 2010). The disease (or diseases) that decimated Native American populations in New England remains unknown. Scholars have proposed smallpox, yellow fever, plague, chicken pox, trichinosis, and leptospirosis.

[5] Nunn and Qian, 165.

[6] Russell Thorton, "Population History of Native North Americans," in Michael R. Haines and Richard H. Steckel (eds.), *A Population History of North America* (New York, NY: Cambridge University Press, 2000), 47–49.

[7] Nunn and Qian, 166–167.

[8] Taylor, 45.

[9] While some cotton varieties are native to the Old World, the most widely used varieties have a New World origin.

[10] Tina Norris, Paula L. Vines, and Elizabeth M. Hoeffel, "The American Indian and Alaska Native Population," *2010 United States Census Brief 10* (January 2012), www.census.gov/prod/cen2010/briefs/c2010br-10.pdf (accessed: August 26, 2014).

[11] The Maya civilization, in present-day southern Mexico and northern Central America, developed the only known written language in the pre-Columbian Americas.

[12] Richard H. Steckel and Jerome C. Rose (eds.), *The Backbone of History: Health and Nutrition in the Western Hemisphere* (Cambridge, UK: Cambridge University Press, 2002).

[13] There is a great deal of uncertainty regarding the peak Native American population in North America prior to European contact. Recent estimates range from 1.8 million to 18 million, with a mid-range estimate of around 5 million people. See Charles Mann, "1491," *The Atlantic* (March 2002).

[14] Taylor, 10.

[15] Daniel K. Richter, *Facing East from Indian Country* (Cambridge, MA: Harvard University Press, 2001), Chapter 2, 41–68.

[16] Philip R.P. Coelho and Robert A. McGuire, *Parasites, Pathogens, and Progress* (Cambridge, MA: The MIT Press, 2011), 15.

[17] Robert L. Cieri, Steven E. Churchill, Robert G. Franciscus, Jingzhi Tan, and Brian Hare, "Craniofacial Feminization, Social Tolerance, and the Origins of Behavioral Modernity," *Current Anthropology* 55, no. 4 (August 2014), 419–443.

[18] Ashraf Quamrul and Oded Galor, "The 'Out of Africa' Hypothesis, Human Genetic Diversity, and Comparative Economic Development," *American Economic Review* 103, no. 1 (February 2013), 6.

[19] Ted Goebel, Michael R. Waters, and Dennis H. O'Rourke, "The Late Pleistocene Dispersal of Modern Humans in the Americas," *Science* 319, no. 5869 (March 14, 2008), 1497.

[20] Goebel, Waters, and O'Rourke, 1497–1502.

[21] Taylor, 9.

[22] Goebel, Waters, and O'Rourke, 1501–1502; and Simon Romero, "Discoveries Challenge Beliefs on Humans' Arrival in the Americas," *New York Times* (March 27, 2014).

[23] Quamrul and Galor, Figure 3, 22.

[24] Quamrul and Galor, 4.

[25] Graeme Baker, *The Agricultural Revolution in Prehistory: Why Did Foragers Become Farmers?* (New York, NY: Oxford University Press, 2006), 1. For at least 95 percent of human history, all humans were hunter-gatherers.

[26] Jared Diamond, *Guns, Germs, and Steel: The Fates of Human Societies* (New York, NY: W. W. Norton & Co., 1997).

[27] Taylor, 8.

[28] Bruce E. Johansen, *The Encyclopedia of Native American Economic History* (Westport, CT: Greenwood Press, 1999), 59; and Taylor, 11.

[29] Enrico Spolaore and Romain Wacziarg, "How Deep Are the Roots of Economic Development?" *Journal of Economic Literature* 51, no. 2 (June 2013), Table 2, 331.

[30] William Cronon, *Changes in the Land: Indians, Colonists, and the Ecology of New England* (New York, NY: Hill & Wang, 1983), 42.

[31] Steckel and Rose, 578.

[32] Neal Salisbury, "The Indians' Old World: Native Americans and the Coming of Europeans," *The William and Mary Quarterly* 53, no. 3 (July 1996), 444.

[33] Taylor, 13.

[34] Johansen, 43–44.

[35] Angus Deaton, *The Great Escape: Health, Wealth, and the Origins of Inequality* (Princeton, NJ: Princeton University Press, 2013), 78.

[36] Steckel and Rose, 578.

[37] Deaton, 74–78.

[38] Gregory Clark, *A Farewell to Alms: A Brief Economic History of the World* (Princeton, NJ: Princeton University Press, 2007), Chapter 3. Clark (p. 66) concludes that "males in these [modern] subsistence societies consume 1,000 hours more leisure per year than in affluent modern Europe."

[39] Steckel and Rose, 575–576.

[40] Daron Acemoglu, Simon Johnson, and James A. Robinson, "Reversal of Fortune: Geography and Institutions in the Making of the Modern World Income Distribution," *The Quarterly Journal of Economics* 117, no. 4 (November 2002), 1231.

[41] Spolaore and Wacziarg, 332–336.

[42] John Kelly, *The Great Mortality: An Intimate History of the Black Death, the Most Devastating Plague of All Time* (New York, NY: HarperCollins, 2005).

[43] Jane Gleeson-White, *Double Entry: How the Merchants of Venice Created Modern Finance* (New York, NY: W.W. Norton & Co., 2012), 20; and www.euronext.com/listings/nyse-paris.

[44] Christopher Columbus owned a copy of Marco Polo's book and wrote many personal notes in its margins.

[45] Taylor, 35.

[46] Frederic C. Lane, "The Economic Meaning of the Invention of the Compass," *The American Historical Review* 68, no. 2 (April 1963), 605–617.

[47] Dave Sobel, *Longitude: The True Story of a Lone Genius Who Solved the Greatest Scientific Problem of His Time* (New York, NY: Walker & Co., 1995).

48 In 1494, with the help of the Pope, the Treaty of Tordesillas was signed, which divided the newly discovered lands outside Europe between Portugal and Spain along a meridian 370 leagues west of the Cape Verde islands (off the west coast of Africa). Spain had claims to the land west of this line of demarcation (most of the Americas), while Portugal received the land east of the line.

49 Tony Horwitz, *A Voyage Long and Strange: On the Trail of Vikings, Conquistadors, Lost Colonists, and Other Adventures in Early America* (New York, NY: Picador Press, 2009).

50 Charles Mann, "1491," *The Atlantic* (March 2002).

51 Karen Ordahl Kupperman, "Apathy and Death in Early Jamestown," *The Journal of American History* 66, no. 1 (June 1979), 24.

52 In 1736, the population of New France was estimated at 39,063. See *Statistics Canada*, www.statcan.gc.ca/pub/98-187-x/4151287-eng.htm (accessed: September 2, 2014). In the thirteen American colonies, the population was over 900,000 by 1740.

53 Johansen, 219.

54 Richter, 43.

55 Richter, 50.

56 The conclusions are based on data from the *Global Price and Income History Group*, which consists of economic historians who are estimating "prices, incomes, and economic wellbeing around the world before 1950." See http://gpih.ucdavis.edu/ (accessed: September 6, 2014).

57 Susan B. Carter, Scott Sigmund Gartner, Michael R. Haines, Alan L. Olmstead, Richard Sutch, and Gavin Wright (eds.), *Historical Statistics of the United States*, Millennial Edition (New York, NY: Cambridge University Press, 2006), series Eg 1–59.

58 Population data from Carter et al., series Eg 1–59; and Carl Bridenbaugh, *Cities in Revolt* (New York, NY: Oxford University Press, 1971), 216–217.

59 Peter H. Lindert and Jeffrey G. Williamson, "American Colonial Incomes, 1650–1774," *Economic History Review* 69, no. 1 (February 2016), 13.

60 Bridenbaugh, 216–217.

61 Lindert and Williamson, 12–13.

62 Computed from Lindert and Williamson, Table 7, Panel B, 41. In 1650, the subsistence ratio was 1.13; by 1770 it had increased to 2.11. The average annual growth rate is:

$$g = \left(\frac{2.11}{1.13} \right)^{1/120} - 1 \approx 0.0052 \text{ or } 0.52 \text{ percent per year.}$$

4

Institutional Foundations

In everyday language, the word "institutions" often conjures up images of buildings, such as banks, courthouses, or universities. To economists, however, institutions are not buildings of brick and mortar, but something different. The economic historian and Nobel Laureate Douglass North defined institutions as "the humanly devised constraints that structure political, economic, and social interaction. They consist of both informal constraints (sanctions, taboos, customs, traditions, and codes of conduct), and formal rules (constitutions, laws, property rights)."[1] It is not the *buildings* of the banks, courthouses, or universities that are institutions, but the "rules of the game" that structure human interaction both inside and outside of these organizations.

Two main questions are addressed in this chapter:

- How and why did American institutions develop and evolve?
- How have institutions affected economic performance throughout American history?

Today, the United States has a tremendous array of institutions dedicated to shaping and regulating economic, political, and social life, and in affecting the distribution of income and wealth. Because institutions establish "the rules of the game," they affect the incentives to save and invest, to become educated, and to invent and innovate.

In Chapter 2, institutions were introduced as one of the potential fundamental causes of economic growth. The purpose of this chapter is to provide a broad overview of institutional development and change throughout American history, and to discuss how institutions influenced growth and development. Many of the concepts and topics introduced in this chapter are elaborated upon in subsequent chapters.

4.1 THE ECONOMICS OF INSTITUTIONAL DEVELOPMENT

Every society and economy is influenced by complex combinations of formal rules and informal constraints, but the key questions concern the particular types and combinations of institutions that are conducive to economic growth and a well-functioning economy, and how these institutions develop.

IMPORTANT CHARACTERISTICS OF INSTITUTIONS

Economists and economic historians have discovered that there is no one-size-fits-all approach to institutional design. Nevertheless, scholars have identified several important characteristics of certain institutions that are positively correlated with economic growth and with many other measures of economic performance. These institutions are called "inclusive" or "open-access" institutions.[2] Inclusive institutions provide a "level playing field" that gives the freedom and opportunity to become educated, to start a business, or to come up with a new invention.[3]

Before individuals or firms can reap the benefits of specialization and exchange in markets, and in order to encourage investment, invention, and innovation, there are several important prerequisites. One is that there must be institutions that protect property and that allow freedom in making contracts. There must also be effective enforcement mechanisms, including a legal system that generally follows the rule of law.

While "property" often refers to tangible assets like land and houses, property rights comprise a far greater range of rights, including:

> control over one's own person and decisions, control over such personal property as automobiles and clothing, control over equipment and capital, and control over such intangibles as ideas, inventions, music, and writings … [and] the exclusive right to use the property, the exclusive right to derive income from use, and the inclusive right to sell the property.[4]

"Freedom to contract" means that parties (individuals or firms) are able to make binding commitments to one another, without interference from government, but in a way that the judicial system can enforce. Finally, "the rule of law" refers to a system of legal codes that are applied equally and without bias to all members of society, including government officials and the wealthy, and upheld by objective and independent courts. Although no legal system has ever met the high standard of true equality before the law, it is crucial to prevent large deviations from the rule of law—such that elites and others do not receive preferential treatment—as these could undermine economic incentives and damage economic performance.

While economists and economic historians do not always agree on the specific types of institutions necessary for economic growth and development, many explanations emphasize the following factors.[5] First, successful economies usually have constitutional governments, which limit the power of government officials, while providing widespread political representation for citizens. Second, successful economies need financial institutions, which should include a stable currency, a central bank, a widespread commercial banking system, and well-functioning markets in financial securities (such as stocks and bonds). Third, successful economies have institutions that foster a high degree of entrepreneurship and innovative activity. Although intellectual property rights are important, so too are institutions that allow "creative destruction" to take place. With creative destruction, new technologies replace old ones, new firms are created while old ones may cease to exist, and new jobs are created while old ones are destroyed. With economic growth, there are both winners and losers in the short run, and institutions must be "adaptively efficient" to allow and indeed to encourage these changes to take place.[6]

THE LEGAL-ORIGINS HYPOTHESIS

The legal-origins hypothesis emphasizes the importance of the legal systems that European settlers brought to the New World in shaping institutional development and economic performance. Scholars make a distinction between Roman civil-law and English common-law systems. Proponents of the legal-origins hypothesis believe that it is the flexibility of common law, which allows it to evolve as the economy changes, that explains why countries based on common-law systems have generally been more successful economically.[7]

Roman civil law was rediscovered during the Middle Ages, and became the basis for most European legal systems.[8] In civil law countries, laws take the form of complex codes such as the Napoleonic code, the French legal code established by Napoleon I in 1804. Spanish and Portuguese legal systems are also based on civil law. In civil-law systems, judges interpret these codes, but do not modify or change laws.[9]

In contrast with civil-law systems was the common-law system developed by the English. In this, laws enacted by Parliament are subject to interpretation by judges. As judges in court make decisions in relation to actual litigants in specific situations, a body of "case law" develops. This in turn may influence how judges interpret the law subsequently, which means that the application of a given law may gradually evolve.

The development of English common law has a long history. In 1215, the Magna Carta was the first document to place restrictions on the English monarch's power. It limited the power to tax without consent and established the principle that the monarch, too, must obey the law. It also protected individual property rights and guaranteed the right to trial by jury. Some scholars have emphasized the importance of the Glorious Revolution in England (1688) in giving Britain's Parliament greater power over the king or queen, in guaranteeing British citizens certain political and civil rights, and in granting the judiciary greater freedom and independence.[10]

Two other important developments in English common law later became part of the American legal system: judicial review and "stare decisis". In the United States, judicial review refers to the principle whereby courts can find the acts of the executive or legislative branches of government unconstitutional. The basic idea of judicial review, however, extends back to the colonial period, when "the laws passed by the assemblies in the colonies were closely watched by the lawyers of the Board of Trade to see that they were not repugnant to the laws of 'this our realm of England,' or at least 'as near as may be.' From 1696, when the Board was established to 1776 some four hundred of these laws were disallowed by this form of judicial review."[11]

In Marbury vs. Madison (1803), the Supreme Court established its powers of judicial review to judge the constitutionality of national and state laws and of decisions made by lower courts. In common law, "stare decisis" is a legal principle whereby courts are generally expected to abide by prior court decisions in similar cases.[12] While judicial review allows judges to interpret and to determine the application of the law, stare decisis ensures that most decisions are constrained by past precedents.

There is a large literature examining the relationships between the types of legal systems, institutional characteristics, and long-run economic performance. Common-law countries generally have:[13]

- more secure property rights and greater freedom in contracting;
- larger and more developed financial markets;
- fewer impediments for new firms to start businesses;
- better-functioning labor markets, with lower unemployment rates;
- more efficient court systems;
- faster economic growth.

The significance of legal origin also becomes evident when one compares the legal origins of U.S. states. Ten states, which were first settled by France, Spain, or Mexico, initially developed civil-law systems. Today, these states have less stable constitutions, a more poorly functioning court system, and a less independent judiciary than states with a common-law heritage.[14]

There is also, however, evidence contrary to the legal-origins hypothesis. First, there are many counterexamples. Numerous former British colonies with a common-law heritage have not experienced rapid economic growth or achieved high standards of living. Civil-law countries also do better than common-law countries on some other measures of economic performance, such as infant mortality and inequality.[15] Finally, there is evidence that a country's institutional developments are also influenced by other factors, including the country's endowments of natural capital (see Chapter 6).

PATH DEPENDENCE AND POSITIVE FEEDBACK

Institutional development is a path-dependent process, such that the initial institutions have affected current institutions and current economic performance. History, however, is not destiny, and there are countless examples of institutional changes throughout U.S. and world history, often precipitated by a shock, such as a war, a depression, or the development of new technologies. Under certain circumstances, the development of political and economic institutions can be mutually reinforcing, producing through the process of positive feedback a "virtuous circle" that strengthens and perpetuates both inclusive political and economic institutions.[16]

MARKET DESIGN

The supply and demand model is the most widely used model in economics, but it assumes a market in which all of the assumptions of perfect competition are met (see Chapter 1). More importantly, perhaps, it assumes the existence of the market itself. While buyers and sellers have found ingenious ways to meet and trade for centuries, a well-functioning market is a social construction that operates according to formal rules and informal constraints. For a market design to be effective, institutions must help to keep transaction costs low and must allow markets to function well.[17] In particular, market design consists of:

> the mechanisms that organize buying and selling; channels for the flow of information; state-set laws and regulations that define property rights and sustain contracting; and the market's culture, its self-regulating norms, codes, and conventions governing behavior. While the design does not control what happens in the market … it shapes and supports the process of transacting.[18]

While the supply and demand model takes the issues of property rights, contract enforcement, and the rule of law as given, those issues are necessary building blocks for a complex market-based economy.

4.2   THE AMERICAN REVOLUTION

Between 1689 and 1763, the French and British waged four large wars throughout the world's oceans and colonies, as well as within Europe. The one with the most direct impact on the American colonies was the final conflict from 1754 to 1763, which is called the "Seven Years War" in Europe and the "French and Indian War" in the United States.[19] Before 1763, the American colonies were given a wide range of freedom by the British government, in what historians have called the "Age of Salutary Neglect."[20]

The end of the French and Indian War, however, marked an important turning point in the relationship between England and the American colonies.

BRITISH POLICIES AFTER THE FRENCH AND INDIAN WAR

In an attempt to prevent further conflict and bloodshed between colonists and Native Americans on the frontier, the first change in British policy, the Proclamation of 1763, prohibited colonists from settling west of the Appalachian Mountains.[21] Many colonies, and colonists who had land claims on the western frontier, were outraged by this change in policy.

The War also caused the British government's debt to nearly double. Prime Minister George Grenville convinced Parliament to raise taxes at home and in the colonies to help pay down the debt. Although taxes were nearly five times higher in England than in the American colonies, many colonists were angered by the prospect of tax increases, believing that only the assemblies in the colonies had the right to raise taxes. They also resented King George III's plan to station 10,000 British soldiers in the American colonies.

Many modest policy changes set in motion a series of events that eventually led to the Revolutionary War. The next of these changes was when Grenville won passage of the Currency Act (1764), which banned the use of paper money as legal tender, thereby forcing American shopkeepers and farmers to pay their debts to British merchants using scarce gold or silver coins. The Sugar Act (1764) imposed tariffs on molasses and sugar, and other imported products like textiles, wine, and coffee.

The Stamp Act (1765), which taxed printed materials and legal documents, sparked the first crisis. This was the first tax on items within the colonies, rather than on imported goods, and therefore challenged the colonial assemblies' exclusive power to levy internal taxes. In protest, nine colonial assemblies sent delegates to the Stamp Act Congress, rioting broke out in several American cities, and there was an organized boycott of British goods.

When news of the rioting and boycott reached Britain in 1766, Parliament was already in turmoil, and King George III dismissed Grenville. Lord Rockingham, who succeeded Grenville as Prime Minister, repealed the Stamp Act and reduced the duty on molasses imposed by the Sugar Act. In order to pacify hardliners, he also passed the Declaratory Act (1766) reaffirming Parliament's "full power and authority to make laws and statutes ... to bind the colonies and people of America ... in all cases whatsoever."[22]

In 1767, Rockingham's government collapsed, and George III replaced him with William Pitt. Pitt was chronically ill and frequently absent, and when away left Charles Townshend in charge. Townshend had strongly supported the Stamp Act and wanted more tax revenues from the colonies. The Townshend Acts (1767) imposed duties on colonial imports of paper, glass, paint, and tea; and also created an American Customs Board, together with admiralty courts in Halifax, Boston, Philadelphia, and Charleston, in an attempt to undermine American political institutions. In 1768, colonial merchants began another boycott of British goods, which had a major impact on the British economy, leading British merchants and manufacturers to petition Parliament to repeal the Townshend duties.

In 1770, Lord North became Prime Minister. He persuaded Parliament to repeal most of the Townshend duties, yet he retained the tax on tea as a symbol of Parliamentary power. Later that year, British soldiers fired into a group of rowdy demonstrators in Boston, killing five men, an event that came to be known as the "Boston Massacre."

While the repeal of the Townshend duties restored some degree of order, conflict ensued again with the passage of the Tea Act (1773), which allowed the East India Company to ship tea directly to the American colonies, bypassing American wholesalers. American merchants feared that if the British could bypass American wholesalers in relation to tea imports, it could do the same with a wide range of other imported products. In protest, tea in port towns was either sent back to England or destroyed in various ways. The most dramatic event was the Boston Tea Party (1773), when a group of protestors boarded a ship from the East India Company and dumped all of the tea on board into the Boston Harbor.

This time the British reaction was harsh. The Intolerable Acts (1774) closed the port of Boston until the East India Company was repaid, placed political power in a Crown-appointed governor, and provided for the quartering of British troops in Boston. The Quebec Act (1774) changed the boundaries of Quebec and eliminated the western land claims of Massachusetts, Connecticut, and Virginia, further infuriating the colonists.

The First Continental Congress met in Philadelphia in 1774 to draft a list of grievances to send to the Crown. While the economic burden of the new taxes and regulations on the colonies after 1763 was modest, the policies were strictly enforced by the British in an autocratic manner, and affected nearly all colonists to varying degrees.[23] Many American colonists believed that they deserved all of the rights of Englishmen, yet the British felt that the colonists and the colonies were created to benefit the Crown and Parliament. American complaints were embodied in the slogan, "No taxation without representation." By 1775, the rising tensions had reached a breaking point.

THE REVOLUTIONARY WAR

The Revolutionary War began on April 15, 1775, when a British commander dispatched troops to arrest Samuel Adams and John Hancock and to seize an arsenal of weapons in Concord, Massachusetts. Militiamen from nearby Lexington intercepted them and fighting ensued. Thereafter, the War dragged on for years and gradually lost public support in England. In 1781, the British commander, General Cornwallis, surrendered at Yorktown, Virginia, surrounded by colonial and French troops. In practice, this effectively ended the War; although the Treaty of Paris, which ended it officially, was not signed until 1783.

The Revolutionary War resulted in a large loss of life and substantial financial costs. In 1780, the colonial population was approximately 2.8 million, and it has been estimated that 25,674 colonists died in service during the War, as a result of either violence or disease. That number represented approximately 0.9 percent of the colonial population, equivalent in 2016 to approximately 3 million Americans dying.[24]

THE ARTICLES OF CONFEDERATION

Shortly after the Declaration of Independence was signed, on July 4, 1776, the delegates of the Second Continental Congress met to draft the Articles of Confederation, the first constitution of the United States. The new federal government was given very little power and authority over the states. It was almost impossible for Congress to enact taxes, since the unanimous consent of all states was required. Unable to raise sufficient taxes to pay for the War, Congress began printing money to pay for military expenditures, and this led to rapid inflation (see Economic History in Action 5.1).

4.3 THE CONSTITUTION

When 55 delegates from nine states met in the summer of 1787 to revise the Articles of Confederation, there were many causes of concern. The new country was in the midst of a serious economic depression, perhaps as severe as the Great Depression of the 1930s.[25] Recent research concludes that "the Revolutionary disaster and Confederation turmoil could have been America's greatest income slump ever, in percentage terms."[26] The effects of the depression and associated discontent manifested themselves in Shay's Rebellion (1786), in which the Revolutionary War hero Daniel Shay led protestors in attacking Massachusetts' courthouses to prevent local judges from foreclosing on farms.

The delegates had their experiences from the Articles of Confederation to guide them; they were also influenced by broader changes, including the Enlightenment, and by the experiences of many delegates in helping to write constitutions in their individual states. In 1690, John Locke, the English philosopher, proposed that people have certain natural rights that belong to every human being from birth. These include the right to life, the right to liberty, and the right to property. These rights were believed to come directly from God, and not just from the monarch. By the 1770s, most educated Americans, too, believed that they were born with certain inalienable rights.

THE CONSTITUTIONAL CONVENTION

While the stated purpose of the Convention was to revise the Articles of Confederation, it was the intention of many from the outset, including James Madison and Alexander Hamilton, to create a completely new constitution and government rather than simply to revise the existing one. Poor economic conditions and Shay's Rebellion may have provided the impetus for the wholesale changes that took place.

As delegates debated throughout the summer of 1787, there were three main issues of conflict. First, some delegates favored a strong national government, while others wanted a weak central government with most of the power residing at the state and local levels. Second, delegates from states with larger populations generally wanted a system of representation based on state populations, while delegates from states with smaller populations favored equal numbers of representatives for all states. Finally, there were disagreements about slavery, including both the legality of the slave trade and how to count slaves when apportioning seats in the legislature.

AN ECONOMIC INTERPRETATION OF THE CONSTITUTION

The Constitution that resulted represented a fundamental restructuring of government in the United States. Instead of a loose confederation of largely independent states with a weak central government, as under the original Articles of Confederation, the new Constitution substantially increased the power and authority of the federal government.

While the experiences of operating under the Articles of Confederation and political ideologies both played important roles in this change, so did the economic self-interests of the delegates who attended the Constitutional Convention. In 1913, Charles Beard first proposed that, "merchants, money lenders, security holders, manufacturers, shippers, capitalists, and financiers" were in favor of the Constitution, while farmers and debtors were not.[27]

In recent decades, several economic historians have tested whether the delegates' specific economic and financial interests significantly influenced the exact structure and design of the U.S. Constitution. This is not to say that self-interested behavior was the only factor that influenced Constitutional design, but that "delegate voting was affected by personal interests at the margin."[28] The influence of personal self-interest was strong enough that the U.S. Constitution "would have been dramatically different had men with dramatically different interests been involved."[29]

CONSTITUTIONAL PROVISIONS

The U.S. Constitution is remarkably succinct, fitting on only four large pages.[30] There are seven articles: Article 1 (legislative branch), Article 2 (executive branch), Article 3 (judicial branch), Article 4 (relations among states), Article 5 (amending the constitution), Article 6 (supremacy of the federal government), and Article 7 (ratification). Ten amendments to the Constitution (the Bill of Rights) were added in 1791, with seventeen further amendments added between 1795 and 2016.

The delegates were able to reach compromises on many important issues. For example, by creating a bicameral legislature, where representation in the House of Representatives is based on state populations but where each state gets two representatives in the Senate, there was an effective compromise on issue of representation. Similarly, federalists were victorious in creating a stronger federal government, but the separation of powers into three branches of government dispersed that power.

FIGURE 4.1 Scene at the Signing of the Constitution of the United States, 1787

Source: Harold Chandler Christy, "Scene at the Signing of the Constitution of the United States" (1940), www.senate. gov/artandhistory/history/common/image/Constitutional_Convention.htm (accessed: April 17, 2016).

Many of the important provisions relating most directly to the economy are contained in Article 1 (Sections 8, 9, and 10). The Constitution gave Congress the power to tax and to pay off debts, including the debts incurred by the states during the Revolutionary War (see Chapter 5). While this decision was controversial, it established the reputation of the United States as a safe borrower, allowing it to borrow vast sums at very low interest rates throughout its history.

Other provisions created the legal structure for a vast common market in the United States, which encouraged specialization, trade, and innovation. While it took many decades before developments in finance and transportation made a national market a reality, institutional barriers were removed by the Constitution. States were prohibited from taxing goods from other states, ensuring the toll-free movement of goods across state borders. There were also no restrictions on the movement of labor (except for slaves) or capital. The U.S. dollar was the common currency and federal taxes had to be uniform among the states. Only the federal government was allowed to enact tariffs and to establish treaties with foreign governments, which ensures uniformity across the states with respect to international law and trade.

The Constitution also encouraged trade and specialization in other ways, by establishing fixed standards for weights and measures, uniform bankruptcy laws, and a post office. Intellectual property rights and rights in tangible property were protected, but in a way that generally served the public interest (see Section 4.4 below), and the contract clause (Article 1, Section 10) ensured that "no state shall pass any ... law impairing the obligation of contracts."

By modern standards, however, the U.S. Constitution fell well short of democracy and equal opportunity. Slavery was legal and constitutional, with a slave counting as three-fifths of a person in the allocation of seats in the House of Representatives, but slaves were given no rights as individuals. The slave trade was allowed to continue for another 20 years, and slavery as a practice could continue indefinitely. Women were not given the right to vote (a change that did not occur until the ratification of the Nineteenth Amendment in 1920).

STATE AND LOCAL GOVERNMENTS

It would be a mistake to conclude that all of the institutional foundations were created in the U.S. Constitution and at the federal level. The Constitution left state and local governments with a great deal of autonomy, and this led to competition among the states. Successful policies in one state were often imitated by other states, while unsuccessful policies were discarded, leading to policy innovations and adaptive efficiency.

State and local governments also promoted economic development aggressively, by encouraging investment in transportation and banking, by investing in education, and by introducing banking laws and general laws of incorporation.[31] Later, by the end of the nineteenth century, states would take the lead in the areas of regulation and social spending.

4.4   LONG-TERM INSTITUTIONAL CHANGES

This section provides a brief survey of some of the major institutional changes since the Constitution, and how these changes affected factor markets (markets for natural capital, markets for physical capital, and markets for human capital and labor), product markets (markets for final goods and services), and technological innovation.

Over the course of the nineteenth century, legislatures and courts generally sided with business and industry, reducing the costs and risks of doing business, making businesses more profitable, and encouraging them to take greater risks than they otherwise might have taken. Beginning in the late nineteenth century, however, the tide turned toward granting more rights and protections to workers and consumers.

NATURAL CAPITAL AND PROPERTY RIGHTS

Both the Jamestown colonists in Virginia (1607) and the Pilgrims in Plymouth (1620) initially suffered high death rates, in part due to lack of food. Both Governor Thomas Dale in Virginia and Governor William Bradford in Plymouth soon made the institutional change from communal property rights to private property rights. Bradford wrote that with communal property, "the young men, that were the most able and fit for labor and service, did repine that they should spend their time and strength to work for other men's wives and children without any recompense."[32]

In 1623, Bradford gave each family private property and made them responsible for their own food. This change "had very good success, for it made all hands very industrious, so as much more corne was planted than other waise would have bene. ... The women now went willingly into the field, and took their little ones with them to set corne; which before would allege weakness and inability."[33]

Private property rights soon became the norm in all the colonies. Throughout U.S. history, however, property rights in land and natural capital have been secure but not absolute, since "[e]conomic development requires both secure property rights and the ability to reallocate property in response to technological and other changes."[34] There is an inherent trade-off between security and reallocation. If property rights are too insecure, then owners will not make investments to improve the value of their property for fear that the property will be confiscated. However, there are times when property needs to be reallocated to serve the public good through "eminent domain", as when land is taken by government (with the owners compensated) to build a highway.

Rights in tangible property have been restricted, modified, and reallocated in several important ways. First, owners of most types of property are required to pay taxes (e.g., property taxes) or to forfeit their property to the government. Second, property is subject to liens, foreclosures, and repossessions in cases of nonpayment. Third, property rights are also limited through zoning restrictions, which can greatly affect the value of property and the incentives to improve it.

The Fifth Amendment (1791) and the Fourteenth Amendment (1868) to the Constitution prevented the taking of private property by federal, state, and local governments for "public use" without "just compensation" and "due process of law." "Just compensation" has been interpreted to mean the fair market value of the property, but the phrase "public use" has been the subject of much debate and litigation. In the nineteenth century, courts strictly interpreted "public use" to mean "literally *use by the public*."[35] In the nineteenth century, the government's power of "eminent domain" was used to make possible the building of roads, dams, and railroads.

Over time, however, the courts' interpretation of "public use" broadened to include taking property for irrigation projects (1896) and mining projects (1906).[36] After World War II, courts allowed eminent domain to be used to eliminate urban blight by allowing redevelopment (1954) and, in Hawaii, to transfer property from landlords to renters to break up concentrated land ownership.[37]

In Kelo et al. vs. the City of New London (2005), the Supreme Court allowed several (non-blighted) private homes to be transferred to another private owner for a large-scale redevelopment project. The Court ruled that this taking was justified, even if it was largely for the benefit of a private entity, as long as it advanced a public purpose, such as the creation of jobs or enhanced tax revenues.[38] In dissent, Justice Sandra Day O'Connor argued that this decision had set a dangerous precedent and that nothing would prevent "the State from replacing … any home with a shopping mall."[39]

Property rights have also changed throughout U.S. history with respect to the "ancient lights doctrine." Under English common law, the "ancient lights doctrine" meant that property rights included unobstructed views and scenery, tranquility, and clean air. As the population expanded and industrialization occurred in the United States, courts abandoned the concept of ancient lights. In the New York case of Parker vs. Foote (1838), the judge wrote that the concept of ancient lights "cannot be applied in the growing cities and villages of this country without working the most mischievous consequences."[40] That is, in the nineteenth century if one property owner inflicted a negative externality on others (pollution, noise, or similar), those affected by the externality did not typically have recourse through the legal system. This was good for economic growth and industrialization, but bad for the lungs and the environment.

By the latter part of the twentieth century, however, there was a move back toward the doctrine of ancient lights as widespread environmental laws and regulations became part of public policy. The 1970s were a particularly active time for environmental policy regulations with the establishment of the Environmental Protection Agency (1970) and the passing of relevant legislation: the Clean Air Act (1970), the Water Pollution Control Act (1972), the Toxic Substances Control Act (1976), and the Comprehensive Environmental Response, Compensation, and Liability Act or Superfund Act (1980). This legislation is discussed in detail in Chapter 19.

PHYSICAL CAPITAL, FINANCE, AND INCORPORATION

Physical capital accumulation depends on new investment. The financial system channels funds from those who save to those who borrow for investment. Some scholars believe that the most important institutional changes in the United States' history occurred in banking and finance. The "finance-led" growth hypothesis argues that the early development of financial markets (markets for stocks, bonds, derivatives, etc.) and of financial institutions (central banks, commercial banks, insurance firms, and so on) was a prerequisite for sustained economic growth. The government has an active role to play in terms of creating central banks, regulating the financial system, and conducting monetary policy (see Chapters 5 and 18).

While firms can obtain funds for investment indirectly from banks and other financial intermediaries, they can also seek funds directly in financial markets by borrowing (issuing bonds) or by selling stock in an initial public offering. Early corporations in the United States required special state legislative charters. Beginning in 1811, however, New York introduced general rules of incorporation that no longer required a special legislative act. While Connecticut passed a similar law in 1837, it was not until the 1870s that generalized incorporation laws became common throughout the United States.

Corporations have several advantages over other forms of business organization, such as proprietorships or partnerships. First, a corporation is treated as a legal person, but one with perpetual life. Second, investors in the corporation have limited liability, in that they can lose no more than the amount they paid for the stock. The division of ownership into thousands or millions of shares allows investors to diversify risk and allows firms to obtain investment in large quantities from many different sources.

HUMAN CAPITAL, TECHNOLOGY, AND INTELLECTUAL PROPERTY

The institutional environment influences education and the creation of new ideas. In the colonial period, there was nearly universal male literacy in New England, in part due to public schools and mandatory attendance laws. In the mid-nineteenth century, the "common school" movement spread to other northern states to satisfy the demands of industry. This was followed by the American high school movement (1910–1940). In the post-World War II period, high schools and universities have continued to expand (see Chapter 11).

Article 1, Section 8 of the Constitution protects intellectual property rights "To promote the progress of science and the useful arts, by securing for limited times to authors and inventors the exclusive right to their respective writings and ideas." Patents protect inventions; copyrights protect creative works; and trademarks cover brand names and the recognizable signs, designs, and expressions of firms. In the United States today, a patent gives an inventor exclusive rights in that invention or idea for a period of 20 years. Copyrights last for the life of the author, artist, or musician, plus an additional 70 years.

If property rights in ideas did not exist, inventors would often be unable to recover their costs of invention and then less invention would take place. While inventors may sometimes be driven by motivations other than money, including intellectual curiosity and professional prestige, the existence of intellectual property rights does provide greater financial incentives to create, invent, and innovate.

Intellectual property rights, however, represent a trade-off between encouraging the creation of new ideas and allowing the full use of existing ideas. While the granting of monopoly rights in ideas succeeds in rewarding the creator, it does this at the cost of increasing the price of the idea and thereby restricting its use. As with any monopoly, it also creates deadweight losses: that is, to encourage a greater rate of invention over the long run, society trades off the inefficiency of monopoly in the short run.

The Patent Act of 1836 was the beginning of the modern U.S. patent system, in which there is an examination of each patent application by a trained technical expert.

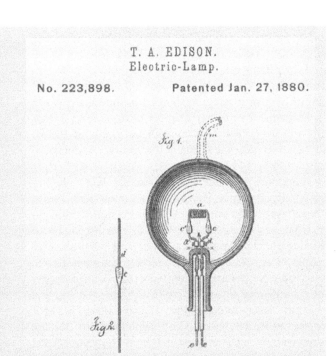

T. A. EDISON.
Electric-Lamp.

No. 223,898.   Patented Jan. 27, 1880.

FIGURE 4.2 Thomas Edison's Patent Application for the Electric Lightbulb, 1880
Source: Records of the U.S. Patent and Trademark Office; Record Group 241; National Archives, www.archives.gov/historical-docs/document.html?doc=11 (accessed: April 18, 2016).

Many nineteenth century observers and modern scholars have credited the low cost of patent applications and the examination system with helping to create the incentives for the high rate of technological progress in the U.S. during the nineteenth century. This interpretation, however, is disputed by others.[41]

The legal criteria for granting a patent are that the idea should be new, useful, and nonobvious, but economists would add an additional constraint: that the social benefits from awarding the patent should outweigh the social costs (the marginal principle from Chapter 1). This last criterion, of course, is sometimes difficult to evaluate, and it undoubtedly differs for each patent application, but it is an instructive issue to consider.

The current copyright system in the United States almost certainly violates the marginal principle. In 1998, the Copyright Term Extension Act extended the copyright length from 50 years after the death of an author or artist to 70 years after death, and the Act applied this retroactively to works that had already been created and to authors and artists who had already died.

There is a cost in keeping these works out of the public domain for another 20 years, since non-copyrighted materials are more available and less expensive to the public. It is difficult to believe that the extension provided much of an incentive to create new works, particularly for those no longer living. Critics called this Act "The Mickey Mouse Protection Act" because without it the early works featuring Mickey Mouse were set to come into the public domain, and the Disney Corporation, alongside others with valuable copyrights, lobbied for this Act.[42]

There are concerns now that current intellectual property rights in the United States are not optimal, with copyright protection that is too strong and patent protection that is too weak.[43]

LABOR

Labor-market institutions have also changed dramatically throughout American history. During the colonial period, indentured servitude contracts enabled hundreds of thousands of people of modest means to travel from England and elsewhere to the American colonies. Individuals sold their labor for a given time period to an owner in the colonies in exchange for passage across the Atlantic, food, clothing, shelter, and often "freedom dues" (in the form of land or money) at the end of indenture. While indentured servants voluntarily sold themselves into a form of enslavement, indentured servants were not slaves. Most were British citizens with the rights of British subjects. For example, if the owner failed to meet the terms of the contract, indentured servants could use the colonial court system.

The institution of slavery developed and operated very differently. Not only was slavery a form of labor relations and a political regime, it was also a set of property rights, and it has been argued that the "legal aspects of slavery and their economic implications ... are where we should look in trying to understand the place of slavery in American economic development."[44] Legal rules underpinned the existence and persistence of slavery in the United States. African slaves were kidnapped and forcefully transported to the New World. They had no rights as individuals; instead, they were the private property of someone else, and the court system enforced this principle from soon after the first slaves arrived in Jamestown in 1619 until slavery ended in the American South in 1865. Slaves could be purchased, sold, or bequeathed; they could be assigned any task that the master saw fit; they could be punished without legal recourse; they could be accumulated as a form of wealth, and used as collateral in credit transactions.[45]

After emancipation in 1865, southern blacks were unwilling to work as wage laborers on large plantations. Instead, the institution of sharecropping developed, in which former plantation owners divided their lands and rented each plot (or share) to a single African-American family. The family farmed its own crops in exchange for giving a percentage of the yield to the landowner. Many landless whites also became sharecroppers. In the agricultural South, sharecropping remained an important labor-market institution from the 1870s to the 1950s.

During the late nineteenth century, at-will employment gradually became the norm under the common law of employment contracts in most states. That is, in the absence of a written employment contract, at any time an "employer can terminate the employee for good cause, bad cause, or no cause at all" and employees, similarly, are free to quit their jobs at any time and for any reason.[46] The employment-at-will doctrine, however, is not absolute, and courts have allowed several exceptions, including protections for whistle-blowers and the ability of groups of workers to bargain collectively with employers through labor unions.[47] Chapters 7, 12, and 14 discuss other aspects of indentured servitude, slavery, and at-will employment.

PRODUCT MARKETS

As in factor markets, legal decisions and the institutional framework tilted toward business and enterprise during the nineteenth century, where the prevailing legal concept in product markets was that of "caveat emptor" (let the buyer beware). In exchanges between buyers and sellers, and provided that the buyer had a fair chance to inspect a good prior to purchase, the buyer assumed all responsibility for the quality of a good once the property right had been transferred by the sale. In cases of negligence, the seller could be sued in civil courts for damages, but generally the seller was absolved from any liability unless negligence could be proven in court.

While regulations regarding the safety of food and health date from colonial times, the first federal law was passed in 1813. It addressed the reliable provision of smallpox vaccines. In 1848, federal inspection of imported drugs was introduced. More widespread federal regulations were not introduced until the twentieth century, however. In response to Upton Sinclair's shocking depiction of the meatpacking industry in his novel, *The Jungle*, the Meat Inspection Act (1906) and the Pure Food Drug Act (1906) were passed. The Pure Food Drug Act created the Food and Drug Administration. While some consumer safety laws were passed during the New Deal of the 1930s, the postwar period has witnessed the enactment of a tremendous array of consumer health and safety laws (see Chapter 16).

The growth of big business with monopoly power in the decades after the Civil War led to antitrust laws and regulations, including the Sherman Act (1890) and the Clayton Act (1914). As discussed in Chapter 17, there have been several prominent antitrust cases, including those against Standard Oil (1911), American Tobacco (1911), IBM (1982), AT&T (1982), and Microsoft (2001).

4.5   CONCLUSIONS

This chapter has provided an overview of institutional development and change from colonial times to the present. On balance, the institutional framework of the United States has been "inclusive," contributing to economic growth and opportunity, but also limiting the rights of African Americans and other groups.

Some scholars are fearful that the United States has entered a period of "institutional decay," where inclusiveness and opportunity are on the decline.[48] There have been other periods in the past where it appeared that institutional decay had set in, but instead institutional changes led to increased resiliency.[49] It remains to be seen whether the institutional framework in the United States can continue to provide a sufficient degree of inclusiveness and sufficient equal opportunity, both of which will be necessary for sustained, broad-based growth in the coming decades.

QUESTIONS

1. Explain in intuitive terms what kinds of institutions are "inclusive institutions." How can inclusive institutions help economic growth?

2. What are judicial review and stare decisis? How do they affect legal and institutional changes?

3. The Copyright Term Extension Act, which is informally called the "Sonny Bono Copyright Term Extension Act" (1998) increased copyright terms in the United States from 50 years after the death of an author or artist to 70 years after death. One of the initial advocates for extending copyright terms was Representative Sonny Bono, who was killed in a ski accident. After he died, his wife Mary was elected to fill his seat. Speaking on the floor of the House of Representatives, Mary Bono said, "Actually, Sonny wanted the term of copyright protection to last forever. I am informed by staff that such a change would violate the Constitution." (http://en.wikipedia.org/wiki/Mary_Bono, accessed November 4, 2014 .) Using the marginal benefit–marginal cost principle, explain why extending copyright protection to last forever is both unconstitutional and bad public policy.

4. To what extent was the American Revolution due to economic factors and concerns? What specific British policies impacted the American colonies, and what was the magnitude of this impact?

5. Read the original text of the U.S. Constitution (available at www.archives.gov/exhibits/charters/constitution_transcript.html). Write an essay describing the most important parts of the Constitution in terms of stimulating U.S. economic growth. Be as specific as possible.

NOTES

[1] Douglass C. North, "Institutions," *Journal of Economic Perspectives* 5, no. 1 (Winter 1991), 97.

[2] Daron Acemoglu and James A. Robinson, *Why Nations Fail: The Origins of Power, Prosperity, and Poverty* (New York, NY: Crown Business, 2012), 74–75, use the term "inclusive;" whereas Douglass C. North, John Joseph Wallis, and Barry R. Weingast, *Violence and Social Orders: A Conceptual Framework for Interpreting Record Human History* (New York, NY: Cambridge University Press, 2009), use the term "open-access." While there are some differences between the two concepts, both stress the importance of private property rights, the freedom to make contracts, and the rule of law.

[3] Acemoglu and Robinson, 74–75.

[4] Price Fishback, "Government and the Economy," in *Government and the American Economy: A New History* (Chicago, IL: University of Chicago Press, 2007), 4–5.

[5] This discussion is based on Douglas A. Irwin and Richard Sylla, "The Significance of the Founding Choices: Editors' Introduction," in *Founding Choices: American Economic Policy in the 1790s* (Chicago, IL: University of Chicago Press, 2011), 5–7.

6 Douglass C. North, *Understanding the Process of Economic Change* (Princeton, NJ: Princeton University Press, 2005).

7 Rafael La Porta, Florencio Lopez-de-Silanes, and Andrei Shleifer, "The Economic Consequences of Legal Origins," *Journal of Economic Literature* 46, no. 2 (June 2008), 285–332.

8 Other legal systems include German and Scandinavian legal systems, which are also based on Roman civil law.

9 See Lawrence M. Friedman, *Law in America: A Short Introduction* (New York, NY: Modern Library, 2002), 7–15, for a discussion of the differences between civil law and common law.

10 Acemoglu and Robinson, 102–103.

11 J.R.T. Hughes, *Social Control in Colonial America* (Charlottesville, VA: The University of Virginia Press, 1976), 13.

12 William Blackstone, *Commentaries on the Laws of England*, 4 vols. (Oxford, UK: Clarendon Press, 1765–1769).

13 See La Porta, Lopez-de-Silanes, and Shiefer, 285–332; Nathan Nunn, "The Importance of History for Economic Development," *Annual Review of Economics* 1, no. 1 (2009), 65–92; and Niall Ferguson, *The Great Degeneration: How Institutions Decay and Economies Die* (New York, NY: Penguin Books, 2012), 86–88.

14 Daniel Berkowitz and Karen Clay, "American Civil Law Origins: Implications for State Constitutions," *American Law and Economics Review* 7, no. 1 (Spring 2005), 62–84; and Daniel Berkowitz and Karen Clay, "The Effect of Judicial Independence on Courts: Evidence from the American States," *Journal of Legal Studies* 35, no. 2 (June 2006), 399–440.

15 David Collison, Stuart Cross, John Ferguson, David Power, and Lorna Stevenson, "Legal Determinants of External Finance Revisited: The Inverse Relationship between Investor Protection and Societal Well-Being," *Journal of Business Ethics* 108, no. 3 (July 2012), 393–410.

16 Acemoglu and Robinson, 319–334.

17 Transaction costs can include the costs of negotiation, search, monitoring, and enforcement.

18 John McMillan, *Reinventing the Bazaar: A Natural History of Markets* (New York, NY: W.W. Norton & Co., 2002), 9.

19 The astute reader will recognize that the "Seven Years' War" actually lasted nine years, but the main conflicts took place in the seven years between 1756 and 1763.

20 This term "salutary neglect" comes from Edmund Burke, "Speech on the Conciliation with the Colonies," *House of Commons*, March 22, 1775.

21 Conflicts between colonists and Native Americans continued for several years after 1763, in fact, as colonial farmers continued moving westward in search of new land.

22 The text of the Declaratory Act can be found at www.constitution.org/bcp/decl_act.htm (accessed: June 6, 2016).

23 Robert Paul Thomas, "A Quantitative Approach to the Study of the Effects of British Imperial Policy upon Colonial Welfare: Some Preliminary Findings," *Journal of Economic History* 25, no. 4 (December 1965), 615–638.

24 Howard H. Peckham (ed.), *The Toll of Independence: Engagements and Battle Casualties of the American Revolution* (Chicago, IL: University of Chicago Press, 1974), 132–133.

25 Peter H. Lindert and Jeffrey G. Williamson, "American Incomes Before and After the Revolution," *Journal of Economic History* 73, no. 3 (September 2013), 725–765.

26 Lindert and Williamson, 741.

27 Charles A. Beard, *An Economic Interpretation of the Constitution* (New York, NY: Macmillan, 1913), 7.

[28] Jac C. Heckelman and Keith L. Dougherty, "An Economic Interpretation of the Constitutional Convention of 1787," *Journal of Economic History* 67, no. 4 (December, 2007), 846.

[29] Robert A. McGuire, "The Founding Era, 1774–1791," in *Government and the American Economy: A New History* (Chicago, IL: University of Chicago Press, 2007), 77. See also Robert A. McGuire, *To Form a More Perfect Union: A New Economic Interpretation of the United States Constitution* (New York, NY: Oxford University Press, 2003).

[30] The original U.S. Constitution contained only 4,543 words, including the signatures, and it fit on four large sheets of paper. In 2016, the Constitution, including the 27 Amendments, contains 7,591 words. The U.S. National Archives has the full text of the Constitution, the Amendments, and other supplementary information, www.archives.gov/exhibits/charters/charters.html (accessed: November 14, 2014).

[31] John Joseph Wallis, "The National Era," in *Government and the American Economy: A New History* (Chicago, IL: University of Chicago Press, 2007), 148–187.

[32] William Bradford (1623), http://press-pubs.uchicago.edu/founders/documents/v1ch16s1.html (accessed: November 16, 2014).

[33] Bradford. To understand the incentives under communal ownership to shirk and to free-ride on the labor of others, consider the following example. Suppose there are 20 individuals who together produce 100 bushels of corn each day when everyone is working. With communal ownership and shared consumption, each person gets 5 bushels per day (100 bushels/20 people). Now, suppose that one person decides to take the day off and not produce anything. The total bushels produced by the group fall from 100 to 95, so that there are only 95 bushels available for consumption among the 20 people. This is a huge windfall for the person who took the day off. His consumption, and that of everyone who worked, falls from 5 bushels to 4.75 bushels (95 bushels/20 people). Under communal ownership, however, every worker faces these same incentives, so that when many workers shirk and free-ride on the labor of others, total production and consumption collapse. The incentives to shirk and to free-ride become larger as the size of the group increases.

[34] Naomi R. Lamoreaux, "The Mystery of Property Rights: A U.S. Perspective," *Journal of Economic History* 71, no. 2 (June 2011), 275.

[35] Errol Meidinger, "The 'Public Uses' of Eminent Domain: History and Policy," *Environmental Law* 11, no. 1 (Spring 1980), 24.

[36] Price Fishback, "Seeking Security in the Postwar Era," in *Government and the American Economy: A New History* (Chicago, IL: University of Chicago Press, 2007), 508.

[37] Fishback, 509.

[38] Ilya Somin, *The Grasping Hand: Kelo v. City of New London & the Limits of Eminent Domain* (Chicago, IL: The University of Chicago Press, 2015).

[39] For the Supreme Court dissenting opinion, see www.law.cornell.edu/supct/html/04-108.ZD.html (accessed: November 17, 2014).

[40] Morton Horwitz, *The Transformation of American Law 1780–1860* (Cambridge, MA: Harvard University Press, 1977), 46.

[41] See B. Zorina Khan and Kenneth L. Sokoloff, "History Lessons: The Early Development of Intellectual Property Institutions in the United States," *Journal of Economic Perspectives* 15, no. 3 (Summer 2001), 233–246. Note that all scholars do not agree, however, about the importance of the patent system in stimulating technological advance and economic growth. For example, see Petra Moser, "Patents and Innovation: Evidence from Economic History," *Journal of Economic Perspectives* 27, no. 1 (Winter 2013), 23–44.

[42] See Timothy B. Lee, "15 Years Ago, Congress Kept Mickey Mouse Out of the Public Domain, Will They Do It Again?" *Washington Post* (October 25, 2013), www.washingtonpost.com/blogs/the-switch/wp/2013/10/25/15-years-ago-congress-kept-mickey-mouse-out-of-the-public-domain-will-they-do-it-again/ (accessed: October 23, 2014).

[43] B. Zorina Khan, "Looking Backward: Founding Choices in Innovation and Intellectual Property Protection," in Douglas A. Irwin and Richard Sylla (eds.), *Founding Choices: American Economic Policy in the 1790s* (Chicago, IL: University of Chicago Press, 2011), 315–343.

[44] Gavin Wright, *Slavery and American Economic Development* (Baton Rouge, LA: Louisiana State University Press, 2006), 7.

[45] Wright, 7.

[46] Charles J. Muhl, "The Employment-At-Will Doctrine: Three Major Exceptions," *Monthly Labor Review* (January 2001), 3.

[47] See Chapter 12 for a more detailed description of these exceptions.

[48] See, for example, Niall Ferguson, *The Great Degeneration: How Institutions Decay and Economies Die* (New York, NY: Penguin Books, 2012); and David Kennedy and Joseph E. Stiglitz, *Law and Economics with Chinese Characteristics: Institutions for Promoting Development in the Twenty-First Century* (Oxford, UK: Oxford University Press, 2013).

[49] Acemoglu and Robinson, 319–334.

5
The Financial System and Capital Accumulation

On April 30, 1789, when George Washington was inaugurated as the first president of the United States, the federal government was essentially bankrupt and the country's financial system was virtually nonexistent. However, by the end of Washington's first term, largely through the efforts of his Secretary of Treasury Alexander Hamilton, a "financial revolution" had taken place in commercial banking, securities markets, and central banking, and the federal government was on a firm financial footing.

By 1825, the U.S. financial system was arguably the most developed in the entire world, with bank capital per capita over twice that of Great Britain. Stock markets were more important in the United States as well, with corporate stock as a percentage of financial assets larger in the United States than in Great Britain, Germany, and France in both 1800 and 1850.[1]

The story of the U.S. financial system, however, is not one of continuous progress. For example, in many ways the financial system in the decades after the Civil War functioned less well than it had in the early nineteenth century. "Reversal of fortune" is a common theme throughout American history, with the financial system functioning better in some periods than in others, and with both progress and regression over time.[2]

In Chapter 2 we saw that growth in physical capital per hour of work is an important determinant of labor productivity growth, accounting for about one-third of labor productivity growth since 1800. Physical capital accumulation depends on the decisions of savers and borrowers, and on the efficiency of the financial system in allocating funds from savers to borrowers. A well-functioning financial system also spreads risks and transfers them to those most willing and able to bear the risks, which is also important to economic growth.

In the financial system, savers can provide funds directly to investors (direct finance) by buying securities like stocks and bonds in financial markets. Alternatively, savers can deposit funds into banks which then lend to investors (indirect finance). Throughout U.S. history, both direct and indirect finance have played key roles. In a financial world like this, borrowers are able to obtain funds at low interest rates for investment projects which can lead in turn to greater capital accumulation and economic growth.

It is easy to take the financial system for granted, yet without a modern financial system it is hard to imagine how there could have been, throughout U.S. history, such massive investments in canals, railroads, roads, machines, factories, education, and new technologies and products.

5.1 FEDERAL GOVERNMENT FINANCES

There are four potential ways of financing government spending: taxation, borrowing through issuing bonds, selling assets such as land, and printing money. During and after the Revolutionary War, the United States operated under the Articles of Confederation, whereby the states were a loose confederation and largely independent. This made it very difficult for the federal government to enact and collect taxes, since any national-level tax legislation required the unanimous consent of all states. With state governments weak and newly formed, individual states also struggled to raise revenue through taxes.

As a result, the federal government and state governments borrowed heavily from private investors and from Holland and France to finance military expenditures, and in consequence accumulated substantial debt. During the Revolutionary War, and similarly unable to tax or borrow enough, the Continental Congress issued large quantities of paper currency, known as the Continental, to help pay for the war effort, and this led to rapid inflation (see Economic History in Action 5.1). By 1790, outstanding government debt was estimated at more than $79 million or about 42 percent of GDP.[3] While in 2015 the debt-to-GDP ratio exceeded 100 percent, the burden of debt after the Revolutionary War was likely an even more daunting issue because the ability of the federal government to tax was so limited. For example, during the last three months of 1790, customs revenues, the main source of federal tax revenue, amounted to only $162,000—not nearly enough to cover even the *interest* on the debt.[4]

After the War ended in 1783, Alexander Hamilton and other Federalists embarked on a wide-ranging plan for a stronger central government, the principles of which are embodied in the U.S. Constitution. The Constitution was put into effect on March 4, 1789, giving the new government both taxing and monetary powers.

One of the first priorities was raising sufficient tax revenues to pay for government expenditures and to pay off the debt. Tariffs on imported goods and duties on ship tonnage were supplemented by domestic excise taxes. Domestic taxes proved highly unpopular, however, culminating in the Whiskey Rebellion in 1794; nevertheless, federal tax revenues roughly tripled between 1792 and 1805, with more than 90 percent coming from tariffs.

ECONOMIC HISTORY IN ACTION 5.1

The Quantity Theory of Money and Inflation

The quantity theory of money can be used to explain the causes of inflation. It begins with the quantity equation of money, which helps to link the money supply to the aggregate price level. The quantity equation is:

$$M_t V_t = P_t Y_t$$

where M_t is the money supply in year t, P_t is the aggregate price level in year t, Y_t is real GDP in year t, and V_t is the velocity of circulation. $P_t Y_t$ is nominal GDP in year t. For example, if the money supply (M_t) is $200 and nominal GDP ($P_t Y_t$) is $1,000, then velocity ($V_t$) must be 5. That is, on average each dollar must circulate five times to allow a money supply of $200 to facilitate $1,000 in the purchases of final goods and services.

The equation above applies when variables remain in levels, but we are usually more interested in growth rates. Using the growth rate rules from Chapter 2 (Economic History in Action 2.2), we can write the equation above in terms of growth rates:

$$g_M + g_V = g_P + g_Y$$

The equations above are true by definition, but to convert the quantity equation to the quantity theory of money, we need to make three additional assumptions. First, in the long run, the velocity of money is assumed to be constant: that is, the growth rate of velocity is assumed to be zero ($g_V = 0$). Second, it is assumed that the growth rate of real GDP (g_Y) is largely independent of the growth rate of the money supply. (This is consistent with Chapter 2, where we saw that the growth of real GDP depended on the growth of inputs and the growth of total factor productivity.) Finally, it is assumed that causation runs primarily from the growth rate of the money supply to the growth rate of prices. The growth rate of prices (g_P) is the rate of inflation, and is commonly written as π.

We can now solve for the inflation rate:

$$\pi = g_M - g_Y$$

That is, the quantity theory of money predicts that the inflation rate in the long run is equal to the difference between the growth rate of the money supply and the growth rate of real GDP. If the growth rate of the money supply is higher, then so too is the long-run rate of inflation.

The quantity theory of money is consistent with the rapid monetary growth and inflation during the Revolutionary and Civil Wars.[5]

Historical Episodes of High Inflation			
Episode	Dates of Episode	Duration	Annual Rate of Inflation (Percent)
Revolutionary War	Feb. 1777–Jan. 1780	36 months	203.7
Civil War (Confederate South)	Feb. 1861–Apr. 1865	51 months	189.2
Civil War (Union North)	1862–1864	3 years	29.4

Sources and Notes: Computed from Stanley Fischer, Ratna Sahay, and Carlos A. Végh, "Modern Hyper- And High Inflations," *Journal of Economic Literature* 40, no. 3 (September 2002), Table 1, 838.

While inflation rates of 200 percent per year are extreme when compared to the 2 or 3 percent inflation rates that the United States has typically experienced recently, U.S. hyperinflations are very modest by world standards. The biggest hyperinflation in world history occurred in Hungary in 1945 and 1946, when the cumulative inflation rate was more than 13,000,000,000,000,000,000,000,000,000,000,000 percent![6]

Hamilton's plan went beyond just financing current expenditures: he also wished to restructure and pay off the debts incurred by both the federal and state governments during the War. Three new types of bonds were issued to pay off past debts. While this was controversial at the time, in retrospect it established the United States as a creditworthy nation, allowing it throughout its history to regularly borrow vast sums at very low interest rates.

5.2   BANKS AND FINANCIAL INTERMEDIARIES

THE ROLE OF COMMERCIAL BANKS

Commercial banks are financial intermediaries that match savers and borrowers. Banks raise capital from investors, accept deposits from customers, and then use those funds to make loans to individuals and businesses. With home mortgages, student loans, debit cards, automatic teller machines, and over 80,000 bank branches nationwide in 2015, banking is an integral part of the economy.

This was not always the case, however. During the colonial period, the British government *prohibited* banks in the colonies. Without banks, lending volumes were low and little lending activity occurred outside close kinship networks, because of problems of information asymmetry.[7] For example, consider borrowing and lending activity between individuals, without commercial banks serving as intermediaries. Adverse selection is a problem of information asymmetry that occurs before a transaction takes place. Individual potential borrowers will naturally know more about their creditworthiness than will individual potential lenders. Lenders, on the other hand, will not be able to determine good credit risks from bad credit risks. Moreover, the potential borrowers who are the most unlikely to pay back a loan will also be the borrowers most likely to seek a loan. From the potential lenders' perspectives, therefore, there is an adverse selection, or adverse sorting: the least creditworthy are the most likely to seek funds through borrowing. Lenders will soon learn that borrowers are "bad risks". In extreme cases, if they are unable to distinguish between good and bad credit risks, they may refuse to make *any* loans.

Moral hazard, in contrast, occurs after the transaction has occurred. Moral hazard results whenever a borrower does anything to limit his or her obligation to pay back a loan. One example is when a borrower uses the proceeds from a loan for a different and perhaps more risky purpose than was agreed upon.

THE ORIGINS OF COMMERCIAL BANKING

Banks and other financial intermediaries are able to reduce these information asymmetries by creating private information about borrowers through procedures such as screening and monitoring, by requiring collateral, and by requiring borrowers to agree to enforceable restrictive covenants that induce borrowers to put the loans to their intended uses.

The first commercial bank in the United States was the Bank of North America, which opened in 1782. Robert Morris, a Philadelphia businessperson and our nation's first Superintendent of Finance, petitioned the Continental Congress for a bank charter. Although the bank was a private corporation, it provided some of the functions of a central bank. In 1787, however, the Bank of North America received a charter from Pennsylvania, which converted it to a state-chartered bank. The next commercial bank to open was The Bank of New York, established in 1784 by Alexander Hamilton; and this bank is still in existence today as The Bank of New York Mellon.

THE ROLE OF CENTRAL BANKS

Modern central banks, such as the Federal Reserve System in the United States, serve many important functions. The best-known role of central banks is monetary policy, whereby central banks influence the money supply and interest rates in the economy to reduce the severity of economic fluctuations and to promote a low and stable inflation rate. In addition, during financial crises and other emergencies, central banks lend to private commercial banks when those banks need loans to survive and cannot get the funds from private sources. By providing such loans, the central bank prevents further financial crises. That is, central banks serve as the lender of last resort. Modern central banks also have supervisory powers that allow them to regulate private commercial banks by restricting their activities, and can use these powers to reduce the risk of bank failures and bank runs. Finally, central banks serve as the bank for private commercial banks and for the government.

Many developed countries in the world today have had a central bank in continuous operation for 150 years or more. The first central bank was the Swedish Riksbank (1668), which was followed by the Bank of England (1694). By the mid-nineteenth century, many other countries had established central banks, including France (1800), Finland (1811), Netherlands (1814), Norway (1816), Austria (1816), Denmark (1818), Germany (1846), and Spain (1856).[8]

In contrast, the history of central banking in the United States is the notable exception to this general pattern, with the United States establishing three central banks in its history while dismantling two of them. From the demise of the Second Bank of the United States in 1836 to the establishment of the Federal Reserve System in 1913, the United States was almost the only industrializing country without a central bank.

FIRST BANK OF THE UNITED STATES

The First Bank of the United States (FBUS) is usually regarded as the country's first central bank, opening in 1791 with a 20-year charter.[9] The FBUS issued $10 million in stock to capitalize the bank, with 20 percent of it owned by the federal government and the remaining 80 percent sold to private investors.

While five states had chartered commercial banks by the end of 1791, the FBUS was the only nationally-chartered bank, and as a result it was the only bank that could operate branches anywhere in the country. Headquartered in Philadelphia, the bank almost immediately opened branches in New York, Boston, Baltimore, and Charleston. By 1804, additional branches were in operation in New Orleans, Norfolk, Savannah, and Washington, DC.

One important function of the FBUS was to limit private banks from issuing too many notes (money) by redeeming these notes at the state-chartered banks. This provided banks with an incentive not to issue notes beyond their supply of specie.

By the time the charter was set to expire, the Federalist administrations of Washington and Adams had given way to the anti-Federalist administrations of Jefferson and Madison. Most of Congress was also anti-Federalist, so the FBUS charter was not renewed.

As a result, the lack of a central bank and the War of 1812 led to a period of rapid monetary expansion followed by a widespread banking panic in August 1814. The Secretary of the Treasury, Albert Gallatin, blamed the excessive expansion and later panic on the failure to renew the FBUS charter.

SECOND BANK OF THE UNITED STATES

Even before the panic in 1814, proposals were circulating for another central bank. President James Madison signed into law the charter of the Second Bank of the United States (SBUS). Like the FBUS, the SBUS had a 20-year charter and the federal government owned 20 percent of it. Bank capital, however, was larger ($35 million, compared with $10 million for the FBUS). In 1817, 18 branches were open throughout the country, growing to 25 branches by 1830.

As the only bank with a national presence, the SBUS helped to control the money supply by quickly returning notes to state banks. The SBUS also acted as a lender of last resort by directly extending loans to private banks during times of crisis.

Despite the success of the SBUS in promoting financial stability and controlling inflation, the election of Andrew Jackson in 1828, and his re-election in 1832, signaled the end of central banking in the United States for more than 75 years. Jackson campaigned against the SBUS because he had a deep distrust of financial elites. Many banks, farmers, and businesses also resented the restraint that the SBUS had imposed on credit creation and inflation, while others mistrusted banks and corporations, or continued to believe that banking was a state and not a federal responsibility.[10]

As before, after the charter expired there was a period of rapid monetary expansion and inflation, which was soon followed by financial panics in 1837 and 1839 and a severe recession. While scholars continue to debate whether the demise of the SBUS was directly responsible for the financial panics, in 1841 Congress passed a bill to establish a third central bank, only to have the bill vetoed by President John Tyler.

THE FREE BANKING AND NATIONAL BANKING ERAS

The closing of the SBUS, which had accepted deposits, issued notes, and made loans throughout its 25 branches nationwide, meant a substantial reduction in the nation's banking services. States immediately recognized the need to establish new banks to fill the void. The period from 1837 to 1863 is known as the Free Banking Era, or State Banking Era, since U.S. states made entry into banking easier. New York proposed the first free banking law, which allowed anyone to open a bank as long as all notes issued were backed by state bonds deposited in the state auditor's office, with all notes redeemable on demand at face value. A special legislative charter was no longer needed. By 1860, a majority of U.S. states had some form of free banking laws.[11] While this period has been portrayed as one of unscrupulous "wildcat" banking, recent evidence suggests that it was not detrimental to economic growth, and actually had positive effects on manufacturing and urbanization.[12]

FIGURE 5.1 The Second Bank of the United States in Philadelphia, 1831

Source: Charles Burton, Library of Congress, www.loc.gov/pictures/collection/cph/item/2015650264/ (accessed: April 2, 2016). Published originally by I.T. Hinton & Simpkin & Marshall, London, March 1, 1831.

The Free Banking Era ended with the passage of the National Banking Acts of 1863 and 1864, when the federal government attempted to gain some control over the banking system, without the formation of another central bank, by creating a system of nationally-chartered commercial banks. The result was the dual banking system that we continue to have today, in which some banks are nationally chartered, while others are chartered by individual U.S. states.

Under these laws, the federal government was given the right to issue notes to banks in return for a deposit of federal government bonds. In 1865, a tax on state-chartered bank notes was imposed, as a result of which only national banks issued notes (money), which were of uniform design and printed by the federal government.

Another feature of this system was the prevalence of unit banking. A unit bank is a small, single bank with no branches. National-chartered banks were restricted to operating in one state only, with a single office and no branches (a unit bank). The restrictions on state-chartered banks varied. Although state-chartered banks could only operate in the state that granted the charter, some states permitted branches, while others did not (unit banks). In the years after 1863, unit banking was the norm for both federal and state-chartered banks, but by 1900 seventeen states allowed within-state branch banking, while twenty-eight states did not allow any branch banking.[13] After 1900, more states allowed branch banking, with roughly 75 percent of U.S. states allowing branch banking by 1940. In addition, the Banking Act of 1933 (the Glass-Steagall Act) allowed national banks to open branches in states that already permitted their own banks to branch.

The prevalence of unit banking in the United States during this period was detrimental both to banks and to customers, and contributed to instability in the U.S. banking system. Branch banking has several advantages over unit banking. First, with unit banking, a bank can only operate in one location, and the bank's health is wholly dependent on the local economy in that area. Second, branching allows for greater diversification. Branch banking allowed banks to diversify across communities, enabling them to tie their loans to a multitude of different businesses.

Third, branch banking also allows for economies of scale, such that larger banks can operate more efficiently than smaller banks because they can offer services at lower costs per customer. In addition, branching allows commercial banks to serve sometimes as their own lenders of last resort, because in times of crisis they can reallocate funds from branch to branch.

The Free Banking and National Banking Eras were periods of tremendous financial instability. The prevalence of unit banking and the absence of a central bank, along with other institutional features of the U.S. banking system, contributed to its instability. While the United States had twelve financial crises since 1840, Canada, for example, has had none.[14]

This does not imply that bigger banks are always better. Many economists have argued that the large commercial banks and financial institutions in the United States today have become too large, too interconnected, and "too big to fail." Many have argued that unless strict regulations are imposed the massive bailouts of the financial system during the financial crisis of 2008 will lead to excessive risk-taking on the part of banks and other financial intermediaries in the future, as they will believe that government will bail them out if they get into trouble again.

THE FEDERAL RESERVE SYSTEM

In response to the Panic of 1907, in 1913 Congress created the Federal Reserve (the Fed). Unlike the FBUS and the SBUS, the Fed charter is permanent, and commercial banks are the shareholders instead of private investors. The legislation included twelve regional Federal Reserve Banks and a seven-member Board of Governors.[15]

At times, the Fed has helped stabilize the economy, but there have also been dramatic policy failures like the Fed's role in the Great Depression of the 1930s and the Great Inflation of the 1970s. The economic history of financial crises and monetary policies under the Federal Reserve is examined in Chapter 18.

COMMERCIAL BANKING SINCE THE GREAT DEPRESSION

The largest financial crisis in American history occurred during the Great Depression, when nearly 10,000 banks failed or suspended operations (see Figure 5.2). Many economic historians blame the Federal Reserve for standing idly by while the banking system nearly crumbled.

Because of the experiences during the Great Depression, the commercial banking industry was a highly regulated one from 1933 to the early 1980s. Deposit insurance through the Federal Deposit Insurance Corporation was introduced in 1933, and there were regulations that limited the formation of banks and branches, and that capped the interest rates banks could pay depositors and charge borrowers. From the 1950s to the 1980s, banking was referred to as a "3-6-3" business: bankers, it was said, had a comfortable and boring existence, paying depositors 3 percent, lending money out at 6 percent, and being on the golf course by 3 p.m.[16]

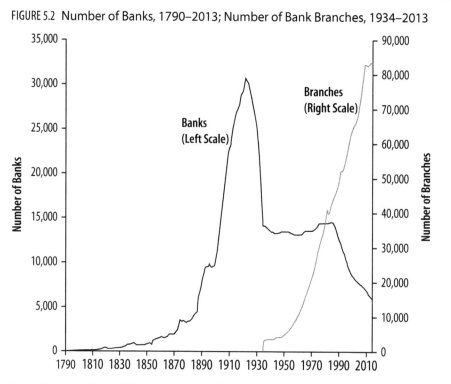

FIGURE 5.2 Number of Banks, 1790–2013; Number of Bank Branches, 1934–2013

Sources: Data from 1790 to 1833: J. Van Fenstemaker, *The Development of American Commercial Banking, 1782–1837* (Kent, OH: Kent State University Press, 1965). Data from 1834 to 1931: *Annual Report of the Comptroller of the Currency*, Table No. 96 (December 7, 1931). Data from 1932 and 1933: *Federal Reserve Bulletin*, Table 1, 1087 (November 1937). Data from 1934 to 2013: Federal Deposit Insurance Corporation, www2.fdic.gov/hsob/HSOBRpt.asp (accessed: September 27, 2014).

Since the 1980s, many of the New Deal regulations on banking and the financial sector have been eliminated, leading to tremendous growth in the financial sector, but also to greater instability. There are now far fewer banks, with fewer than 6,000 banks in 2013, yet the number of branches has skyrocketed (Figure 5.2). Historical restrictions on interstate branch banking were abolished completely in 1994 with the Riegle-Neal Interstate Banking and Branching Efficiency Act. Commercial banking is even more concentrated than Figure 5.2 suggests: in 2014 the four largest banks in the United States—J.P. Morgan Chase, Bank of America, Citigroup, and Wells Fargo—together owned over 40 percent of all commercial bank assets, compared with less than 10 percent in 1990.

INVESTMENT BANKING

In the late nineteenth and early twentieth centuries, there was a great merger movement in which large, modern corporations emerged in railroads, mining, and manufacturing. Because of the branch banking restrictions described above, commercial banks were too small to help these massive industrial corporations, such as U.S. Steel.

As a result, investment banks developed. These served as important financial intermediaries. An investment bank is not really a bank at all, in the sense that it does not accept deposits. Investment banks, however, served many other important functions, such as acting as an underwriter when corporations issued new stocks and bonds. They also provided advice regarding mergers and acquisitions, whereby two or more corporations consolidate to become one. By 1900, the investment banking industry was a highly concentrated oligopoly, dominated by J.P. Morgan and Company, Kuhn, Loeb and Company, Brown Brothers, and Kidder, Peabody and Company.[17]

Throughout the twentieth century, investment banking remained highly concentrated. By 2004, the biggest investment banks were Goldman Sachs, J.P. Morgan Stanley, Merrill Lynch, Lehman Brothers, and Bear Stearns. The financial crisis of 2008, however, led to the collapse and reorganization of the investment banking industry. Lehman Brothers collapsed and declared bankruptcy, while Bear Stearns was purchased by J.P. Morgan Chase and Merrill Lynch by Bank of America. Surviving investment banks like Goldman Sachs and J.P. Morgan Chase converted to bank holding companies, in order to be eligible for government bailouts.[18]

OTHER FINANCIAL INTERMEDIARIES

As late as 1950, depository institutions (commercial banks and thrift institutions) accounted for almost two-thirds of financial intermediary assets (see Table 5.1). Thrift institutions have a long history in the United States: they include mutual savings banks (1816); building and loans (1831), later called savings and loans; and credit unions (1908). Like commercial banks, thrift institutions also accept deposits, but they are usually owned cooperatively by the individual depositors.

In 1950, commercial banks, thrift institutions, and life insurance companies held over 85 percent of total financial intermediary assets. By 2013, the share of these three types of intermediaries had fallen to 26.4 percent. In the post-World War II period, many other types of financial intermediaries have grown in relative importance, including public and private pension funds (20.1 percent of total financial intermediary assets), mutual funds (14.2 percent of total assets), and government-sponsored enterprises like Fannie Mae and Freddie Mac (7.8 percent).

Pension funds provide income to retired workers. Employers, both private firms and governments, contribute money (often with contributions from workers too) to buy securities, such as stocks and bonds, and the earnings from these securities provide retirement benefits. While retirement plans started as government promises to fund old-age pensions to veterans of the Revolutionary and Civil Wars, such plans began to be offered to state and local government employees during the Progressive Era at the end of the nineteenth century, and to federal workers in 1920. Private pension funds expanded greatly during World War II, when wage controls prevented wage increases and led firms to look for other ways to compete for workers, such as offering retirement (and health) benefits.

The first mutual fund in the United States started in 1924. Mutual funds are financial intermediaries which hold diversified portfolios of securities and sell shares of these portfolios to savers. Mutual funds allow small investors to hold a much more diversified portfolio to reduce the investor's risk than would be possible from just buying a small set of individual securities. Hedge funds, in contrast, accept funds only from a limited number of wealthy individuals or large institutions.

TABLE 5.1 Financial Intermediaries' Shares of Financial Assets (Percent)				
Year	Commercial Banks	Thrift Institutions	Life Insurance Companies	All Other Intermediaries
1880	62.6	23.9	10.5	3.1
1900	62.9	18.2	10.7	8.2
1922	63.2	12.5	11.6	12.7
1950	50.8	13.3	21.1	14.8
1990	27.0	12.8	11.1	49.1
2013	15.7	3.9	7.4	73.6

Sources and Notes: Computed from Eugene White, "Were Banks Special Intermediaries in Late Nineteenth Century America?" *Federal Reserve Bank of St. Louis Review* 80, no. 3 (May/June 1998), Table 1, 14; and Federal Reserve, *Financial Accounts of the United States* (First Quarter 2014).

5.3   MONEY

WHAT IS MONEY?

Economists define money in terms of the functions it serves, and the three main functions of money are as a medium of exchange, as a unit of account, and as a store of value. The medium of exchange function is perhaps the most important function of money. Something is a medium of exchange if it is routinely used to purchase goods and services. A medium of exchange is critically important in an economy, since it avoids the "double coincidence of wants" problem that arises with barter exchange. With barter, in order to buy something you have to find someone who is willing to sell you what you want to buy, and who is simultaneously willing to buy what you have to sell in exchange. This is often a very difficult challenge.

Another important function of money is that it serves as the unit of account. That is, nearly everything is quoted in terms of dollars, from how much it costs for a cup of coffee to how much a professional athlete earned last year. Without money, there would be a nearly infinite number of relative prices (that is, the price of any one product in relation to any other single product). For example, a typical Walmart store contains 120,000 different products and thus over 7 million relative prices.[19]

Money is also a store of value: it holds its value over time. That is, you can store money in your sock drawer today and spend it next year, when—provided inflation has been minimal—it will buy approximately the same amount of goods and services. While money is a store of value, it is not a particularly *good* store of value, because most money, such as currency and most checking accounts, does not pay an interest rate. Assets such as stocks and bonds, in contrast, typically grow more in value over time, and are therefore a better way to store value.

While currency has been a common medium of exchange throughout most of U.S. history, another important medium of exchange is checking account deposits, which can be accessed through written, paper checks, and through electronic payments using debit cards and other forms of electronic transfers. While checking account deposits are ubiquitous today, personal checks were very uncommon prior to the Civil War, and then used only for large transactions.

The Federal Reserve publishes two definitions of the money supply: M1 and M2. M1 emphasizes the medium of exchange functions of money and includes currency and checking account deposits.[20] The Fed also reports a broader measure of the money supply which includes other assets that can easily be converted to M1. M2 consists of all of M1 plus savings account deposits; small time deposits of less than $100,000, like certificates of deposit (CDs); and money-market mutual funds of less than $50,000 that hold bonds with maturities of less than one year (see Section 5.4 below).

COMMODITY AND FIAT MONEY

Throughout its history, the United States has alternated between commodity money and fiat money. Commodity money is a valuable good that also serves as a medium of exchange, like gold, which has value in jewelry and in other uses. Fiat money, in contrast, has no intrinsic value beyond its value as a medium of exchange. Dollar bills today are money simply because the government has decreed them to be so "by fiat." We use dollars because we trust that others will accept them when we purchase goods and services.

During the colonial period, many things served as a medium of exchange, including wampum, furs, tobacco, coins from many countries (but particularly England or Spain), book credit, and bills of exchange.[21] These were generally forms of commodity money since the goods—such as fur and tobacco, as well as the gold and silver in coins—had value beyond their value as money.

The first national currency was the Continental dollar, which was fiat money created by the Continental Congress in 1776. During the Revolutionary War, Congress printed large amounts of Continentals, causing them to become nearly worthless as inflation spiraled out of control.

The Coinage Act of 1792 established the United States Mint. The Mint adopted a decimal system for currency (instead of relying on the complicated British system, in which one pound was divided into 20 shillings, and each shilling into 12 pence). The Mint also created a bimetallic standard, creating both silver and gold coins. The decision to implement a bimetallic standard proved to be a controversial one, and debates over gold and silver continued throughout the nineteenth century.

In the decades leading up to the Civil War, paper money became more common as well. Both the First and Second Banks of the United States issued "national bank notes" which were backed by gold and silver coins. Commercial banks issued bank notes and promised to exchange their notes for coins. By 1860, there were more than 10,000 different types and denominations of bank notes in circulation, issued by nearly 1,600 state-chartered banks.

During the Civil War, fiat money returned. The Union currency, called "Greenbacks" because it was the first currency of that color, was printed in large amounts to help pay for the War. Rapid inflation ensued in the North, while in the Confederate South the experience was even worse, with huge quantities of Confederate dollars leading to even more rapid inflation (see Economic History in Action 5.1).

After the Civil War, there was a return to a commodity money standard based on gold at prewar rates. The Coinage Act of 1873 (also known as the "Crime of 1873") removed the silver dollar from circulation and only allowed silver in coins of less than 1 dollar. In 1879, the United States reestablished commodity money by linking the value of the dollar to gold: 20.67 dollars was equal to one ounce of gold. The primary form of paper money was gold certificates, redeemable in gold.

Without a central bank, the government did not control the money supply, but passively issued gold certificates to anyone who turned in gold, and paid gold to anyone who redeemed gold certificates. Because the money supply was tied to the quantity of gold, the quantity of money (and aggregate prices) depended on the supply of gold. Prices generally fell until 1896, and then increased as the result of gold discoveries in Alaska and elsewhere.

In the twentieth century, the United States gradually returned to fiat money. After 1913, the Fed was required to hold gold reserves equal to 40 percent of the money it created, although the Fed still allowed people and institutions to trade dollars for gold and vice versa. The United States temporarily broke the link between gold and dollars in 1933, but reestablished the gold standard in 1934 at a reduced value of the dollar relative to gold, allowing the money supply to increase substantially. In addition, Americans could no longer trade dollars for gold, and between 1934 and 1974 it was illegal for private citizens to own gold, except in small amounts for jewelry.

In 1945, the Fed reduced the gold reserve requirement to 25 percent, and eliminated this requirement entirely in 1965. The final transition to a pure fiat currency occurred in 1971, when President Richard Nixon prohibited foreign governments from exchanging dollars for gold.

5.4   SECURITIES

A security is a tradable financial asset. There are many types of securities, including stocks, bonds, and derivative securities (such as futures and options). The initial sale of a security is called a primary market transaction; examples include the U.S. Treasury conducting an auction of newly issued bonds, or a corporation going public with an initial public offering (IPO) of stock. Most trading in financial markets, however, occurs in secondary market transactions, in which previously issued securities are exchanged with the help of brokers.

BONDS

When governments or corporations need to borrow funds, they can issue bonds. A bond is called a fixed-income security: it is a promise to pay to the holder of the bond a predetermined amount of money at one or more specified times in the future. The firms or governments that issue the bonds are borrowers, while those that purchase the bonds are savers.

The first federal bonds were issued by the Department of the Treasury to pay off state and federal debts after the Revolutionary War. From then to the present, governments have borrowed extensively to fund wars and to fund infrastructure projects, such as canals, roads, bridges, and schools. Since the late 1800s, corporations too have borrowed extensively; their bonds, issued in what is called the commercial paper market, have maturities from 90 days and to 270 days. In recent years, the bond market has been by far the largest financial market in the United States, far exceeding the size of stock markets.[22]

STOCKS

Stocks are known as equity securities, since a stock certificate is a legal document that certifies ownership of a fraction of a corporation. If, for example, the corporation has issued 10,000 stock shares and you own 100 of them, then you own 1 percent (100/10,000) of the corporation.

The first shareholder-owned company may have been the East India Company, founded by Dutch merchants in 1602. During the colonial period, eight corporations were formed, but by 1800 there were over three hundred corporations in the United States, with two-thirds of these engaged in the building of transportation improvements such as turnpike roads, canals, and bridges. Almost 10 percent were banks.[23]

The trading of stocks and bonds started in several U.S. cities around 1790. In 1792, the Buttonwood Agreement was signed, signaling the beginning of what was to become the New York Stock Exchange. Historically, stock markets are auction markets where stocks are traded on a bustling trading floor, with traders motioning frantically to each other to signal prices. Today, however, all major stock exchanges operate primarily or exclusively through electronic auctions rather than face-to-face auctions on a trading floor. The New York Stock Exchange (NYSE) and NASDAQ (formerly known as the National Association of Securities Dealers Automated Quotation System) are currently the two largest in the world, accounting for nearly half of all stock exchange trading worldwide.[24]

Until the early 2000s, the overwhelming majority of stock trading occurred in formal stock exchanges, and the volume and price of every trade was public information. However, both technological and regulatory changes have since allowed trading to occur outside such exchanges, making it possible for traders to operate in secrecy. It has been estimated that by 2013 around 15 percent of U.S. stock trading occurred in approximately 50 so-called "dark pools."[25]

DERIVATIVES

Derivatives are financial instruments whose values are tied to underlying assets, such as commodities, stocks, or bonds. They consist of futures, options, and more complex derivatives.

A futures contract is an agreement to trade a certain commodity or financial asset for a certain price at a particular future point in time. Futures are used for both hedging and speculation. When someone hedges, they reduce risk by taking two opposing positions, allowing them to make money in futures markets when they lose money elsewhere (in a spot market), and vice versa. In contrast, someone who speculates is simply betting on the direction of price changes in markets.

Commodity futures in wheat, corn, cotton, and other agricultural commodities have been traded in the United States since the mid-nineteenth century. Financial futures, based on future prices of stock indexes, bonds, interest rates, or other financial assets, are more recent, with the first traded in 1972. In recent decades, many unregulated "exotic" derivatives have emerged, and these played a large role in the 2008 financial crisis (see Chapter 18).

SECURITIZATION

Securitization refers to the process in which individual loans are aggregated into securities that can be sold in financial markets. These securities are valuable because they represent claims on the cash flows from a pool of loans, most often mortgage loans on residential property. A mortgage-backed security (MBS) is a type of derivative: its value derives from the value of the underlying assets, the pool of mortgage loans.

The Federal National Mortgage Association (1938), known as Fannie Mae, was originally a U.S. government agency that established a secondary market in mortgages. Since 1957, banks have been permitted to buy and sell mortgages. Pass-through certificates, first issued in 1970, were the first modern mortgage-backed securities.

In recent decades, mortgage-backed securities and other asset-backed securities have exploded in volume, and these are now the largest debt securities behind U.S. Treasury bonds.[26]

5.5 INTEREST RATES AND THE THEORY OF LOANABLE FUNDS

The loanable funds theory provides a framework for understanding the factors that influence real interest rates and investment spending. While central banks can affect real interest rates in the short run, the forces of supply and demand determine real interest rates in the long run. The loanable funds market is not a physical location but the set of exchanges and banks, including bond markets, stock exchanges, mutual funds, investment banks, and commercial banks, where savers and borrowers interact.

Like any model, the theory of loanable funds is an abstraction because it assumes only one type of loan and only one interest rate. It also ignores the role of banks and other financial intermediaries in matching savers and borrowers. Nevertheless, it provides a useful framework for better understanding the determinants of saving, investment, and interest rates.

NOMINAL AND REAL INTEREST RATES

Interest rates are both the reward for saving and the cost of borrowing. Suppose you deposit $1 into an account with the promise that you will receive $1.05 in one year. We can use the growth rate rules from Chapter 2 to write this as:

$$\$1(1 + 0.05) = \$1.05$$

That is, in one year, you receive back your original principal of $1, plus 5 cents in interest as a reward for saving.

What rational savers and borrowers care about, however, is not the nominal or money interest rate, but the real or inflation-adjusted interest rate. A rational saver wants to know what she will be able to buy with the $1.05 received in one year. Is the purchasing power of $1.05 one year from now greater or less than the purchasing power of $1 today, and if so, by how much?

Let r denote the real or inflation-adjusted interest rate, i the nominal interest rate (0.05, or 5 percent, in the example above), and π the inflation rate, which measures the increase (or decrease) in the prices of all goods and services. The real interest rate is:

$$r = i - \pi$$

That is, the real interest rate is equal to the difference between the nominal interest rate and the inflation rate.[27] Suppose you earn a nominal interest rate of 5 percent ($i = 0.05$) over the next year: your $1 will grow to $1.05. However, if over the same period there was inflation of 5 percent ($\pi = 0.05$), then the $1.05 would buy the same amount of goods and services next year as the $1 buys now. In other words, the *real* interest rate would be 0 percent.

On the other hand, if the prices of goods and services increased over that period by only 2 percent ($\pi = 0.02$), then you would be able to purchase about 3 percent more goods and services next year ($r = 0.03$). In that case, the real interest rate would be 3 percent.

THE THEORY OF LOANABLE FUNDS

The theory of loanable funds posits that the real interest rate is simply a price, and like any other price it can be examined using the tools of supply and demand. Domestic households and governments, as well as foreign households and governments, are the suppliers of saving or loanable funds. The supply of saving flows to loans for borrowers, who use these proceeds for investment projects.

We can write the supply of saving as:

Saving = S = Private saving + Public saving + Net foreign saving

Private saving is the saving done by households, while public saving is the saving done by government. Public saving is positive if tax revenues are greater than spending (budget surplus), and negative if tax revenues are less than spending (budget deficit). The real interest rate is the reward for saving. As real interest rates increase, the amount of saving increases also: the supply curve of saving is upward-sloping.[28]

As with any supply curve, there are also exogenous shift variables which cause the quantity supplied of saving to change at any given real interest rate. The supply of saving will increase (shift right) if there is:

• an increase in consumer income or wealth;
• a decrease in the rate of time preferences (such that savers become more oriented toward the future);
• a decrease in foreign interest rates; and/or
• a decrease in the perceived risks of saving.

The demand for loans is equal to the demand for investment. Like any demand curve, the demand curve is downward-sloping: the quantity demanded increases as the cost of borrowing (the real interest rate) decreases. The demand curve for investment will increase (shift right) if there is:

• an increase in the productivity of capital; and/or
• an increase in investor confidence.

With the real interest rate on the vertical axis and the quantity of saving and investment on the horizontal axis, market equilibrium is determined by the intersection of the supply of saving and the demand for investment. In equilibrium, saving equals investment.

5.6 INVESTMENT, CAPITAL ACCUMULATION, AND ECONOMIC GROWTH

The theory of loanable funds can be used to help explain long-run decreases in real interest rates coupled with greater investment spending.

REAL INTEREST RATES AND INVESTMENT IN THE LONG RUN

From 1800 to 2015, real interest rates in the United States fell substantially. Between 1800 and 1849, long-run real interest rates averaged 6.2 percent per year. From 1850 to 1899, they fell to an average annual rate of 4 percent; and since 1900, real interest rates have averaged around 2.4 percent per year.[29] Lower real interest rates coupled with higher investment spending mean that the supply of saving has increased at a greater rate than the demand for investment, as shown in Figure 5.3.

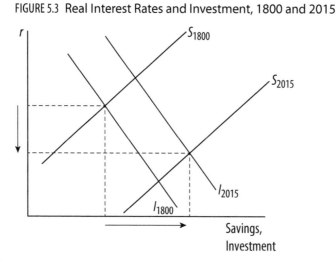

FIGURE 5.3 Real Interest Rates and Investment, 1800 and 2015

The demand for investment has increased (shifted right) tremendously, due to increased productivity of capital as a result of technological innovations, but saving must have shifted out even more to have led to a decrease in real interest rates.

Recall that total saving is the sum of private saving by domestic households, public savings by federal, state, and local governments, and foreign saving by foreign households and governments. There is no evidence that public saving has increased in the long run. In fact, public saving has become more negative in recent decades as governments have run larger budget deficits. By itself, this would reduce saving, drive up interest rates, and crowd out private investment. The long-run increase in saving must therefore be primarily due to some combination of higher private saving and higher foreign saving, which together have shifted the saving curve from S_{1800} to S_{2015}.

Private saving rates increased in the nineteenth century and remained high in the United States until the 1970s, when private saving rates began to fall. Foreign saving (capital inflows) have allowed the United States to maintain high rates of domestic investment spending in recent decades, and throughout much of American history. Between 1800 and 1900, foreign saving was positive and accounted for about 5 percent of total saving. While the magnitude is not large, foreign saving was particularly important in certain sectors of the economy, such as in financing railroads, and at certain time periods of rapid growth and structural change, particularly during the 1830s and 1880s. From World War I to the early 1980s, net foreign saving was negative, but since the early 1980s, net foreign saving has increased, largely offsetting the decreases in the domestic private and public saving in the United States.[30]

CAPITAL ACCUMULATION AND ECONOMIC GROWTH

The change in the capital stock in each period is the net effect of new investment less the depreciation of capital. If the economy accumulates more capital through investment than the amount of capital wearing out each period, then the capital stock is growing. Mathematically, we can show this as:

$$K_{t+1} = K_t + I_t - \bar{d}K_t$$

The expression above says that the capital stock next year K_{t+1} is equal to the capital stock this year K_t, plus the amount of new investment this year I_t, and less the amount of capital depreciation $\bar{d}K_t$. A constant fraction $\bar{d}$ of the capital stock is assumed to depreciate each year. For example, if the depreciation rate is 5 percent ($\bar{d} = 0.05$), then capital in an economy lasts an average of 20 years ($1/0.05 = 20$).

Next, subtract K_t from both sides of the equation above:

$$K_{t+1} - K_t \equiv \Delta K_{t+1} = I_t - \bar{d}K_t$$

Finally, divide sides by K_t to write it in terms of growth rates:

$$g_K = \frac{\Delta K_{t+1}}{K_t} = \frac{I_t}{K_t} - \bar{d}$$

Put simply, the growth rate of capital (g_K) is positive if the investment-to-capital ratio exceeds the depreciation rate. Over the long run, the growth rate of the stock of physical capital has averaged close to 3 percent per year, which helped to contribute to long-run economic growth.

5.7 CONCLUSIONS

A well-functioning financial system is a necessary precondition for sustained economic growth. The United States developed a monetary system, commercial banks, bond and stock markets, and central banking during the "Founding Era," and by 1825 may have had the most advanced financial system in the world. However, after the charter of the Second Bank of the United States expired in 1836, the rest of the nineteenth century and up to the Panic of 1907 was a period of frequent financial panics and instability. Despite this turbulence, however, the United States continued to grow and develop.

This instability led in 1913 to the creation of the Federal Reserve. In Chapter 18 we will return to discussing the importance of central banking and monetary policy in reducing the frequency and severity of economic fluctuations. While the Fed has been successful in some periods, as for example in preventing the Great Recession of 2008 from turning into another Great Depression, we will learn that at times the Fed has also made things worse either through inaction or through poorly conceived or ill-timed policies. For example, poor Federal Reserve policies contributed to the length and severity of the Great Depression of the 1930s, and also led to the Great Inflation of the 1970s.

QUESTIONS

1. Using the loanable funds theory, show on a graph how each of the following events affects savings (supply) and/or investment (demand). In each case, what happens to the real interest rate and the quantity of investment in the economy? Consider each case separately and explain your answer.

A. A war causes the government to increase spending on the military. (Assume that taxes do not change.)

B. Suppose that an increase in life expectancy causes a general decrease in the rate of time preference for individuals in this economy.

C. The introduction of railroads throughout the United States after 1830, and particularly after 1865, increased the productivity of capital in nearly all sectors of the economy.

2. Consider an economy in which physical capital lasts an average of 10 years. If the current level of investment this year is $1 million, and the value of the capital stock is $9 million, is the growth rate of the capital stock positive, negative, or zero? Explain.

3. Imagine that the nominal interest rate on your savings account is 1 percent a year and that inflation is 2 percent a year. After one year, would the money in your account buy more goods and services than it does today, the same, or less than today? Is the real interest rate positive, zero, or negative? Briefly explain.

4. Suppose that an economy is described by the quantity theory of money. Assume that velocity is constant and that real GDP grows at 3 percent per year in the long run. If the money supply grows by 100 percent, what is the approximate rate of inflation? Why might the money supply grow this quickly? Include examples from American history in your answer.

5. The chapter notes that the United States has had twelve financial crises since 1840, while Canada has had none. Why is there such a large discrepancy between these two countries in the prevalence of financial crises?

6. What are adverse selection and moral hazard? Why are these problems particularly common in the financial system, and how do financial intermediaries reduce them? Provide one example of adverse selection and one example of moral hazard not described in this chapter

NOTES

[1] Richard Sylla, "U.S. Securities Markets and the Banking System, 1790–1840," *Federal Reserve Bank of St. Louis Review* 80, no. 3 (May/June 1998), 83–98.

[2] Richard Sylla, "Reversing Financial Fortunes: Government and the Financial System since 1789," in *Government and the American Economy: A New History* (Chicago, IL: University of Chicago Press, 2007), 115–147.

[3] Estimates of nominal debt from Richard S. Grossman, *Wrong: Nine Economic Policy Disasters and What We Can Learn from Them* (New York, NY: Oxford University Press, 2013), 41; and estimates of nominal GDP from Louis Johnston and Samuel H. Williamson, "What Was the U.S. GDP Then?" *MeasuringWorth*, 2016.

[4] Grossman, 41.

[5] Hugh Rockoff, "War and Inflation in the United States from the Revolution to the First Iraq War," National Bureau of Economic Research Working Paper, no. 21221 (May 2015), www.nber.org/papers/w21221.

[6] Stanley Fischer, Ratna Sahay, and Carlos A. Végh, *Journal of Economic Literature* 40, no. 3 (September 2002), 837–880.

[7] Robert E. Wright, *The Wealth of Nations Rediscovered: Integration and Expansion in American Financial Markets, 1780–1850* (New York, NY: Cambridge University Press, 2002).

[8] Grossman, 34.

[9] The Bank of North America, which first operated as a nationally-chartered bank under the Continental Congress, performed some of the functions of a central bank.

[10] Federal Reserve Bank of Philadelphia, *The Second Bank of the United States: A Chapter in the History of Central Banking*, December 2010, www.philadelphiafed.org/publications/economic-education/second-bank.pdf (accessed: June 2, 2014).

[11] Arthur J. Rolnick and Warren E. Weber, "Free Banking, Wildcat Banking, and Shinplasters," *Federal Reserve Bank of Minneapolis Quarterly Review* 6, no. 3 (Fall 1982), Table 1, 12.

[12] Matthew Jaremski and Peter L. Rousseau, "Banks, Free Banks, and U.S. Economic Growth," *Economic Inquiry* 51, no. 2 (April 2013), 1603–1621.

[13] Rajeev Dehejia and Adriana Lleras-Muney, "Financial Development and Pathways of Growth: State Branch Banking and Deposit Insurance Laws in the United States, 1900–1940," *Journal of Law and Economics* 50, no. 2 (May 2007), 239–272.

[14] Charles W. Calomiris and Stephen H. Haber, *Fragile by Design: The Political Origins of Banking Crises and Scarce Credit* (Princeton, NJ: Princeton University Press, 2014).

[15] The twelve Federal Reserve District Banks are in Atlanta, Boston, Chicago, Cleveland, Dallas, Kansas City, Minneapolis, New York, Philadelphia, Richmond, St. Louis, and San Francisco.

[16] John R. Walter, "The 3-6-3 Rule: An Urban Myth?" Federal Reserve Bank of Richmond *Economic Quarterly* 92, no. 1 (Winter 2006), 51–78.

[17] David Stowell, *An Introduction to Investment Banks, Hedge Funds, and Private Equity: The New Paradigm* (Burlington, MA: Academic Press, 2010), 22.

[18] Alan S. Blinder, *After the Music Stopped: The Financial Crisis, the Response, and the Work Ahead* (New York, NY: Penguin, 2013), Table 6.1, 166–167.

[19] Walmart, http://news.walmart.com/news-archive/2005/01/07/our-retail-divisions (accessed: June 5, 2014). With n goods, there are $[n(n-1)]/2$ relative prices or $[120,000(119,999)]/2 = 7,199,940,000$.

[20] M1 also includes traveler's checks, although in 2015 traveler's checks were less than one-third of one percent of M1.

[21] Peter L. Rousseau and Caleb Stroup, "Monetization and Growth in Colonial New England, 1703–1749," *Explorations in Economic History* 48, no. 4 (December 2011), 600–613.

[22] Securities Industry and Financial Markets Association, www.sifma.org/research/statistics.aspx (accessed: April 8, 2016).

[23] Robert E. Wright, "Rise of the Corporation Nation," in Douglas A. Irwin and Richard Sylla (eds.), *Founding Choices: American Economic Policy in the 1790s* (Chicago, IL: Chicago University Press, 2011), Table 7.1, 220–221.

[24] Marc Levinson, *Guide to Financial Markets: Why They Exist and How They Work*, Sixth Edition (New York, NY: The Economist), 180.

[25] Levinson, 185.

[26] Securities Industry and Financial Markets Association, www.sifma.org/research/statistics.aspx (accessed: April 8, 2016).

[27] This is an approximation. The exact formula is:

$$1 + r = \frac{1 + i}{1 + \pi}$$

This can be simplified to:

$$r = i - \pi - r\pi$$

Since the last term, $r\pi$, is approximately zero for small values of r and π, it is usually ignored.

[28] An upward-sloping supply curve for savings assumes that the substitution effect is larger than the income effect.

29 The nominal interest rate is the long-term rate (contemporary series) from Lawrence H. Officer, "What Was the Interest Rate Then?" *MeasuringWorth*, www.measuringworth.com/interestrates/ (accessed: June 14, 2014). The inflation rate is from Samuel H. Williamson, "Seven Ways to Compute the Relative Value of a U.S. Dollar Amount, 1774 to present," *MeasuringWorth*, April 2013, www.measuringworth.com/inflation/ (accessed: June 14, 2014). The real rate is the difference between the nominal interest rate and the inflation rate.

30 Lance E. Davis and Robert J. Cull, "International Capital Markets, Domestic Capital Markets, and American Economic Growth, 1820–1914," in *Cambridge Economic History of the United States*, Volume 2 (New York, NY: Cambridge University Press, 1996), 733–812.

6
Natural Capital

Although numerous scholars have stressed the importance of natural capital to America's success, the growth accounting exercises from Chapter 2 suggested that natural capital has in fact been an insignificant contributor to economic growth. There are, however, three main reasons to question the growth accounting results.

The first reason focuses on measurement issues. In Chapter 2, the growth of natural capital was measured by the growth of the land area of the United States, whereas natural capital actually encompasses a far broader range of natural assets, including the quality of agricultural land, pasture land, and forests. Natural capital also includes subsurface resources like metals, minerals, oil, coal, and natural gas, and above-ground resources such as the potential for water, solar, and wind power. The climate and navigable waterways are also part of natural capital stock. Since it is almost impossible to quantify the true value of this broader measure of natural capital, the growth accounting exercises may have underestimated the importance of natural capital.

Second, there was often a long delay between the time of a territorial acquisition and the time when an area contributed to economic growth. As late as the Civil War, two-thirds of the area of the United States was still in the public domain and largely unoccupied, yet natural capital without people and production cannot contribute to economic growth. For example, while Texas was granted statehood in 1845, it wasn't until 1901 that the Lucas gusher at Spindletop started the decades-long oil boom in Texas that helped drive the American economy.[1] Here again, measurement issues make it difficult to fully quantify the magnitude and timing of natural capital in simple growth accounting exercises.

The third possible explanation for how natural capital could have been more important to economic growth than growth accounting suggests focuses on ways in which the quantity and type of natural capital may have indirectly affected the growth and development of the United States. Examples include the effects of natural capital on:

- institutional developments
- human capital accumulation and work effort
- market growth (through encouraging high rates of population growth, transportation improvements, and the location, size, and density of cities)
- manufacturing and industrialization.

The use of natural capital (particularly the burning of fossil fuels) and the production of goods and services both lead to environmental damages (negative externalities) that harm the natural capital stock. Chapter 19 will discuss the negative consequences for the environment of industrialization and economic growth, and potential policy responses that might mitigate these impacts. The purpose of this chapter, however, is to focus on the possible direct and indirect ways in which natural capital can help to stimulate economic growth.

6.1   NATURAL CAPITAL AND INSTITUTIONAL DEVELOPMENTS

In Chapter 4, the impact of the English common-law heritage on institutional development in the U.S. was examined. While empirical evidence is consistent with the legal-origins hypothesis, there is also substantial empirical evidence that the type of natural capital in a country helps shape institutional developments. It does this through two main channels.[2]

SETTLER-MORTALITY HYPOTHESIS

The settler-mortality hypothesis focuses on the disease environment at the time of the initial European settlement in the New World.[3] The hypothesis is based on three main premises.

First, different types of colonization policies in the New World led to different sets of institutions. In some places, such as Mexico, Europeans set up "extractive institutions": these did not protect private property rights, nor did they provide proper checks and balances against government appropriation. At the other extreme, in places such as Australia, New Zealand, Canada, and the United States, Europeans established "inclusive institutions": these protected private property, fostered freedom and enforcement of contracting, and resulted in legal systems that generally followed the rule of law and that provided checks and balances to limit government power and appropriation.

The second premise of the settler-mortality hypothesis is that colonization policies were influenced by the feasibility of settlement in a particular area. In locations where the disease environment was favorable to European settlement (places with temperate climates and better health conditions), Europeans settled in greater numbers and inclusive institutions were far more likely to develop. In places where European settler mortality was high, in contrast, there was relatively little European settlement and colonizers were more likely to adopt extractive institutions and to enslave indigenous populations or import African slaves.

The third premise is that colonization strategies and initial institutions continue to influence current institutions and current economic performance. That is, institutional development is a path-dependent process: decisions made hundreds of years ago, based on the disease environment at that time, continue to influence modern-day institutions and living standards.

FACTOR-ENDOWMENT HYPOTHESIS

The factor-endowment hypothesis emphasizes the importance of natural capital endowments such as climate and soil type in determining the suitable mix of crops, and of the mineral endowments of an area in shaping institutions. For example, because crops like corn and wheat could be profitably grown on small parcels of land, the northern U.S. developed institutions that led to widespread ownership of land and many small family farms. Widespread ownership resulted in institutions that protected private property, expanded voting rights, and gave rise to early public investment in education.[4]

In contrast, because of the different climate and soil types in the American South, cash crops like tobacco and cotton were more profitably grown on large-scale plantations because of economies of scale. This led to the introduction and growth of slavery, and to greater differences between rich and poor. It also put the American South on an institutional path that inhibited long-run growth and development throughout most of American history. The prior existence of the instition of slavery has also been correlated with lower levels of economic development that continue for many decades, or even longer, after slavery has been abolished.[5]

These three theories to explain institutional developments in the New World—the legal-origins hypothesis, the settler-mortality hypothesis, and the factor-endowment hypothesis—are not mutually exclusive. Further, they all stress that institutions are path-dependent and are an important determinant of long-run economic growth.[6]

6.2 HUMAN CAPITAL ACCUMULATION AND WORK EFFORT

While discussions today of human capital accumulation typically focus only on the education and experience of the workforce, the *health* of the workforce is also an important component of human capital, particularly prior to the twentieth century when the vast majority of jobs required more physical effort than mental effort. Simply put, healthy people can work longer and harder than unhealthy people.

Land abundance contributed to the health of the American workforce in several ways. With abundant food and wood supplies, most Americans were well fed and able to keep warm during the winter. The rural nature of the population meant that epidemic diseases were less common in the United States than in other parts of the world that were more densely populated.

A favorable climate promotes human health in other ways. Relative to areas with tropical and desert climates, areas with temperate climates, which include most of the United States, have been shown to yield higher agricultural productivity, have a more favorable disease environment, and make it possible for individuals to work longer and harder.[7] In the modern world, the introduction of antibiotics and air conditioning have reduced the importance of climate on human health and work effort, particularly in developed countries.[8]

6.3 TERRITORIAL EXPANSION AND FEDERAL LAND POLICIES

Westward expansion began when the first European settlers moved inland from the small settlements of Jamestown, Cape Cod, Boston, and Salem on the Atlantic coast. With the signing of the Treaty of Paris in 1783, which ended the Revolutionary War, Great Britain ceded to the United States all land south of Canada, north of Florida, and east of the Mississippi River. This area produced a new western frontier for the United States, and this was just the beginning. Between 1803 and 1853, several land purchases and war treaties increased the size of the United States to include the land area that would become the lower 48 states. The acquisition of this massive amount of territory required the federal government to develop policies determining how these lands were to be surveyed, sold, settled, and governed.

FEDERAL LAND POLICIES

Before 1785, private property lines often followed waterways or meandered along tree lines, with physical features such as prominent rocks or trees marking the boundaries. Over time, however, these physical features sometimes changed—trees died and streams changed course or dried up, making it difficult to determine property boundaries and titles to land.

With Congress wanting to sell the vast public domain it had acquired from Britain in 1783, the Land Ordinance of 1785 established a system of rectangular surveys to create unambiguous property lines through the creation of square townships (Figure 6.1). Each township consisted of 36 numbered sections, each of one square mile or 640 acres, and each township was given a unique description so that it could never be confused with another township. Each section in a township could later be subdivided into half sections (of 320 acres), quarter sections (of 160 acres), or quarter-quarter sections (of 40 acres). The process of surveying townships moved westward without respect to any physical features of the land, creating a distinctively American pattern of rectangular fields and straight roads that is amazingly evident even today from the window of any airplane flying across the Midwest.

FIGURE 6.1 System of Public Land Survey, 1796

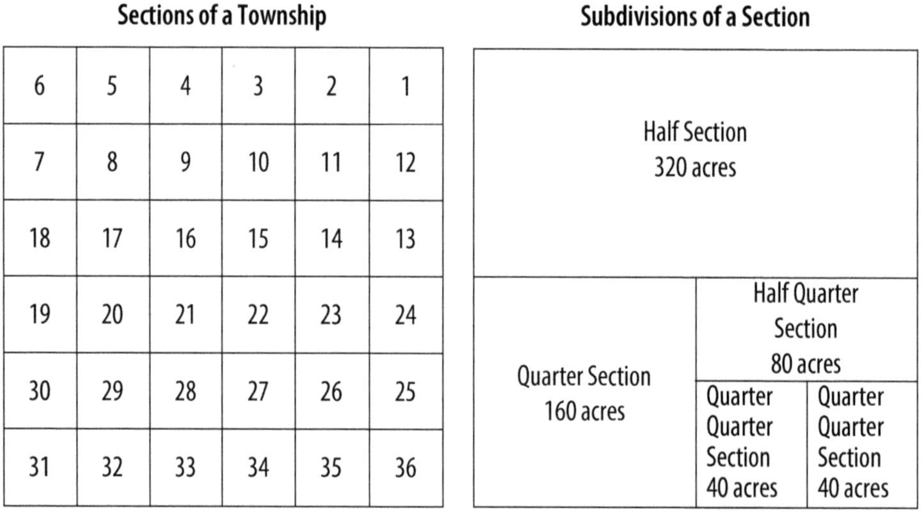

Sections of a Township

6	5	4	3	2	1
7	8	9	10	11	12
18	17	16	15	14	13
19	20	21	22	23	24
30	29	28	27	26	25
31	32	33	34	35	36

A township is 6 miles long and 6 miles wide (36 square miles) and it contains 36 sections.

Subdivisions of a Section

Half Section
320 acres

Quarter Section
160 acres

Half Quarter Section
80 acres

Quarter Quarter Section
40 acres

Quarter Quarter Section
40 acres

A section is 1 square mile and it contains 640 acres, which can be divided into smaller parcels.

Sources and Notes: Based on Charles O. Paullin, *Atlas of Historical Geography of the United States* (Washington, DC, and New York: Carnegie Institution of Washington and the American Geographical Society of New York, 1932), Plate 48A. Surveys under the Land Act of 1796 followed the principles from the Land Ordinance of 1785.

After parcels had been surveyed, they were offered for sale at public auctions, subject to minimum acreage requirements and to minimum prices set through a succession of land acts. Under the Land Ordinance of 1785, the minimum price was $1 per acre, with a minimum acreage of 640 acres (one section), paid in cash. If no one bid at least the minimum price at auction, then the land remained for sale at the legal minimum price until sold. Section 16 of each township was set aside for a public school, while other sections were set aside to compensate veterans of the American Revolutionary War for their service.

Economic historians have considered areas of the United States where the rectangular, grid-based, land-demarcation system under the Land Ordinance of 1785 was used, and compared them with other areas where land boundaries and plot sizes were irregular and varied with topography.[9] They observe that the grid-based system of land demarcation led to "higher land values, fewer border and title disputes, and more land transactions."[10]

The Northwest Ordinance (1787) dealt with how areas in the Northwest Territory were to be admitted as U.S. states. It called for the creation of between three and five states in the area north of the Ohio River and east of the Mississippi River. Once the population in an area had reached 60,000, the territory could join the Union and would have complete equality with existing states. The first state created in the Northwest Territory was Ohio (1803). Indiana (1816), Illinois (1818), Michigan (1837), and Wisconsin (1848) followed. A significant part (about one-third) of Minnesota (1858) was also part of the Northwest Territory.

Another important feature of the Northwest Ordinance was the prohibition of slavery in the Northwest Territory. As a result, the Ohio River came to mark the boundary between free and slave regions, from the Appalachian Mountains to the Mississippi River. The dividing line led to a series of compromises and conflicts, and eventually to the Civil War. In 1820, the Missouri Compromise attempted to settle the question of whether slavery would be permitted in the Louisiana Territory. Missouri was admitted as a slave state, while Maine as a free state. Slavery was also banned in the Louisiana Territory north of the 36° 30' N boundary. In 1854, the Kansas–Nebraska Act served to repeal the Missouri Compromise by allowing people in the territories of Kansas and Nebraska to decide whether to allow slavery.

While the causes of the Civil War are still debated, a large part of the story is the uncompromising differences between slave and free states over slavery in the territories that had not yet become states. With the election in 1860 of Abraham Lincoln, who had campaigned on a platform of prohibiting slavery in the territories that had not yet become states, seven states in the South seceded and formed a new nation, the Confederate States of America. Lincoln and most northern whites refused to accept this secession and feared that it would fragment the United States into several small countries in constant conflict. Between 1861 and 1865, the Union and the Confederacy waged the bloodiest war in American history, with almost 2.4 percent of the population killed—the equivalent in 2016 of more than 7.5 million Americans.[11]

After 1862, many landowners acquired land from the government through the Homestead Act (Figure 6.2), but there were subsequent amendments to the Act and other federal land policies were introduced. The Timber Culture Act (1873) granted 160 acres of land to anyone who would plant and cultivate trees on at least one-quarter of the land acquired. In 1878, this Act was amended to require trees on only one-sixteenth of the land. The Desert Land Act (1877) allowed for purchases of land if the land would be irrigated; and the Timber and Stone Act (1878) sold parcels for accessing timber and stone to be used for personal use (but not commercial use).

FIGURE 6.2 Family in Nebraska in Pursuit of a Homestead, 1866

Source: U.S. National Archives, https://research.archives.gov/id/518267 (accessed: April 4, 2016).

By 1900, most of the good land near rivers had been claimed, leaving only drier and less productive areas that were generally not viable for agriculture on only 160-acre parcels. The Kincaid Act (1904) granted, for a small filing fee, 640-acre parcels of land in western Nebraska; while a new Homestead Act (1909) doubled the allotment elsewhere to 320 acres. Finally, the Stock Raising Homestead Act (1916) granted 640-acre parcels on land suitable only for ranching purposes. In total, over one billion acres of land in the public domain was transferred by the federal government to the private sector. While land sales were the most important, homesteading was a close second, followed by land grants to railroads (see Chapter 8).

Since the federal government sold relatively small parcels of land at low prices (or gave it away), land ownership in the United States was widespread, particularly in the northern states. In 1910, 75 percent of Americans owned land, compared to only 2.4 percent in Mexico.[12] It is easy to take this outcome for granted. If the federal government had instead maintained ownership of this land and granted only limited access, or had bestowed large estates to political and economic elites, the structure and development of the American economy might have been very different.

Although auctioning land to the highest bidder should have allowed the government to capture the full market values of the land sold, in practice corruption, bribery, and favoritism were widespread. Sometimes bidders would collude or would coerce others into withholding competitive bids. With access to credit sometimes limited, and with information imperfect regarding the quality and productivity of land, the auction system did not necessary result in land going to the bidder who valued it most, even in the absence of corruption, collusion, and bribery. Finally, beginning in 1830, Congress passed a series of preemption laws, made permanent in 1841, which allowed squatters to bypass the auction process and to obtain land at the minimum price by settling on land that was unoccupied. This, too, contributed to an inefficient allocation of land.[13] Overall, however, the abundance and availability of land likely spurred both population growth and economic growth.

Land sales remained quite modest until the 1830s, when crop and commodity prices rose significantly.[14] Crop prices increased both because of a business cycle expansion and because of a series of poor harvests caused by rust (a type of fungus) and the Hessian fly, which destroyed wheat, barley, and rye. Throughout the nineteenth and early twentieth centuries, fluctuations in land sales and homestead applications appear to have followed changes in agricultural prices associated with overall economic fluctuations in the United States.[15]

TERRITORIAL ACQUISITIONS

Because of the importance of the Mississippi River and competing claims to it from France (and Spain), President Jefferson desired permanent and exclusive rights to the Mississippi. In 1803, the Louisiana Purchase from France, which included almost all of the land between the Mississippi River and the Rocky Mountains, almost doubled the size of the United States. To explore this vast territory, a group led by Meriwether Lewis and William Clark left from St. Louis in 1804 and crossed the continental divide of the Rocky Mountains, eventually reaching the Pacific Coast.

While the Louisiana Purchase eliminated French claims to the Mississippi, Spain maintained control of some coastal regions bordering the Mississippi. A revolt by settlers in 1810 provided the impetus for President Madison to occupy the area. By 1819, Spain had ceded these coastal areas and all of Florida to the United States.

The Texas Republic won independence from Mexico in 1836, but it remained an independent nation for nine years. In 1845, John L. Sullivan, an editor at *United States Magazine and Democratic Review*, wrote that it was "the fulfillment of our manifest destiny to overspread the continent allotted by Providence for the free development of our yearly expanding millions." While Sullivan used the term "manifest destiny" to advocate for the annexation of Texas, the general conviction that Americans had a divine right to spread across the continent can be traced back to colonial times. In the mid-nineteenth century, however, "manifest destiny" was used as a justification for annexing Texas (1845) and Oregon in a treaty with Great Britain (1846); and also, following the Mexican–American War (1846–1848), for gaining control of the American Southwest by means of the Mexican Cession (1848) and the Gadsden Purchase (1853).

By 1853, the United States controlled all of the territory that would eventually become the "lower 48" states (Figure 6.3). These new territories became states through the process first established in the Northwest Ordinance (1787), with New Mexico (1912) and Arizona (1912) the last of the lower 48. Alaska, purchased from Russia in 1867, and Hawaii, annexed in 1898, became the 49th and 50th U.S. states in 1959.

LAND POLICIES AND NATIVE AMERICANS

Federal policies regarding the legal recognition of tribes and their rights to tribal lands have a complex history. Federal land policies appear initially to have respected the

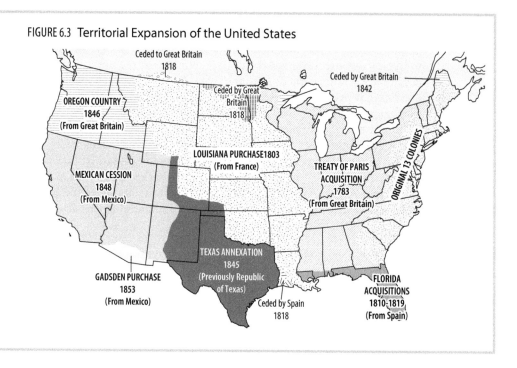

FIGURE 6.3 Territorial Expansion of the United States

property rights of Native Americans. Section 14, Article 3, of the Northwest Ordinance (1787) states:

> The utmost good faith shall always be observed toward the Indians; their land and property shall never be taken from them without their consent; and in their property, rights, and liberty, they shall never be invaded or disturbed, unless in just and lawful wars authorized by Congress, but laws founded in justice and humanity shall from time to time be made, for preventing wrongs being done to them, and for preserving peace and friendship with them.[16]

This policy, however, was more rhetoric than reality. In 1789, Congress gave the Department of War responsibility for dealing with issues concerning Native Americans. Jefferson's decision to purchase Louisiana from France (1803) was made without consulting the indigenous populations who inhabited this area. The War of 1812 with Great Britain (1812–1815) occurred, in part, because of British support for Native American tribes in stemming American expansion.[17]

With the discovery of gold on Cherokee lands in 1828 and continued westward expansion by American settlers, there was increasing pressure to relocate tribes. In 1830 Congress passed the Indian Removal Act, which forcibly moved Cherokee, Choctaw, Chickasaw, Creek, and Seminole tribes to lands west of the Mississippi River, in what is now Oklahoma. An estimated 4,000 people, or nearly one-fourth of the Cherokee, died on the "Trail of Tears."[18]

In 1834, Congress passed an Act that granted almost all land west of the Mississippi to Native Americans.[19] Once again, however, westward expansion continued to encroach on Native American lands, with wars and relocations of tribes a common theme throughout the remainder of the nineteenth century. Because of the collapse of the indigenous populations (see Chapter 3), due largely to lack of immunity from European diseases, European Americans viewed the land as empty and thought it wasteful to let it remain uncultivated. As a result, they continually pushed westward to settle it.

The Dawes Act (1887), however, represented a change in policy. It authorized the President of the United States to survey remaining tribal lands and to divide it into small parcels to be granted to individual Native Americans. Those who chose to live separately from tribes were granted U.S. citizenship. This policy was intended to reduce the power of tribes, to encourage individual initiative through private ownership, and to instill "American values" in Native Americans.[20]

Under the Dawes Act, however, unallocated land was sold to white settlers. More than 90 million acres, nearly two-thirds of reservation land, was sold to non-Native American settlers, usually without any compensation being given to Native Americans.[21] In 1924, all Native Americans were made citizens of the United States; but they were second-class citizens, often suffering extreme poverty and hardship on reservations with little opportunity for upward mobility.

Some lands have since been regained through court battles, and today there are over three hundred Native American reservations, with a collective geographic area amounting to 2.3 percent of the United States.[22]

6.4 NATURAL CAPITAL AND MARKET GROWTH

In a world with constant technological knowledge and constant capital (physical, human, and natural), a larger population with more workers leads to lower levels of output per capita and output per worker because of the diminishing marginal product of labor. This is what Thomas Malthus (1798) envisioned: population growth leads to more people per acre of land, and this drives individual incomes down to subsistence levels.[23]

A larger population, however, need not lead to misery at bare subsistence. Adam Smith (1776) wrote, "The division of the labor is limited by the extent of the market."[24] Larger markets with more people allow for greater specialization and exchange, which contributes to economic growth. Larger populations and markets may also encourage the growth of total factor productivity by stimulating technological progress through scale effects.[25] Since ideas (inventions) are nonrival, one person can use an idea without diminishing the ability of anyone else to use the same idea at the same time. With more people, there is also a greater possibility that there will be more geniuses who will create new inventions and innovations, and entrepreneurs who will make them widely available, so that all can benefit.

A larger population and population growth may also contribute to economic growth through positive human capital externalities and agglomeration economies, whereby external benefits accrue from living and working closer to others, and these lead to economic growth.[26] As population grows in an economy and as population densities increase, so too do the possibilities of positive spillovers.

THE LOCATION OF CITIES AND ECONOMIC ACTIVITY

The locations of rivers and other geographical features often determined where settlements, and later cities, originated. Many cities in the United States "formed at obstacles to water navigation, where continued transport required overland hauling or portage. Portage sites attracted commerce and supporting services, and places where the fall provided water power attracted manufacturing during early industrialization."[27]

In 1900, the twenty largest American cities were all located on major waterways.[28] New York City, for example, has a large harbor along a major river, the Hudson. With the completion of the Erie Canal in 1825, the locational advantages of New York were enormous. Between 1790 and 1850, New York's population increased from 33,000 to over 800,000. The location of rivers and oceans also influenced the borders of U.S. states. Before Colorado entered the Union in 1876, all U.S. states had at least one border delineated by rivers or oceans. Of the fifty states today, only four (Colorado, Montana, Utah, and Wyoming) do not have waterways defining any of their borders.

POPULATION GROWTH

In the eighteenth and nineteenth centuries, the United States experienced rapid population growth. Although there were many causes for rapid population growth (see Chapter 7), perhaps the most important factor was an abundance of high-quality land available at low prices. Land abundance promoted high rates of population growth through natural increase because it encouraged high birth rates and fostered relatively low mortality rates.

Land abundance and availability also led to high rates of immigration from abroad. Tens of millions of immigrants have come to the United States for a variety of reasons, but the lure of land was an important inducement. Cheap land on the western frontier, as well as the prospects of discovering gold and silver, also induced massive westward migration. The population of Illinois, for example, increased from less than 2,500 in 1800 (excluding Native Americans), to almost 900,000 in 1850, and to close to 5 million by 1900.

TRANSPORTATION AND TRADE

One of the most important determinants of the ability to trade, both internally and internationally, is proximity to navigable rivers and to the ocean. The United States has a considerable coastline, and in many ways the American landscape is dominated by rivers: the Hudson, the Missouri, the Mississippi, the Ohio, the Colorado, and the Columbia, to name a few. With proximity to oceans and an abundance of navigable rivers, it was possible to develop an extensive transportation network in the United States, even prior to the widespread proliferation of railroads. The Mississippi River, in particular, allowed the transport of goods to a degree matched by few other rivers in the world.

While oceans and rivers did not by themselves lead to market growth, they certainly contributed to it. The development of the market was reinforced by rapid population growth and by improvements in transportation and communication, beginning with the introduction of steam boats in 1807, which was followed in turn by the canal-building era in 1817, the start of railroad construction in the 1830s, and the introduction of the telegraph in the 1840s (see Chapter 8).

6.5 NATURAL CAPITAL, MANUFACTURING, AND INDUSTRIALIZATION

Largely because of the relative abundance and early exploitation of natural capital, but stimulated also by the relative scarcity of labor, manufacturing and industrialization in the United States developed along distinct lines. Both relied on an intensive use of natural capital, but they also depended on the early development of specialized machines that economized on labor, machines that eventually led to the "mass production" processes of assembly-line manufacturing.

FROM THE AMERICAN SYSTEM OF MANUFACTURING TO MASS PRODUCTION

While the United States was neither the technological nor the industrial leader throughout most of the nineteenth century, contemporary observers observed something unique about American manufactured goods. By the 1850s, the term "American system of manufactures" was in use to describe goods that were highly standardized and produced with specialized machines and interchangeable component parts.[29]

The supply and demand framework can help us understand how and why the American system of manufacturing developed.[30] Land abundance and a rapidly growing population meant that demand for manufactured goods was increasing at a high rate. In addition, land abundance also meant that food prices were relatively low in the United States, so that for any given income or family size there was more money left over to spend on nonfood products, and this led to further increases in demand for manufactured goods. Widespread land ownership and a relatively egalitarian social structure implied a similarity of tastes and incomes, which was met with standardized products. Finally, the rural isolation of those living at or close to the frontier demanded products that were simply designed, durable, and easy to fix.

On the supply side, land abundance meant that wages in manufacturing had to be kept high enough to prevent potential workers from heading west. High wages and low-priced natural resources provided incentives for firms to develop machines: the firms "traded off abundant natural-resource inputs for labor, as well as machines which were wasteful of natural resources yet could be constructed more cheaply."[31] Goods produced with specialized machines and interchangeable component parts allowed firms to use fewer workers.

The American system of manufacturing gradually evolved into mass production. The move to true interchangeability of parts took time, but there was a greater and earlier standardization of parts in the United States than elsewhere, first in firearms, and then in clocks and watches, agricultural machinery, sewing machines, typewriters and office machines, bicycles, and automobiles.[32] The Ford Model T merged true interchangeability of parts with a moving assembly line, introduced in 1913, making it possible for Ford to produce large quantities of a standardized product at low prices. The Model T was so standardized that Henry Ford wrote in 1922, "Any customer can have a car painted any color that he wants so long as it is black."

The assembly line and mass production allowed millions of cars to be made cheaply using largely unskilled labor, producing affordable automobiles for millions of Americans. After World War I, a Ford Model T cost less than $400, which was only about three months' pay for a typical worker. In the long run, however, the lack of industrial diversity and the dependence on a low-skilled labor force both hampered Detroit and the surrounding area.[33]

FUELS AND MINERALS

Early factories in New England relied on power from water wheels. Beasts of burden and human beings were also important early sources of power. Over time, however, abundant wood, coal, oil, and natural gas provided the United States with cheap and plentiful sources of power.

Throughout most of the nineteenth century, America depended on an abundant supply of wood for building homes, furniture, tools, and wagons, and also as a source of energy (Figure 6.4). In the iron and steel industry, for example, charcoal (made from wood) was the primary energy source prior to the Civil War.[34] Wood and charcoal were initially used to power steam engines for railroads and industry. In 1860, the lumber industry was the second largest industry in the United States, second only to cotton textiles, and per-capita wood consumption in the U.S. was five times greater than that of England and Wales.[35]

As Figure 6.4 indicates, wood use per capita began to decrease after 1850 as coal use per capita began to increase, with coal surpassing wood in the 1880s. Coal remained the dominant source of energy in the United States from the 1880s to 1950, peaking around 1920. In the post-World War II period, per-capita coal use waned and then rebounded somewhat, but by then petroleum and natural gas had overtaken coal as the most important sources of power. After the oil price shocks in the 1970s, nuclear power and renewable sources of power (hydroelectric, solar, and wind) grew somewhat in importance.

After 1900, when the United States became the "world's preeminent manufacturing nation," the United States also became the world leader in the production of coal, petroleum, iron ore, copper, lead, and many other important minerals used in manufacturing (Figure 6.5).[36] American leadership in manufacturing appears to be primarily the result of early developments in resource extraction rather than greater relative natural endowments.[37] Between 1823 and 1869, 31 U.S. states introduced geographical surveys to assess and promote their endowments of subsurface resources, and the U.S. Geological Survey was created in 1879.[38]

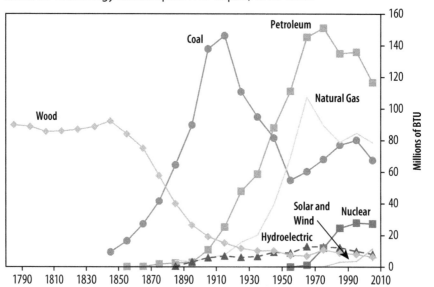

FIGURE 6.4 U.S. Energy Consumption Per Capita, 1790–2010

Sources: Calculations based on data from the United States Energy Information Administration and the United States Census Bureau. Data for wood consumption per capita prior to 1850 are computed from interpolations between benchmark years.

FIGURE 6.5 U.S. Fuel and Mineral Output, 1913 (Percentage of World Total)

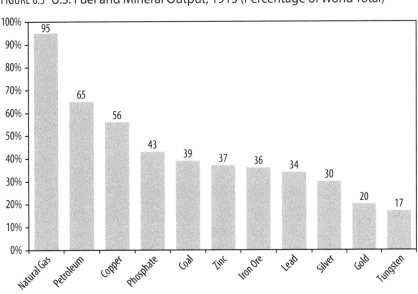

Source: George Otis Smith, *The Strategy of Minerals* (New York, NY: Appleton & Co., 1919). Computed using data from the U.S. Geological Survey, *Mineral Resources of the United States* (Washington, DC: Government Printing Office, 1913).

A wide range of subsurface endowments is not a necessary component for growth in the modern world because of very low transportation costs. In 1900, however, international transport costs were much higher and so subsurface endowments were an important factor in U.S. growth and development.

Coal, iron, and oil were of particular importance. In 1840, Canadian geologist Abraham Gesner discovered how to distill kerosene from oil or coal to light lamps. People skimmed oil from the surface of creeks or other places where it had surfaced. It was not until 1859, however, when Edwin L. Drake successfully used a steam engine to drill for oil, that subsurface oil extraction became practical. Soon oil wells spread to Kentucky, Ohio, Illinois, and Indiana, and petroleum-refining industries developed in Cleveland and Pittsburg as entrepreneurs rushed to transform oil into kerosene. Gasoline, a byproduct of the refining process, was originally discarded—only with the arrival of the automobile did gasoline become a valuable commodity.

Extraction of coal and iron was also important in the development of the steel industry. In 1887, prospectors discovered rich iron ore deposits in the Mesabi Range of Minnesota. Coal production increased dramatically during the late nineteenth century, from 33 million tons in 1869 to more than 250 million tons by 1899.[39] Although iron is strong, it is also heavy and brittle, and it rusts when it gets wet. Around 1850, British manufacturer Henry Bessemer and American iron maker William Kelly developed the first inexpensive industrial process for the mass production of steel from molten pig iron. By 1880, over 90 percent of American steel was being produced using the Bessemer process. In 1886, the open-hearth process was invented, which allowed production of high-quality steel from raw materials as well as from scrap metal.

Steel, which is harder, more malleable, and less brittle than iron, was soon widely used to build rails, barbed wire, and farm machinery. It also made innovative construction possible. One example is the Brooklyn Bridge, completed in 1883, which spans almost 2,000 feet of the East River in New York City. In addition, steel-framed skyscrapers became commonplace in American cities in the late nineteenth and early twentieth centuries.

New discoveries of oil and minerals, together with falling transportation costs, made the exploitation of fuel and mineral endowments less important as the twentieth century progressed, but the United States was able to use its resource-based industrial prosperity to invest in a well-educated workforce and to lead the world in scientific research and technology.[40]

6.6 RESOURCE CURSE OR BLESSING?

For many countries of the world, an abundance of natural capital has not been a blessing but a curse. Empirical studies, which examined countries around the world since 1970, found that natural capital abundance was in fact associated with lower rates of economic growth, even after controlling for other factors.[41] This result has led many to conclude that there exists a "resource curse" such that countries that are relatively well endowed with natural capital tend to grow more slowly than those with less natural capital.

Does the economic history of the United States represent a curious exception to the "resource curse," or does the U.S. experience fit into a more general pattern? One study suggests that the economic history of the United States is not unique. By examining sixteen advanced economies, including that of the United States, over a much longer period of time (1870–2006), the authors found that it is the *type* of natural capital that is critically important to economic growth.[42] By considering land and mineral abundances separately, they found that land abundance is bad for growth, while mineral abundance is good for growth. In the United States, the amount of cultivatable land per capita fell substantially after 1870, whereas by 1950 the United States had become the leading mineral-dominated economy.[43] By moving labor out of agriculture and into mineral production and other pursuits, the United States was able to grow relatively quickly among a cohort of other fast-growing economies. The authors found that mineral abundance is associated with the creation of new knowledge, as measured by the number of patents issued.[44] The same is not true of land abundance.

The effect of abundant natural capital on economic growth also seems to depend on whether the exploitation of natural capital stimulates or impedes the development of other sectors of the economy. Natural capital can lead to economic growth if its discovery and extraction stimulates production elsewhere in the economy, through backward and forward linkages. In the United States, natural capital exploitation led to substantial linkages of both kinds. The economy needed agricultural machinery to harvest crops; canals and railroads to move them to markets and to ports; and a banking system to finance these endeavors. The discovery of domestic iron and coal deposits stimulated the growth of railroads, manufacturing, and other sectors as well. In the modern world, the "resource curse" is identified with poor countries that do not diversify beyond the extraction of a particular mineral or the exports of a particular cash crop.

6.7 MARKETS, SCARCITY, AND NATURAL CAPITAL DEPLETION

Some types of natural capital, like many lakes and streams, are renewable resources: they are replenished each year. However, fossil fuels, like oil, natural gas, and coal are considered to be nonrenewable resources, since there is some finite amount in the Earth. With a nonrenewable resource, once it has been used, it is essentially gone forever—it would take millions of years for the Earth to create more oil, natural gas, or coal.

When economists talk of "supply," however, they are referring to the amount offered for sale at a given price. In markets, supply curves for nonrenewable resources can shift out over time as more resources are discovered and as new extraction technologies are developed. Even so, the possibility remains that our increasing demand for nonrenewable natural capital may exceed our ability to discover and extract supplies of natural capital, and that could limit economic growth. Thus far, however, and considered over the very long run, costs of even "nonrenewable" natural capital have not increased faster than overall prices. Figure 6.6 shows nearly a century's retail gasoline prices, adjusted for inflation; while the price of gasoline is volatile, there is no evidence that the price of gasoline has risen more than the prices of other goods and services. The price of gasoline in 2015 dollars was the highest in 1918, at $3.92 per gallon, while the next most expensive year was 2012, when the average annual price of a gallon of gas averaged $3.74. The year 1998 was the cheapest year on record, with real gas prices averaging only $1.50 per gallon.

PROPERTY RIGHTS AND MARKETS

Let's first consider the case where property rights to a nonrenewable natural resource are well defined, meaning that ownership claims are well established and owners have

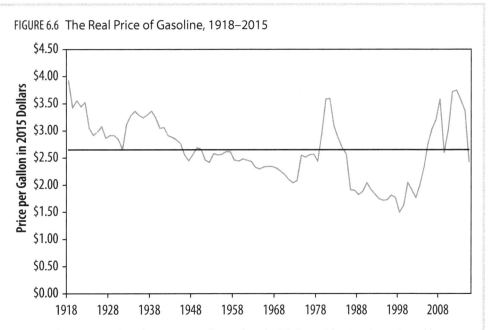

FIGURE 6.6 The Real Price of Gasoline, 1918–2015

Sources and Notes: Nominal gasoline prices per gallon are from the U.S. Energy Administration, various tables. Consumer prices (CPI-U) are from the U.S. Bureau of Labor Statistics.

the right to sell the resource. In such an instance, increasing scarcity of a natural resource leads to two mutually reinforcing responses. As increasing scarcity of the resource drives up its price, this creates incentives for demanders to conserve the resource or to reduce their quantity demanded of it. It also creates incentives for suppliers to discover new reserves and to develop substitutes.

For example, consider the history of energy sources used for heating, lighting, and propulsion throughout American history (see Figure 6.4). Until the late nineteenth century, wood was the main source of energy in the United States, but then deforestation reduced the available supplies of wood. By 1875, coke (made from coal) had replaced charcoal (from wood) as the primary energy source for iron blast furnaces, which were used to make steel. By the end of the nineteenth century, coal too was beginning to be used to generate electricity for factories and homes. Per-capita coal use began to decline after 1920, as coal was overtaken by petroleum (oil) by 1950, and by natural gas by 1960. As oil prices increased in the 1970s and again in the 2000s, petroleum and natural gas use per capita declined, while coal made a comeback and nuclear power and renewable energy sources (solar, wind, and hydroelectric) grew in importance.

Many economists are optimistic about the power of human ingenuity and substitutability: they believe that suppliers and demanders will respond to price signals and deal with issues of scarcity. While the world may soon run out of cheap oil, expensive oil will be around for a long time, and we will never run out of oil altogether. More importantly, there are strong incentives to develop entirely new technologies that can provide abundant and cheap sources of energy. Even so, it is possible that new technologies and new discoveries may not save us in the future as they have saved us in the past.

Technological innovation and substitutability have come to the rescue repeatedly throughout American history. Consider the case of rubber during World War II. In 1941, 99.6 percent of the rubber consumed in the United States was natural rubber, produced from the sap of rubber trees, but most of the rubber tree plantations were located in Southeast Asia. After the Japanese attack on Pearl Harbor on December 7, 1941, this source of rubber was cut off. By 1945, however, rubber consumption in the United States had increased again, but by this time 85 percent of the rubber consumed no longer came from rubber trees: instead, it was synthetically produced from petroleum byproducts.[45]

What are the prospects for the future? Widespread solar energy, nuclear fusion (which does not produce nuclear waste or contribute to global warming), or some other energy source that has not yet been discovered, may continue to provide plentiful and clean energy to power the United States and other world economies.

It is not the scarcity and imminent depletion of fossil fuels that likely pose the greatest risk: a far greater danger is the *abundance* of relatively cheap fossil fuels, because consumption of these is contributing to global climate change.

In short, optimists believe that human ingenuity and the possibilities of substitution will allow us to overcome any problems that come our way; while pessimists feel that current and future environmental issues are more intractable than any we have confronted in the past (see Chapter 19).

TRAGEDY OF THE COMMONS AND RESOURCE DEPLETION

In many cases, market outcomes do not in fact lead to an efficient use of natural capital. There are also many instances where property rights are not well defined, leading to genuine concerns about overuse, depletion, and extinction. The use of a natural resource also creates negative consequences (negative externalities) for others when the market participants do not pay the full costs of their decisions. The history of environmental protection and conservation in the United States is covered in detail in Chapter 19, but "tragedy of the commons" problems have occurred throughout American history when resources have been scarce and owned in common. Even if ownership claims are assigned, overuse can still occur if the property rights are not enforceable (see Economic History in Action 6.1).

A "tragedy of the commons" problem occurs when individuals, each following his or her self-interest, overuse a common-property resource and thereby behave in a way that is contrary to the long-term interests of the group as a whole. The "commons" can include the Earth's atmosphere, oceans, rivers, forests, animals, the office refrigerator, or any other shared resource without private property rights. In the absence of legally defined and enforceable property rights, there is a tendency for overuse, and, in some cases, complete extinction or depletion.

ECONOMIC HISTORY IN ACTION 6.1

Barbed Wire, Property Rights, and Agricultural Development[46]

During the colonial period, legal codes were adopted that required farmers to construct fences to keep out the livestock of others. Without a "lawful fence," farmers were not legally entitled to compensation for damage caused by the livestock of others. Later, U.S. states adopted comparable codes, which also required farmers to fence out livestock.

While the eastern half of the United States had abundant wood supplies for fencing, the "fencing out" doctrine proved to be an impediment to agricultural development on the Great Plains because of a relative scarcity of timber and other natural fencing materials.

The development and use of barbed wire, however, solved this problem. In timber-scarce areas, barbed wire was cheaper and its use required far less labor in constructing a fence. After 1880, the use of barbed-wire fencing increased dramatically as the price of barbed wire dropped from more than $200 a ton to less than $50.[47]

Barbed-wire fencing allowed farmers to enforce their property rights, and the efficiency gains from this were substantial. Between 1880 and 1900, "average crop productivity increased relatively by 23% in counties with the least woodland . . ."[48]

6.8 CONCLUSIONS

Natural capital has had an important and widespread impact on the growth and development of the United States. By discovering and exploiting minerals and fuel sources relatively early in its history, the U.S. was able to become the leading industrial nation in the world by the early twentieth century. The income and wealth created by a vibrant industrial sector allowed the U.S. to invest heavily in education, science, and technology, and to thereby remain the leading economy in the world throughout the twentieth century.

QUESTIONS

1. Describe the major land acquisitions of the United States from 1803 to 1853 that allowed the U.S. to extend from coast to coast, and eventually to establish 48 states in the contiguous United States.

2. What are the main similarities and differences between the settler-mortality hypothesis and the factor-endowment hypothesis?

3. What is the "American system of manufactures" and how did natural capital, broadly conceived, influence its development? Be sure to distinguish between supply and demand factors.

4. How did natural capital help the United States become the world's leading industrial country by 1900?

5. Provide and explain two examples of the "tragedy of the commons" problem that are not mentioned in the chapter.

NOTES

[1] David Halberstam, *The Reckoning* (New York, NY: William Morrow & Company, 1986). Halberstam (82) wrote, "If, as Naohiro Amaya of Japan's Ministry of International Trade believed, the American century and the oil century were one and the same thing, then the century began on January 10, 1901, in a field just outside of Beaumont, Texas. The field was named Spindletop ..."

[2] Ross Levine, "Law, Endowment, and Property Rights," *Journal of Economic Perspectives* 19, no. 3 (Summer 2005), 61–88. See also Raphael A. Auer, "Geography, Institutions, and the Making of Comparative Development," *Journal of Economic Growth* 18, no. 2 (June 2013), 179–215.

[3] Daron Acemoglu, Simon Johnson, and James A. Robinson, "The Colonial Origins of Comparative Development: An Empirical Investigation," *The American Economic Review* 91, no. 5 (December 2001), 1369–1401.

[4] Kenneth L. Sokoloff and Stanley L. Engerman, "History Lessons: Factor Endowments, and Paths of Development in the New World," *Journal of Economic Perspectives* 14, no. 3 (Summer 2000), 217–232.

[5] Nathan Nunn, "Slavery, Inequality, and Economic Development in the Americas: An Examination of the Engermann-Sokoloff Hypothesis," in Elhanan Helpman (ed.), *Institutions and Economic Performance* (Cambridge, MA: Harvard University Press, 2008), 148–180.

[6] Nathan Nunn, "The Importance of History for Economic Development," *Annual Review of Economics* 1, no. 1 (2009), 65–92.

[7] John Luke Gallup, Jeffrey D. Sachs, and Andrew D. Mellinger, "Geography and Economic Development," *International Regional Science Review* 22, no. 2 (August 1999), 179–232.

[8] Jeff E. Biddle, "Making Consumers Comfortable: The Early Decades of Air Conditioning in the United States," *Journal of Economic History* 71, no. 4 (December 2011), 1078–1094. After 1900, air conditioning was first introduced in industries that were humidity-sensitive, like tobacco, textiles, and gunpowder. Air conditioning spread to movie theaters, department stores, and other retailers in the 1920s and 1930s. In 1940, nearly 90 percent of the country's "air conditioning capacity was devoted to commercial comfort air conditioning" (1080). After World War II, air conditioning was routinely installed in office buildings, hotels, and other commercial establishments. The boom in home air conditioning did not occur until after the late 1950s.

[9] Gary D. Libecap and Dean Lueck, "The Demarcation of Land and the Role of Coordinating Property Institutions," *Journal of Political Economy* 119, no. 3 (June 2011), 426–467.

[10] Libecap and Lueck, 460.

[11] J. David Hacker, "A Census-Based Count of the Civil War Dead," *Civil War History* 57, no. 4 (December 2011), 307–348. Hacker estimates that 752,000 Americans died during the Civil War.

[12] Levine, 74.

[13] Mark Kanazawai, "Possession is Nine Points of the Law: The Political Economy of Early Public Land Disposal," *Explorations in Economic History* 33, no. 2 (April 1996), 227–249.

[14] Arthur H. Cole, "Cyclical and Sectional Variations in the Sale of Public Lands, 1816–60," *Review of Economics and Statistics* 9, no. 1 (January 1927), 41–53. Cole concludes (45) that "consideration of the general course of land sales indicates that the speculative fever so widely prevalent in the United States during these decades was chiefly responsible for variations in the movement of sales. Less significant … were the factors of immigration and the improvement of transportation." For a more complete account of the impact of real estate speculation on the American economy throughout history, see Edward L. Glaser, "A Nation of Gamblers: Real Estate Speculation and American History," *American Economic Review* 103, no. 3 (May 2013), 1–42.

[15] Randy McFerrin, Stephen Norman, and Douglas Wills, "Determinants of Homestead Claims and the Expansion of Western Settlement," *Applied Economic Letters* 19, no. 18 (2012), 1927–1932. While Cole (1927) and others examined the period prior to 1860, McFerrin et al. examine the 1881–1907 period and found that lagged wheat prices and current and lagged interest rates affected homestead land claims. Higher homestead claims were associated with higher wheat prices and lower real interest rates.

[16] The complete ordinance is available online at the U.S. National Archives, www.ourdocuments.gov/doc.php?flash=true&doc=8&page=transcript (accessed: October 4, 2014).

[17] The War of 1812 was, in many ways, "the second War of Independence." See A.J. Langguth, *Union 1812: The Americans Who Fought the Second War of Independence* (New York, NY: Simon & Schuster, 2010). By 1814, the British were raiding and burning towns all along the Atlantic coast of the United States, including the White House, the Capitol, and other federal buildings, causing President James Madison and other federal officials to flee from their own capital.

[18] John Ehle, *Trail of Tears: The Rise and Fall of the Cherokee Nation* (New York, NY: Anchor Books, 1988).

[19] Statute I of this Act (June 30, 1834) stated "that all that part of the United States west of the Mississippi, and not within the states of Missouri and Louisiana, or the territory of Arkansas … [is] deemed to be the Indian country." See Library of Congress, *A Century of Lawmaking for a New Nation: U.S. Congressional Documents and Debates, 1774–1785*, http://memory.loc.gov/cgi-bin/ampage?collId=llsl&fileName=004/llsl004.db&recNum=776 (accessed: October 9, 2014).

[20] Leonard A. Carlson, *Indians, Bureaucrats, and Land: The Dawes Act and the Decline of Indian Farming* (Westport, CT: Praeger, 1981).

[21] National Congress of American Indians, *An Introduction to Indian Nations in the United States*, 3, www.ncai.org/about-tribes/indians_101.pdf (accessed: October 10, 2014).

[22] A map of Indian Reservations in the United States can be found at the United States National Park Service website, www.nps.gov/nagpra/documents/RESERV.PDF (accessed: October 14, 2014).

[23] Thomas Malthus, *An Essay on the Principle of Population as it Affects the Future Improvement of Society* (London: J. Johnson, 1798).

[24] Adam Smith, *An Inquiry into the Nature and Causes of the Wealth of Nations* (London: W. Strahan & T. Cadell, 1776), Book I, Section III, Section 1.

[25] Charles I. Jones and Paul M. Romer, "The New Kaldor Facts: Ideas, Institutions, Population, and Human Capital," *American Economic Journal: Macroeconomics* 2, no. 1 (January 2010), 224–245.

[26] See Jeffrey Lin, "Geography, History, Economies of Density, and the Location of Cities," *Federal Reserve Bank of Philadelphia Business Review*, no. 3 (2012), 18–24, for an accessible survey.

[27] Hoyt Bleakley and Jeffrey Lin, "Portage and Path Dependence," *Quarterly Journal of Economics* 127, no. 2 (May 2012), 587.

[28] Edward Glaeser, *Triumph of the City: How Our Greatest Invention Makes Us Richer, Smarter, Greener, Healthier, and Happier* (New York, NY: Penguin, 2011), 43.

[29] Nathan Rosenberg, "Why in America?" *Exploring the Black Box: Technology, Economics, and History* (Cambridge, UK: Cambridge University Press, 1994), 110.

[30] Rosenberg, 109–120.

[31] Rosenberg, 117.

[32] David A. Hounshell, *From the American System to Mass Production, 1800–1932: The Development of Manufacturing Technology in the United States* (Baltimore, MD: Johns Hopkins University Press, 1984).

[33] Glaeser, 41–67.

[34] Peter Temin, *The Iron and Steel Industry in Nineteenth-Century America: An Economic Study* (Cambridge, MA: MIT Press, 1964).

[35] Nathan Rosenberg, *Technology and American Economic Growth* (New York, NY: Harper & Row, 1972), 28.

[36] Gavin Wright, "The Origins of American Industrial Success, 1879–1940," *American Economic Review* 80, no. 4 (September 1990), 651.

[37] Wright, 664.

[38] Karen Clay, "Natural Resources and Economic Outcomes," in Paul W. Rhode, Joshua L. Rosenbloom, and David F. Weiman (eds.), *Economic Evolution and Revolution in Historical Time* (Stanford, CA: Stanford University Press, 2011), Table 2.1, 32.

[39] *Fourteenth Census of the United States*, Vol. XI, *Mines and Quarries*, 1922, Tables 8 and 9, pp. 258 and 260.

[40] Wright, 665.

[41] Jeffrey D. Sachs and Andrew Warner, "The Curse of Natural Resources," *European Economic Review* 45, no. 4–6 (May 2001), 827–838, is perhaps the most cited paper in this area.

[42] David Greasley and Jakob B. Madsen, "Curse and Boon: Natural Resources and Long-Run Growth in Currently Rich Countries," *Economic Record* 86, no. 274 (September 2010), 311–328.

[43] Greasley and Madsen, Table 1, 315, and 317.

[44] Greasley and Madsen, Table 7, 322.

[45] David C. Mowery and Nathan Rosenberg, *Paths of Innovation: Technological Change in 20th-Century America* (New York, NY: Cambridge University Press, 1998), 90.

[46] This case study is based on Richard Hornbeck, "Barbed Wire: Property Rights and Agricultural Development," *Quarterly Journal of Economics* 125, no. 2 (May 2010), 767–810.

[47] Hornbeck, Figure 1, 777.

[48] Hornbeck, 769.

7

Population and Population Growth

Population levels and population growth not only *affect* economic growth: they also *depend on* economic growth. That is, the relationship between population growth and economic growth is endogenous. The decision to have children or to migrate to the United States depends, in part, on economic conditions, including the rate of economic growth.

While other chapters have focused on how population and population growth influence economic growth, this chapter emphasizes how population growth is itself contingent upon economic growth and other economic conditions. First, it explores the determinants of U.S. population growth, including the relative importance of natural increase and rates of net migration at different times throughout U.S. history. Second, it examines both migration from abroad (both voluntary immigration and forced migration through slavery) and internal migration (from westward expansion to the change from a rural to an urban economy). Finally, it discusses the demographic transition: the transition from high birth and high death rates in the pre-industrial period to low birth and low death rates in the modern world. The U.S. experience deviates in many ways from the standard European pattern, and several theories and empirical contributions are considered to help explain the changes in birth rates and death rates over more than two hundred years of American history.

7.1 POPULATION GROWTH

Population growth in any country is the result of some combination of natural increase and net international migration. Both have contributed to the tremendous population growth in the United States, from the initial colonial settlement to the present.

THE POPULATION GROWTH EQUATION

The population growth equation makes it possible to determine the proportion of population growth that is due to natural increase (or decrease) and the proportion that is the result of net international migration (which can also be positive or negative). The population in any country one year from now is equal to the population today plus the number of births that occur during the year, minus the number of deaths, plus net migration from abroad. Net migration is the difference between the number of immigrants who arrived during the year and the number of residents of the country who departed for other countries (emigration).

This can be shown mathematically as:

$$POP_{t+1} = POP_t + (B_t - D_t) + (IM_t - EM_t)$$

where POP_{t+1} is the population at the beginning of next year, POP_t is population at the beginning of the current year, B_t is the number of births during the current year, D_t is the number of deaths during the current year, IM_t is the number of immigrants during the current year, and EM_t is the number of emigrants during the current year.

If the current population is subtracted from both sides of the equation and if both sides are then divided by the current population, then the equation above can be written in terms of the growth rate of the population:

$$g_{POP} = \frac{POP_{t+1} - POP_t}{POP_t} = \left(\frac{B_t}{POP_t} - \frac{D_t}{POP_t} \right) + \left(\frac{IM_t}{POP_t} - \frac{EM_t}{POP_t} \right)$$

This can be written more succinctly as:

$$g_{POP} = (CBR_t - CDR_t) + (CIR_t - CER_t)$$

That is, the growth rate of the population (g_{POP}) is equal to the difference between the crude birth rate (CBR_t) and the crude death rate (CDR_t), plus the difference between the crude immigration rate (CIR_t) and the crude emigration rate (CER_t)—that is, the crude rate of net migration. A positive difference between the crude birth rate and the crude death rate is called "natural increase", while a negative difference is called "natural decrease". The term "crude" is used by demographers to denote that the rates describe the frequency of a demographic event across the total population, without regard to the age structure or gender composition of the population. In many instances these rates are reported per 1,000 people, but to maintain consistency with the notation in Chapter 2, the rates below are generally reported relative to the total population in decimal or percentage form.[1]

LONG-RUN POPULATION GROWTH

Over the past two centuries, population growth in the United States has been considerably faster than in many other countries. Between 1820 and 2014, the U.S. population increased from fewer than 10 million people to about 320 million, more than a 32-fold increase in population (Figure 7.1). In contrast, populations in France, Germany, Italy, United Kingdom, and Spain experienced no more than a 4-fold increase between 1820 and 2014. In 1820, the United States had a smaller population than any one of these European countries; by 2014, the United States had a population larger than the combined populations of all five of them.

FIGURE 7.1 Population by Country, 1820 and 2014

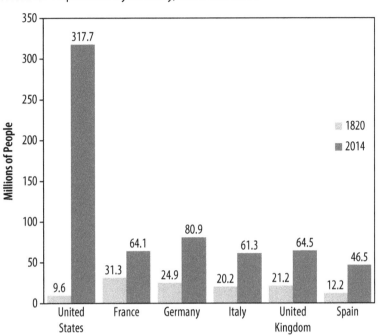

Sources: U.S. data for 1820 are from the United States Bureau of the Census (www.census.gov/history/www/through_the_decades/fast_facts/1820_fast_facts.html, (accessed: February 2, 2015); 1820 data for France, Germany, Italy, Spain, and the United Kingdom are from Angus Maddison, *The World Economy: A Millennial Perspective* (Paris: OECD) and the Maddison Project, 2013 version, www.ggdc.net/maddison/maddison-project/home.htm (accessed: February 2, 2015). All 2014 data are from the Population Reference Bureau, *2014 World Population Data Sheet*, www.prb.org/pdf14/2014-world-population-data-sheet_eng.pdf (accessed: February 2, 2015).

In 2014, the United States was the third most populous country in the world, behind China (1,364.1 million) and India (1,296.2 million), yet the rate of population increase since 1820 has been far faster in the United States than it has been in China or India over the past two centuries. By 1820, both China and India were already large countries with populations of 381 million and 209 million, respectively.[2] Between 1820 and 2014, world population increased from around 1 billion to more than 7 billion, but this worldwide 7-fold increase in population is still far less than the increase experienced by the United States.

As rapid as population growth has been in the United States since 1820, it was even faster *before* 1820. Between 1620 and 1700, the nonindigenous population increased from 2,302 people to over 250,000. This represents an annual rate of increase of about 6 percent per year, which resulted in the population size doubling at intervals of less than 12 years.[3]

During the initial years of European settlement, and following the establishment of Jamestown in 1607, the rate of natural increase was negative during what became known as the "starving time," but waves of new immigrants more than replaced those who had perished, so that there was still net growth (see Chapter 3). By the decade of the 1640s, however, the rate of natural increase was positive in the colonies as a whole (see Figure 7.2). More important, however, were rapid rates of net migration to the colonies, primarily consisting of (white) indentured servants and (black) slaves from

FIGURE 7.2 Population Growth, Natural Increase, and Net Migration: Annual Averages by Decade, 1640s–2010s

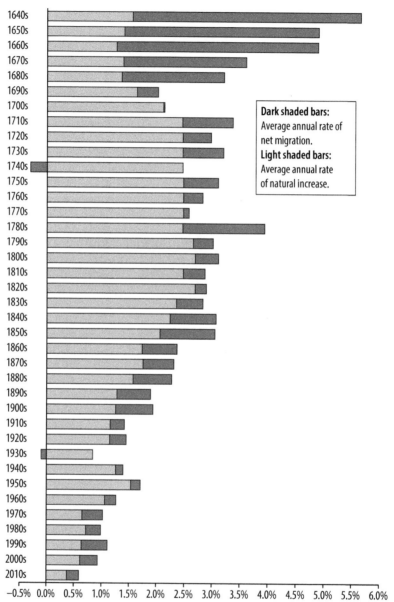

Dark shaded bars: Average annual rate of net migration.
Light shaded bars: Average annual rate of natural increase.

Sources and Notes: For the decades from the 1620s to the 1780s, the data above pertain only to the white population and are computed from Henry A. Gemery, "The White Population of the Colonial United States, 1607–1790," in Michael R. Haines and Richard H. Steckel (eds.), *A Population History of North America* (Cambridge, UK: Cambridge University Press, 2000), Table 5.10, 178. For the decades from the 1790s to the 1990s, data are computed from Susan B. Carter, Scott Sigmund Gartner, Michael R. Haines, Alan L. Olmstead, Richard Sutch, and Gavin Wright (eds.), *Historical Statistics of the United States*, Millennial Edition (New York, NY: Cambridge University Press, 2006), series Aa19 (for natural increase) and series Aa20 (for net migration). For the decades 2000s and 2010s, data are computed from U.S. Bureau of the Census, *Estimating Net International Migration for 2010 Demographic Analysis: An Overview of Methods and Results*, www.census.gov/popest/data/national/totals/2013/NST-EST2013-alldata.html (accessed: February 13, 2015). Note that the 2010s only include 2010–2013.

Africa (see Section 7.2 below). From the 1640s through the 1680s, the rates of net migration were greater than the rates of natural increase. In every decade after 1690, however, right up to the present, natural increase has been the dominant source of population growth.

While the relative importance of net migration has fluctuated substantially from decade to decade, it is evident from Figure 7.2 that the rate of natural increase began to diminish in the early nineteenth century and has continued to diminish over time, with the exception of the post-World War II "Baby Boom."

The downward trend in the rate of natural increase has caused overall population growth to slow over time as well. Annual population growth exceeded 3 percent per year during the eighteenth century, leading to a doubling of the population every generation. While the rate of natural increase fell throughout the nineteenth century, net international migration became an important source of population growth from the 1840s to World War I. During the nineteenth century as a whole, population growth averaged 2.7 percent per year.

Population growth rates continued to fall to less than 2 percent per year in each decade of the twentieth century, and have slowed to less than 1 percent per year in the twenty-first century. While the decade of the 2010s is not yet over, the period since 2010 represents the slowest population growth in American history, although some of this decline is most likely transitory, the result of the Great Recession and slow recovery.

7.2 INTERNATIONAL AND INTERNAL MIGRATION

During the colonial period, the majority of immigrants from Europe came as indentured servants. In addition, African slaves were forcibly transported across the Atlantic in large numbers from around 1700 to 1808, when the U.S. Constitution ended the legal slave trade (but not slavery). Changing economic and political conditions in the U.S. and abroad, together with U.S. immigration policies, have caused immigration to ebb and flow, yet the United States remained a major destination for immigrants throughout most of the nineteenth and twentieth centuries, and continues to be so in the twenty-first.

INDENTURED SERVITUDE AND REDEMPTION CONTRACTS

Despite high rates of natural increase, labor remained a relatively scarce factor of production throughout the colonial period. The costs to Europeans of immigrating to the American colonies were high, greater than a typical worker's annual income early in the seventeenth century. In the absence of a well-developed financial system and the ability to borrow, an alternative institutional arrangement developed, called an indenture contract, which allowed and encouraged emigration to the American colonies.

Indentured servants contracted to do certain work for a specified number of years, usually between three and seven, in exchange for ocean transportation across the Atlantic, and usually food, housing, and clothing, and often also training in a specific skill or craft. At the end of the contract, workers typically received "freedom dues" of money and/or land. In short, an indentured contract was a form of a loan and a job training program as well. Indentures proved popular: between 1650 and 1780, net white migration to the colonies is estimated to have been around 600,000, with more than half of these immigrants coming as indentured servants.

The market for indentured servants appears to have been a highly competitive labor market based on rational behavior. While indentured servants were not paid wages, their implicit wage was the inverse of their length of indenture. That is:

$$w = \frac{1}{T}$$

where w is the implicit wage and T is the length of an indentured contract. Individuals who were able to negotiate shorter lengths of indenture were workers who were more valuable to the employer per hour of work and, therefore, commanded a higher implicit wage. That is, workers with higher productivity and higher implicit wages signed shorter contracts since they were able to "pay back" their employer for the costs of passage, food, housing, clothing, etc. with fewer hours of work.

For example, literate workers, and those with desirable skills such as abilities in metal-working or making textiles, were able to negotiate shorter contracts. Women typically served a shorter period of indenture because of a greater scarcity of women in the colonies. In addition, areas that had poor climates and disease environments, like the Caribbean, offered shorter periods of indenture in order to attract the workers they needed.[4]

While indentured contracts were used by English immigrants, those from continental Europe (mostly from Germany) arrived using a slightly different institutional arrangement called a redemption contract. Under this arrangement, the ship's captain provided passage, and upon arrival in the Americas immigrants were given a short time to repay the captain by borrowing from friends and relatives or by self-contracting themselves or their children into servitude for a given number of years. Redemptioners often had to pay a portion of the costs of transport to the ship's captain in advance, as a "down payment" prior to departure.

By the early nineteenth century, however, indentured and redemption contracts had largely vanished as a result of economic changes. Rising wages in Europe and falling ocean transportation costs made it easier for workers to self-finance transatlantic voyages. By this time, extensive kinship networks in the United States meant also that it was often possible to find someone willing and able to help pay for the costs of passage. As a result, the market for indentured servants collapsed after 1819.[5] The end of indentured servitude "was a watershed event in the history of European emigration to America and in the history of American social and economic development."[6]

SLAVERY

Slavery has existed in many parts of the world throughout history, including in ancient Greece and Rome. During the voyages of discovery, African slaves were first brought to the New World by the French and Spanish. The first group of about twenty slaves in British North America arrived near Jamestown, Virginia, aboard a Dutch ship in 1619.

Although slavery was soon legal in all of the American colonies, the share of slaves in the northern colonies was typically less than 5 percent of the total population. There were few slaves in New England, but relatively more in the Middle colonies of New York, New Jersey, and Pennsylvania. Between 1777 and 1804, the northern states, one by one, voted to abolish slavery. Emancipation, however, was not immediate. Most states adopted a system in which slaves were not freed until well into adulthood. By not granting freedom to slaves until they reached their mid-twenties, slave owners ensured that the slaves, through years of labor, compensated them for the costs of their upbringing. As a result, slaves in northern states largely bore the costs of emancipation themselves.

In contrast, slavery became increasingly important to the southern economy. Large-scale expansion of slavery did not occur until the end of the seventeenth century, in the tobacco-growing regions of Virginia and Maryland. Tobacco had become a valuable crop, and in the seventeenth century depended on white indentured servant labor from England. In the 1690s, however, there was an increased availability of slaves, due to reduced demand for the sugar produced by slaves in Brazil and the Caribbean; and at the same time there was a reduced supply of indentured servants, because of slower population growth in England and greater opportunities there for laborers.[7] As a result, there was a substitution of slave labor for indentured labor in the Chesapeake region. Plantations of ten to twenty slaves became the norm in the tobacco-producing regions in the eighteenth century. After 1700, slave labor was used to grow rice in South Carolina and Georgia.

By the late eighteenth century, slaves were about 40 percent of the population in the South and about 20 percent of the total national population. The rapid expansion of cotton textiles in England led to a surge in cotton production in the American South and thus to an increased demand for slaves. By 1850, almost 75 percent of agricultural slaves worked in cotton production.[8] Slaves moved southward and westward as cotton eventually spread into Louisiana and Texas.

The transatlantic slave trade lasted for three centuries, and between 10 and 12 million Africans were forcibly transported to the New World. North America, however, received only about 7 percent of the slaves transported across the Atlantic, and the United States was among the first to end the slave trade by legislation in 1808.[9] While the United States was a relatively small player in the transatlantic slave trade, by 1825, 36 percent of all slaves in the Western Hemisphere were in the United States.[10] Unlike Brazil and the Caribbean, slave fertility in the American South was high (see Figure 7.7) and death rates were comparatively low, with the consequence that the U.S. slave population grew tremendously, largely as the result of natural increase. Just before the onset of Civil War in 1860, there were nearly 4 million slaves in the American South.

While slaves in the American South fared better than their counterparts in Brazil and the Caribbean, there is substantial evidence of malnutrition in young children. The evidence from one study suggests that American slave children at 4.5 years of age were taller, on average, than only 2 of 1,000 children today at the same age.[11] Child mortality rates were also extremely high, at over twice the rate of white American children at the time. Only 45 percent of slave children lived to their 5th birthday, compared to 63 percent for the United States as a whole.[12] For those who survived to adulthood, the heights and mortality rates of American slaves had mostly converged to those of free whites, but there is substantial evidence of extreme deprivation during childhood.

IMMIGRATION

By 1820, transatlantic flows of people and labor consisted almost entirely of workers not bound to any master, either temporarily or permanently. While net migration was

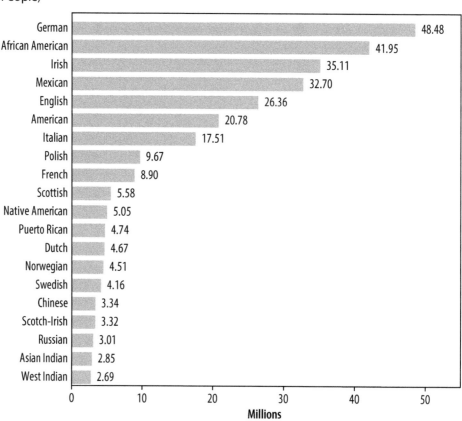

FIGURE 7.3 Twenty Largest Ancestry Groups in the United States, 2012 (Millions of People)

Sources and Notes: United States Bureau of the Census, *2008–2012 American Community Survey 5-Year Estimates,* available through factfinder2.census.gov (accessed: February 17, 2015). The figure above is computed from the following series: B02006 (Asia Alone by Selected Groups), B02009 (Black or African American Alone or in Combination with One or More Other Races), B02010 (American Indian and Alaska Native Alone or in Combination with One or More Other Races), B03001 (Hispanic or Latino Origin by Specific Origin), and B04003 (Total Ancestry Reported). Note that ancestry is self-reported and respondents can select more than one ancestry group; therefore, the sum of the totals for all ancestry groups exceeds the total U.S. population. The U.S. Census Bureau defines ancestry "as a person's ethnic origin or descent, 'roots,' or heritage, or the place of birth of the person or the person's parents or ancestors before their arrival in the United States." www.census.gov/population/ancestry/ (accessed: February 17, 2015). "Native American" in the figure above refers to both American Indians and Alaska Natives. "American" is self-reported and is an unknown compilation of the other ancestry groups.

very low in the 1820s, contributing only about 0.2 percent per year to population growth during this decade (Figure 7.2), immigration from Europe accelerated in the 1840s and 1850s.

While subsequent chapters will discuss slavery (Chapters 9 and 14) and immigration (Chapter 15) in greater detail, it is evident from Figure 7.3 that the United States today is a true "melting pot", with a population representing a tremendous range of ethnic and racial backgrounds from all over the world.

INTERNAL MIGRATION

Two long-term trends characterize internal migration within the United States: westward expansion and urbanization. In 1800, the U.S. population was split almost evenly between the Northeast and the South, with only 1 percent of the population in the Midwest, primarily in Ohio (Figure 7.4). A century later, in 1900, the Midwest was the most populous region in the United States as it had become a hub of both agriculture and manufacturing. In 1900, however, the West remained largely unsettled, with barely 1 in 20 Americans living in the thirteen states west of North Dakota, South Dakota, Nebraska, Kansas, Oklahoma, and Texas.

Over the twentieth and the start of the twenty-first centuries, the population shares of the South and West increased substantially. Push factors included the decline of the manufacturing sector in the Northeast and the Midwest, which began in the 1970s, and pull factors included job opportunities and better weather for retiring baby boomers and others in the Sun Belt states. By 2010, over 60 percent of Americans lived in the South and West.

URBANIZATION

In 1790, only one in twenty of the U.S. population lived in urban areas, defined as towns and cities with populations of 2,500 or more; and by 1860, only one in five Americans lived in urban areas. It was not until 1920 that over half of Americans lived in urban areas, and by 2010 over 80 percent of Americans were urban residents (Figure 7.5).

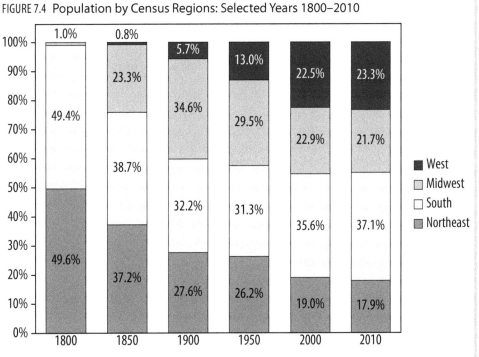

FIGURE 7.4 Population by Census Regions: Selected Years 1800–2010

Sources: U.S. Bureau of the Census, various sources. Computed using state-level population data sources aggregated into Census regions.

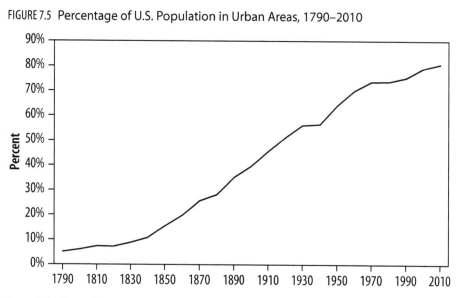

FIGURE 7.5 Percentage of U.S. Population in Urban Areas, 1790–2010

Source: United States Census Bureau. Data for 1790–1990 are available at www.census.gov/population/censusdata/table-4.pdf (accessed: February 20, 2015). Data for the years 2000 and 2010 are available at www.census.gov/newsroom/releases/archives/2010_census/cb12-50.html (accessed: February 20, 2015). Note that the definition of urban population changed in 1950.

American cities since the mid-nineteenth century have attracted relatively large numbers of immigrants. Within many cities, ethnic enclaves developed, with names such as "Little Italy" or "Chinatown" that reflected their origins. The "Great Migration" of southern blacks to northern cities between 1910 and 1970, with the largest migration between 1940 and 1970, was also an important source of internal migration from rural to urban areas.

Within urban areas, there was also a decrease in the proportion of residents living in the centers of cities: more and more residents moved out to the suburbs, particularly in the decades after World War II (see Chapter 8). In 1910, only 7.1 percent of the U.S. population lived in suburbs, but by the year 2000, half of Americans were suburban residents.[13] Most suburbs were first populated by middle-class whites, but over time suburbs became increasingly diverse, both economically and ethnically.

7.3 THE FERTILITY TRANSITION

Every industrialized country in the world has experienced a demographic transition from a regime in the pre-industrial period of high birth and high death rates, with little population growth, to a regime in the modern world of low birth and low death rates, again with little population growth from natural increase. For many European countries, mortality rates fell first and then, after a lag, so too did fertility rates. With mortality rates falling first, the positive difference between birth and death rates causes an increase in population growth rates and in the size of the population during the transition. Over time, however, birth rates fall to meet death rates, population growth rates diminish, and the size of the population stabilizes once again.

The demographic transition in the United States, however, seems to deviate from this standard pattern in several ways. First, the fertility transition in the United States began earlier than it did in most other countries.[14] Fertility began to fall in the United States after 1800, while it was still a largely agricultural and rural economy, so the fertility transition in the U.S. cannot simply have been due to a transition from a rural to an urban economy. Second, the fertility decline in the United States well preceded any decline in mortality rates. Mortality rates rose over much of the nineteenth century and did not begin to fall until after 1880. Finally, high rates of immigration, continuous expansion on the western frontier, and the relative growth of cities and suburbs all influenced the U.S. fertility transition in unique ways.

U.S. FERTILITY RATES IN THE LONG RUN

At the beginning of the nineteenth century, the U.S. birth rate was among the highest in the world and close to the estimated biological maximum. The crude birth rate, however, is affected by the age distribution, gender composition, and marriage patterns of the population. A better measure of fertility is the total fertility rate (TFR), which is the number of births a woman would have in her lifetime if, at each year of her age, she experienced the average birth rate occurring by age in the female

FIGURE 7.6 Large Frontier Family in the Nineteenth Century

Source: Photographer and date are unknown. Image courtesy of the Beale Memorial Library, Bakersfield, Kern County, CA.

population in that year. It is also easier and more intuitive to consider the total fertility rate (e.g., seven children per woman) rather than the crude birth rate (e.g., 55 births per 1,000 people).

In 1800, the total fertility rate for white women exceeded seven children, but by 1900, it had fallen in half (Figure 7.7). Fertility rates continued to decline across the twentieth century, but with far greater fluctuations in fertility rates from period to period, such as the declines in rates during the Great Depression of the 1930s and the post-World War II "Baby Boom" from 1946 to 1964.

African-American women also experienced a fertility transition, but with a lag of 40 or 50 years after white women in the nineteenth century, probably because of the lower average incomes for African Americans. Over time, however, the gap in fertility rates between white and black women narrowed; and in recent years the gap has vanished completely, with the two groups experiencing almost identical fertility rates by 2010.

While data on fertility rates for Hispanic and Asian women are not available for the years prior to 1980, fertility rates for Hispanic women since then are somewhat higher than for the overall population, while fertility rates for Asian women are somewhat lower. The post-1980 fertility rates of these groups in the U.S. are strongly influenced by the high rates of immigration since 1965 from Latin America and Asia, and by the fertility patterns in those source countries.

FIGURE 7.7 Total Fertility Rates in the United States, 1800–2010

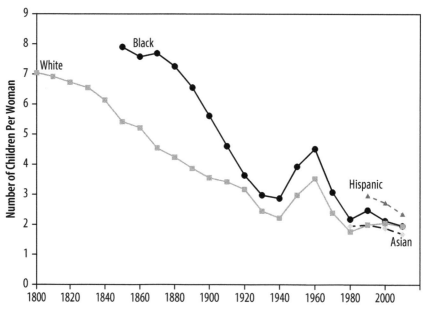

Sources: 1800–1970 from Michael Haines, "Fertility and Mortality in the United States," in Robert Whaples (ed.), *EH.Net Encyclopedia* (March 19, 2008), Table 1, http://eh.net/encyclopedia/fertility-and-mortality-in-the-united-states/ (accessed: February 26, 2015). 1980–2010 from U.S. Centers for Disease Control and Prevention, "Births: Final Data for 2013," *U.S. National Vital Statistics Reports* 64, no. 1 (January 15, 2015), Table 4, www.cdc.gov/nchs/data/nvsr/nvsr64/nvsr64_01.pdf (accessed: February 26, 2015).

REPLACEMENT FERTILITY

For long-run stability of the population, in the absence of net migration, women have to have, on average, just over two children per woman. This is called "replacement fertility" since fertility rates of about 2.1 children per woman in effect replace both the mother and father and allow for some mortality prior to and during child-bearing years. In 2012, almost 100 countries worldwide had total fertility rates below 2.1.[15]

Note, however, that replacement fertility is a long-run concept because of population momentum. Suppose that a country has experienced above-replacement fertility, but that fertility suddenly then declines to replacement levels or below. Momentum occurs because of the different sizes of older and younger cohorts: this affects the current rate of natural increase, because of the influence of cohort sizes by age on current birth rates and death rates. A change from above replacement fertility to replacement fertility or below will not cause the population to stabilize immediately, even in the absence of net migration: the change will occur only after the relatively larger cohorts of children born when fertility was above replacement have passed through their child-bearing years. In addition, for particularly large cohorts, there can be a "baby boom echo" that can persist for several generations, even at replacement fertility rates. In the long run, however, population growth will cease and the population will stabilize with replacement fertility rates.

EXPLAINING THE U.S. FERTILITY TRANSITION

There is no simple and complete theory to explain the fertility transition in the United States. There are, however, several explanations that, taken together, largely account for the timing and magnitude of the fertility transition. Most of them focus on reasons why the demand for children decreased over time, but changes in the supply of technologies to control fertility, including birth control and abortion, are also part of the story.

Many factors caused the demand for children to start to decrease in the United States around 1800. One set of explanations focuses on the availability of land (i.e., the land-availability hypothesis). On the expanding frontier, land was relatively cheap and abundant, while labor was relatively expensive and scarce. One way to secure a captive source of labor was to have a lot of children. Then, as the availability of land decreased, the demand for children started to fall. Evidence suggests that fertility declines were particularly large when less than 40 percent of the potential cultivatable land remained available.[16]

The relationship between land availability and fertility can be explained by the desire of farmers to leave bequests to their children. In the "target bequest" model, parents desire to pass along at least as much wealth to each of their children as they themselves had inherited from their parents. As land became relatively more scarce and expensive, the only way for couples to reach this target bequest was to have fewer children.

An alternative model also focuses on bequests, but emphasizes the *strategic* behavior of parents and children. In the "strategic bequest" model, there is an implicit bargain between parents and children: children will take care of parents in their old age in exchange for a share of the family wealth.[17] As labor-market opportunities outside the agricultural sector improved with the rise of industrialization and urbanization, the bargaining power shifted toward the younger generation: because there were now other ways in which they could build wealth, they could expect and demand greater compensation for providing old-age security for their parents. The only way for parents to provide a larger bequest to each child was to have fewer children.

The land-availability hypothesis, however, fails to explain fertility patterns in the American South, because slaves provided an alternative type of old-age insurance.[18] There is, however, some indirect evidence for the old-age security hypothesis in explaining the U.S. fertility transition. During the nineteenth century, U.S. counties with more banks and greater financial development were also counties with fewer children per woman. A more developed financial system allowed parents to save more effectively for retirement by themselves, with the result that they had less incentive to have as many offspring to provide care and support to their parents in old age.[19]

Another set of demand-side explanations emphasizes increasing education and greater labor-market opportunities for women. Education can increase women's earning potential, thereby increasing the opportunity costs of having children, which in turn can lead to fewer children. More education can also change attitudes towards fertility as women choose to do other things with their time instead of bringing up a large number of children.

While decreases in the demand for children are likely to be the primary cause for the fertility transition, changes in the supply of technologies to control fertility, including access to birth control and the availability of abortion, probably played a part as well. This explanation assumes that couples wanted to have smaller families, and that improvements in contraceptive methods and availability made that goal easier to achieve. There is some evidence in support of such supply-side explanations. For example, birth rates during the nineteenth century were 4–15 percent higher in states that had laws restricting women's access to abortion.[20]

The supply-side explanation is unlikely to have been a major part of the story prior to the post-World War II period, for several reasons. First, modern contraceptive methods did not become available until after 1850, long after the fertility transition had begun in the United States. After the invention of vulcanized rubber in 1844, modern condoms were invented in 1855, and the diaphragm in the 1880s. Contraceptives were expensive, though, and not widely available in the United States in the nineteenth century, because of "Comstock Laws," a collection of state and local laws making it illegal to distribute contraceptive devices such as condoms and diaphragms.[21] In addition, simulation models of lifetime fertility show that the withdrawal method alone was "sufficient to produce voluntary reductions [in fertility] of the magnitude we observe in the nineteenth and early twentieth centuries."[22]

An increase in the supply of technologies to control fertility probably became more important after the introduction of the birth-control pill in 1957. One study estimates that approximately 40 percent of the decline in marital fertility rates between 1955 and 1965 was due to the birth-control pill.[23]

THE BABY BOOM

Given the decline in fertility rates that had continued for more than two hundred years, the post-World War II "Baby Boom" (1946–1964) is particularly challenging to explain. It was a time of rapidly rising incomes, increased rates of urbanization, greater opportunities for women in terms of education and employment, and the increasing availability of the birth control pill, all of which should have caused fertility rates to fall rather than to increase. The start of the "Baby Boom" was not predicted by economists and demographers, and nor was its end.[24]

Many explanations focus on the impact of the Great Depression and World War II on the United States (and other countries). During the Depression and War, marriages and births were postponed, but the postwar period was one of optimism and growth, and this spurred an increase in marriage and fertility. While this may explain the rise in fertility in the years immediately after World War II had ended, it is more challenging to explain the relatively high fertility rates during the late 1950s to mid-1960s.[25]

Another explanation stresses the importance of "relative income," the ratio of actual income to expected income. Those who grew up in the 1930s and 1940s had quite modest material aspirations because of the Depression and the War. The unexpectedly high rates of economic growth in the 1950s and 1960s caused actual incomes to exceed what people were expecting. That is, relative income was high in the decades after World War II. As a result, it was easier to marry young and to have more children, and still to maintain or even surpass the standard of living they had expected.[26]

At a proximate level, the fertility boom is largely accounted for by a marriage boom, since the proportion of American women marrying at all and the proportion marrying at a young age (20–25) were both increasing after World War II, when fertility within marriage was also on the upswing. Prior to the widespread use of the birth-control pill, early marriage is likely to have led to more "unintended" pregnancies and children.[27] However, the causes of the postwar "Baby Boom" are not fully understood and cannot be explained by economic factors alone.[28]

THE SECOND FERTILITY TRANSITION

Some scholars argue that the post-1960 period is unique and must represent a second fertility transition. The post-1960 period is characterized by three main changes in fertility patterns: (1) relatively few women chose not to have children at all, and the variation of childbearing converged around a two-child mode, meaning that more women chose to have two children; (2) there was an increase in the proportion of children born out of wedlock; and (3) highly-educated women became more likely to delay motherhood and childbearing within marriage.[29]

Another important change in the fertility behavior of women has been the large decline in U.S. teen birth rates in the last 25 years. Between 1991 and 2013, the birth rate for every 1,000 women aged 15–19 fell from 61.8 births to 26.6 births, a reduction of almost 57 percent.[30] The decline in teenage birth rates is not the result of higher rates of abortion but of fewer teens getting pregnant. While the teen birth rate for 2013 was "a historic low for the nation," it was still higher than that of any other industrialized country of the world, with the possible exception of Russia.[31] For example, teenage birth rates in the United States are at least three times higher than in Italy, Sweden, Denmark, Netherlands, Japan, and Switzerland.[32]

Although sexual activity of U.S. teens is lower than in many other countries, the use of contraceptives by American teens is at a lower rate too, which more than offsets the lower level of sexual activity.[33] While it is a common belief that having a child as a teenager leads to poor outcomes for both mother and child, recent research supports the view that teen childbearing does not in fact have an important causal impact on inferior outcomes for mother and child. Instead, for teenage girls with low incomes and limited future opportunities there are relatively low opportunity costs in having children while young, so they often choose to have children as teenagers. As a result, a high teen birth rate in the United States is mostly a consequence of other social and economic problems, like high inequality and lack of opportunity, rather than "the underlying social problem itself."[34]

7.4 THE MORTALITY TRANSITION

In a stable population without population growth, life expectancy at birth (e_0) is simply the inverse of the crude death rate (CDR): $e_0 = 1/CDR$. While the expression is more complicated with population growth, life expectancies increase when death rates fall, and vice versa.

During the colonial period, life expectancies at birth ranged from the mid-20s to around 40 years of age, depending on time, place, and race, with life expectancies for blacks near the lower bound.

While fertility rates have displayed long-term decreases since 1800, throughout most of the nineteenth century mortality rates in the United States were either stable or increasing. Increasing urbanization across the nineteenth century probably reduced fertility rates, but it also almost certainly increased mortality rates and reduced life expectancies. Although income per capita growth was rapid from 1820 to 1870, the best available evidence suggests that mortality increased and life expectancies decreased until the 1870s.

Cities in mid-nineteenth century America were especially unhealthy places. The combination of increased urban crowding and a lack of clean water and basic sanitation in these relatively new urban areas led to a greater spread of diseases.[35] Water-borne and food-borne diseases such as typhoid, cholera, dysentery, and non-respiratory tuberculosis were common in mid-nineteenth-century American cities, with an overall mortality rate from these diseases of 214 per 100,000 from 1848 to 1854.[36]

After 1880, however, mortality rates began to fall and life expectancies at birth started to increase. In the late nineteenth and early twentieth centuries, increases in life expectancies were mostly the result of decreases in infant and child mortality, although mortality also decreased across the entire age spectrum.

PROGRESS AGAINST INFECTIOUS DISEASES

The mortality declines from the late nineteenth century to the middle of the twentieth century were largely due to progress against infectious diseases. Headway against such diseases was first made as a result of public health measures, including the provision of community water and sewage systems, garbage and waste removal, and the control of animals and insects that carry and transmit diseases. Malaria, for example, was largely eradicated from the U.S. during this time.

By the end of the nineteenth century, widespread acceptance of germ theory led to public health campaigns to advocate hand washing and the washing and safe handling of food. By 1890, the largest cities in the United States began to introduce piped water, sewer systems, filtration and chlorination of water supplies, and garbage disposal. In 1895, New York City became the first large U.S. city with a public-sector garbage service.

Starting in the 1890s, many new vaccines were developed to prevent particular diseases. They included vaccinations against rabies (1885), plague (1897), diphtheria (1923), pertussis (1926), tuberculosis (1927), tetanus (1927), yellow fever (1935), polio (1955 and 1962), measles (1964), mumps (1967), rubella (1970), and hepatitis B (1981).[37]

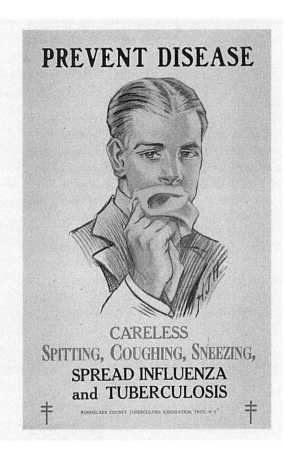

FIGURE 7.8 Public Health Poster, 1925
Source: U.S. National Library of Medicine, www.nlm.nih.gov/
exhibition/visualculture/infectious01.html (accessed: April 13, 2016).
Reprinted with permission: © 2016 American Lung Association.

Public health interventions, however, went well beyond providing clean water, sanitation, and vaccinations. Another important aspect of public health interventions included providing information and education to help prevent the spread of diseases (Figure 7.8). For example, public education programs in the 1920s reduced infant mortality rates by providing expectant mothers with visits from nurses and by establishing health clinics.[38]

Beginning in the late 1930s with the development of sulfa drugs and of penicillin (discovered in 1928 but not developed for medical use until 1942), the focus shifted from preventing infectious diseases towards curing them. Other important medical developments included better ways of detecting and monitoring infectious diseases, including blood tests, tissue cultures, and molecular techniques to detect and identify infectious pathogens.[39]

Between 1900 and 1980, the mortality rate from infectious diseases declined from 797 deaths per 100,000 people to only 36 deaths per 100,000 people. From 1938 to 1952, the decline was particularly rapid, with mortality rates from infectious diseases falling over 8 percent per year.[40] However, death rates from infectious diseases have begun to inch upward since 1980. One factor has been the emergence of acquired immune deficiency syndrome (AIDS), first identified in 1981 and later determined to be caused by infection with the human immunodeficiency virus (HIV). Another has been the appearance of new drug-resistant strains of tuberculosis, and other diseases too have become increasingly resistant to antibiotics. Thus far, death rates from such diseases remain very low when compared to those in the early part of the twentieth century, but many experts fear that medical science will not be able to keep pace with the challenges brought by new bacteria, viruses, fungi, or parasites, or by changes in known organisms that may affect the efficacy of current approaches to treatment.

THE LONGEVITY TRANSITION

In recent decades, further reductions in mortality and gains in life expectancy have not primarily been the result of lower death rates for infants and children, but instead largely represent a longevity transition, in which most of the gains in life expectancy are occurring later in life. Of the gains in life expectancy for the 1900–1920 birth cohorts, only about 30 percent were gains in life expectancy realized after the age of 65. In contrast, for the life expectancy gains from the 1980–2000 birth cohorts, it is estimated that over 60 percent relate to gains in life expectancy after the age of 65.[41]

In 1900, one in five Americans died before reaching the age of 18.[42] In contrast, government projections forecast that only one in five children born in the United States in 2000 will die prior to the age of 65.[43]

The longevity transition is due to several factors. Primary among these is the almost 60 percent decrease in age-adjusted mortality rates from heart disease. One reason for the decline in heart disease is the reduction in smoking. In 1965, 42 percent of adult Americans smoked, but by 2012, only 18.1 percent of adults were smokers. Dietary changes, with reduced consumption of saturated fats and cholesterol, have also helped to reduce heart disease. Modern medicine has played an important role too. Many drugs have been developed to control cholesterol and high blood pressure, and there have been important surgical and technological innovations, including heart bypass surgery and the development of implantable heart pacemakers. The second leading cause of death is cancer, and death rates from cancer have also decreased, falling 22 percent from 1991 to 2014.[44]

Figure 7.9 compares the overall death rates, along with the ten leading causes of death, in 1900 and 2010. Overall, death rates have decreased by more than 50 percent, with age-adjusted decreases being even larger. In 1900, the two leading causes of death were infectious diseases: influenza/pneumonia and tuberculosis. By 2010, heart disease and cancer were the top two causes, accounting for almost half of all deaths.

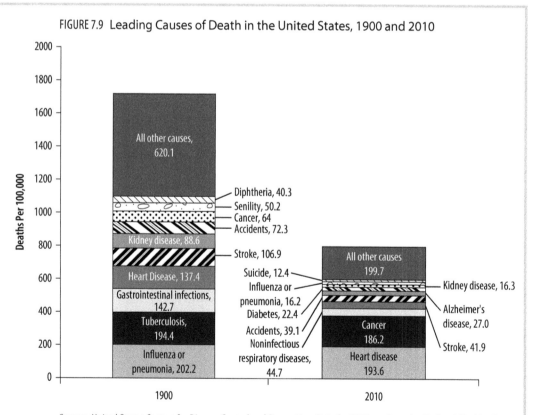

FIGURE 7.9 Leading Causes of Death in the United States, 1900 and 2010

Sources: United States Centers for Disease Control and Prevention. Data for 2010 are from the *National Vital Statistics Report* 61, no. 4 (May 8, 2013), Table B, 5. Data for 1900 are from *Leading Causes of Death 1900 to 1998*, 67, www.cdc.gov/nchs/data/dvs/lead1900_98.pdf (accessed: March 1, 2015).

Projections of future life expectancies in the United States are fraught with uncertainty. On the one hand, there is the possibility of discovering ways to slow or stop the aging process, to cure cancer, and to eliminate most heart disease: those developments would have the potential to increase life expectancies well beyond the current 79 years of age. However, it is also possible that rising rates of obesity may slow or reverse the increases in life expectancies that Americans have come to expect. One study concludes that the effects of obesity could reduce life expectancies by two to five years; another concludes that reductions in smoking rates will more than offset the increases in obesity, so that by 2040 life expectancies will have increased, though by less than one year.[45]

One unexpected finding is that after decades of decline U.S. mortality rates for white non-Hispanics aged 45–54 *increased* between 1998 and 2013, due almost entirely to higher rates of "suicide, drug and alcohol poisoning (accidental and intent undetermined), and chronic liver diseases and cirrhosis."[46] While this increase in midlife mortality rates does not extend to other ethnicity or age groups in the United States or to those in other rich, industrialized countries, it illustrates the difficulties in accurately predicting future trends in mortality rates and life expectancies.

7.5 CONCLUSIONS

Demographic changes have profoundly affected the way Americans live. Compared to 1900, Americans can now expect to live more than 30 years longer. The chances of dying from an infectious disease are far lower, but the aging population now suffers from far more chronic conditions, and the majority succumb to heart disease or cancer.

Family sizes are also smaller and a lower proportion of children are born to married couples. The population of the United States is over four times larger than it was in 1900, but population growth is much slower. The population is also far more urban, with a greater proportion of the population living in the South and the West. Although immigration was an important determinant of population growth in 1900 and remains so today, immigrants are no longer predominantly from Europe but mostly from Latin American and Asian countries.

QUESTIONS

1. What are the similarities and differences between indentured contracts and redemption contracts? What factors led to the demise of the market for indentured servants and redemptioners?

2. Suppose that on January 1, 2020, the population of a country is 100 million. During 2020, there are 1 million births and 500,000 deaths. In addition, 2 million people immigrate to the country, while 500,000 emigrate. What is the population on January 1, 2021? What is the population growth rate of this country, as a percentage? What proportion of the population growth is the result of natural increase? Show your calculations and explain.

3. What is the fertility transition and when did it take place in the United States? What explanations have been proposed to account for this transition? Critically evaluate each of these explanations.

4. Life expectancy at birth in the United States increased from approximately 41 years of age in 1880 to almost 69 years of age by 1950. Discuss the causes for this dramatic increase in life expectancy and assess their relative importance.

5. What do you suspect will be the life expectancy of Americans born in the year 2100? Be sure to use evidence from the past and present to support your answer.

NOTES

[1] In some instances, the denominator used to compute crude birth rates, death rates, immigration rates, and emigration rates is the average of the population at the beginning and end of the one-year period, rather than the population at the beginning of the year.

[2] Angus Maddison, "Historical Statistics on the World Economy, 1–2008 A.D.," www.ggdc.net/maddison/Historical_Statistics/vertical-file_02-2010.xls (accessed: February 2, 2015).

[3] Susan B. Carter, Scott Sigmund Gartner, Michael R. Haines, Alan L. Olmstead, Richard Sutch, and Gavin Wright (eds.), *Historical Statistics of the United States*, Millennial Edition (New York, NY: Cambridge University Press, 2006), series Z1.

[4] David W. Galenson, *White Servitude in Colonial America* (Cambridge, UK: Cambridge University Press, 1981), Table 7.1.

[5] Farley Grubb, "The End of European Immigrant Servitude in the United States: An Economic Analysis of Market Collapse, 1772–1835," *Journal of Economic History* 54, no. 4 (December 1994), 794–824. Grubb (p. 800) concludes: "The meager volume of servants after 1819 represented more than just a fall in immigration. It represented a permanent shift by immigrants away from servitude as a means of financing transatlantic migration."

[6] Grubb, 795.

[7] Stanley L. Engerman, "Slavery and Its Consequences for the South," in Stanley L. Engerman and Robert E. Gallman (eds.), *The Cambridge Economic History of the United States: The Long Nineteenth Century* (Cambridge, UK: Cambridge University Press, 1996), 333.

[8] Engerman, 337–338.

[9] Engerman, 330.

[10] Robert William Fogel, *Without Consent or Contract: The Rise and Fall of American Slavery* (New York, NY: W.W. Norton & Co., 1989), 34.

[11] Richard H. Steckel, "A Peculiar Population: The Nutrition, Health, and Mortality of American Slaves from Childhood to Maturity," *Journal of Economic History* 46, no. 3 (September 1986), 721–741.

[12] Steckel, Table 4, 733.

[13] Frank Hobbs and Nicole Stoops, "Demographic Trends in the 20th Century," *2000 Census Special Report* (Washington, DC: U.S. Bureau of the Census, 2002), 33.

[14] Until recently, scholars thought that the U.S. fertility transition had begun by 1800. More recent estimates, however, show that the decline may not have started prior to the mid-nineteenth century. Even the mid-nineteenth century precedes the fertility transition for most European countries. See David J. Hacker, "Rethinking the 'Early' Decline of Marital Fertility in the United States," *Demography* 40, no. 4 (November 2003), 605–620.

[15] According to the World Bank, 99 countries had total fertility rates below 2.1 in 2012, http://data.worldbank.org/indicator/SP.DYN.TFRT.IN (accessed: February 6, 2015). Replacement fertility, however, differs somewhat by country, depending on the mortality rates of women prior to and during childbearing years.

[16] Richard Easterlin, "Population Change and Farm Settlement in the Northern United States," *Journal of Economic History* 36, no. 1 (March 1976), 45–75.

[17] William Sundstrom and Paul David, "Old-Age Security Motives, Labor Markets, and Family Farm Fertility in Antebellum America," *Explorations in Economic History* 25, no. 2 (April 1998), 164–197.

[18] Sundrom and David, 164–197. See also Susan Carter, Roger Ransom, and Richard Sutch, "Family Matters: The Life-Cycle Transition and the Antebellum Fertility Decline," in Timothy Guinnane, William Sundstrom, and Warren Whatley (eds.), *History Matters: Essays on Economic Growth, Technology, and Demographic Change* (Stanford, CA: Stanford University Press, 2004), 271–327.

[19] Alberto Basso, Howard Bodenhorn, and David Cuberes, "Fertility and Financial Development: Evidence from U.S. Counties in the 19th Century," *National Bureau of Economic Research Working Paper*, no. 20491 (September 2014).

[20] Joanna N. Lahey, "Birthing a Nation: The Effect of Fertility Control Access on the Nineteenth-Century Demographic Transition," *Journal of Economic History* 74, no. 2 (June 2014), 482–508.

[21] Timothy W. Guinnane, "The Historical Fertility Transition: A Guide for Economists," *Journal of Economic Literature* 49, no. 3 (September 2001), 600–602.

[22] Guinnane, 602. This quote refers to the model developed by Paul A. David and Warren C. Sanderson, "Rudimentary Contraceptive Methods and the American Transition to Marital Fertility Control," in Stanley L. Engerman and Robert E. Gallman (eds.), *Long-Term Factors in American Economic Growth* (Chicago: University of Chicago Press, 1986), 307–389.

[23] Martha J. Bailey, "'Momma's Got the Pill': How Anthony Comstock and *Griswald vs. Connecticut* Shaped U.S. Childbearing," *American Economic Review* 100, no. 1 (March 2010), 123.

[24] Jan Van Bavel and David S. Reher, "The Baby Boom and Its Causes: What We Know and What We Need to Know," *Population and Development Review* 39, no. 2 (June 2013), 257.

[25] Van Bavel and Reher, 269.

[26] Richard A. Easterlin, "The Conflict between Aspirations and Resources," *Population and Development Review* 2, no. 3-4 (September and December 1976), 417–425. For empirical support for the relative income hypothesis, see Matthew J. Hill, "Easterlin Revisited: Relative Income and the Baby Boom," *Explorations in Economic History* 56, no. 2 (April 2015), 71–85.

[27] Van Bavel and Reher, 282.

[28] Van Bavel and Reher, 282.

[29] Martha J. Bailey, Melanie E. Guldi, and Brad J. Hershbein, "Is There a Case for a 'Second Demographic Transition'? Three Distinctive Features of the Post-1960 U.S. Fertility Decline," *National Bureau of Economic Research Working Paper*, no. 19599 (October 2013).

[30] Brady E. Hamilton, Joyce A. Martin, Michelle J.K. Osterman, and Sally C. Curtin, "Births: Preliminary Data for 2013," *National Vital Statistics Report* 63, no. 2 (May 29, 2014).

[31] Hamilton et al., 2; and Melissa S. Kearney and Phillip B. Levine, "Why is the Teen Birth Rate in the United States So High and Why Does It Matter?" *Journal of Economic Perspectives* 26, no. 2 (Spring 2012), Figure 1, 144. In 2009, the U.S. teen birth rate was 37.9 births per 1,000 women aged 15–19, compared with 30.2 births in Russia. Between 2009 and 2013, the U.S. teen birth rate fell from 37.9 to 26.6, but 2013 data are not available for the Russian Federation. In 2012, the World Bank reported a teen birth rate for the Russian Federation of 26 births per 1,000 women aged 15–19, http://data.worldbank.org/indicator/SP.ADO.TFRT (accessed: February 22, 2015).

[32] Hamilton et al., Figure 1, 144.

[33] Hamilton et al., 150.

[34] Kearney and Levine, 163.

[35] David Cutler, Angus Deaton, and Adriana Lleras-Muney, "The Determinants of Mortality," *Journal of Economic Perspectives* 20, no. 3 (Summer 2006), 102.

[36] Cutler et al., 102.

[37] Cutler et al., 103.

[38] Carolyn M. Moehling and Melissa A. Thomasson, "Saving Babies: The Impact of Public Education Programs on Infant Mortality," *Demography* 51, no. 2 (April 2014), 367–386.

[39] Centers for Disease Control, "Achievements in Public Health, 1900–1999," *Morbidity and Mortality Weekly Report* 48, no. 29 (July 30, 1999).

[40] Gregory L. Armstrong, Laura A. Conn, and Robert W. Pinner, "Trends in Infectious Disease Mortality in the United States during the 20th Century," *Journal of the American Medical Association* 281, no. 1 (January 6, 1999), 65.

[41] Karen N. Eggleston and Victor R. Fuchs, "The New Demographic Transition: Most Gains in Life Expectancy Now Realized Late in Life," *Journal of Economic Perspectives* 26, no. 3 (Summer 2012), 143.

[42] Felicitie C. Bell and Michael L. Miller, "Life Tables for the United States Social Security Area 1900–2010," *Actuarial Study No. 120*, Social Security Administration (August 2005), Figure 5, www.ssa.gov/oact/NOTES/as120/images/LD_fig5.html (accessed: February 23, 2015).

[43] Bell and Miller, Figure 5, www.ssa.gov/oact/NOTES/as120/images/LD_fig5.html (accessed: February 25, 2015).

[44] "U.S. Cancer Deaths Fell 22% Since 1991," *Scientific American* (December 31, 2014), www.scientificamerican.com/article/u-s-cancer-deaths-fell-22-since-1991/ (accessed: February 25, 2015).

[45] S. Jay Olshansky, Douglas J. Pasaro, Ronald C. Hershow, Jennifer Layden, Bruce A. Carnes, Jacob Brady, Leonard Hayflick, Robert N. Butler, David B. Allison, and David S. Ludwig, "A Potential Decline in Life Expectancy in the United States in the 21st Century," *New England Journal of Medicine* 352, no. 11 (2005), 1138–45. These authors project a decline in future life expectancy, whereas Samuel H. Preston, Andrew Stokes, Neil K. Mehta, and Bochen Cao, in "Projecting the Effect of Changes in Smoking and Obesity on Future Life Expectancy in the United States," *Demography* 51, no. 1 (February 2014), 27–49, project a small gain by 2040.

[46] Anne Case and Angus Deaton, "Rising Morbidity and Mortality in Midlife Among White Non-Hispanic Americans in the 21st Century," *Proceedings of the National Academy of Sciences of the United States of America* 112, no. 49 (December 8, 2015), 15079, www.pnas.org/content/112/49/15078.full.pdf (accessed: June 9, 2016).

8
Transportation and Communication

Throughout American history there has been a seemingly never-ending revolution in transportation and communication—a revolution that has helped to transform the economy. By wagon, by steamboat, by railroad, by automobile, and most recently by airplane, Americans have been on the move for centuries. So too they have become more interconnected: by mail, by telegraph, by telephone, and now by the Internet. From the printing press to motion pictures, television, and the Internet, information and entertainment too have helped shape the economy.

Although the U.S. Constitution provided the institutional framework for a "common market," a truly nationwide common market was not possible until transportation and communication developments allowed for the rapid, widespread, and inexpensive exchange of goods and information throughout the country. Improvements in transportation and communication have been a combination of both technological breakthroughs and large infrastructural investments. As new forms of transportation and communication developed and expanded, transaction costs fell, lowering prices of goods to consumers, and allowing for greater specialization and division of labor as markets grew and flourished. Larger markets also encouraged technological innovations in other parts of the economy.

Private entrepreneurs, motivated by profits, were instrumental in these developments, but state governments and the federal government also played important roles in subsidizing and regulating the transportation and communication sectors. While government involvement helped in encouraging the building of the transportation and communication networks, rent-seeking behavior by potential recipients of government subsidies was also prevalent, as was corruption.

8.1 TOLL ROADS AND WAGON TRAILS

In 1800 there were already 20,000 miles of post roads, yet the road system in the United States was far from adequate.[1] Travel times from New York City to western Pennsylvania took longer than one week, while parts of western Ohio were a month away (Figure 8.1). In 1803, President Jefferson, who was eager to explore the Louisiana

FIGURE 8.1 Rates of Travel from New York City, 1800 and 1857

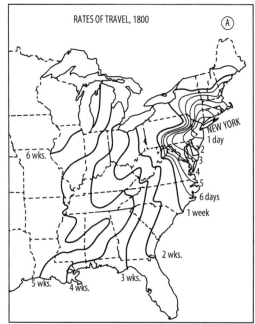

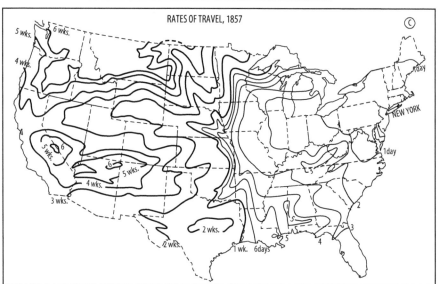

Source: Charles O. Paullin, *Atlas of the Historical Geography of the United States* (Washington, DC: Carnegie Institution, 1932), Plates 138A and 138C.

Purchase, sent Meriwether Lewis and William Clark on an expedition from St. Louis to the Pacific coast. It took them 863 days, between 1804 and 1806, to make the 7,000-mile round-trip journey.[2]

Although steamboats, canals, and railroads were the dominant forms of transportation throughout the nineteenth century, toll roads and wagon trails, such as the Oregon Trail, were also important. Most roads in the nineteenth century were built by private companies, in three episodes of toll road construction: the turnpike era in eastern states from 1792 to 1845, wooden plank roads from 1847 to 1853, and toll roads in western states from 1850 to 1902.[3] The federal government, however, did complete one major road project: the 620-mile National Road.

TOLL ROADS

The first major transportation improvements in the United States were turnpikes: intercity toll roads paved with gravel and stone. They were constructed by private companies and financed mostly from private sources, with $25 million of the total $30 million coming from private capital invested in several hundred turnpike companies. The total investment in turnpikes (private and public) over many years is likely to have been less than 10 percent of one year's GDP, and was equivalent to about 60 percent of the total amount invested in canals. There was, however, far greater private investment in turnpikes compared to canals, with private investment in turnpikes more than twice the amount of canals.[4]

The first turnpike was the 62-mile Lancaster Turnpike (1795) between Lancaster and Philadelphia; but it was New England that initially led the way, with more than 60 percent of the nationwide mileage in 1810. By 1830, however, New York and Pennsylvania contained 7,000 miles of the almost 12,000 miles nationwide.[5] By way of comparison, there are over 4 million miles of roads in the United States today, so the turnpike mileage of 12,000 represents about one-third of 1 percent of the road miles today.[6]

Despite the collection of tolls, very few turnpikes were profitable and almost all earned a rate of return that was less than the opportunity cost of capital.[7] There were several reasons for the lack of profitability. One was the existence of "shunpikes"—side roads around toll booths that allowed their users to avoid paying tolls. In some cases, state charters were overly restrictive, which reduced profitability. Other explanations include high construction costs and population densities too low to generate sufficient traffic and revenue. Some scholars have argued that turnpikes were not sufficiently better than free roads to justify the tolls charged.[8]

If the profitability of turnpikes was so low, even from the beginning, what explains the high rate of private investment needed to build 12,000 miles of such roads over the course of several decades? Researchers point to a civic-minded culture that encouraged investment for long-term community gain: investors did not necessarily expect private gain through stock ownership.[9] As with modern fundraising for charities, community spirit and social pressure led to investment in private road companies.

Many investors also positioned themselves to gain indirectly from the building of such roads, and evidence shows that "the vast majority of the stockholders in turnpikes were farmers, land speculators, merchants or individuals and firms invested in commerce."[10] While these investors lost money in the turnpike company itself, it is likely that in other ways they gained sufficiently from having a road nearby to make the investment both rational and profitable.

Eventually, competition from steamboats, canals, and railroads spelled the end for turnpike companies. Many turnpikes became part of the growing public road system, having been purchased by local governments or simply adopted after they had been abandoned.

By the 1840s, however, there was still a need for shorter feeder routes that would allow travelers to reach the canals and railroads, and plank roads (toll roads built with wooden planks) filled this need. Between 1845 and 1860, around 9,000 miles of plank roads were built, with the top lumber-producing states of New York and Pennsylvania leading the way.[11]

The last phase of private road construction occurred in the West after 1850, particularly in California, Colorado, and Nevada. In California, at least 159 companies built and operated toll roads, while 117 companies operated roads in Nevada.[12] Between 1850 and 1902, roughly 7,000 miles of toll roads were built in western states.[13] Ideological changes associated with the Progressive period (1890–1920) turned the tide against private roads and toward the public operation and ownership of roads. This became national policy with the Federal Highway Act (1916), which prohibited tolls on highways that received federal funds.[14]

THE NATIONAL ROAD

In 1807, to prevent the U.S. from becoming entangled in the Napoleonic Wars between England and France, Congress and President Thomas Jefferson passed the Embargo Act, which prohibited American ships from trading in foreign ports. As a result of the decline in international trade, attention turned toward internal improvements.

In 1808, the Secretary of the Treasury, Albert Gallatin, presented to Congress a wide-ranging and comprehensive plan calling for $20 million in federal spending over 10 years to build roads and canals. This was at a time when the entire annual federal budget was less than $10 million. The plan was never carried out in full, due to financial constraints and concerns about the constitutionality of such an undertaking, but one major project was completed: the National Road.

Construction started in 1811, in Cumberland, Maryland, and the road headed west across the Allegheny Mountains, reaching Wheeling, West Virginia, on the Ohio River, in 1818. In 1839 it was extended to Vandalia, Illinois, 70 miles northeast of St. Louis and the Mississippi River. The National Road cost $7 million (about $150 million in 2015 dollars) and served as the gateway to the west.[15] Today U.S. Route 40 follows the course of various portions of the National Road.

WAGON TRAILS

The wagon routes of westward migration usually followed paths used by Native Americans, which were often adjacent to streams and rivers because these provided the easiest lines of travel. Beginning around 1810, the route that became the Oregon Trail was traveled by mountain men employed as trappers, but it was not passable by wagon until the 1830s. Settlement to Oregon increased dramatically in the 1840s, particularly after the Oregon Treaty (1846) was signed. This agreement with Great Britain gave the U.S. undisputed claim to the Pacific Northwest.

There were several other important wagon routes. The Mormon Trail was the route followed by Brigham Young and the Mormon settlers on their way to what was to become Salt Lake City, Utah. For much of the way it paralleled the Oregon Trail along the Platte River, but in western Wyoming the Mormons split from the Oregon Trail to drop into the Salt Lake Valley in 1847.

The California Trail departed from the Oregon Trail farther west, providing a route for settlers going to Sacramento and San Francisco; while the Santa Fe Trail and the Spanish Trail provided routes from Independence, Missouri, to Santa Fe, New Mexico, and on to southern California. Several hundred thousand settlers used these routes, on often perilous and sometimes deadly journeys that lasted between 4 and 6 months. An estimated 10 percent of settlers died along the way.

Between 1840 and 1848, almost 19,000 settlers made their way to Oregon, Utah, and California using overland wagon trails, with over 11,500 going to Oregon, 4,600 going to Utah, and less than 3,000 traveling to California.[16] The discovery of gold in the Sierra Nevada Mountains of northern California in 1848 led to dramatically greater numbers during the California Gold Rush. From 1849 to 1860, overland migration to Oregon, Utah, and California exceeded 250,000 (more than 10 times the amount in the previous decade), with more than 200,000 destined for California.[17]

8.2 WATER TRANSPORTATION

Whereas transporting heavy goods on wooden wagons along dirt roads was extremely difficult, moving goods on rivers, oceans, and canals was far easier and also less costly.

STEAMBOATS AND RIVER TRANSPORTATION

The shipping of goods downstream was a cheap and common form of transportation in 1800, but returning upstream was time-consuming and expensive, involving the use of keelboats, propelled by crews of twenty or more men pushing long poles into the riverbed, or flatboats, pulled by draft animals on paths at the side of the river. The introduction of steamboats on western rivers caused dramatic reductions in upstream freight rates, and led to tremendous increases in the volume of goods shipped up and down the Mississippi, the Missouri, the Ohio, and other major rivers.

In 1712, Englishman Thomas Newcomen invented a steam engine that used a piston to pump water out of mines. A more efficient and more useful method of harnessing steam power became available when James Watt, a Scottish inventor, developed a continuous-motion rotary steam engine in 1781.[18]

Applying steam power to navigation, however, required an efficient method of transmitting the power generated so that it could propel a boat through water. Some early attempts tried pumping water in at the front of the boat and expelling it at the stern, while others tried to imitate the feet of a duck, but the most promising method was the paddle wheel.[19]

Americans Robert Livingston and Robert Fulton developed the first commercially successful steamboat operation. In 1807, Robert Fulton's 142-foot long steamboat, equipped with two paddle wheels, made the 150-mile trip from New York City to Albany, New York, in 32 hours and commercial service soon started on the North River (now called the Hudson River).

The first steamboat on the Mississippi River, the *New Orleans* (1811), was owned by Fulton and Livingston, and ushered in an era of commercial steamboat navigation on western rivers. Starting with that one steamboat on the Mississippi River in 1811, there were over 150 on western rivers by 1830, and more than 1,000 by 1865. Not until the 1880s did the number of steamboats register an absolute decline.[20]

For steamboats between 1815 and 1860, total factor productivity (TFP) growth, the growth of output relative to the growth of inputs (see Chapter 2), averaged around

5 percent per year and "exceeded that of any other major transportation medium for a period of similar length in the nineteenth century."[21]

The primary reason for TFP growth was a more than threefold increase in the carrying capacity of steamboats relative to their tonnage. Changes in hull design, along with a reduction in the weight of steam engines and other equipment, allowed steamboats to carry substantially more cargo. The same design changes also allowed boats to operate in shallower waters, thereby increasing the length of the navigation season. Reductions in port times and passenger journey times greatly increased the average number of roundtrip voyages per year and thus contributed to productivity gains as well.[22]

Productivity changes were reflected in large decreases in shipping costs. Upstream rates from New Orleans to Louisville decreased in real terms by more than 90 percent between 1815 and 1860, while downstream rates fell by almost 40 percent.[23] By the mid-1820s, both upstream and downstream freight rates on steamboats were only about 3 percent of the costs of transporting goods overland by wagon.[24]

OCEAN TRANSPORTATION

Steamboats were common on American rivers long before steam engines powered ships across the Atlantic. For most of the nineteenth century, a sailing vessel, the clipper ship, was the preferred mode of transatlantic travel. Fast and maneuverable, clipper ships carried mail, passengers, and highly-valued cargo on journeys that took about 30 days.

The invention of the screw propeller, which replaced the paddle wheel, and of riveting techniques, which enabled the production of iron-hulled ships, together made it possible for steam power to be used on ocean-going vessels.[25] It was not until the 1880s, however, that steamships outnumbered sailing vessels on transatlantic voyages.[26] Economic historians have argued that large decreases in the costs of ocean shipping from 1850 to 1913, in part due to the advent of the steamship, ushered in the first era of globalization.[27] In addition, when immigration surged in the late nineteenth century, steamships were the primary means of transporting people from Europe to the United States.[28]

World War II, in particular, was a catalyst to the U.S. shipbuilding industry. More than 4 million men and women together built more than 5,000 ships; and by the end of the war, over 60 percent of the worldwide tonnage of ocean-going vessels was American.[29] U.S. dominance in shipping waned in the postwar period, and the industry has become increasingly dominated by China, South Korea, Japan, and Greece.

CANALS

In places where natural waterways did not exist, Americans created artificial waterways by digging canals. Among the first were the Santee Canal (1800) in South Carolina and the Middlesex Canal (1802) in Massachusetts. By 1816, however, the United States had a mere 100 miles of canals. The canal era (1817–1843) began in earnest with the construction of the Erie Canal. A quarter century later, the country had more than 3,300 miles of canals, largely the result of the success of the Erie Canal.

The 363-mile-long Erie Canal between the Hudson River in Albany, New York, and Buffalo, New York, on Lake Erie took over eight years to complete. It was 40 feet wide and 4 feet deep, with 83 locks that in total raised and lowered boats 565 feet. The canal was an immediate financial success and tolls repaid construction costs fully within twelve years of opening.

Before the Erie Canal, freight charges between Buffalo, New York, and New York City averaged 19 cents per ton-mile. By 1830, costs had fallen to less than 2 cents per ton-mile, and they continued to fall below 1 cent per ton-mile by the 1850s.[30] The Erie Canal greatly increased the volume of goods shipped in and out of New York City, and by 1840 the city was firmly established as the center of the expanding U.S. economy.

The completion of the Erie Canal in 1825 sparked a canal-building boom, but no other canals matched the success of the Erie. Although extensive canal systems were built in Pennsylvania, Ohio, and Indiana, profits on these canal projects proved disappointing.

Unlike road building, financing for canal investment mostly came from public sources, with U.S. states providing over 60 percent of the funds between 1817 and 1860.[31] Federal land grants pushed the public share to 75 percent of total investment.[32]

8.3 RAIL TRANSPORTATION

Rail transportation had several advantages over water transportation: railroads could operate year round, long after canals, rivers, and lakes had frozen during the winter months in northern states; passengers and products could move at much greater speeds by rail; and railroads could be built in areas without navigable waterways or where canal construction was difficult or impossible.

RAIL MILES

In 1830, only five years after railroads were introduced in England, the first railroad opened in the United States. The Baltimore & Ohio opened with only 13 miles of track from the Baltimore Harbor. Railroad construction was rapid in the 1830s, and remained so until the Panic of 1837. Throughout the nineteenth century, booms and busts in railroad construction closely mirrored U.S. business cycle fluctuations (see Chapter 18).

By 1860, over 30,000 miles of railroads had been constructed in the United States, exceeding the combined mileage of railroads in the United Kingdom, France, and Germany. Total investment in railroads up to 1860 was five times greater than the amount invested in canals.[33]

Expansion after the Civil War was even more impressive. While Congress had instructed engineers to survey potential transcontinental routes in 1853, it was the Pacific Railroad Act in 1862 that led to action. The first transcontinental was the largest publicly-funded project of the nineteenth century.[34] The federal government provided construction loans and massive land grants to two private companies: the Central Pacific, which built a railroad eastward from Sacramento, California; and the Union Pacific, which built west from Omaha, Nebraska. The transcontinental was completed on May 10, 1869, when the two rail lines met at Promontory Summit, Utah (Figure 8.2).

From 1865 to 1900, however, the greatest percentage of track was laid in the Great Plains states, with Chicago becoming the major terminus and St. Louis, Kansas City, Omaha, Minneapolis, and Denver becoming secondary hubs of the growing railway network. By 1910, there were 266,000 miles of main track nationwide, almost 9 times the amount in 1860. In 1910, only Canada had more rail miles per capita than the United States.[35]

FIGURE 8.2 The Completion of the First Transcontinental Railroad, 1869

Source: U.S. National Archives, www.archives.gov/global-pages/download.php?f=/historical-docs/doc-content/images/promontory-point-utah-xl.jpg (accessed: April 21, 2016).

RAILROAD OUTPUT AND PRODUCTIVITY

Table 8.1 shows the growth rates of total output (freight tonnage and passenger miles) and total factor productivity for American railroads. Total output growth averaged 10.57 percent per year from 1839 to 1910, and output doubled roughly every 7 years.[36]

The most rapid gains occurred from 1839 to 1859, with output increasing more than 18 percent per year and total factor productivity growth of almost 4 percent

TABLE 8.1 Output and Productivity Growth in Railroads, 1839–1910 (Percent Per Year)		
Time Period	Output Growth g_Y	Total Factor Productivity Growth g_A
1839–1859	18.05%	3.76%
1859–1890	9.09%	2.24%
1890–1910	5.73%	2.05%
1839–1910	**10.57%**	**2.61%**

Sources: Computed using data from Albert Fishlow, "Internal Transportation in the Nineteenth and Early Twentieth Centuries," in Stanley L. Engerman and Robert E. Gallman (eds.), *The Cambridge Economic History of the United States: The Long Nineteenth Century,*. (Cambridge, UK: Cambridge University Press, 2000), Table 13.11, 582, and Table 13.14, 594.

per year. The rapid growth of output and total factor productivity was reflected in falling prices for freight and passengers. During the 1830s, freight rates per ton-mile were about 7.5 cents and passenger fares per mile averaged 5 cents. By 1859, freight rates had fallen to 2.58 cents per ton-mile, while passenger rates fell to 2.44 cents per mile.[37]

Most of the increase in total output was due to growth in the factors of production, and not to total factor productivity growth. Although total factor productivity increased more than six-fold between 1839 and 1910, the inputs of labor, capital, and fuel all witnessed more than 100-fold increases.

Annual TFP growth from 1839 to 1910 averaged 2.61 percent per year, and over 2 percent in each of the sub-periods listed in Table 8.1. This was more rapid than TFP growth in the overall economy, which was less than 1 percent economy-wide during this period (see Chapter 2, Table 2.3).

About one-half of the TFP growth in railroads was due to economies of scale in the operation of railroads, while the other half was due to technological improvements. Steel rails (1864), instead of iron, permitted heavier loads, while locomotives and freight cars increased in size and efficiency. Air brakes (1868) and automatic couplers (1873) improved the speed and safety of railroads. Other innovations played a role as well, including the introduction of the sleeping coach (1872) and the refrigerated boxcar (1876).[38]

THE "AXIOM OF INDISPENSABILITY" AND AGGREGATE ECONOMIC GROWTH

Generations of scholars have debated the importance of railroads to U.S. economic growth. Many early scholars believed that railroads were indispensable to economic growth, but they did not have a way to test their argument empirically. In the 1960s, economic historians developed an approach called the "social savings" method, which attempted to measure the gains in consumer surplus from railroads by comparing the cost and quantity of shipping goods by rail to the next best alternative form of transportation (canals, rivers, wagons, etc.). Two prominent studies concluded that U.S. GDP would have been only a few percentage points lower in 1860 or 1890 if railroads had never existed.[39]

While these studies overturned the "axiom of indispensability" argument of earlier scholars, the measured social savings of railroads seemed surprisingly small. Since the 1960s, economic historians have investigated how railroads indirectly influenced economic growth and development, beyond the direct transportation savings captured by the social savings methodology. Railroads have been shown to increase the value of agricultural land and to help stimulate agricultural productivity. Railroads also encouraged growth in manufacturing, investment in education, and urbanization in the Midwest.[40]

In addition, railroads precipitated changes in finance and banking. The spread of railroads (along with the telegraph system) led to dramatic growth in stock and bond markets, and proximity to a railroad resulted in lower bank failure rates and better balance-sheet management by commercial banks.[41] While it is difficult to precisely quantify the impact of these indirect effects, most scholars now believe that railroads were more important to U.S. economic growth than the early social savings literature suggested, although still not absolutely indispensable to nineteenth-century economic growth.

STANDARD TIME

Railroads altered the way we measure and conceptualize time. Time was once a local matter, where noon occurred when the sun was directly overhead. Measured by this standard, the time in Boston, for example, is almost 12 minutes later than the time in New York. Railroad travelers from Maine to California had to reset their watches at least 20 times.

With coast-to-coast railroads, the problem of local time came to the forefront. Great Britain had already faced this problem and had decided to introduce a standard time nationally. Railroads throughout Canada and the United States agreed in 1883 to follow this principle, but with the continent divided into four standard time zones. After 1883, many communities reported both railroad time and local time. Detroit, for example, continued to post both local and standard time until 1900. Standard time, however, did not become U.S. law until Congress passed the Standard Time Act in 1918.

LAND GRANTS AND THE CRÉDIT MOBILIER SCANDAL

Between 1850 and 1871, nearly 250 million square miles of public lands were transferred to private railroad ownership, an amount almost equal to the size of Texas. This policy was very controversial at the time, and the question of whether land grants were necessary for the completion of the transcontinental railroad has been a subject of debate ever since.[42]

The land grants were associated with widespread corruption. The most famous incident involved the construction company of the Union Pacific, called Crédit Mobilier, which sold bonds worth $150 million, a sum far in excess of what it needed to construct the transcontinental. In 1867, Congress considered investigating Crédit Mobilier, and this prompted the company to pay bribes to many members of Congress and to Vice President Schuyler Colfax, either by giving away stock or by selling stock at prices far below market prices. As stockholders in the Union Pacific, members of Congress benefitted financially from the land grants since these drove up stock prices. When the scandal became public in 1872, it fueled hostility toward the railroads and government from farmers and others (see Chapter 9).

TROLLEYS AND SUBWAYS

Prior to the late nineteenth century, getting around growing cities was as challenging as finding a decent place to live and a steady job. Innovations in mass transit, however, soon enabled large numbers of workers to go to and from their jobs more easily. Cable cars, driven by large underground cables, were introduced in San Francisco in 1873. In contrast, streetcars or trolleys are powered by overhead electric wires. The first practical electric streetcar began operation in Richmond, Virginia, in 1888. Boston introduced electric subways beneath the city's busy streets in 1897, while the first underground line of the New York subway opened in 1904.

Around 1900, mass-transit networks in many cities resulted in some urban sprawl, with outlying city neighborhoods being linked to central business districts. The decline of streetcars or trolleys was almost as rapid as their rise, although many underground subways continue to thrive. Between 1921 and 1939, nearly 75 percent of the mileage "fell into disuse" because of competition from automobiles and buses.[43]

8.4 HIGHWAYS AND AUTOMOBILES

To generations of Americans who came of age during the twentieth century, the automobile was more than a means of transportation: it defined a way of life. From cruising on Saturday night to the development of shopping malls, motels, drive-in movie theaters, and fast food, and to the growth of suburbs, the automobile impacted American life and the economy perhaps as much as the railroad had done a century before.

THE AUTOMOBILE AGE

The first steam-powered vehicles operated on roads in the eighteenth century, and steam carriage services were common in England by the 1830s.[44] The gasoline-powered automobile, however, was not developed until the late nineteenth century, in Germany and France. By 1895, however, the French had taken the lead in the production and design of automobiles.[45]

Although several Americans managed to build experimental cars by 1895, few Americans had ever seen a car, and American automobiles "were exceptionally primitive in comparison with the best contemporary French designs."[46] This soon changed. News coverage of the 732-mile Paris–Bordeaux–Paris auto race in 1895 had an immediate impact in the United States, with most of the 500 patent applications relating to automobiles at the U.S. Patent Office filed less than two months after the race.[47]

By 1900, more than thirty companies in the United States were making automobiles, but it was not yet clear that gasoline-fueled cars were the future of the automobile industry. While electric and steam-powered cars set records at short distances, gasoline-powered cars excelled in "virtually all early endurance and reliability runs over public roads," and were soon the most common automobiles.[48] There were several other reasons for their dominance. The discovery of massive oil reserves at Spindletop, Texas (1901), and elsewhere provided cheap and abundant fuel. The introduction of the Ford Model T (1908) and the moving assembly line at Ford (1913) greatly reduced the cost of production and thus the cost of owning a gasoline-powered car. Lastly, the invention in 1911 of the electronic starter, which replaced the hand crank, improved the safety, convenience, and desirability of gasoline-powered automobiles.[49]

The early decades of the automobile industry in the United States witnessed tremendous growth and competition, with hundreds of companies producing cars. American automobile production surpassed that of France by 1905, and exceeded the combined production of France, Germany, and Great Britain in 1907.[50] In 1929, there were 26.7 million motor vehicles registered in the United States, one automobile for every 4.5 persons.[51]

Over time, mergers and bankruptcies led to a far more concentrated industry. By 1929, the "Big Three"—General Motors, Ford, and Chrysler—controlled 75 percent of the U.S. auto industry and had become an oligopoly (Chapter 17). By the mid-1950s, the Big Three controlled almost 95 percent of the U.S. market for automobiles, and close to 50 percent of the worldwide share.[52]

Between the mid-1950s and 2008, however, the Big Three lost over 40 points in U.S. market share.[53] The Volkswagen (VW) Beetle was the first successful import, but far more damaging to the Big Three was increased competition from Japanese automakers (Nissan, Honda, and Toyota). In 2008, Toyota became the largest producer of vehicles worldwide, a position that had been previously held by GM for 77 consecutive years.[54]

ROADS AND HIGHWAYS

The success of the automobile depended on massive investments in the building and paving of roads. The initial impetus for paved roads in the United States was the invention in 1887 of the first practical pneumatic tire for bicycles (the modern tire, made of reinforced rubber and filled with air). Cycling groups provided the spark for the "good roads movement," which secured state aid for paved-road construction in several states during the 1890s, prior to the widespread use of automobiles.[55]

Bicyclists were later joined by automobile manufacturers and enthusiasts, and also farmers, who together crusaded for the improvement of the country's rural roads.[56] Although the "good roads movement" led to more paved local roads, the quality of long-distance roads remained poor. In 1919, an Army caravan of 79 trucks needed 62 days to drive from Washington, DC to San Francisco, averaging only 50 miles a day.[57] On one of those trucks was a young Lieutenant Colonel named Dwight D. Eisenhower.

While from 1912 the federal government provided some funds for roads, the Federal Highway Act (1921) represented the first large-scale support, with federal matching funds on a 50–50 basis to each state for nonurban "primary" roads. During the 1920s, federal, state, and local spending for roads averaged about $2 billion a year, or more than 2 percent of GDP.[58]

More support for intercity and interstate roads came from the Federal Highway Act (1944), but the federal government took a much bolder step when the Highways Act (1956) was signed into law by President Dwight D. Eisenhower. The bill authorized $25 billion for more than 40,000 miles of multi-lane, toll-free interstate highways (Figure 8.3). Taxes on gasoline, diesel fuel, tires, lubricants, and auto parts paid for the

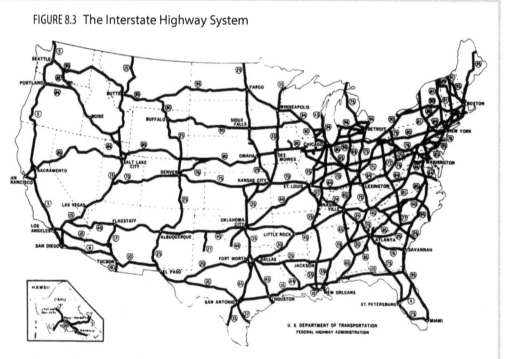

FIGURE 8.3 The Interstate Highway System

Source: U.S. Department of Transportation, Federal Highway Administration, www.fhwa.dot.gov/interstate/finalmap.cfm (accessed: March 23, 2016).

project, with 90 percent of the funds coming from the federal government and 10 percent from state governments.[59]

Table 2.3 (in Chapter 2) showed that the 1950s and 1960s had the highest rates of labor productivity and total factor productivity growth in American history. Evidence suggests that the "massive road-building of the 1950's and 1960's offered a one-time boost to the level of productivity ... [and] contributed about 1 percentage point more to total factor productivity growth before 1973 than after."[60] The impact of the interstate highway system is large enough to explain much of the unusually robust performance during the 1950s and 1960s, as well as the productivity slowdown after 1973.

8.5 AIR TRANSPORTATION

Orville and Wilbur Wright made the first flights in a heavier-than-air vehicle near Kitty Hawk, North Carolina, in 1903. Further improvements in their aircraft soon convinced the Wright brothers that they had a commercially viable product. In 1911, the Wright Company had the capacity to produce two planes a month, which were sold to the army and other customers.[61] In 1918, production in the U.S. topped 14,000, with almost all planes purchased by the military for World War I, compared to just 49 airplanes in 1914.[62]

One important boost to the airline industry after the War was the Kelly Airmail Act (1925), which shifted airmail from government planes to private contractors, and led to the development of both aircraft and companies to carry mail and passengers. Technological improvements during the 1920s and 1930s laid the groundwork for the modern airline industry. During the 1920s, the monoplane replaced the biplane, and by the 1930s, aluminum had replaced wood as the material of choice. The 1930s also witnessed the introduction of cabin pressurization, retractable landing gear, and improved instrumentation and navigation. In 1933, United Airlines introduced the Boeing 247, which allowed passengers to fly coast-to-coast without changing planes or stopping overnight.

U.S. leadership in airplane construction was largely the result of World War II, however. Between 1940 and 1946, more than 300,000 military aircraft were produced in the United States, including almost 95,000 in 1944 alone.[63] During World War II, the aircraft industry was the largest producer and employer in the United States, with 1.35 million employed in the industry in 1943.[64]

After World War II, the U.S. airline industry became a highly-regulated industry dominated by Eastern, American, United, Trans World Airlines (TWA), Western, and Pan-American Airlines, each firm having been given a regional monopoly. Introduced into service by Pan-American Airlines in 1958, the Boeing 707 was the first commercially successful jetliner, and is generally credited with starting the modern era of commercial aviation.[65] Beginning in 1978, airline deregulation allowed more entrants and led to mergers, increased competition, and bankruptcies. As Table 8.2 shows, during this period of deregulation from the 1970s to the 2000s, the average number of passenger air miles per capita almost tripled.

During the 2000s, the typical American drove almost 11,000 miles a year, flew 1,852 miles by airplane, yet traveled only 53 miles on railroads. A hundred years previously, in the decade of the 1900s, the typical American traveled 278 miles by rail each year and 19 miles by automobile, but had never flown in an airplane.

TABLE 8.2 Average Passenger Miles Per Capita Per Year, 1890s–2000s			
Decade	Private Automobiles	Commercial Airlines	Railroads
1890s	<0.1		193
1900s	19		278
1910s	458	<0.01	358
1920s	2,327	0.1	320
1930s	3,118	2	166
1940s	3,553	25	418
1950s	5,184	111	181
1960s	6,509	285	92
1970s	8,317	651	47
1980s	9,200	1,105	48
1990s	8,728	1,506	51
2000s	10,821	1,852	53

Sources and Notes: Decade averages based on annual data, computed from the following sources: U.S. Department of Transportation, Bureau of Transportation Statistics, Table 1-40 U.S. Passenger Miles; Susan B. Carter, Scott Sigmund Gartner, Michael R. Haines, Alan L. Olmstead, Richard Sutch, and Gavin Wright (eds.), *Historical Statistics of the United States, Millennial Edition* (New York, NY: Cambridge University Press, 2006), Series Df 39, Df 42, Df340, Df1120; Harold Barger, *The Transportation Industries 1889–1946* (New York: National Bureau of Economic Research, 1951), Table B-1, 184–185; and U.S. Bureau of the Census, various sources.

8.6 COMMUNICATION

Throughout most of human history, the speed of communication was no faster than the speed of travel, and both were painfully slow. There were a few exceptions, through the use of smoke signals, beacons, drums, passenger pigeons, and optical telegraphs sent from tower to tower, but it was not until the 1830s that electrical telecommunication technologies began to emerge. Since that time, the speed of communication has far exceeded the speed of travel, with virtually instantaneous communication worldwide in the modern age.

POSTAL SERVICE

In the nineteenth century, the U.S. Post Office was the most prominent evidence of the federal government in most communities. The U.S. Constitution made it a federal responsibility "To establish Post Offices and post [*sic*] Roads." In 1789, there were 75 post offices in coastal towns, connected by 1,875 miles of postal roads.[66]

A few decades later, the United States had the most well-developed postal system in the world. In 1828, there were 74 post offices for every 100,000 people in the United States, compared to only 17 per 100,000 in Great Britain and 4 per 100,000 in France.[67] By 1831, three-quarters of all federal employees worked for the U.S. Postal Service, and there were more postmasters (8,764) than soldiers in the U.S. Army (6,332).[68]

The U.S. Postal Service has long subsidized the newspaper, magazine, and book industries by charging very low postal rates. Although the Post Office Act (1792) first established this subsidy, the Postal Act (1879) allowed for the free distribution of newspapers within the county in which they were produced and, for the first time, set low national rates for mailing magazines. It also established fourth-class rates for mailing books.

These subsidies, along with technological breakthroughs in the making of paper and in printing, led to a boom in newspaper and magazine circulation. In 1800, there were 24 daily newspapers (with a combined circulation of 50,000) and 40 magazines, but by 1900 there were hundreds of newspapers (with a combined circulation of over 15 million) and more than 5,500 magazines.[69]

After the Civil War, mail-order catalogs from Montgomery Ward (1872), from Sears, Roebuck and Company (1888), and from other department stores brought big-city merchandise to farmers in rural areas and to residents of small towns. The United States provided a boost to the mail-order business in 1896 by starting the rural free delivery (RFD) system, which was soon able to deliver packages to every home in America.[70]

TELEGRAPH

The telegraph marked the beginning of modern communication: for the first time, the speed of communication far exceeded that of transportation. Although many individuals worked on sending electromagnetic signals over wires, Samuel Morse is credited with having invented the telegraph, in 1837. Telegraphs and railroads became complementary technologies. Railroad managers found that telegraphs were an invaluable aid to the safe and efficient operation of railroads; and if telegraphs were built alongside rail lines, they were easy to repair when wires went down.[71]

By 1860, 50,000 miles of wire had been used in constructing the U.S. telegraph system. The next year telegraph lines extended from coast to coast, and the first permanent line across the Atlantic was completed in 1866. In 1867, fewer than 6 million messages were sent by telegraph in the United States, but that number increased rapidly, exceeding 25 million messages in 1879 and more than 50 million in 1888.[72]

TELEPHONE

As with the telegraph, many people are credited with inventing the telephone, but it is generally attributed to Alexander Graham Bell. The telephone relies on a steady stream of electricity, rather than electrical bursts, to transmit the human voice. By allowing direct person-to-person communication, the telephone likely had a social value well beyond its direct economic impact.

The early years of the telephone industry involved fights over patent rights, but in 1885, the American Telephone and Telegraph Company (AT&T) was formed, as a subsidiary of American Bell, to build a long-distance telephone network. In 1892, AT&T connected New York to Chicago; and in 1915, service was established from New York to San Francisco. A three-minute coast-to-coast call cost $20.70 in 1915 (about $500 in 2015 dollars).[73]

Although long-distance phone calls were expensive in the 1910s, local calls were much more affordable and the proportion of households with telephones increased from 8 percent in 1910 to 35 percent in 1920. The 1920s witnessed rapid growth as well, but the Great Depression of the 1930s caused telephone ownership to fall. Rapid growth took off again after World War II, and in recent decades the proportion of households with telephones (including both landlines and cellular) has been around 98 percent (Figure 8.4).

FIGURE 8.4 Percentage of U.S. Households with Telephones, Radios, Televisions, Computers, and/or the Internet, 1900–2010

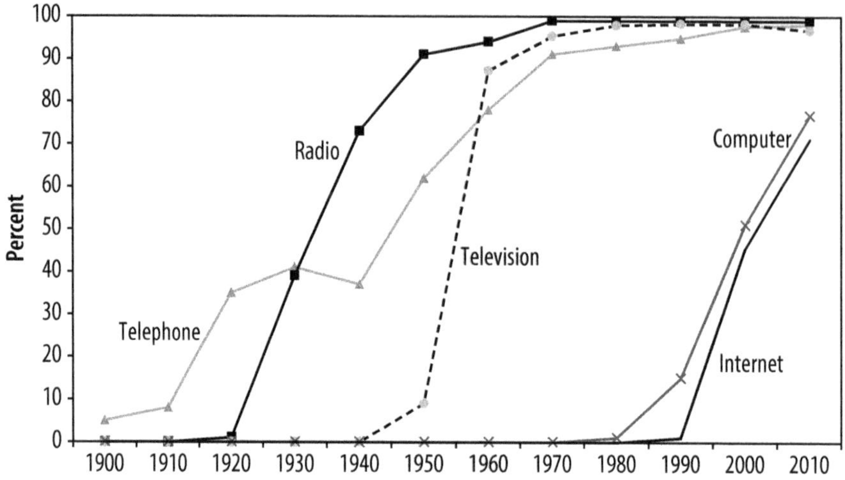

Sources: Constructed from U.S. Bureau of the Census data, www.census.gov/statab/hist/HS-42.pdf (accessed: November 4, 2015) and www.census.gov/hhes/computer/ (accessed: November 4, 2015).

MOTION PICTURES

Motion pictures changed entertainment from a rival and labor-intensive good to a largely nonrival good allowing spectators to watch movies simultaneously on thousands of screens nationwide. In 1900, spectator entertainment was provided by live performers, but by 1938, live entertainment's share was less than 3 percent of all performances.[74]

Improvements in picture quality and the spread of theaters nationwide increased entertainment output (measured as one person consuming one hour of entertainment) 27-fold from 1900 to 1938, corresponding to an average annual growth rate of 8.6 percent per year and a 7.2 percent annual per capita increase.[75] Three-quarters of the per capita increase was due to growth in total factor productivity (TFP).[76]

While motion pictures did not have the impact of steam, railways, or electricity, their influence on the aggregate economy was not insignificant: from 1900 to 1938, motion pictures contributed almost 2 percent of aggregate GDP growth and over 3 percent of aggregate TFP growth.[77]

RADIO

Many individuals are responsible for the development of radio and the radio industry, beginning with the discovery of electromagnetic waves by the German physicist, Heinrich Rudolf Hertz (1887). In 1902, Canadian-born Aubrey Fessenden became the first person to transmit voice and music using continuous waves.[78] Although radios were used by hobbyists in the 1910s and by the Navy during World War I, the radio industry began only after World War I.

The first U.S.-licensed radio station was KDKA, a Pittsburgh station which began broadcasting music in 1920. In 1921, there were 5 radio stations in the United States, but by 1923, there were 556.[79] The 1920s and 1930s were the Golden Age of radio, with nationwide broadcast companies like the National Broadcasting Company (NBC) and Columbia Broadcasting System (CBS) producing drama and comedy shows that were heard by millions. In 1943, the American Broadcasting Company (ABC) was established. The diffusion of radio was extremely rapid, with 91 percent of households owning a radio in 1950, compared with virtually none in 1920 (Figure 8.4).

TELEVISION

Although television was invented in the 1920s, it was not until 1931 that CBS became the first radio network to launch an experimental TV station; NBC followed a year later. The American television industry, however, did not begin to take off until the 1950s. As the prices of television sets plunged, television ownership surged, from 9 percent of American households in 1950 to 87 percent in 1960 (Figure 8.4). In 1950, a Philco set with a 12-inch screen cost $499, but by 1955, a consumer could buy a 21-inch Admiral set for only $149.[80]

By 1960, there were more than 500 licensed, local television stations in the United States, and most were affiliated with NBC, CBS, or ABC, the three companies that dominated television broadcasting from the 1950s to the 1970s. The dominance of the Big Three in broadcasting began to wane in the 1980s because of deregulation, the rise of cable television, satellite broadcasting, and hundreds of new television stations broadcasting nationwide.

COMPUTERS AND THE INTERNET

The most recent advances in communication involve personal computers and smart-phones, both of which rely on the Internet. The Internet consists of three parts. First, there is the hardware of the Internet, consisting of innumerable fiber-optic cables, routers, and servers, which link computers together.

The second component of the Internet is the software, including protocols of communication that allow devices with different operating systems to communicate with one another. The best known of these is the Transmission Control Protocol and Internet Protocol (TCP/IP). In 1969, the Advanced Research Projects Agency Network (ARPANET) was the first network to implement TCP/IP, which constitutes the basis of communication that makes the Internet possible.

The third part of the Internet is the World Wide Web, an information system of interlinked hypertext documents (web pages) that allows the display of, and easy access to, text, pictures, video, sound, and other files from distant computers. In 1993, the Mosaic web browser was introduced, a software application which displays web pages; Mosaic is credited with having popularized the World Wide Web. From a single website in 1991, the Web had grown to include over 1 billion websites in 2016.[81] Household access to the Internet grew rapidly, in tandem with personal computers (Figure 8.4). In 2016, 88.5 percent of Americans had Internet access, placing the United States 20th in the world, well behind 100 percent of households in Iceland and 98 percent in the Netherlands.[82]

8.7 CONCLUSIONS

Innovations in transportation and communication have collapsed both time and distance, and made the exchange of goods, services, and information far easier and less costly, encouraging market growth and technological progress.

The historical distinctions between telephones, radios, televisions, and computers have blurred almost completely with the proliferation of smartphones and other devices that serve multiple purposes. With smartphones, we can make phone calls, play music, read newspapers and magazines, send e-mail, watch television and movies, play games, and do literally millions of other things.[83]

Next time you step onto a coast-to-coast airplane flight or glance down at your smartphone, think about the extraordinary extent to which things have changed since Lewis and Clark departed from St. Louis in 1804.

QUESTIONS

1. Available evidence shows that few, if any, turnpikes were ever profitable. If profitability of turnpikes was so low, even from the beginning, what explains the high rate of private investment needed to build 12,000 miles of roads over the course of several decades?

2. What mode of transportation had the greatest rate of total factor productivity growth during the nineteenth century, and what factors caused TFP to increase?

3. Some studies estimate that railroads had only a modest impact on the U.S. economy, arguing that real GDP would have been only a few percentage points lower in 1860 and 1890 if railroads had never been invented. Other scholars, however, believe that the impact of railroads on the economy during the nineteenth century was far greater than is indicated by the "social savings" estimates. How important were railroads to U.S. economic growth and development? (A good essay will use evidence from the notes listed at the end of this chapter.)

4. Consider two hypothetical worlds: (1) one with modern transportation technology, but communication technology from 1800; (2) the other with modern communication technology, but transportation technology from 1800. Which world would you rather live in, and why? Which world do you think would generate a higher standard of living for the typical citizen? Write an essay, using evidence from this chapter and other sources to support your arguments.

5. Consider the various communications improvements discussed in Section 8.6. Which one do you think was most important, and why?

NOTES

[1] Albert Fishlow, "Internal Transportation in the Nineteenth and Early Twentieth Centuries," in Stanley L. Engerman and Robert E. Gallman (eds.), *The Cambridge Economic History of the United States: The Long Nineteenth Century*, Volume II (Cambridge, UK: Cambridge University Press, 2000), 548.

[2] United States National Park Service, www.nps.gov/lecl/faqs.htm (accessed: October 20, 2015).

3 Daniel Klein and John Majewski, "Turnpikes and Toll Roads in Nineteeth-Century America," in Robert Whaples (ed.), *EH.Net Encyclopedia* (February 10, 2008), http://eh.net/encyclopedia/turnpikes-and-toll-roads-in-nineteenth-century-america (accessed: October 26, 2015).

4 Fishlow, 550.

5 Fishlow, 549.

6 U.S. Department of Transportation, *National Transportation Statistics*, Table 1.4, www.rita.dot.gov/bts/sites/rita.dot.gov.bts/files/publications/national_transportation_statistics/html/table_01_04.html (accessed: October 27, 2015).

7 Daniel B. Klein, "The Voluntary Provision of Public Goods? The Turnpike Companies of Early America," *Economic Inquiry* 28, no. 4 (October 1990), 782–812. Klein concludes (792) that "fragmentary evidence and, more importantly, the impressions of contemporary observers, suggest that throughout the states under consideration, turnpikes on average paid no more than two percent per year, not counting the loss of capital value."

8 Fishlow, 551.

9 Klein and Majewski.

10 Joseph Austin Durrenberger, *Turnpikes: A Study of the Toll Road Movement in the Middle Atlantic States and Maryland* (Valdosta, GA: Southern Stationery & Printing, 1931), 104.

11 Klein and Majewski.

12 California figures from Daniel B. Klein and Chi Yin, "Use, Esteem, and Profit in Voluntary Provision: Toll Roads in California, 1850–1902," *Economic Inquiry* (1996), 678–692; Nevada figures from David T. Beito and Linda Royster Beito, "Rival Road Builders: Private Toll Roads in Nevada, 1852–1880," *Nevada Historical Society Quarterly* 41 (1998), 71–91.

13 Klein and Majewski.

14 Klein and Majewski.

15 Carter Goodrich, *Government Promotion of American Canals and Railroads, 1800–1890* (New York, NY: Columbia University Press, 1960), 65.

16 John D. Unruh, Jr., *The Plains Across: The Overland Emigrants and the Trans-Mississippi West, 1840–1860* (Urbana, IL: University of Illinois Press, 1979), Table 1, 119.

17 Unruh, Table 2, 120.

18 Richard L. Hills, *Power from Steam: A History of the Stationary Steam Engine* (Cambridge, UK: Cambridge University Press, 1989), 63.

19 John Steele Gordon, *An Empire of Wealth: The Epic History of American Economic Power* (New York, NY: HarperCollins Publishers, 2004), 132–134.

20 Erik F. Haites, James Mak, and Gary M. Walton, *Western River Transportation: The Era of Early Internal Development, 1810–1860* (Baltimore, MD: Johns Hopkins University Press, 1975), 130–131.

21 James Mak and Gary M. Walton, "Steamboats and the Great Productivity Surge in River Transportation," *Journal of Economic History* 32, no. 3 (September 1972), 623. Mak and Walton computed TFP using two different methods, with one method yielding an average annual growth rate of 4.6 percent and the other method resulting in an annual increase of 5.5 percent.

22 Mak and Walton, 619–640.

23 Mak and Walton, 625.

24 Douglass C. North, *Growth and Welfare in the American Past* (Englewood Cliffs, NJ: Prentice Hall, 1973), 108.

25 C. Knick Hartley, "Ocean Freight Rates and Productivity, 1740–1913: The Primacy of Mechanical Invention Reaffirmed," *Journal of Economic History* 48, no. 4 (December 1988), 851–876.

[26] Louis P. Cain, "Transportation," in Susan B. Carter et al. (eds.), *Historical Statistics of the United States, Millennial Edition* (New York, NY: Cambridge University Press, 2006), 4-768.

[27] Hartley, 851–876. See also Kevin H. O'Rourke and Jeffrey G. Williamson, *Globalization and History: The Evolution of a Nineteenth-Century Atlantic Economy* (Cambridge, MA: MIT Press, 1999).

[28] Drew Keeling, "Transport Capacity Management and Transatlantic Migration, 1900–1914," *Research in Economic History* 25 (2008), 225–283.

[29] Andrew Gibson and Arthur Donovan, Cain, 4–770.

[30] Fishlow, 2000, 563.

[31] Susan B. Carter, Scott Sigmund Gartner, Michael R. Haines, Alan L. Olmstead, Richard Sutch, and Gavin Wright (eds.), *Historical Statistics of the United States, Millennial Edition* (New York, NY: Cambridge University Press, 2006), series Df 684 and 685.

[32] Approximately 4.5 million acres in federal land grants were given to encourage the building of canals, compared to 130 million acres given to railroads. See John Bell Rae, "Federal Land Grants in Aid of Canals," *Journal of Economic History* 4, no. 2 (November 1944), 167.

[33] Computed using the data from Albert Fishlow, Table 13.2, 560, and Table 13.8, 579.

[34] Xavier Duran, "The First Transcontinental Railroad: Expected Profits and Government Intervention," *Journal of Economic History* 73, no. 1 (March 2013), 177–200.

[35] Daniel E. Bogart, "Modern Transport Since 1700: A Momentous Achievement" (June 11, 2012), Table 1, 6–7, http://papers.ssrn.com/sol3/papers.cfm?abstract_id=2082161 (accessed: November 3, 2015).

[36] Note that this is an application of the "Rule of 70" from Chapter 2. If you divide 70 by the growth rate in percent, you get $70/10.57 = 6.62$ years.

[37] Fishlow, 581.

[38] Cain, Table Df-A, 4–762.

[39] Albert Fishlow, *American Railroads and the Transformation of the Ante-bellum Economy* (Cambridge, MA: Harvard University Press, 1965); and Robert W. Fogel, *Railroads and American Economic Growth: Essays in Econometric History* (Baltimore, MD: Johns Hopkins Press, 1970).

[40] See Jeremy Atack, "On the Use of Geographic Information Systems in Economic History: The American Transportation Revolution Revisited," *Journal of Economic History* 73, no. 2 (June 2013), 313–338, for a survey of several recent papers by Atack and many co-authors.

[41] Jeremy Atack, Matthew S. Jaremski, and Peter L. Rousseau, "Did Railroads Make Antebellum Banks More Sound?" *National Bureau of Economic Research Working Paper*, no. 20032 (April 2014).

[42] Duran, 177–200.

[43] Fishlow, 625.

[44] Rudi Volti, *Cars and Culture: The Life Story of a Technology* (Baltimore, MD: The Johns Hopkins University Press, 2004), 7.

[45] James J. Flink, *The Automobile Age* (Cambridge, MA: The MIT Press, 1988), 15.

[46] Flink, 15.

[47] Flink, 19.

[48] Flink, 10–11.

[49] The self-starter or electric starter was invented by Charles F. Kettering. In 1912 Henry Leland, head of the Cadillac Motor Company, introduced the electric starter into his cars for safety reasons. In 1910, one of Leland's friends had stopped to help a motorist whose car had stalled. While trying to turn the hand crank at the front of the car, the crank had kicked back, breaking the man's jaw, and he later died from the injury.

50 Flink, 25; and U.S. Department of Commerce, *Highway Statistics, Summary to 1955* (Washington, DC: Government Printing Office, 1957), 28.

51 Flink, 188.

52 Thomas H. Klier, "From Tail Fins to Hybrids: How Detroit Lost Its Dominance of the U.S. Automarket," *Economic Perspectives* Q2 (Federal Reserve Bank of Chicago, 2009), Figure 1, 3.

53 Klier, 2.

54 Klier, 2.

55 Fishlow, 626.

56 Jason Lee, "An Economic Analysis of the Good Roads Movement," *Institute of Transportation Studies Research Report* 12–18, (Davis, CA: University of California, Davis, September 2012), vi.

57 M.G. Lay, *Ways of the World: A History of the World's Roads and the Vehicles that Used Them* (New Brunswick, NJ: Rutgers University Press, 1992), 172.

58 Volti, 46–47.

59 Volti, 106–107.

60 John G. Fernald, "Roads to Prosperity? Assessing the Link Between Public Capital and Productivity," *American Economic Review* 89, no. 3 (June 1999), 620–621.

61 Donald M. Pattillo, *Pushing the Envelope: The American Aircraft Industry* (Ann Arbor, MI: University of Michigan Press, 1998), 7.

62 Pattillo, Table 2, 32.

63 Roger E. Bilstein, *The American Aerospace Industry: From Workshop to Global Enterprise* (New York: Twayne Publishers, 1996), Table 1, 225–227.

64 Glenn E. Bugos, "History of the Aerospace Industry," in Robert Whaples (ed.), *EH. Net Encyclopedia* (August 28, 2001), http://eh.net/encyclopedia/the-history-of-the-aerospace-industry/ (accessed: November 10, 2015).

65 Bilstein, 143.

66 Alexander J. Field, "Communication," in Carter et al., 4–981.

67 Richard John, *Spreading the News: The American Postal System from Franklin to Morse* (Cambridge, MA: Harvard University Press, 1995), 5.

68 John, 3.

69 Dan Lacy, *From Grunts to Gigabytes: Communications and Society* (Urbana, IL: University of Illinois Press, 1996), 65, and Carter et al., series Dg256.

70 Although RFD began in 1896, it was not a permanent and widespread service throughout the United States until 1902. See United States Postal Service, https://about.usps.com/who-we-are/postal-history/rural-free-delivery.pdf (accessed: November 14, 2015).

71 Alfred D. Chandler, Jr., *The Visible Hand: The Managerial Revolution in American Business* (Cambridge, MA: Harvard University Press, 1977).

72 U.S. Bureau of Statistics, *Statistical Abstract of the United States*, no. 12 (Washington, DC: Government Printing Office, 1889), Table 188, 256.

73 Carter et al., Series Dg59. Consumer Price Index (CPI) from U.S. Bureau of Labor Statistics, *Detailed Report*, February 2015, Table 24.

74 Gerban Bakker, "How Motion Pictures Industrialized Entertainment," *Journal of Economic History* 72, no. 4 (December 2012), 1037.

75 Bakker, 1059.

76 Bakker, 1059.

77 Bakker, 1060.

[78] Charles E. Scott, "The History of the Radio Industry in the United States to 1940," in Robert Whaples (ed.), *EH.Net Encyclopedia* (March 26, 2008), http://eh.net/encyclopedia/the-history-of-the-radio-industry-in-the-united-states-to-1940/ (accessed: November 22, 2015).

[79] Christopher H. Sterling and John M. Kittross, *Stay Tuned* (Belmont, CA: Wadsworth, 1978), 510.

[80] Simon Winchester, *The Men Who United the States: America's Explorers, Inventors, Eccentrics, and Mavericks, and the Creation of One Nation, Indivisible* (New York, NY: HarperCollins, 2013), 412.

[81] Internet Live Statistics, www.internetlivestats.com/total-number-of-websites/ (accessed: November 23, 2015).

[82] Internet Live Statistics, www.internetlivestats.com/internet-users-by-country/ (accessed: November 23, 2015).

[83] In 2013, the number of applications on Apple's App Store exceeded 1 million.

9
Agriculture

The huge decline in the share of the population employed in agriculture is one of the most dramatic and important structural transformations in American economic history. During the colonial period, close to 90 percent of the working-age population were involved in agricultural production. In 1800, almost 75 percent of the workforce were still employed in agriculture, but this proportion has steadily declined over time, from 50 percent in 1870 to less than 1.5 percent in 2015 (Figure 9.1).

If the overwhelming majority of the workforce were still needed to provide the crops and livestock to feed and clothe Americans, there would be far fewer people available to work in health care, information technology, education, manufacturing, finance, construction, and other sectors of the economy. High productivity growth in agriculture has resulted in the ability of each farm to provide enough food for more than 150 people worldwide today. Productivity gains have not been without costs, however: the transition out of agriculture has often resulted in tremendous hardship as cherished ways of life have been abandoned.[1]

To a large extent, the economic history of the United States is the story of the transformation from a largely rural, agricultural economy to an urban, industrial, and service economy. Growth accounting exercises show that the transfer of labor from agriculture to manufacturing and services accounts for as much as 50 percent of the increase in aggregate labor productivity observed in the U.S. economy between 1870 and 1990.[2] While growth accounting is a statistical decomposition that does not necessarily imply causation, it suggests that the massive exodus of labor out of agriculture to pursue occupations in other sectors of the economy is an essential part of the growth and development of the economy.

This chapter focuses on the potential causes for the dramatic productivity gains in agriculture and for the transition of the workforce out of the agricultural sector. It also traces the differential development of agriculture in the North and the South. Because of differences in soil and climate, agriculture in northern states developed quite differently from agriculture in the South.

Another essential feature of U.S. agricultural history is the myriad of policy responses by government to help farmers, many of which started during the New Deal to lessen the impact of the Great Depression in the 1930s. Although these programs were intended to provide temporary relief, farm programs have since become permanent features of the U.S. economy. While these programs have helped farmers, many of them have harmed consumers and taxpayers far more than they have benefitted farmers.

FIGURE 9.1 U.S. Agricultural Employment Share by Decade, 1800–2010

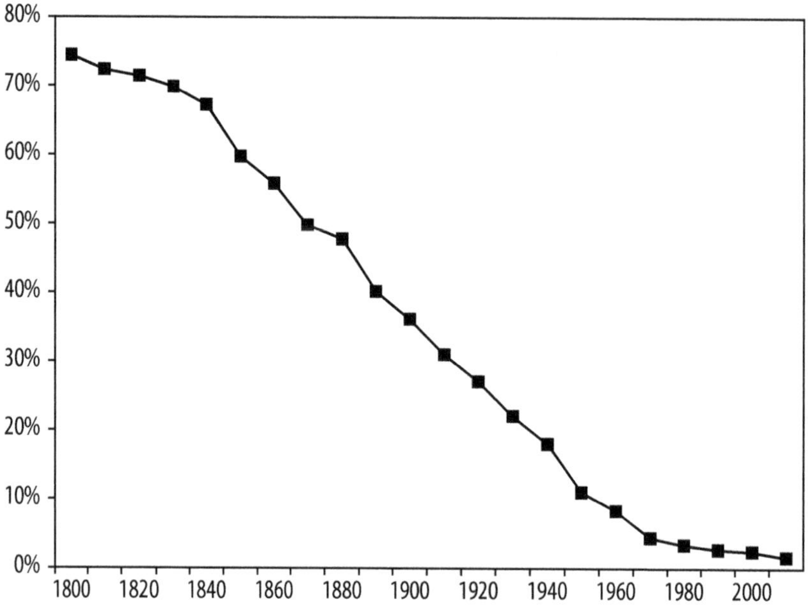

Sources: 1800–2000 data from Benjamin N. Dennis and Talan B. Iscan, "Engel versus Baumol: Accounting for Structural Change Using Two Centuries of U.S. Data," *Explorations in Economic History* 46, no. 2 (April 2009), 186–202. The data are available at http://myweb.dal.ca/tiscan/research/data/account.xls (accessed: May 12, 2015). 2010 data from the Federal Reserve Economic Data (FRED), Federal Reserve Bank of St. Louis, https://research.stlouisfed.org/fred2/series/USAPEMANA (accessed: May 12, 2015).

Many other government policies, however, have been tremendously successful, including government investments in research and experiment stations, as well as land-grant colleges and universities (see Chapter 11). Government policies have also been instrumental in disseminating information, in developing new varieties of crops, and in successfully combatting many animal and crop diseases.

9.1 FARM OUTPUT

For farmers truly on the frontier, there was no choice but to be self-sufficient. This isolation, however, did not last for long. One farm on the frontier soon attracted others to the same area, and soon after that farmers were going to markets to sell much of what they produced.

NORTHERN AGRICULTURE BEFORE THE CIVIL WAR

During the colonial period, farmers in Massachusetts and throughout New England were active market participants as price differences between local markets converged.[3] With the advent of river steamboats, canals, and, most importantly, railroads (see Chapter 8), agricultural production and markets continued to grow and expand geographically throughout the nineteenth century. Grains and livestock from western farmers led to declines in the production of grains by eastern farmers. While many farmers in New England and the Middle Atlantic states left farming or moved west, some switched from the production of grains to dairy farming and to growing fruits and vegetables.

During the first half of the nineteenth century, large numbers of people from New England and the Middle Atlantic states moved to Ohio, Indiana, and southern Michigan. This migration was not at a constant rate, but occurred in surges when corn and wheat prices were high. In percentage terms, the decades of greatest western migration occurred in the 1810s and 1830s, although the 1850s were the largest in absolute numbers.[4]

By the 1850s, the best land in southern Michigan, northern Illinois, and southern Wisconsin had been settled. By 1860, the frontier moved farther west, with settlement throughout Iowa and into southern Minnesota and eastern Nebraska. By this time, California had been a state for a decade and Oregon had been admitted to the Union, but most of the vast area between the western frontier and the Pacific coast would remain largely unsettled for another half century.

Throughout the nineteenth century, markets for products, labor, and capital became increasingly integrated, both domestically and internationally, as price differences between locations narrowed and market fluctuations became more synchronous.[5] After the Civil War, the Midwest and the West became the leaders in the production of wheat and corn. From 1875 to 1879, the East Coast produced about half of the wheat it consumed, but its production relative to consumption fell to only 23 percent from 1910 to 1913. By the early twentieth century, the production of wheat in Iowa, Kansas, Minnesota, Missouri, Nebraska, North Dakota, and South Dakota was more than three times more than the amount they consumed.[6]

Not only was wheat transported to other regions throughout the United States, but it was also exported. U.S. exports of wheat increased more than *fourfold* between 1870 and 1892. From the mid-1850s to World War I, the freight cost of transporting a bushel of wheat from Chicago to New York fell from 20.8 cents to 5.4 cents, and transatlantic shipping costs declined from 14.3 cents per bushel to 4.9 cents. By World War I, the prices of wheat in Chicago and in Liverpool, England, were nearly identical.[7]

While the Great Depression and World War II led to an interruption of international trade, American agricultural exports continued to expand in the post-World War II era. In every year since 1960, the United States has had a trade surplus in agriculture, and this has helped to offset persistent trade deficits in nonagricultural U.S. trade.[8]

SOUTHERN AGRICULTURE BEFORE THE CIVIL WAR

Because of differences in soil and climate, the development of agriculture in the South was quite different from that in the North. While agriculture in the South did include many small family farms, the distinguishing features of agriculture in the South prior to the Civil War were large plantations and their use of slave labor.

Although the South lagged behind the North in terms of manufacturing, transportation, communication, banking and finance, and education in the nineteenth century, the economy in the South was also market-oriented, primarily because of the growing importance of cotton as a cash crop. Between 1820 and 1860, cotton production in the South increased between 1,100 and 1,200 percent, with 86 percent of the production occurring on agricultural units of 100 acres or more, which also contained 90 percent of the slave population in the South.[9]

While the growth of the South in the antebellum period was largely due to a surging British demand for cotton, cultivation on plantations also included tobacco, sugar, indigo, and rice, and, to a lesser extent, okra, yams, sweet potatoes, and watermelons.

The relative productivity of plantation agriculture in the South using slave labor has been a hotly debated and contentious issue in U.S. economic history. There are several main hypotheses, although the validity and relative importance of each is still a matter of considerable debate. One explanation argues that large plantations with slave labor benefitted from specialization, division of labor, and economies of scale associated with the gang labor system. In this view, the gang labor system resulted in increased speed and intensity of work. Large plantations also operated much like factories, with extensive specialization within gangs, and were able to produce more output per hour of work than smaller farms in either the North or the South.[10]

Other scholars believe that large plantations had high levels of labor productivity, but for reasons other than slave labor or the gang system. Between 1801 and 1862, the amount of cotton picked per slave quadrupled, increasing at an average annual rate of 2.3 percent per year, and this was largely the result of the development and diffusion of new cotton varieties.[11] Large plantations with slaves were better able to afford new and more expensive cotton seeds, and this resulted in taller plants with more cotton per boll, greatly increasing labor productivity on large plantations relative to that on smaller farms.

Plantations with slaves likely produced more output per slave, but perhaps not more output per hour of work (that is, labor productivity may not have been higher). There is some evidence that slaves simply worked more hours per day (including night work) and more days per year, along with a higher proportion of women on plantations working in the fields compared to free agricultural workers in the South.[12] In this view, the greater output with slaves is mostly due to a greater input of labor, but not to greater output per hour of work.

An even more difficult question to answer is whether plantations in the South were more productive than farms in the North. One problem is that different crops were grown in the North and the South. Because of differences in climate, cotton could not be grown in the North, whereas cotton was an agricultural staple in the South. Most comparisons have used the year 1860, but some scholars have argued that this was an unusually good year for growing cotton, and that the measured higher productivity in 1860 of plantation agriculture in the South relative to the family farms in the North may be partly, if not entirely, a statistical artifact.[13]

AGRICULTURE IN THE NORTH AND SOUTH AFTER THE CIVIL WAR

After the Civil War, differences between the North and the South persisted for many decades. Agriculture in the North continued to spread westward, with growth in California and other western states as the railroad network continued to expand.

In contrast, sharecropping and tenant farming became standard features of agriculture in the South (Chapter 4). For a century after the Civil War, the South remained more agricultural and substantially poorer than other regions of the country (Chapter 14).

CHARACTERISTICS OF AGRICULTURAL MARKETS

Agricultural markets display a rare combination of features affecting supply and demand which can help to explain why the agricultural employment share has fallen so much in the long run, and why price supports and other forms of government intervention in agricultural markets are so prevalent. The best way to understand these features is to consider the market for food as a whole, rather than considering just the market for one individual crop.

As discussed below, the supply of food has been subject to large productivity improvements in the long run, primarily as the result of mechanical and biological innovations. In the short run, the supply of food is also extremely sensitive to weather changes. This implies that the supply of food has increased tremendously over the long run, yet supply changes are quite variable from year to year.

ECONOMIC HISTORY IN ACTION 9.1

Elasticity

Economic theory usually predicts the direction of the relationships between variables. For example, the law of demand posits that there is a negative or inverse relationship between the price of a product and the quantity demanded of that product, holding all else equal. When the price falls, the quantity demanded increases, and vice versa. The law of demand, however, says nothing about how much the quantity demanded will change. Does the quantity demanded change a little or a lot?

The answer to this question in any particular market relies on calculating the *price elasticity of demand*, ε_D, which is defined as:

$$\varepsilon_D = \left| \frac{\% \; change \; in \; quantity \; demanded}{\% \; change \; in \; price} \right|$$

Price elasticity of demand is usually reported as a positive number. That's why absolute value notation is used (the vertical bars). Economists make the distinction between inelastic, elastic, and unit elastic demand. A product is *elastic* if the price elasticity of demand is *greater* than 1. That is, if the price of a product changes by 1 percent, then the quantity demanded of that product changes (in the opposite direction) by more than 1 percent, implying a high degree of responsiveness to price changes. If a product is price *inelastic*, then a given percentage change in price yields a proportionally smaller change in the quantity demanded. That is, quantity demanded is not very responsive to changes in price. In the rare case that the percentage change in quantity demanded equals the (inverse) of the percentage change in price, demand is said to be *unit elastic*.

The price elasticity of demand depends on many factors, including the number of substitute goods and whether the good is a necessity or a luxury. In general, price elasticity of demand is lower (more inelastic) when there are few substitutes and when the good is a necessity. Food, in general, certainly qualifies as a necessity with no substitutes.

While price elasticity of demand represents the relationship between a change in the price of a good or service and the quantity demanded of that good or service, the concept of elasticity can be applied to anything. It is simply the measure of the responsiveness of one variable to a change in another variable, holding all else constant.

With other elasticities, however, the *direction* of the relationship is important, so they are not reported using absolute values. Another important elasticity is the *income elasticity of demand*, which is defined as:

$$\varepsilon_Y = \frac{\% \; change \; in \; quantity \; demanded}{\% \; change \; in \; income}$$

Income elasticity of demand can be positive or negative. Engel's law, named after the statistician Ernst Engel (1821–1896)—not the Marxist theorist Frederich Engels—is the observation that as income rises, the proportion of income spent on food falls, even if actual expenditures on food increase. That is, the income elasticity of demand for food is between zero and one, but far closer to zero. Recent estimates show that for every 1 dollar change in consumer incomes, the demand for food increases by only 6 cents.[14]

On the demand side, the market for food is characterized by another pair of features: a very low price elasticity of demand and a very low income elasticity of demand (see Economic History in Action 9.1). A low price elasticity of demand implies that the quantity demanded is not very sensitive to changes in price. As supply increases, a low price elasticity of demand means that the price of food falls by a proportion greater than the proportion of the increase in the quantity of food demanded.

While economic growth has greatly increased consumer incomes, the low income elasticity of demand for food means that income growth has only a small influence on the demand for food. In the long run, increases in supply outpace the small increases in demand, leading to falling total revenue for farmers. In any market, the total revenue available to producers is equal to the price times the quantity sold. Huge productivity improvements have caused large increases in supply, but with a low price elasticity of demand and a low income elasticity of demand, the total revenue available to farmers has decreased, causing many would-be farmers to pursue other occupations in the long run.[15]

Consider Figure 9.2 below, which is initially in equilibrium with a price P_0 and a quantity Q_0. Over time, productivity improvements increase supply from S_0 to S_1. Economic growth in the rest of the economy increases consumer incomes, but because of the low income elasticity of demand, demand increases relatively little from D_0 to D_1.

FIGURE 9.2 The Market for Food

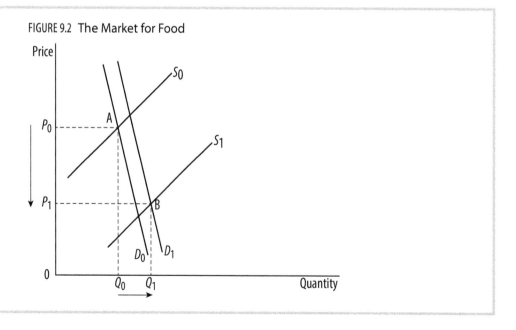

The increases in supply and demand lead to a new equilibrium at P_1 and Q_1. Note, however, that total revenue at the new equilibrium (equal to the rectangle P_1BQ_10) is less than total revenue at the original equilibrium (equal to the rectangle P_0AQ_00), because of a low price elasticity of demand and a low income elasticity of demand. Because price has decreased proportionally more than quantity has increased, the total revenue available to farmers has decreased. While this is bad for farmers, it is good for consumers, because farmers' total revenue equals consumers' total spending on food.

9.2 GROWTH IN THE FACTORS OF PRODUCTION

Like any production process, output in agriculture is produced using the four factors of production: natural capital (such as land, soil, and climate), physical capital, human capital, and labor.

LAND AND NATURAL CAPITAL

With the Gadsden Purchase from Mexico in 1853, the United States controlled all of the land that would eventually become the lower 48 states, but most of this land was unimproved. In 1850, "improved land" accounted for 38 percent of total land in farms, but this increased substantially over time to 77 percent in 1900 and 85 percent in 1940.[16]

Between 1850 and 1910, land in farms more than tripled and the proportion of all U.S. land devoted to farming increased from 16 percent to 39 percent.[17] Along with the increase in the *quantity* of farmland, the real *price* of farmland also more than doubled during this period.[18]

The amount of land per worker was very high in the United States during the late nineteenth and early twentieth centuries, an amount perhaps only surpassed by Canada.[19] Total farmland in the United States continued to gradually increase until 1950, peaking at just over 1.2 billion acres. In contrast, between 1950 and 2010, total U.S. farmland decreased by over 23 percent, while output and productivity soared (Figures 9.3 and 9.7).

PHYSICAL CAPITAL

While territorial acquisition and federal land policies were instrumental in expanding the available farmland in the United States (see Chapter 6), the acquisition and distribution of land is only the first step. For land to be used productively, large capital investments are needed as well. Agricultural capital consists of five main types: (1) improvements to land, such as clearing, fencing, planting trees, terracing, and irrigation; (2) agricultural buildings, such as barns, stables, and sheds; (3) farm tools and machinery; (4) draft animals, used for the planting and harvesting of crops; and (5) working capital purchases of inputs from outside of the farm sector, such as the purchases of seeds and fertilizers.[20]

During the nineteenth century, the growth rate of the capital stock increased more than 2 percent per year in the United States, and exceeded growth rates in all countries except Canada. The vast majority of this capital investment involved land improvements.[21]

The growth rate of physical capital accumulation, however, slowed markedly from 1900 to 1940, increasing only 0.5 percent per year (Figure 9.3). During and after

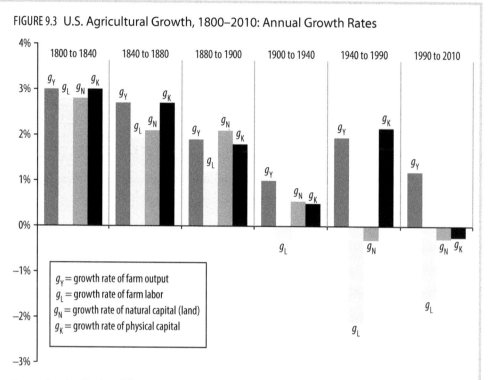

FIGURE 9.3 U.S. Agricultural Growth, 1800–2010: Annual Growth Rates

g_Y = growth rate of farm output
g_L = growth rate of farm labor
g_N = growth rate of natural capital (land)
g_K = growth rate of physical capital

Sources: Based on Yair Mundlak, "Economic Growth: Lessons from Two Centuries of American Agriculture," *Journal of Economic Literature* 43, no. 4 (December 2005), Figure 1, 992. The figure above was created with the same data sources and time periods as described in Mundlak (2005), Figure 1, with the exception of the 1990–2010 period, which was computed using data from the United States Department of Agriculture, Economic Research Service, Table 1 www.ers. usda.gov/datafiles/Agricultural_Productivity_in_the_US/National_Tables/table01.xls (accessed: May 15, 2015). See Chapter 2 for a detailed description of growth accounting.

World War II, the capital stock increased by over 2 percent per year from 1940 to 1990, largely because of large capital investments in farm machinery, such as tractors.

Since 1990, the growth rate of the capital stock has been slightly negative. Measures of the value of physical capital, however, do not fully take into account the technological improvements embodied in the capital stock. These improvements are captured in total factor productivity growth.

LABOR AND HUMAN CAPITAL

Although the number of American farmers increased from 1.3 million in 1800 to 11.8 million in 1910, population growth was far more rapid, causing the agricultural employment share to plummet.[22] In the twentieth century, both the number of farmers and the proportion of the population in farming decreased substantially. Although there were still 9.6 million farmers in 1938, only 3 million remained in farming by 2000.[23]

Measuring the increase in the human capital of agricultural workers is a difficult task. Agricultural states led the way in the high school movement by the 1920s (see Chapter 11), and the impact of farm journals, newspapers, and radios contributed to the spread of knowledge to farmers. The growth accounting exercises reported in this chapter do not directly measure any changes in human capital, but are captured in the estimates of total factor productivity growth.

9.3 PRODUCTIVITY GROWTH

During the nineteenth century, farm output increased rapidly, averaging more than 2.5 percent per year from 1800 to 1900 (Figure 9.3). The overwhelming majority of this output growth is accounted for by growth in the factors of production, implying very low rates of growth of labor productivity and total factor productivity.

Estimates suggest that total factor productivity in the nineteenth century increased far less in the farm sector than in the nonfarm sector (Figure 9.4). It would be a mistake, however, to conclude that nineteenth-century agriculture must have been largely devoid of innovations. On the contrary, as farmers moved westward into drier and more extreme climates, substantial biological and mechanical innovations prevented farm output from decreasing.

While estimated total factor productivity growth in agriculture was also modest during the first several decades of the twentieth century, between 1940 and 1990 TFP growth in agriculture was quite rapid and indeed exceeded the rate in the rest of the economy. There is some evidence that TFP growth has slowed since 1990, but the period from 1940 to 2010 as a whole is one of remarkable productivity growth.

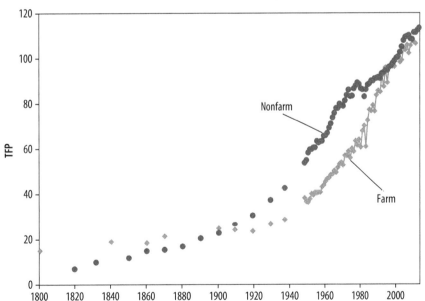

FIGURE 9.4 Farm and Nonfarm Total Factor Productivity (TFP), 1800–2013 (Year 2000 = 100)

Sources and Notes: 1800–2000 data from Benjamin N. Dennis and Talan B. Iscan, "Engel versus Baumol: Accounting for Structural Change Using Two Centuries of U.S. Data," *Explorations in Economic History* 46, no. 2 (April 2009), Figure 3, 189. See Dennis and Iscan for a description of the original data sources. Data kindly provided by Talan B. Iscan. 2000–2011 data from U.S. Department of Agriculture, Economic Research Service, *Farm Multifactor Productivity from United States*, Table 1, www.ers.usda.gov/datafiles/Agricultural_Productivity_in_the_US/National_Tables/table01.xls (accessed: May 19, 2015). 2000–2013 data from U.S. Bureau of Labor Statistics, *Nonfarm Multifactor Productivity*, Table 3, www.bls.gov/news.release/prod3.t03.htm (accessed: May 19, 2015).

Although rapid TFP growth in agriculture is most evident after 1940, there were many notable technical innovations between 1900 and 1940 that for the most part diffused throughout the farm sector only after 1940. Innovations can be grouped into four main categories: (1) biological innovations, including "new" plants and animals; (2) improved cultivation and land-use practices, such as terracing, the optimal timing of operations, and crop rotation patterns; (3) chemical innovations, including fertilizers and pesticides; and (4) new and improved machinery.[24]

CROPS

New varieties of crops were imported to the United States from other parts of the world. In addition, extensive crossbreeding led to the creation of completely new hybrid crops. The process of finding suitable crops that would thrive in new climates involved trial and error, and there were countless failures. For example, Agoston Haraszthy, a pioneer in the California wine industry, changed locations five times, after investing a large sum in each location, before finally finding a suitable environment for grapes in the Sonoma Valley.[25]

The varieties of wheat, corn, cotton, tobacco, and fruit grown in the United States by 1900 were far different from those grown a hundred years earlier.[26] For example, the discovery and importation of new varieties of wheat (together with the development of hybrids) allowed the U.S. "wheat belt" to move hundreds of miles northward and westward into drier and harsher climates. In 1919, 80 percent of the acreage in U.S. wheat consisted of varieties that had not been grown in the United States before 1873, and only 8 percent of the wheat acreage was planted with varieties that were grown in the U.S. prior to 1840.[27] Many of these varieties were imported from Europe and southern Russia. The diffusion of hybrid varieties of cotton from Mexico helped dramatically increase labor productivity in the U.S. South as discussed above.

The development and spread of hybrid corn is another success story. In 1930, there was hardly any acreage devoted to hybrid corn in Iowa, but this rapidly increased to 90 percent of corn acreage by 1940. Although other areas of the country lagged behind Iowa, the adoption of hybrid corn occurred nationwide by 1960.[28] Rapid scientific advances led to the growth of the high-fructose corn-syrup industry in the 1970s, and also to the use of corn to provide the fuel ethanol. In recent decades these developments helped corn to remain, in terms of acreage, the largest crop in the United States.

By experimenting with hybrids and new varieties from Europe and elsewhere, researchers and farmers also discovered new ways to combat insects and plant diseases. Without these biological innovations, scholars estimate that commercial losses due to pests and diseases could have been "disastrous," with losses between 50 and 80 percent.[29]

LIVESTOCK

The only livestock indigenous to the Americas were the llama, the dog, and the turkey. The introduction of horses, cattle, and oxen provided power to American farmers. In addition, the importation of pigs, chickens, goats, and sheep were important sources of food and clothing.[30]

FIGURE 9.5 The Transformation of American Livestock: Dairy Cow in 1800–1830 (Above) and Dairy Cow in 1940 (Below)

Sources and Notes: Dairy cow in 1800–1830 is from New York State Agricultural Society, *Annual Report*, vol. 10 (Albany, NY, 1851), 321, http://hdl.handle.net/2027/njp.32101050721891 (accessed: April 4, 2016). Dairy cow in 1940 is from the Library of Congress, www.loc.gov/pictures/item/fsa2000017645/PP/ (accessed: April 4, 2016).

Through selective breeding, livestock were transformed (Figure 9.5) and became substantially larger, with the result that "the sheep, swine, and cattle of 1940 bore little resemblance to those of 1800."[31] After 1940, the transformation continued with the widespread use of artificial insemination, which enabled selective breeding to be used to develop desirable characteristics.[32]

The 1950s and 1960s witnessed the widespread use of antibiotics in manufactured feeds, along with growth hormones. By the 1980s, scientists were able to produce large quantities of synthetic hormones and to alter animals genetically.[33] Between 1800 and the mid-1990s, the quantity of milk produced per cow increased more than sixteenfold.[34] Not all of these developments, however, are beneficial to human health. For example, the widespread use of antibiotics in animals has contributed to antimicrobial resistance that has made antibiotics less effective in combatting diseases in humans.[35]

Recent developments include embryo transplants, cloning, and genetic engineering. Although these developments have not yet generated large gains in measured productivity growth, the promise remains for continuing productivity improvements in the future.[36]

COMBATTING ANIMAL DISEASES

Throughout the nineteenth century, there was an increasing threat and prevalence of livestock diseases.[37] Greater specialization and increasing trade, along with transportation improvements, led to a proliferation of contagious diseases that affected the health of both livestock and humans. An increasing concentration of animals in dairies and stockyards resulted in more intermingling of animals. In addition, the expansion of railroads and improvements in ocean transportation allowed livestock to travel greater distances, which also reduced the time in transit relative to the incubation period of diseases. Both of these developments contributed to the spread of diseases among livestock.

By 1900, however, the United States had emerged as the world leader in controlling contagious animal diseases. The Bureau of Animal Industry (BAI), created in 1884 as part of the U.S. Department of Agriculture (USDA), led the way in this fight. By the 1940s, through quarantines, slaughter, trade restrictions, and other regulations, the BAI had been instrumental in eradicating seven major animal diseases in the United States: bovine pleuropneumonia (1892), fowl plague (1929), foot-and-mouth disease (1929), glanders (1934), bovine tuberculosis (1940), dourine fever (1942), and Texas fever (1943).[38]

FERTILIZERS AND PESTICIDES

The history of modern fertilizers began in Germany in the 1840s with the commercial use of phosphates extracted from dissolved bones, but mineral phosphate soon replaced that from bones. The first artificial nitrogen fertilizer, ammonium sulfate, became available in the 1860s; but it was the invention in 1909 of the Haber-Bosch method of producing ammonium sulfate that was the "real breakthrough."[39]

During World War I, President Woodrow Wilson tried to boost agricultural output by subsidizing the importation of nitrates from Chile.[40] In the United States, the purchases of nitrogen, phosphorus, and potassium doubled from 1910 to 1940.[41] After World War II, the use of commercial fertilizers really skyrocketed, growing at an annual rate of 4.5 percent between 1940 and 1980.[42]

This increase was due to several factors. First, the use of manure was leading to soil exhaustion in many regions. Second, the real price of fertilizer fell substantially during the first few decades after World War II, largely because of increased capacity and competition in the fertilizer industry. Third, many new crop varieties, including hybrid corn, were bred to be more responsive to fertilizers.[43]

The other major uses of agricultural chemicals are herbicides and pesticides. Although various poisons have been used for centuries to combat weeds, insects, and other agricultural pests, the use of chemical pesticides became much more widespread after World War II. In 1952, only 5–10 percent of corn, wheat, and cotton acres were treated with herbicides; by 1980, 90–99 percent of corn, wheat, and soybean acres received herbicides.[44]

MECHANIZATION

Mechanization refers to the process of changing from working by hand or with animals to doing that work with machinery. Mechanization did not happen overnight, however, but involved countless innovations over more than two hundred years.

Perhaps the first machine to have a substantial impact on agriculture was the cotton gin, invented by Eli Whitney and others around 1793. The cotton gin removed a bottleneck in production by allowing one worker to remove the seeds from 50 pounds of short-staple cotton per day instead of only 1 pound a day by hand. The lower cost of American cotton and the tremendous growth of cotton textiles in England caused cotton exports, as a proportion of all U.S. exports, to increase from 38 percent in 1815–1819 to 65 percent by 1840, and incidentally contributed to the rapid growth of slavery in the American South.

Machines also affected the growth and development of agriculture in the North. When farmers first moved into the Midwest in the early nineteenth century, they used relatively simple and primitive tools. A plow was nothing more than a curved tree limb with a piece of iron attached at the end with rawhide.[45] Seeds were scattered by hand; grains were cut by a cradle scythe; and handheld flails were used for threshing, to help separate grains from their husks.

During the nineteenth century, the quality of plows improved dramatically. Wooden and iron plows were replaced first by cast-iron plows and eventually by steel plows.[46] Although John Deere produced the first all-steel plow in 1837, steel plows did not become commonplace until the price of steel fell in the 1850s.[47]

Along with the steel plow, the grain thresher and the mechanical reaper were the most important mechanical inventions during the first half of the nineteenth century. A thresher separated the grain from the chaff, while a reaper cut and gathered crops at harvest time. The reaper, in particular, solved a major bottleneck in production, since a family farm could only plant as much as it could harvest. By dramatically increasing the amount that could be harvested, the reaper allowed farmers to plant much more.

In 1833, Obed Hussey patented a horse-powered reaper and started selling it, but Cyrus McCormick was eventually far more successful. His reaper was patented in 1834, but it was not until 1840 that he believed it was sufficiently improved to offer for sale. By 1860, over 100 companies were selling reapers, but McCormick adopted several business practices that made his company by far the largest.[48] He moved production to Chicago to be closer to farmers, and he offered farmers a free trial period on every machine, along with a money-back guarantee. McCormick also advertised the price of reapers widely, in farm journals and newspapers. His ability to produce reapers in large quantities, along with his ability to market his machines, led to the dominance of McCormick reapers. By 1870, over 80 percent of U.S. wheat was harvested by machine.[49]

Other important inventions helped tame the prairie, including the steel windmill (1854), which pumped water from underground for irrigation, and barbed wire (1867), which prevented animals from trampling crops in areas where there was little wood for fences.

In the second half of the nineteenth century, perhaps the most significant mechanical innovation was the combine harvester (or combine), which was commercially developed in the 1880s. The combine merged a reaper and a thresher into one machine. The first self-propelled combine was invented in 1911, and over time combines evolved to become smaller and more versatile, allowing for the harvesting of corn, beans, peas, and other crops. From 4,000 combines on American farms in 1920, the number quickly increased to 61,000 in 1930 and 190,000 in 1940.[50] By the 1980s, the combine had become the dominant method for harvesting for almost every grain and legume.[51]

The twentieth century also witnessed the introduction and spread of the gasoline-powered tractor. The general-purpose tractor was invented in 1924, and the emergence in the 1930s of pneumatic tires (tires made of reinforced rubber and filled with compressed air) greatly increased its usefulness and effective power (Figure 9.6).

Gasoline-powered tractors were further enhanced by the invention of the power-take-off shaft (or PTO). This converted the pulling power of the engine into a rotary movement, greatly increasing the range of possible uses for a tractor and leading also

FIGURE 9.6 A Fleet of Ford Tractors, 1925

Source: Library of Congress, www.loc.gov/pictures/item/det1994023011/PP/ (accessed: April 6, 2016).

to smaller machines.[52] Tractors accounted for 11 percent of total American draft power in 1920, a figure that increased to 40 percent in 1930, to 65 percent in 1940, and to 100 percent in 1960.[53]

From 1,000 tractors in 1910 to 920,000 in 1930, the number of tractors on American farms continued to increase, reaching 4 million tractors in 1953. Between 1910 and 1955, the three largest producers of tractors in the United States were International Harvester, Ford, and John Deere, which had a combined market share of almost 65 percent. No other manufacturer had more than a 9.1 percent market share.[54]

Since the 1950s, the number of tractors has remained relatively constant, at around 4.5 million.[55] While the number of tractors has not increased, continued innovations in design and size have occurred, with tractor horsepower on farms more than doubling from the mid-1950s to the mid-1980s.[56] More recently, tractors have offered greater comfort, with enclosed air-conditioned cabs, improved safety features, greater power, and improved fuel efficiency.

Larger farms in the Great Plains and California were the first adopters of tractors, with the South being the last region of the country to adopt tractors widely. The rise of the tractor also led to the decline of farm horses and mules, from 26.5 million in 1915 to only 3.1 million by 1960.[57] While the use of the tractor greatly increased the power available to farmers, it also saved farmers considerable amounts of time and land which had been devoted to caring for horses and mules. Nearly 25 percent of U.S. cropland was converted from growing feed for draft animals to growing products for human consumption.[58]

The increasing use of electricity in powering motors also contributed to mechanization between 1920 and 1960.[59] Electric motors were used in fans for ventilation and hay drying, in refrigeration, in augers, grinders, and other feed-handling equipment, and in mechanized dairy farming.

Two other mechanical inventions were critically important to the agricultural sector in the twentieth century: the mechanical cotton picker and the vacuum-driven milking machine. Prior to mechanization, picking cotton and milking cows were both very labor-intensive activities. After a long history of attempts to mechanize the picking of cotton, the first successful machine was invented in 1928. Diffusion was very slow, with only 107 machines in operation in 1945.[60] The diffusion of mechanical cotton pickers became quite rapid after World War II, however, with almost the entire U.S. cotton crop being mechanically harvested by 1970.[61]

The milking machine follows a similar history. Although a milking machine employing the intermittent suction principle was invented in 1905, lack of electricity, unsanitary practices, and "hard times" on the farm slowed its adoption. At the beginning of World War II, "perhaps 90 percent of all cows were milked by hand."[62] This situation changed quite rapidly, however, with half of all cows milked mechanically by 1950, and nearly all dairy cows in commercial operations by the mid-1960s.[63]

FARM SIZE AND ECONOMIES OF SCALE

Between 1850 and 1870, the average farm size in the United States decreased from 203 acres to 153 acres, primarily as the result of the Civil War and the demise of plantation agriculture and slavery in the South (Figure 9.7). Between 1870 and 1940, average farm sizes barely changed, with farms having fewer than 175 acres on average in 1940, and only 2 percent of farms having 1,000 acres or more.[64]

FIGURE 9.7 Number of Farms, Total Farmland, and Size of Farms by Decade, 1850–2010

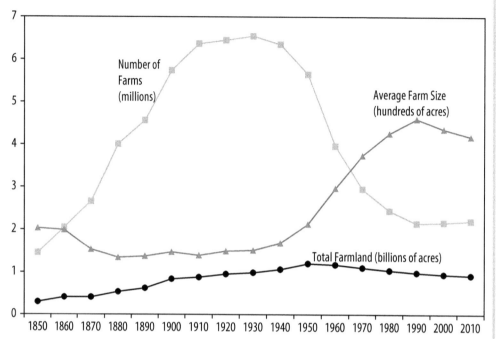

Sources and Notes: Susan B. Carter, Scott Sigmund Gartner, Michael R. Haines, Alan L. Olmstead, Richard Sutch, and Gavin Wright (eds.), *Historical Statistics of the United States, Millennial Edition* (New York, NY: Cambridge University Press, 2006), for Number of Farms, 1850–1920 (series Da16) and 1930–1980 (series Da4); Average Farm Size, 1850–1920 (series Da19) and 1930–1980 (series Da6); and Total Farmland, 1850–1920 (series Da17) and 1930–1980 (series Da5). For 1990, 2000, and 2010, data for all three variables are from U.S. Census Bureau, *Statistical Abstract of the United States 2012*, Table 824, www.census.gov/compendia/statab/2012/tables/12s0824.pdf (accessed: May 27, 2015).

After 1940, however, farm sizes more than doubled. There are several reasons why farms got bigger. One factor was the increased opportunities for farmers and their children in nonfarm occupations. Those with opportunities would often leave agriculture unless agricultural incomes and living standards increased fast enough to keep pace with growth in the nonfarm economy. For those who remained in farming, larger farm sizes produced higher incomes. Although the incomes of farm households lagged well behind those of nonfarm households throughout most of the twentieth century, in recent decades farm household incomes have exceeded nonfarm incomes.[65] Another reason for larger farm sizes was increased mechanization, since the high fixed costs of machinery could be spread over more acres.

In addition to farms getting larger, farms have also become more specialized over the past century or more. In 1910, for example, nearly 90 percent of farms reported raising chickens, while over 80 percent had dairy cows, and more than 75 percent grew their own corn. By the 1980s, these percentages had fallen to 10 percent, 15 percent, and 32 percent, respectively.[66]

9.4 AGRARIAN DISCONTENT

Between 1865 and 1900, American farmers protested and organized through four major reform movements: Granger, Greenback, Alliance, and Populist. Farmers complained about falling prices and incomes, and believed that they were being harmed by the monopoly power of railroads, grain-elevator operators, milling companies, commodity buyers, meat packers, and money lenders.

In the late nineteenth century, there was a shortage of gold relative to real GDP, so that the U.S. money supply was shrinking relative to the economy. As a result, the U.S. experienced deflation: that is, prices were gradually falling from 1873 to 1896. This was bad for farmers. Consider a farmer who had borrowed to purchase a farm by taking out a mortgage. Since the price of selling corn or wheat was falling over time, but the monthly mortgage payment remained fixed in dollars, this made it increasingly difficult to make the mortgage payment. Farmers recognized that this circumstance was not an accident but the result of the country following a gold standard. In 1896, William Jennings Bryan ran for President and advocated for a bimetallic standard of both silver and gold, which would have put more money into circulation and led to higher prices.

It was not only deflation that was bad for farmers: they were also upset about the greater risks and uncertainties associated with greater commercialization and market integration of farming.[67] The degree of farmers' discontent in northern U.S. states is positively correlated with greater variability in farm prices, yields, and incomes, and farm protests were more severe in states with higher rates of farm foreclosures.[68]

Although Bryan lost the election of 1896, prices began to rise again anyway, because of discoveries of gold in Alaska and the development of a new cyanide process to extract gold from lower-quality ores. In many ways, the first couple of decades of the twentieth century were particularly good for American farmers, with the period 1910–1914 labeled the "golden age of agriculture."[69] This prosperity, however, vanished with remarkable speed after World War I and the recession of 1920 and 1921.

The 1920s were particularly hard times for American farmers. Between 1921 and 1929, about one-sixth of U.S. farms faced foreclosure.[70] The fear that prices would continue to fall led farmers to lobby for government support. Throughout the 1920s, Congress passed several McNary-Haugen bills, only to have them vetoed by President Calvin Coolidge. The Great Depression in the 1930s marked a watershed in agricultural policies, and introduced an era of large-scale interventions in many agricultural markets that has persisted to the present day.

9.5 AGRICULTURAL POLICIES

Land policies, taxes, and tariffs have affected agriculture since the founding of the Republic. During the late nineteenth and early twentieth centuries, however, government policies focused specifically on agricultural research and extension programs in an attempt to increase agricultural productivity. Policies also addressed public goods issues such as animal and crop diseases, and sought to maintain competitive markets.[71] The United States Department of Agriculture (USDA) was created in 1862 to serve as an information agency for American farmers. Congress also passed the Morrill Acts (1862 and 1890) to encourage the establishment of agricultural and mechanical colleges and universities in each state.

A nationwide system of state agricultural experiment stations, associated with land-grant colleges and universities, was the result of the Hatch Act (1887). The Smith-Lever Act (1914) offered financial support to states to encourage the dissemination of research from the experiment stations to farmers, while the Smith-Hughes Act (1917) provided federal support to high schools for the teaching of vocational agriculture.

Public health interventions to combat livestock and crop diseases, as discussed in Section 9.3 above, were also crucial to the health and productivity of the agricultural sector. However, it was not until the Great Depression of the 1930s that the federal government became actively and extensively involved in increasing crop prices and incomes for farmers.

During the Great Depression, prices received by farmers fell 55 percent between 1929 and 1933, and in 1932, almost 4 percent of all U.S. farms faced foreclosure.[72] Roosevelt's New Deal included legislation and programs to help farmers, including the Agricultural Adjustment Act (1933), the Farm Security Administration (1935, 1937), the Soil Conservation Service (1935), the Rural Electrification Administration (1935), and many others. Since the 1930s, the United States has experienced frequent changes in its agricultural policies, with major acts approved in 1954, 1956, 1965, 1970, 1973, 1977, 1985, 1996, 2002, 2008, and 2014.[73]

While there have been a wide array of mechanisms to intervene into agricultural markets since the 1930s, the majority of farm output, measured by value, is not subject to price supports or other direct market interventions.[74] Interventions have primarily focused on wheat, corn, cotton, peanuts, and milk, with most fruits, vegetables, and livestock receiving only small-scale and sporadic support.[75]

The complex history of government interventions in agricultural markets can be organized into six broad categories: (1) price supports; (2) supply controls; (3) demand-expansion policies; (4) direct payments; (5) deficiency payments; and (6) crop insurance.[76] The effects of these policies are summarized in Table 9.1 below.

From the Agricultural Adjustment Act (1933) to the mid-1950s, the primary policy tools consisted of price supports and supply controls in the form of acreage restrictions.[77] A price support is a government policy that maintains a price above the market price.[78] With a price support, both the farmer and consumer face higher prices. One way to keep prices above what would have occurred in market equilibrium without the price support is to practice a purchase and removal policy, in which the government agrees to purchase, at a specified support price, whatever quantity farmers want to

TABLE 9.1 Summary of U.S. Farm Policies

Policy	What the government does	Effect on — Farmers	Consumers	Quantity
Price support	Buys the crop at a support price	Higher price	Higher price	More
Supply control	Reduces the quantity planted or sold	Higher price	Higher price	Less
Demand-expansion	Promotes demand by subsidizing crop purchases	Higher price	Higher price	More
Direct payment	Pays farmers based on historical production	Higher income	—	—
Deficiency payment	Pays farmers the difference between a target price and the market price	Higher price	Lower market price	More
Crop Insurance	Pays farmers if they suffer losses	Avoids losses	—	—

sell. Another way to guarantee prices paid to farmers is to use "nonrecourse loans." Under the Commodity Credit Corporation (CCC), farmers could borrow money based on high agricultural prices from the 1910–1914 period. Farmers would borrow money based on these high "parity" prices by using their crops as collateral. If the market price of the crop at the time of harvest fell below the parity price, the farmer would "default" on the loan by forfeiting the crop to the CCC, but with no other negative ramifications for the farmer. As a result, the government guaranteed farmers at least the parity price for their crop. With both purchase and removal and nonrecourse loans, the government acquired the surpluses.

The Agricultural Adjustment Act (1933) also included supply controls in the form of acreage allotments, which restricted farmers to planting only a specified number of acres for each crop, the acreage being based on a portion of each farmer's historical plantings of the crop. Over time, however, these policies also resulted in large surplus problems. Acreage restrictions were not particularly effective in reducing supply, for two primary reasons. First, farmers took their least productive land out of production and used their remaining land more intensively by increasing the quantity of chemical fertilizers and water. Second, productivity improvements, through better seed varieties, mechanization, and fertilizers, led to large increases in supply (see Section 9.3).

In response, the federal government introduced demand-expansion policies. U.S. demand for agricultural products was increased through federal school lunch programs (1946) and the permanent food stamp program (1964). Programs were also implemented to increase foreign demand for U.S. agricultural products by providing subsidies. Another demand-expansion policy in recent decades has been the ethanol program, in which the federal government has provided subsidies to farmers to produce corn that is converted into a biofuel additive in gasoline.

To avoid problems of overproduction, the federal government has moved toward direct payments to farmers, much like issuing a Social Security check or welfare check. With direct payments, government support is decoupled from current production and based on historical production. While direct payments can be costly, an advantage for government is that such payments are predictable from year to year.

Under the deficiency payment or target price method, the government establishes target prices for wheat, cotton, and feed grains. When market prices fall below target prices, the government pays farmers a deficiency payment, thereby ensuring that they receive the target prices for their crops. While deficiency payments do not raise prices for consumers, they can be very costly when prices fall well below target prices, and they encourage overproduction.

Finally, with federal crop insurance programs, the government subsidizes premiums to private insurers to insure farmers against shortfalls in crop yields or revenues (that is, prices multiplied by yields). The primary problem with insurance programs is the moral hazard problem (see Chapter 5): the existence of insurance reduces farmers' incentive to avoid bad outcomes, and thus encourages them to engage in riskier farming practices.

Along with market inefficiencies, one frequent criticism of farm programs is that while the stated purpose is to help the small family farm, most government payments go to relatively rich farmers on big farms.[79] Although 85 percent of economists agree that agricultural subsidies should be completely eliminated, such subsidies are remarkably persistent.[80]

The growth and continuing existence of farm subsidies is consistent with the theory of collective action.[81] Relatively small, homogeneous groups with a lot to gain

FIGURE 9.8 Total Direct Federal Government Payments to Farmers as a Percentage of GDP, 1933–2015

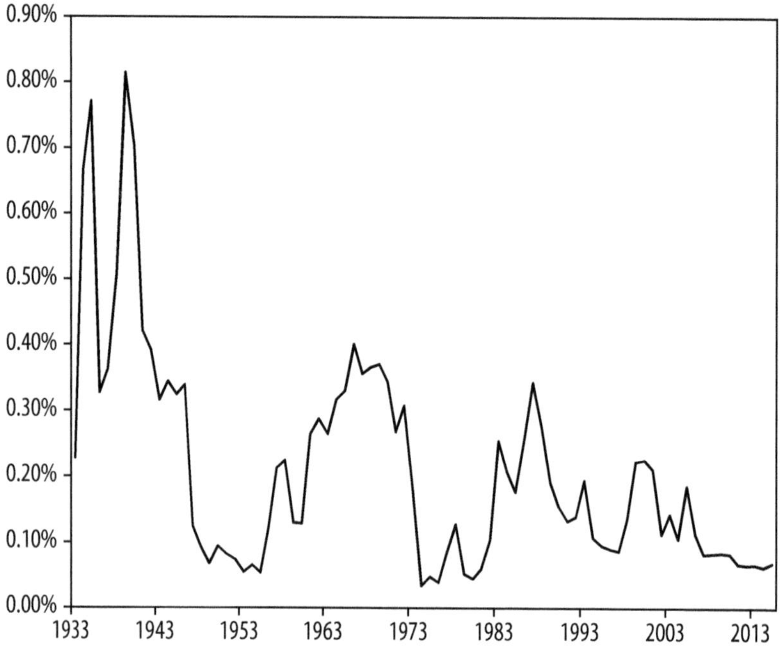

Sources: United States Department of Agriculture, Economic Research Service, "Total Direct Government Payments to Farmers," www.ers.usda.gov/data-products/farm-income-and-wealth-statistics/government-payments-by-program.aspx (accessed: June 1, 2015). Real GDP from Louis Johnston and Samuel H. Williamson, "What Was the U.S. GDP Then?" MeasuringWorth, www.measuringworth.org/usgdp/ (accessed: June 1, 2015).

(such as farmers) tend to be more effective in lobbying government to enact policies in their interests than larger groups that are more diffuse (such as consumers). The members of smaller groups, who have greater individual stakes in policy decisions, can organize at lower cost and can more successfully control the free-rider problems associated with larger groups.

Figure 9.8 shows the history of direct federal payments to farmers from 1933 to 2015. Although payments to farmers have averaged considerably less than one-half of 1 percent of GDP since the 1930s, the most notable feature of Figure 9.8 is the variability of payments from year to year. These are a result of transitory changes in prices, due to shocks such as droughts, aggregate economic fluctuations, and changes in farm policies. For example, payments decreased from over $26 billion in 2005 to little more than $12 billion by 2007.

9.6 CONCLUSIONS

The history of American agriculture is often portrayed in two seemingly contradictory ways. On the one hand, it is a remarkable success story, in which fewer and fewer farmers have been able to feed and clothe a growing population in the United States and worldwide. On the other hand, the image of the struggling farmer, in need of help to withstand market forces, is also part of our agricultural history. The combination of huge productivity improvements (due to biological and mechanical innovations), low price elasticity, and low income elasticity of demand for food, reconciles these two competing visions of American agriculture.

QUESTIONS

1. Use the tools of supply and demand to explain why the agricultural employment share has decreased so dramatically in the long run.

2. Consider a sector of the economy that experiences rapid technological change. Suppose that the price elasticity of demand for goods produced in this sector is high (elastic) and that the income elasticity of demand is high as well (greater than 1, so that goods in this sector are luxury goods). Using the tools of supply and demand, what would you expect to happen to total revenue and the number of workers employed in this sector over time? Explain.

3. What are the potential reasons why larger plantations using slave labor in the South had higher productivity than smaller farms in the South? Why is it difficult to compare the relative labor productivity of agriculture in the South and in the North?

4. Consider Figure 9.3. In which periods of U.S. history was output growth in agriculture the highest? In which periods of U.S. history was labor productivity growth in agriculture the highest? (Recall that labor productivity growth is approximately equal to $g_Y - g_L$.) Are these generally the same periods? What factors can account for the differences between output growth rates (g_Y) and labor productivity growth rates ($g_Y - g_L$) at different time periods in U.S. history? Explain.

5. One type of intervention in agricultural markets, which began during the New Deal, was supply controls. Explain why supply controls that require farmers to take land out of production are often not very effective in restricting the supply of food or in increasing farm prices and income.

6. In the decades after 1940, average farm sizes in the United States more than doubled, while the number of workers employed in agriculture fell. Explain the potential causes of the decline in agricultural employment and the increase in average farm sizes.

7. Between 1865 and 1896, farmers organized themselves through four major reform movements. What were the likely causes of agricultural discontent in the late nineteenth century?

NOTES

[1] United States Department of Agriculture, *Briefing on the Status of Rural America*, www.usda.gov/documents/Briefing_on_the_Status_of_Rural_America_Low_Res_Cover_update_map.pdf (accessed: March 26, 2015).

[2] Stephen Broadberry, "How Did the United States and Germany Overtake Britain? A Sectoral Analysis of Comparative Productivity Levels, 1870–1990," *Journal of Economic History* 58, no. 2 (June 1998), 375–407.

[3] Winifred Rothenberg, *From Market Places to a Market Economy: The Transformation of Rural Massachusetts, 1750 to 1850* (Chicago, IL: University of Chicago Press, 1992).

[4] Douglass C. North, *The Economic Growth of the United States, 1790–1860* (Englewood Cliffs, NJ: Prentice Hall, 1961).

[5] C. Knick Harley, "Transportation, the World Wheat Trade, and the Kuznets Cycle, 1850–1913," *Explorations in Economic History* 17, no. 3 (July 1980), 218–250.

[6] C. Knick Harley, "Western Settlement and the Price of Wheat, 1872–1913," *Journal of Economic History* 38, no. 4 (December 1978), 865–878.

[7] Harley (1980), 246–247.

[8] United States Department of Agriculture, Economic Research Service, "Value of U.S. Agricultural Trade by Calendar Year," www.ers.usda.gov/datafiles/Foreign_Agricultural_Trade_of_the_United_States_FATUS/Calendar_Year/By_Year/XMScy1935.xls (accessed: March 28, 2015).

[9] Gavin Wright, *The Political Economy of the Cotton South: Households, Markets, and Wealth in the Nineteenth Century* (New York: Norton, 1978), 28.

[10] Robert W. Fogel and Stanley L. Engerman, *Time on the Cross: The Economics of American Slavery* (Boston, MA: Little, Brown, 1974), 285.

[11] Alan L. Olmstead and Paul W. Rhode, "Biological Innovation and Productivity Growth in the Antebellum Cotton Economy," *Journal of Economic History* 68, no. 4 (December 2008), 1123–1171.

[12] Gavin Wright, *Slavery and American Economic Development* (Baton Rouge, LA: Louisiana State University Press, 2006), 24–26.

[13] Gavin Wright, "The Relative Efficiency of Slave Agriculture: Another Interpretation," *American Economic Review* 69, no. 1 (March 1979), 219–226.

[14] Andrew Muhammad, James L. Seale, Jr., Birgit Meade and Anita Regmi, "International Evidence on Food Consumption Patterns: An Update Using 2005 International Comparison Program Data," in United States Department of Agriculture, Economic Research Service, *Technical Bulletin no. 1929* (March 2011), iii, www.ers.usda.gov/media/129561/tb1929.pdf (accessed: April 16, 2015).

[15] Benjamin N. Dennis and Talan B. Iscan, "Engel versus Baumol: Accounting for Structural Change Using Two Centuries of U.S. Data," *Explorations in Economic History* 46, no. 2 (April 2009), 186–202.

[16] Giovanni Federico, *Feeding the World: An Economic History of Agriculture 1800–2000* (Princeton, NJ: Princeton University Press, 2005), 33.

[17] Alan L. Olmstead and Paul W. Rhode, "Farms and Farm Structure," in Susan B. Carter, Scott Sigmund Gartner, Michael R. Haines, Alan L. Olmstead, Richard Sutch, and Gavin Wright (eds.), *Historical Statistics of the United States*, *Millennial Edition* (New York, NY: Cambridge University Press, 2006), 4–11.

[18] Olmstead and Rhode (2006), 4–11.

[19] Federico, 65.

[20] Federico, 40.

[21] Federico, 40.

[22] Federico, Table 4.16, 57.

[23] Federico, 57.

[24] Federico, 84.

[25] Olmstead and Rhode (2008), 232–233.

[26] Olmstead and Rhode (2008), 3.

[27] Olmstead and Rhode (2008), 391.

[28] Wallace E. Huffman and Robert Evenson, *Science for Agriculture* (Ames, IA: Iowa State University Press, 1993), Chapter 6.

[29] Olmstead and Rhode (2008), Table 13.1, 388.

30 Alfred W. Crosby, "The Columbian Exchange: Plants, Animals, and Disease between the Old and New Worlds," National Humanities Center (2001), http://nationalhumanitiescenter. org/tserve/nattrans/ntecoindian/essays/columbian.htm (accessed: May 15, 2015).

31 Olmstead and Rhode (2008), 3.

32 R.H. Foote, "The History of Artificial Insemination: Selected Notes and Notables," *Journal of Animal Science* 80 (2002), 3.

33 Bruce L. Gardner, *American Agriculture in the Twentieth Century: How it Flourished and What It Cost* (Cambridge, MA: Harvard University Press, 2002), 26.

34 Olmstead and Rhode (2006), 4–18.

35 U.S. Centers for Disease Control and Prevention, "Antibiotic Use in Food-Producing Animals," www.cdc.gov/narms/animals.html (accessed: June 12, 2016).

36 Gardner (2002), 20.

37 Alan L. Olmstead and Paul W. Rhode, *Arresting Contagion: Science, Policy, and Conflicts Over Animal Disease Control* (Cambridge, MA: Harvard University Press, 2015), Chapter 2, 19–41.

38 Olmstead and Rhode (2015), 5.

39 Federico, 89.

40 Gardner (2002), 22.

41 Olmstead and Rhode (2006), 4–14.

42 Gardner (2002), 22.

43 Olmstead and Rhode (2006), 4–14.

44 Jorge Ferandez-Cornejo et al., "Pesticide Use in U.S. Agriculture: 21 Selected Crops, 1960–2008," *Economic Information Bulletin*, no. 124 (U.S. Department of Agriculture, Economic Research Service, May 2014), iv.

45 Louis P. Cain, "Entrepreneurship in the Antebellum United States," in David S. Landes, Joel Mokyr, and William J. Baumol (eds.), *The Invention of Enterprise: Entrepreneurship from Ancient Mesopotamia to Modern Times* (Princeton, NJ: Princeton University Press, 2010), 347.

46 Peter D. McClelland, *Sowing Modernity: America's First Agricultural Revolution* (Ithaca, NY: Cornell University Press, 1997), 16–63.

47 Cain, 348.

48 Cain, 349.

49 Federico, 100.

50 Carter et al., series Da629.

51 Olmstead and Rhode (2006), 4–13.

52 Federico, 92.

53 Federico, 100.

54 William J. White, "Economic History of Tractors in the United States," in Robert Whaples (ed.), *EH.Net Encyclopedia* (March 2008), https://eh.net/encyclopedia/economic-history-of-tractors-in-the-united-states/ (accessed: May 21, 2015).

55 Olmstead and Rhode (2006), 4–13.

56 Olmstead and Rhode (2006), 4–13.

57 Carter et al., series Da983 and Da985.

58 Carter et al., series Da663.

59 Gardner (2002), 15.

60 Olmstead and Rhode (2006), 4–14.

[61] Moses S. Musoke and Alan L. Olmstead, "The Rise of the Cotton Industry in California: A Comparative Perspective," *Journal of Economic History* 42, no. 2 (June 1982), 385–412.

[62] Olmstead and Rhode (2006), 4–14.

[63] Olmstead and Rhode (2006), 4–14.

[64] Olmstead and Rhode (2006), 4–11.

[65] Gardner (2002), Figure 3.12, 78.

[66] Olmstead and Rhode (2006), 4–12.

[67] Anne Mayhew, "A Reappraisal of the Causes of the Farm Protest Movement in the United States, 1870–1900," *Journal of Economic History* 32, no. 2 (June 1972), 464–475.

[68] Robert A. McGuire, "Economic Causes of Late Nineteenth Century Agrarian Unrest: New Evidence," *Journal of Economic History* 41, no. 4 (December 1981), 835–852; and James H. Stock, "Real Estate Mortgages, Foreclosures, and Midwestern Agrarian Unrest, 1865–1920," *Journal of Economic History* 44, no. 1 (March 1984), 89–105.

[69] Gardner (2002), 1.

[70] Lee J. Alston, "Farm Foreclosures in the United States during the Interwar Period," *Journal of Economic History* 43, no. 4 (December 1983), 885–903.

[71] Randall R. Rucker and E.C. Pasour, Jr., "The Growth of U.S. Farm Programs," in *Government and the American Economy: A New History* (Chicago, IL: University of Chicago Press, 2007), 456.

[72] Rucker and Pasour, 461.

[73] Gardner (2002), 216–218.

[74] Bruce Gardner, "U.S. Agriculture in the Twentieth Century," in Robert Whaples (ed.), *EH.Net Encyclopedia* (March 20, 2003), http://eh.net/encyclopedia/u-s-agriculture-in-the-twentieth-century/ (accessed: May 28, 2015).

[75] Gardner (2003).

[76] Parke Wilde, *Food Policy in the United States: An Introduction* (New York, NY: Routledge, 2013), 23.

[77] Rucker and Pasour, 469.

[78] Wilde, 23.

[79] "Farm Subsidies: Milking Taxpayers," *The Economist* (February 14, 2015).

[80] N. Gregory Mankiw, "Newsflash: Economists Agree" (February 14, 2009), http://gregmankiw.blogspot.com/2009/02/news-flash-economists-agree.html (accessed: June 4, 2015).

[81] Mancur Olson, *The Logic of Collective Action: Public Goods and the Theory of Groups* (Cambridge, MA: Harvard University Press, 1965).

10 Manufacturing and Industrialization

During the colonial period, high costs of labor and capital, along with limited and scattered domestic markets, meant that most manufactured goods were either imported from England or made at home. Alexander Hamilton, in his *Report on Manufactures* (1791), estimated that between two-thirds and four-fifths of all clothes were produced at home. Although the United States had lumber mills, shipyards, iron works, and many other industrial establishments in 1791, these firms were small and the country was still overwhelmingly agricultural.

A century later, however, the United States had become the leading manufacturing and industrial nation in the world. By 1890, the value of manufacturing output exceeded that of agricultural output for the first time, and a decade later it more than doubled agricultural output. It was also during this time that the United States surpassed the United Kingdom to become the world's leading industrial power. Several factors contributed to the success of manufacturing and industry in the United States, including an abundance and early exploitation of natural capital; a growing population, along with transportation and communication improvements to expand markets; financial developments, including the growth of commercial banks and financial markets; mass education; and tariff protection.[1]

After decades of dominance in the twentieth century, manufacturing in recent decades has been increasingly subject to automation and to foreign competition, and the proportion of the workforce employed in manufacturing has decreased from more than 25 percent in the 1960s to less than 9 percent in 2016. No area of the United States has fared worse than the "Rust Belt," the historically manufacturing region bordering the Great Lakes.

This chapter traces the growth, dominance, and relative decline (by some measures, at least) of U.S. manufacturing from its beginnings to the present. It examines the reasons why the United States was able to overtake the rest of the world by the end

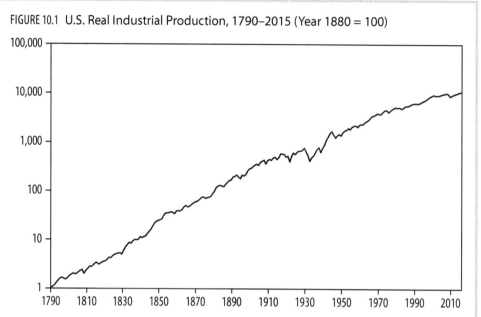

FIGURE 10.1 U.S. Real Industrial Production, 1790–2015 (Year 1880 = 100)

Sources: 1790–1915 data from Joseph H. Davis, "An Annual Index of U.S. Industrial Production, 1790–1915," *The Quarterly Journal of Economics* 119, no. 4 (November 2004), 1177–1215, www.nber.org/data/industrial-production-index/ip-total.xls (accessed: June 12, 2015). 1916–1918 data from Solomon Fabricant, *The Output of Manufacturing Industries, 1899–1937* (New York: National Bureau of Economic Research, 1940), 44 (accessed: June 12, 2015). 1919–2015 data from Federal Reserve Economic Data (FRED), Industrial Production, Total Index, series IPB50001N, annual averages of monthly data (accessed June 12, 2015). The series are ratio spliced in 1915 and 1919.

of the nineteenth century, and how the U.S. was able to maintain leadership throughout most of the twentieth century. It also discusses the extent to which declining employment in manufacturing in recent decades should be a cause of concern. Evidence shows that the United States is not alone in this regard, as other high-income economies are experiencing the same phenomenon. Finally, prospects for the future are discussed.

Figure 10.1 shows the long-term increase in U.S. industrial production from 1790 to 2015, which includes manufacturing along with mining and utilities. Figure 10.1 uses a ratio scale, so the slope of the line indicates the growth rate. The first striking feature is the tremendous growth over time, with production more than 10,000 times greater in 2015 than in 1790. It is evident from Figure 10.1 that the growth rate of industrial production begins to increase after 1830 (the slope of the line gets steeper) and this higher rate of growth is maintained throughout the rest of the nineteenth century.

In the twentieth century growth rates slowed, although they remained robust. The big events of the twentieth century are also apparent in Figure 10.1. The Great Depression of the 1930s is the cause of the largest downward spike in the figure; while the marked upturn thereafter occurs during World War II, from 1941 to 1945. Also clearly visible in the figure is the Great Recession, which started in December 2007.

10.1 EARLY MANUFACTURING AND THE EMERGENCE OF FACTORIES

The first industrial revolution began in England in the mid-eighteenth century and centered on the cotton textile industry, and specifically the mechanical production of woven fabrics made with cotton thread (see Economic History in Action 10.1). After the Revolution War had ended, it did not take long for the cotton textile industry to flourish in the United States as well.

The first factories in the United States were cotton textile mills in New England. Machines in factories, powered by water, steam, electricity, or some other power source, allowed the production process to become largely mechanized. Division of labor and specialization occurred as workers were subjected to an organizational discipline, and standardized products were sold in a wide market rather than a strictly local one.

COTTON TEXTILES

The first American cotton textile mill, Almy and Brown, opened in Pawtucket, Rhode Island, in 1790. It was built by Samuel Slater, who had arrived from England in 1789. Slater had memorized the construction of textile machinery that the British had hoped to keep secret. He later made improvements to these machines, successfully mechanizing both weaving and cotton carding (the disentangling, cleaning, and intermixing of fibers into a continuous web of cotton prior that was then spun into yarn). This was the beginning of the textile industry in New England and provided a new market for Southern cotton.

ECONOMIC HISTORY IN ACTION 10.1

Three Industrial Revolutions

While some scholars believe that the long-run growth rate of technological progress is relatively steady, others argue that technological progress is better described as a series of "industrial revolutions," in which clusters of new inventions appeared over relatively short periods of time, each followed by a period in which the new ideas slowly diffused throughout the economy. Since 1750, there have been three such industrial revolutions.[2]

The first one, from about 1750 to 1830, depended upon steam power, which was applied in powering steam engines in cotton textile factories, locomotives, and many other types of machinery.

The second industrial revolution was, by most accounts, the most transformative in terms of improving standards of living. Between 1870 and 1900, there were five main clusters of inventions: (1) electricity and all of its "spin-offs," from electric lights to electric motors; (2) the internal combustion engine, with its uses in automobiles, tractors, and airplanes; (3) clean water, indoor plumbing, and central heating; (4) the ability to rearrange molecules, including the developments in the petroleum, chemical, plastics, and pharmaceutical industries; and (5) communication and entertainment devices, including the telephone, phonograph, motion pictures, and photography. As is evident in this chapter and throughout the book, the full impact of these inventions and innovations often took decades to impact aggregate economic growth (see Section 10.3, for example, for a discussion of the slow diffusion of electricity as a power source in American factories).

The magnitude and impact of the third industrial revolution is subject to substantial controversy. It started around 1960 with the commercial development of mainframe computers, and it includes the personal computer, robotics, the Internet, smartphones, and other more recent developments in information and communication technology. Although aggregate productivity and productivity in manufacturing increased for a time after 1989, they have not yet approached the productivity gains realized during and after the second industrial revolution (see Tables 2.3 and 10.1). While some believe that the third industrial revolution has largely run its course, others feel that its impact is only just beginning and that it may lead to a world in which computers and robots replace many workers, while other workers have dramatically greater productivity levels.[3] Some argue that recent developments, from self-driving cars to the merging of computers and robots to produce machines that can outperform humans in a wide range of tasks, portend a future of ever-rising productivity growth rates. If so, however, these changes may be accompanied by ever-increasing inequality.

A number of small textile mills like the Slater mill soon followed, but mills did not become numerous until after the Embargo Act of 1807, which restricted the importation of cotton textiles from England. Between 1805 and 1814, 94 new cotton mills were built in New England.

In 1814, in Waltham, Massachusetts, the Boston Associates built the first mechanized factory that combined spinning and weaving to produce cotton fabric. Eight years later, the Boston Associates began construction on a mill located at the intersection of the Concord and Merrimack rivers, renaming the settlement Lowell in honor of Francis Cabot Lowell, who had improved on the British model for a spinning machine and power loom. When the factory opened in 1823, it employed young women from New England farm families, who lived in dormitories provided by the company, and this way of working soon became known as the Lowell system.

Before 1820, the U.S. cotton textile industry was concentrated in three regions. The area around Providence, Rhode Island dominated, and this was followed by the Boston area. Both of these regions focused mostly on mechanized spinning. The region around Philadelphia, Pennsylvania focused on hand spinning and weaving. After 1820, however, the Boston area became for the next several decades the leading center for cotton-textile manufacturing in the United States.[4]

Scholars have shown that the areas to first industrialize in the United States were those where the wages (the value of the marginal products) of women and children were the lowest relative to those of adult males.[5] The relative productivity of women and children in the dairy, wheat, and hay-growing regions of the North was lower than that of women and children in the plantation areas of the South. As a result, women and children were largely "redundant" labor in agriculture in the Northeast. In 1810, the percentage of young women (aged 10–29) employed in wage work was quite small; over the next two decades, however, as factories became more common, the percentage of female factory workers increased. By 1832, 40 percent of the industrial workforce in the Northeast consisted of young women and children.

Labor productivity growth in cotton textiles was quite rapid during the antebellum period in New England, averaging between 2.2 percent and 3.3 percent per year between 1820 and 1860.[6] The vast majority of the labor productivity growth was due to increases in total factor productivity. Mechanization was only part of the story. The number of workers per firm almost tripled between 1820 and 1850, to an average of 97.5 workers per firm by 1850, allowing greater division of labor and economies of

FIGURE 10.2 Spinning Room in Chace Cotton Mill, Burlington, Vermont, 1909

Source: Lewis Wickes Hine, U.S. National Archives and Records Administration, 1909, catalog.archives.gov/id/523189 (accessed: June 18, 2015).

scale.[7] There is also evidence that organizational changes led to greater intensity of work, which further contributed to productivity gains.[8]

The emergence of a specialized machine-tool industry, which evolved out of the machine shops associated with New England textile mills in the 1820s and 1830s, was an important development.[9] During the nineteenth century, steady improvements in speed, power transmission, gearing mechanisms, precision metal-cutting, and many other aspects of performance all helped to stimulate growth in other industries, including firearms, boots and shoes, farm machinery, sewing machines, locomotives, cigarettes, and bicycles.[10]

By 1910, labor productivity in the U.S. cotton textile industry was remarkably high, with the typical worker in New England performing "as much work as 1.5 British, 2.3 German, and nearly 6 Greek, Japanese, Indian, or Chinese workers."[11] Despite high labor costs in the United States, New England cotton textile workers were willing and able to tend to far more machines per worker than workers in other countries (Figure 10.2).

THE AMERICAN SYSTEM OF MANUFACTURING

By the mid-nineteenth century, contemporary observers in other countries were recognizing something distinctive about many American-made goods. In the production of textiles, firearms, clocks, agricultural machinery, sewing machines, and many other items, the ideas of standardization, interchangeable parts, and division of labor in factory production were being widely implemented.[12] American goods were simple in design and easy to repair. They were not elegant or expensive, but practical, cheap, and functional.

Both supply and demand factors, which stemmed largely from the natural capital endowments in the United States, accounted for the development of the American System (see Section 6.5 for a detailed discussion of these factors). It is important to note, however, that the American System described only a small subset of industries prior to 1860. At that time, many industries were clearly inferior to their European counterparts.[13] Not until the end of the nineteenth century would the U.S. manufacturing sector assume broad-based world leadership.

IRON

Iron, too, was important to industrial development during the nineteenth century. Steam engines, made from iron, powered water pumps that revolutionized coal mining. Iron steam engines powered steamboats on western rivers, and iron rails made railroads an efficient and extensively used form of transportation. Later in the century, iron pipes allowed for construction of urban water and sewer systems in American cities.

Evidence suggests that productivity growth in iron was not as high as in cotton textiles between 1820 and 1860, with estimates of labor productivity growth between 1.5 percent and 1.7 percent per year.[14] Before the Civil War, the primary culprit for the relatively lower productivity growth was not technological backwardness but the low quality of the iron ore, which contained high levels of the mineral silica. After 1870, productivity in iron increased tremendously due to the discovery of better sources of iron ore, in the deposits at Lake Superior.[15]

THE RISE OF MODERN CORPORATIONS

By 1810, corporations were common for banking, insurance, and turnpike companies, but early corporations did not have certain advantages that corporations enjoy today. First, corporations in the early nineteenth century required special state charters which had to be granted by legislatures. While those who were politically connected might have little trouble getting a corporate charter from a U.S. state, others could spend years futilely attempting to form a corporation.

As a result, there was political pressure to implement "general" laws of incorporation that would make it possible for any group to obtain a corporate charter, provided that the group adhered to the specified regulations and met the requirements. In 1811, New York passed a law that permitted general incorporation for many types of manufacturing with capitalization less than $100,000. In 1837, Connecticut passed the Connecticut General Incorporation Act, the first general act that made incorporation the right of anyone; and by 1861, the constitutions of thirteen states allowed incorporation under general laws.

Investors in early corporations did not enjoy limited liability. For example, stockholders of English joint-stock companies typically assumed "double liability," meaning that in the case of bankruptcy stockholders were liable for twice their initial investments. Some U.S. states experimented with double liability or unlimited liability.

After 1830, however, states started passing statutes providing limited liability: a stock-holder was not personally liable for any of the debts of the company beyond the value of the stockholder's initial investment in that company. By 1860, the principle of lim-ited liability had become common throughout the United States.

TARIFF PROTECTION

In Chapter 3, the concepts of specialization based on comparative advantage and gains from trade were introduced (see Economic History in Action 3.1). It was shown that the best possible outcome is one in which countries specialize in the goods in which they have a comparative advantage (a lower opportunity cost) and voluntarily trade with other countries: this exchange makes the citizens of both countries better off.

In reality, international trade is seldom unfettered: governments often intervene. One way of doing so is by imposing tariffs. A tariff is a tax on imported goods; and, like any tax, a tariff prevents some mutually beneficial exchanges from taking place, thereby reducing the benefits of exchange. Figure 10.3 shows the welfare implications for the domestic market of imposing a tariff. The supply and demand curves represent those of domestic firms and consumers. Let's first consider the case of free trade,

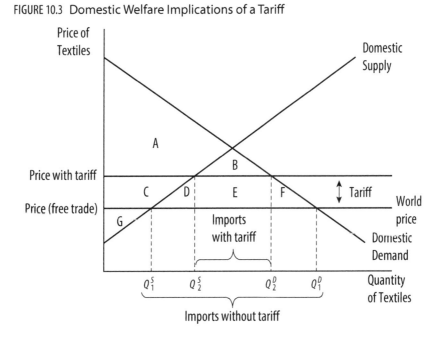

FIGURE 10.3 Domestic Welfare Implications of a Tariff

	Consumer Surplus	Producer Surplus	Tax Revenue	Total Surplus
Free Trade	A+B+C+D+E+F	G	—	A+B+C+D+E+F+G
Tariff	A+B	C+G	E	A+B+C+E+G
Change	−(C+D+E+F)	+C	+E	−(D+F)

where the world price is below the intersection of domestic supply and demand. At the world price, domestic demand is Q_1^D and domestic supply is Q_1^S. When domestic quantity demanded exceeds domestic quantity supplied, the difference must be provided through imports.

At the world price, the consumer surplus to domestic consumers is the area A+B+C+D+E+F. Recall that consumer surplus reflects the area between consumers' maximum willingness to pay and the price that consumers actually have to pay, up to the quantity purchased (see Chapter 1). Producer surplus for domestic firms is the area G, the difference between the price sellers receive and the supply curve up to the quantity supplied. With free trade, the total surplus (the sum of consumer and producer surplus) is the area A+B+C+D+E+F+G.

Now consider the implementation of a tax on imports. Provided that the country is a small country whose actions do not affect world prices, the price in the domestic market increases by the amount of the tariff. At the higher price, domestic consumers are worse off. Consumers buy less (Q_2^D) and consumer surplus is now only the area A+B. Domestic producers, however, are better off. Because domestic prices are higher, domestic producers are able to sell more to domestic consumers, and producer surplus with the tariff is now the area C+G. The government also benefits from the tariff through the collection of tax revenue equal to the amount of imports multiplied by the size of the tariff (area E). Note, however, that the area D and the area F are both lost. Areas D and F represent the deadweight loss of the tariff. That is, the deadweight loss is the loss in total surplus that results from some mutually beneficial exchanges no longer taking place because of the tariff.

If tariffs generate deadweight losses, then why have tariff rates been so high (Figure 10.4) throughout most of American history?

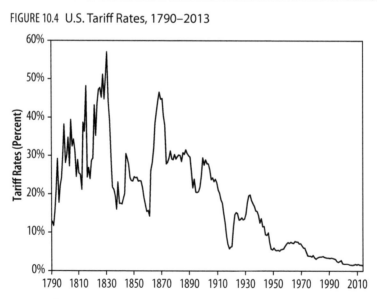

FIGURE 10.4 U.S. Tariff Rates, 1790–2013

Sources and Notes: 1790–1836 from Douglas A. Irwin, "New Estimates of the Average Tariff of the United States, 1790–1820," *Journal of Economic History* 63, no. 2 (June 2003), Table 1, column 6, 508–509; 1837–1970 from U.S. Bureau of the Census, *Historical Statistics: Colonial Times to 1970,* series U211, 888; 1971–1995 from U.S. Census Bureau, *Statistical Abstract of the United States,* various years; and 1996–2013 from the World Bank, data.worldbank.org/indicator/TM.TAX.MRCH.SM.AR.ZS (accessed: April 3, 2016).

One reason for high tariff rates was the need to raise tax revenues. Without a permanent income tax until 1913, tariffs were an important source of federal tax revenues. Another justification for tariffs is the infant industry argument.[16] Protecting new (infant) industries from foreign competition can allow time for these industries to grow and mature. Without this protection, it might prove impossible for the domestic industry to flourish. While protectionism has costs in the short run (deadweight losses), in the long run the creation and development of domestic industries may yield substantial benefits to the country and its citizens. Opponents, however, stress that once this idea is accepted, special interest groups of all kinds will lobby for tariff protection, whether or not the protectionism will ever benefit the general public.

In the antebellum period, U.S. cotton textiles, iron, and many other industries were protected from foreign competition, primarily from England, by high tariff rates. Evidence suggests that tariff protection was particularly important for the development of the domestic iron industry. In each year between 1827 and 1846, tariff rates on imported iron were over 40 percent, peaking at 70.8 percent in 1831.[17] It is estimated that tariff protection allowed U.S. iron production to be about 30 to 40 percent greater than it would have been with free trade.[18]

The development of cotton textiles may have been less dependent on tariff protection. There is widespread agreement that the Jeffersonian Embargo from 1808 to 1815 aided the development of the New England textile industry, and the Tariff of 1816 may have been necessary to allow domestic output to continue to expand.[19] Although tariff rates for textiles increased from less than 20 percent in 1816 to more than 50 percent by the early 1830s, tariff protection may not have been necessary in the cotton textile industry by the late 1820s, although this conclusion is subject to debate.[20]

It is clear, however, that high tariff rates remained in place for over a century more, well beyond what could possibly have been necessary to protect "infant industries." The country was highly protectionist after the Civil War, and despite the strength and dominance of American manufacturers, import barriers were increased by the Fordney-McCumber Tariff (1922) and the Smoot-Hawley Tariff (1930).

MANUFACTURING IN 1860

Cotton textile and iron industries are symbolic of the first industrial revolution, but they were not typical of U.S. manufacturing in 1860. While cotton goods were the most important, ranked by value added, and iron ranked sixth, both cotton and iron were geographically concentrated, with textiles concentrated in New England and iron in Pennsylvania. Throughout the United States, the more typical manufacturing establishment was a lumber mill, a flour mill, or a boot and shoe maker (Table 10.1).

Although cotton textile mills and iron foundries were not large by modern standards, they were large firms for the time. For example, while the average cotton textile mill had almost 100 employees in 1850, the typical flour mill had only one or two employees.[21]

By 1860, New England and the Middle Atlantic produced 68 percent of the manufactured goods in the United States. The Midwest was next with almost 19 percent. Prior to the Civil War (and for many decades after), the South well lagged behind the rest of the country.

TABLE 10.1 Manufacturing in the United States in 1860 (Ranked by Value Added)			
Item	Value Added (Dollars)	Percent of Total Manufacturing Value Added	Number of Employees
Cotton Goods	$54,671,082	6.40%	114,955
Lumber	$53,569,942	6.27%	75,595
Boots and Shoes	$49,161,124	5.75%	123,026
Flour and Meal	$40,083,056	4.69%	27,682
Men's Clothing	$36,680,803	4.29%	114,800
Iron	$35,689,276	4.18%	48,975
Machinery	$32,565,843	3.81%	41,223
Woolen Goods	$25,032,489	3.00%	40,597
Carriages and Wagons	$23,654,560	2.77%	37,102
Leather	$22,785,715	2.67%	22,679

Source: Computed using United States Census Office, *Manufacturers of the United States in 1860* (Washington, DC: Government Printing Office, 1865), 733–742. Value added is computed as the difference between the value of output and the value of raw material in each industry.

10.2 THE RISE OF BIG BUSINESS

Between 1865 and 1914, the American economy assumed many of its modern characteristics, including the emergence of large-scale enterprises that dominated their industries. One of the main issues in the debate over the rise of big business is the extent to which it reflected efficient responses to technological changes and economies of scale, or whether the pursuit of monopoly power and market control were the real driving forces.

RAILROADS

Before the Civil War, there was only one industry in the United States that could be considered "big business," and that was the railroad industry. During the 1850s, the largest east–west rail routes were capitalized at values from between $17 million to $35 million. In contrast, only a few of the largest textile, iron-making, and metal-working factories had capital values over $1 million.[22]

While railroads do not produce manufactured goods but only transport goods and people, they had a profound influence on the development of manufacturing in the United States. Large manufacturing corporations later adopted several of the innovations in finance and operations that were introduced by railroads from the 1850s to the 1870s.

Because of their scale and scope, the demands of railroads on financial intermediaries and financial markets stimulated development of the U.S. financial sector. The huge increase in railroad securities (bonds and stocks) brought trading and speculation to the New York Stock Exchange. For example, prior to the railroads, on one day in March 1830 only 31 shares of stock were traded. By the mid-1850s, however, hundreds of thousands of shares were traded weekly. After the Civil War, large manufacturers started to rely on New York markets and banks for financing, as well.

The operational complexity of multiple lines operating in different states demanded the creation of the first administrative hierarchies in American business. Daniel

C. McCallum, superintendent of the New York and Erie Railroad in the 1850s, developed an organizational chart to show the structure of the railroad company.[23] Early organizational hierarchies in railroads were later modified for use in other corporations. In most large corporations, there is a Chief Executive Officer at the top, and also a Board of Directors. Below are the Vice Presidents of the various divisions, with Department Heads below them, and so on.

The size and complexity of railroads also required new ways of measuring costs and revenues. Railroads developed modern methods of accounting in terms of financial, capital, and cost accounting. The ability of railroads to measure marginal and average costs, along with marginal and average revenues, allowed for rational, profit-maximizing behavior with accurate information. In the decades after the Civil War, these methods were quickly adopted in many other industries.

INFORMATION PROCESSING

Before the Civil War, the typical manufacturing establishment was quite small, generally consisting of one or more owners or managers, a small number of skilled artisans, and perhaps a few unskilled workers.[24] In small firms, owners and workers could coordinate and manage production through informal oral communication. Any external transactions were recorded in simple ledgers using double-entry bookkeeping.

The tremendous increase in the size of firms and the complexity of operations, particularly during the period 1880–1920, was contingent upon developing new ways of recording, storing, retrieving, analyzing, and communicating information within the firm. The rapid growth of manufacturing encouraged, and was also built upon, the creation and diffusion of information-processing technologies, including both office equipment and bureaucratic systems. The increased demand for information led to an explosion in the number of clerical workers, from fewer than 75,000 in 1870 to almost 3 million in 1920, an increase of 3,700 percent.[25]

In 1874, Remington introduced the first mass-produced typewriter, and in 1886, *Scientific American* estimated that more than 50,000 typewriters had been sold. Almost 150,000 typewriters were sold in 1900 alone. Typewriters allowed trained typists to record information several times faster than was possible with handwriting. In addition, the use of carbon paper allowed typists to produce several copies at once.

Early adding machines used dials and levers to enter numbers. In the mid-1880s, adding machines that used keys instead were developed, and the Burroughs Adding Machine Company introduced a machine that could print out numbers as they were entered, providing a way to record and verify calculations. By the 1920s, many other important office appliances were in use, including billing machines, cash registers, dictating machines, and rotary mimeographs. The mimeograph allowed for the rapid and inexpensive production of hundreds of copies at once.

The proliferation of documents required new ways to store and organize this information. The first commercially successful vertical filing cabinets were made by the Library Bureau, a firm founded by Melvin Dewey, to store the card indexes developed for use with the Dewey Decimal System (DDC). Dewey introduced his system in 1876, and today it is one of the most widely used classification system in the world, utilized in libraries throughout the world, including the Library of Congress.

Vertical filing was introduced to the business community at the 1893 Chicago World's Fair, where it won a gold medal: it was an effective solution to the problem of how best to organize, store, and retrieve paper documents. Vertical filing entailed more than just file drawers and folders to hold papers; it also included methods of organizing papers into folders and folders into drawers in a way that organized all documents (incoming, outgoing, and internal) in a single logical system arranged by subject, by location, or by any other categorization appropriate to the business.

Another important innovation, and a precursor to modern computers and information technology, was punched-card tabulating. Herman Hollerith developed a mechanical tabulator based on punched cards, which could tabulate statistics from millions of pieces of data. He founded the Tabulating Machine Company, which later became the International Business Machines Corporation (IBM). Punched cards allowed the rapid sorting and tabulation of quantitative data. Hollerith first used his machine to help the U.S. Census Bureau tabulate the 1890 Census more rapidly than had been done previously. After he lost the business of the U.S. Census, around 1900, Hollerith moved into the commercial market, working with, among others, several insurance companies, the New York Central Railroad, Edison Electric, and the department store Marshall Fields. IBM was founded in 1911; by 1930 it dominated the tabulating market, outdistancing its nearest competitor, Remington Rand, eight to one in installations.[26] In the 1950s, tabulating companies, led by IBM, were the first commercial adopters of computers.

MERGERS AND CONSOLIDATIONS

Between 1879 and 1904, the emergence of giant corporations was largely due to mergers and consolidations of existing firms. Integration can occur in two general ways: horizontally or vertically (Figure 10.5).

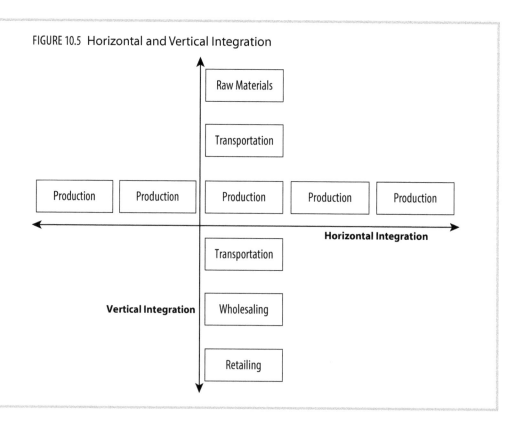

FIGURE 10.5 Horizontal and Vertical Integration

With horizontal integration, consolidation takes place at the same stage of the production process, where all of the firms are engaged in identical or similar activities. John D. Rockefeller's Standard Oil initially dominated through horizontal integration in the oil-refining industry, although it also integrated vertically. Rockefeller entered the business in 1862, and acquired oil refineries that produced kerosene for lighting and heating in Pittsburg, Philadelphia, New York, Ohio, and elsewhere. By 1890, Standard Oil controlled 88 percent of the refined-oil flows in the United States.

Legal changes made it easier for firms to merge and consolidate. Under a trust agreement, the stockholders of several corporations that were previously in competition with each other turned over their shares to a group of trustees and received "certificates of trust" in exchange. The trustees then assumed voting control over the companies and the former stockholders received dividends on their trust certificates. In 1881, Rockefeller combined Standard Oil with 39 allied companies to establish the Standard Oil Trust.[27] Trusts soon dominated many of the nation's key industries, from meatpacking to sugar refining to the manufacture of copper wire.

When trusts were declared illegal in several states, the New Jersey legislature revised its statues of incorporation in 1889 to allow corporations to hold the stocks of one or more subsidiary corporations, forming holding companies. In order to have absolute control, a holding company would have to own more than 50 percent of the voting stock in each of the subsidiary corporations; but in practice, especially as shares became widely dispersed, it was possible to maintain effective control with a far smaller percentage of the voting stock.

A vertically integrated company is one that owns and controls each stage of the production process, from acquiring raw materials to the production, marketing, and sales of the final product. In steel, the Carnegie Company was formed primarily through vertical integration. When Andrew Carnegie merged the Carnegie Company with J.P. Morgan's companies in 1901 to form United States Steel, this became by far the largest corporation in the world. It controlled two-thirds of the nation's furnaces and mills; and it also owned a large proportion of the vast ore reserves in the Lake Superior region, more than 50,000 acres of land with coal, more than 1,100 miles of railroad, and a fleet of lake steamers and barges.

During the first phase of the concentration movement (1879–1893), there were many technological innovations. A partial list of innovations in the 1870s and 1880s includes the roller mill, used to process oatmeal and flour; refrigerated cars, used in meatpacking; food-preparation and can-sealing machinery, used in mass-producing canned foods; the Bessemer and open-hearth processes, used in steel-making; and improved metal-working machinery.[28]

Many of these new technologies permitted mass production and generated lower average costs per unit through economies of scale. Factories grew much more rapidly in size in the 1870s and 1880s than in later decades, due to the exceptional pace of technological change. While there were certainly many instances of consolidation to gain market power and reduce price competition during the first phase of consolidation, opportunities for increased efficiency through economies of scale were also important.

However, during the Great Merger Wave (1898–1902), which consisted mostly of horizontal integration, the primary motives were to reduce price competition and to increase market power.[29] During the Great Merger Wave, of the 93 consolidations for which it is possible to estimate market share, 72 were cases in which the consolidation controlled at least 40 percent of the market. In 40 cases, the market share of the consolidated firm controlled 70 percent or more of the market.[30] Scholars conclude that the Great Merger Wave "cannot be explained by unreaped economies of scale."[31]

RAILROADS AND ANTITRUST POLICIES

In the decades after the Civil War, the growth of the size of the railroad industry, and later of the manufacturing industry, provoked a public outcry, and for the first time the federal government stepped in to regulate transportation and industry. In 1887, the federal government passed the Interstate Commerce Act and created the Interstate Commerce Commission (ICC), which was charged with ensuring that railroad rates were "reasonable and just." Similarly, Congress passed the Sherman Antitrust Act (1890), which outlawed "Every contract, combination in the form of trust or otherwise, or conspiracy, in restraint of trade or commerce ..."[32]

Although there have been many court cases and much further legislation, these acts marked the beginning of the federal government's involvement in maintaining market competition. In Chapter 17, the rationale, history, and effectiveness of regulations and antitrust policies are examined.

THE START OF INDUSTRIAL LEADERSHIP

By the mid-1890s, the United States produced more manufactured goods than any other country in the world; and by the start of World War I in 1914, production in the United States exceeded that of its three nearest rivals combined (Britain, France, and Germany).

American manufacturing firms were not only natural-capital intensive and physical-capital intensive, but they were also much larger than their counterparts in the United Kingdom and the rest of Europe. Large-scale operations in the United States were due, in part, to a large and affluent domestic market for products. In 1900, total national income in the United States was twice that of the United Kingdom and four times greater than either France or Germany.[33]

After 1895, the U.S. industrial leadership was based on three main factors: (1) cheap and abundant sources of energy (see Chapter 6); (2) universal public schooling (see Chapter 11); and (3) high rates of capital accumulation, learning by doing, and invention.[34]

10.3   THE INTERWAR YEARS

Between the two World Wars, the manufacturing sector of the United States experienced very rapid rates of labor productivity and total factor productivity growth. The years from 1919 to 1929, in particular, stand out as a historically unprecedented period of growth in manufacturing.

THE ROARING TWENTIES

While growth rates for the economy as a whole were not unusually fast during the 1920s, the "Roaring Twenties" can certainly be used to describe the manufacturing sector. In manufacturing, both labor productivity growth and total factor productivity growth exceeded 5 percent per year (Table 10.2). During this time, 83 percent of the nonfarm total factor productivity growth in the U.S. economy was due to growth in manufacturing.[35] Because labor productivity growth of 5.45 percent barely exceeded total factor productivity growth of 5.12 percent, almost all of the labor productivity growth was due

TABLE 10.2 Growth of Labor and Total Factor Productivity in Manufacturing, 1919–2012 (Annual Growth Rates in Percent)

Time Period	Labor Productivity ($g_Y - g_L$)	Total Factor Productivity (g_A)
1919–1929	5.45	5.12
1929–1941	2.16	2.60
1941–1948	0.20	−0.52
1948–1973	2.51	1.49
1973–1989	2.42	0.57
1989–2000	3.56	1.58
2000–2007	4.60	1.90
2007–2013	2.30	−0.20

Sources: For time periods from 1919 to 2000: Alexander J. Field, "Technological Change and U.S. Productivity Growth in the Interwar Years," Journal of Economic History 66, no. 1 (March 2006), Table 3, 214. For 2000–2007 and 2007–2013: U.S. Bureau of Labor Statistics, "Multifactor Productivity Trends in Manufacturing 2013," Economic News Release (July 28, 2015), Table A, www.bls.gov/news.release/prod5.nr0.htm (accessed: August 27, 2015).

to total factor productivity growth (technological and organizational changes), with only 0.33 percent per year the result of more capital per hour of work (capital deepening).

The extraordinary total factor productivity growth in manufacturing during the 1920s is attributable to several factors. First was the development and widespread use of small electrical motors.[36] In the factory, the replacement of centralized steam power with many small electric motors allowed factories to be organized in a manner that better utilized existing floor space and that substantially improved the speed and flow of production. Electricity was probably first used to power machinery in factories in 1883, but electricity diffused relatively slowly—it was not until 1920 that electric power eclipsed steam power in factories. Adoption subsequently accelerated, and by 1929 nearly 80 percent of factory power was electric.[37]

Electric motors were also important on the output side, and are associated with a "consumer revolution" in the 1920s. Many new consumer products that relied on small electric motors became important household appliances, including refrigerators, washing machines, and vacuum cleaners. Radios, indoor lighting, and toasters also relied on electricity. While virtually no American households owned radios in 1920, 40 percent did by 1930. Between 1920 and 1930, the proportion of American households with electric lighting increased from 35 percent to 68 percent; those with washing machines increased from 8 percent to 24 percent; and those with vacuum cleaners increased from 9 percent to 30 percent.[38]

Other industries contributed substantially to the productivity growth of manufacturing during the 1920s, including the petroleum and automobile industries.[39] The automobile industry thrived as the result of mass-production methods, inexpensive materials, and fuels. Just 26 percent of American households owned a car in 1920, but 60 percent did a decade later. By 1929, there were 26.7 million automobiles in the United States, one car for every 4.5 Americans.[40] U.S. automobiles also dominated American manufactured exports, with the U.S. share of worldwide automobile exports exceeding 70 percent by 1928.[41]

The success of electric household appliances and automobiles was helped by the development of consumer credit and by widespread advertising.[42] The majority of consumer credit during the 1920s was provided by consumer finance companies. Before 1924, sales finance companies purchased installment contracts from automobile dealers on a "full recourse" basis, meaning that if the buyer failed to meet his or her contractual obligations, the automobile dealer was fully responsible. Beginning in 1924, however, many finance companies began to purchase installment contracts on a "no recourse" basis, absolving automobile dealers of all financial responsibility should a buyer default on the loan, although dealers were obligated to repurchase any cars that finance companies had repossessed following nonpayment.[43]

The automobile industry was not the only industry that benefitted from installment credit plans that allowed purchasers to take immediate possession—to "buy now, and pay later." Such plans extended to the purchases of other consumer durables, including electric appliances and furniture. At the same time, advertising became an increasingly important way to stimulate demand for consumer durable goods.

MANUFACTURING DURING THE GREAT DEPRESSION

According to the National Bureau of Economic Research, there were actually two severe contractions during the Great Depression. The first contraction was from August 1929 to March 1933, and there was a second from May 1937 to June 1938.[44] Many economic historians refer to the entire period from 1929 to 1941 as the "Great Depression," since the economy fell below its long-run trend in mid-1929 and did not return to its long-run trend until at least 1941. If workers on New Deal work relief programs are excluded, the U.S. unemployment rate in every year between 1931 and 1940 exceeded 14 percent.[45]

One would not normally think of an extended period of low output and high unemployment as one in which there was a great deal of technological and organizational change, but research suggests that the 1930s also experienced historically rapid total factor productivity growth in manufacturing. While total factor productivity growth from 1929 to 1941 was only half what it was from 1919 to 1929 (2.60 percent compared with 5.12 percent), it was still more rapid than it has been in any period since (Table 10.2).

One important cause for productivity growth in manufacturing during the 1930s was an expansion of privately-funded research and development (R&D), a practice that began with Thomas Edison at Menlo Park, New Jersey, in 1876. Total R&D employment in U.S. manufacturing increased from 6,274 in 1927 to 10,918 in 1933, and to 27,777 in 1940.[46] Other measures also suggest an increasing emphasis on research and development, with inflation-adjusted spending on R&D more than doubling during the 1930s, and more research labs created between 1929 and 1936 (73) than in the 1919–1928 period (66).[47] Other developments played a role too, including a trend toward larger-capacity equipment, the use of new materials (particularly plastics and alloy steel), improved chemical processes, and a variety of innovations that increased thermal efficiency.[48]

10.4 DECADES OF DOMINANCE

After World War II, the U.S. economy was the world's most productive by virtually any measure, with the manufacturing sector leading the way. "American-made" signaled a trademark of excellence, whether in automobiles, consumer electronics, or clothing.

The dominance of American firms was clearly visible across virtually all manufacturing industries. The U.S. share of worldwide industrial production reached almost 45 percent in 1953.[49] Two years later, U.S. automobile manufacturers produced 9 million cars, more than four times more than Canada, Germany, France, and Italy combined.[50]

In the quarter century after World War II, the global dominance of the U.S. manufacturing sector was the result of several factors. Although labor productivity and total factor productivity growth in manufacturing were both near zero from 1941 to 1948, the United States was the only major power whose factories were not bombed extensively during World War II, and this provided an advantage to U.S. firms for many years after the War had ended. Manufacturing also benefitted from the expansion of the "military–industrial complex" after World War II.[51] During and after the Cold War, large government contracts to produce machinery, aircrafts, and weapons aided U.S. manufacturers for decades.

Higher educational attainment in the United States contributed to the high rates of productivity growth in American manufacturing, particularly between the 1920s and the 1960s. The United States was decades ahead of most other countries in both high school and college graduation rates. By the mid-1950s, due to the high school movement (1910–1940) and post-World War II increases in college enrollment, the United States had the best-educated workforce in the world (see Chapter 11).

10.5 THE DECLINE OF MANUFACTURING?

While it is true that the share of employment in manufacturing declined from over 30 percent of the U.S. workforce after World War II to less than 10 percent of the workforce by 2010, the growth rate of manufacturing output since the end of World War II has matched growth rates in the rest of the economy.

Figure 10.6 illustrates both the decline in the manufacturing share of employment and the steady manufacturing share of real GDP. A constant manufacturing share of real GDP means that manufacturing output has grown at roughly the same rate as GDP.

When growing output is combined with falling employment, labor productivity, by definition, must increase. As shown in Table 10.2, labor productivity growth in American manufacturing averaged almost 4 percent per year between 1989 and 2007, which is faster than the "golden age" (1948–1973) figure of 2.51 percent. Although labor productivity growth slowed to 2.3 percent between 2007 and 2013, this growth was wholly due to capital deepening, with total factor productivity growth slightly negative from 2007 to 2013.

It is too early to conclude whether low total factor productivity growth is the new norm or a short-run phenomenon, due to the global financial crisis in 2007–2008 and its aftermath. U.S. manufacturers continue to spend far more on research and development than those in any other country, but manufacturers' R&D spending is rising more rapidly in China, Korea, and Taiwan.

The stability of manufacturing output to GDP ratio may be more fragile than it appears, as it relies almost exclusively on very rapid growth in one narrow sector of manufacturing: computers and electronics.[52] With computers and electronics excluded from the calculations, total factor productivity between 1987 and 2011 falls from 1.3 percent per year to only 0.3 percent per year.[53]

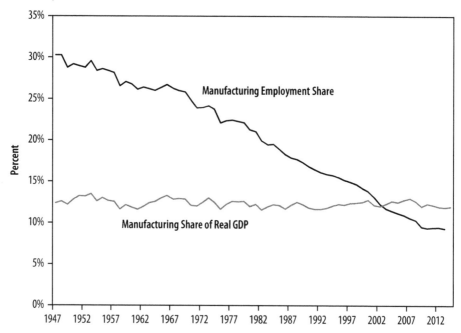

FIGURE 10.6 Manufacturing Value Added and Employment as a Share of the Total U.S. Economy, 1947–2014

Sources and Notes: U.S. Bureau of Economic Analysis, Industry Accounts, various files, www.bea.gov/industry/gdpbyind_data.htm (accessed: July 2, 2015). Output is measured as value added in 2009 prices, while employment is measured as full-time equivalent employees.

The United States saw a disproportionally large decline in manufacturing employment between 2000 and 2007, which is likely to have been the result of lower tariffs for imported products from China after it had joined the World Trade Organization in 2001.[54] The long-term decline, however, is in line with what the other G-7 countries have experienced in recent decades (Figure 10.7). The long-term decline in the manufacturing share of employment has meant that there are fewer jobs available at good wages for those who lack advanced education. It has also caused harm to cities, and their residents, where job losses have been particularly severe. The bankruptcy of Detroit in 2013, the largest municipal bankruptcy in American history, is emblematic of the disruptions that have occurred. While structural change is a common theme in American economic history, this does not lessen the pain for the individuals most affected.

10.6 CONCLUSIONS

The long-run decline of the agricultural share of employment (Chapter 9) and the rise and decline of the manufacturing share of employment (this chapter) are important structural transformations that have many similarities—as well as some differences—in comparison with what most other high-income countries in the world today have

FIGURE 10.7 Manufacturing Employment Shares: G-7 Countries, 1970–2012

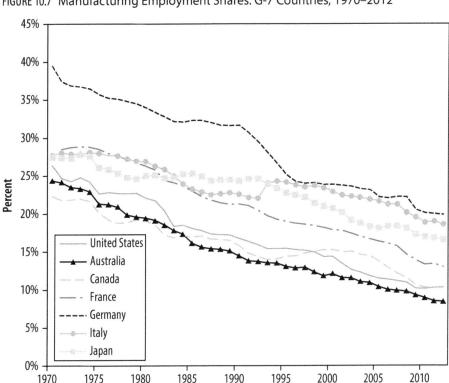

Source: U.S. Bureau of Labor Statistics, "International Comparisons of Annual Labor Force Statistics, 1970–2012," *International Labor Comparisons* (June 7, 2013), www.bls.gov/fls/flscomparelf/lfcompendium.xls (accessed: July 5, 2015). Data in the figure above are computed as the ratio of manufacturing employment (Table 2.4) to total employment (Table 2.1).

experienced. While the manufacturing sector has been an engine of growth throughout almost all of American history, recent developments paint a somewhat contradictory picture of the present and the future of the manufacturing sector in the United States.

QUESTIONS

1. New England was the first region of the country to industrialize. Why did it happen there first and not in other parts of the country?

2. A survey of Ph.D. economists who are members of the American Economic Association shows that over 83 percent of respondents agree with the following statement: "The U.S. should eliminate remaining tariffs and other barriers to trade."[55] Why do most economists support "free trade"? How do you reconcile this with the fact that the U.S. manufacturing sector thrived during the nineteenth century, when there were high tariffs on imported manufactured goods?

3. Explain the difference between horizontal and vertical integration. When was the "Great Merger Wave," and was it largely one of vertical integration or of horizontal integration? Overall, was this wave of mergers good for the U.S. economy or not? Explain.

4. Throughout all of the twentieth century and up to 2010, the United States was the world's leading manufacturing economy. Explain the factors that allowed the U.S. to overtake Great Britain by 1900 and to maintain that lead for so long.

5. Since the end of World War II, the share of employment in manufacturing has declined from more than 30 percent of the workforce to less than 10 percent by 2010. What factors have caused the proportion of manufacturing workers to decline so precipitously, and to what extent should this decline be of concern to policymakers and others? Explain.

NOTES

[1] Robert C. Allen, *Global Economic History: A Very Short Introduction* (New York, NY: Oxford University Press, 2011), 79–83.

[2] Robert J. Gordon, "Is U.S. Economic Growth Over? Faltering Innovation Confronts the Six Headwinds," National Bureau of Economic Research Working Paper, no. 18315 (August 2012), www.nber.org/papers/w18315.pdf.

[3] See, for example, Erik Brynjolfsson and Andrew McAfee, *Race Against the Machine: How the Digital Revolution is Accelerating Innovation, Driving Productivity, and Irreversibly Transforming Employment and the Economy* (Digital Frontier Press, 2012).

[4] David R. Meyer, *The Roots of American Industrialization* (Baltimore, MD: Johns Hopkins University Press, 2003).

[5] Claudia Goldin and Kenneth Sokoloff, "Women, Children, and Industrialization in the Early Republic: Evidence from the Manufacturing Censuses," *Journal of Economic History* 42, no. 4 (December 1982), 741–774; and Claudia Goldin and Kenneth Sokoloff, "The Relative Productivity Hypothesis of Industrialization: The American Case, 1820 to 1850," *Quarterly Journal of Economics* 99, no. 3 (August 1984), 461–487. Empirical support for this hypothesis can be found in Lee A. Craig and Elizabeth B. Field-Hendry, "Industrialization and the Earnings Gap: Regional and Sectoral Tests of the Goldin-Sokoloff Hypothesis," *Explorations in Economic History* 30, no. 1 (January 1993), 60–80.

[6] Kenneth Sokoloff, "Productivity Growth in Manufacturing during Early Industrialization: Evidence from the American Northeast, 1820–1860," in Stanley Engerman and Robert Gallman (eds.), *Long-Term Factors in American Economic Growth* (Chicago, IL: University of Chicago Press, 1986), 698.

[7] Kenneth L. Sokoloff, "Was the Transition from the Artisan Shop to the Nonmechanized Factory Associated with Gains in Efficiency? Evidence from the U.S. Manufactures Censuses of 1820 and 1850," *Explorations in Economic History* 21, no. 4 (October 1984), 354.

[8] William Lazonick and Thomas Brush, "The 'Horndal Effect' in Early U.S. Manufacturing," *Explorations in Economic History* 22, no. 1 (January 1985), 53–96.

[9] Nathan Rosenberg, "Technological Change in the Machine Tool Industry, 1840–1910," *Journal of Economic History* 23, no. 4 (December 1963), 414–443.

[10] Richard R. Nelson and Gavin Wright, "The Rise and Fall of American Technological Leadership: The Postwar Era in Historical Perspective," *Journal of Economic Literature* 30, no. 4 (December 1992), 1937.

[11] Gregory Clark, "Why Isn't the Whole World Developed? Lessons from the Cotton Mills," *Journal of Economic History* 47, no. 1 (March 1987), 141.

12 David A. Hounshell, *From the American System to Mass Production, 1800–1932: The Development of Manufacturing Technology in the United States* (Baltimore, MD: Johns Hopkins University Press, 1984).

13 John James and Jonathan S. Skinner, "The Resolution of the Labor-Scarcity Paradox," *Journal of Economic History* 45, no. 3 (September 1985), 513–540.

14 Sokoloff (1986), 698.

15 Robert C. Allen, "The Peculiar Productivity History of American Blast Furnaces, 1840–1913," *Journal of Economic History* 37, no. 3 (September 1977), 605–633.

16 Alexander Hamilton first articulated the infant industry argument in his *Report on Manufactures* (1791), but it was more fully articulated by Daniel Raymond in *Thoughts on Political Economy* (1820). Infant industry arguments are part of modern strategic trade theory.

17 Joseph H. Davis and Douglas A. Irwin, "The Antebellum U.S. Iron Industry: Domestic Production and Foreign Competition," *Explorations in Economic History* 45, no. 3 (July 2008), Table 3, 262.

18 Davis and Irwin, 254.

19 Douglas A. Irwin and Peter Temin, "The Antebellum Tariff on Cotton Textiles Revisited," *Journal of Economic History* 61, no. 3 (September 2001), 797.

20 Irwin and Temin, Figure 1, 781. Irwin and Temin (791) conclude, "even if the tariff had been abolished in the late 1820s, the results suggest that domestic production would not have fallen by a substantial amount." Other scholars, however, disagree with this assessment. C. Knick Harley, "The Antebellum Tariff: Different Products or Competing Sources? A Comment on Irwin and Temin," *Journal of Economic History* 61, no. 3 (September 2001), 802, argues otherwise: "if the tariff had been removed, British cloth would have been significantly cheaper than the American and a dramatic switch of American purchases from American cloth to the now cheaper, identical, imported cloth would have occurred."

21 Sokoloff (1984), 354.

22 Unless otherwise noted, the material from this section is based on Alfred D. Chandler, Jr., *The Visible Hand: The Managerial Revolution in American Business* (Cambridge, MA: The Belknap Press of Harvard University Press, 1977).

23 Rebecca Onion, "The First Modern Organizational Chart is a Thing of Beauty," *Slate* (February 5, 2014), www.slate.com/blogs/the_vault/2014/02/05/the_first_modern_organizational_chart_is_a_thing_of_beauty.html (accessed: July 9, 2015).

24 This section draws from JoAnne Yates, "Business Use of Information and Technology during the Industrial Age," Chapter 4 in Alfred D. Chandler, Jr., and James W. Cortada (eds.), *A Nation Transformed by Information. How Information Has Shaped the United States from Colonial Times to the Present* (New York, NY: Oxford University Press, 2003), 107–135.

25 Yates, 112.

26 Yates, 134.

27 Alfred D. Chandler, "The Enduring Logic of Industrial Success," *Harvard Business Review* (March–April 1990), 131.

28 Anthony Patrick O'Brien, "Factory Size, Economies of Scale, and the Great Merger Wave of 1898–1902," *Journal of Economic History* 48, no. 3 (September 1988), 648–649.

29 Naomi R. Lamoreaux, *The Great Merger Movement in American Business, 1895–1904* (New York, NY: Cambridge University Press, 1985), Chapters 5 and 6, 118–186.

30 Lamoreaux, 1–5.

31 O'Brien, 646.

32 For the full text of the Sherman Antitrust Act, see www.ourdocuments.gov/doc.php?flash=true&doc=51&page=transcript (accessed: June 23, 2016).

33 Nelson and Wright, 1939.

34 Robert C. Allen, "American Exceptionalism as a Problem in Global History," *Journal of Economic History* 74, no. 2 (June 2014), 339.

35 Alexander J. Field, "Technological Change and U.S. Productivity Growth in the Interwar Years," *Journal of Economic History* 66, no. 1 (March 2006), 211.

36 Field, 227.

37 Warren D. Devine, Jr., "From Shafts to Wires: Historical Perspectives on Electrification," *Journal of Economic History* 43, no. 2 (June 1983), 349 and 353.

38 Stanley Lebergott, *The American Economy: Income, Wealth, and Want* (Princeton, NJ: Princeton University Press, 1976), 248–299.

39 Field, 227.

40 James J. Flink, *The Automobile Age* (Cambridge, MA: The MIT Press, 1988), 10–11.

41 James Foreman-Peck, "The American Challenge of the Twenties: Multinationals and the European Motor Industry," *Journal of Economic History* 42, no. 4 (December 1982), 868.

42 Martha Olney, *Buy Now, Pay Later: Advertising, Credit, and Consumer Durables in the 1920s* (Chapel Hill, NC: University of North Carolina Press, 1991).

43 Olney, 107. The repurchase feature reduced moral hazard problems of dealers extending loans to poor credit risks.

44 National Bureau of Economic Research, "U.S. Business Cycle Expansions and Contractions," www.nber.org/cycles.html (accessed: July 11, 2015).

45 Robert Margo, "Employment and Unemployment in the 1930s," *Journal of Economic Perspectives* 7, no. 2 (Spring 1993), 41–59.

46 Field, 214.

47 David Mowery and Nathan Rosenberg, "Twentieth Century Technological Change," in Stanley Engerman and Robert Gallman (eds.), *Cambridge Economic History of the United States*, Volume 3 (Cambridge, MA: Cambridge University Press, 2000), 814 and 819.

48 Field, 216.

49 Larry Schweikart, *The Entrepreneurial Adventure: A History of Business in the United States* (Fort Worth, TX: Harcourt College Publishers, 2000), 385.

50 John Rae, *The American Automobile Industry* (Woodbridge, CT: Twayne Publishers, 1985), 174.

51 In President Dwight D. Eisenhower's farewell address in 1961, he warned the nation about the dangers of the power and influence of a "military–industrial complex."

52 Martin Neil Baily and Barry P. Bosworth, "U.S. Manufacturing: Understanding Its Past and Its Potential Future," *Journal of Economic Perspectives* 28, no. 1 (Winter 2014), 8–9.

53 Baily and Bosworth, Table 3, 9.

54 See Justin R. Pierce and Peter K. Schott, "The Surprisingly Swift Decline of U.S. Manufacturing Employment," *Yale Department of Economics Working Paper* (February 2015), http://faculty.som.yale.edu/peterschott/files/research/papers/pierce_schott_pntr_20150301.pdf (accessed: April 16, 2016); and Daron Acemoglu et al., "Import Competition and the Great U.S. Employment Sag of the 2000s," http://economics.mit.edu/files/9811 (accessed: April 16, 2016).

55 Robert Whaples, "The Policy Views of American Economic Association Members: The Results of a New Survey," *Econ Journal Watch* 6, no. 3 (September 2009), Table 1, Question 1, 340, http://econjwatch.org/file_download/9/ejw_derc_sep09_whaples.pdf (accessed: July 14, 2015).

11
Education

Throughout most of its history, the United States led the world in educational attainment. An early emphasis on education, particularly in New England, caused literacy rates throughout the colonies to exceed rates in England and elsewhere. By the late nineteenth century, the United States had the highest enrollment rates in the world, as publicly funded "common schools" became the norm. In the twentieth century, the United States was the first nation to provide a high school education for the majority of its population, with high school graduation rates increasing from 9 percent in 1910 to 51 percent by 1940.[1] The tremendous increase in high school graduation laid the foundation for the dramatic expansion of higher education in the decades after World War II.

The supply of educated Americans increased tremendously over the first three-quarters of the twentieth century. Between 1900 and 1975, the educational attainment of young adults increased by 6.2 years or 0.82 years per decade. During the last 25 years of the twentieth century, however, increases in educational attainment for young adults slowed considerably, only increasing by 0.50 years in total.[2] The slow-down in the growth of educational attainment in the United States, along with rapid increases in schooling in many European and Asian countries, has caused the United States to lose its lead in terms of the quantity of education.

There are also widespread concerns about educational quality. American students do not perform particularly well on standardized tests in comparison with students in many other countries. In 2012, U.S. 15-year olds ranked 24th worldwide in reading, 28th in science, and 36th in math on the OECD Program for International Student Assessment Tests.[3] While some blame the primary and secondary school systems for this performance, others believe that other factors, such as high rates in equality and child poverty in the United States, are more likely to be the primary causes.

In contrast, the system of higher education in America is generally considered to be the best in the world. For example, according to one recent ranking, 8 of the top 10 and 32 of the top 50 universities in the world are in the United States.[4] Higher education has been under fire in recent decades as well, however, with tuition costs increasing far faster than the rate of inflation and with 6-year college graduation rates below 60 percent nationwide. Although the international reputation of American colleges and universities remains high, U.S. young adults also tend to perform relatively poorly on international assessments.[5]

The growth accounting exercises from Chapter 2 showed that educational attainment explains between 10 and 20 percent of labor productivity growth during the twentieth century, and this is consistent with what other scholars have reported.[6] Growth accounting, however, does not take into account potential spillovers or positive externalities of education that can positively impact growth beyond the private returns to education. It may also be the case that increased human capital is a complement to technological change. Overall, therefore, the impact of education may have been larger, and perhaps much larger, than the growth accounting exercises suggest.

The stagnation of growth in educational attainment since 1980 and the relatively poor performance of American students on international assessments have led many to conclude that the educational system is no longer an engine of growth, and may even be an impediment to growth.[7] In recent decades, a great deal of experimentation has led to many policy changes in education, particularly at the primary and secondary levels, to encourage greater competition and accountability. These include educational voucher programs, greater public school choice, publicly-financed charter schools, "virtual" online schools, and incentive programs for public schools based on student performance on standardized tests. Thus far, however, educational reforms have not resulted in widespread and substantial improvements in student performance.

11.1 EDUCATION AND GOVERNMENT

Throughout American history, education has been primarily financed and provided by the public sector, although private institutions have played a secondary role. In recent years, 90 percent of primary and secondary school students are enrolled in public educational institutions, and over 70 percent of college students attend public colleges and universities.[8] Many students who attend private colleges and universities also receive federal financial aid to help pay for their education, so that the government presence is larger than the enrollment figures for higher education suggest.

Education is not a pure public good (education is not nonrival and nonexcludable), so it is not immediately obvious why government should be so involved. Education is a rival good, since one student's consumption of the good does reduce another student's enjoyment and quality of the same good in the form of crowded classrooms and less individual attention from the teacher. It is also excludable in that students can be suspended from school for disciplinary reasons and private and public schools do not necessarily have to accept all students. There are, however, several reasons which explain why the government has played such a large role in the financing and provision of education from colonial times to the present.[9]

POSITIVE EXTERNALITIES

Given that a private market will underprovide goods in the presence of positive externalities (see Chapter 19), there are a number of positive externalities (public benefits) to education that could justify its public provision. If more education leads to higher labor productivity that is not fully reflected in higher wages received by an individual worker, then there is a positive external benefit to society. That is, the effect of aggregate education on aggregate earnings is likely larger than the effect of individual education on individual earnings.

Education can also provide positive externalities to society beyond the direct impacts on labor productivity. For example, educated citizens are more informed and tend to vote more frequently. This could lead, through the democratic process, to better public policies. Education is also associated with lower rates of crime, and individuals with more education also tend to have better health. Since health insurance, by definition, involves paying into a common pool, lower medical expenditures by any one individual have benefits beyond that individual. Lower crime and better health are both conducive to economic growth.

CREDIT MARKET FAILURES

Because education is a costly and long-term investment, in a private-education-only world many families would have to borrow to pay for their children's education. Consider a talented child from a poor family who, if educated, could earn a comfortable living as an adult. While it would be socially optimal to borrow money to pay for this child's education, private lenders might be unwilling to make such loans if there are no sources of collateral.

Private markets for mortgages, for example, depend on the fact that the value of the house can serve as collateral. In the event of default, the lender is able to foreclose on the property and sell it to recoup the unpaid balance on the loan. In contrast, a poor family likely has no collateral to back a loan for education. Since a bank cannot claim a family's child if the family does not pay back a loan (or garnish the child's wages when an adult), banks would be unwilling to make educational loans to those without sufficient collateral. In the United States today, federal student loans for higher education partially mitigate this problem, since the federal government can legally garnish wages or take proceeds from federal tax refunds if student loans are not repaid.

FAILURES TO MAXIMIZE FAMILY UTILITY

Even without the existence of positive externalities or credit market failures, some parents would still be likely to choose to provide less education for their children than the amount that would maximize long-term family utility. Parents might not be sufficiently altruistic to provide the optimal amount of education for their children, and children (if given the choice) might be too myopic to attend school. In this case, making loans to parents will not solve the problem, and public provision of education, along with compulsory school attendance and child labor laws, is a better alternative.

PROVIDING OPPORTUNITY AND MOBILITY

Because education is a normal good (demand increases with income), if all education were privately financed, then higher-income families would provide more education to their children than would lower-income families. More education is associated with higher incomes later in life, but a privately-financed system would limit opportunities to children who just happen, through no fault of their own, to be born to lower-income families. The widespread desire for a level playing field, such that any child has an equal opportunity to achieve the "American Dream," is another reason to provide a free education to all, regardless of family circumstances. Note, however, that while providing opportunity may require public financing, this does not necessarily imply the public provision of education.

CULTURAL VALUES

Throughout American history, public education has commonly been viewed as an effective means of assimilating millions of immigrants into mainstream American society. Public elementary and secondary schools undoubtedly help children to learn how to read, write, and calculate, but they also provide a set of common experiences that help define what it means to be an American. Throughout countless communities in the nineteenth and twentieth centuries, when nearly all students in a given location attended the same school regardless of family income levels or place of birth, the public school system helped to teach millions of children to speak English and to learn about American institutions and society.

11.2   EDUCATION IN THE AMERICAN COLONIES

By the time of the American Revolution, basic literacy rates were quite high throughout the colonies. Male literacy rates in the New England colonies were the highest, with an estimated rate of 60 percent in 1660, 70 percent in 1710, 85 percent in 1760, and 90 percent in 1790.[10] Outside New England, male literacy among non-slaves in the colonies averaged 67 percent throughout the 1700s, but this rate was higher than the 60 percent literacy rate for males in England during this time.[11] Female literacy rates in the American colonies were not as high, with most studies reporting rates about one-half that of males.[12]

The dependence of economic success in colonial America on trade and foreign markets meant that the ability to read, write, and calculate were rewarded. To navigate the institutional and legal system, one also needed the ability to draft and to understand contracts and land titles, so there were strong economic incentives to be literate and numerate in colonial America, particularly for males.[13]

In the seventeenth century, many different groups settled in what was to become the United States, but it was the Puritans and the Pilgrims who had the largest impact on American education. The Pilgrims and Puritans arrived in the New World in 1620 and 1630, respectively, but the two groups converged in their religious and political beliefs, which allowed them to effectively work together in establishing Massachusetts and the other New England colonies.

The early educational accomplishments in New England were the result of two primary factors: (1) a belief in the importance of education in fostering religion; and (2) peaceful relations with Native Americans for many decades, which allowed schools to function without fear of being attacked.[14] At the core of Puritan faith was the belief that worshippers had a direct connection to God, and that this direct connection meant that believers needed to be able to read the Bible for themselves.[15]

There were several notable educational achievements in New England during the colonial period. In 1635, just five years after Boston was founded, the public voted to establish the Boston Latin School, the first secondary school in the colonies. The Puritans and Pilgrims also established primary education in a less formal manner than at the secondary level. Initially, primary education took the form either of parents teaching their children at home or of young and widowed women teaching children for a small fee. While education stressed the importance of learning spiritual truths, instruction also focused on reading, writing, and arithmetic.

Over time, primary education became more formalized. The Massachusetts Compulsory Schooling Law (1642) was the first compulsory education law in America. It required the head of every household to teach all children in his or her home to read and to understand religious principles. In 1647, the "Old Deluder Satan" Law (so named because of the law's first sentence) required each community of 50 or more households to assign at least one person to teach all the children in the community to read and write, in exchange for payment from the townspeople. For towns of 100 or more households, the legislation required the establishment of a formal grammar school.[16] By 1689, there were laws requiring grammar schools in Connecticut and New Hampshire as well.[17]

Other groups also contributed to formal education in colonial America. Like their New England counterparts, the Dutch in New York and the Quakers in Pennsylvania and New Jersey established religious schools to teach children how to read the Bible. In the South, education tended to occur within the home, and few formal schools were established.

Massachusetts was also at the forefront of higher education in America. Many Puritan ministers were graduates of Oxford University or Cambridge University. Harvard University was founded in 1636 and was modeled after these English universities, with the primary aim of providing training for ministers. For many decades, Harvard was the only institution of higher learning in the colonies, but several other colleges were later established. Throughout the colonial period, almost all institutions of higher education were private, religious institutions. In 1693, the College of William and Mary in Williamsburg, Virginia, was founded by Anglicans. This was followed by the establishment of Yale College (1701); Princeton College (1746); and Columbia College (1754), which until 1787 was named Kings College. In another example of the importance of path dependence, Princeton, Harvard, Yale, and Columbia were ranked in 2015 as the top four national universities in the United States.[18]

11.3   THE COMMON SCHOOL MOVEMENT

After the Revolutionary War ended, many individuals thought that schools had an important role to play in building the new nation. Thomas Jefferson was an early advocate for public education, believing that it was essential to a well-functioning democracy. As the author of the Land Ordinance of 1785, Jefferson set aside one section of each township for educational purposes. Jefferson was also instrumental in founding the publicly-supported University of Virginia (1819).

ORIGINS OF THE COMMON SCHOOL MOVEMENT

Public education in America did not become widespread until the common school movement from 1830 to 1900. Advocates such as Horace Mann, the first Secretary of Education for Massachusetts and the first such official in any U.S. state, are strongly identified with the common school movement, but it was largely a grassroots and decentralized effort that played out in thousands of communities throughout the country.[19] The primary goals of the common school movement were not to increase basic literacy, since it was already quite high, but to level the playing field for rich and poor, and to provide all children with a moral education that would instill a set of common values and so help to unite the country during a period of high immigration in the mid-nineteenth century.[20]

To help achieve these goals, communities built more schools and lengthened the school year.[21] Improved training of teachers was also emphasized, and in 1839 Horace

Mann opened the first public teacher-training institute, in Lexington, Massachu-setts.[22] After the Civil War, "normal schools," now called teachers' colleges, became the primary means of educating teachers.

The common school movement had many features that subsequently became the hallmarks of the American educational system, including public funding and provi-sion, the separation of church and state, a decentralized system with thousands of fis-cally independent districts, and an "open and forgiving" structure.[23] "Open" meant that almost all children could attend school, while "forgiving" meant that students could advance to higher grades and institutions even after mediocre performance at lower grade levels. Another feature of common schools was gender neutrality, with nearly equal participation by boys and girls.[24]

Although enrollment rates varied by region, with the South and the industrial North lagging behind the rural areas in the northern states, by the end of the nine-teenth century enrollment rates in the United States exceeded 90 percent for children between the ages of 5 and 14 and were the highest in the world (Figure 11.2).

PUBLIC AND PAROCHIAL SCHOOLS

For Horace Mann and others, the separation of church and state did not preclude the teaching of religion in schools.[25] States did, however, ban the use of state and local school funds in church-run schools. New Hampshire was the first to do so in 1792, and several other states soon followed suit. Almost all of the states that entered the

FIGURE 11.1 Williams School in Brush, Colorado, 1915

Source: Lewis Wickes Hine, Library of Congress, www.loc.gov/pictures/item/ncl2004004418/PP/ (accessed: March 29, 2016).

FIGURE 11.2 Primary School Enrollment Rates by Country: Children Ages 5–14, 1830–1900

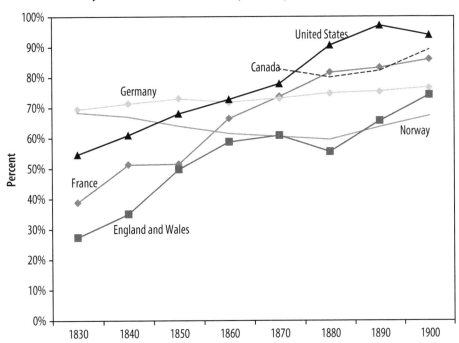

Sources and Notes: Computed from Peter H. Lindert, *Growing Public: Social Spending and Economic Growth Since the Eighteenth Century*, Volume 1 (Cambridge, UK: Cambridge University Press, 2004), Table 5.1, 91–93. Unless stated otherwise, data include enrollment in both public and private schools. Data for Germany are only from Prussia. Canada includes only public school enrollment; while data for the United States are for public school enrollment from 1830 to 1870, and for both public and private enrollments thereafter. Data for the United States for 1840 are missing in Lindert, so 1840 data are estimated by linearly interpolating using 1830 and 1850 data.

Union prior to 1876 had written constitutional provisions banning the use of school funds by religious organizations. In 1876, Congress required that all future U.S. states must include the same restriction in their constitutions.[26]

Many Roman Catholics (and some Protestant groups) strongly objected to the creation of supposedly "nonsectarian" schools. When repeated attempts to gain a share of public funds for religious schools failed to get legislative approval, many Catholics rejected the nondenominational public school compromise and created their own separate and parallel system of parochial schools. Enrollment in Catholic elementary and secondary schools reached nearly 2 million by 1920, but this was less than one-tenth of the enrollment in public schools.[27]

LEADERSHIP IN THE COMMON SCHOOL MOVEMENT

By the latter part of the nineteenth century, the rural parts of the northern states led the nation and the world in education through the creation of public common schools. Over 70 percent of the nation's students and teachers were in the rural North, although the rural North actually spent far less per pupil than other areas of the United States.[28]

Rural northern leadership was due to several factors.[29] First, education in the rural North was relatively more affordable than elsewhere. Wages for the typical worker were higher in the North than in the South or in Western Europe. In addition, there was an abundant and elastic supply of female and part-time teachers in the rural North, which kept the costs of education low. As a result, the costs of providing education relative to the wages for the typical worker were much lower in the rural northern United States than in England or in other regions of the U.S.[30]

Rural parts of northern states also had decentralized local governments with greater autonomy, and political voice was spread more broadly within these communities. Consequently, residents were willing and able to tax themselves to provide public education, and there was a great deal of competition between communities which further fueled educational expansion. In 1850, 90 percent of free children aged 5–14 were enrolled in school in the rural North, compared to 67 percent in the urban North and below 40 percent in the rural and urban South.[31]

The Civil War (1861–1865) had a profoundly negative impact on education in the American South. Between 1860 and 1870, school attendance in the South dropped by one-third, leading to school attendance rates only one-half of those in the North in 1870. In total, the shock of the Civil War left the South about three decades behind its pre-Civil War trend.[32]

SCHOOL FUNDING

In the North, the major sources of funding were local taxes, along with some state support. Private tuition was a very small source of revenue in the North, but the major source of funding in the rural South prior to the Civil War.[33] Public funding for education varied substantially by region, and the degree of inequality between areas appears to have been an important determinant of the level of public funding. Between 1850 and 1930, there was a significant negative relationship between the degree of inequality and the level of school funding.[34] In areas where the differences between rich and poor were smaller, the populace were more willing to tax themselves to provide funding for schools. Moreover, greater public funding is also associated with increased school attendance rates, particularly for poor, native-born, and rural children.[35]

EDUCATION FOR AFRICAN AMERICANS

Although the South lagged behind the North in terms of educating free white children before the Civil War, the situation for African-American children was far worse. By the 1820s, all southern states made it illegal to teach slaves how to read or write, fearing that literacy skills would make it more likely that slaves would communicate and revolt.[36] In 1860, almost 60 percent of white Americans aged 5–19 were enrolled in school, compared to less than 2 percent of black Americans. Of those black Americans who were enrolled, most were free black Americans living in northern states.[37]

Educational opportunities for free black children in the North were also very limited. In the 1840s, for example, black primary school children in Boston were restricted to two segregated schools.[38] In 1855, however, Massachusetts passed a law abolishing segregation in schools, which was the first such law in the country.[39]

It was not until after the Civil War that the South had free schools, and that led to an increase in enrollment rates for African Americans.[40] In 1880, black enrollment rates nationwide for those aged 5–19 were 33.8 percent, compared to 62 percent for whites. By 1950, black enrollment rates had almost converged, with 74.8 percent of black Americans in schools compared to 79.3 percent of white Americans.[41] While there were only small differences in enrollment rates by 1950, segregation and discrimination led to lower-quality and separate schools for African-American children (see Chapter 14).

11.4 THE AMERICAN HIGH SCHOOL

In 1900, the overwhelming majority of both white and black children were enrolled in elementary school for at least part of the year. Education beyond the eighth grade, however, was still relatively uncommon, with barely more than 10 percent of all 14- to 17-year-olds enrolled in a private or public secondary school.[42] Beginning around 1910, both high school enrollment and graduation rates began to increase dramatically, largely because of the spread of the public high school.

THE ORIGINS OF PUBLIC HIGH SCHOOLS AND PRIVATE ACADEMIES

Public high schools in urban areas were established in the decades prior to the Civil War. By 1841, there were 26 public high schools in Massachusetts. Other areas soon followed, with public high schools opening in Philadelphia (1838) and New York (1848). By 1860, there were over 320 public high schools in the United States.[43]

In the nineteenth century, most areas outside cities could not yet support a public high school. In the absence of such schools, private academies developed. Because academies generally taught students who came some distance, many academies boarded their students. Some academies taught vocational subjects, while others prepared students for college.

Public high schools and academies were not particularly widespread in the nineteenth century, however. In 1870, only 6.5 percent of 15- to 18-year-olds nationwide were attending a public high school or a private academy, with 60 percent or more of those students attending private academies.[44] By 1910, most towns with populations greater than 10,000 had at least one public high school, but still relatively few students nationwide had access to a high school education.[45]

One reason for the low enrollment rates was the fact that the vast majority of jobs did not require a high school degree. In 1870, many Americans worked in agriculture (53 percent), in manufacturing, as unskilled laborers and operatives (13 percent), or as domestic servants (10 percent). Only about 10 percent of jobs required an education beyond elementary school.[46]

This changed rapidly, however, as by the end of the nineteenth century the demand for educated workers had increased dramatically. With the rise of big business, there was tremendous growth in white-collar occupations. The emergence of large firms in manufacturing, utilities, communication, and transportation led to an increasingly complex division of labor. Jobs in banking, insurance, real estate, communication, and retail trade also increased. The invention of office machinery such as typewriters, adding machines, dictation machines, and complex filing systems increased the demand for workers with clerical skills. Many blue-collar workers now required greater education and skills also, including electricians, plumbers, printers, machinists, and auto mechanics.[47]

THE HIGH SCHOOL MOVEMENT

The increased demand for skilled workers raised the returns to education, and helped spur the high school movement in the twentieth century. Between 1910 and 1940, enrollment and graduation rates increased rapidly, and thereafter graduation rates continued to increase in most parts of the country until the 1970s (Figure 11.3).

At the beginning of the high school movement in 1910, New England states led the way and had the nation's highest enrollment and graduation rates. By 1928, however, many other states had graduation rates that exceeded those in New England. The educational leaders then included states in the Midwest, such as Iowa, Kansas, and Nebraska, as well as states on the Pacific coast, such as California, Oregon, and Washington.

The states that were the educational leaders by the late 1920s had several common characteristics.[48] First, these states had high levels of (taxable) wealth per capita, and this wealth was distributed relatively equally across the population. Second, they also had relatively large agricultural, ranching, and/or mining sectors, and comparatively small manufacturing sectors. In manufacturing states, the availability of high-paying jobs for teenagers increased the opportunity costs of attending school, with the result that enrollment rates were lower where manufacturing jobs were more prevalent. Leading areas were also places that had large numbers of competing school districts and a strong sense of community.

FIGURE 11.3 U.S. High School Graduation Rates, 1870–2010: Public and Private Graduates as a Percentage of the 17-Year-Old Population

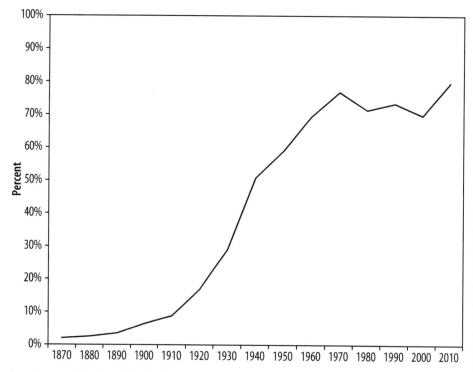

Source: Thomas N. Snyder and Sally A. Dillow, Digest of Educational Statistics 2012 (Washington, DC: U.S. Department of Education, National Center for Educational Statistics, 2013), Table 122, 189.

Two areas lagged the rest of the country during the high school movement: the industrial North and the South. Enrollment and graduation rates were low in the South, even if one excludes African Americans. In the 1910s and 1920s, young people in industrial areas often dropped out of school between the ages of 14 and 16 because of abundant and relatively well-paying job opportunities in factories and elsewhere.

This changed, however, with the massive rise in unemployment during the Great Depression of the 1930s. In addition to the general lack of employment opportunities for teenagers, the passage in 1933 of the National Industrial Recovery Act (NIRA), which prohibited the employment in manufacturing of young people under the age of 16, further contributed to increased enrollment in education and to increased graduation rates. Between 1929 and 1936, high school graduation rates more than doubled in the relatively industrial Middle Atlantic region.[49] The South, however, continued to lag well behind the rest of the country until the 1970s.

The high school movement went beyond just greater enrollment and graduation rates. There were also substantial changes in the curriculum. In 1910, in preparation for college, the typical high school student was taking a classical curriculum, rich in English, history, foreign languages, geometry, and algebra.[50] By the 1930s, however, the high school curriculum had changed substantially: it now emphasized a wide range of business subjects such as typing, stenography, and bookkeeping, as well as other vocational subjects such as woodworking, electrical work, metal-working, and farming (in rural areas) for boys, and cooking, sewing, and other household subjects for girls. In addition, courses in the arts and for life skills were added, including classes in music, dance, personal hygiene, and physical education.[51]

ECONOMIC HISTORY IN ACTION 11.1

Education and Unified Growth Theory

Unified growth theory links together many of the concepts and ideas presented in this book, including the emerging role of education in economic growth.[52] A single framework is used to explain all of human history. In early human history, there are low levels of income per capita and population, accompanied by no schooling and no income growth. As population increases, a larger population living in greater densities leads to technological change, which increases incomes and induces parents to allocate some of their income to the education of their children.

Technological change increases the returns to investments in education, and education in turn results in further technological change. At some point, the complementarity between technological change and human capital accumulation allows the world to escape the Malthusian trap.

Crucial to the model is the idea of the demographic transition (see Chapter 7), whereby the growth process creates incentives for families to have fewer and more highly-educated children. Eventually, rapid technological progress and increases in education do indeed trigger such a transition, and fertility rates then decrease permanently.

11.5 HIGHER EDUCATION

Although higher education in the United States has a long history, stretching back to the early colonial era (see Section 11.2), widespread expansion of higher education was not possible until graduation from high school became the norm. There were, however, several important developments prior to World War II that laid the groundwork for the massive increases in enrollment and graduation rates at American colleges and universities in the decades after World War II.

HIGHER EDUCATION BEFORE WORLD WAR II

The University of Georgia and the University of North Carolina were the first public universities in the United States. While the University of Georgia was the first to receive a state charter in 1785, it did not begin admitting students until 1801. The University of North Carolina was not chartered until 1789, but it started admitting its first students in 1795, prior to the University of Georgia. At least a dozen other states had opened public universities by 1819, and by 1860 nearly one-quarter of colleges and universities were public.[53]

In most states, private and public institutions coexisted, but there were exceptions to this general pattern. In many eastern states, which had longstanding and prestigious private colleges and universities, there was little room for public institutions. In contrast, the newer and more sparsely populated West introduced public institutions early in their history and never had many private colleges and universities.

The Morrill Land-Grant Act (1862) set aside federal public lands for support of state colleges and universities that emphasized agricultural, mechanical, and technological subjects, including engineering. Among the many land-grant schools established under this act were the state universities of Kansas, Michigan, Minnesota, Wisconsin, Missouri, and Vermont.[54]

The second Morrill Act (1890) was targeted at the former Confederate states. To obtain funds from the federal government, each state had either to show that race was not an admissions criterion or to designate a separate land-grant institution for African Americans. This provision led to the creation of several of today's historically black colleges and universities.

The creation of state colleges and universities peaked between 1865 and 1895, and this period was also the peak for new private colleges and universities. In 1876, Johns Hopkins University established the prototype graduate-school curriculum; this was soon taken up by many other universities, and is still the basic template for graduate education today. The University of Chicago (1890) and Stanford University (1891) were also established during this period.

By 1910, there were over 1,000 colleges and universities, including more than 100 co-educational black colleges, but only 3 percent of the college-age population nationwide attended college.[55] Although colleges and universities were relatively plentiful, by modern standards the sizes of both private and public institutions were very small. In 1900, the median private institution had only 130 students, while the median public institution had 240 students.[56] The period after World War II was accompanied by many more colleges and universities, but also much bigger ones. Modern universities—like Arizona State University with more than 80,000 students, or the 23-campus California State University system with nearly 475,000 students—would have been difficult to comprehend for someone attending college in 1900.

THE POSTWAR BOOM

By the middle of the twentieth century, the growth in U.S. education shifted from high schools to higher education. Of Americans born in 1900, only about 10 percent attended college and 4 percent graduated with a bachelor's degree. However, of those born in 1950, half attended college and 24 percent graduated.[57]

In June 1944, Congress passed the Serviceman's Readjustment Act (also called the GI Bill of Rights), which provided a wide range of benefits to returning World War II veterans, including cash payments for college tuition and living expenses. While the GI Bill did not *cause* the postwar boom in higher education, it did cause it to happen sooner.[58]

The postwar boom was largely due to an increase in public higher education. In 1900, only about 20 percent of college students attended a public university, but the percentage who attended a public institution increased to 70 percent in the postwar era.[59] However, the growth of both private and public institutions, accompanied by the geographic mobility of the college-aged population, led to vigorous competition among both private and public institutions for quality students.

By the mid-1950s, as a result of the high school movement and postwar increases in college enrollment, the United States was well ahead of other countries in terms of providing an education to its citizenry. In 1955, the average American had close to 11 years of schooling (Figure 11.4); Canadians were second, with less than 9 years of education, and most other countries of the world provided less than 8 years of education.

By 2010, however, the United States had largely lost its lead in terms of educational attainment. While Americans had 13.73 years of education on average in 2010, several other countries, including Canada, Germany, Japan, and the United Kingdom, also provided more than 13 years of education on average.

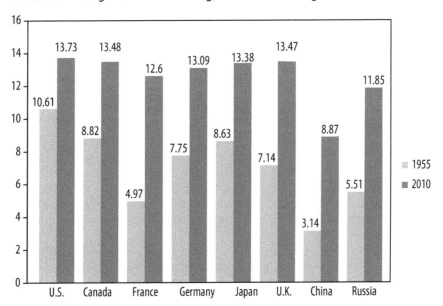

FIGURE 11.4 Average Years of Schooling, 1955 and 2010: Ages 25–29 in Each Country

Source: Computed using data from Robert Barro and Jong-Wha Lee, "A New Data Set of Educational Attainment in the World, 1950–2010," *Journal of Development Economics* 104 (April 2010), 184–198. June 2014 version available at www.barrolee.com/ (accessed: June 28, 2015).

11.6 EDUCATIONAL REFORMS SINCE WORLD WAR II

There have been critics of American schools since before the common school movement in the nineteenth century, but beginning in the 1950s the public school system became the focus of intense scrutiny. A series of articles and books criticized the "anti-intellectualism" and "watered down curriculum" of American schools.[60] The most important of these books were Arthur Bestor's *Educational Wastelands* (1953) and Rudolph Flesch's *Why Johnny Can't Read* (1955).

When the Soviet Union launched the first Sputnik rocket in 1957, beating America into space, the nation's educational system became the scapegoat. Congress reacted by passing the National Education Defense Act (1958), which provided federal funding for the training of graduate students in mathematics, sciences, and foreign languages, and in addition provided money for new school construction.[61] There were also calls for higher standards in primary and secondary schools (much like the recent school standards movement), but the political and social turbulence of the 1960s soon dominated discussions of school reform.

THE INCLUSIVENESS MOVEMENT

From the 1950s to the 1970s, there were several changes in public schools that made them more open and accommodating to students who had previously been marginalized. In 1950, African-American students were segregated by law in 17 states; Mexican-American students received less than 6 years of formal education, on average; and 72 percent of disabled students were not enrolled in school.[62]

The Supreme Court decision in Brown vs. Board of Education of Topeka (1954) outlawed segregation in American schools, overturning Plessy vs. Ferguson (1896). To enforce the decision in the South, President Dwight Eisenhower deployed federal troops in 1957 to impose integration of Central High in Little Rock, Arkansas. This, however, was only part of a longer struggle to integrate schools. The Civil Rights Act (1964) threatened the loss of federal funds if school districts refused to desegregate, while the Elementary and Secondary Education Act (1965) provided $4 billion to aid disadvantaged students. By 1972, these efforts had proved largely successful, with 91 percent of black students in the South in integrated schools.[63]

The 1960s and 1970s also witnessed the rise of bilingual education in response to the increase in immigrants from Latin America and Asia (see Chapters 7 and 15). By 1974, the federal government had allocated $68 billion for bilingual education and teaching materials had been published in nearly 70 languages.[64]

Legislation in the 1970s also included provisions for students with disabilities. Section 504 of the Rehabilitation Act (1973) required every school district to provide a "free appropriate public education" to each student, regardless of the nature and severity of the disability.

Civil rights legislation also extended to promote gender equality in education, particularly in higher education. Title IX (1972), an amendment to the Higher Education Act (1965), required that: "No person in the United States shall, on the basis of gender, be excluded from participation in, be denied the benefits of, or be subjected to discrimination under any education program or activity receiving federal financial assistance." Title IX is credited with increasing opportunities for and participation of women in high school and college athletics, as well as providing greater educational opportunities in higher education.

While Title IX may only be one of many reasons (see Chapter 14), enrollment and graduation rates for women in law, medicine, and graduate business programs began to increase substantially thereafter. For example, in 1971 less than 10 percent of medical school graduates were women, while in recent years nearly 50 percent of graduates have been women.[65]

THE STANDARDS MOVEMENT

The school standards movement started when the National Commission on Educational Excellence published a report in 1983 entitled *A Nation at Risk: The Imperative for Educational Reform*, which painted a dire picture of the state of education in America. In the "Standards and Expectations" section, the Commission recommended that "standardized tests of achievement (not to be confused with aptitude tests) should be administered at major transition points from one level of schooling to another." [66]

Since the publication of this report, standardized tests given to students have played an increasing role in terms of ranking, rewarding, and punishing students, teachers, and schools. The use of standardized tests was strengthened by the No Child Left Behind Act (2001) and "Race to the Top," the $4.35 billion contest funded as part of the American Recovery and Reinvestment Act (2009). The Common Core curriculum, a nationwide set of curricular standards adopted by almost all U.S. states by 2014, also involves the assessment of these standards through tests.

The standards movement encompasses a combination of high-stakes testing, state- or nationally-imposed curriculum standards, and various accountability measures for students, teachers, schools, and school districts.[67] The primary focus is on content, both in determining what material students should learn and then in setting up mechanisms to ensure that students have really learned this material.[68]

Critics of the school standards movement counter that a true education encompasses far more than just test performance, and that "teaching to the test" narrows the curriculum and stifles imagination and creativity in both teaching and learning.

THE SCHOOL CHOICE MOVEMENT

A related set of reforms has focused on providing more competition between schools and more choices for students and parents at the primary and secondary levels. The two main ways used to expand choices have been educational voucher programs and the proliferation of charter schools.

Educational vouchers are certificates of funding issued by the government to parents to pay for the tuition of their child at a public or private school of their choosing. While voucher programs have been introduced in many places, starting with Milwaukee, Wisconsin in 1990, only a very small percentage of students nationwide are participating in voucher programs today.

Charter schools have become far more widespread, with 4.2 percent of public school students attending such schools by 2011–2012.[69] Charter schools are publicly-funded schools of choice within the public school system, in which schools form a contract or "charter" with a public entity and are given autonomy from state and local regulations in exchange for accountability for results, typically based on students' test scores. The first charter-school law was passed in Minnesota in 1991, and by 2012 charter legislation had been adopted in 41 states and in Washington, DC.[70] Charter schools are often for-profit ventures run by private entities.

While there are some success stories, there are also instances of incompetence and corruption. Overall, "some studies in some locations find charters outperform traditional public schools, some find they are no different than the traditional ones, and some find they perform worse."[71]

STUDENT PERFORMANCE

Dissatisfaction with the performance of American schools has been a recurring theme throughout American history, even during periods when most modern scholars, looking back, believe that the educational system performed quite well.

Student achievement depends on both school factors (teacher quality, spending per pupil, etc.) and non-school factors (individual characteristics, family circumstances, local neighborhoods, etc.). In influencing student performance, teacher quality is likely the most important school factor; but overall, the non-school factors of individual and family characteristics are far more important, with an impact on student achievement that is between 4 to 8 times larger than that of teacher quality.[72]

To many critics of the reform movement, the widespread attacks on public education and public school teachers have been misplaced.[73] Neither vouchers nor charter schools have been a silver bullet, and many scholars agree that the best way to improve student performance would be to directly tackle the non-school issues of poverty and income inequality. Poverty and inequality, however, are far more difficult and costly to address than school factors like teacher quality.

Most scholars agree that the recruitment, motivation, and retention of high-quality teachers are important determinants of favorable student outcomes. Beginning in the early twentieth century, school districts introduced a single-scale salary system, where teachers' pay was based solely on years of experience and educational attainment. A single-salary scale was introduced to equalize pay between male and female teachers. However, paying the same salary to all teachers with the same education and experience, regardless of their on-the-job performance, removes all monetary incentives for doing a better job.

While the basic principle of paying teachers based on performance seems reasonable to most teachers and to the general public, in practice the accurate measurement of teacher performance is fraught with challenges. Any merit-pay system based on student test scores cannot simply reward high scores; if it did, it would simply reward teachers in wealthy neighborhoods with students who arrived at school with excellent skills. Similarly, it cannot simply reward improvements in test scores. If it did, it would unfairly penalize teachers whose students are already scoring too well to post large gains on standardized tests.

A further complication of merit pay is that teacher success depends heavily on the active cooperation and abilities of students. Teachers must devote an enormous amount of skill and energy in "motivating the client [student] to cooperate, and still the outcome is far from certain. The client may choose to spurn the practitioner's [teacher's] offer of improvement—out of apathy, habit, principle, spite, inattention, or whim. In such a field, success rates are likely to be low ..."[74] Physicians are not held monetarily accountable for their patients' obesity or neuroses, but merit-pay systems in education may hold teachers accountable for the shortcomings of their students. While statistical models can control for student differences, many teachers fear that models to measure performance will unfairly reward some teachers while penalizing others for factors outside of their control, and for reasons that have little or nothing to do with their actual on-the-job performance.

CHANGES IN SCHOOL FINANCING

Historically, education was a local concern, with most funding coming from local property taxes. Until 1930, over 80 percent of school funding was local, with states contributing the other 20 percent. Prior to recent decades, federal involvement in financing primary and secondary education was essentially nil. In recent decades, however, the local–state–federal ratios have been roughly 45–45–10, most recently with the federal share rising above 10 percent (Figure 11.5) as control and financing have shifted toward federal and state governments as a result of more broad-based reform efforts.

REFORM IN HIGHER EDUCATION

From the early 1980s to 2013, college tuition increased much faster (+440 percent) than the rate of inflation (+110 percent) or median family income (+150 percent).[75] In part because of these dramatic increases in costs, and given that the federal government provides a substantial amount of financial aid to students, the school standards movement looks poised to extend to higher education.

In 2014, the U.S. Department of Education released plans to tie federal financial aid to colleges' performance. The performance rankings will attempt to measure the net costs of colleges and universities, as well as including measures of performance and opportunity. Performance measures will likely include retention rates, graduation

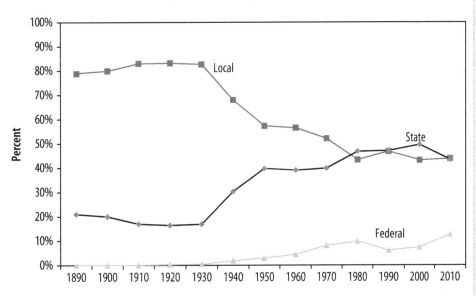

FIGURE 11.5 Share of U.S. Primary and Secondary Public School Funding, 1890–2010

Source: Computed from U.S. Department of Education, National Center for Education Statistics data, various tables, https://nces.ed.gov/ (accessed: June 14, 2015).

rates, and after-graduation measures like students' job-market performance and the ability of graduates to pay back student loans. Opportunity measures could include the percentage of first-generation college students at each institution and the proportion receiving Pell grants and other indicators of lower socioeconomic status.

Many observers, though, are concerned that an aggregate measure for more than 5,000 U.S. colleges and universities in the country will undoubtedly leave much out and will penalize some for no cause. One college president said, "You just cannot compare [the broad variety of schools] coherently. You need to compare them in a mission-specific way."[76] Others are concerned that the rankings will provide perverse incentives to colleges and universities. For example, schools could boost retention and graduation rates by watering down the curriculum and standards, or they could increase graduates' average incomes by eliminating those majors that are not typically associated with higher-earning jobs.

11.7   CONCLUSIONS

Education is perhaps the biggest sector of the United States economy today. During a typical school day, more than one-quarter of the U.S. population is directly engaged in primary, secondary, and post-secondary education, whether as students, teachers, support staff, administrators, or professors. Once you add in the parents of all the students, perhaps half of all Americans have either direct or indirect exposure to the educational system on a daily basis. This close proximity leads to strong opinions regarding the performance of education in America. While the overwhelming majority of Americans are satisfied with the school their children attend, Americans are far less satisfied with the educational system in general.[77] With hindsight, it is clear that the common school and high school movements were transformative and beneficial. Whether recent reforms will ultimately prove to have been as effective remains to be seen.

QUESTIONS

1. What arguments are typically used to justify the funding and provision of education by government?

2. Why did the New England colonies have higher literacy rates than the other American colonies?

3. In both the common school movement and the high school movement, there is a positive relationship between public school funding and the degree of income equality. Why might greater equality of income lead to more funding for public education?

4. Claudia Goldin and Lawrence F. Katz have called the period from 1910 to 1940 the "Rise of the American High School," since high school graduation rates increased from 9 percent in 1910 to 51 percent by 1940. Which U.S. states led the way in public high school education (be specific), and what were the general characteristics of these states that caused them to be the educational leaders in secondary education?

5. Compare and contrast the history of educational attainment and opportunity for white Americans and African Americans.

6. Since the 1950s, public schools have faced a great deal of criticism. What types of reforms have occurred in American public schools since the 1950s? To what extent have these reforms been necessary and successful? Explain.

7. Assess and evaluate the relative importance of school versus non-school factors in explaining the relative performance of American students in primary and secondary schools in recent decades. Why is it, do you suspect, that American students score so poorly in international tests of student performance?

8. Explain how unified growth theory brings together some of the main concepts explored in this chapter and in Chapter 7 (on population growth and the fertility transition).

NOTES

1 Thomas N. Snyder and Sally A. Dillow, *Digest of Educational Statistics 2012* (Washington, DC: National Center for Educational Statistics, U.S. Department of Education, 2013), Table 122, 189.

2 Claudia Goldin and Lawrence F. Katz, *The Race Between Education and Technology* (Cambridge, MA: Harvard University Press, 2009), 19.

3 Office of Economic Cooperation and Development, Programme for International Student Assessment, *Country Note: United States*, 7, www.oecd.org/pisa/keyfindings/PISA-2012-results-US.pdf (accessed: February 19, 2015). The rankings for 2012 include results from 65 countries and regions. Among the 34 countries who are members of the OECD, students in the United States rank 27th in math, 17th in reading, and 20th in science.

4 U.S. News and World Report, *Best Global Universities Ranking*, www.usnews.com/education/best-global-universities/rankings (accessed: November 26, 2014). Other rankings, like the *Times Higher Education World University Rankings*, are similar.

5 *OECD Skills Outlook 2013: First Results from the Survey of Adult Skills* (OECD Publishing), http://dx.doi.org/10.1787/9789264204256-en (accessed: November 27, 2014). U.S. young adults, aged 16–24, perform "significantly below OECD averages" in terms of literacy and numeracy, with U.S. young adults ranked 22 of 24 countries in numeracy and 18 of 24 in literacy.

6 The results from Chapter 2 are in line with what other scholars have reported. Goldin and Katz estimate that 13.6 percent of labor productivity growth between 1915 and 2005 is explained by growth in educational attainment. See Goldin and Katz, Table 1.3, 39. Robert J. Gordon, "The Demise of U. S. Economic Growth: Restatement, Rebuttal, and Reflections," (January 2014), 9, http://economics.weinberg.northwestern.edu/robert-gordon/NBER%20P383F%20Sequel_140126.pdf (accessed: May 24, 2015), reports results that are "almost identical to those of Goldin and Katz."

7 Robert J. Gordon, "Is U. S. Economic Growth Over? Faltering Innovation Confronts the Six Headwinds," *National Bureau of Economic Research Working Paper*, no. 18315 (August 2012).

8 According to the National Center for Education Statistics (NCES), in Fall 2011, 90.3 percent of elementary and secondary school students attended public institutions, while 72.0 percent of college students attended public institutions. Enrollment projections by the NCES through Fall 2021 predict almost the same split between public and private education: http://nces.ed.gov/programs/digest/d12/tables/dt12_003.asp (accessed: December 2, 2014).

9 Section 11.1 draws from David Franklin Mitch, "Market Forces and Market Failure in Antebellum American Education: A Commentary," *Social Science History* 32, no. 1 (Spring 2008), 135–139; and from Jonathan Gruber, *Public Finance and Public Policy*, Fourth Edition (New York, NY: Worth Publishers, 2013), 294–296.

10 Kenneth Lockridge, *Literacy in Colonial New England: An Enquiry into the Social Context of Literacy in the Early Modern West* (New York, NY: Norton, 1974), 13.

[11] Lockridge, 77.

[12] Lockridge reports that male literacy rates in New England increased from 60 percent in the late seventeenth century to 90 percent by 1790; and estimates that female literacy rates rose from 31 percent to 48 percent over the same period, roughly half the rate for males.

[13] Robert C. Allen, *Global Economic History: A Very Short Introduction* (New York, NY: Oxford University Press, 2011), 72.

[14] William H. Jeynes, *American Educational History: School, Society, and the Common Good* (Thousand Oaks, CA: Sage Publishing, 2007), 1.

[15] David F. Labaree, *Someone Has to Fail: The Zero-Sum Game of Public Schooling* (Cambridge, MA: Harvard University Press, 2010), 45.

[16] Jeynes, 13. For the full text of the Act, see www.constitution.org/primarysources/deluder.html (accessed: June 22, 2015).

[17] *The New York Public Library American History Desk Reference* (New York, NY: Stone Song Press, 2003), 356.

[18] The *U.S. News and World Report Rankings* for 2015 can be found at: http://colleges.usnews.rankingsandreviews.com/best-colleges (accessed: June 24, 2015).

[19] Goldin and Katz, 148.

[20] Jeynes, 146–150.

[21] Goldin and Katz, 147.

[22] Jeynes, 157.

[23] Goldin and Katz, 5.

[24] Goldin and Katz, 129 and 154.

[25] Mondale and Patton, 33.

[26] Goldin and Katz, 149.

[27] In 1919–1920, total enrollment in Catholic schools was 1,925,521, with the overwhelming majority of this enrollment in elementary schools (1,795,673). In contrast, total enrollment in public elementary and secondary schools was 21,678,016. See U.S. Department of Education, National Center for Education Statistics, *120 Years of American Education: A Statistical Portrait* (Washington, DC: Government Printing Office, 1993), Table 11, 42–43, and Table 15, 49.

[28] Sun Go and Peter Lindert, "The Uneven Rise of American Public Schools to 1850," *Journal of Economic History* 70, no. 1 (March 2010), Table 1, 4.

[29] Go and Lindert, 7–14.

[30] Go and Lindert, 9.

[31] Go and Lindert, 4.

[32] Hoyt Bleakley and Sok Chul Hong, "When the Race between Education and Technology Goes Backwards: The Postbellum Decline of White School Attendance in the Southern U.S." (April 2013), 1–49, www-personal.umich.edu/~hoytb/Bleakley_Hong_Backwards.pdf (accessed: June 25, 2015).

[33] Go and Lindert, 4.

[34] Dietrich Vollrath, "Inequality and School Funding in the Rural North," *Explorations in Economic History* 50, no. 2 (April 2003), 267–284. See also Rodney Ramcharan, "Inequality and Redistribution: Evidence from U.S. Counties and States, 1890–1930," *Review of Economics and Statistics* 92, no. 4 (November 2010), 729–744.

[35] Christiana Stoddard, "Why did Education Become Publicly Funded? Evidence from the Nineteenth-Century Growth of Public Primary Schooling in the United States," *Journal of Economic History* 69, no. 1 (March 2009), 172–201.

[36] Claudia Goldin, "Human Capital," in Claude Diebolt and Michael Halpert (eds.), *Handbook of Cliometrics* (Heidelberg, GER: Springer-Verlag, 2015).

37 U.S. Department of Education, Table 2, 14.

38 Mondale and Patton, 41.

39 Mondale and Patton, 45.

40 Goldin and Katz, 142.

41 U.S. Department of Education, Table 2, 14.

42 U.S. Department of Education, Table 9, Column 13, 36.

43 Goldin and Katz, 159.

44 Goldin and Katz, 188.

45 Goldin and Katz, 195.

46 Goldin and Katz, 167.

47 Goldin and Katz, 170–171.

48 Goldin and Katz, 210–217.

49 Goldin and Katz, 205.

50 Goldin and Katz, Table 6.5, 233. In 1910, about half of high school graduates intended to continue on to colleges and other institutions of higher learning. By 1937, less than 30 percent of high school graduates planned to go to college.

51 Goldin and Katz, 235.

52 For technical expositions of unified growth theory, see Oded Galor, *Unified Growth Theory* (Princeton, NJ: Princeton University Press, 2011); and Oded Galor and David N. Weil, "Population, Technology, and Growth: From Malthusian Stagnation to the Demographic Transition and Beyond," *American Economic Review* 90, no. 4 (September 2000), 806–828. For a more intuitive treatment, built around many of the same ideas and applied to world economic history, see Gregory Clark, *A Farewell to Alms: A Brief Economic History of the World* (Princeton, NJ: Princeton University Press, 2009).

53 Goldin and Katz, 255.

54 *The New York Public Library American History Desk Reference*, 361.

55 *The New York Public Library American History Desk Reference*, 365.

56 Goldin and Katz, 262.

57 Goldin and Katz, 283.

58 Goldin and Katz, 247.

59 Goldin and Katz, 278.

60 Mondale and Patton, 68–69.

61 Mondale and Patton, 69.

62 Mondale and Patton, 133.

63 Mondale and Patton, 149.

64 Mondale and Patton, 158.

65 Diana M. Lautenberger, Valerie M. Dandar, Claudia L. Raezer, and Rae Anne Sloane, *The State of Women in Academic Medicine: The Pipeline and Pathways to Leadership, 2013–2014* (Washington, DC: Association of American Medical Colleges, 2014), Table 1, www.aamc.org/download/411782/data/2014_table1.pdf (accessed: June 27, 2015).

66 The Report can be found at www2.ed.gov/pubs/NatAtRisk/index.html (accessed: July 1, 2015).

67 Labaree, 183.

68 Labaree, 185.

69 U.S. Department of Education, National Association of Education Statistics, http://nces.ed.gov/programs/coe/indicator_cgb.asp (accessed: July 1, 2015).

[70] Eugenia Toma and Ron Zimmer, "Two Decades of Charter Schools: Expectations, Reality, and the Future," *Economics of Education Review* 31, no. 2 (April 2012), 209.

[71] Toma and Zimmer, 210–211.

[72] RAND Corporation, *Teachers Matter: Understanding Teachers' Impact on Student Achievement*, www.rand.org/education/projects/measuring-teacher-effectiveness/teachers-matter.html (accessed: July 3, 2015).

[73] See, for example, Diane Ravitch, *The Reign of Error: The Hoax of the Privatization Movement and the Danger to America's Public Schools* (New York, NY: Alfred A. Knopf, 2013).

[74] Larabee, 136.

[75] Edward N. Wolff, William J. Baumol, and Anne Noyes Saini, "A Comparative Analysis of Education Costs and Outcomes: The United States vs. Other OECD Countries," *Economics of Education Review* 39, (April 2014), 2.

[76] Douglas Belkin, "Obama Spells Out College-Ranking Framework," *Wall Street Journal* (December 19, 2014), www.wsj.com/articles/obama-spells-out-college-ranking-framework-1418965261 (accessed: July 7, 2015).

[77] In recent years, the PDK/Gallup Poll has indicated that over two-thirds of parents give an A or B grade to the public school that their own oldest child attends, but less than 20 percent of Americans give A or B grades to "public schools nationally." See Tables 14 and 16 of the *46th Annual PDK/Gallup Poll of the Public's Attitudes toward the Public Schools*, http://pdkintl.org/noindex/PDK_Poll46_2014.pdf (accessed: July 9, 2015).

12

Labor and Labor Markets

For almost all of us, the labor market is the most important market in which we participate. Not only will our success in this market largely determine our material standards of living, but the jobs we do will also help to shape our identities as human beings. The musician, Bruce Springsteen, explained the importance work can have:

> You get up in the morning, at a certain time. You prepare yourself. You get yourself ready to go to a job. You walk down the street and you're there at a particular time of day. And you interact with your co-workers. And that's a big part of your social life, your work life, and your place in the world. You're doing something that has a purpose. There's a reason you're there besides just feeding your family. You're part of the social fabric. You're what's holding the world together. You're what's holding the town together, what's holding your family together.[1]

While many of us are lucky enough to feel this way about what we do, others are not as fortunate, suffering long periods of unemployment, low wages, or unrewarding working lives. While different individuals have different labor-market experiences, much about work in general has changed in dramatic ways since the nineteenth century.

In 1870, more than half of employed Americans still worked on farms. The other half of the jobs were divided almost equally between industry and services. Most jobs were much more physically demanding than the jobs held by workers today, and the hours were much longer, generally exceeding 60 hours a week. Employees were not entitled to vacations, sick leave, unemployment compensation, or reimbursement for injuries on the job, even though workplace injuries were far more commonplace.

This chapter focuses on voluntary exchange in labor markets; indentured servitude and slavery are discussed in other chapters. The chapter emphasizes issues such as participation in the labor market, the rise and fall of labor unions, changing working conditions and job safety, and unemployment. Relative wages and distributional issues are discussed in Chapter 13, while labor market discrimination and segregation are covered in Chapter 14.

12.1 LABOR MARKETS

In labor markets, workers exchange their time and effort for wages. Unlike markets for goods, where individuals are the demanders, in labor markets individuals supply labor, and it is firms that are the primary demanders of labor. Although workers and firms are the primary actors in labor markets, there are often two other actors: labor unions and governments. A labor union is a group of workers who bargain collectively for better wages, better working conditions, and sometimes for broader social and economic goals. In the twentieth century, governments also became much more involved in influencing labor market outcomes through a wide variety of policies, including laws that protected labor unions, established minimum wages, and created unemployment insurance, old-age insurance, and disability insurance systems. The growth in the size of governments in the twentieth century also meant that they themselves—federal, state, and local governments—became sizable employers of labor.

MARGINAL PRODUCTIVITY THEORY

The usual starting part for analyzing labor market outcomes is marginal productivity theory, where the labor market is modeled as a perfectly competitive one. Recall the assumptions of perfect competition from Chapter 1, here applied to labor markets:

- There are so many buyers (firms) and sellers (workers) that each market participant takes the market price (in this case, the wage rate) as given. That is, both firms and workers are price takers.
- Workers are assumed to be homogeneous (i.e., the same).
- Employers and workers both have perfect information regarding wages and job opportunities.
- There are no externalities.
- There are no barriers to entering or leaving the labor market (freedom of entry and exit).

Let's first consider labor demand for a profit-maximizing firm. The profit-maximizing condition is that a firm should hire workers as long as the value of the marginal product of labor ($VMPL$) exceeds the nominal wage rate (W). The profit-maximizing number of workers that a firm should hire is that number for which the value of the marginal product is equal to the nominal wage rate (W). That is:

$$VMPL = W$$

This is just another example of the marginal principle from Chapter 1. The value of the marginal product is the *marginal revenue* (the marginal benefit) that a firm receives from hiring one more worker. That is, the $VMPL$ is the marginal change in output of each additional worker (called the marginal product of labor or MPL) multiplied by how much that output can be sold for (P_Q). The wage rate is the *marginal cost* to the firm of hiring that worker. As long as an additional worker yields benefits greater than the additional cost, a profit-maximizing firm will increase profits by hiring that worker.

The equation above is measured in money wages, but rational actors care about *real* wages. That is, they care not about the dollars themselves (since those are just pieces of paper), but rather about what the dollars can buy in terms of goods and services. We can write this profit-maximizing condition in terms of the real wage by dividing each side by the aggregate price level (P):

$$\frac{P_Q \cdot MPL}{P} = \frac{VMPL}{P} = \frac{W}{P}$$

Firms will hire workers until the real value of the marginal product ($VMPL/P$) is equal to the real wage (W/P). The market demand curve for labor is simply the sum of all of the firms' individual demand curves for labor, and it is downward-sloping due to diminishing marginal product of labor.

There are several factors that will shift the market demand curve for labor. The labor demand curve is called a derived demand curve, since demand for labor depends in part on the price of the output that the labor produces (P_Q). Labor demand will increase (shift right) if:

*   The price of what labor produces can be sold for more in output markets (that is, if P_Q increases). If what workers produce becomes more valuable, then firms will want to hire more workers at any given wage rate.
*   There is an increase in the marginal product of labor (MPL). If there is an improvement in technology or more factors of production per worker, then labor demand will increase since labor productivity has increased.

Let's now consider the labor-supply decisions of individuals. Labor supply is modeled as a labor–leisure choice decision, where "leisure" denotes all activities that are not work for pay. Suppose that the real wage increases. This has two effects on the decision to supply labor. At higher wages, the opportunity cost of leisure is higher, since taking an hour of leisure means giving up more money. As a result, as the wage increases, the number of leisure hours falls and the number of work hours increases. This is called the *substitution effect*: as real wages increase, workers substitute away from leisure and toward work.

Higher real wages may lead to less work, however. Leisure is a normal good, so as wages increase, so too do individuals' incomes. With higher income, workers want to consume more of most goods, including leisure. By consuming more leisure, the number of hours worked falls. This is known as the *income effect*.

So, as the real wage increases, ceteris paribus, the substitution effect predicts that work hours will increase, while the income effect predicts that work hours will decrease. Labor supply curves are typically drawn as upward-sloping, which assumes that the substitution effect is stronger than the income effect. Empirically, this is the case for most workers most of the time. The market supply of labor is simply the sum of all individual supplies of labor.

Several factors will shift the market supply curve of labor, including:

*   A change in alternative employment opportunities. (If there are better opportunities in other labor markets, they will attract workers to those markets, thereby reducing the supply of labor in this market.)
*   A change in the cost of acquiring human capital. (In markets that require more human capital, higher costs of acquiring human capital will decrease labor supply on those markets.)
*   Population changes. (More people of working age increases labor supply.)
*   Changes in tastes and social norms regarding work versus leisure.

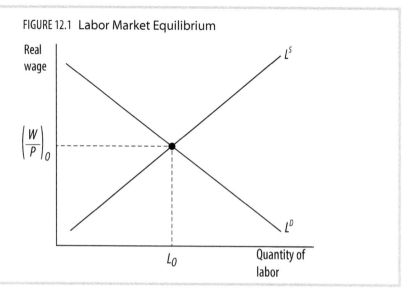

FIGURE 12.1 Labor Market Equilibrium

Like any competitive market, equilibrium occurs where the labor supply curve (L^S) and the labor demand curve (L^D) intersect, as shown in Figure 12.1.

12.2   LABOR FORCE PARTICIPATION RATES

The labor force participation rate (LFPR) is the percentage of the adult population (16 years and older) who are either employed or unemployed—that is, the percentage of the adult population who are either working for pay or actively seeking work. For a fixed population, labor force participation rates will rise if there is an increase in labor demand, or an increase in labor supply, or some combination of the two. There have been several important trends in labor force participation rates since the end of the eighteenth century.

CHILD LABOR

After the arrival of the first colonists, children worked to help their families. Before 1870, the majority of Americans were farmers and as late as 1900 more than one-third of the workforce was in agriculture. On farms, children performed a wide range of tasks, such as collecting eggs, milking cows, cleaning barns, caring for animals, and picking crops.

Throughout the nineteenth century, children were also important sources of labor in the growing manufacturing sector. In 1820, 23 percent of the manufacturing labor force in the industrializing Northeast consisted of children aged 15 and under.[2] Evidence suggests, however, that the child-labor share of industrial employment may have started to decline as early as 1840, although child labor continued to be an important source of labor until the early twentieth century. The first national statistics on child labor are available for 1880. For children aged 10–15 years of age, 32.5 percent of males were in the labor force in 1880, compared to just 12.2 percent of females. By 1930, these percentages had fallen to 6.4 percent and 2.9 percent, respectively.[3]

The continued use of child labor in the late nineteenth and early twentieth centuries sparked controversy and led to legislative reforms: many states passed minimum-age laws to restrict child labor. There were also federal attempts to reduce child labor, culminating in the Fair Labor Standards Act (1938), which prohibited full-time employment for those aged 16 and under and which also established a nationwide minimum wage that made it unprofitable to employ most children.

Available evidence, however, suggests that changing economic conditions were more important for the decrease in child labor than were federal and state legislation.[4] Industrialization and rising incomes provided parents with the luxury of keeping their children out of the labor force. In addition, the expansion of schooling and the increasing rates of return to education reduced child labor. Finally, technological progress increased the skill requirements for many jobs, to the detriment of children (who typically had lower human capital). In addition, mechanization replaced some jobs that had previously been done by children, leading to a decrease in the labor demand for children. It is likely the case that the U.S. states where demand for child labor decreased the most were the ones most likely to pass child labor laws, in which case the legislation may have been largely symbolic.[5]

MALE LABOR FORCE PARTICIPATION RATES

The most notable long-run feature of male labor force participation rates has been the withdrawal of older men from the paid labor force. While labor force participation rates (LFPRs) for males aged 25–44 have remained above 90 percent throughout American history, increasing years in school has reduced participation rates for younger males and the participation rates for older males have plummeted. Between 1850 and 1880, LFPRs for males aged 65 and over were between 76 and 78 percent (Figure 12.2). After 1880, rates began to decline, reaching levels at or below 20 percent from 1980 onwards. In recent decades, the labor force participation of somewhat younger men (aged 55–64) has also been decreasing.

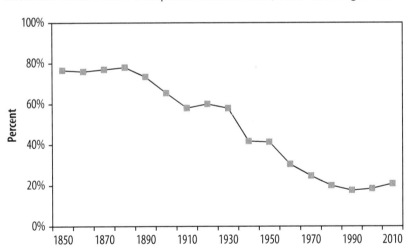

FIGURE 12.2 Labor Force Participation Rates for Men, 1850–2010: Ages 65 and Older

Sources and Notes: 1850–1980 from Dora L. Costa, *The Evolution of Retirement: An American Economic History 1880–1990* (Chicago, IL: University of Chicago Press, 1998), Table 2A.1, 29. 1990–2010 from Braedyn Kromer and David Howard, "Labor Participation Rates and Work Status of People 65 and Older," *American Community Survey Briefs* (U.S. Census Bureau, January 2013), www.census.gov/prod/2013pubs/acsbr11-09.pdf (accessed: July 24, 2015). For the period 1850–1930, the series for men aged 65 and older are the percentage "gainfully employed," while the data from 1940 and after are based on the current definition of the labor force.

In contrast, the proportion of women over the age of 65 who do paid work has remained consistently low over time. In the late nineteenth century, about 8 percent of women aged 65 and older were in the workforce; and this proportion was still at only 8.4 percent by 1990, although it inched up to 12.5 percent by 2010.[6]

At first glance, it is paradoxical that an increasing proportion of older men should have withdrawn from formal paid employment after 1880. While retirement was becoming more common, life expectancies were also increasing and the health of older men was improving. In addition, work hours were decreasing and jobs were becoming physically less demanding as service-sector jobs became a larger proportion of all jobs. These changes suggest that labor force participation rates for older men should have been increasing and not dramatically decreasing. What, then, can explain the change from more than 75 percent of older men in the labor force in 1880 to less than 20 percent a century later?

The most likely explanations for the increase in retirement focus on the overall increase in incomes (because of economic growth) and on the development and spread of pensions. Real GDP per capita was almost seven times higher in 1980 than in 1880.[7] More income per person made it possible for individuals and society to save and to accumulate enough wealth for an extended period of retirement.

Pensions provided the mechanism. In the United States, public (government-provided) pensions originated with military pensions to disabled Revolutionary War veterans and their widows. Public pensions grew in scale and scope after the Civil War (see Section 20.2). The Union Army pension program expanded tremendously as a result of the Pension Act of 1890, which provided pensions to all Union Army veterans aged 65 and older who had served more than 90 days and who were honorably discharged. In addition to Civil War pensions, many states began providing old-age assistance to the elderly poor even before the Social Security Act (1935), which extended old-age pensions to most Americans. After the Social Security Act, the rate of decrease accelerated, with the labor force participation rate of men aged 65 and older decreasing from 58 percent in 1930 to 41.8 percent by 1940.

Private pension plans were also important. The first private pension plan was established by American Express in 1875, but by 1900 still only twelve private pensions existed.[8] In 1930, about 10 percent of all private-sector workers were covered by employer-provided pensions.[9] The tax incentives in the Revenue Act of 1942 led to an expansion of private pensions after World War II, with 41 percent of workers covered by 1960 and almost 50 percent by the mid-1980s.[10] Many private pension plans also stipulated a mandatory retirement age, typically 65.

For the typical household, however, Social Security is more important than employer-provided pension plans or individual retirement accounts. For the median household aged 65–69 in 2008, net worth was $731,100, with the present-value of Social Security benefits accounting for $315,300 or 43 percent of the total. The median household did not have any money in an employer-provided, defined-benefit pension plan, and had only $5,000 in a private retirement account. Real estate and financial assets accounted for most of the remaining wealth. For households aged 65–69, Social Security represents 52 percent of net worth at the 30th percentile in the distribution, but only 31 percent at the 90th percentile.[11]

FEMALE LABOR FORCE PARTICIPATION RATES

The changes in the labor force participation rates given above—due to increasing education; to increased retirement; and, more recently, to a decrease in labor force participation for men at younger ages—together led to a decrease in male labor force participation rates.

In contrast, female labor force participation rates have skyrocketed. In 1870, fewer than 15 percent of females aged 16 and over were in the labor force; but by the year 2000, more than 60 percent of adult women were part of the labor force (Figure 12.3).

The increase in female LFPRs could not have been possible without huge increases in participation rates by married females, since the majority of adult women were married during the increase in participation rates. In 1900, only 4.3 percent of married women were in the labor force; by 2000, the proportion was more than 60 percent and greater than the participation rate for all females (Figure 12.3).

The expansion of high school education (1910–1940) for young women, and the rise of the clerical and sales sectors in the 1920s, were the first changes that led to increases in married female labor force participation, particularly for white women.[12] The growth of teaching, office work, and nursing also increased the demand for female labor.

Before 1940, however, most of the increases were due to shifts in labor supply and not labor demand. The fertility transition (see Chapter 7), with women having fewer children, together with the growth of electric appliances in the home, freed up time for women to work in paid employment. From 1940 to 1960, however, shifts in labor demand accounted for almost all of the increases in labor force participation. The period since 1960 has included a combination of labor supply and labor demand factors, with labor demand factors becoming more important since 1980 as the gender wage gap has substantially narrowed (see Chapter 14).[13]

FIGURE 12.3 Male and Female Labor Force Participation Rates, 1800–2010

Sources and Notes: 1800–1900 data for males (16 and over) and females (16 and over) from Thomas Weiss, "Estimates of the White and Nonwhite Gainful Workers in the United States by Age Group, Race, and Sex: Decennial Census Years, 1800–1900," *Historical Methods* 32, no. 1 (Winter 1999), Table 2, 23. 1880–1990 data for married females and 1910–1990 data for males (16 and over) and females (16 and over) from Matthew Sobek, "New Statistics on the U.S. Labor Force, 1850–1990," *Historical Methods* 34, no. 2 (Spring 2001), Table 8, 78. 2000 and 2010 data are from the U.S. Bureau of Labor Statistics, various sources.

12.3 LABOR UNIONS

It is difficult to identify the beginnings of union activity in America since informal arrangements between workers and employers have existed since early colonial times. For example, the Massachusetts Bay Company granted charters to shoemakers and coopers (workers who made and repaired casks and barrels) in Boston in 1648.[14] Although these charters were quite different from modern unions, they demonstrate that the desire of workers to organize to improve their condition—as any group of sellers might do—has a very long history.

CRAFT UNIONS

The earliest craft unions were typically short-lived, with the longest-lived union being that of the Philadelphia shoemakers, called the Federal Society of Journeymen Cordwainers (1794–1806). Skilled shoemakers had seen their wages and status threatened by low-paid, unskilled workers that employers were hiring in increasing numbers. In 1799, the union went on strike to protest against a wage cut. The employers responded by taking the union to court, on charges of conspiring to interfere with employers' rights to operate freely in the labor market. The court ruled against the union, finding the shoemakers guilty of criminal conspiracy. That is, it ruled that a union organizing to promote a collective interest was a criminal act.

The criminal conspiracy doctrine dictated court decisions until the Commonwealth vs. Hunt decision in 1842, which ruled that unions per se were not illegal. Although Commonwealth vs. Hunt provided some scant legal protection for unions, craft union membership waned in the decades before the Civil War. It is estimated that 300,000 workers belonged to unions in 1830, but union membership by 1860 may have been as low as 5,000 workers, only about 0.1 percent of all nonfarm workers.[15]

Employers had many tools with which they could limit union activity. Workers who joined unions, or who were suspected of trying to organize unions, could be, and usually would be, fired. New employees were often required to sign "yellow-dog" contracts, in which they promised not to join a union.[16] These contracts then served as the basis for civil suits against unions that persuaded employees to violate their labor contracts. Another useful weapon against unions was an injunction, in which a court could forbid practices such as picketing and secondary boycotts. Employers also engaged in widespread intimidation and violence to suppress union activity.

INDUSTRIAL UNIONS

Union activity increased during the Civil War because of plentiful job opportunities and low unemployment rates, but it was not until after the war that industrial unions emerged. In 1869, the Knights of Labor was the first union to organize workers across all skills, industries, and regions. Not only was it interested in higher wages, but it also promoted worker-owned cooperatives and campaigned against the abuse of child labor. Membership peaked in 1886 at around 700,000 members, but thereafter it soon collapsed. The Knights suffered from costly and ill-advised strikes, and lost money from financing poorly-conceived cooperatives.

The late nineteenth century was a period of frequent strikes and violence. In 1886, police fired into a crowd of striking workers at the McCormick factory in Chicago, killing four. When anarchists protested in Haymarket Square, a bomb exploded, killing seven policemen (Figure 12.4). In the melee that followed, several protesters were also

FIGURE 12.4 Haymarket Riot, Chicago, May 4, 1886

Source: T. de Thulstrup, from sketches and photos furnished by H. Jeaneret. Originally published in *Harper's Weekly* (May 15, 1886), 312–313. Library of Congress, www.loc.gov/pictures/item/99614182/ (accessed: August 2, 2015).

killed. Eight anarchists were later executed for conspiracy. Although the Knights of Labor were not directly involved, this incident also contributed to the collapse in membership.

The year 1890 witnessed over 1,200 strikes, the most in any single year in American history. Other confrontations between unions and employers soon followed. In 1892, the private Pinkerton militia was called in to break a strike at Andrew Carnegie's steel plant in Homestead, Pennsylvania, and seven workers were killed. Two years later, the American Railway Union went on strike at the Pullman factory outside Chicago, threatening to disrupt travel across the country. A federal court issued an injunction, forbidding interference with interstate commerce, and federal troops were called in to enforce the court order, but not before 13 workers were killed and more than 50 wounded. Railroad workers in 26 states protested, with additional violence and death. Although the Haymarket incident (1886), the Homestead strike (1892), and the Pullman strike (1894) are among the most notable in American history, confrontations between business and labor occurred frequently.

By the end of the nineteenth century, workers had largely organized along craft lines (unions for welders, unions for shipbuilders, etc.). Disenchanted with the Knights of Labor, Samuel Gompers, an official of the Cigar Makers' Union, left the Knights of Labor in 1881. In 1886, his union, along with many other unions, formed the American Federation of Labor (AFL), which was set up as a blanket organization of highly autonomous craft unions and excluded most of the country's unskilled workers.

As technology continued to change, traditional craft distinctions blurred. Many in the AFL came to see its craft organization as an impediment to dealing effectively with large corporations based on assembly-line production and advocated for union membership based on representation of all workers within a particular industry, regardless of their craft. In 1935, a number of industrial unionists, frustrated by the AFL's refusal to restructure along industrial lines, created the Congress of Industrial Organizations (CIO).

The competitive struggles between the AFL and the CIO continued throughout the Great Depression of the 1930s, the World War II years of the 1940s, and into the 1950s. In 1955, however, at near the height of union membership in the United States (Figure 12.5), the AFL and CIO merged to form the AFL-CIO.

CHANGES IN LABOR LAWS

The New Deal represented a watershed for American workers that resulted in a large increase in unionization rates after the 1930s (Figure 12.5). The most important piece of New Deal labor legislation was the National Labor Relations Act of 1935, which is also known as the Wagner Act, after the New York Senator Robert F. Wagner. The Wagner Act gave labor the rights to organize, to elect (by secret ballot) union officers who would

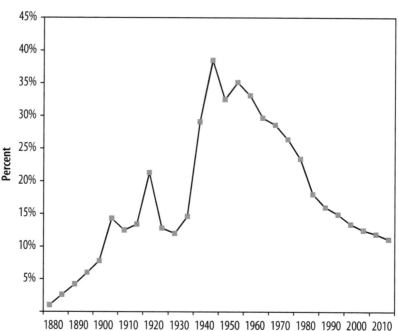

FIGURE 12.5 Percentage of Nonagricultural Workforce in Unions, 1880–2014

Sources and Notes: 1880–1980 are from Stanley Lebergott, *The Americans: An Economic Record* (New York, NY: W.W. Norton & Company, 1984), Table 29.5, 386. Note that data between 1880 and 1900 are linearly interpolated. The numerator is union members, while the denominator is workers in nonfarm enterprises, so the self-employed and agricultural workers are excluded. 1985–2014 are from the U.S. Bureau of Labor Statistics, Table 1, www.bls.gov/webapps/legacy/cpslutab1.htm (accessed: August 5, 2015).

serve as their bargaining agents, and to bargain collectively with employers. The Wagner Act allowed for closed-shop agreements—agreements in which firms undertook only to hire union labor. It was also made illegal for employers to interfere in this process by firing or punishing workers for union activity. Finally, it created the National Labor Relations Board to make sure that the provisions of the Wagner Act were enforced.

In 1946 and 1947, after the end of World War II, as workers' overtime disappeared and real wages fell due to rising prices, there were widespread strikes and work stoppages. These were not popular with much of the electorate. In 1946, Republicans gained control of Congress and responded with the Labor Management Relations Act (1947), more commonly known after its sponsors as the Taft-Hartley Act.

Taft-Hartley contained many provisions that eventually weakened unions. It outlawed closed shops and replaced these with union-shop agreements. With union-shop agreements, firms could hire nonunion labor, but with the stipulation that nonunion workers would be required to join the union within a specified period of time. It also required unions to bargain in good faith and prohibited unions from striking in support of other union strikes. Most importantly in the long run, perhaps, it allowed individual states to pass "right-to-work" laws, which were laws that prevented the exclusion of nonunion workers from workplaces represented by a union. These statutes also prevented unions from requiring employees to pay union fees, which increased free rider problems. In 2015, 25 U.S. states had "right-to-work" laws. Most of these were states in the South and West, but the Midwestern states of Indiana, Michigan, and Wisconsin also had such laws.[17]

In 1959, Congress passed the Labor Management Reporting and Disclosure Act, also known as the Landrum-Griffin Act, in response to growing concerns about criminal activity by unions. This Act required full financial disclosures of union revenues and expenditures, including the salaries of union officials. It also sought to ensure fair elections and specified penalties for union leaders found guilty of misusing union funds.

THE IMPACT OF UNIONS

There are many ways in which unions affect labor markets. On the one hand, unions are a source of market power that enables them to garner higher wages for their members by restricting entry. Since the 1970s, the union wage gap (the difference between union jobs and similar jobs not represented by a union) has fluctuated between 15 and 20 percent.[18] Not only do unions produce higher wages for their members, but there is also some evidence that even the threat of unionization has led to higher wages for nonunion workers as employers paid higher wages to reduce the probability of unionization.[19] It is also possible that unions in one occupation might have spillover effects on other occupations that lower wages in those occupations. For example, if unions artificially restrict entry, then wages increase in the union sector, but with the spillover of causing an increase in the supply of labor for nonunion jobs, and that drives down wages in the nonunion sector.

Unions may also have positive impacts through the exit-voice channel.[20] Without unions, workers have no mechanism for airing grievances without risking demotion or dismissal, so their only option in response to poor working conditions is to quit or "exit." Unions, however, provide workers with a "voice" for airing grievances and suggesting better ways of doing the job. Union-backed jobs typically have lower rates of job turnover than nonunion jobs. The greater stability of employees represented by unions constitutes one way in which unions can have a favorable impact on firms' productivity and profits. Dozens of studies have concluded that, in general, workers in unionized firms are more productive. This could be because workers have a voice; but it could also be because if entry is restricted, firms can be more selective and can choose to hire more productive workers. However, the increase in productivity is generally not sufficient to justify the higher wages negotiated by unions.[21]

THE DECLINE OF UNIONS

Since the mid-1950s, the proportion of the U.S. workforce who belong to unions has declined from more than one in three workers in 1955 to only one in nine workers by 2014 (Figure 12.5). The decline in the private-sector workforce has been even more precipitous. In 2014, only 6.6 percent of private-sector workers belonged to a union, compared to 35.7 percent of public-sector workers.[22] While union growth in the public sector since 1960 has been strong, the increase in public-sector unionization rates has not been sufficient to compensate for the collapse of union membership in the private sector.

Scholars have investigated many potential causes for the decrease in private-sector unionization rates. One explanation simply ties the decline in unions to the decline in the manufacturing jobs that were a traditional stronghold for union activity (see Chapter 10). As the manufacturing employment share fell, so too has the rate of unionization in the United States. While the decline of manufacturing is certainly a contributing factor, other advanced economies have also seen manufacturing employment fall without the same decline in union membership that the United States has experienced. While only 11.1 percent of U.S. workers belonged to unions in 2015, unionization rates are much higher elsewhere, including Canada (27.2 percent), Denmark (67.2 percent), Finland (68.6 percent), Norway (53.3 percent), Sweden (67.5 percent), and the United Kingdom (25.8 percent).[23]

Another possibility is that American workers have come to rely on the government, rather than unions, for pensions, health care, protection against discrimination, and a whole range of other labor benefits that were only primarily provided by unions in the past. In this view, unions no longer have an important role to play in ensuring the prosperity and safety of labor. However, in recent decades wages for lower-skilled workers have stagnated, at best, while inequality has soared, which suggests that government has not been as effective as unions were in the past.

Unions also have a poor public image: they are often seen as institutions that are corrupt, inefficient, and more liberal than the politics of many Americans. Many workers do not want their union dues going to politicians or to causes they do not support. Many government policies and court decisions have also been detrimental to organized labor, from "right-to-work" laws to the message sent to unions by President Ronald Reagan in 1981 when he fired 11,000 federal air-traffic controllers two days after their union, PATCO, had declared a strike. Some historians believe that Reagan's actions laid the groundwork for an assault on organized labor.

12.4 WORKING CONDITIONS AND THE NATURE OF WORK

Since the beginning of industrialization, the changing types of jobs held by Americans and the changing conditions of employment have fundamentally altered what work means. While many of these changes were precipitated by economic growth and market forces, public policy also played an important role.

WORK HOURS

During the early decades of industrialization, New England factory workers often labored 12–14 hours a day. Work in agriculture was also long and backbreaking. Since the early nineteenth century, however, labor hours have declined considerably. First, the desire was for a 10-hour workday; then for an 8-hour workday; and finally for a 5-day, 40-hour week.

Between 1830 and 1950, average hours fell every decade, at varying rates of decline, from 67.5 hours per week in 1830 to 41.1 hours by 1950.[24] New Hampshire passed the first law regarding labor hours in 1847, but it only applied to women and children. By 1910, 58 percent of U.S. states had laws regarding work hours, yet these only applied to 7 percent of all employees.[25] By the late nineteenth century, the 10-hour workday was the norm. In the 1890s, 50 percent of all men and 30 percent of all women in manufacturing worked exactly 10 hours per day.[26]

Henry Ford adopted the 5-day workweek in 1926, but it remained uncommon prior to the Fair Labor Standards Act (1938), which required overtime payments (equal to 1.5 times normal wages) for work in excess of 40 hours per week. This provided an incentive to employers to reduce hours. Both union activity and government policy made something close to an 8-hour workday and 40-hour workweek the norm for full-time workers in the post-World War II period.

JOB SAFETY

The workplace is far safer today than it was more than a century ago. Part of the reason is the long-run shift away from the dangerous processes used to produce goods,

FIGURE 12.6 Difficult and Dangerous Work: Gary, West Virginia, 1908

Source: Lewis Wickes Hine, Library of Congress, www.loc.gov/pictures/item/ncl2004000118/PP/ (accessed: March 29, 2016).

FIGURE 12.7 Distribution of the Labor Force by Sector, 1840–2010

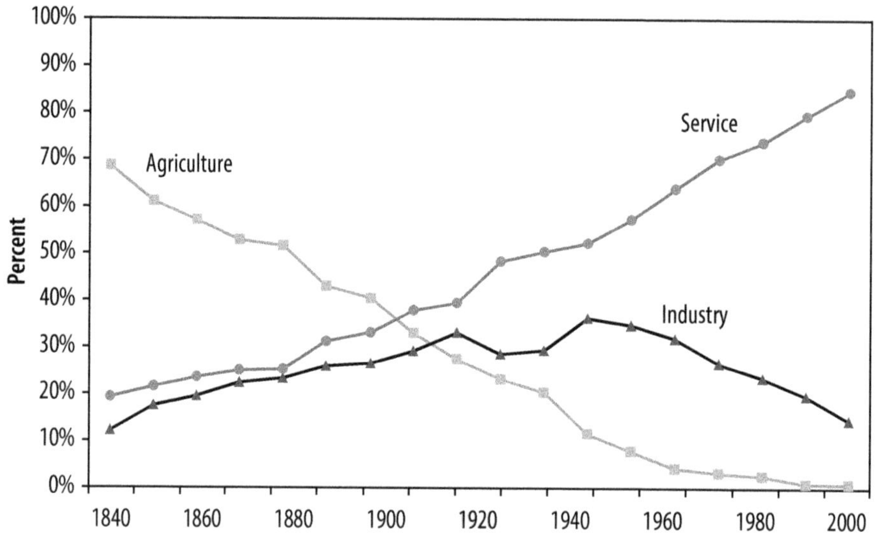

Sources: 1840–1990: Louis Johnston, "The Growth of the Service Sector in Historical Perspective: Explaining Trends in U.S. Sectoral Output and Employment, 1840–1890," April 2001. Data kindly provided by Louis Johnston. 2000 and 2010 data computed from U.S. Bureau of Economic Analysis, *National Income and Product Accounts Tables*, Table 6.5D. Industry includes the sum of manufacturing, mining, and construction. Agriculture also includes fishing and forestry.

such as farming, logging, mining, and manufacturing, to safer production processes such as service in clerical and professional occupations (Figure 12.7). Even the dangerous jobs that remain, however, have become far less dangerous. For example, in 1900 the annual fatality rate for miners was about 300 per 100,000 miners employed, while in recent years better safety measures have reduced it to around 25 per 100,000, a decrease of over 90 percent.[27]

With workers' compensation laws and with courts more willing to award large damages in relation to workers killed or injured on the job, firms had greater incentives to make the workplace safer. As life expectancy rose and incomes increased, workers demanded safer workplaces as well. In 1900, workplace accidents were very cheap for employers, with only about half of the families of all fatally injured workers recovering anything and average compensation amounting to only about 6 months of pay.[28] In contrast, workplace fatalities today can sometimes cost employers tens of millions of dollars.

THE RISE OF THE PROFESSIONS

Between 1900 and 2000, the percentage of the labor force employed in technical and professional occupations increased from 4 percent of the workforce to more than 20 percent.[29] In the late nineteenth century, only medicine, law, and theology were considered "learned professions," but the tremendous growth of scientific knowledge about the physical, chemical, biological, and social worlds during the nineteenth and twentieth centuries led to an expansion of professional occupations: engineers, dentists, professors, teachers, accountants, physicians, veterinarians, and architects, to name a few.

The rise of the professions was also accompanied by occupational licensing regulations. Some states began to regulate occupations as early as the 1870s, but widespread occupational licensing did not occur until the twentieth century. By the early 1900s, most states had adopted medical and dental licensing regulations, but it was not until the 1910s and 1920s that most states had regulations for accountants, architects, nurses, and other occupations.

There are two primary motivations for occupational licensing regulations. First, occupational licensing constitutes a barrier to entry, so members of a profession may lobby government for occupational licensing in order to restrict entry into an occupation, thereby creating monopoly power, which increases wages and salaries. Second, the sale and purchase of professional services is frequently subject to asymmetric information problems, in which potential sellers of professional services know more about the quality of their services than potential buyers. In extreme cases of information asymmetry, the "lemons" problem may arise as lower-quality services drive out higher-quality services from the marketplace.[30] In the case of asymmetric information, occupational licensing may also be welfare-enhancing as it may eliminate incompetent and untrained providers and protect the safety and welfare of consumers.

The growth in population and increasing urbanization made the market exchange of professional services more anonymous, and at the same time the increasing sophistication of these jobs made it more difficult for consumers to adequately judge quality. Because of these changes, the market mechanism could not eliminate all unqualified providers from the market. As a result, during the Progressive Era state governments enacted regulations that set standards of qualifications to practice these occupations.

Evidence suggests that when states had stricter licensing requirements for physicians, this resulted in lower mortality rates for conditions where physician quality really mattered, such as dealing with complications during childbirth or operating to cure appendicitis.[31] By the mid-twentieth century, there were more than 1,200 state occupational licensing statutes for at least 75 different occupations.[32] While occupational licensing can indeed effectively protect consumers from frauds and charlatans, critics have argued that the vast majority of these regulations are unnecessary and that, by increasing prices and restricting entry, the regulations only benefit sellers, and at the expense of buyers.[33]

12.5 UNEMPLOYMENT

Consider the competitive labor market equilibrium depicted in Figure 12.1. In that diagram, equilibrium is characterized by the point where quantity supplied equals quantity demanded. That is, in equilibrium there is neither a surplus nor a shortage of workers (i.e., there are no unemployed workers).

In the real world, however, the unemployment rate is never equal to zero. Even when the economy is growing along its long-run growth path, the U.S. unemployment rate is around 6 percent, which is called the natural rate of unemployment. The natural rate of unemployment reveals that, in the real world, there must in fact be some deviation from the assumptions of perfect competition.

THE NATURAL RATE OF UNEMPLOYMENT

Economists typically distinguish between three types of unemployment: frictional unemployment, structural unemployment, and cyclical unemployment. The actual unemployment rate at any time is the combination of all three types:

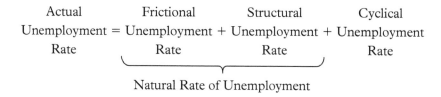

Frictional unemployment is the short-term mismatch between potential workers and firms. Frictional unemployment is desirable if it results in a better match between employees and employers. *Structural unemployment* depends on the context: the laws and regulations that affect the incentives of employees and employers. It also reflects the functioning of labor markets, including long-term mismatches between the skills workers possess and the skills firms demand.

The combination of frictional and structural unemployment determines the economy's natural rate of unemployment. The nearly horizontal line in Figure 12.8

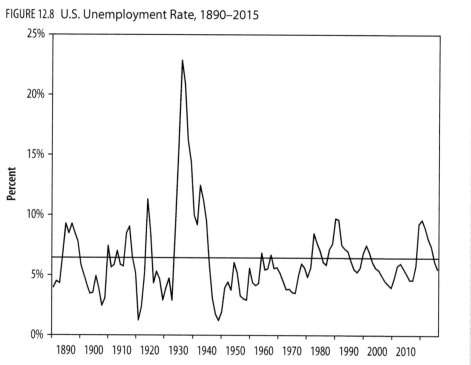

FIGURE 12.8 U.S. Unemployment Rate, 1890–2015

Sources and Notes: 1890–1947 data from David R. Weir, "A Century of U.S. Unemployment, 1890–1990: Revised Estimates and Evidence for Stabilization," *Research in Economic History* 14 (1992), Table D3, 341–343. 1948–2015 data from U.S. Bureau of Labor Statistics, http://data.bls.gov/timeseries/LNS14000000 (accessed: August 12, 2015), computed as annual averages of monthly data.

represents the long-run trend of unemployment of about 6 percent per year, which is a simple estimate of the natural rate of unemployment.

The most striking feature of Figure 12.8, however, is the volatility of unemployment from year to year. Deviations from the natural rate are called *cyclical unemployment*, since these deviations are due to the business cycle (also called economic fluctuations). When the economy is below its long-run growth trend, unemployment rises and there is positive cyclical unemployment. When the economy is above its long-run growth trend, unemployment falls and there is negative cyclical unemployment. The negative relationship between real GDP relative to its long-run trend and cyclical unemployment is called Okun's Law, named after Arthur Okun. Cyclical unemployment is discussed in Chapter 18; the emphasis here is on explaining the natural rate of unemployment.

There are two main types of explanations to account for the natural rate of unemployment: job-search explanations and job-rationing explanations. Job-search explanations emphasize features of labor markets that reduce the probability that workers will be successful in finding jobs, including lack of information, long-term mismatches between worker skills and labor demand (because of technological changes), and public policies that reduce the incentives to find jobs (such as unemployment insurance and other social-welfare programs). Many European countries, for example, have higher natural rates of unemployment, which are at least partly the result of more generous and longer-lasting unemployment insurance.

Job-rationing explanations focus on reasons why real wages in many labor markets may stay above the perfectly competitive, equilibrium wage, thereby generating a surplus of workers or unemployed workers that contributes to overall unemployment rates (Figure 12.9). Unions, occupational licensing, and minimum-wage laws all result in higher wages than would have occurred in a perfectly competitive market, and thus contribute to unemployment.

It might also be in the interests of workers and firms for real wages to be in excess of the perfectly competitive level. Suppose that there is a decrease in labor demand, resulting in a surplus of labor, as depicted in Figure 12.9. One option then would be for real wages to fall. As wages fell, there would be an increase in the quantity demanded of labor and a decrease in the quantity supplied of labor—because of the lower real wages, fewer workers would be interested in working. Under perfect competition, this process would continue until labor supply and labor demand were equal, and there would be no unemployment in equilibrium.

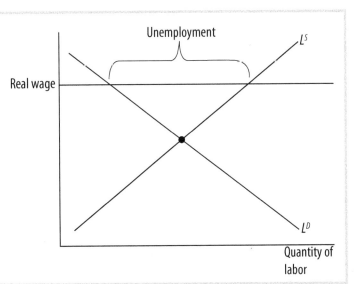

FIGURE 12.9 Job Rationing

In markets that are not perfectly competitive, however, real wages do not always adjust; workers may just be laid off or fired instead. From the firm's perspective, an across-the-board wage cut in this example would be likely to cause the most productive workers to leave the firm, and that would reduce productivity and profits. Selective layoffs and firing the least productive workers might be better for the firm. In addition, workers too might prefer this. Given the choice between a 10 percent across-the-board wage cut and 10 percent of workers being fired, individual workers might opt for the latter, each thinking that she or he would not be one of the 10 percent to be fired. A 10 percent wage cut would make all of the workers unhappy, whereas letting 10 percent go might have a smaller negative impact on the remaining workers and on the firm. Finally, real wages above competitive equilibrium levels might enhance worker productivity, and thus the profits of the firm, through efficiency wage channels (see Economic History in Action 12.1).

ECONOMIC HISTORY IN ACTION 12.1

Henry Ford and Efficiency Wages

Efficiency wages are one possible explanation for unemployment in the long run. With efficiency wages, an employer pays its workers *more* than the equilibrium wage rate, thereby causing an excess supply of labor (i.e., unemployment). Efficiency wage theory suggests that the reason why some employers pay wages in excess of equilibrium wages is because profits are then higher. Above-equilibrium wages provide an incentive for workers not to shirk, since losing their jobs is more costly to workers if they are being compensated well. Efficiency wages may also cause workers to work harder, and thus increase labor productivity; and it may reduce worker turnover, which can also enhance labor productivity since training new workers is costly.[34] Another possible reason for paying higher-than-equilibrium wages is to reduce the possibility of strikes, which could be damaging to profitability.[35]

In 1914, Henry Ford instituted a $5-per-day minimum wage for his assembly-line workers, which more than doubled the wages of most of his workers.[36] He also decreased the workday from 9 hours to 8 hours. Ford's goal was to reduce labor turnover because of the monotonous and difficult nature of assembly-line work.

After the wage increase was announced, crowds of more than 12,000 potential workers lined up outside of Ford's factory in Highland, Michigan.[37] The higher wage and the surplus of workers had two effects. First, with a huge surplus of workers to choose from, the Ford Motor Company was able to hire the most productive of these workers. Second, since each worker knew that thousands were lined up to take his or her job, workers had a more than ample incentive to work hard. In 1913, the annual turnover rate at Ford was 370 percent, but by 1915 it had declined to only 16 percent.[38] The resulting labor productivity increases more than offset the higher cost of labor, and profits soared.

12.6   CONCLUSIONS

The types of jobs and the conditions of employment have fundamentally changed over the past two hundred years. Instead of doing outdoor work on a farm, the typical American spends his or her day indoors, often sitting at a desk for only 8 or 9 hours instead of 12–14 hours. Vacations are now nearly universal, and the physical demands of work have decreased over time, just as the mental requirements have increased. Jobs are also far less dangerous than in the past, and for those unlucky few who *are* injured, workers' compensation and disability insurance help soften the impact. Dramatically higher wages mean that workers, through Social Security and private-pension plans, often enjoy many years of travel and leisure in retirement.

Not all is well, however. While fewer Americans lose their jobs each year, for those that do the duration of unemployment is longer. As jobs have become more specialized, requiring greater human capital investments, the prospects of finding a new job after losing one are often dimmer than a century ago. Finding a new job may require substantial retraining, and some workers are only able to find work at substantially lower wages.

While the focus of this chapter has been on the changing nature of work over time, differences in the wages received by workers are taken up in the next chapter on income and wealth inequality.

QUESTIONS

1. In the essay, "Economic Possibilities for Our Grandchildren," written in 1930, John Maynard Keynes predicted that, as a result of economic growth, we would "in a hundred years … [be] eight times better off in the economic sense than we are today." In 2015, U.S. real GDP per capita was 6.4 times larger than in 1930, and with 15 years to 2030, it looks as though he made a very good prediction. The second part of his prediction has proved less accurate. Keynes envisioned that we would be so rich by 2030 that it would only be necessary to work "three-hour shifts or a fifteen-hour week," yet the average American still works about 35 hours a week. Using the labor demand and labor supply model, and substitution and income effects, explain what Keynes assumed about the relative importance of substitution and income effects that caused this prediction about very short work weeks to be inaccurate.

2. Using the perfectly competitive labor demand and labor supply model, what would happen, all else being equal, to the real wage and the number of workers in each of the cases below?

   A. There is an increase in the amount of physical capital as a result of positive net investment in the economy.

   B. In a particular occupation, workplace safety regulations are effective in lowering the rate of workplace accidents and injuries.

   C. In a particular occupation, the good that workers are producing is no longer as popular as it once was, leading to a decrease in the price of the good that workers help produce.

   D. Social Security retirement benefits are cut and the retirement age is increased.

3. Discuss the potential reasons for the long-run decrease in labor force participation rates for older males.

4. During the twentieth century, female labor force participation increased dramatically, particularly for married women. In explaining why labor force participation rates increased, distinguish between labor demand and labor supply factors.

5. In 1955, 1 in 3 workers were represented by a labor union, while by 2015 only 1 in 9 were represented. What factors explain the decrease in unionization rates in the United States during this time?

6. What is a "yellow-dog" contract and how and when did this affect the formation of unions?

258 Chapter 12

7. What is the difference between an open shop and a closed shop? Which did the Taft-Hartley Act make illegal, and how did this affect union membership?

8. Explain why and how the real wage may stay above the market-clearing wage, thereby contributing to the natural rate of unemployment.

NOTES

[1] *Charlie Rose* television interview, Charlie Rose, Inc., December 20, 1998.

[2] Robert Whaples, "Child Labor in the United States," in Robert Whaples (ed.), *EH.Net Encyclopedia* (October 7, 2005), http://eh.net/encyclopedia/child-labor-in-the-united-states/ (accessed: July 16, 2015).

[3] Whaples (accessed: July 16, 2015).

[4] Carolyn Moehling, "State Child Labor Laws and the Decline of Child Labor," *Explorations in Economic History* 36, no. 1 (January 1999), 72–106.

[5] Moehling, 72–106.

[6] Braedyn Kromer and David Howard, "Labor Participation Rates and Work Status of People 65 and Older," *American Community Survey Briefs* (U.S. Census Bureau, January 2013), Figure 2, 2, www.census.gov/prod/2013pubs/acsbr11-09.pdf (accessed: August 5, 2015).

[7] Louis Johnston and Samuel H. Williamson, "What Was the U.S. GDP Then?" *MeasuringWorth* (2015), www.measuringworth.org/usgdp/ (accessed: August 9, 2015).

[8] Dora L. Costa, *The Evolution of Retirement: An American Economic History, 1880–1990* (Chicago, IL: University of Chicago Press, 1998), 16.

[9] Costa, 17.

[10] Costa, 17.

[11] James Poterba, Steven Venti, and David Wise, "The Composition and Drawdown of Wealth in Retirement," *Journal of Economic Perspectives* 25, no. 4 (Fall 2011), Table 2, 99.

[12] Claudia Goldin, "Labor Markets in the Twentieth Century," in Stanley L. Engerman and Robert E. Gallman (eds.), *The Cambridge Economic History of the United States: The Twentieth Century*, Volume 3 (Cambridge, UK: Cambridge University Press, 2000), 579.

[13] For a more complete discussion of labor demand and labor supply factors, see Claudia Goldin, *Understanding the Gender Gap: An Economic History of American Women* (New York, NY: Oxford University Press, 1990), Chapter 5, 119–158.

[14] Stanley Lebergott, *The Americans: An Economic Record* (New York, NY: W.W. Norton & Co., 1984), 383.

[15] Lebergott, Table 29.5, 386.

[16] Although the origin of the phrase "yellow dog" is unknown, it began appearing in articles and editorials in 1921 and it likely refers to a sickly dog that no one would want. See Joel I. Seidman, *The Yellow Dog Contract* (Baltimore, MD: Johns Hopkins Press, 1932), 11–38.

[17] See National Conference of State Legislatures, www.ncsl.org/research/labor-and-employment/right-to-work-laws-and-bills.aspx (accessed: August 16, 2015).

[18] Barry T. Hirsch and David A. MacPherson, *Union Membership and Earnings Data Book: Compilations from the Current Population Survey*, 2013 Edition (Washington, DC: Bureau of National Affairs, 2013), Table 2a.

[19] Sherwin Rosen, "Trade Union Power, Threat Effects, and the Extent of Organization," *Review of Economic Studies* 36, no. 2 (April 1969), 185–196.

[20] Richard B. Freeman and James L. Medoff, *What Do Unions Do?* (New York, NY: Basic Books, 1984).

21 George J. Bojas, *Labor Economics*, Seventh Edition (New York, NY: McGraw-Hill, 2016), 446.

22 U.S. Bureau of Labor Statistics, "Union Members Summary 2014," *Economic News Release* (January 23, 2015), www.bls.gov/news.release/union2.nr0.htm (accessed: August 22, 2015).

23 Office of Economic Cooperation and Development, "Trade Union Density," https://stats.oecd.org/Index.aspx?DataSetCode=UN_DEN (accessed: September 3, 2015). Note that data are for the year 2012.

24 Roderick Floud, Robert W. Fogel, Bernard Harris, and Sok Chul Hong, *The Changing Body: Health, Nutrition, and Human Development in the Western World since 1700* (New York, NY: Cambridge University Press, 2011), Table 6.7.

25 Hans-Joachim Voth, "Labor Time," in Joel Mokyr (ed.), *The Oxford Encyclopedia of Economic History*, Volume 3 (New York, NY: Oxford University Press, 2003), 257.

26 Voth, 257.

27 For 1900 data, see Mark Aldrich, *Safety First: Technology, Labor and Business in the Building of Work Safety, 1870–1939* (Baltimore, MD: Johns Hopkins University Press, 1997), Appendix 1-3. Recent data from the U.S. Bureau of Labor Statistics, www.bls.gov/iif/oshwc/osh/os/osar0012.htm (accessed: August 31, 2015).

28 Mark Aldrich, "History of Workplace Safety in the United States, 1880–1970," in Robert Whaples (ed.), *EH.Net Encyclopedia* (August 14, 2001), http://eh.net/encyclopedia/history-of-workplace-safety-in-the-united-states-1880-1970/ (accessed: September 7, 2015).

29 This section draws from Marc T. Law and Sukoo Kim, "Specialization and Regulation: The Rise of Professions and the Emergence of Occupational Licensing Regulation," *Journal of Economic History* 65, no. 3 (September 2005), 723–756.

30 George Akerlof, "The Market for 'Lemons': Quality Uncertainty and the Market Mechanism," *Quarterly Journal of Economics* 84, no. 3 (August 1970), 488–500.

31 Law and Kim, 754.

32 Law and Kim, 725–726.

33 See, for example, Milton Friedman, *Capitalism and Freedom* (Chicago, IL: University of Chicago Press, 1962), Chapter 9.

34 For a more detailed description of efficiency wage theories, see Lawrence F. Katz, "Efficiency Wage Theories: A Partial Evaluation," *National Bureau of Economic Research Macroeconomics Annual* 1 (1986), 235–276.

35 Daniel M.G. Raff, "Wage Determination Theory and the Five-Dollar Day at Ford," *Journal of Economic History* 48, no. 2 (June 1988), 387–399. Raff discounts the usual efficiency-wage explanations for paying wages above market equilibrium and concludes that Ford paid $5 a day because of "a desire to buy peace" (398).

36 Raff, 387.

37 Raff, 389.

38 Sumner H. Slichter, *The Turnover of Factory Labor* (New York, NY: D. Appleton & Co., 1919), 244.

13

The Distribution of Income and Wealth

Like the rate of economic growth, the degree of economic inequality affects our well-being. Some inequality is inevitable and economically desirable. Individuals are not born with the same talents and abilities, and some inequality is necessary to provide the proper incentives to invest in human capital, to work hard, to take risks, to invent, and to innovate. Most would agree that hard work, sacrifice, and ingenuity should be rewarded with greater income and wealth. Without the incentive of trying to "get ahead," it is hard to imagine how the U.S. economy could have achieved the high rates of growth it has experienced throughout its history.

Beyond some point, however, the inequality becomes too great and starts to undermine the ideals of equality of opportunity and representative democracy. There is increasing evidence that inequality of outcome in one generation negatively affects equality of opportunity for the next generation. High inequality is also associated with poor consequences for society, including lack of social cohesion, increased crime, ill-health, and obesity.[1] The degree of inequality has varied substantially throughout American history, and so too has the extent of economic mobility: the ability of an individual, a family, or some other group to change their relative economic status over time.

In 1774, the distribution of income and wealth in the United States was probably more equal than in any other country in the Western world, and was certainly far more equal than today. During the first 150 years of American history, inequality increased substantially, but because of data limitations the exact timing of this increase is not completely understood.

By 1928, however, inequality in the United States was at historic highs, and slightly greater than in England. Between 1929 and the early 1950s, the United States experienced the "Great Compression", during which the levels of inequality fell dramatically and then remained low until the 1970s, when inequality began to increase once again during the "Great Divide."[2] By 2007, inequality was nearly as high as it had been in 1928; and relative to similarly-developed economies, income and wealth inequality in the United States were the highest in the world. In recent years, the top 1 percent in the United States have earned more than 20 percent of the total income and have owned more than 40 percent of the total wealth.

As inequality in recent decades has surged to near historic highs, economic mobility in the United States has fallen. While there was once exceptionally high mobility, as in the nineteenth and early twentieth centuries, recent studies have shown that intergenerational mobility in the United States is no longer exceptional and is markedly lower in the United States than in many European countries.

The purpose of this chapter is to document and explain the long-run patterns of economic inequality and mobility in the United States and to compare the U.S. experience with the experience of other countries for which we have comparable data. The focus in this chapter is on aggregate measures and trends, while differences by race, gender, and region are emphasized in Chapter 14.

13.1 MEASURING INEQUALITY

There is no single measure of inequality that captures all of its dimensions, and there are various ways to account for it. Before we can examine and understand the history of inequality in the United States, a brief discussion of measurement issues is warranted.

WAGES, EARNINGS, INCOME, AND WEALTH

In many contexts, the words "wages" and "earnings" are used interchangeably. In this chapter, "wages" refer to payments specifically tied to some unit of time worked (e.g., a wage rate of $20 per hour). "Earnings" represent a broader concept and include salaries paid per month or per year that are not directly linked to worker hours. In some instances, "earnings" may also refer to the "total compensation" that employees receive, which will include not only monetary payments but also in-kind benefits, such as employer-provided health insurance. In contrast, while wages and earnings come from participation in the labor market, "income" includes not only income from labor but also income from owning the other factors of production, and it may come in the form of profits, rents, dividends, interest payments, capital gains, or royalties. In addition, income is usually measured for the household or family (rather than for the individual), in recognition of the fact that multiple wage-earners may contribute to overall household incomes.

Another issue is whether to focus on market income or the income that remains after taxes and government transfers (called disposable income). In this chapter, market incomes are emphasized for reasons of historical comparability; before the twentieth century, taxes and transfers in the United States were negligible. Disposable income in the United States today is more equally distributed than market income because of progressive taxes and social welfare programs. However, when disposable income is used instead of market income, and since the United States redistributes relatively less than most other advanced democracies, the U.S. is relatively more unequal than other similarly-developed economies.

Wages, earnings, and income are *flow* variables that are measured relative to some unit of time, whether hourly, weekly, monthly, or yearly. In contrast, wealth is a *stock* variable that can be measured at any given point in time. Wealth, or net worth, is the difference between the value of someone's assets (what they own) and the value of their liabilities (what they owe) at any given point in time. While earnings and income can never be negative, wealth can be negative if someone has negative net worth. Many households at the bottom of the wealth distribution have negative wealth: the value of what they own is less than the value of what they owe.

SUMMARY MEASURES OF INEQUALITY

In this chapter, three common measures of inequality are used: (1) group shares; (2) interpercentile ratios; and (3) Gini coefficients and Lorenz curves.

Group shares have an intuitive appeal in that they are easy to understand. An example of a group share measure is to say that the top 1 percent of households own 40 percent of the wealth.[3] The primary disadvantage of group share measures is that they describe only a portion of the overall distribution.

Interpercentile ratios are also intuitive but are somewhat more informative, since they compare two parts of the distribution. For example, the P90/P10 ratio compares the ratio of someone at the 90th percentile in the distribution of income, wealth, or some other measure to someone at the 10th percentile of that distribution. As with group shares, however, the entire distribution is still not represented.

In contrast, Lorenz curves and Gini coefficients take the entire distribution into account. Figure 13.1 illustrates the Lorenz curve for household incomes in the United States in 2014. On the horizontal axis, in this case, is the cumulative proportion of households; on the vertical axis is the cumulative proportion of income. In other applications, the horizontal axis might instead measure the cumulative proportion of individuals or families, while the vertical axis might instead measure the cumulative proportion of earnings or wealth.

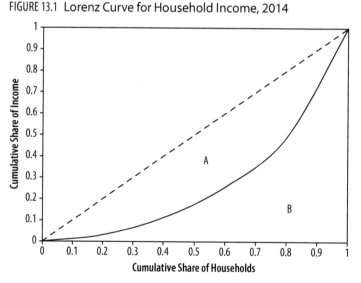

FIGURE 13.1 Lorenz Curve for Household Income, 2014

Sources and Notes: Computed from U.S. Census Bureau, Table H-2 "All Races," www.census.gov/hhes/www/income/data/historical/inequality/ (accessed: May 15, 2015).

The diagonal line in Figure 13.1 represents the line of perfect equality. Along this line, the bottom 20 percent of households receive 20 percent of the total income, while the bottom 40 percent receive 40 percent of the income, and so on. With perfect equality, every household receives the same amount.

The curved line in Figure 13.1 represents the actual Lorenz curve for U.S. household incomes in 2014. The poorest 20 percent earned 3.2 percent of the total income, and the bottom 40 percent together earned 11.6 percent of the income, and so on.

The Gini coefficient (G) is a numerical measure that summarizes the Lorenz curve. It is defined as:

$$G = \frac{\text{Area A}}{\text{Area A} + \text{Area B}}$$

In an economy with inequality, the Lorenz curve will always be curved in the middle, although it will start and end at the same points as the line of perfect equality (since, by definition, the poorest 0 percent of the households have 0 percent of the income, and 100 percent of the households must have 100 percent of the income). As the Area A increases, so does the divergence from perfect equality. The more bowed out the Lorenz curve, the greater the Area A and the greater the Gini coefficient. With perfect equality, the Gini coefficient is 0 since Area A is 0. The other extreme is the hypothetical case in which one household earns all of the income: in this case, Area A would be equal to Area A + Area B, and the value of the Gini coefficient would be 1. That is:

$$0 \leq G \leq 1$$

Although an increase in the Gini coefficient represents an increase in inequality, there are problems in summarizing the entire shape of the income distribution into a single number. For example, consider the impact of a shift in income from the poorest 5 percent of households to the richest 5 percent of households. Such a shift would obviously increase the Gini coefficient. However, an identical increase in the Gini coefficient could be obtained, for example, by transferring income from the 40th percentile to the 60th percentile of the distribution. Although the increase in the Gini coefficient would be the same in both cases, the welfare implications of these two transfers would be quite different.

In countries across the world today, Gini coefficients for income range from just above 0.20 for the most equal economies to about 0.60 for the most unequal. Inequality of wealth is greater, with Gini coefficients ranging from around 0.55 to almost 0.85.[4] In recent years, the U.S. Gini coefficient for household income is near 0.50, while for wealth it exceeds 0.80.[5]

Because Lorenz curves are nonlinear, computing exact areas requires the use of integral calculus. These areas, however, can be approximated by computing the areas of triangles or trapezoids instead.[6]

13.2 LABOR MARKETS AND EARNINGS INEQUALITY

For most American households, the primary source of income comes from household members' participation in labor markets. In Chapter 12, the model of the perfectly competitive labor market was introduced. While this model is not sufficient to explain all of the reasons for changes in earnings inequality over time, it does provide a useful framework in understanding many of the important reasons why workers are compensated very differently in different labor markets. Many labor markets, however, are not perfectly competitive, and deviations from perfect competition lead to additional reasons for earnings inequality.

A HYPOTHETICAL WORLD

To better understand why wages differ among workers in the real world, consider a hypothetical world with the following three characteristics:

- Except for differences in wages, all jobs are equally desirable to all workers.
- All workers are equally able to do any job.
- All labor markets are perfectly competitive.

In such a world, every worker would earn an identical wage in the long run, and there would be no wage inequality. To understand why, consider Figure 13.2, which illustrates the labor market for two occupations. The wage rates (W) in each occupation are on the vertical axes, and the quantity of labor (L) on the horizontal axes. The labor demand (L^D) curves in each occupation are downward-sloping, due to diminishing marginal product of labor; while the labor supply (L^S) curves are upward-sloping, implying that the substitution effect is larger than the income effect (see Chapter 12).

Suppose that initially wages are higher in Occupation 1 (W_1), for some reason, than in Occupation 2 (W_2). If this were to occur in a perfectly competitive world where everyone was equally able to do every job, then workers from Occupation 2 would change careers and move into Occupation 1. As a result, labor supply in Occupation 1 would increase, driving down wages, while labor supply in Occupation 2 would decrease, driving up wages. This process would continue until real wages in both occupations were the same (W_E).

In the real world, of course, these three conditions are never satisfied, so workers are not all paid the same. Let us examine some important departures from this hypothetical world.

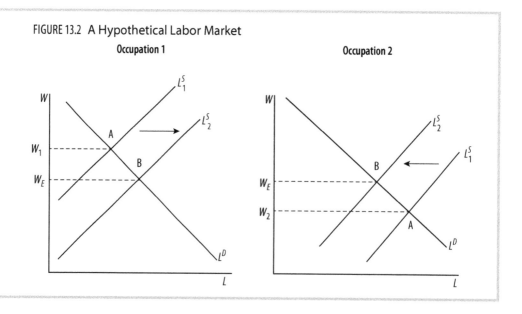

FIGURE 13.2 A Hypothetical Labor Market

COMPENSATING WAGE DIFFERENTIALS

One reason why different workers are paid differently is that not all jobs are equally desirable. Some jobs are more dangerous, more unpleasant, more stressful, or more monotonous than others. If the characteristics of certain jobs make those occupations unattractive, labor supply will be lower and those jobs will pay higher wages, all else being equal. That is, workers must be compensated with higher wages to offset the unpleasant characteristics of the job. In this case, the compensating wage difference—the difference in wages offered to offset or to compensate for the undesirability of the job—is positive.

Compensating wage differentials can also be negative when jobs are very desirable. Some jobs are more fun, more flexible, more stimulating, or more prestigious than other jobs. Labor supply in these occupations will be higher and wages will be lower as a result, all else being equal.

THE DEMAND AND SUPPLY FOR SKILLS

Another reason why workers are paid differently has to do with differences in the supply of, and demand for, worker skills in labor markets. Consider two labor markets: one market for "high-skilled" workers and another for "low-skilled" workers. The wage gap (the ratio of wages for those with high skills to those with low skills) will widen if the demand for high-skilled workers increases more than the demand for low-skilled workers or if the supply of low-skilled workers increases more than the supply of high-skilled workers. If the opposite occurs, then wage gaps will narrow.

One common and intuitive paradigm is to view inequality as a "race between education and technology."[7] Technological change tends to be "skill-biased," in the sense that it increases the demand for high-skilled workers more than the demand for low-skilled workers. This, by itself, would cause wage gaps between high-skilled and low-skilled workers to widen over time. However, individuals and society often respond to the increased demand for high-skilled workers by increasing education in order to increase the *supply* of high-skilled workers.

The high school movement in the first half of the twentieth century (see Chapter 11) was, in part, a labor supply response to skill-biased technological change. At times when technology races ahead of education, inequality increases, since labor demand for skilled workers increases faster than the labor supply of skilled workers. When the supply of skilled workers outpaces the demand for skilled workers, inequality decreases.

OTHER FACTORS THAT AFFECT THE DEMAND AND SUPPLY OF LABOR

There are many other factors that affect the supply and demand for labor in different labor markets and that can contribute to changes in aggregate inequality over time. On the supply side, population growth, whether through natural increase or net immigration, leads to changes in labor supply. For example, newly-arrived immigrants have generally had less human capital than native-born individuals, often due to both language barriers and to fewer years of formal education. As a result, increases in immigration have sometimes caused the supply of lower-skilled workers to increase faster than the labor supply of higher-skilled workers, thereby increasing inequality.

On the labor demand side, international trade and other changes in product markets can have a differential impact on certain types of jobs, leading to an increase in labor demand in industries where exports are growing and a decrease in labor demand in sectors where imports are replacing domestic production. Because labor demand is a derived demand (derived in part from the price of the products workers produce), anything that increases the demand for certain products, all else being equal, will increase the labor demand for workers in that market, and vice versa.

DEPARTURES FROM PERFECT COMPETITION

While shifts in labor demand and labor supply in competitive markets are certainly part of the reason for changes in inequality, they do not tell the whole story. In many occupations there are substantial barriers to entry that restrict the supply of workers and increase real wages. For example, the existence of stringent occupational licensing regulations or strong unions may reduce labor supply and lead to higher wages (see Chapter 12).

A more complete view of labor markets also recognizes the impact of discrimination and segregation throughout American history. Discrimination involves treating people differently solely on the basis of their membership of a group. In labor markets, discrimination refers to employment (both hiring and hours worked), pay, and promotion practices that result in workers who are equal with respect to their productivity being treated differently because of their race, gender, age, ethnicity, or any other characteristic unrelated to job performance. A result of discrimination is "segregation," in "which a (natural or legal) person separates other persons on the basis of one of the enumerated grounds without an objective and reasonable justification."[8] Segregation and discrimination are discussed in Chapter 14.

13.3   INCOME AND WEALTH INEQUALITY IN HISTORICAL PERSPECTIVE

Estimating the degree of inequality and attempting to explain the causes of inequality have been two very active areas of research in recent decades. This work has resulted in a much better understanding of when and why inequality has changed throughout American history.

THE COLONIAL PERIOD

On the eve of the Revolutionary War, the American colonies likely had the most equal distribution of income in the Western world, even when the slave population is included.[9] In 1774, the Gini coefficient for household income was 0.437 (see Table 13.1). For the free population as a whole, the estimated Gini coefficient in 1774 was 0.400, but there was substantial variation by region. Overall, including both free and slave populations, the Gini coefficient was 0.354 in New England, 0.381 in the Middle colonies, and 0.464 in the South. Among the free population in the South, the Gini coefficient was only 0.328.

Relatively abundant and high-quality data on labor and property income allow scholars to estimate inequality by region in 1774, but attempts to determine inequality prior to this are more speculative. Between 1650 and 1774, inequality among whites may have diminished because frontier settlement of yeoman farmers outpaced the growth of cities and towns.[10] Overall, however, inequality likely increased from 1650 to 1774 because the growth of slavery more than offset the increasing importance of

TABLE 13.1 Income Inequality at Benchmark Years, 1774–2014		
Year	Gini Coefficient	Top 1 Percent Share
1774	0.437	7.1 percent
1860	0.510	10.0 percent
1928	0.490	23.9 percent
1953	0.390	9.9 percent
1975	0.397	8.9 percent
2007	0.463	23.5 percent
2014	0.476	21.1 percent

Sources and Notes: Estimates for 1774 and 1860 are from Peter H. Lindert and Jeffrey G. Williamson, "American Incomes, 1774–1860," *National Bureau of Economic Research Working Paper*, no. 18396 (September 2012), Tables 6 and 7. Estimates for the top 1 percent income shares (including capital gains) for the years 1928–2014 are from Thomas Piketty and Emmanuel Saez, "Income Inequality in the United States, 1913–1998," *Quarterly Journal of Economics* 68, no. 1 (February 2003), 1–39, Table A3. Series updated through 2014 and available at http://eml.berkeley.edu/~saez/TabFig2014prel.xls (accessed: August 20, 2015). The Gini coefficient labeled "1928" above is actually for 1929 and it is from Peter H. Lindert, "Three Centuries of Inequality in Britain and America," in *Handbook of Income Distribution*, Volume 1 (Amsterdam, NL: Elsevier, 2000), Table 4, 198–199. Gini coefficients for 1953 and thereafter are from the U.S. Census Bureau, Table H-4, www.census.gov/hhes/www/income/data/historical/inequality/ (accessed: August 20, 2015). The estimates for Gini coefficients and the top 1 percent shares for 1774 and 1860 are for households. For 1928 and after, the top 1 percent estimates are derived from income tax returns, which represent tax filers who may be married, single, or married but filing separately.

the egalitarian frontier. Given the extremely low incomes of slaves, the increase in the slave population from 4 percent of the colonial population in 1650 to 21 percent in 1774 almost certainly resulted in an increase in overall inequality across the colonial period.

THE LONG NINETEENTH CENTURY

Earnings, income, and wealth inequality all increased during the first 150 years of U.S. history. The picture of when and why inequality increased is not completely clear, however, because of fragmentary data, particularly for the period before 1913.

There is little doubt, however, that the United States was a much more unequal place by 1860 than it had been at the end of the colonial period (Table 13.1). Recent evidence suggests that inequality increased in every region in the United States: among free households alone and among free and slave households combined, although the increase was most pronounced in the South.[11] In the United States as a whole, the Gini coefficient rose from 0.437 in 1774 to 0.51 in 1860, and the share of income going to the top 1 percent of households increased from 7.1 percent to 10 percent between 1774 and 1860.[12] The growth of factories, manufacturing, and urbanization contributed to the increase in inequality between 1774 and 1860. In addition, new forms of transportation differentially affected land values based on the proximity of the land to canals and railroads.

Evidence on earnings and wealth is broadly consistent with the pattern in income inequality for the period prior to the Civil War. Between 1820 and 1860, wages of skilled and white-collar workers increased more rapidly than for unskilled laborers, which led to greater wage inequality.[13] Wealth inequality also increased substantially by 1860, although the increase was most marked from the 1820s to the late 1840s.

In 1860, the distribution of wealth in the rural North was more equal than it was in urban areas or in the rural South.[14] It was also more equally distributed in the rural North than it would be later. Westward migration was largely composed of middle-income farm families who had similar incomes and wealth. There was still substantial inequality in the agricultural areas in the North, with households headed by women, recent immigrants, young people, and the aged typically being poorer than the average farm family. As one study summarized, "to be wealthy in this egalitarian society of historical tradition was to be a middle-aged, native, white, literate, male farmer."[15]

The best available evidence shows that inequality continued to increase in the decades after the Civil War. Between 1850 and 1880, wage inequality in manufacturing increased, which is consistent with the "de-skilling hypothesis."[16] The continued spread of the factory and the increase in the size of firms (see Chapter 10) also simplified many tasks "to the point where tasks might be learned in a matter of days or even hours—as well as lessening the degree of skills and dexterity required."[17] As a result, there were relatively more workers clustered in low-wage jobs in 1880 as compared to 1850, which stretched out the distribution of earnings. At the same time, the larger size of firms and the increasing complexity of operations increased the demand for more specialized and educated workers, which also contributed to rising inequality.

Inequality fluctuated over time but continued its upward trend between 1880 and World War I. Although evidence is somewhat fragmentary, what there is suggests that by the late nineteenth century, in the so-called Gilded Age, there was a great deal of inequality in the United States. The great mansions and estates of the Vanderbilts, the Astors, the Rockefellers, and the Carnegies on Fifth Avenue in New York City, along with the palatial summer homes in Newport, Rhode Island, are symbols of the extreme wealth that was created and concentrated at the upper end of the distribution. During the Gilded Age, inequality in the United States exceeded inequality in Great Britain for the first time. While World War I led to a temporary decrease in inequality, by the end of the 1920s inequality was at an all-time high in terms of both income and wealth.

THE GREAT COMPRESSION

Between 1929 and 1953, income and wealth inequality in the United States diminished substantially. The shocks of the Great Depression and World War II played important roles, but so too did New Deal policy changes in response to the Great Depression of the 1930s (see Chapters 16 and 20). The strengthening of unions, highly progressive income taxes, and wage and price controls imposed by the National War Labor Board during World War II together increased the incomes of the poor and tempered those of the top earners. Strong demand for labor during World War II (particularly low-skilled labor) and the migration of millions of African Americans from the South to industrial cities in the North also helped to reduce inequality. Finally, massive investments in secondary and postsecondary education increased the supply of skilled workers, which reduced the skill premium in labor markets and contributed to lower levels of inequality.

MIDDLE CLASS AMERICA

Income inequality and wealth inequality remained low and stable between the early 1950s and the mid-1970s. After World War II, the American Dream included a stable and well-paying job, a nuclear family with two or three kids, a house in the suburbs with a new car in the garage, and a two-week summer vacation. Television broadcast this ideal throughout the country in programs such as *Leave it to Beaver* and *Father Knows Best*. Although this ideal exceeded reality for many Americans, a prosperous middle-class lifestyle was accessible for an increasing number of Americans.

While average incomes soared, income inequality barely changed between 1953 and 1975 (Table 13.1 and Figure 13.3). As a result, there was robust income growth in all parts of the income distribution. Between 1947 and 1979, income growth for those in the bottom 20 percent of the income distribution averaged 2.5 percent per year, which well exceeded the 1.9 percent growth rate of incomes for those in the top 5 percent (Figure 13.3).

THE GREAT DIVERGENCE

In recent decades, the magnitude of both income inequality and wealth inequality has increased to levels not seen since the Gilded Age of the late nineteenth century, and near to being historic highs. Depending on the data series examined, inequality began to increase sometime between 1974 and 1980.[18] While overall economic growth slowed after the mid-1970s, income growth has been fastest for those at the upper end of the distribution. Between 1979 and 2013, real incomes for those in the bottom 20 percent fell at an annual rate of 0.3 percent per year, while for those in the top 20 percent annual growth exceeded 1 percent per year (Figure 13.3).

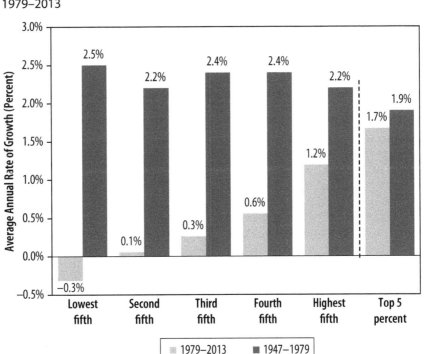

FIGURE 13.3 Average Annual Rates of Growth by Income Quintiles, 1947–1979 and 1979–2013

Sources and Notes: Computed from the U.S. Census Bureau, *Historical Income Tables: Income Inequality*, Tables F-2, F-3, and F-5. The growth rates above refer to the growth of family income by quintile and within the top 5 percent.

There is an immense literature examining the potential causes for the increase in income and wealth inequality in the United States since the mid-1970s. Economists have identified several potential factors, including:

- increased skill-biased technological change (due to computers and information technology)
- increased globalization (international trade and immigration)
- a slowdown in the growth of educational attainment and human capital accumulation
- the growth of financial services and financial deregulation
- changes in pay norms
- the reduced role of unions
- changes in government redistributive tax-and-transfer policies.[19]

There is little doubt that in recent decades there has been substantial growth in the wage premium associated with higher education and cognitive ability.[20] Demand for workers with high levels of human capital has increased at a greater rate than labor demand for lower-skilled workers, the result of both skill-biased technological change and increasing international trade.

Labor supply factors contributed as well. The growth in educational attainment slowed (see Chapter 11), so that in the "race between education and technology," the impact of skill-biased technological change took the lead. The increase in immigration that began after 1965 (see Chapter 15) led to faster growth in labor supply for lower-skilled workers than in higher-skilled workers, which also contributed to rising inequality.

In the view of many economists, however, there is much more going on than just a race between education and technology. There has been an increasing realization that most of the increase in income inequality and in wealth inequality has taken place at the very top of the distribution, where the vast majority of those in the top 1 percent are college graduates.

Some economists have stressed the proliferation of "winner-take-all" labor markets to explain the rising incomes in the top 1 percent of the distribution. Recall from Chapter 12 that the real wage (W/P) in competitive markets is equal to:

$$\frac{W}{P} = \frac{VMPL}{P} = \frac{P_Q \cdot MPL}{P}$$

where MPL is the marginal product of labor, and $VMPL$ is the value of the marginal product of labor, which is equal to the marginal product multiplied by the price of the quantity that a worker produces (P_Q). P is the aggregate price level.

In winner-take-all markets, consumers are willing to pay tremendously more to superstars who might only be slightly better than their next-best competitors. That is, small differences in MPLs can mean a big difference in the VMPLs. Developments in transportation and communications allow superstars to reach ever-larger audiences. Since buyers of music, books, sporting events, and entertainment want to read, hear, and watch the very best, individuals at the top of these professions are able to command an ever-increasing share of the market. The combination of technology, scale, luck, and the erosion of social pressures for fairness are leading to the U.S. economy becoming more of a winner-take-all economy.[21]

Between 1975 and 2014, the share of income going to the top 1 percent more than doubled, from less than 9 percent in 1975 to over 21 percent by 2014. The top

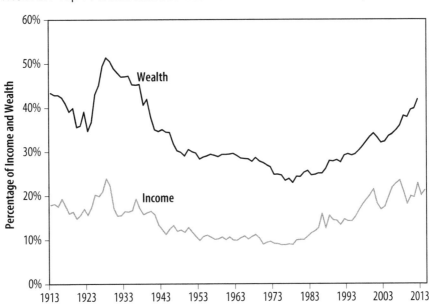

FIGURE 13.4 Top 1 Percent Share of Income and Wealth: United States, 1913–2014

Source: The top 1 percent share of income is from Thomas Piketty and Emmanuel Saez, "Income Inequality in the United States, 1913–1998," *Quarterly Journal of Economics* 68, no. 1 (February 2003), 1-39, Table A3. Series updated through 2014 and available at http://eml.berkeley.edu/~saez/TabFig2014prel.xls (accessed: August 20, 2015). The top 1 percent share of wealth is from Emmanuel Saez and Gabriel Zucman, "Wealth Inequality in the United States Since 1913: Evidence from Capitalized Income Tax Data," *National Bureau of Economic Research Working Paper,* no. 20625 (October 2014), Table B1: "Top Wealth Shares," available at http://eml.berkeley.edu/~saez/SaezZucman2014FullData.zip (accessed: August 22, 2015).

1 percent wealth share has exhibited a similar pattern, increasing from a low of 23 percent in 1978 to almost 42 percent by 2013 (Figure 13.4).

At the very top of the distribution, inflation-adjusted incomes have skyrocketed since the mid-1970s (Table 13.2). Between 1975 and 2014, real GDP per capita more than doubled, while real incomes increased far more for those in the top 1 percent. In contrast, real incomes less than doubled for every group outside the top 1 percent.

For those in the bottom 90 percent, real income per capita actually decreased slightly from 1975 to 2014. In contrast, for those in the top 0.01% (the top 1 in 10,000), real incomes went up over seven-fold, from $3.8 million in 1975 to more than $29 million in 2014. In general, the higher up the distribution, the larger have been the gains in income over the past four decades.

In almost all countries for which we have comparable data, income inequality was high in the early part of the twentieth century and narrowed during the Great Depression and World War II. Only in some countries did the share going to the top 1 percent increase after the 1970s. The United States, Australia, Canada, and the United Kingdom (Anglo-Saxon countries) are "U-shaped countries" in that the top 1 percent share displays a U-shaped pattern over the past century (Figure 13.5).[22] Although the U-shape is most pronounced for the U.S., these other countries do exhibit a similar pattern.

TABLE 13.2 Real Income in 2014 Dollars by Income Share, 1975 and 2014 (Including Capital Gains)			
Income Share	1975	2014	Ratio (2014/1975)
Bottom 90%	$33,300	$33,068	0.993
90%–95%	$103,115	$143,202	1.388
95%–99%	$147,543	$245,484	1.664
99%–99.5%	$252,552	$507,883	2.011
99.5%–99.9%	$394,322	$994,638	2.522
99.9%–99.99%	$859,381	$3,537,677	4.117
Top 0.01%	$3,811,459	$29,032,034	7.617

Sources and Notes: Computed from Thomas Piketty and Emmanuel Saez, "Income Inequality in the United States, 1913–1998," *Quarterly Journal of Economics* 68, no. 1 (February 2003), 1-39, Table A3. Series updated through 2014 and available at eml.berkeley.edu/~saez/TabFig2014prel.xls (accessed: August 20, 2015), Table A6.

FIGURE 13.5 Top 1 Percent Share of Income, 1913–2013: U-Shaped Countries

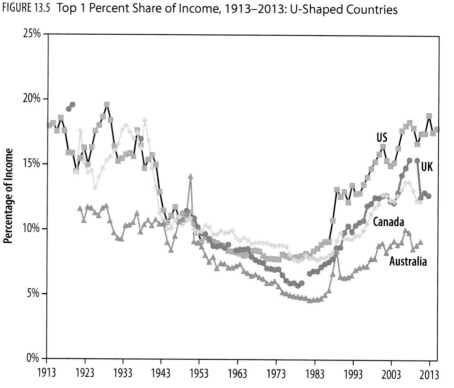

Sources and Notes: Computed using data from Facundo Alvaredo, Anthony B. Atkinson, Thomas Piketty, Emmanuel Saez, and Gabriel Zucman, *WID—The World Wealth and Income Database*, www.wid.world/ (accessed: April 28, 2016). Data for income exclude capital gains.

In contrast, in Japan and in most of continental Europe, the top 1 percent share over the past century has displayed an L-shaped pattern, without an increase in equality at the top in recent decades (Figure 13.6).

FIGURE 13.6 Top 1 Percent Share of Income: L-Shaped Countries

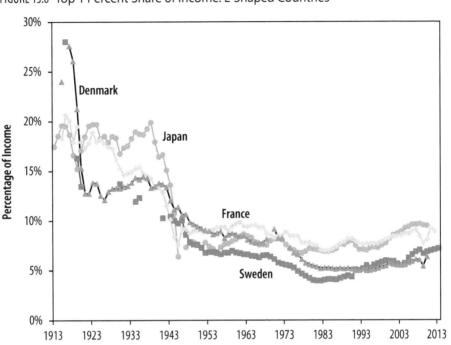

Sources and Notes: Computed using data from Facundo Alvaredo, Anthony B. Atkinson, Thomas Piketty, Emmanuel Saez, and Gabriel Zucman, *WID—The World Wealth and Income Database*, www.wid.world/ (accessed: April 28, 2016). Data for income exclude capital gains.

Many scholars believe that explanations based on changes in the supply and demand for skills in labor markets and those based on "winner-take-all" are both insufficient in accounting for the dramatic rise in inequality at the very top of the distribution, since this rise has occurred in some countries and not in others. While highly developed countries throughout the world have been subject to the same skill-biased technological change, transportation improvements, communication improvements, and globalization, not all countries have witnessed an increase in the share of income going to the top 1 percent.

Instead, many economists focus on changes in policies that have disproportionally benefitted the very rich.[23] One possible explanation is differences in tax policies between countries. International evidence, based on 18 countries since 1960, "shows that there is a strong correlation between the reductions in top (income) tax rates and the increases in top 1 percent pre-tax income shares."[24] In the United States, as the share of income going to the top 1 percent more than doubled, top income-tax rates were slashed by more than 50 percentage points, from a top marginal tax rate of 91 percent in 1960 to a top rate of 39.6 percent in 2013.[25]

The negative correlation between top tax rates and top 1 percent income shares can be explained in a number of ways. One possible scenario is that tax cuts led to more work and greater entrepreneurship by top earners, leading to both a greater concentration of income at the very top and faster economic growth. The problem with this explanation, however, is that countries that slashed marginal tax rates the most, like the United States and the United Kingdom, experienced growth rates that were no faster than those in countries that *did not* cut top marginal tax rates, such as Germany and Switzerland.[26]

An alternative explanation focuses on changes in bargaining incentives for highly paid workers. With marginal tax rates over 90 percent, top earners had little incentive to bargain for raises, as they would receive less than 10 cents for every dollar increase in earnings. As tax rates fell, however, the incentives to bargain more aggressively also increased. In this story, the cuts in tax rates helped cause the increase in inequality at the top of the distribution.

Finally, the observed correlation between tax cuts and rising inequality could just be a coincidence and be due to omitted variables. For example, cuts in top marginal tax rates in the United States—and in some other countries, including the United Kingdom—were part of other policy changes collectively termed the "Washington Consensus."[27] In these countries, tax cuts were accompanied by widespread deregulation of financial and other markets and an increasing faith in the efficiency of markets. Some scholars argue that the increasing concentrations of income and wealth at the very top are the result of the growth of financial services due to financial deregulation.[28]

The proportions of income and wealth going to the top 1 percent, the top 0.1 percent, and the top 0.01 percent have all increased tremendously in recent decades. Even so, high inequality in the United States also extends outside the top 1 percent. Figure 13.7 reports the P90/P10 income ratios after taxes and transfers have been taken into account. Even excluding the top 10 percent of the distribution the U.S. still stands out, with the inequality in the U.S. exceeding all countries in Figure 13.7 except Mexico. While U.S. households at the 90th percentile make 6.2 times as much as households at the 10th percentile, the ratios are only half as large for several European countries.

13.4 POVERTY

The measures of inequality presented thus far are measures of *relative* inequality. For example, consider two hypothetical economies with the same aggregate prices: one where half of the individuals earn $5,000 a year and the other half earn $10,000, and a second economy where half earn $5 million a year and the other half earn $10 million. In this example, the Gini coefficient is the same in both of these economies, even though clearly everyone is much better off in an absolute sense in the second economy.

In contrast, the poverty rate measures the percentage of individuals (or households, or families) who fall below a certain minimum *absolute* threshold of real income. The poverty rate is not influenced by the incomes of those above the threshold.

THE OFFICIAL POVERTY RATE

The poverty thresholds were developed in 1963 and 1964 by economist Mollie Orshansky in the Social Security Administration, and were officially adopted, with revisions, in 1969.[29] Poverty thresholds are based on the cost of the Department of Agriculture's "economy food plan" for families of different sizes. Since evidence at the time showed that the average family in the United States spent about one-third of their after-tax income on food, the poverty thresholds for different family and household

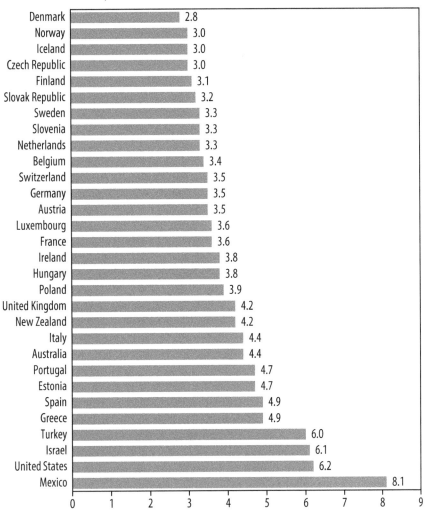

FIGURE 13.7 Income Inequality in Developed Economies, 2012: P90/P10 Ratios (After Taxes and Transfers)

Sources and Notes: Organization for Economic Cooperation and Development, https://data.oecd.org/inequality/income-inequality.htm (accessed: July 21, 2015).

sizes were constructed by multiplying the costs of the "economy food plan" by three.[30] While these thresholds are adjusted each year using the Consumer Price Index (CPI) to reflect changes in the cost of living, the official methodology has changed little since 1969.

POVERTY TRENDS

Official poverty rates extend back to 1959, but scholars have extended the series back to 1914 using multiple regression analysis (see Figure 13.8). In the century from 1914, economic growth caused real GDP per capita to increase more than eightfold.[31]

FIGURE 13.8 U.S. Poverty Rates Among Persons, 1914–2013

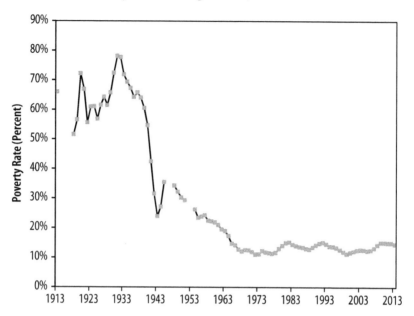

Sources and Notes: Data for the years 1914–1958 are from Robert D. Plotnick, Eugene Smolensky, Eirik Evenhouse, and Siobhan Reilly, "The Twentieth-Century Record of Inequality and Poverty in the United States," in Stanley L. Engerman and Robert E. Gallman (eds.), *Cambridge Economic History of the United States: The Twentieth Century,* Volume 3 (Cambridge, UK: Cambridge University Press, 2000), Table 4.4, 293–294. Poverty rates for the years 1914–1946 are estimated using a multiple regression model (see 291–292). Data for the years 1959–2013 are from the U.S. Census Bureau, *Table 2: Poverty Status, by Family Relationship, Race, and Hispanic Origin,* www.census.gov/hhes/www/poverty/data/historical/hstpov2.xls (accessed: September 4, 2015).

In the long run, economic growth has reduced poverty rates from more than 60 percent in the interwar period to less than 15 percent by 2013. In 2013 the poverty threshold for a two-parent, two-child family was $23,624.

A careful examination of Figure 13.8, however, reveals that aggregate poverty rates have changed very little since the mid-1960s. While rates have increased modestly during economic contractions and decreased during expansions, the long-run trend has been extremely stable over the past 50 years. In 1965, the year after President Lyndon Johnson declared the "War on Poverty," 14.7 percent of Americans fell below the poverty threshold. By 2013, the poverty rate was still 14.5 percent, down slightly from 15 percent of Americans in 2012. With real GDP per capita almost two and a half times greater in 2013 than in 1965, why have poverty rates not declined?

In large part, the lack of improvement in poverty rates is due to increasing inequality and to the lack of real wage growth for the median worker and for those below the median.[32] While the increasing labor force participation of women, all else being equal, should have reduced poverty rates, the increase in the share of female heads of families worked in the opposite direction. Increased immigration may have played a small role, too, but the number of immigrants is simply not sufficiently large to account for the aggregate patterns. Changes in the generosity of government antipoverty programs do not appear to be an important factor.[33]

For decades, there have been criticisms of the official poverty measure and calls to improve it.[34] One problem is that the poverty thresholds are the same for the entire contiguous United States, even though costs of living are far higher in San Francisco than in St. Louis, for example. Another concern is that a figure roughly three times the cost of the food budget from fifty years ago may no longer adequately measure any meaningful threshold corresponding to "poverty." American families now spend a far smaller fraction of their incomes on food; and while food prices have decreased substantially, other costs, such as out-of-pocket medical expenses, utilities, and housing, have increased. Finally, the official poverty rate only takes into account before-tax money income: it does not include in-kind government benefits such as food stamps, housing subsidies, or money from the Earned Income Tax Credit (which provides cash subsidies to low-income working families through the income tax system).

THE SUPPLEMENTAL POVERTY MEASURE

To address some of these issues and concerns, in 2011 the U.S. Census Bureau began to publish the Supplemental Poverty Measure (SPM), which accounts for geographic differences in costs of living and which is based on the costs of food, clothing, shelter, and utilities (FCSU). The SPM also redefines family income to include both cash income and in-kind benefits that families can use to meet their FCSU needs.[35] Although the new poverty measure leads to differences in poverty rates by age, region, race, and gender (see Chapter 14), the overall poverty rate in recent years is quite similar using either measure. However, broader measures of poverty, similar to the SPM, show a larger decrease in poverty rates since the 1960s than are shown by the official poverty rate (see Chapter 20).

13.5 ECONOMIC MOBILITY

Americans have always thought of the United States as the "land of opportunity," and throughout American history there are countless examples of rags-to-riches stories.

While such stories are often interesting and inspirational, they say little about the everyday lives and experiences of most Americans. While spectacular success stories are still possible in the United States, recent evidence strongly suggests that the probability of moving up the economic ladder has diminished, and current trends point to the likelihood that there will be even less mobility in the future.

MEASURING MOBILITY

The most common measure of economic mobility reflects the intergenerational elasticity of earnings between fathers and sons. Recall from Chapter 9 that elasticity measures the responsiveness of one variable to a change in another variable. For example, consider a group of 30-year-old fathers in 1985 who have newborn sons. In 2015, these newborn sons will now themselves be 30 years old. In this case, an intergenerational earnings elasticity measures the relationship between the fathers' earnings in 1985 and their sons' earnings in 2015 (when the sons are the same age as their fathers were in 1985). Typically, these elasticities are measured as deviations from the average, so this statistic removes the factors that influences average incomes over time, and provides a measure of relative (and not absolute) mobility from one generation to the next.

FIGURE 13.9 The Great Gatsby Curve: Income Inequality and Intergenerational Mobility

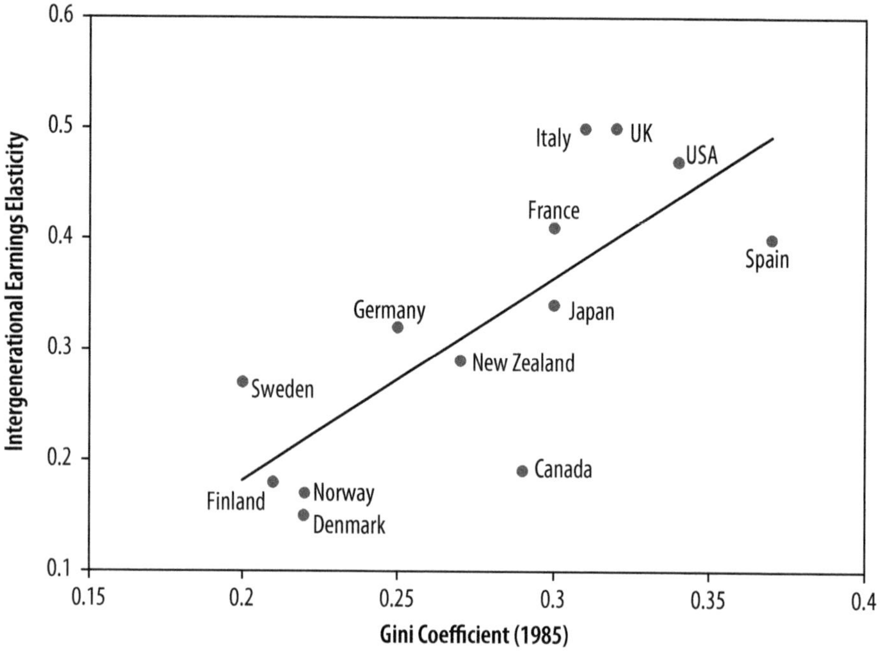

Sources and Notes: Gini coefficients for 1985 are from the Organization for Economic Cooperation and Development (OECD); and intergenerational earnings elasticity data are from Miles Corak, "Inequality from Generation to Generation: The United States in Comparison," Figure 1, 10, http://nws-sa.com/rr/Inequality/inequality-from-generation-to-generation-the-united-states-in-comparison-v3.pdf (accessed: August 24, 2015).

An earnings elasticity of 0 implies that there is no relationship between the relative earnings of fathers and sons. In contrast, an earnings elasticity of 1 implies that fathers' and sons' relative incomes are the same. In general, the larger is the earnings elasticity, the lower is the income mobility from one generation to the next. Among high-income countries, recent estimates of international earnings elasticities range from below 0.20 in Denmark, Norway, and Finland to near 0.50 in the United States, Italy, and the United Kingdom (Figure 13.9).

A LAND OF OPPORTUNITY

In recent decades, the United States has had nearly the lowest level of intergenerational mobility (highest earnings elasticity) among rich countries in the world today, but there was a time when economic mobility was "exceptional."[36] Before 1900, the U.S. had far higher economic mobility than Great Britain, for example, but the U.S. lead in mobility vanished by 1950 as economic mobility in the U.S. fell from the levels experienced throughout the nineteenth century.

During the nineteenth century, high economic mobility appears to have been associated with a high rate of geographic mobility also. Americans were always on the move in search of more valuable land and better labor-market opportunities. The decline in economic mobility likewise coincides with a fall in U.S. residential mobility. After 1910, "economic activity across locations become more homogeneous [and] may have reduced the ability of families and individuals to 'invest through migration' and foster occupational mobility across generations."[37]

ECONOMIC INSECURITY

Paradoxically, while long-run mobility from generation to generation has likely decreased in recent decades, year-to-year fluctuations in incomes have become more volatile. Jobs have become more unstable, and greater numbers of homeowners have faced foreclosure. Since the mid-1970s, there has been an increase in lower-paying jobs with little stability. These are often part-time jobs with few, if any, benefits.

The short-run volatility in economic fortunes is reflected in home ownership rates. By the age of 55, 89 percent of Americans have purchased a home at some point in their adult lives. While nearly 90 percent of Americans will become homeowners, there is remarkable fluidity as individuals move into and out of home ownership. Over a 25-year period, 52 percent of Americans ceased to be homeowners for some period of time.[38]

THE GREAT GATSBY CURVE

The Great Gatsby Curve measures the cross-country relationship between economic inequality in one generation and the level of economic mobility in the next generation. On the horizontal axis is the Gini coefficient from a generation ago (from 1985, in Figure 13.9). On the vertical axis is the intergenerational earnings elasticity, as described above. In Figure 13.9, the intergenerational earnings elasticity for the United States is 0.47. This means that if a father earns twice the average, his son is predicted to earn 47 percent more than average a generation later. Recall that the higher the intergenerational elasticity of earnings, the more closely are fathers' and sons' incomes related, and the lower is the level of economic mobility from one generation to the next.

The United States is very unequal and also has especially low economic mobility. In addition, because inequality in the United States is greater now than it was a generation ago, the Great Gatsby Curve predicts that, as the United States moves up the Great Gatsby Curve, economic mobility in the next generation will be even lower.

13.6 CONCLUSIONS

Rising inequality, along with diminished upward mobility for many Americans, has been an increasingly important public policy issue in recent years. Politicians on both sides of the aisle express concerns about the direction in which the United States appears to be heading. In 2011, the "Occupy Wall Street" movement protested against economic and social inequality in New York City's Wall Street financial district, using the slogan "We are the 99 percent." Protests erupted in over a hundred cities and nearly 8,000 people were arrested.[39] While the movement has become more subdued, for many Americans the issues raised by this movement continue to match their own deep concerns about whether the U.S. can deliver on the promise to provide opportunity and a realistic prospect of upward mobility for all.

QUESTIONS

1. Describe the level and trends in income and wealth inequality during the following periods: the colonial period, 1820–1860, 1870–1928, 1928–1953, 1953–1975, and 1975–2015.

2. How is economic mobility typically measured? Why was nineteenth-century economic mobility in the United States "exceptional"?

3. What factors likely account for the increase in income inequality that the United States has experienced since the 1970s? Why have some similarly advanced economies not experienced dramatic increases in inequality of the kind experienced in the U.S.?

4. Describe the differences between how the official poverty rate is computed and how the Supplemental Poverty Measure (SPM) is computed.

5. When did the "Great Compression" occur, and what were its causes? Use the labor demand and supply framework to address this question.

6. What is the "Great Gatsby Curve" and what does it imply about the future of economic mobility in the United States?

7. What does it mean for a country to be "U-shaped" versus "L-shaped"? Which countries are U-shaped and which are L-shaped? What factors are most likely to account for the differences between U-shaped and L-shaped countries? Explain.

NOTES

[1] For a survey of the literature on this topic, see Kate Pickett and Richard Wilkinson, *The Spirit Level: Why Greater Equality Makes Societies Stronger* (New York, NY: Bloomsbury Press, 2010).

[2] The name "Great Compression" was first coined by Claudia Goldin and Robert Margo in "The Great Compression: The Wage Structure in the United States at Mid-Century," *Quarterly Journal of Economics* 107, no. 1 (February 1992), 1–34. The name "Great Divide" comes from a book of the same title by Joseph Stiglitz. See Joseph E. Stiglitz, *The Great Divide: Unequal Societies and What We Can Do About Them* (New York, NY: W.W. Norton & Co., 2015).

[3] For example, see U.S. Census Bureau, *Historical Income Tables: Households*, Table H-2 (All Races), www.census.gov/hhes/www/income/data/historical/household/2013/h02AR.xls (accessed: August 20, 2015).

[4] For Gini coefficients by country for wealth, see James B. Davies, Susanna Sandström, Anthony B. Shorrocks, and Edward N. Wolff, "The Level and Global Distribution of Household Wealth," *National Bureau of Economic Research Working Paper*, no. 15508 (November 2009), Appendix V, 56–60, www.nber.org/papers/w15508.pdf (accessed: August 26, 2015).

[5] For the Gini coefficient for U.S. household incomes, see the U.S. Census Bureau, *Historical Income Tables*, Table H-4, www.census.gov/hhes/www/income/data/historical/inequality/ (accessed: August 20, 2015). For the wealth Gini coefficient, see Davies et al., Appendix V, 56–60.

[6] John Golden, "A Simple Geometric Approach to Approximating the Gini Coefficient," *Journal of Economic Education* 39, no. 1 (Winter 2008), 68–77.

[7] Claudia Goldin and Lawrence F. Katz, *The Race Between Education and Technology* (Cambridge, MA: Harvard University Press, 2009).

[8] European Commission against Racism and Intolerance, www.coe.int/t/dghl/monitoring/ecri/activities/GPR/EN/Recommendation_N7/Recommendation_7_en.asp (accessed: July 19, 2015). By this definition, voluntary separation does not constitute segregation.

9 This section relies heavily on Peter H. Lindert and Jeffrey G. Williamson, "American Incomes, 1774–1860," *National Bureau of Economic Research Working Paper*, no. 18396 (September 2012).

10 A yeoman farmer is someone who owns a modest farm and works it primarily with family labor.

11 Lindert and Williamson, 27.

12 Lindert and Williamson, Tables 6 and 7.

13 Robert Margo, *Wages and Labor Markets in the United States, 1820 to 1860* (Chicago, IL: University of Chicago Press), 72–73, 158.

14 Jeremy Atack and Fred Bateman, "The 'Egalitarian Ideal' and the Distribution of Wealth in the Northern Agricultural Community: A Backward Look," *Research in Economics and Statistics* 63, no. 1 (February 1981).

15 Jeremy Atack and Fred Bateman, *To Their Own Soil: Agriculture in the Antebellum North* (Ames, IA: Iowa State University Press, 1987), 129.

16 Jeremy Atack, Fred Bateman, and Robert Margo, "Skill Intensity and Rising Wage Dispersion in Nineteenth-Century American Manufacturing," *Journal of Economic History* 64, no. 1 (March 2004), 172–192.

17 Atack et al., 173.

18 Peter H. Lindert, "Three Centuries of Inequality in Britain and America," in *Handbook of Income Distribution*, Volume 1 (Amsterdam, NL: Elsevier, 2000), 201.

19 Many of these factors are discussed in Anthony B. Atkinson, *Inequality: What Can Be Done?* (Cambridge, MA: Harvard University Press, 2015); and in Joseph E. Stiglitz, *The Price of Inequality: How Today's Divided Society Endangers Our Future* (New York, NY: W.W. Norton & Co., 2012).

20 See David H. Autor, "Skills, Education, and the Rise of Earnings Inequality Among the 'Other 99 Percent,'" *Science* 344, no. 6186 (May 23, 2014), 843–851, for an accessible introduction to the broad literature on this topic.

21 See Alan B. Krueger, "Land of Hope and Dreams: Rock and Roll, Economics and the Rebuilding of the Middle Class" (June 12, 2013), www.whitehouse.gov/sites/default/files/docs/hope_and_dreams_-_final.pdf (accessed: June 15, 2015).

22 Facundo Alvaredo, Anthony B. Atkinson, Thomas Piketty, and Emmanuel Saez, "The Top 1 Percent in International and Historical Perspective," *Journal of Economic Perspectives* 27, no. 3 (Summer 2013), 3–20.

23 Alvaredo et al., 6.

24 Alvaredo et al., 8.

25 For U.S. income tax rates from 1913, see http://taxfoundation.org/sites/default/files/docs/fed_individual_rate_history_nominal.pdf (accessed: July 5, 2015).

26 Alvaredo et al., 9–11.

27 This term was coined in 1989 by the English economist John Williamson to describe the "standard" set of reforms that the International Monetary Fund, the World Bank, and the United States Treasury Department implemented in countries beset by instability and slow growth.

28 Thomas Philippon and Ariell Reshef, "Wages and Human Capital in the U.S. Finance Industry, 1909–2006," *Quarterly Journal of Economics* 127, no. 4 (November 2012), 1551–1609.

29 Gordon Fisher, "The Development and History of the Poverty Thresholds," *Social Security Bulletin* 55, no. 4 (Winter 1992), 3–14, www.socialsecurity.gov/policy/docs/ssb/v55n4/v55n4p3.pdf (accessed: July 7, 2015).

30 Three was not the exact multiplier, and a higher multiplier was used for families with fewer than three persons to account for the relatively higher costs of housing.

31 In 1914, U.S. real GDP per capita (measured in 2009 U.S. dollars) was $6,036.50, while in 2014 it was $50,397. See Louis Johnston and Samuel H. Williamson, "What Was the U.S. GDP Then?" *MeasuringWorth* (2015), www.measuringworth.org/usgdp/ (accessed: July 10, 2015).

32 Hilary W. Hoynes, Marianne E. Page, and Ann Huff Stevens, "Poverty in America: Trends and Explanations," *Journal of Economic Perspectives* 20, no. 1 (Winter 2006), 47–68.

33 Hoynes et al., 66.

34 Natalia Kolesnikova and Yang Liu, "Understanding Poverty Measures and the Call to Update Them," *The Regional Economist* (Federal Reserve Bank of St. Louis, July 2012), 4–5, www.stlouisfed.org/~/media/Files/PDFs/publications/pub_assets/pdf/re/2012/c/poverty.pdf (accessed: September 18, 2015).

35 Kolesnikova and Liu.

36 Jason Long and Joseph Ferrie, "Intergenerational Occupational Mobility in Great Britain and the United States since 1850," *American Economic Review* 103, no. 4 (June 2013), 1109–1137.

37 Long and Ferrie, 1133.

38 Hirschl and Rank, 2010.

39 See occupyarrests.com (accessed: September 22, 2015).

14

Segregation and Discrimination

While the forces of supply and demand can account for much of the inequality between groups and over time, a more complete account of distributional differences must depart fundamentally from the perfectly competitive paradigm. Prejudice, discrimination, and segregation are defining features of both contemporary policy discussions and American economic history. In this chapter, the history of educational and occupational segregation, and the role of discrimination in accounting for differences in earnings, income, and wealth by region, race, ethnicity, and gender are examined.

The shocks of the World Wars, court decisions, government policies, and market competition, together with changing social norms, have all played important roles in reducing, but not eliminating, segregation and discrimination. In this chapter, several theories and empirical methods are introduced to help explain the existence and persistence of both discrimination and segregation, and to measure their impacts.

14.1 THE ECONOMICS OF DISCRIMINATION

Explaining the causes and consequences of discrimination and empirically measuring the magnitude of discrimination are both difficult and complex tasks. Nevertheless, in recent decades economists and other social scientists have developed models and empirical methods to help them.

DISCRIMINATION, PREJUDICE, AND SEGREGATION

Discrimination occurs in a market when participants face terms of trade that are determined, at least in part, by personal characteristics that do not appear directly relevant to the transaction. In labor markets, discrimination takes place if there are differences in the probability of being hired, in pay, and/or in promotion practices that result in workers who are equal with respect to their productivity being treated differently because of their race, ethnicity, gender, age, sexual orientation, or any other characteristic unrelated to job performance.

Prejudice, in contrast, refers to dislike, distaste, or misperceptions based on innate characteristics such as race or gender. While prejudice often leads to discrimination, one does not necessarily cause the other. Prejudice may not result in discrimination if prejudiced employers, employees, or customers are unable to act on their prejudices because of either legal enforcement or market competition. It is also possible for there to be discriminatory outcomes even in the absence of prejudice, as in cases of statistical discrimination, which are discussed below.

Finally, segregation refers to the action or state of certain groups being set apart from other groups in an establishment, a community, or a country. While segregation is usually the result of past or present discrimination, it is also possible for segregation to occur, at least conceptually, without discrimination.

TASTE-BASED MODELS OF DISCRIMINATION

The first economic models of discrimination depended on prejudice.[1] These models showed that workers of minority groups may be paid lower wages than other equally productive workers because of a "taste for discrimination" on the part of employers, fellow employees, or customers who do not like hiring, working alongside, or buying from certain groups, based on characteristics unrelated to job performance.[2]

First consider taste discrimination on the part of employers. For simplicity, assume that labor markets are perfectly competitive and that there are only two sectors in this economy: Sector A and Sector B. Suppose all workers have the same qualifications and the occupations in both sectors are equally attractive to all workers. Under these conditions, if there is no discrimination, then both sectors will pay the same wage, denoted as W_1 in Figure 14.1.

Now suppose that firms in Sector A choose not to employ members of some particular group, say women, because of taste discrimination. Initially, this will cause women to leave Sector A (where firms refuse to hire women) and to begin looking for

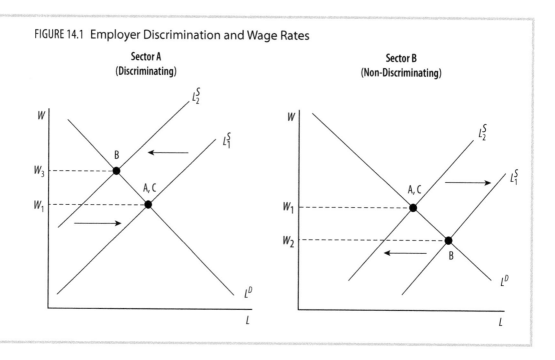

FIGURE 14.1 Employer Discrimination and Wage Rates

jobs in the non-discriminating Sector B. This will increase the labor supply in Sector B (from L_1^S to L_2^S) and reduce the labor supply in Sector A (from L_1^S to L_2^S), leading to a gender wage differential equal to $W_3 - W_2$.

If labor markets are perfectly competitive, however, this gap is only temporary. With wage rates lower in Sector B, some men employed in Sector B will exit that market and seek jobs in Sector A, thereby decreasing the labor supply in Sector B and increasing the labor supply in Sector A. These movements will reverse the changes in labor supply that had occurred previously; and, in equilibrium, the wage rate in both sectors will again be the same, at W_1. In this example, with perfect competition, employer discrimination does not lead to wage gaps in the long run, but it does lead to segregation with only men working in Sector A.

Instead of two sectors, however, suppose that there are many sectors and that employers in most of these sectors refuse to hire women because of taste discrimination. In this case, large numbers of women are crowded into just a few occupations and the exit of men from those occupations may not be enough to equalize wages. With occupational crowding, persistent wage gaps can exist.[3] Occupational crowding can also occur due to the voluntary choices of employees, who may make career decisions for reasons other than just the level of wages.

Next, consider taste discrimination where the source of prejudice comes instead from fellow workers. For example, suppose that male workers dislike being supervised by women. If non-discriminating employers decide to hire female supervisors, then this could lead to lower productivity by male workers, who may shirk and do other things to reduce their performance. This will cause firms who hire female supervisors to have lower profits, and, in the extreme, will cause non-discriminating firms to be driven out of business. In this case, market forces do not eliminate wage gaps but encourage them.

The same general result can occur with taste-based customer discrimination. Suppose customers do not like purchasing products from female salespeople. If some firms hire females anyway, those firms would have lower sales and profits. Customers would be willing to pay higher prices to buy from men just because they prefer to do so.

In summary, with taste-based models of discrimination, employer discrimination will be eliminated with perfect competition, but when prejudice comes from fellow employees and/or customers, market forces can encourage, rather than discourage, discrimination and can result in persistent wage gaps between favored and unfavored groups.

STATISTICAL DISCRIMINATION

Models of statistical discrimination predict that there will be discriminatory outcomes, even when no prejudice exists, if there is imperfect information about workers' training or productivity. Suppose that employers accurately predict that members of certain groups, on average, have objectively lower human capital. Assume, however, that employers cannot observe the qualifications, motivations, and productivity of each job candidate with perfect accuracy at the time of hiring, so that hiring decisions are made on the basis of imperfect signals observed in tests, interviews, and résumés of individual job applicants.

For example, suppose two job candidates apply to work at a large firm (one a member of the purple group, the other a member of the green group). The firm decides to hire both workers, but a decision has to be made on the wage to offer each worker. After reviewing each applicant's résumé and cover letter, and after conducting screening assessments and a job interview, each person receives an overall "test" score of 16 (T). If this test score is perfectly correlated with productivity, then each person will be paid the same.

Suppose, however, that this test score measure is imperfect—some high-score applicants later turn out to have low productivity, and vice versa. A rational employer might link the applicant's wage offer not only to the applicant's score, but also to the average score of the applicant's group ($\overline{T}$). In this case, the wage offer would be:

$$w = \alpha T + (1 - \alpha)\overline{T}$$

The parameters α and $(1 - \alpha)$ represent the relative weights that the employer puts on the individual score versus the group average score. Initially, assume that $\alpha = 0.5$, and that the average score for purple applicants is 10, while it is 14, on average, for green applicants. Then the wage offers to these candidates are:

$$w_P = (0.5 \cdot 16) + (0.5 \cdot 10) = \$13$$

$$w_G = (0.5 \cdot 16) + (0.5 \cdot 14) = \$15$$

Although each applicant has the same individual score, the green applicant benefits by being associated with a higher-scoring group, while the purple applicant receives a lower wage because of his or her association with a lower-performing group. In this case, the wage gap is:

$$\frac{w_P}{w_G} = \frac{\$13}{\$15} = 0.87$$

That is, the purple worker in this example only makes 87 percent as much as the green worker. Although statistical discrimination such as this may lead to better assessments of worker productivity, and may therefore result in higher profits, it is still discriminatory.

Now suppose that the screening process is more accurate in determining on-the-job productivity for green applicants than it is for purple applicants, perhaps because of biases in the screening procedures. If the tests are a worse predictor for the productivity of individual purple workers, then employers will put a smaller weight on individual purple performance during screening compared to the individual performance of green applicants. That is, $\alpha_P < \alpha_G$. For example, suppose that $\alpha_P = 0.2$ and $\alpha_G = 0.8$. In this case, the resulting wage gap will be even wider:

$$w_P = (0.2 \cdot 16) + (0.8 \cdot 10) = \$11.20$$

$$w_G = (0.8 \cdot 16) + (0.2 \cdot 14) = \$15.60$$

$$\frac{w_P}{w_G} = \frac{\$11.20}{\$15.60} = 0.72$$

In summary, a purple worker's wage in this example is based primarily on the group average, while the green worker's wage is largely determined by the worker's own qualifications. Even though both workers are identical in terms of measured attributes related to productivity, imperfect information leads to differences in pay between purple and green workers, even when employers are not prejudiced.

PRE-MARKET DISCRIMINATION

Unequal outcomes in labor markets can also occur in competitive markets if discrimination in housing or education causes certain groups to have lower human capital, less well-developed social networks, or more limited information or access to jobs. In the case of pre-market discrimination, even when there is no discrimination occurring in the labor market per se, discrimination in other markets or institutions prior to this market exchange can lead to lower productivity, on average, among members of a group who have suffered discrimination in other aspects of their lives.

ESTIMATING DISCRIMINATION

Estimating the existence and extent of discrimination is challenging. There are two main empirical methods used to measure discrimination: (1) multiple regression analysis; and (2) audit studies.

Multiple regression analysis is a statistical technique used to indicate how a number of different factors that act together, as well as separately, influence a particular outcome. The example below describes how multiple regression analysis can be applied to employment discrimination. Suppose female attorneys at several large firms file an employment discrimination lawsuit claiming that they are being paid less than similar male attorneys are paid. As part of the lawsuit, a random sample is collected of the annual salaries, the years of experience, and the gender of attorneys at these law firms. These data are entered into a computer and a standard statistical program is used to estimate an equation that best fits the relationship between salary, experience, and gender. Suppose the estimated equation is:

$$\widehat{Salary_i} = \$100{,}000 + \$10{,}000 \cdot Experience_i + \$3{,}000 \cdot Male_i$$
$$+ \$5{,}000(Male_i \cdot Experience_i)$$

This equation predicts the salary of an attorney, denoted $Salary_i$, based on the number of years of experience and the gender of the attorney, where $Male_i$ is a variable that takes on a value of 1 if the attorney is male, and 0 otherwise. The last term is an interactive term that multiplies $Male$ and $Experience$ together to determine whether or not experience is rewarded differently for male attorneys.

The regression output provides information indicating the probability of whether or not the results from the sample are just due to random variation from sample to sample. This information is usually in the form of standard errors or t statistics, which indicate whether or not the results for a variable are statistically significant. In the social sciences, results are generally considered statistically significant if the likelihood that they occurred by chance is less than one in twenty, or 0.05, which corresponds to the 95 percent confidence level.

Statistical significance, however, only measures the likelihood of one variable affecting another variable: it says nothing about the magnitude or *size* of the effect. A female attorney who is predicted to earn $50,000 less is far more economically important than one predicted to earn $5 less, yet both of the effects can be statistically different from zero.

Consider the predicted salaries for a male attorney and a female attorney just starting out (with zero years of experience) using the equation above. In this case, a female attorney is predicted to earn $100,000 a year, while the male attorney is predicted to earn $103,000. Next, consider the predictions for female and male attorneys each with 10 years of experience. The predicted salary for a female attorney is now $200,000, whereas for a male it is $253,000.[4] Note, in this example, that the wage gap between female and male attorneys widens as experience increases.

For the estimated coefficients on the gender variables to be interpreted as discrimination, the regression model must include all variables that systematically influence salary. In this simple example, the only other variable besides gender is experience. In actual applications, researchers would collect information on each attorney's education (such as her or his law school grade-point average and LSAT scores, and the ranking of the law school attended), on the specialization chosen (such as corporate law or family law), on the number of hours worked, and on any other variables available that are likely to be correlated with salary.

However, some factors that determine salary are very difficult, if not impossible, to quantify, and these factors may be known only to the employer and not to the researcher. For example, if there are any measured differences between men and women, the researcher cannot be sure that these differences are not attributable to some unobserved factor or factors. For example, it might be that men, on average, are more willing to work nontraditional work hours (that is, more willing to come in nights and weekends), and that the researcher is unaware of this. Even if the researcher *is* aware of such a factor, it still may not be possible to account for it in the regression model. In these cases, then, after controlling for many but perhaps not all of the factors that determine salaries, it could be that there are some observed differences in salaries between men and women that are not due to discrimination after all, but are simply the result of omitted variables.

As a result of these issues, researchers have attempted to examine market outcomes through controlled experiments using audit studies. With in-person audits, the participants in the study take the roles of job applicants, bank customers, housing buyers, etc. The auditors are paired with one another, and are provided with carefully constructed résumés and histories. They are coached so that the paired individuals are as similar to one another as possible. The only observable difference between the two in each pair is either race or gender. From the outcomes of many paired groups, investigators can measure whether there are systematic differences in the probabilities of being hired, getting an apartment, etc. In cases where job offers are extended, in-person audit studies can measure whether there are any differences in the salaries offered. Because the pairs are identical by construction in all respects except race or gender, any differences can be attributed to discrimination.

Some audit studies eliminate the human element. For example, fictitious résumés are paired together and are then sent to different employers, separately and at different times. In one well-known study, the only difference between paired résumés was the name, with one name chosen in each pair to be a "white" name, such as Emily Walsh, and the other name a "black" name, such as Lakisha Washington.[5] The résumés with white names were 50 percent more likely to elicit an offer of a job interview. Other audit studies have shown systematic differences in the treatment of men and women.[6] The results from audit studies and multiple regression analysis demonstrate that discrimination continues to influence a wide range of market outcomes.

14.2 AFRICAN-AMERICAN CONVERGENCE

Since the end of the Civil War, the dominant long-run theme of the economic history of African Americans is convergence with whites. This convergence has not been continuous, however, but has largely occurred during four time periods: (1) Reconstruction after the Civil War (1865–1877); (2) World War I (1917–1918); (3) World War II (1941–1945); and (4) the period from the early 1960s to the early 1970s, which coincides with the Civil Rights Movement and federal legislation banning discrimination in education, public accommodations, voting, and labor and housing markets.[7] The convergence, however, has slowed considerably in recent decades and is far from complete. Although racial differences have narrowed considerably over the very long run, large differences persist between blacks and whites in terms of earnings, income, wealth, health, and opportunity.

THE ECONOMIC LEGACY OF SLAVERY

Estimates of the education, income, and wealth of African Americans in the immediate aftermath of the Civil War reflect the extreme deprivations of slavery. Most African Americans had no or little formal education, and the overwhelming majority were illiterate. In the 1870 U.S. Census, only 13 percent of white Americans aged 10 and older reported that they were illiterate. In contrast, the black illiteracy rate was 81 percent nationwide; and 83 percent in the South, where more than 90 percent of African Americans lived.[8]

The 1870 Census also reveals huge wealth gaps between blacks and whites, with a wealth ratio of only 0.025, meaning that for every dollar of wealth held by whites, blacks held only 2.5 cents.[9] With little education and wealth, and relatively few marketable skills, newly freed slaves earned low wages. Based on contemporaneous reports of agricultural incomes, the ratio of average black income to average white income in 1865 was about 0.25.[10]

RECONSTRUCTION

"Reconstruction" refers to the period after the Civil War (1865–1877) when federal troops occupied the South. The purposes of Reconstruction were to provide a means whereby former Confederate states could be readmitted to the Union, and to define and enforce an institutional framework in which free blacks and whites could peacefully coexist. Many whites in the South, however, saw Reconstruction as a humiliating and vengeful imposition.

The Emancipation Proclamation (1863) by President Abraham Lincoln legally freed slaves, and this was reaffirmed by the ratification of the Thirteenth Amendment (1865). The Fourteenth Amendment (1868) granted citizenship and equal protection under the law to African Americans, while the Fifteenth Amendment (1870) prohibited the denial of the vote due to "race, color or previous condition of servitude."

Southern state legislatures reacted by passing laws to limit the rights and political power of African Americans. These "Black Codes," which were modeled after earlier slave statutes, ranged in severity and outlawed everything from interracial marriages to loitering in public places. In most cases, they prevented blacks from owning property and from conducting business. A key element of the Black Codes were vagrancy laws, which criminalized black men who were out of work or not working in jobs recognized as appropriate by whites.

Even under these constraints, former slaves could and did make decisions to invest in human capital, to choose occupations, to accumulate wealth, and to change locations in pursuit of better economic opportunities. African Americans also made large political gains during Reconstruction in terms of voting and holding political offices. Literacy rates increased and educated blacks began to populate state legislatures, to open schools, and to start successful businesses. By 1870, at least 15 percent of all Southern elected officials were black, which was almost twice the percentage of black elected officials in the South a century later.[11]

THE DECLINE OF THE SOUTHERN ECONOMY

Before the Civil War, per capita incomes in the South were similar to those in other parts of the United States, although inequality was far greater due to slavery. However, for a century after the Civil War, the South remained a relatively poor region. In 1860, per capita incomes, even with slaves included in the total, were nearly 90 percent of the U.S. average. In 1880 and 1900, however, per capita incomes in the South were only 54 percent of the U.S. average. For decades, the South as a region was far below the rest of the country, and substantial convergence of Southern incomes did not occur until after 1940 (see Figure 14.2).

Since 90 percent of African Americans still lived in the South as late as 1910, the poor economic performance of the region disproportionally affected black incomes and opportunities.

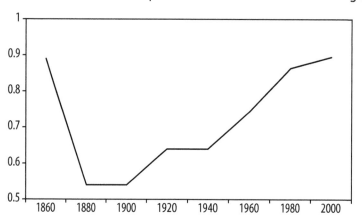

FIGURE 14.2 Southern Per Capita Income Relative to the U.S. Average, 1860–2000

Sources and Notes: The South consists of the South Atlantic, the East South Central, and the West South Central regions. The 1860 ratio is computed from Peter H. Lindert and Jeffrey G. Williamson, "American Incomes, 1774–1860," *National Bureau of Economic Research Working Paper*, no. 18396 (September 2012), Table 1, 33. Population figures from the 1860 U.S. Census are used to compute the weighted average to yield per capita income for the entire South. 1880–1940 data are from Kris James Mitchener and Ian W. McLean, "U.S. Regional Growth and Convergence, 1880–1980," *Journal of Economic History* 59, no. 4 (December 1999), Table 1, 1019. 1960–2000 data are computed from U.S. Bureau of Economic Analysis, www.bea.gov/regional/index.htm (accessed: August 15, 2015).

There are many explanations for this sustained period of relative Southern backwardness. One theory emphasizes the slowdown in demand for Southern cotton in the decades after the War as other regions of the world began to compete with the South in growing cheap cotton. There is also substantial evidence that labor supply decreased substantially after the War as black women and children, in particular, no longer worked in the formal sector as free individuals.[12] Because measures of income typically only include goods and services purchased in markets, the move from market to non-market production, as well as the increase in leisure, caused measured incomes to fall. However, since these choices were voluntary, former slaves must have been better off.

Some scholars have also blamed the change from gang labor under slavery to sharecropping after the Civil War as an important cause of relative Southern decline. Newly freed blacks were resistant to working as wage laborers on large plantations, but instead desired more autonomy and independence. With little capital, land, or access to borrowing from banks, former slaves had only limited options. As a result, sharecropping developed. With sharecropping, former plantation owners divided their lands and rented each plot (or share) to a single black family. The family farmed its own crops and in exchange gave a percentage of the crop as "rent" to the landowner. Many landless whites also became sharecroppers in the decades after the Civil War.

Sharecropping is often portrayed as the cause of poverty in the South after the Civil War, with blacks being unable to escape from ruthless landlords, yet records show that state-to-state migration rates of sharecroppers were high, as were year-to-year movements within local areas.[13] Over time, many black farmers were able to move up the agricultural ladder, often eventually owning small parcels of land.

While slaves did not earn money incomes, scholars have attempted to estimate or impute what their incomes would have been had they been free workers. Compared to the imputed incomes of slaves on large plantations in 1859, by 1879, the value of real per capita incomes and leisure time had increased nearly threefold for African-American sharecroppers.[14] The larger problems that held back African Americans were educational barriers, widespread discrimination, and lack of competition in local labor markets, which together severely limited job opportunities outside the agricultural sector.[15]

DISENFRANCHISEMENT AND JIM CROW LAWS

For at least ten years after the end of Reconstruction in 1877, African Americans continued to vote and to hold political offices. By the end of the nineteenth century, however, states in the South had adopted a wide range of laws and policies that severely restricted the political rights and economic opportunities of African Americans through a system of overt racial discrimination.

All Southern states imposed new voting restrictions for African Americans. In some states, officials administered literacy tests at voter registration. Officials frequently asked blacks more difficult questions than they asked whites; in practice, they could pass or fail applicants as they wished. Another common requirement was the poll tax, an annual tax that had to be paid in order to vote. Poor whites were excluded from these poll taxes by "grandfather" clauses written into these laws.

At the same time that blacks had voting rights taken from them, state and local governments throughout the South passed laws that separated whites and blacks in public and private facilities, which were known as Jim Crow laws.[16] Racial segregation was

FIGURE 14.3 Segregation on Beale Street in Memphis, Tennessee, 1939
Source: Marion Post Wolcott, Library of Congress, www.loc.gov/pictures/collection/fsa/item/fsa1998013755/PP/ (accessed: April 3, 2016).

imposed in relation to schools, hospitals, parks, restaurants, lodging, transportation systems, restrooms, and drinking fountains. With the Supreme Court decision of Plessy vs. Ferguson (1896), the Court established the "separate but equal" doctrine which allowed segregated facilities, and these were then maintained until the Civil Rights Movement sixty years later. In practice, the "separate" part of the law was enforced but not the "equal" part, and facilities labeled as "colored" rapidly declined in quality (Figure 14.3).

African Americans faced not only extensive legal discrimination but also an entire institutional structure of informal rules and customs based on fear, intimidation, and punishment. Between 1882 and 1960, almost 4,000 African Americans were executed by white mobs, often by hanging, in order both to "punish" those suspected (but not convicted) of crimes and to create an atmosphere of fear and intimidation.[17]

In education, disenfranchisement and segregation in the South also led to increasing gaps in per pupil spending by race. In 1890, in several Southern states spending per black pupil had nearly reached parity with spending per white pupil. Just twenty years later, however, spending on black pupils relative to that on white pupils ranged from 75 percent in Delaware to only 17 percent in Louisiana.[18]

In spite of these barriers, blacks continued to make slow progress along several dimensions. Public health measures and infrastructure investment helped. For example, a public health campaign eradicated hookworm, a parasitic disease that affected as many as 40 percent of school-age children in the South, and this soon helped to increase school enrollment, attendance, and literacy.[19] Public investments in water filtration and sewage systems reduced the incidence of typhoid and diarrhea in many Southern cities, benefitting both blacks and whites.[20]

The New Deal programs of the 1930s also improved health and living standards. Research has shown that counties in the South with higher expenditures by New Deal agencies experienced larger declines in infant mortality.[21] The Tennessee Valley Authority and the Rural Electrification Administration brought electricity to many parts of the South. In 1933, only 2 percent of households in the Tennessee Valley had electricity, but 75 percent did by 1945. Electric lights and refrigerators improved living standards, while radios reduced isolation and provided greater awareness of the outside world.[22]

Blacks, however, continued to be underrepresented in the growth of nonfarm employment in the South during the first half of the twentieth century.[23] Segregation and discrimination operated mostly through job classifications and industries, rather than through location.[24] In 1930, in industries such as furniture, textiles, shoes, printing, cars and railroad shops, more than 90 percent of operatives were white; while in jobs related to tobacco manufacture, iron and steel, fertilizers, and turpentine, more than 75 percent of workers were black.[25] There was also extensive discrimination against black workers, particularly in their ability to obtain higher-paying jobs.[26]

THE GREAT MIGRATION

Between 1915 and 1970, six million African Americans left the South in pursuit of job opportunities and a better way of life (Figure 14.4). They moved to large cities like New York, Detroit, Chicago, Philadelphia, and Los Angeles, but also to smaller cities such as Milwaukee, Newark, Gary, and Oakland.[27]

Although the Great Migration began with the increased demand for labor to work in northern manufacturing jobs during World War I, it was not until World War II that the Great Migration began in earnest. With the labor supply from Europe largely cut off, due to immigration laws passed in 1921 and 1924 (see Chapter 15) and the Great Depression, the onset of World War II led manufacturing firms to seek out new sources

FIGURE 14.4 Family Moving North during the Great Migration, 1940

Source: Jack Delano, Library of Congress, www.loc.gov/pictures/item/fsa2000022285/PP/ (accessed: April 27, 2016).

of labor. This increased labor demand was the primary pull factor luring African Americans northward and westward into manufacturing cities.

There were also important push factors. The infestation of the boll weevil beetle decimated cotton crops in the 1920s, and the impact of the Great Depression further worsened economic conditions in the South.[28] Falling agricultural incomes and high unemployment, coupled with the long history of segregation and discrimination in the South, "pushed" millions of African Americans out of the South in search of better opportunities. Another important push factor was the Fair Labor Standards Act (1938), which for the first time imposed a nationwide minimum wage.[29] Because wages in the South were so low, the minimum wage led to increased unemployment in the South, and provided an unintended reason for African Americans to move north.

Between 1940 and 1960, roughly one-fourth of Southern blacks migrated out of the South. Since the black–white wage differential was smaller in the North, and since wages were far higher there as well, the migration of millions of African Americans narrowed the U.S. racial wage gap substantially. This was particularly true during the 1940s, when black–white wage gaps for both male and female workers converged more rapidly than in any other decade of American history.[30]

THE CIVIL RIGHTS MOVEMENT

Scholarship convincingly argues that the Civil Rights Movement "was a true revolution, that is, a fundamental break with past trends and behavior that cannot be explained away as an inevitable consequence of market forces or modernization."[31] The Civil Rights Movement broke down barriers in education, public accommodations, employment, and voting.

Landmark federal legislation in 1964 and 1965 was essential for its success.[32] The two most important pieces of legislation were the Civil Rights Act (1964) and the Voting Rights Act (1965). Title II of the Civil Rights Act prohibited discrimination in public accommodations (restaurants, hotels, etc.), while Title III gave the U.S. Attorney General the power to intervene on behalf of those who had been denied access to public facilities.

The 1954 Supreme Court decision in Brown vs. The Board of Education of Topeka struck down segregation of local schools, but desegregation of schools occurred only gradually. Title IV of the Civil Rights Act formally desegregated public schools and strengthened the U.S. Attorney General's ability to support and enforce the law. It also outlawed discrimination in all "federally assisted programs." Since nearly all colleges and universities receive some federal support, if only through the federal student loan programs, the scope of the Act has been extremely wide in education.

Title VII prohibited employment discrimination on the basis of race, color, religion, gender, or national origin, and also of pregnancy, childbirth, or any related medical conditions (added in 2000). In addition, it specifically covered hiring, firing, compensation, terms, conditions, and privileges of employment.

The Voting Rights Act prevented states and local governments from imposing any law or policy that results in discrimination against racial or language minorities. It explicitly outlawed literacy tests and similar devices that had long been used, contrary to the guarantee in the Fifteenth Amendment, to prevent blacks and other minorities from voting.

After making very little economic progress during the 1950s, African Americans throughout the United States experienced substantial gains from the early 1960s to

FIGURE 14.5 Black Median Income by Region, 1953–2013 (2013 U.S. Dollars)

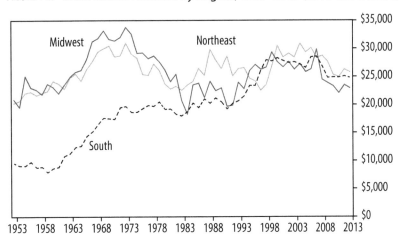

Sources and Notes: Computed from United States Bureau of the Census, *Historical Income Tables*, Table P-5, www.census.gov/hhes/www/income/data/historical/people/2013/p05B.xls (accessed: August 1, 2015).

1973 (Figure 14.5). Although black median income increased in all regions during the Civil Rights era, the gains were largest in the South. Measured in 2013 dollars, median black incomes in the South increased from $7,926 in 1959 to $19,687 by 1973, an average annual increase of 6.7 percent per year.

While convergence in the quantity and quality of African-American education predates the Civil Rights Movement, between 15 and 20 percent of the gains made by African Americans between 1960 and 1980 were due to increases in school quality. The black–white test score gap decreased markedly during the 1980s, and this decline was concentrated in cohorts born in the South between 1963 and the early 1970s.[33]

The South as a region prospered during the Civil Rights era, even though many white southerners, and especially white businessmen, strongly resisted desegregation (incidentally providing evidence that "firms do not always know best how to maximize profit").[34] The desegregation stimulated retail sales, in fact; contrary to the concerns of many white businessmen, new black customers did little to discourage white patronage. Desegregation also led to outside investment in the region, from the movement of professional sports franchises to manufacturing firms eager to benefit from lower wages and lower rates of unionization. Real estate was also given a boost, as many areas of the South became destinations for retirees and those on vacation.

In every decade between 1880 and 1960, more whites and blacks left the South than moved into the South. Since 1970, however, net migration rates for both whites and blacks into the South have been large and positive each decade, with more people moving into the South than leaving.[35]

Southern per capita incomes continued to converge toward the U.S. average, reaching almost 90 percent by the year 2000 (Figure 14.2). From the mid-1970s to the early 1990s, black–white median income ratios were relatively constant for men, but fell for women (Figure 14.6). From the end of the recession in 1991 to the onset of the Great Recession in December 2007, black–white income ratios began to

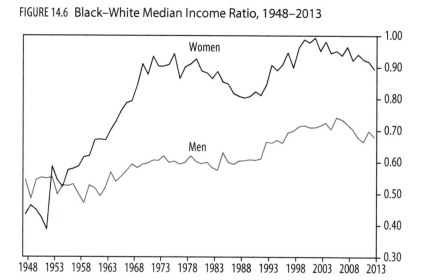

FIGURE 14.6 Black–White Median Income Ratio, 1948–2013

Sources and Notes: Computed from U.S. Bureau of the Census, *Historical Income Tables*, Table P-2, www.census.gov/hhes/www/income/data/historical/people/2013/p02.xls (accessed: August 8, 2015). The figure above reports the ratio of median black income divided by median white income in current dollars.

converge again, leading to less inequality between blacks and whites. The impact and the aftermath of the Great Recession, however, have erased many of the gains over the past twenty years. In 2013, the ratio of black–white median income was still only 69.8 percent for men; while for women the racial wage gap stood at 89.4 percent, down from a near-parity ratio of 99.4 percent in 2002.

WHY DOES THE INCOME GAP PERSIST?

There are two broad sets of explanations for why the black–white income gap remains wide. One view attributes persistent inequality to the path-dependent legacy of slavery and segregation. During the Great Migration, as large numbers of African Americans migrated into northern and western cities from the South, cities that had previously tolerated small African-American populations became increasingly segregated as their black populations grew.

Many scholars have argued that residential segregation is at least partly responsible for the continuing income gaps between blacks and whites. Although residential segregation is well below peak levels, high levels of segregation have persisted in most American cities to the present day.

Segregation negatively affects disadvantaged individuals through various channels, including reduced exposure to role models and successful peers, decreased funding for public goods including schools, and increased distance from available jobs. Segregation can also lead to different cultural norms between groups, which foster discriminatory attitudes and social distance between groups. In the United States, cities where residential segregation is higher are also cities where black poverty and inequality are higher, and where white poverty and inequality are lower, in comparison with cities that are less segregated.[36]

The second broad view identifies recent changes in labor markets and lingering racial discrimination as the major factors. African Americans have been disproportionally affected by the factors that have increased income inequality in the United States since the 1970s (see Chapter 13), including the shift from manufacturing to services, the diminished power of unions, skill-biased technological change, and globalization. Because of the well-documented shift in labor demand toward workers with higher skills, the bottom third of the white wage distribution and the bottom half of the black wage distribution have been unable to keep pace with high-skilled workers. In this view, the majority of the persistent wage gap is due to "race neutral" factors that have adversely affected both blacks and whites, but which have disproportionally affected blacks since blacks were more likely than whites to be living in the manufacturing areas and central cities that have been particularly hard hit since the 1970s.

In recent decades, social surveys report large decreases in discriminatory attitudes. In 1958, only 4 percent of Americans "approved" of marriages between blacks and whites, but by 2013, the approval rate was 87 percent.[37] Rates of intermarriage have increased as well in the last half century. Civil Rights legislation has also made discrimination illegal.

Nevertheless, discrimination—in labor markets, credit markets, housing markets, education, and the criminal justice system, as well as in other avenues of life—continues to limit the opportunities and outcomes for African Americans. One study concludes that discrimination in labor markets accounts "for at least one third of the black–white wage gap."[38]

Table 14.1 reports recent differences by race and gender for a wide variety of economic and social outcomes. By almost any measure, African Americans, on average, lag behind white Americans. Blacks have higher unemployment, poverty, and incarceration rates, along with lower marriage rates, life expectancy, income, and wealth. African-American males are imprisoned in the criminal justice system more than six

TABLE 14.1 Racial and Gender Differences, 2013	White		Black		Hispanic		Asian	
	Male	Female	Male	Female	Male	Female	Male	Female
Bachelor's Degree or More (Percent)	32.4	31.6	19.8	23.3	13.9	16.2	56.1	50.8
Unemployment Rate (Percent)	6.8	6.2	14.2	12.1	8.8	9.5	5.6	4.8
Median Full-Time Weekly Earnings (Dollars)	$884	$722	$664	$606	$594	$541	$1,059	$819
Life Expectancy at Birth (Years)	76.7	81.4	72.3	78.4	79.1	83.8	83.1	85.8
Incarceration Rates (Percent in 2010)	0.678	0.091	4.347	0.260	1.775	0.133	NA	NA
Median Annual Household Income (Dollars)	$58,270		$34,598		$40,903		$67,065	
Gini Coefficient for Household Income	0.467		0.493		0.472		0.453	
Poverty Rate (Percent)	9.6		27.2		23.5		10.5	
Median Family Wealth (Dollars)	$134,008		$11,184		$13,900		$91,440	
Percent of Families in Upper Half of the Wealth Distribution	59		23		25		51	
Percent Never Married (Age 25 and Older)	16		36		26		19	

Sources and Notes: Data are from various official U.S. government sources, including the Census Bureau, the Bureau of Labor Statistics, the Centers for Disease Control and Prevention, the Federal Reserve, and the Bureau of Justice Statistics. All data are for the year 2013, except where noted.

times as frequently as their white counterparts. The wealth gap remains large and persistent, with white median family wealth of $134,008, compared to only $11,184 for black families.

ECONOMIC MOBILITY

Economic mobility in the United States has likely decreased in recent decades (see Chapter 13), but rates of mobility vary tremendously by location and by race. In comparison with whites, African Americans in recent decades have experienced substantially less upward intergenerational mobility and substantially more downward intergenerational mobility. The higher probability of downward mobility applies to blacks across all income groups. About 61 percent of black children whose parents had incomes in the top half of the income distribution fall into the bottom half as adults, compared with only 36 percent for whites.[39]

The causes for the relative lack of upward mobility for African Americans seem to be closely related to the areas where African Americans live. Areas where the probability of a child starting in the bottom 20 percent of the income distribution rising to the top 20 percent by the age of 30 is greatest in areas that have less residential segregation, less income inequality, better primary schools, greater social networks and engagement in community organizations, and greater family stability. Mobility is lowest "in areas with larger African American populations, such as the Southeast."[40] For example, the chance that a child of any race will reach the top 20 percent of the national income distribution after starting from a family in the bottom 20 percent is only 4.4 percent in Charlotte, North Carolina, but almost 13 percent in San Jose, California.[41]

14.3 HISPANIC AND ASIAN AMERICANS

While Hispanic and Asian Americans have long contributed to the success of the United States, large increases in immigration since the mid-1960s have greatly increased the proportion of Americans with Latino and Asian heritage. The magnitude and importance of the most recent wave of immigration over the past half century, and the impact of this on Latinos, Asians, and the United States as a whole, are discussed in detail in Chapter 15.

The experiences of Hispanic and Asian Americans have been profoundly affected by U.S. immigration policies, and there is also a long history of discrimination and limited opportunities for U.S.-born Latino and Asian Americans.

The figures presented in Table 14.1 show that Hispanic men and women fare quite similarly to African-American men and women along many dimensions, but with even lower levels of educational attainment and incomes. In contrast, Asian Americans have long been considered the "model minority" and tend to have higher levels of educational attainment and income and longer life expectancy than white Americans. There is, however, a great deal of heterogeneity among Asian Americans. Some groups, such as Asian Indian, Filipino, Japanese, and Chinese Americans, typically have high levels of education and median household incomes well above those of white Americans and the national average. In contrast, Southeast Asian populations, such as Cambodian, Hmong, and Laotian Americans, who mostly came to the U.S. as refugees with low levels of education, have median household incomes below those of white Americans and the national average, in addition to higher levels of poverty.[42]

Although some of the current gaps are still likely to be the result of discrimination, "there is general agreement that most or all of the earnings differential ... [between white and Hispanic men and between white and Asian men] can be explained by differences in education and language knowledge."[43] For example, one recent study found no evidence of discrimination against second-generation Asian Americans, although there were small, but statistically significant, discrimination coefficients for first-generation Asian Americans.[44]

14.4 GENDER CONVERGENCE

While progress has not been continuous, the relative wages of women have increased substantially over the course of American history, and perhaps most dramatically since around 1980. In many instances, changes in the gender wage gap have not followed trends in overall inequality. For example, between 1955 and 1980, the gender wage gap remained quite constant, with women making about 60 percent of what men made. This period, however, was one of fast wage growth and low inequality in the economy as a whole. Since 1980, as overall inequality has increased dramatically, the wage gap between women and men has narrowed substantially with women "swimming against the tide" of rising inequality.

Chapter 12 (Section 12.2) discussed the large increase in female labor force participation rates since the late nineteenth century. In the late nineteenth century, fewer than 15 percent of all adult women were part of the labor force, and similarly fewer than 5 percent of married women. Today, about 60 percent of adult women are in the labor force and there are virtually no differences between married and single women.

Increases in both labor demand and labor supply for women can account for the increases in labor force participation, but the gender wage gap narrows only if the labor demand for women increases more than the labor demand for men, or if the labor supply of women increases less than the labor supply of men.

The ratio of female earnings to male earnings by those in full-time work increased throughout the nineteenth century until the 1880s (Table 14.2), from 0.371 in 1820 to 0.559 in 1885. During industrialization, the substitution of machinery for human strength and the increasing division of labor enhanced the relative productivity of women and caused the ratio of female–male earnings to increase.[45]

Although participation rates have risen dramatically since the late nineteenth century, the wage gap barely changed between 1885 and 1980, increasing only from 0.559 to 0.628 in nearly a century. Since 1980, however, the ratio has increased, reaching 0.805 by the year 2000. The nearly 20-percentage-point decrease in the wage gap since 1980 is the fastest rate of convergence in American history. There are several possible explanations for the convergence and continued existence of gender wage gaps, and these explanations have varied in importance at different times in American history.

TABLE 14.2 Ratio of Female-to-Male Full-Time Earnings, 1820–2010

Year	Ratio
1820	0.371
1832	0.441
1850	0.460
1885	0.559
1900	0.554
1920	0.559
1939	0.539
1955	0.639
1965	0.599
1980	0.628
1990	0.721
2000	0.745
2010	0.805

Sources and Notes: 1820–1965 from Claudia Goldin, Understanding the Gender Gap: An Economic History of American Women (New York: Oxford University Press, 1990), Table 3.1, 60–61. The data prior to 1955 refer to women in the manufacturing sector and are based on full-time, year-round employees. The data for the years from 1980 to 2010 are computed from the U.S. Bureau of the Census, Median Usual Weekly Earnings of Full Time Wage and Salary Workers by Sex, Table 649, www.census.gov/compendia/statab/2012/tables/12s0649.xls (accessed: August 4, 2015).

DIFFERENCES IN HUMAN CAPITAL

One reason why women earn less than men is that women tend to have less labor market experience. Historically, women provided the majority of household work and childcare, and participated in labor markets less continuously and less intensively than men. Periods of absence from the labor force are also associated with a depreciation of skills. In addition, with the customary division of labor within the family, there was also less incentive for women to develop skills that would be rewarded through continuous labor market participation.

While women's labor market experience and attachment have increased substantially in recent decades, many believe that the source of the current gender pay gap extends beyond the workplace and into the typical American household. Although men, on average, spend more time on household activities than they used to, women still spend far more time each week taking care of children, cooking, cleaning, shopping for groceries, and doing laundry. Because women, on average, demand more flexibility to take care of children and to tend to family responsibilities, they are more likely to seek jobs that offer this flexibility and are more likely to work part-time.

Women are also more likely to leave the workforce temporarily, to work fewer hours, or to turn down promotions, often so that they can care for children or other family members. All of these choices can lead to lower earnings for women. While there certainly are biological differences between men and women, many argue that differences in perceptions regarding home and work responsibilities are mostly, if not entirely, cultural.

Scholars have identified differences across countries in cultural beliefs regarding gender attitudes and female behaviors, and have traced these differences to differences in traditional agricultural practices.[46] Agricultural practices in some societies in the pre-industrial period are described as "shifting cultivation;" they depend on labor rather than machines, with both men and women using handheld tools like hoes in their farming. In contrast, "plough cultivation," in which a plough is used to prepare the soil, depends on machines rather than labor (that is, they rely on physical capital). Because ploughs require "significant upper body strength, grip strength, and bursts of power ... men have an advantage in farming relative to women."[47]

Societies characterized by plough cultivation, and by the gender-based division of labor, developed cultural beliefs that a woman's place "is within the home." Even as economies moved away from agriculture, these beliefs persisted. Countries like the United States, where plough cultivation was the norm, exhibit greater gender inequality and lower levels of female labor force participation today.

LABOR MARKET DISCRIMINATION

Many of the changes that eventually resulted in large increases in married women's employment, including increased education, reduced birth rates, and the rising importance of the clerical sector, were evident as early as the 1920s. Before 1950, however, married women, in particular, faced substantial barriers. Prior to the 1930s, the typical workweek was 5.5 or 6 days and 50 hours long, and part-time work was virtually non-existent.[48]

It was common practice to prohibit married women from employment in school districts and firms, and these prohibitions, called "marriage bars," included both rules against hiring married women and policies against retaining existing female workers when they married. At their peak, marriage bars were in place in 87 percent of all local school districts and probably about 50 percent of all office work.[49]

In the 1950s, because of increased demand for labor, and a relative shortage of young unmarried women, marriage bars were eliminated and part-time employment developed, although many other types of discrimination continued. Nearly all studies show a decrease in discrimination against women over time, and some recent research shows little or no gender wage gap between young working women and young working men after other controls are added to the regression models.[50]

OCCUPATIONAL SEGREGATION

Even casual observation discovers that women are more likely than men to be in certain occupations, and less likely in others. The overwhelming majority of elementary school teachers, nurses, receptionists, flight attendants, and house cleaners are women; while men are far more likely to be construction workers, truck drivers, police officers, surgeons, chemical engineers, or pilots.

Women are still underrepresented in the STEM (science, technology, engineering, and math) majors and in the occupations that require those skills. Figure 14.7 plots the gender composition of college majors on the horizontal axis and the mid-career annual salaries by major on the vertical axis. It is clear that the higher the female concentration in any college major, the lower the mid-career earnings. While this correlation is not necessarily causal, women are not choosing the highest-paying majors in large numbers.

FIGURE 14.7 Mid-Career Salary and Gender Composition by College Major

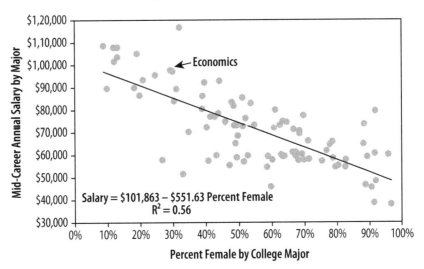

Sources and Notes: Percentage Female by College Major computed from National Center for Education Statistics, Digest of Education Statistics 2013, Table 318.30, https://nces.ed.gov/programs/digest/d13/tables/dt13_318.30.asp (accessed: September 7, 2015). Mid-Career Annual Salary by Major computed from *2013–2014 PayScale College Salary Report*, www.payscale.com/college-salary-report-2014/majors-that-pay-you-back (accessed: September 7, 2015).

LINEAR vs. NONLINEAR OCCUPATIONS

While occupational segregation by gender is a feature of many U.S. labor markets, most of the unexplained wage gap may be the result of the choices men and women make within similar occupations.[51] Among high-earning occupations, many are non-linear with respect to hours worked and pay earned. For occupations in finance and law, for example, those who are willing to put in very long hours at any time of day or night are often rewarded handsomely. Figure 14.8 shows a "nonlinear" occupation, like law or finance. If males are more likely to cluster in the top right quadrant, while women, particularly after having children, are more likely to cluster in the bottom left, then this could account for some of the earnings gap in these occupations.

In contrast, some occupations have a linear pay structure. With a linear occupation, working twice the hours results in twice the pay (but not *more* than twice the pay, as with a nonlinear occupation). Consider women with children who want to work part-time: in a linear occupation, such as being a pharmacist, there is no part-time penalty—with standardized drugs and computer records, pharmacists can easily step in for one another throughout the day. As a result, 65 percent of new pharmacists are women, and there is almost no pay gap between male and female pharmacists.[52] Figure 14.9 illustrates a linear pay structure.

MALE GENDER GAPS

The decreasing gap in wages between men and women in recent decades is a story of increasing opportunities and outcomes for women, but also one of stagnation and struggles for many men. In the past few decades the return to education has been

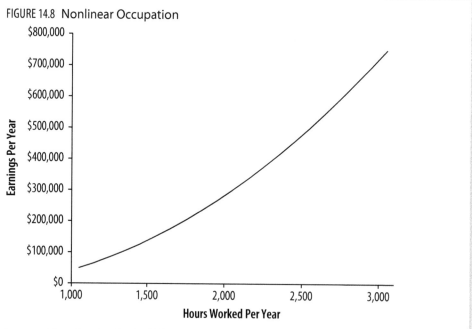

FIGURE 14.8 Nonlinear Occupation

Sources and Notes: Based on Claudia Goldin, "A Grand Gender Convergence: Its Last Chapter," *American Economic Review* 104, no. 4 (April 2014), Figure 4, 1105.

FIGURE 14.9 Linear Occupation

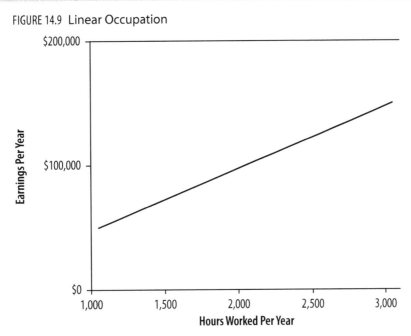

Sources and Notes: Based on Claudia Goldin, "A Grand Gender Convergence: Its Last Chapter," *American Economic Review* 104, no. 4 (April 2014), Figure 4, 1105.

increasing, yet male educational attainment, and therefore income, has stagnated. In recent years, only 42 percent of bachelor's degree recipients are male.

Most one-parent households are headed by mothers, not fathers; and in these families boys appear to do relatively worse. The decrease in unionization rates and the decline in manufacturing employment have also caused male earnings to fall, particularly for men with relatively little human capital.

14.5 CONCLUSIONS

While discrimination and segregation still influence many economic outcomes in the United States, the long-run history is one of convergence for women and for African Americans. When compared to the 1950s, there have been dramatic gains in outcomes and opportunities, although economic progress by African Americans has slowed since the 1970s. In contrast, income and wage convergence by gender has accelerated in recent decades.

QUESTIONS

1. A large employer gives each new hire an aptitude test, which is scored from 1 to 20. Let T be a worker's score on the test. The firm then pays the new worker a wage of $W0.5T + 0.5G$ where G is the average score for the worker's gender: 16 for women and 12 for men. What is the wage for a male who scores 16 on the test? Now, suppose that the employer still uses the same formula, but that the wages paid to male workers and to female workers are identical. In this case, is anyone facing discrimination? Explain.

2. Consider the predicted multiple regression equation in Section 14.1. What are the predicted salaries for a female attorney and a male attorney, both with 20 years of experience at the firm? Are the differences in salaries necessarily the result of discrimination? Why or why not?

3. Discuss the changing economic role of African Americans in the United States from 1865 to the present. What were the major factors and processes that kept African Americans, on average, relatively poor after the Civil War? To what extent are these processes still operating today? Explain.

4. Using the labor demand and supply framework, explain why the gender wage gap was relatively constant between 1885 and 1980, and why the ratio of female–male earnings has increased from 0.628 in 1980 to 0.805 in 2010.

5. What are linear and nonlinear occupations? Explain what this distinction means and why it is important.

NOTES

[1] Gary Becker developed the first economic models of discrimination. See Gary S. Becker, *The Economics of Discrimination* (Chicago, IL: University of Chicago Press, 1957), based on his 1955 Ph.D. dissertation.

[2] The models in this section are described in more detail in Kevin Lang, *Poverty and Discrimination* (Princeton, NJ: Princeton University Press, 2007), Chapter 10; and in George J. Borjas, *Labor Economics*, Seventh Edition (New York, NY: McGraw Hill, 2015), Chapter 9.

[3] Barbara R. Bergmann, "Occupational Segregation, Wages and Profits When Employers Discriminate by Race or Sex," *Eastern Economic Journal* 1, no. 2 (April 1974), 103–110.

[4] For a female attorney with 10 years of experience, the predicted salary is $100,000 + $10,000 · 10 = $200,000. For a male attorney with 10 years of experience, the predicted salary is $100,000 + $10,000 · 10 + $3,000 · 1 + $5,000(1 · 10) = $253,000.

[5] Marianne Bertrand and Sendhil Mullainathan, "Are Emily and Greg More Employable than Lakisha and Jamal? A Field Experiment on Labor Market Discrimination," *American Economic Review* 94, no. 4 (September 2004), 991–1013.

[6] David Neumark, Roy J. Bank, and Kyle D. Van Nort, "Sex Discrimination in Restaurant Hiring: An Audit Study," *Quarterly Journal of Economics* 111, no. 3 (August 1996), 915–941. The authors found that men were more likely to be interviewed and hired by high-price restaurants, while women were more likely to be interviewed and hired by low-price restaurants. Since servers depend primarily on tips, this implies that males earn more than females as a result of discrimination.

[7] Robert A. Margo, "Government and the American Dilemma," in *Government and the American Economy: A New History* (Chicago, IL: University of Chicago Press, 2007), 232–254.

[8] Robert A. Margo, 240.

[9] Robert A. Margo, 239–240.

[10] Robert Higgs, *Competition and Coercion: Blacks in the American Economy, 1865–1914* (New York, NY: Cambridge University Press, 1977).

[11] Michelle Alexander, *The New Jim Crow: Mass Incarceration in the Age of Colorblindness* (New York, NY: The New Press, 2012), 29.

[12] Roger L. Ransom and Richard Sutch, *One Kind of Freedom: The Economic Consequences of Emancipation*, Second Edition (New York, NY: Cambridge University Press, 2001).

[13] Gavin Wright, *Old South, New South: Revolutions in the Southern Economy since the Civil War* (New York, NY: Basic Books, 1986).

[14] Kenneth Ng and Nancy Virts, "The Value of Freedom," *Journal of Economic History* 49, no. 4 (December 1989), 959.

[15] Wright, 37.

[16] These laws appear to have been named after a minstrel-show character who sang a song ending in the words "Jump Jim Crow." See Melvin I. Urofsky, "Jim Crow Law," *Encyclopedia Britannica*, www.britannica.com/event/Jim-Crow-law (accessed: July 16, 2015).

[17] *Lynching in America: Confronting the Legacy of Racial Terror*, Economic Justice Initiative (2015), 4–5, www.eji.org/files/EJI%20Lynching%20in%20America%20SUMMARY.pdf (accessed: August 25, 2015).

[18] Robert A. Margo, *Disenfranchisement, School Finance, and the Economics of Segregated Schools in the U.S. South, 1890–1910* (New York, NY: Garland Press, 1985), Table I-1.

[19] Hoyt Bleakley, "Disease and Development: Evidence from Hookworm Eradication in the American South," *Quarterly Journal of Economics* 122, no. 1 (February 2007), 73–117.

[20] Werner Troesken, *Water, Race, and Disease* (Cambridge, MA: MIT Press, 2004).

[21] Price V. Fishback, Michael R. Haines, and Shawn Kantor, "The Impact of the New Deal on Black and White Infant Mortality in the South," *Explorations in Economic History* 38, no. 1 (January 2001), 93–122.

[22] Wright, 59–60.

[23] Wright, 6.

[24] Wright, 38.

[25] Wright, 38.

[26] William A. Sundstrom, "Half a Career: Discrimination and Railroad Internal Labor Markets," *Industrial Relations* 29, no. 3 (September 1990), 423–440.

[27] Isabel Wilkerson, *The Warmth of Other Suns: The Epic Story of America's Great Migration* (New York, NY: Random House, 2010), 9.

[28] Fabian Lange, Alan L. Olmstead, and Paul W. Rhode, "The Impact of the Boll Weevil, 1892–1932," *Journal of Economic History* 69, no. 3 (September 2009), 685–718.

[29] Wright, 15, 216–225.

[30] James P. Smith and Finis R. Welch, "Black Economic Progress After Myrdal," *Journal of Economic Literature* 27, no. 2 (June 1989), Table 6, 526.

[31] Gavin Wright, *Sharing the Prize: The Economics of the Civil Rights Revolution in the American South* (Cambridge, MA: The Belknap Press of Harvard University, 2013), 4.

[32] Wright, 4.

[33] Kenneth Y. Chay, Jonathan Guryan, and Bhashkar Mazumder, "Birth Cohort and the Black–White Achievement Gap: The Roles of Access and Health Soon After Birth," *National Bureau of Economic Research Working Paper*, no. 15708 (June 2009).

[34] Wright, 19.

[35] Wright, 143.

[36] Elizabeth Ananat, "The Wrong Side(s) of the Tracks: The Causal Effects of Racial Segregation on Urban Poverty and Inequality," *American Economic Journal: Applied Economics* 3, no. 2 (April 2011), 58.

[37] Gallup Poll, www.gallup.com/poll/163697/approve-marriage-blacks-whites.aspx (accessed: September 12, 2015).

[38] Roland G. Fryer, Jr., Devah Pager, and Jorg L. Spenchuch, "Racial Disparities in Job Finding and Offered Wages," *National Bureau of Economic Research Working Paper*, no. 17462 (September 2011).

[39] Bhashkar Mazumder, "Black–White Differences in Intergenerational Economic Mobility in the United States," *Economic Perspectives*, Quarter 1 (2014), Federal Reserve Bank of Chicago, 7, www.chicagofed.org/~/media/publications/economic-perspectives/2014/1q2014-part1-mazumder-pdf (accessed: September 14, 2015).

[40] Chetty, Hendren, Kline, and Saez, 1605.

[41] Chetty, Hendren, Kline, and Saez, 1554.

[42] Karthick Ramakrishnan and Farah Z. Ahmad, "Income and Poverty: Part of the 'State of Asian Americans and Pacific Islanders' Series," (Center for American Progress, July 21, 2014), https://cdn.americanprogress.org/wp-content/uploads/2014/08/AAPI-IncomePoverty.pdf (accessed: June 17, 2016).

[43] Lang, 301.

[44] G. Reza Arabsheibani and Jie Wang, "Asian–White Male Wage Differentials in the United States," *Applied Economic Letters* 17, no. 1 (January 2010), Table 4, 42.

[45] Claudia Goldin, *Understanding the Gender Gap* (New York, NY: Oxford University Press, 1990), 63–67.

[46] Alberto Alesina, Paulo Guiliano, and Nathan Nunn, "On the Origins of Gender Roles: Women and the Plough," *Quarterly Journal of Economics* 128, no. 2 (May 2013), 469–530.

[47] Alesina et al., 470.

[48] Goldin, 159.

[49] Goldin, 161.

[50] Claudia Goldin, "A Grand Gender Convergence: Its Last Chapter," *American Economic Review* 104, no. 4 (April 2014), 1091–1119.

[51] Goldin, 1094, makes the distinction between linear and nonlinear occupations.

[52] Goldin, 1115.

15

Immigration and Immigration Policies

The Old World arrived in the New World in three distinct ways: colonization, coercion, and immigration.[1] Colonists from England, France, Spain, Sweden, and the Netherlands established colonies in North America during the voyages of discovery. Coercion also contributed to population growth and economic development through the importation of African slaves (who were 19 percent of the U.S. population by 1790) and the incorporation of Native American, French, Spanish, and other populations as the U.S. expanded westward through conquest and purchase. The third way depended on immigration; that is, on the voluntary decisions of tens of millions of people to migrate to the United States. Since 1820, more than 80 million people have made the decision to come to the United States, which is more than have migrated to any other country in the world.[2]

Many factors contributed to the large number of immigrants over the last two centuries.[3] Rapid economic growth and technological progress have dramatically lowered transportation costs and made ocean voyages faster and safer. Technological progress led to improved communication, which has made people more aware of opportunities elsewhere. Because the rate of economic growth has varied considerably from country to country since 1800, the "Great Divergence" in average living standards across countries has provided increased incentives for those from poorer countries to move to richer countries. Finally, the twentieth-century surge in population growth in developing countries has greatly increased the young, working-age populations in those countries, the age group most likely to emigrate.

The focus of this chapter is on the causes and effects of immigration, as well as on how U.S. policies have affected immigration flows. Immigration waves in the nineteenth century are connected to economic changes taking place on both sides of the Atlantic. While immigration was largely unrestricted before 1875, limitations on Chinese immigrants and other groups became increasingly common. By 1924, there were strong restrictions on immigration that lasted until 1965. Finally, the causes and effects of the resurgence of immigration—due in part to immigration reform in 1965, which led to large flows of migrants from Latin America and Asia—are examined.

15.1 THE DETERMINANTS OF INTERNATIONAL MIGRATION

The decision to leave one's country of birth is undoubtedly one of the most difficult and complex choices a person can make. While the expected costs and benefits are different for each person, many economic historians categorize the decision to migrate in terms of both push and pull factors.[4]

PUSH FACTORS

Push factors are conditions in a person's home country (the source country) that encourage emigration. In many instances, poor economic performance that results in low incomes and high unemployment are the primary push factors. In other cases, wars, natural disasters, discrimination, and political or religious persecution can be important push factors that cause people to leave a source country to find better opportunities and better conditions in a destination country.

PULL FACTORS

Pull factors are conditions in a destination country that attract immigrants. Greater economic opportunities, and religious and political freedom, are often the primary pull factors. Throughout much of American history, one of the most important pull factors was the availability of high-quality and low-cost land. Pull factors can manifest themselves in many ways, such as the pull of the California Gold Rush after 1848.

There are often large fluctuations from year to year in the number of immigrants coming to the United States, and these are associated with business cycles or economic fluctuations. During the Great Depression of the 1930s, for example, the number of immigrants coming to America fell dramatically as economic conditions in the United States deteriorated. In general, the number of immigrants decreases during recessions and increases during expansions.

Another important pull factor is the presence of known individuals from the source country who have already migrated to the destination country. There are numerous instances in American history where a relatively small group of early immigrants has provided the information, kinship, and connections to encourage many others to follow (Economic History in Action 15.1).

ECONOMIC HISTORY IN ACTION 15.1

Somali Immigrants in Lewiston, Maine

Lewiston, Maine, was once home to thriving textile and shoe factories, which attracted immigrants in large numbers. Bates Mill was the city's largest employer from the 1850s to the mid-twentieth century, and it developed into a huge industrial complex of over 1 million square feet. Irish immigrants began arriving during the Irish Potato Famine in the late 1840s. In the late 1860s, large numbers of French Canadians began moving to the city. By 1880, 35 percent of Lewiston's population was foreign-born.[5]

By the late 1950s, however, Lewiston's textile mills had begun to close, and stores abandoned the downtown area. In 1982, the city's largest department store, the four-story B. Peck & Company, closed after more than a century in business.[6] From a population of almost 42,000 in 1970, Lewiston's population fell to less than 36,000 by 2000.

Things were soon about to change in ways no one could have expected. In 1999, thousands of Somali refugees, fleeing civil war, had migrated to the U.S. as refugees, and were relocated in several large American cities. Some refugees were unhappy and began looking elsewhere for places to live—places with employment opportunities, low crime, good schools, and cheap housing. As one writer noted, "A family of Somali refugees discovered Lewiston in 2001 and began spreading the word to immigrant friends and relatives that housing was cheap and it looked like a good place to build new lives and raise children in peace."[7] Soon other African immigrants followed, including those from the Sudan, the Democratic Republic of the Congo, and other African countries. By 2015, almost 10 percent of the Lewiston population consisted of African immigrants and their children. While there have been some conflicts, most observers agree that immigration has helped revitalize Lewiston.

A SELF-SELECTION MODEL OF IMMIGRATION

While an examination of push and pull factors can help to explain changes in the number of immigrants and determine which countries may be source countries for migration to the United States, another important issue involves the self-selection of who decides to migrate from each country.[8] The self-selection model of immigration is based on two premises: (1) workers in source and destination countries are not the same in terms of their abilities, education, age, and so on; and (2) the migration decision for any worker depends on how the specific skills of a would-be immigrant are rewarded in both the source and destination countries. This decision depends on the entire distribution of the relationship between skills and earnings for workers in each country. The decision rule is a simple maximizing one: migration to a destination country will occur whenever the earnings in the destination country minus the costs of immigration exceed earnings in the source country, all else being equal.

Consider a hypothetical distribution of skills in a source country, as shown in Figure 15.1. Assume that skills follow a normal distribution in the population. Recall that the peak of a normal distribution represents the average skill level in the source country, denoted as μ_S. If the migrant flow consists mostly of those with higher-than-average skills, this type of selection, from the perspective of a destination country, will be positive. From the source country's perspective, this situation is sometimes called a "brain drain." In contrast, there can also be negative selection, where workers in a source country who have lower-than-average skills decide to migrate to a destination country.

To determine how this sorting takes place, and whether there is positive or negative selection, consider Figure 15.2. In this example, the payoff for workers with higher skills is larger in the destination country than it is in the source country, while the payoff for those with lower skills is higher in the source country. A steeper line indicates greater inequality in a country, since those with higher skills will earn relatively more than those with lower skills. If the destination country has a higher premium for skills, then there will be positive selection as workers with higher-than-average skills will decide to migrate, since their high skills will be more highly rewarded in the destination country.

FIGURE 15.1 The Distribution of Skills in the Source Country

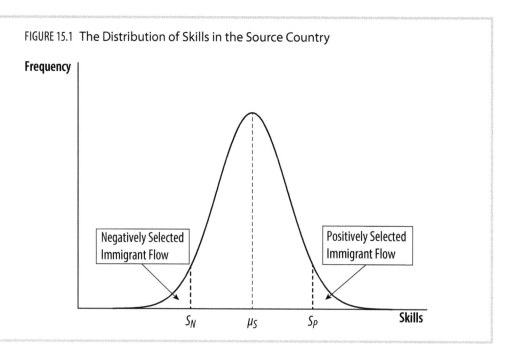

FIGURE 15.2 Positive Selection

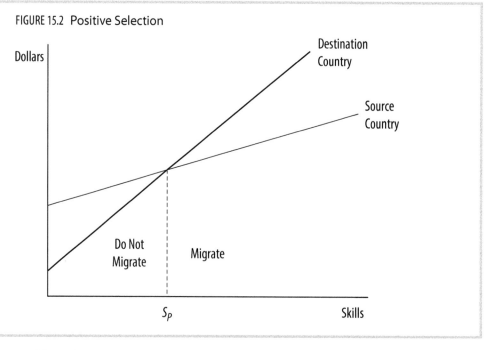

The volume and sorting of immigrants can change if one (or more) of the exogenous variables changes. If inequality in the source country increases, then the source-country line gets steeper. If inequality increases enough in the source country, or decreases enough in the destination country, such that the relative slopes of the two lines reverse, then there will be negative selection instead of positive selection (see Figure 15.3).

FIGURE 15.3 Negative Selection

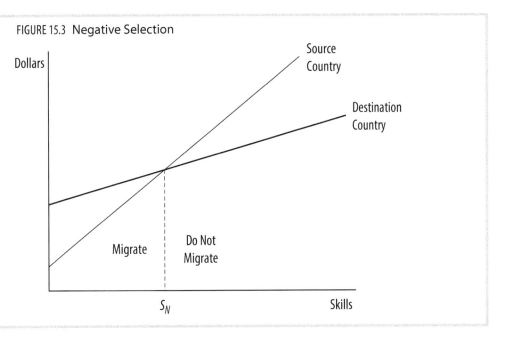

The lines in the diagram can also shift up or down. Consider an increase in incomes in the destination country due to economic growth, all else being equal. This will cause the destination-country line to shift up in a parallel manner (if relative inequality is held constant). An upward shift in the destination-country line lowers the skill level at which individuals in the source country will decide to migrate; it also leads to more migration, since the gap between dollars earned in the destination country and in the source country is now larger at any given level of skills than before the upward shift. The destination-country line represents the earnings in the destination country, but these are earnings net of migration costs, so a decrease in migration costs will increase the returns in the destination country (since it is now less costly to get to that country). Like an increase in incomes in the destination country, a decrease in migration costs will also cause the destination-country line to shift up. Finally, note that even if the lines shift up or down, as long as the relative slopes of the two lines do not reverse, and as long as the slope of the destination-country line is steeper, there will still be positive selection.

Figure 15.3 represents the case of negative selection. The return to skills in the destination country is lower for those with higher skills. In this case, those with high skills will not migrate, since they can earn more by staying in the source country. At the lower end of the skills distribution, however, the return on skills is higher in the destination country than in the source country: as a result, workers with lower-than-average skills will decide to migrate, and immigrants to the destination country will be negatively selected from the source country.

15.2 U.S. IMMIGRATION PATTERNS AND POLICIES

Immigration policy has varied greatly throughout American history. From Independence in 1776 to 1875, the policy was one of almost complete openness. Between 1875 and 1924, a rigid system of ethnic quotas was implemented in a series of policy changes that eventually ended the Age of Mass Migration. From 1965, there has been a move back toward a more open but highly complex and regulated set of immigration policies.

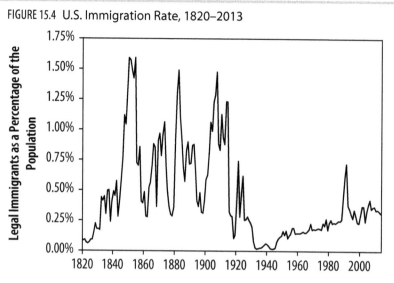

FIGURE 15.4 U.S. Immigration Rate, 1820–2013

Sources and Notes: Annual number of legal immigrants is from Department of Homeland Security, *2013 Handbook of Immigration Statistics*, Table 1, www.dhs.gov/sites/default/files/publications/table1_3.xls (accessed: October 28, 2015). Annual population is from Louis Johnston and Samuel H. Williamson, "What Was U.S. GDP Then?" *MeasuringWorth*, www.measuringworth.org/usgdp/ (accessed: October 28, 2015).

TABLE 15.1 Legal Immigration by Decade, 1820s–2000s

Decade	Number of Immigrants (Thousands)	Immigration Rate per 1,000 Population
1820s	129	1.1
1830s	538	3.6
1840s	1,427	7.0
1850s	2,815	10.8
1860s	2,081	5.9
1870s	2,742	6.3
1880s	5,249	9.5
1890s	3,694	5.4
1900s	8,202	9.8
1910s	6,347	6.6
1920s	4,296	3.8
1930s	699	0.6
1940s	857	0.6
1950s	2,499	1.5
1960s	3,214	1.7
1970s	4,248	2.0
1980s	6,244	2.6
1990s	9,775	3.7
2000s	10,299	3.5

Sources and Notes: Computed from the same sources as Figure 15.4.

IMMIGRATION BEFORE 1860

The Naturalization Act of 1790 established the principle that an immigrant could acquire U.S. citizenship after a period of residence in the U.S. The Act stipulated a period of two years and established that immigration was open to "free white persons." Since 1802, the length of residency required before applying for citizenship has been five years.

In 1819, in an effort to improve conditions on ships and to reduce mortality, Congress passed the first immigration law, which required ship captains to report passenger lists to port authorities. These lists are the basis for most of the annual historical data on immigration. Figure 15.4 reports annual immigration rates, while Table 15.1 presents decade totals on immigration and immigration rates (measured as the number of immigrants per 1,000 residents) for each decade from the 1820s to the 2000s.

During the 1820s, an average of fewer than 13,000 immigrants per year came to the United States, a rate of only 1.1 immigrants per 1,000 residents. Immigration began to pick up in the 1830s, but the 1840s and 1850s were the most important decades for immigration prior to the Civil War, with net migration responsible for 27 percent of the population growth in the 1840s and over 32 percent in the 1850s.[9]

Both push and pull factors were responsible for the surge in immigration, which peaked from 1847 to 1854. In the 1840s, the primary source country was Ireland, where the Irish Potato Famine (1845–1849) pushed migrants from their homeland to escape poverty and death. Although the British government offered bargain fares to help Irish migrants settle in Canada, nearly 650,000 Irish moved to the United States during the 1840s, often first arriving in Canada and then moving to the nearest large city in the United States, usually Boston or New York.[10] The influx of male workers from Ireland displaced the predominantly female workforce in cotton textiles, woolen textiles, and shoe production.[11]

Although Ireland remained the most important source country during the 1850s, with just over 1 million immigrants coming to the U.S., Germany was a close second with more than 976,000 immigrants.[12] A failed revolution in Germany (1848–1849) was the primary push factor. Most Germans settled on farms in the Midwest, but almost one-third of German immigrants populated growing cities in the Midwest, such as Chicago, Cincinnati, Milwaukee, and St. Louis.

While poor conditions in Europe pushed people out, pull factors in the United States also contributed to the surge in immigration. Between 1840 and 1850, the land area of the United States increased by 68 percent with the annexation of Texas (1845), the Oregon Territory (1846), and the Mexican Cession (1848) after the Mexican–American War (1846–1848). Not only was there the promise of new land, but in early 1848 James W. Marshall discovered gold at Sutter's Mill in Coloma, California, which led to the California Gold Rush, attracting tens of thousands from all over the world.

Most immigrants, however, did not make the journey to California but settled in the East and Midwest. In a study linking the records of passenger ship arrivals in New York City to the 1850 and 1860 U.S. Censuses, only about a third remained in New York City.[13] More than half settled in New York, Ohio, and Pennsylvania, and these immigrants were more likely than native-born citizens to settle in urban areas. They were also much more geographically mobile than native-born citizens, with nearly 70 percent changing counties between 1850 and 1860, compared to only 43 percent of the native-born population.

During their first two decades in the United States, immigrants were upwardly mobile, accumulating wealth at an average annual rate of almost 15 percent among the most recent arrivals. The immigrants who fared best were those who migrated to fast-growing regions in the Midwest. Immigrants who moved to cities such as Milwaukee and St. Louis were several times wealthier by 1860 than their counterparts who remained in the East.

Immigration peaked in 1854, increasing the U.S. population that year by 1.6 percent—an annual rate of increase that has never been surpassed (Figure 15.4). The surge in immigration, however, abruptly ended in 1855, with immigration less than one half of what it had been in 1854.[14] Scholars have proposed many explanations for the sudden drop, including improving economic conditions in Europe, the outbreak of the Crimean War (which caused European governments to stem the flow of emigrants in order to increase the supply of potential soldiers), and a recession in the United States.[15]

While all of these explanations are likely to be part of the story, more recent scholarship suggests that a "rise of nativism was the initiating cause of the decline."[16] Nativism refers to prejudice and discrimination against immigrants, who typically belong to a different ethnic group than the majority of native-born citizens.

The response against immigrants was both political and physical. A secret society, called the Order of the Star-Spangled Banner, had over a million white males as members by the mid-1850s, which amounted to about one-eighth of all eligible voters.[17]

They were more commonly referred to as the Know-Nothings, since when questioned about their organization they would say, "I know nothing." Rising nativist feelings led to the dramatic growth and success of the Know-Nothing Party, with seventy members elected to Congress in the 1854 election.[18]

Attacks against Irish Catholics began in late 1853 and soon led to violence against both Irish and German immigrants. In 1855, there were riots in Baltimore, Cincinnati, Louisville, New Orleans, and St. Louis, with more than twenty killed and hundreds wounded in Louisville, Kentucky. Consistent with the nativist explanation for the decline in immigration, empirical evidence confirms that immigration decreased the most in U.S. states where the Know-Nothing Party was the strongest.[19] Slavery and the Civil War, however, soon replaced immigration as the most important political issues.

IMMIGRATION FROM THE CIVIL WAR TO WORLD WAR I

The Civil War (1861–1865) and a long recession in the 1870s temporarily stemmed the high flows of immigrants to the United States, but immigration rates increased substantially from the 1880s to World War I. Before the 1890s, the vast majority of immigrants were from northwest Europe, primarily Great Britain, Ireland, Germany, and Scandinavia.

From 1880 to 1914, more than 22 million immigrants arrived.[20] Not only were the flows of immigrants large relative to the population, but the source countries also changed:

FIGURE 15.5 Recent Immigrants in New York City, 1889

Source: Jacob Riis, "Lodgers in a Crowded Bayard Street Tenement – 'Five Cents a Spot,'" https://commons.wikimedia. org/wiki/File:Jacob_Riis,_Lodgers_in_a_Crowded_Bayard_Street_Tenement.jpg (accessed: February 22, 2016).

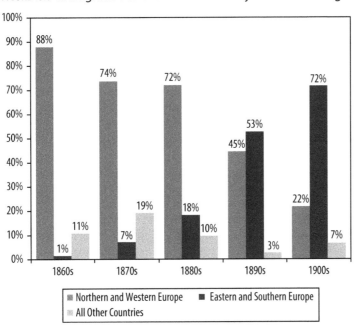

FIGURE 15.6 Immigration to the United States by Decade and Region, 1860s–1900s

Sources and Notes: Computed using data from James A. Dunleavy and Henry A. Gemery, "Economic Opportunity and the Responses of the 'Old' and 'New' Migrants to the United States," *Journal of Economic History* 38, no. 4 (December 1978), Table 1, 902.

from northern and western European countries to southern or eastern European countries, such as Hungary, Poland, Russia, Greece, and Italy (Figure 15.5). The change was due to two main factors. First, economic growth in England, Germany, and Scandinavian countries reduced income differences and made the United States a less attractive destination for immigrants from those countries than it had been previously. Second, the introduction of the steamship and the expansion of railroads in both Europe and the United States made it less costly for generally poorer migrants from southern and eastern European countries to travel to the East coast and then to the interior of the United States.

During the 1870s, 72 percent of all immigrants were from northern and western European countries, and only 18 percent were from southern and eastern Europe (the remaining 10 percent were from countries outside of Europe). By the 1900s, these percentages had almost completely reversed, with 72 percent from southern and eastern Europe and only 22 percent from northern and western Europe (Figure 15.6). Large numbers of these immigrants were from Jewish and Eastern Orthodox religions. As well as speaking different languages, these "new" immigrants also brought different religions and different cultural backgrounds that were viewed by some Americans as threatening. These nativist fears eventually manifested themselves in substantial restrictions on immigration from southern and eastern Europe (see below).

Most of the "new" immigrants from Europe moved to urban areas in the United States, and in 1910 more than one-half of all workers in New York, Chicago, and Detroit were immigrants.[21] Not only were European immigrants more likely to settle in urban areas, but they also avoided moving to the South. By 1890, the foreign-born share had surged to 14.7 percent of the population as a whole, but only 2.6 percent in the South. One explanation for the lack of immigration to the South focuses on the unwillingness of immigrants to work and live with African Americans. English and German immigrants, in particular, avoided states with a high percentage of African Americans.[22] An alternative explanation emphasizes the low wages and lack of opportunity in the South. In this view, the choices of immigrants simply reflected their decisions to move to the places where the opportunities open to them were the best.

While much smaller in magnitude, there was also immigration from China and Japan, with several hundred thousand immigrants coming to the United States and settling mostly in California. Chinese immigration began during the California Gold Rush, with nearly 300,000 immigrants arriving from China between 1849 and 1882. With travel costs several times larger than average annual wages in China, the trip to the United States was quite costly.

Six large Chinese-owned companies lent money to these immigrants, so most immigrants arrived in debt. These companies held title to the debts and used or rented out the immigrants in gangs to work on the first transcontinental railroad, in mines, and in other capacities, deducting money from the laborers' wages until the debts were repaid in an arrangement somewhat akin to indentured servitude.[23] While over 90 percent of Chinese immigrants were male, a small number of Chinese women arrived, mostly to work as concubines and prostitutes under extreme conditions that contemporary and more recent observers have described as "debt slavery."[24]

After legislation in 1882 had substantially reduced the flows of immigrants from China (see below), immigration from Japan began to increase. In 1884, the Japanese government allowed Hawaiian planters to recruit Japanese workers, and an emigration boom began. After the U.S. annexed Hawaii in 1898, Japanese immigration to the U.S. West Coast increased, with migrants being attracted by high wages. The annual rate of immigration to the West Coast peaked at around 10,000 per year. By 1930, approximately 140,000 Japanese immigrants lived in the United States, with over 70 percent in California.[25]

Other groups also migrated to the United States during this period. Between 1880 and 1919, and in search of better economic opportunities, over 280,000 immigrants arrived in the eastern and southeastern U.S. from Jamaica, Cuba, Puerto Rico, and other islands in the Caribbean.[26]

The Mexican immigrant population in the United States surged as well. In 1902, the National Reclamation Act (also known as the Newlands Act) encouraged the irrigation of arid land, and this created new farmland in many U.S. states, including Texas, Arizona, and California. This new farmland drew Mexican farm workers northward to seek jobs. During and after the Mexican Revolution (1910–1920), both push and pull factors prompted even more migration from Mexico. In the decade of the 1890s, there were only 734 immigrants from Mexico, but between 1900 and 1929 over 700,000 immigrants arrived from Mexico, with nearly 70 percent of this total coming during the 1920s.[27]

IMMIGRATION RESTRICTIONS

The first immigration restrictions targeted immigrants from Asian countries. During the 1870s, there was increasing momentum to stop immigration from China. With the completion of the first transcontinental railroad (1869), thousands of Chinese laborers returned to California, and their return was later accompanied by high rates of unemployment. Although the increase in unemployment was actually associated with the national recession that started in 1873, Chinese immigrants were increasingly blamed for adversely affecting the wages and employment opportunities of white laborers in California. Another important reason given for excluding Chinese workers during the 1870s "was a widespread and growing belief among Americans that this immigration constituted a new form of slavery."[28]

The first federal law restricting immigration was the Page Act (1875), named after its sponsor Horace F. Page, a member of the U.S. House of Representatives from California. The Page Act prohibited immigration of "any subject from China, Japan, or any Oriental Country, without their free and voluntary consent."[29] The Act also excluded prostitutes, convicts, and "obnoxious persons." This law had little impact, however, since there was scant enforcement.

The first effective law to prohibit immigrants from a particular country was the Chinese Exclusion Act (1882), which banned immigration from China except for members of the immediate families of Chinese already in the U.S. It was not repealed until 1943, when China became an ally of the United States during World War II, but the annual quota thereafter was set at only 105 people per year.

By the early 1900s, the same fears that had led to anti-Chinese discrimination and restrictive legislation had spread to include Japanese and other Asian people. The segregation of Japanese and Korean students from the public school system was made possible by the San Francisco earthquake of 1906. Because many Chinese families moved to other areas or were relocated to temporary refugee camps, enough space became available in the segregated Chinese school system to include Japanese and Korean students as well. In 1906 the Chinese Primary School in San Francisco was renamed the "Oriental Public School", and this fueled a diplomatic crisis between Japan and the United States as anti-American protests erupted in Japan in response to the segregation.

President Theodore Roosevelt intervened and persuaded the San Francisco Board of Education to withdraw the segregation order. In exchange, the Japanese government agreed in 1907 to limit further migration to the United States in an informal "Gentlemen's Agreement."

Although immigration of Asians to the West Coast slowed after 1907, millions of Europeans continued to come to the United States. In a series of steps, however, the flows from southern and eastern Europe were severely curtailed as well. The growing numbers of immigrants from eastern and southern Europe stirred nativist sentiment, fear, and hostility among the overwhelmingly Protestant American population with northern European ancestry. To many native-born Americans, the "new" immigrants were inferior in terms of intelligence, ability, and culture.

In 1917, Congress passed a new law that barred immigrants from all Asian countries and made literacy a requirement for all immigrants over the age of 16. After World War I ended, immigration legislation became even more restrictive. Several factors likely contributed to the laws in the 1920s. The rise of communism in Russia, rising anti-Semitism, a return to the gold standard after the War (which led to contractionary monetary policy and to a severe recession in 1920 and 1921), and a move toward economic isolation in response to World War I, together moved immigration policy toward increasingly stringent barriers.[30]

In 1921, Congress enacted the Emergency Immigration Act, which limited the number of southern and eastern Europeans by pegging the number of immigrants permitted into the United States each year at 3 percent of the number of people from that country living in the United States in 1910. The Immigration Act of 1924 made American policy even more restrictive by setting the nationality quotas at 2 percent of the number of people from each country living in the United States in 1890, with an overall limit of 150,000 each year. The 1921 and 1924 quota laws applied only to immigrants from the Eastern Hemisphere, and immediate family members and other close relatives were exempt from the overall limits. Since in 1890 there were hardly any immigrants from southern and eastern European countries in the United States, the Immigration Act of 1924 dramatically reduced immigration from southern and eastern Europe.

Immigration fell from 706,896 in 1924 to only 294,314 in 1925. Between 1925 and 1929, immigration averaged 304,182 people per year. While the legislation of the 1920s reduced immigration, the impact of the Great Depression and World War II caused immigration to fall well below the quota limits. Between 1931 and 1945, an average of fewer than 50,000 immigrants entered the U.S. each year. The fewest immigrants arrived at the depths of the Great Depression in 1933, when only 23,068 emigrated to the U.S., and during the middle of World War II—23,775 arrived in 1943. The totals for 1933 and 1943 are each less than 2 percent of the number that arrived in 1907 (1,285,349), at the peak of the Age of Mass Migration.

Immigration remained relatively low between 1925 and 1964, averaging fewer than 175,000 immigrants per year, and never exceeding the 335,176 immigrants in 1927. Because of the nationality-based quota system, immigrants came increasingly from other source countries, not in southern and eastern Europe. From 1925 to 1964, about 60 percent of immigrant visas went to citizens of Germany and the United Kingdom.[31]

The next policy changes occurred during World War II. After the Japanese attack on Pearl Harbor, Hawaii, and U.S. entry into the War, there was substantial fear of, and hostility toward, those with Japanese ancestry in the U.S. In 1942, the U.S. government evacuated all persons of Japanese descent from the West Coast and involuntarily relocated them to ten remote internment camps in the interior regions of the U.S. About 110,000 people were incarcerated in these camps until the end of the War, and 65 percent of those incarcerated were American citizens.[32]

Internment led to several detrimental long-run effects. For young people who attended low-quality schools in internment camps, it lowered their likelihood of completing college and receiving postgraduate education.[33] For adults, the forced withdrawal from the paid labor force and the missed labor force experience during the War had a lasting impact on their working lives: in comparison with Japanese Americans in Hawaii (who were not involuntarily relocated), males earned between 9 and 13 percent less, 25 years after internment, and were more likely to work in lower-status jobs and to be self-employed.[34] Internment also reduced wealth, since farms and property were confiscated from Japanese Americans.

The other important development that started during World War II was the Bracero program (1942–1964), an agreement between the U.S. and Mexican governments that permitted Mexican male citizens (the braceros) to work temporarily in the United States. While the agreement stipulated certain benefits and protections for Mexican workers, these conditions were rarely met and Mexican workers often experienced poor conditions and harsh treatment.

The initial impetus for this agreement was a shortage of labor in the U.S. due to the massive mobilization efforts during World War II. While U.S. farms needed workers, the Mexican government hoped that the braceros would learn new agricultural skills that could benefit agriculture in Mexico, and also that they would earn higher wages which when brought back to Mexico would help to stimulate the Mexican economy.

THE POST-1965 IMMIGRATION RESURGENCE

After the Civil Rights Act (1964), the discriminatory immigration laws of the 1920s came under attack. In 1965, the Immigration and Nationality Act represented a fundamental change in U.S. immigration policy: it abolished nationality quotas and

TABLE 15.2 U.S. Foreign-Born Population by Region of Birth: 2010		
Region of Birth	Population (Millions)	Percent
Latin America	17.49	43.8
Asia	11.28	28.2
Europe	4.82	12.1
Caribbean	3.73	9.3
Africa	1.61	4.0
North America	0.81	2.0
Oceania	0.22	0.5
TOTAL	39.96	100

Sources and Notes: U.S. Census Bureau, "The Foreign-Born Population in the United States: 2010," *American Community Survey* Reports ACS-19 (May 2012), Table 2, 2, www.census.gov/prod/2012pubs/acs-19.pdf (accessed: November 3, 2015). Due to rounding, percentages do not sum to 100.

established family reunification as the primary goal of U.S. immigration policy. Although this Act is widely believed to have led to mass migrations from both Asia and Latin America as a direct result of eliminating past discriminatory policies, there is evidence that while "this may be true for Asians, it is not the case for Latin Americans, who faced more restrictions to legal migration after 1965 than before."[35]

In absolute numbers, immigration in recent decades is similar to that during the Age of Mass Migration; compared to the size of the population, however, the immigration rate was higher in every decade from the 1840s to the 1920s than it has been in recent decades. The major source countries changed once again, this time to countries in Latin America, particularly Mexico, and to several in Asia. In 2010, over 70 percent of the U.S. foreign-born population were from Latin America and Asia (Table 15.2).

The group referred to as "Hispanics" includes all immigrants from Latin American countries and their offspring. In 2002, Hispanics became the largest ethnic minority group in the United States, surpassing African Americans. According to the U.S. Census Bureau, there were 54 million Hispanics in the U.S. in 2013, or 17 percent of the U.S. population. By 2060, the Hispanic population is expected to have more than doubled, to 128.8 million, and it is estimated that this will be 31 percent of the U.S. population.[36] In 2013, 64 percent of Hispanics and nearly 30 percent of all foreign-born residents of the United States were from Mexico.

The Asian population has grown tremendously as well. In 1970, only three-fourths of 1 percent of the U.S. population were of Asian ancestry, but by 2013, over 6 percent of the U.S. population were Asian, nearly 20 million in total.

The United States may be undergoing yet another change in the composition of the immigrant population. The year 2013 was the first in which more immigrants came from China and India than from Mexico. In recent years, there have been far fewer Mexican immigrants, particularly undocumented ones; while the number of immigrants from China and India, who often arrive on student and work visas, has soared.

15.3 THE ECONOMIC IMPACTS OF IMMIGRATION

There are many issues regarding the economic consequences of immigration. Some of the most important and most studied questions are these:

- How much do immigrants themselves gain from migration?
- How have immigrants fared in U.S. labor markets over time?
- Has immigration increased or decreased the rate of economic growth in the United States?
- Has immigration, on average, hurt or benefitted native-born workers?
- What have been the distributional impacts of immigration? Who wins and who loses from immigration?
- What are the fiscal impacts of immigration? Do immigrants pay their fair share toward government services?

INCOME GAINS TO MIGRANTS

There is widespread agreement that migrants, on average, gain from immigration. One study showed that recent Mexican immigrants around 30 years of age who had some high school education earned $8.70 per hour in the U.S. in 2000, compared to $2.40 per hour for those of similar age and education who remained in Mexico—a difference of more than $12,000 a year for a full-time worker putting in 40 hours a week.[37] Comparing immigrants from developing countries who had moved to high-income countries like the U.S., a 2013 study estimated a gain of "more than $10,000 a year for a randomly selected worker from a less-developed country."[38]

The gains to immigrants in percentage terms are likely to have been larger in recent decades than the gains were during the Age of Mass Migration. For example, Norwegian immigrants to the U.S. in the late nineteenth century earned only about 70 percent more in the U.S., in part due to negative selection of Norwegian immigrants.[39]

ECONOMIC GROWTH AND THE WAGES OF NATIVE-BORN WORKERS

The impacts of immigration on the rate of U.S. economic growth and on the growth rate of wages of U.S.-born workers are unresolved issues, although the weight of the evidence suggests that the effects of immigration have been mostly favorable.

The simple labor demand and supply model predicts that an influx of immigrants, all else being equal, will increase labor supply along a given labor demand curve and reduce wages in the market. However, there are other channels that can lead to immigration causing higher wages for native-born workers and faster economic growth.

Consider the Cobb-Douglas production with constant returns to scale from Chapter 2. Recall that at any time t, the function links the levels of the factors of production to the amount of real GDP:

$$Y_t = A_t K_t^a H_t^b N_t^c L_t^{1-a-b-c}$$

where Y_t stands for real GDP, and K_t, H_t, N_t, and L_t represent the four factors of production: physical capital, human capital, natural capital, and labor, respectively. A_t, called total factor productivity (TFP), measures the productivity of the factors of production in creating real GDP. The exponents above the factors of production represent elasticities.

If the labor market is perfectly competitive, the real wage rate will equal the marginal product of labor, with prices normalized to one. To find the marginal product of labor, take the partial derivative of the production function with respect to labor and rearrange the equation:

$$\text{real wage} = \frac{\partial Y_t}{\partial L_t} = (1 - a - b - c) A_t \left(\frac{K_t}{L_t}\right)^a \left(\frac{H_t}{L_t}\right)^b \left(\frac{N_t}{L_t}\right)^c$$

It is clear that an increase in L, perhaps due to immigration, will lead to lower capital per worker hour, lower human capital per worker hour, lower natural capital per worker hour, and lower real wages, if all that changes is L. As one paper noted in the title, "The Labor Demand Curve is Downward Sloping."[40]

Richer models of labor markets and the production process, however, do not necessarily lead to lower wages and lower output per worker hour because of immigration. It is possible for immigration to affect the growth rates of the other factors of production and total factor productivity growth as well. Immigrants can contribute to economic growth and increasing wages for native-born workers through a variety of mechanisms, including increased national savings rates (leading to physical capital accumulation), higher rates of inventive activity and technological progress, and population growth that allows for greater economies of scale and division of labor, which can also contribute to total factor productivity growth.[41]

Despite protectionist trade policies throughout the nineteenth century (see Chapter 10), the United States was able to grow rapidly, without taking advantage of the full benefits of international trade, because immigration and high rates of natural population increase made the domestic economy sufficiently large. The large economy encouraged inventive activity and allowed the U.S. to enjoy the benefits of specialization, division of labor, and economies of scale.

Evidence on the impacts of immigration in recent decades paints a similar picture. In the Cobb-Douglas case above, there is an implicit assumption that workers are homogeneous—that is, that each worker is a perfect substitute for every other worker. It may be the case, instead, that native-born and foreign-born workers are imperfect substitutes for one another; and perhaps they are even complements, who often do not compete against each other in the same labor markets. For recent immigrant cohorts, empirical evidence supports this interpretation.

While some lower-skilled native-born workers may be hurt by immigration, immigration has on average increased both total factor productivity growth and the wages of native-born workers.[42] Immigration has encouraged the "efficient specialization of immigrants and natives in manual-intensive and communication-intensive tasks, respectively (in which each group has a comparative advantage), resulting in a gain in overall efficiency [and] immigration is significantly associated with [higher] total factor productivity growth."[43]

SELF-SELECTION

While the self-selection model of immigration in Section 15.1 emphasized the relationships between skills and earnings in the source country and the destination country, immigrants are self-selected on many other characteristics as well, including education, occupation, age, ambition, social networks, and gender.

The United States has clearly benefitted from positive self-selection along many dimensions throughout its history. Historically, most immigrants were young, working-age individuals. With few children and few elderly people migrating to the United States, the U.S. was able to save on education costs and the costs of caring for those in old age, while benefitting from a young and productive workforce. Throughout American history, labor-force participation rates for immigrants have exceeded those of native-born workers.[44]

While some aspects of self-selection are difficult to measure (such as ambition), educational attainment data have allowed scholars to measure self-selection in terms of education. In a recent study of 32 immigrant groups from the 1960s to the 1990s, there was positive selection in 31 of the 32 groups, with the only exception being Puerto Rico.[45] Immigrants from Mexico had the lowest degree of positive self-selection, but the average Mexican immigrant still had a higher-than-average level of education compared to the similar population in Mexico.[46] In general, there has been a greater degree of positive self-selection of immigrants from Asia compared to those from Latin America.[47] Note, however, that an immigrant group may display positive self-selection yet still arrive in the U.S. with lower levels of educational attainment than native-born U.S. citizens, particularly if the source country lags well behind the U.S. in terms of educational attainment.

While there are instances of negative self-selection, such as the Norwegian immigrants to the U.S. in the late nineteenth century, the available evidence strongly suggests that the United States has benefitted throughout its history from immigrants who were relatively young and brought with them relatively high levels of human capital.

CONVERGENCE

Until recently, the conventional wisdom was that immigrants initially earned substantially less than native-born workers but then rapidly converged, with immigrants sometimes surpassing native-born workers, on average, within their working lives. This conclusion, however, was based on cross-sectional data at a given point in time. Since immigrants who had been in the United States a long time (and were typically older) made more money—closer to the earnings of native-born workers—than younger, newly-arrived immigrants, scholars erroneously concluded that the earnings of immigrants must over time converge with those of native-born workers.

If immigrant skills by age were constant over time, then this would be a valid conclusion. These studies, however, used data for younger, newly-arrived immigrants who were less skilled, on average, than their older counterparts had been when they arrived in the U.S. decades earlier. What appeared to be convergence over time was just the result of younger immigrants arriving with fewer skills than earlier waves of arrivals. Another reason for the apparent convergence was negative selection of returning immigrants. That is, those who did not do well in the United States were more likely to return to their country of birth.

Recent studies have used panel data, in which the same individuals are interviewed at multiple points in time. These studies have led to a different picture of immigrants' labor-market experiences. During the Age of Mass Migration, the average immigrant earned, from arrival, close to what native-born workers earned, and then experienced occupational advancement at the same rate as native-born workers. Initial gaps often persisted into the second generation and gaps varied "substantially across sending countries."[48]

During both their first 5 years and their first 30 years in the United States, immigrants from England, Wales, Russia, Scotland, France, and Ireland earned *more* than native-born workers. In contrast, during their first 5 and 30 years in the United States, immigrants from Nordic countries (Norway, Denmark, Finland, and Sweden) and from Portugal, Belgium, and Switzerland earned *less* than native-born workers.[49]

While there appears to have been little convergence over time during the Age of Mass Migration, other panel studies show very long-run convergence, particularly for groups who strongly maintained their cultural identity. Between 1865 and 1930, approximately 1 million French Canadians migrated to the United States, settling mostly in New England. While French-Canadian immigrants maintained their cultural identity—including speaking French and maintaining a separate school system—by the year 2000, the descendants of these immigrants had largely achieved parity with native-born workers in terms of educational attainment.[50]

Earlier waves of Mexican immigrants also experienced long-run convergence. For first-generation Mexican immigrants who were born around 1900, the average educational attainment was only 3.81 years.[51] The children of these immigrants, however, received 7.88 years of education in the United States, and 12.61 years of education in the United States as third-generation immigrants, which is quite close to the overall level of educational attainment. Later birth cohorts also show increases in educational attainment from the first to the second generations, and from the second to the third.

There are currently concerns that the large numbers of Hispanic immigrants into the United States in recent decades will not converge economically, but will maintain a separate language and culture that will discourage such convergence. Hispanic immigrants today, on average, lag well behind non-Hispanic white Americans in terms of educational attainment, earnings, income, and wealth (see Chapter 14, Table 14.1). While the future might not repeat the past, the long-run convergence of previous immigrant groups with native-born workers suggests eventual convergence for more recent groups of immigrants.

THE FISCAL IMPACTS OF IMMIGRANTS

Fiscal concerns were not an issue throughout most of American history, since government was small and the overwhelming majority of immigrants were in their prime working years. In recent decades, however, with the growth of government and with a greater proportion of older and younger immigrants, debate has often focused on the fiscal consequences of immigration. One of the most debated questions surrounding immigration is whether immigrants pay enough in taxes to cover the costs of the public services they use, such as schools, health care, and welfare benefits. Many studies have examined this issue, and, although they have used different methods and data, all have shown the net fiscal impact of immigration to be quite small, with estimates typically in "the range of ±1 percent of GDP."[52]

More highly-skilled immigrants generally make a positive fiscal contribution, while the fiscal impact of low-skilled immigrants is often negative, but the positive and negative contributions largely offset each other to make the overall impact small. There are, however, larger negative impacts on particular states and municipalities, particularly in the short run, as immigrants tend to cluster in certain locations. In 2010, nearly 56 percent of all foreign-born individuals lived in four states: California, New York, Texas, and Florida. These states, along with the municipalities with large concentrations of immigrants, have likely experienced negative fiscal impacts, but the magnitude of such impacts is difficult to quantify.

15.4 CONCLUSIONS

In many ways, the United States is a nation of immigrants, but immigration has also frequently been a source of controversy. At times when immigration has surged, fears that immigrants will adversely affect native-born workers and taxpayers, or that they will fundamentally change American culture, have been at the forefront of public policy debates.

Overall, the United States has gained from immigration both present and past, although recent gains are likely not as large as they were during the nineteenth and early twentieth centuries. The main economic impacts of immigration in recent decades are distributional, although other factors—skill-biased technological change, increased international trade, and government tax and expenditure policies—have been far more important in influencing the overall distribution of income and wealth.

QUESTIONS

1. Consider two hypothetical countries: Inequalia and Egalitaria. In Inequalia, workers with high levels of human capital make far more than workers with lower levels of human capital. In Egalitaria, high-skilled workers make only a little more than those with lower skills. Using the self-selection model of immigration, graphically illustrate each of the situations below and explain what you predict will occur.

   A. Consider those who decide to migrate from Egalitaria to Inequalia. Is the immigrant flow one of positive selection or negative selection? Explain.

   B. Now, suppose that there is a recession in Inequalia, but not in Egalitaria. What do you predict will happen to the number of immigrants to Inequalia? Based on your answer to Part A, has there been a change from positive selection to negative selection or vice versa? Explain.

2. Using the self-selection model of immigration, assume initially that there is a positive selection of migrants from a source country to the United States. Also, assume that the income lines for the source country and for the United States intersect at $100,000 per year. Suppose that the United States passes legislation stipulating a maximum income of $300,000 per year: that is, the income tax rate for any money earned beyond $300,000 is 100 percent. How will this legislation likely affect who decides to migrate to the United States from this source country? What is likely to happen to the average skills of those who decide to migrate to the United States from this source country? Explain.

3. Explain the ways in which immigration can potentially decrease the earnings of native-born workers, and explain also how immigration can potentially increase the earnings of native-born workers. What is the empirical evidence for the impact of immigration on the earnings of native-born workers in the United States, both past and present?

4. Explain how the 1921 and 1924 immigration acts were discriminatory against immigrants from southern and eastern European countries.

5. Compare and contrast the Age of Mass Migration with the recent wave of immigration (since 1965). In what ways are they similar? In what ways are they different?

NOTES

[1] This distinction is from Philip Martin and Elizabeth Midgley, "Immigration: Shaping and Reshaping America," *Population Bulletin* 61, no. 4 (December 2006), 8.

[2] According to the Department of Homeland Security, *2013 Handbook of Immigration Statistics*, Table 1, www.dhs.gov/sites/default/files/publications/table1_3.xls (accessed: September 2, 2015), nearly 79.4 million people immigrated to the United States between 1820 and 2013. With annual rates of immigration near 1 million per year, by the year 2014 the number of immigrants had exceeded 80 million.

[3] Orn B. Bodvarsson and Hendrik Van den Berg, *The Economics of Immigration: Theory and Policy*, Second Edition (New York, NY: Springer, 2013), 9.

[4] See Brinley Thomas, *Migration and Economic Growth*, Second Edition (Cambridge, UK: Cambridge University Press, 1973) for a discussion that emphasizes push factors; and Jeffrey Williamson, "Migration to the New World: Long Term Influences and Impact," *Explorations in Economic History* 11, no. 4 (Summer 1974), 357–387, for one that stresses the importance of pull factors.

[5] James S. Leamon, *Historic Lewiston: A Textile City in Transition* (Auburn, ME: Lewiston Historical Commission, 1976), 17.

6 https://en.wikipedia.org/wiki/Lewiston,_Maine (accessed: September 4, 2015).

7 Jesse Ellison, "Lewiston, Maine, Revived by Somali Immigrants," *Newsweek* (January 16, 2009), www.newsweek.com/lewiston-maine-revived-somali-immigrants-78475 (accessed: September 5, 2015).

8 The self-selection model presented here is based on Andrew D. Roy, "Some Thoughts on the Distribution of Earnings," *Oxford Economic Papers* 3, no. 2 (June 1951), 135–146; and George J. Borjas, "Self-Selection and Earnings of Immigrants," *American Economic Review* 77, no. 3 (September 1987), 531–553. Borjas was the first to apply the model to the immigration decision. More complete textbook treatments of the model can be found in George J. Borjas, *Labor Economics*, Seventh Edition (New York, NY: McGraw-Hill, 2016), 331–335. Bodvarsson and Van den Berg, 40–49, also discuss the model and some recent extensions of it.

9 Calculated from Susan B. Carter, Scott Sigmund Gartner, Michael R. Haines, Alan L. Olmstead, Richard Sutch, and Gavin Wright (eds.), *Historical Statistics of the United States*, Millennial Edition (New York, NY: Cambridge University Press, 2006), series Aa19 for natural increase and series Aa20 for net migration.

10 United States Department of Homeland Security, *2013 Yearbook of Immigration Statistics* (Washington, DC: U.S. Department of Homeland Security, Office of Immigration Statistics, 2014), Table 2.

11 Pamela J. Nickless, "Changing Labor Productivity and the Utilization of Native Women Workers in the American Cotton Textile Industry, 1825–1866," *Journal of Economic History* 38, no. 1 (March 1978), 288.

12 United States Department of Homeland Security, Table 2.

13 Joseph Ferry, *'Yankeys Now': European Immigrants in the Antebellum U.S., 1840–1860* (New York, NY: Oxford University Press, 1999).

14 In 1854, there were 427,833 immigrants, but this number fell to 200,877 in 1855.

15 For a discussion of potential explanations, see Raymond L. Cohn, "Nativism and the End of the Mass Migration of the 1840s and 1850s," *Journal of Economic History* 60, no. 2 (June 2000), 361–383.

16 Cohn, 361.

17 Bodvarsson and Van den Berg, 380.

18 Cohn, 374.

19 Cohn, Table 4, 378.

20 United States Department of Homeland Security, Table 1.

21 Vernon J. Briggs, *Mass Migration and the National Interest* (Armonk, NY: M.E. Sharp, 1992), 56–57.

22 James A. Dunleavy and Henry A. Gemery, "Economic Opportunity and the Responses of 'Old' and 'New' Migrants to the United States," *Journal of Economic History* 38, no. 4 (December 1978), 901–917.

23 Patricia Cloud and David W. Galenson, "Chinese Immigration and Contract Labor in the Late Nineteenth Century," *Explorations in Economic History* 24, no. 1 (January 1987), 22–42.

24 Cloud and Galenson, 26.

25 Roger Daniels, *Coming to America: A History of Immigration and Ethnicity in American Life*, Second Edition (New York, NY: Perennial, 2002), Table 9.2, 250.

26 Department of Homeland Security, Table 2, 5-11.

27 Department of Homeland Security, Table 2, 5-11.

28 Cloud and Galenson, 34.

29 For the text of the Page Act, see http://library.uwb.edu/guides/usimmigration/1875_page_law.html (accessed: November 13, 2015).

30 Bodvarsson and Van den Berg, 387.

[31] Martin and Midgley, 12.

[32] Aimee Chin, "Long-Run Labor Market Effects of Japanese American Internment during World War II on Working-Age Male Internees," *Journal of Labor Economics* 23, no. 3 (July 2005), 493.

[33] Martin Saavedra, "School Quality and Educational Attainment: Japanese American Internment as a Natural Experiment," *Explorations in Economic History* 57, no. 3 (July 2015), 59–78.

[34] Chin, 491–525.

[35] Douglas S. Massey and Karen A. Pren, "Unintended Consequences of U.S. Immigration Policy: Explaining the Post-1965 Surge from Latin America," *Population and Development Review* 38, no. 1 (March 2012), 1–29.

[36] U.S. Census Bureau, www.census.gov/newsroom/facts-for-features/2014/cb14-ff22.html (accessed: September 6, 2015).

[37] Gordon H. Hanson, "Illegal Immigration from Mexico to the United States," *Journal of Economic Literature* 44, no. 4 (December 2006), 869–924.

[38] John Kennan, "Open Borders," *Review of Economic Dynamics* 16, no. 2 (April 2013), L1-L14.

[39] Ran Abramitzky, Leah Platt Boustan, and Katherine Eriksson, "Europe's Tired, Poor, Huddled Masses: Self-Selection and Economic Outcomes in the Age of Mass Migration," *American Economic Review* 102, no. 5 (August 2012), 1832–1856.

[40] George J. Borjas, "The Labor Demand Curve is Downward Sloping: Reexamining the Impact of Immigration on the Labor Market," *Quarterly Journal of Economics* 118, no. 4 (November 2003), 1335–1374.

[41] For a discussion of these channels, see Susan B. Carter and Richard Sutch, "Historical Perspectives on the Economic Consequences of Immigration into the United States," *NBER Working Paper on Historical Factors in Long Run Economic Growth*, no. 106 (December 1997).

[42] Frederic Docquier, Caglar Ozden, and Giovanni Peri, "The Labor Market Effects of Immigration and Emigration in OECD Countries", *Economic Journal* 124, no. 3 (September 2013), 1106–1145.

[43] Giovanni Peri, "The Effect of Immigration on Productivity: Evidence from U.S. States," *Review of Economics and Statistics* 94, no. 1 (February 2012), 357.

[44] Carter and Sutch, Table 1.

[45] Cynthia Feliciano, "Educational Selectivity in U.S. Immigration: How Do Immigrants Compare to Those Left behind?" *Demography* 42, no. 1 (February 2005), 131–152.

[46] Feliciano, Table 1, 140.

[47] Feliciano, Table 1, 140.

[48] Ran Abramitzky, Leah Platt Boustan, and Katherine Eriksson, "A Nation of Immigrants: Assimilation and Economic Outcomes in the Age of Mass Migration," *Journal of Political Economy* 122, no. 3 (June 2014), 467.

[49] Abramitzsky et al., Figure 3, 490.

[50] Mary MacKinnon and Daniel Parent, "Resisting the Melting Pot: The Long-Term Impact of Maintaining Identity for Franco-Americans in New England," *Explorations in Economic History* 49, no. 1 (January 2012), 30–59.

[51] James P. Smith, "Immigrants and the Labor Market," *Journal of Labor Economics* 24, no. 2 (April 2006), Table 6, 224.

[52] For a survey of the literature on the fiscal consequences of immigration, see Robert Rowthorn, "The Fiscal Impact of Immigration on Advanced Economies," *Oxford Review of Economic Policy* 24, no. 3 (Autumn 2008), 560–580.

16
The Growth of Government

From cradle to grave, Americans are affected in countless ways by the activities of government. At birth, Americans receive from government a birth certificate and a Social Security number, which come with a myriad of obligations and privileges. Nearly 90 percent of Americans attend public schools, and almost everyone pays taxes. Travel occurs on public roads and through publicly owned airports. In most communities, government provides water, sewer, garbage, fire, and police services.

At some point in their lives, almost all Americans will receive money from government, whether in the form of student loans and grants, unemployment or disability payments, antipoverty cash payments or in-kind benefits, Social Security or Medicare. The U.S. military is engaged throughout the world in defending and promoting U.S. interests; it is also involved in massive surveillance efforts that some feel undermine individual liberties guaranteed by the Constitution.

Government employs more than one-sixth of the workforce, and government policies affect the working conditions of everyone in the workforce. Not only are labor markets influenced by government policies, but government also influences all markets by providing the legal structure and regulations under which market exchange takes place.

Many of these modern functions of government did not exist 150 years ago. The scale and scope of the federal government, as well as that of state and local governments, have increased dramatically over the last century and a half. Government expenditures relative to GDP have grown from less than 5 percent in 1850 to almost 40 percent by 2016. At the federal level, the growth in expenditures has been primarily the result of growth in spending on national defense, Social Security, Medicare, Medicaid, and interest on the debt. State and local governments have also expanded faster than the economy as a whole. Even with all of these changes, however, the size of government relative to the size of the economy is smaller in the United States than it is in most European countries.

While specific government actions and policies are highlighted throughout the book, the purpose of this chapter is to provide a broad historical overview of the changing scale and scope of government through theories of government growth.

FIGURE 16.1 East Front of U.S. Capitol Building, 1828

CAPITOL, 1826, EAST FRONT.
From a sketch by Charles Bulfinch.

Source: Charles Bullfinch, 1904, Library of Congress, www.loc.gov/pictures/item/2014649264/ (accessed: March 7, 2016).

Some theories of government growth emphasize increasing citizen demands on government to provide public goods, to reduce negative externalities, to provide security, and to redistribute income and wealth. Other theories focus on the supply side, with the growth of government seen as primarily due to the incentives of public officials, to the nature of the U.S. representative form of government, and to inherent inefficiencies in government. The "ratchet" theory of government combines both demand and supply factors as government responds to crises, such as wars and depressions, but predicts that spending rarely returns to pre-crisis levels even long after the crisis has subsided.

Demand versus supply theories of government are related to public-interest versus public-choice views of government. In the public-interest view, politicians and bureaucrats are assumed to be neutral arbiters who are doing their best to serve the public interest, as represented through majority voting. While government policies do not all improve upon market outcomes—because of lack of understanding, unintended consequences, and imperfect information on the part of public officials—with the public-interest view, the *goal* of government officials is to improve social welfare.

In contrast, the public-choice view applies to the collective decision-making process the same principles that economists use in analyzing private decisions in markets. Economists generally assume that rational individuals are motivated by self-interest and strive to maximize utility when purchasing goods and services. In the public-choice view of government, the assumption of maximizing social welfare is replaced by self-interested maximizing behavior on the part of bureaucrats and politicians. That is, politicians and bureaucrats maximize their own individual welfare, not social welfare. Politicians and bureaucrats are able to do so because voters find it difficult to monitor government effectively and voters also have little incentive to do so.

Some believe that government has become too expansive, infringing on individual liberties through high taxes and in many other ways too, from unnecessary consumer protection laws to mandatory health insurance. Others feel that government has not gone far enough. The United States, for example, remains one of the few high-income countries without universal health insurance, although the Affordable Care Act (2010) was a move toward wider provision of health insurance.

This chapter also examines what the future may hold in terms of the role of government and markets throughout the remainder of the twenty-first century. Aside from ideological battles, the challenges of an aging population are likely to continue to affect the economy for decades to come.

16.1 DEMAND-SIDE THEORIES OF GOVERNMENT

Well-functioning markets, close to perfectly competitive, are extraordinarily efficient mechanisms for allocating society's scarce resources (physical capital, natural capital, technology, labor, and human capital) to where they are most productive and valued. Competitive markets also supply the goods and services that consumers want. Prices coordinate economic activity by providing information about scarcity and by incentivizing behavior that tends to make the most productive use of scarce resources.

In many instances, however, markets perform quite poorly—they are "market failures." Markets do not work well in providing public goods, or when there are externalities, monopolies, imperfect information, departures from rationality, or macroeconomic problems, such as financial crises and recessions. While market failures are departures from the efficiency of perfect competition, efficiency is only one of several, possibly competing, social goals. Government policies may also redistribute income to provide greater equity and equality of opportunity, even at the expense of efficiency.

"Citizen over state" theories about the growth of government emphasize the demands of citizens in wanting government to do more as the economy has changed from a rural and agricultural economy to a much larger-scale, urban, industrial, and service economy.[1] Economic growth and population growth have resulted in many changes that have caused citizens to demand more from government. While governments have always provided public goods such as national defense, technological change has led to a greater frequency of wars, and wars have become much more costly as weaponry has advanced.[2]

Population growth, technological change, industrialization, urbanization, and globalization have together led to much greater interaction between people and have increased the prevalence of both negative and positive externalities.[3] In addition, negative externalities are much more likely to affect a greater number of people, making resolution through private bargaining and litigation through the court system much more difficult. As a result, the government has become more involved in regulating firms. Government has also implemented taxes and subsidies, and has created new markets to address negative externalities.

In addition, economic growth has provided Americans with higher incomes, leading to an increased demand for environmental quality. Environmental quality is an income-elastic good: the demand for environmental quality increases proportionally more than the increase in consumer incomes.

There has also been a tendency for citizens to demand that government provide greater economic security and stability. The twentieth century witnessed federal provision of both social assistance and social insurance programs to help reduce the impacts of poverty, unemployment, poor health, disability, and age. During recessions and depressions, monetary and fiscal policies have been used in an attempt to reduce the length and severity of economic downturns.

PROVIDING PUBLIC GOODS AND NATIONAL DEFENSE

One function of government, spelled out in the Preamble of the U.S. Constitution, is to "provide for the common defence [sic]." While national defense has always been a government responsibility, the cost of the military has varied substantially throughout American history, with costs rising both during times of war and also over time, as weaponry has become increasingly sophisticated and expensive.

Public goods like national defense will either not be supplied at all by the market, or, if supplied, will be produced in quantities below the optimal level. Pure public goods are defined by two characteristics: nonrivalry and nonexcludability. National defense is a nonrival good—that is, individuals can consume the good simultaneously without diminishing the ability of others to consume the same good at the same time. As a result, once the good exists, there is a zero marginal cost in providing it to one more person. Public goods like national defense are also nonexcludable: once national defense is provided, it is not practically possible to prevent someone from consuming it. If national defense is successful in stopping an attack, then everyone benefits, whether or not they have helped to pay for it.

Suppose that a private firm tried to provide national defense by charging users a price for it. Because rational individuals would correctly believe that they would benefit from the good regardless of whether or not they personally paid for it, they would have no incentive to pay for it voluntarily. That is, there would be a free rider problem. Government is the one institution in society that can compel people to pay taxes or face further fines and imprisonment.

Many other goods, such as water and sewage treatment, sanitation, research and development, parks, and highways, are partial public goods and are generally provided by government. Spending on these goods has become more common and widespread since the late nineteenth century, as technological change has resulted in the ability to provide clean water, sanitation, and modern highways.

ENCOURAGING COMPETITION

For markets to be allocatively efficient, there must be perfect competition. One departure from perfect competition occurs when there is an insufficient number of firms, because then each firm is able to affect the market price. When a single firm supplies the market, economists refer to this market structure as a monopoly. When a few firms dominate most of the market, it is called an oligopoly.

When there is perfect competition, markets maximize the cumulative benefits to buyers and sellers. Firms, however, do better either if they are the only seller of a product (a monopoly) or if they can somehow agree with other firms to set prices (collusion). While sellers gain through monopoly or collusion, the loss to consumers exceeds the gains to producers: because potential gains from trade are not all realized, this results in what is called a deadweight loss.

Government enforces antitrust laws and regulates industries to ensure that markets are competitive and to prevent firms from colluding. In cases where there is a natural monopoly—that is, when it is cheaper for one firm to produce the entire output in the market than for several firms each to produce part of it—governments often regulate the firm to ensure that consumers are paying a fair price. Many local utilities are natural monopolies. The fixed costs of establishing the means to produce power and provide it to each household can be very high, which serves as a strong deterrent for possible competitors. Society also benefits from having natural monopolies, since multiple firms operating in such industries are more costly.

From the latter part of the nineteenth century to World War I, the federal government started to regulate railroads and other industries, typically after state laws had been ruled unconstitutional by the Supreme Court. Regulation and enforcement of antitrust laws, beginning with the Sherman Antitrust Act (1890), has waxed and waned since the late nineteenth century. In some periods, government authorities and the court system have been more aggressive; at other times, enforcement has been lax, as when the financial system was insufficiently regulated in the years leading up to the Great Recession. Antitrust laws and regulations are covered in Chapter 17.

EXTERNALITIES

The rising prevalence of externalities provides another reason for the growth of government. Externalities can be either negative or positive. A negative externality occurs when an individual or a firm engages in some activity that imposes a cost on others that does not have to be paid by the party generating the cost. Many social problems, including nearly all environmental challenges, are the result of negative externalities. A negative externality creates a situation in which rational individuals and firms do "too much" of an activity from the perspective of maximizing social welfare.

For example, consider a coal-burning steel factory which emits carbon dioxide (CO_2) and sulfur dioxide (SO_2) into the air, both gases that cause pollution and contribute to global climate change. When making production and consumption decisions, neither the steel company nor the purchasers of the steel take the costs of this pollution into account. As a result, there will be an overproduction of steel compared to the socially efficient amount.

While private parties may be able to solve or to internalize an externality problem under certain conditions (see Chapter 19 for a discussion of the Coase Theorem), in most cases the coercive power of government is needed to improve social welfare. Governments can potentially improve social welfare by regulating the company, by placing a tax on steel to discourage production, or by creating a market in tradeable emission permits.

A positive externality, in contrast, is an external benefit of an activity received by people other than those who pursue the activity. Examples include education, basic scientific discoveries, and home improvements like painting your house (as this also increases the value of the homes nearby). The market by itself will not produce enough of the good or service that generates the positive externality, so governments often subsidize those goods and services in order to gain more of the positive externality.

REDISTRIBUTING INCOME AND WEALTH

Almost every government policy involves some degree of redistribution of income, even if redistribution is not the primary motivation for the policy. In the case of user fees (such as a fee charged to cross a bridge or to enter a park), the same person both pays for and benefits from the activity. In most other instances, however, the people who finance a particular activity through taxes are not exactly the same people who benefit from that activity; and even if they are, the benefits each experiences are probably not in proportion to how much each pays. In these cases, therefore, there is in effect some redistribution from one group to another.

The fact that a market outcome may be efficient says nothing about distributional implications. A competitive market outcome may result in a very unequal distribution of income and wealth, and this inequality may leave some individuals unable to afford adequate food and shelter. While almost all societies have always provided some support for the poor and destitute, social assistance programs provided by government grew in scale and scope in the United States during the Great Depression of the 1930s and in the Great Society programs of the 1960s.

The Social Security Act (1935) introduced Aid to Dependent Children (ADC), which provided some relief to poor, single mothers. In 1962, this was changed to Aid to Families with Dependent Children (AFDC); and in 1996, the program was replaced with Temporary Assistance for Needy Families (TANF).

After World War II, the U.S. economy experienced robust rates of growth and an unprecedented level of prosperity. It became increasingly clear, however, that not all Americans were enjoying the full fruits of this prosperity. In 1964, President Lyndon Johnson declared a "War on Poverty" and many programs were introduced or expanded to provide a more comprehensive "safety net" and greater opportunities for the poor. Some programs provided food, housing, and medical care for the poor, while others focused on job training and preschool education. The history of social assistance programs is the subject of Chapter 20.

IMPERFECT INFORMATION AND INCOMPLETE MARKETS

Public goods are not the only types of goods that markets fail to produce in sufficient quantities. An incomplete market is one where some of the necessary conditions for market formation and exchange exist, but not all of them. As a result, the good or service will be underprovided or not provided at all. Incomplete markets are often the result of imperfect and asymmetric information. For example, because of information asymmetries, private markets may fail to provide insurance for many of the risks that individuals and firms face. Similarly, the expansion of government has been the result of an "increasing demand for security against adverse economic events."[4] In the twentieth century, the federal government implemented a number of social insurance programs, motivated, in part, by this market failure.

The Social Security Act (1935) included social assistance programs like Aid to Dependent Children, but it also introduced several social insurance programs. With social assistance, benefits are provided to needy persons without recipients having contributed to gain entitlement to those benefits. Social insurance, however, requires recipients (or their employers) to make contributions to receive benefits. In 2016, for example, Social Security's Old-Age, Survivors, and Disability Insurance (OASDI) program required that, up to an earnings limit of $118,500, each employee should pay 6.2 percent of his or her earnings to the program each year, with employers contributing a matching sum.

While old-age pensions and disability insurance are types of social insurance, the government is also involved in providing many other types of insurance, including unemployment insurance, medical insurance for the elderly (Medicare), workers' compensation (insurance against on-the-job injuries), and insurance for disabilities that are not job-related. The Federal Deposit Insurance Corporation (FDIC), created by the Banking Act of 1933, insures deposits in banks and thrift institutions.

By providing insurance in areas where the private sector is unwilling to provide it in sufficient quantities, however, the government often compounds the problems of adverse selection and moral hazard. That is, by fixing failures in private insurance markets, government provision of insurance often worsens the problem that is being insured against. Consider insurance provided for workers in case of injuries sustained on the job. Without stringent monitoring and enforcement, such insurance creates an incentive for dishonest workers to feign injury in order to enjoy leisure and to collect benefits without working.

PATERNALISM

Another justification for government intervention comes from a concern that in some markets individuals may not act in their own best interests. Paternalistic policies strive to improve social welfare by discouraging individuals from engaging in behavior that is likely to cause them (and others) harm in the long run. This includes everything from mandatory helmet laws to prohibitions on the consumption of certain substances. In some cases, individuals make poor choices because they do not have the information or knowledge to make better choices; in other cases, though, their choices represent departures from complete rationality.

In the nineteenth century, the prevailing view in the legal system was the rule of "caveat emptor" or "let the buyer beware." As long as consumers had a fair chance to examine a good prior to purchase, the buyer assumed full responsibility for the quality of the good after purchase. In the twentieth century, the seller and government assumed much greater responsibility for the safety and quality of goods. Starting with the Food and Drug Act (1906) and the Meat Inspection Act (1906), government took a more active role in ensuring the safety and quality of the food and medicines we consume.

Many of the Great Society programs of the 1960s were intended to protect people, often from themselves. Many of the most notable acts were the Cigarette Labeling and Advertising Act (1965), the Fair Packaging and Labeling Act (1966), the National Traffic and Motor Vehicle Safety Act (1966), the Flammable Fabrics Act (1967), and the Consumer Credit Protection Act (1968).

Government expanded to ensure safety and standards in many other areas of the economy, passing further legislation, including the Patient Protection and Affordable Care Act (2010) and the Dodd-Frank Wall Street Reform and Consumer Protection Act (2010), and setting up bodies to provide oversight and enforcement, including the National Transportation Safety Board (1967), the National Highway Traffic Safety Administration (1970), and the Consumer Product Safety Commission (1972). Because of concerns that welfare recipients will not use the cash they receive wisely, most social assistance programs offer in-kind benefits, in the form of medical care, food, housing, job training, and early childhood education, rather than cash payments.

STABILIZATION POLICIES

Not only are there market failures in individual markets, but there can also be economy-wide market failures, in the form of recessions and depressions, which can lead to periods of low output and high unemployment that may persist for years. The central banks in the nineteenth century, the First and Second Banks of the United States, engaged in some activities to stabilize financial markets and the economy as a whole (see Chapter 5). While the Federal Reserve was established in 1913, modern stabilization policies are largely the result of the experiences of the Great Depression of the 1930s and of World War II.

The belief that government, through fiscal and monetary policies, could and should help to stabilize the economy became official government policy after World War II. The Employment Act (1946) required "the federal government to use all practicable means … to promote maximum employment, production, and purchasing power." It also created the Council of Economic Advisors to help advise the U.S. President on how best to achieve these goals.

The Employment Act was influenced by the views of John Maynard Keynes, who suggested that the high and persistent unemployment during the Great Depression was the result of insufficient aggregate demand. Fiscal policies (which make use of government spending and taxation) and monetary policies (in which the central bank influences the money supply and interest rates) are used to help increase spending and aggregate demand in order to forestall recessions and depressions. The history and causes of economic fluctuations, and the responses of monetary and fiscal policies in attempting to stabilize the economy, are discussed in Chapter 18.

16.2 SUPPLY-SIDE THEORIES OF GOVERNMENT

In contrast to "citizen over state" theories about the growth of government, "state over citizen" theories stress the incentives of bureaucrats and politicians in expanding government. In this view, the growth of government is primarily a supply-side phenomenon in which politicians and bureaucrats supply more government than the populace desires. Instead of maximizing social welfare by attempting to act in the public interest, self-interested behavior on the part of politicians and bureaucrats instead leads to an overly expansive role of government and to inherent inefficiencies, since voters have little incentive or ability to adequately monitor the actions of government.

RATIONAL IGNORANCE

Individuals consume so many goods and services that they have neither the time nor the incentive to understand the impact of public policies on every one of these goods and services. In addition, as voters, they realize that their vote has only a miniscule probability of affecting the outcome of any public policy choice.

Consider the U.S. sugar industry, which has enjoyed trade protection since 1789, when Congress passed the first tariff on imported sugar. During the 2000s, U.S. sugar prices were more than 10 cents higher per pound than world sugar prices because of U.S. government "loans to sugar processors and a marketing allotment program."[5]

Each American, on average, consumes about 150 pounds of sugar per year. If each pound of sugar costs 10 cents more because of the protectionist policies, then the annual cost of these policies to an average consumer is about $15 per year. This policy, and hundreds of others, imposes small costs on American consumers. Under these circumstances, individuals frequently adopt a position of rational ignorance, since the marginal cost of understanding and voting on a particular policy exceeds the expected marginal benefit from doing so. That is, it is rational to choose not to understand or attempt to change a policy that affects you adversely by only a small amount. Because of rational ignorance, special interest groups can lobby government to enact policies that benefit the few at the expense of the many. These policies also lead to inefficiencies or deadweight losses to society.

Lobbying occurs when special interest groups meet with legislators to urge support of policies preferred by the interest groups. Legislators have an incentive to respond favorably to lobbying, since interest groups engage in activities that benefit legislators, such as making campaign donations, influencing voters through advertising, and increasing voter turnout on Election Day for politicians they support.

DISPERSED COSTS AND CONCENTRATED BENEFITS

While the costs of a particular policy are usually small for each individual consumer, the benefits from the policy are usually far larger for each producer. For example, there are only about 5,000 farms growing sugar beets or sugar cane in the United States. If 320 million people all pay $15 more per year for sugar, the benefit to these 5,000 producers translates to nearly $100,000 per producer. With dispersed costs and concentrated benefits ($15 cost per consumer vs. $100,000 benefit per producer), producers have a far greater incentive to make sure that the policy stays in place (and perhaps even expands), for example by lobbying members of Congress or by contributing to the campaigns of candidates who promise to support sugar producers.

Chapter 9 discusses the long history of all types of agricultural subsidies and price supports. While there is near universal agreement that the overwhelming majority of these policies benefit only a relatively small number of farmers (often with high incomes), these policies impose only small costs on each of the millions of consumers, and so they remain part of the political landscape year after year and decade after decade. Concentrated benefits to special interest groups along with costs distributed over millions of consumers frequently produce economically inefficient outcomes.

REGULATORY CAPTURE

"Regulatory capture" occurs when a regulatory agency, created to act in the public interest, instead advances the interests of the industry that it has been charged with regulating. Sometimes the line between regulatory capture and corruption is difficult to determine. (Corruption is the misuse of government power for personal gain.)

One cause of regulatory capture and corruption is that some regulators may know that catering to the desires of the industry may bring personal rewards after they leave government. Many former regulators serve on the boards of directors of companies, are highly-paid consultants, and receive exorbitant amounts for speaking engagements. The fact that there is a "revolving door" whereby the same people move between government regulation and the industry increases the likelihood of regulatory capture. This risk can be minimized by appointing as regulators career civil servants, academics, or those near the end of their careers, since these individuals are less likely to seek employment in the regulated firms afterwards.

There is considerable debate regarding the importance of regulatory capture. From the late nineteenth century to the 1960s, regulation was not strongly correlated with market failures and was generally "pro-producer" in that regulation tended to increase industry profits.[6] There is also evidence that is inconsistent with the regulatory capture hypothesis. First, there is a long list of regulations and laws that were *not* supported by industry and indeed resulted in lower profits, including oil and natural-gas price regulation, and many environmental, product safety, and worker protection laws. Second, regulatory capture theory does not provide a good explanation of why many industries were first regulated and then later deregulated.[7]

16.3 WARS, CRISES, AND THE RATCHET EFFECT

The "ratchet" theory of government combines both demand and supply factors to explain the growth of government.[8] During crises, such as wars, depressions, and natural disasters, citizens demand that governments do something to combat the crisis, and that causes the government to expand. Once a policy or program is in place, however, it rarely goes away, even after the initial cause has long subsided. Bureaucrats and special interest groups who benefit from the policy will act in ways intended to ensure the continuation of the policy. The crisis itself will also often change beliefs about the role of the appropriate scale and scope of government. That is, once a policy is in place, people soon accept the new policy as the status quo and do not demand that it be repealed.

Consider the creation of the Transportation Security Administration in response to the terrorist attacks on the World Trade Center and the Pentagon on September 11, 2001. Immediately after these tragic events, stringent airport security and passenger screening procedures were implemented. The ratchet theory of government predicts that we will now be screened at airports forever, whether or not there is any substantial future threat.

Before the Civil War, federal expenditures and revenues were usually closely aligned and generally quite small, at only 2 or 3 percent of GDP (Figure 16.2). Both expenditures and revenues appear to ratchet upwards in a series of "stair steps," each associated with a major crisis: the Civil War, World War I, the Great Depression and the New Deal, and World War II. Although more difficult to see in Figure 16.2, the same

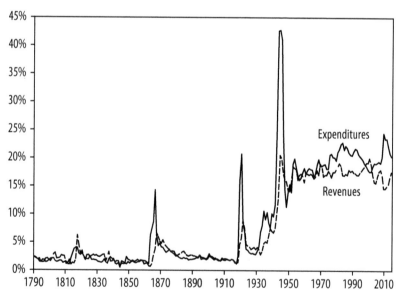

FIGURE 16.2 U.S. Federal Expenditures and Revenues as a Percentage of GDP, 1790–2014

Sources and Notes: For the years 1790–1929, data on federal expenditures and revenues are from Kevin D. Hoover and Mark V. Siegler, "Taxing and Spending in the Long View: The Causal Structure of U.S. Fiscal Policy after 1791," *Oxford Economic Papers* 52, no. 4 (December 2000), 745–773. Data for nominal GDP are from Louis Johnston and Samuel H. Williamson, "What Was the U.S. GDP Then?" *MeasuringWorth*, www.measuringworth.org/usgdp/ (accessed: September 15, 2015). For the years 1930–2014, data are from U.S. Office of Management and Budget, Table 1.2, www.whitehouse. gov/sites/default/files/omb/budget/fy2016/assets/hist01z2.xls (accessed: September 15, 2015).

pattern seems to apply to earlier (and smaller) wars as well, such as the War of 1812, the Mexican–American War (1846–1848), and the Spanish–American War (1898).

WARS AND NATIONAL DEFENSE

National defense expenditures increased dramatically during the twentieth century and contributed to the growth of the federal government. Prior to World War I, less than 2 percent of GDP was spent on national defense (Figure 16.3). Both World War I and World War II, however, led to sharp increases in defense spending. While defense spending peaked at over 20 percent of GDP in World War I, it fell to less than 2 percent of GDP in the 1920s and 1930s. This was not the pattern after World War II. The size of military spending relative to the size of the economy was unprecedented, peaking at over 40 percent of GDP near the end of the War. While military spending fell substantially after the War, it remained relatively high throughout the postwar period.

Between World War I and World War II, American policies were very isolationist, with substantial restrictions on immigration and high trade barriers. As the U.S. emerged from World War II, most policymakers recognized the failures of previous policies and urged the U.S. to become a more active participant in the international economy. Several international institutions were created in the aftermath of World War II (1944–1945), including the United Nations, the International Monetary Fund, the World Bank, and the International Trade Organization. Although the U.S. Senate refused to ratify the charter for the International Trade Organization, the U.S. did enter into the General Agreement on Tariffs and Trade in 1947.

FIGURE 16.3 National Defense Spending as a Percentage of GDP, 1900–2013

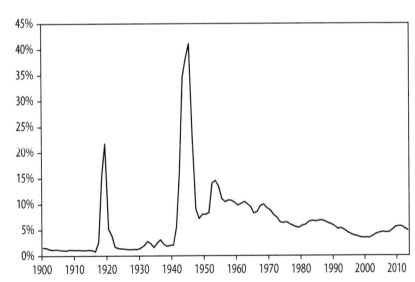

Sources and Notes: Expenditures on national defense for the years 1900–1961 from *Historical Statistics of the United States: Colonial Times to 1970* (Government Printing Office, 1975), Series Y 458, 459, and 463, 1114. For the years 1962–2013, national defense expenditures from Office of Management and Budget, *Historical Tables: Budget of the U.S. Government, Fiscal Year 2016*, Table 3.1, www.gpo.gov/fdsys/pkg/BUDGET-2016-TAB/pdf/BUDGET-2016-TAB.pdf (accessed: March 6, 2016). Nominal GDP for all years from Louis Johnston and Samuel H. Williamson, "What Was the U.S. GDP Then? *MeasuringWorth*, www.measuringworth.org/usgdp/ (accessed: March 6, 2016).

From 1947 to 1991, U.S. foreign policy focused on the containment of communism. In 1947, President Harry Truman made an open-ended pledge, known as the "Truman Doctrine," to aid any country threatened by communists. To help European countries rebuild and to prevent the spread of communism, the United States created the Marshall Plan, committing $13 billion (approximately $140 billion in 2016 dollars) to Western European countries. The Berlin Crisis (1948), the Communist victory in China (1949), the first Soviet nuclear bomb test (1949), the establishment of the North Atlantic Treaty Organization or NATO (1949), and the outbreak of the Korean War (1950) together led to "a policy of active global containment and deterrence of the USSR."[9] This situation was termed the "Cold War" because there was no direct large-scale fighting between the two major powers, the United States and the Soviet Union, although there were major regional wars in Korea, Vietnam, and Afghanistan, in which the United States and the Soviet Union supported opposite sides.

During the Cold War, U.S. defense policy focused on the theory of deterrence. The strategy was to establish a military that was so large and so strong that no other country would contemplate a direct attack on the United States. The Soviet Union followed the same general strategy, and the result was an "arms race," with ever larger, ever more powerful, and ever more expensive weaponry. An arms race is a variation of the prisoner's dilemma game (see Chapter 17). Since the value of your own weapons depends on the weapons possessed by your rival, there is an incentive to spend more than your adversary to gain an advantage. As both the U.S. and Soviet Union had the same incentives, however, the result was that both countries spent increasing amounts on armaments while achieving no change in their relative military strengths, which made both countries worse off in the process.

While defensive expenditures fell to 7 percent of GDP by 1948, they surged to almost 15 percent of GDP by 1953, due to U.S. involvement in the Korean War. From 10 percent of GDP in 1968, at the height of the Vietnam War, national defense expenditures fell to 5.5 percent of GDP by 1979; but they increased again during the Reagan administration, peaking at almost 7 percent of GDP in 1986.

In the late 1980s and early 1990s, the collapse of communist regimes in Eastern Europe and increased openness (*glasnost*) and market reforms (*perestroika*) in the Soviet Union under President Mikhail Gorbachev signaled the end of the Cold War. While many hoped for a large "peace dividend," this hope was short-lived. National defense relative to GDP fell to less than 3.5 percent by 1999, but during the "War on Terror" that followed the attacks on September 11, 2001, it soon exceeded 5 percent of GDP. In 2010, defense expenditures were 5.7 percent of GDP, primarily as the result of conflicts in Iraq and Afghanistan. Although national defense expenditures fell to less than 5 percent of GDP by 2013, they remained a larger share of GDP than in any other country in the OECD, with the exception of Israel.[10]

THE GREAT DEPRESSION

In addition to wars, the Great Depression of the 1930s stands out as a period in which the role of government in the American economy changed permanently. While government expenditures did not increase dramatically during the Great Depression, the regulatory and legal changes during the New Deal laid the foundation for large changes in the scale and scope of government in the decades after World War II. These changes are discussed in several other chapters, but in summary the New Deal led to increased government intervention in agriculture, labor, finance, housing, welfare, retirement, and many other areas.

16.4 FEDERAL, STATE, AND LOCAL GOVERNMENT EXPENDITURES AND REVENUES

The United States has a federal system of government, meaning that responsibilities are shared across all levels of government. The Tenth Amendment to the U.S. Constitution provides the basis for this system of shared governance: "The powers not delegated to the United States by the Constitution, nor prohibited by it to the States, are reserved to the States respectively, or to the people."

THE LONG NINETEENTH CENTURY

Before World War I, and except during times of major wars, state and local governments were responsible for most of government spending and for the collection of most tax revenues. Between 1789 and 1840, state governments invested heavily in internal projects such as banks, canals, and other transportation improvements (Chapter 8). In 1840, state governments owed over 85 percent of government debt.[11] The federal government played a very limited role in these areas, with the exception of the First and Second Bank of the United States (Chapter 5) and the building of the National Road (Chapter 8). Substantial state involvement in infrastructure projects ended in the early 1840s, however, when eight states and the Territory of Florida defaulted on bonds they had issued to build or buy banks, canals, and railroads.[12]

After 1842, local governments took an increasing role in financing internal improvement projects. By 1900, local government spending exceeded spending at the state or federal level (Table 16.1), and local governments were investing in schools, roads,

TABLE 16.1 Federal, State, and Local Government Expenditures as a Percentage of GDP, 1850–2000

Year	Federal	State	Local	Total
1850	1.7	1.3	1.6	4.6
1900	2.9	0.9	3.3	7.1
1950	15.3	3.6	5.7	24.6
2000	17.6	10.5	9.7	37.8

Sources and Notes: State and local expenditures for 1850 from Randall G. Holcombe and Donald J. Lacombe, "The Growth of Local Government in the United States from 1820 to 1870," *Journal of Economic History* 61, no. 1 (March 2001), Table 4, 188. State and local expenditures for 1900 and 1950 from Susan B. Carter, Scott Sigmund Gartner, Michael R. Haines, Alan L. Olmstead, Richard Sutch, and Gavin Wright (eds.), *Historical Statistics of the United States*, Millennial Edition (New York, NY: Cambridge University Press, 2006), series Ea16 and Ea17. Year 2000 state and local expenditures from U.S. Bureau of the Census, *Government Finances 1999–2000*, Table 1 (June 2003), www2.census. gov/govs/local/00allpub.pdf (accessed: September 10, 2015). The sources for federal government expenditures are as given in the sources and notes for Figure 16.2. Nominal GDP data for 1850 and 1900 are from Louis Johnston and Samuel H. Williamson, "What Was the U.S. GDP Then?" *MeasuringWorth*, www.measuringworth.org/usgdp/ (accessed: September 10, 2015). Nominal GDP data for 1950 and 2000 are from the U.S. Bureau of Economic Analysis, www.bea.gov/national/xls/gdplev.xls (accessed: September 10, 2015).

municipal buildings, and public health improvements.[13] By 1913, local governments owed 76 percent of all government debt, which was more than ten times the amount of state debts.[14] Throughout the nineteenth and early twentieth centuries, revenue from property taxes paid for the overwhelming majority of both state and local spending.

While state-level expenditures remained quite modest at around 1 percent of GDP between 1850 and 1900, during the late nineteenth and early twentieth centuries state governments established extensive regulations of labor markets and other types of markets. States had always been responsible for regulating banks, but also began to regulate railroads in the 1870s. While state laws were later found to be unconstitutional, and railroad regulation eventually became a federal responsibility (Chapter 17), state governments often led the way, with the federal government following.

Between 1789 and 1914, federal government expenditures and revenues, relative to GDP, remained very low, averaging less than 3 percent of GDP during this time. The only times when expenditures exceeded 5 percent of GDP occurred during the War of 1812 and during the Civil War (Figure 16.2). The federal government originally focused on the sales and distribution of the land it owned, on national defense and foreign policy, on the post office, and on the establishment of a monetary and financial system. Before the Civil War, the overwhelming majority of federal revenues were from tariffs (taxes on imported goods). In some years, revenues from the sales of public lands were important sources as well. The remainder of federal revenue came from a variety of internal sales taxes.

THE TWENTIETH CENTURY

In 1913, a permanent federal income tax was introduced, which eventually became a major source of federal revenue. In 1929, however, federal revenues and expenditures were still less than 4 percent of GDP, but the Great Depression and World War II caused federal government expenditures and revenues to permanently increase relative to GDP. Many economic historians believe that the Great Depression was a "defining moment" that "altered the basic rules, institutions, and attitudes" regarding the role of government in the economy.[15]

Between 1947 and 2015, federal expenditures averaged 19.2 percent of GDP, while federal revenues were 17.2 percent of GDP. During the 1950s and 1960s, expenditures and revenues were quite close to one another. Since around 1970, however, expenditures have typically exceeded revenues, resulting in persistent budget deficits (see Section 16.5).

Consider the data from Table 16.2, which shows federal expenditures and revenues by type in 1960 and 2010. In 1960, the United States was in the midst of the Cold War and nearly half of all federal expenditures were for national defense. The only other expenditure categories larger than 10 percent of the budget were Social Security and net interest on the debt.

By 2010, national defense expenditures had fallen to only 19 percent of the budget, but the biggest increase was federal expenditures on health, the result of the introduction of Medicare (1965) for the elderly and Medicaid (1965) for the poor and disabled. Medicare costs also increased substantially because of the Medicare Prescription Drug Improvement and Modernization Act (2003), which provided prescription-drug benefits to Medicare recipients. The other notable change in federal expenditures between 1960 and 2010 was an increase from 4

TABLE 16.2 Federal Expenditures and Revenues by Function and Source, 1960 and 2010

	Federal Expenditures	
	1960	2010
Health	3%	25%
National Defense	49%	19%
Social Security	13%	16%
Education, Welfare, and Housing	4%	11%
Unemployment and Disability	9%	9%
Net Interest	10%	8%
Other	12%	12%
	Federal Revenues	
	1960	2010
Income Taxes	44%	42%
Social Insurance Contributions	17%	35%
Corporate Taxes	23%	13%
Excise Taxes	13%	3%
Other	3%	7%

Sources and Notes: Computed using U.S. Bureau of Economic Analysis, National Income and Product Accounts data, various tables.

TABLE 16.3 State and Local Expenditures and Revenues by Function and Source, 1960 and 2010

	State and Local Expenditures	
	1960	2010
Education	39%	33%
Health	8%	22%
Public Order and Safety	10%	13%
Welfare and Social Services	10%	7%
Transportation	12%	6%
Other	21%	19%
	State and Local Revenues	
	1960	2010
Federal Grants	9%	24%
Sales Taxes	27%	22%
Property Taxes	36%	21%
Income Taxes	6%	14%
Other	22%	19%

Sources and Notes: Computed using U.S. Bureau of Economic Analysis, National Income and Product Accounts data, various tables.

percent of the budget to 11 percent of the budget for education, welfare, and housing.

The growth of Medicare and Social Security has led to an increase in payroll taxes for social insurance contributions, from 17 percent of federal tax revenues in 1960 to 35 percent in 2010. Income tax revenues remained the largest source of federal revenues in both periods; and while taxes for social insurance have increased, the shares of revenues coming from the corporate income tax and excise taxes have decreased over the past half century.

By 1950, federal government spending considerably exceeded the combined spending of state and local governments. Fifty years later, the trend had reversed itself once again. In the year 2000, while federal government spending was still larger than state or local government spending, the combined state and local total (20.2 percent of GDP) exceeded the federal total (17.6 percent of GDP).

By 2012, governments in the United States consisted of the federal government, fifty state governments, several territorial governments, and more than 89,000 local governments, including those of counties, municipalities, townships, special districts, and school districts.[16] Most of the growth of government since the 1960s has occurred at the state and local levels. Table 16.3 shows the sources of state and local expenditures and revenues in both 1960 and 2010.

While the size of government in the United States has generally grown over time, the size of the U.S. government relative to the economy is nevertheless relatively small when compared to most other OECD countries (Figure 16.4). In 2013, total government spending as a percentage of GDP was 38.7 percent in the United States, while it was over 50 percent of GDP in several European countries. The difference in the relative size of the government in the United States compared to many European countries is primarily the result of differences in social spending (see Chapter 20).

FIGURE 16.4 Total Government Spending by Country as a Percentage of GDP, 2013

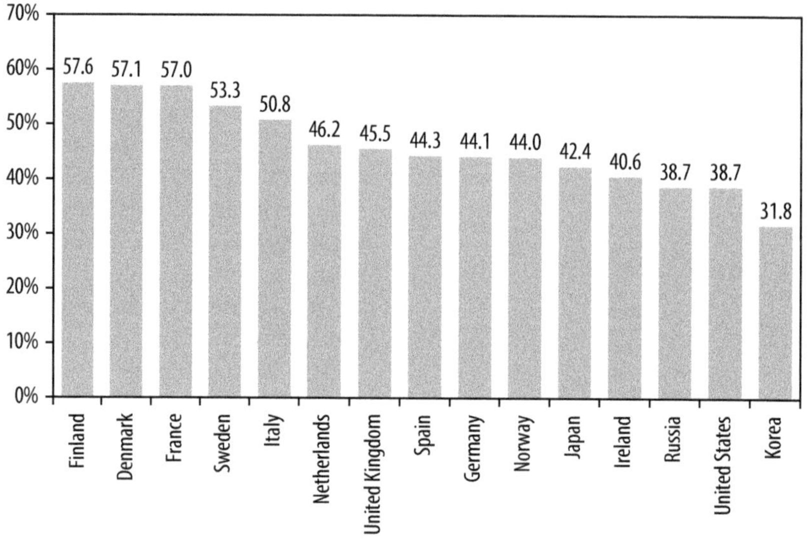

Source: Office of Economic Cooperation and Development, https://data.oecd.org/gga/general-government-spending. htm (accessed: July 2, 2015).

16.5   DEFICITS AND DEBT

A budget deficit occurs when government expenditures (spending) exceed tax revenues in a given year. When taxes are greater than spending, there is a budget surplus. The budget is balanced if taxes and spending are equal. Government debt is the amount a government owes to others who have loaned it money in the past (by buying government bonds). It is the accumulated flow of past deficits that have not yet been repaid.

Until the aftermath of the Great Recession, large deficits in American history primarily occurred during wars—the War of 1812 (1812–1815), the Civil War (1861–1865), World War I (1917–1918), and World War II (1941–1945). The only large peacetime deficits were during the Great Depression, in 1934, when the deficit reached 5.8 percent of GDP; and after the Great Recession in 2009, 2010, and 2011, when deficits exceeded 8 percent of GDP.

Figure 16.5 shows federal budget surpluses and deficits since 1790. Excluding the major wars, the average annual deficit from 1790 to 1970, and from 1947 to 1970, was less than one-fourth of 1 percent of GDP. Since 1970, however, the deficit has averaged over 3 percent of GDP, and expenditures have almost always exceeded revenues. The only budget surpluses since 1970 occurred from 1998 to 2001, a period associated with rapid economic growth prior to the recession of 2001. Deficits also ballooned in the aftermath of the Great Recession.

Evidence suggests that the reason for nearly balanced budgets throughout most of American history was the causal connection between taxes and spending. Before 1970, the dominant causal relationship was that taxes caused spending—if tax revenues changed, the normal response was for spending to fall in line with tax revenues.[17] Since around 1970, however, federal taxes and spending in the United States have

FIGURE 16.5 Federal Government Surplus/Deficit as a Percentage of GDP

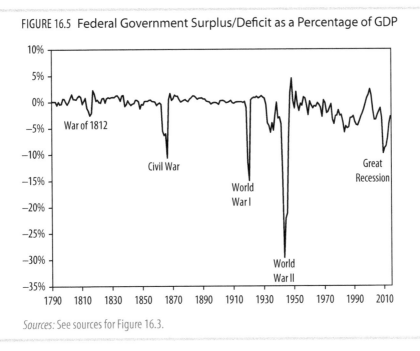

Sources: See sources for Figure 16.3.

been causally independent, perhaps contributing to persistent deficits, with only three small surpluses (1999, 2000, and 2001), between 1970 and 2014.[18]

Many citizens and many politicians believe that the ideal economic (and moral) ideal is a balanced budget every year (a zero deficit) and no public debt. In the 1980s and 1990s, several bills were introduced in Congress as Amendments to the U.S. Constitution which would have required annual balanced budgets, but none passed.

Deficits and debt may sometimes be highly beneficial, though not always. The theory of functional finance provides a way to conceptualize deficits and debt.[19] According to this theory, government budgets should not be judged on whether they balance or not, but instead according to their effects on the economy in both the short run and the long run.

Most college students are running personal budget deficits and accumulating debt. That is, they are spending more on tuition, room, and board each year than they are currently earning. In the case of college, these deficits and the accumulated debt are often a sound investment that leads to substantially higher lifetime earnings, particularly if students do well in college and graduate. While borrowing $60,000 to get a college degree may be a sound investment, borrowing $60,000 to throw the best party ever is likely to be an unwise decision. Functional finance asserts that government budget decisions should be viewed in the same way.

CROWDING OUT OR CROWDING IN?

Many critics of government spending fear that it will "crowd out" private investment spending. The theory of loanable funds (Chapter 5) showed that government budget deficits reduce total savings in an economy and, ceteris paribus, lead to higher real interest rates and lower private investment spending. In the theory of loanable funds, however, it is assumed that incomes are held constant. In richer models of the economy, greater government spending need not always lead to lower investment spending.

Some economists have argued that public infrastructure and educational spending have increased the rate of economic growth (i.e., that they have increased the size of the economic pie) and have instead led to "crowding in", in which government expenditures have increased the resources available to the private sector. During the nineteenth century, infrastructure investment was a mixture of private and public. Government investments in canals and railroads (primarily through land grants) promoted private industry. In modern times, government construction and maintenance of roads, airports, schools, public transportation, and public utilities provide services that are essential to a well-functioning private sector.

When the economy is below potential output, deficit spending through higher government spending and/or lower taxes can help to counter the decrease in private spending associated with recessions and to assist in the return to potential output. While the right timing and the right magnitude of discretionary fiscal policy can reduce the severity and length of contractions, if the actions are of the wrong magnitude or if they affect the economy at the wrong time (due to the recognition, implementation, and transmission lags of fiscal policy), fiscal policy can also exacerbate economic fluctuations (Chapter 18).

The important lesson of functional finance is the need to focus on the effects of particular government expenditures and taxes at particular times, and not necessarily to believe that deficits and debt are always bad.

THE U.S. GOVERNMENT DEBT

Figure 16.6 shows the size of the federal debt relative to GDP. Recall that the debt is the accumulation of past deficits not yet repaid. Historically, large deficits associated with wars increased the national debt, but the debt-to-GDP ratios fell *after* wars

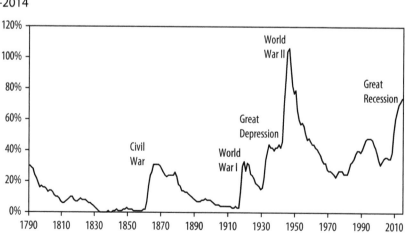

FIGURE 16.6 U.S. Federal Government Debt Held by the Public as a Percentage of GDP, 1790–2014

Source: Computed from Congressional Budget Office, *The 2015 Long-Term Budget Outlook* (June 2015), www.cbo.gov/publication/50250 (accessed: September 12, 2015), data from Figure 1-1, 11.

because of a combination of budget surpluses (or very small deficits), inflation, and real GDP growth. This pattern was repeated again and again, following the Revolutionary War (1775–1783), the War of 1812 (1812–1815), the Civil War (1861–1865), World War I (1917–1918), and World War II (1941–1945). The general pattern of rising debt-to-GDP levels during wars, however, does not appear in the Korean War (1950–1953) or the Vietnam War (1964–1973).

BUDGET AND DEBT FORECASTS

The Congressional Budget Office (CBO) regularly publishes long-run forecasts of future budget deficits and debt. Recent forecasts paint a picture of difficult choices and tradeoffs in the future. The baseline assumptions forecast assumes that current policies and tax laws continue into the indefinite future, and that all future promised entitlement benefits are paid to recipients of Social Security, Medicare, and other government programs. Assumptions regarding three variables are critical: (1) future long-run rates of economic growth; (2) future life expectancies; and (3) future rates of growth of healthcare spending.

The CBO predicts that by the year 2080 the annual deficit will balloon to 17.8 percent of GDP and the debt-to-GDP ratio will be 283 percent, which is four times higher than it was in 2013.[20] While these predictions are dire, they are driven almost entirely by projected increases in healthcare spending, which is expected to reach 46 percent of GDP by 2083, with Medicare and Medicaid spending accounting for 15 percent of GDP. The growth in healthcare spending has slowed in recent years (see Chapter 20), however, and if the growth of healthcare spending turns out to be slower than predicted, the magnitude of future deficits and debts may be substantially lower than the CBO has forecast.

GENERATIONAL ACCOUNTING

Generational accounting measures the net fiscal burden of government taxing and spending policies on past, present, and future generations.[21] It attempts to answer the question: "What is the net benefit to each generation (those born in different years) from the government's spending and tax policies, assuming that the budget is eventually brought into long-run balance?"[22]

In 2010, for current generations of all ages, the expected present value of government benefits is projected to exceed the present value of taxes paid. That is, there is a net transfer (net benefit) from government to current generations. However, most of this transfer will be paid by generations not yet born. The main message of recent estimates of generational accounting is that "current generations are net receivers of public resources, while future generations of Americans are expected to foot the bill."[23]

16.6   CONCLUSIONS

Markets and government have the potential to improve economic welfare, but they can also make things worse. Both government failures and market failures are pervasive, so that policymakers should ideally choose the least problematic option. While a benevolent, all-knowing government has the potential to improve many market outcomes, governments, too, are subject to problems and limitations that can adversely affect markets and economic performance. There are countless instances in American economic history of market failure and of government failure, and often it is the specific incentives and constraints facing market participants and government that will determine the best, if not necessarily the optimal, outcome under any given set of circumstances.

Many of the themes and issues introduced in this chapter are examined in detail in the closing chapters. Chapter 17 focuses on antitrust regulation and other types of regulation. Chapter 18 examines the interrelationships between markets and government during recessions, depressions, and expansions; while Chapter 19 discusses the problems of externalities and common resources. The economic history of social spending, including both social assistance and social insurance, is taken up in Chapter 20.

QUESTIONS

1. What are the main functions of government today? Which of these functions existed in 1850 and which did not? Describe how the roles, responsibilities, and relative sizes of federal, state, and local governments have changed since the mid-nineteenth century.

2. Following a crisis or a war, why does the size of government often not return to its pre-crisis or prewar levels?

3. Do you think the growth of government in the twentieth century was primarily a demand-side phenomenon or a supply-side phenomenon? Explain both views. Take a stand on the issue and provide examples and evidence to support your position.

4. Describe the general features and patterns of federal budget deficits and surpluses since 1790. When did patterns change, and why?

5. How would regulatory practices be affected if there were a law requiring regulatory agencies to include equal representation on behalf of the firms, the workers, and the consumers? More generally, how do you think the members of regulatory agencies should be selected?

NOTES

[1] For a discussion of the theories of government growth, see Thomas A. Garrett and Russell M. Rhine, "On the Size and Growth of Government," *Review* 88, no. 1 (Federal Reserve Bank of St. Louis, 2006), 13–30.

[2] Mark Harrison and Nikolaus Wolf, "The Frequency of Wars," *The Economic History Review* 65, no. 3 (August 2012), 1055–1076. The authors show that the frequency of wars in the world has increased steadily since 1870.

[3] Price Fishback, "Government and the Economy," in *Government and the American Economy: A New History* (Chicago, IL: The University of Chicago Press, 2007), 20.

[4] Fishback, 21.

[5] United States Department of Agriculture, Economic Research Service, "U.S. Sugar Production," www.ers.usda.gov/topics/crops/sugar-sweeteners/background.aspx (accessed: September 2, 2015).

[6] See, for example, William A. Jordan, "Producer Protection, Prior Market Structure and the Effects of Government Regulation," *Journal of Law and Economics* 15, no. 1 (April 1972), 151–176.

[7] W. Kip Viscusi, Joseph E. Harrington, Jr., and John M. Vernon, *Economics of Regulation and Antitrust*, Fourth Edition (Cambridge, MA: The MIT Press, 2005), 380.

[8] See Robert Higgs, *Crisis and Leviathan: Critical Episodes in the Growth of American Government* (New York, NY: Oxford University Press, 1987).

[9] Fishback, 510.

[10] Office of Economic Cooperation and Development, https://data.oecd.org/gga/general-government-spending.htm#indicator-chart (accessed: August 3, 2015).

[11] John Joseph Wallis, "American Government Finance in the Long Run," *Journal of Economic Perspectives* 14, no. 1 (Winter 2000), 66.

[12] Fishback, 26–27.

[13] Fishback, 27.

[14] Wallis, 66.

[15] Michael D. Bordo, Claudia Goldin, and Eugene N. White, "The Defining Moment Hypothesis: The Editors' Introduction," in *The Defining Moment: The Great Depression and the American Economy in the Twentieth Century* (Chicago, IL: University of Chicago Press, 1998), 1.

[16] U.S. Bureau of the Census, "There are 89,004 Local Governments in the United States," *Census Bureau Report* CB12-161 (October 30, 2012), www.census.gov/newsroom/releases/archives/governments/cb12-161.html (accessed: September 17, 2015).

[17] Kevin D. Hoover and Mark V. Siegler, "Taxes and Spending in the Long View: The Causal Structure of U.S. Fiscal Policy, 1791–1913," *Oxford Economic Papers* 52, no. 4 (October 2000), 745–773.

[18] Kevin D. Hoover and Steven M. Sheffrin, "Causation, Spending, and Taxes: Sand in the Sandbox or Tax Collector for the Welfare State?" *American Economic Review* 82, no. 1 (March 1992), 225–248.

[19] Abba Lerner, "Functional Finance and the Federal Debt," *Social Research* 10, no. 1 (Spring 1943), 38–51.

[20] Congressional Budget Office, *The Long-Term Budget Outlook* (June 2009), www.cbo.gov/sites/default/files/111th-congress-2009-2010/reports/06-25-ltbo.pdf (accessed: September 7, 2015).

[21] For a description, see Alan J. Auerbach, Jagadeesh Gokhale, and Laurence J. Kotlikoff, "Generational Accounting: A Meaningful Way to Evaluate Fiscal Policy," *Journal of Economic Perspectives* 8, no. 1 (Winter 1994), 73–94, http://pubs.aeaweb.org/doi/pdfplus/10.1257/jep.8.1.73 (accessed: August 25, 2015).

[22] Jonathan Gruber, *Public Finance and Public Policy*, Fourth Edition (New York, NY: Worth Publishers, 2013), 105–106.

[23] Nicoletta Batini, Giovanni Callegari, and Juia Guerreiro, "An Analysis of U.S. Fiscal and Generational Imbalances: Who Will Pay and How?" *International Monetary Fund Working Paper* 11, no. 72 (April 2011), Table 3, 20, www.imf.org/external/pubs/ft/wp/2011/wp1172.pdf (accessed: August 18, 2015).

17

Regulation and Antitrust Policies

Ever since the colonial period, governments have regulated certain types of economic activities. Throughout much of the nineteenth century, however, the prevailing view was in favor of free enterprise in which there was little, if any, regulation regarding the market structure of industries and the behavior of firms.

Until nearly the end of the nineteenth century, commercial disputes were generally resolved through private litigation in the court system. However, several changes in the economy between the Civil War and the Progressive Era limited the ability of private litigation to adequately address these issues. Following the railroads, the growth of large corporations became the norm in many industries, and waves of mergers and consolidations led to market power and to the concentration of income and wealth in the American economy (see Chapters 10 and 13).

To many contemporary observers, the increasing concentration of wealth and power distorted justice through both legal and illegal forms of influence, including outright bribery, such that "courts did not make the perpetrators pay for the social harm of their actions, at least to the satisfaction of the public."[1] With corruption, bribery, and undue influence the new norm by the late nineteenth century, judicial action by private parties was soon supplemented by regulatory reforms. While many of these reforms began within municipalities and states, the increase in the scale of firms across local and state boundaries eventually led to federal involvement.[2]

The primary concern with monopoly and similar kinds of market concentration is not that being big is necessarily undesirable, but that a firm that has substantial market power can set prices above the competitive equilibrium price, which results in adverse impacts on consumers and efficiency losses to society. There have been two major types of public policies in the United States to deal with the problems of monopoly and market power: antitrust policy for ordinary markets and regulation of natural monopolies. There is a third possibility: public ownership. In the United States, some natural monopolies have been publicly owned, such as the U.S. Postal Service and Amtrak, as have many local utilities, but public ownership of utilities and other natural monopolies is far less common in the United States than in many other countries.

Federal regulation of railroads and other forms of transportation began when Congress passed the Interstate Commerce Act in 1887, while the Sherman Antitrust

Act (1890) introduced antitrust law for almost all other industries. Since 1890, a series of new laws and court cases have shaped antitrust and regulatory policies in the United States, although there is substantial disagreement among economists about the overall desirability and effectiveness of these policies.

17.1 MARKET POWER AND DEADWEIGHT LOSSES

Since exchange is voluntary, both consumers and producers must benefit from participation in a market. The concepts of consumer and producer surplus, which were introduced in Chapter 1, allow us to measure the benefits to consumers and firms from market participation.

MONOPOLY AND BARRIERS TO ENTRY

If a monopoly exists, it must be due to some barrier to entry—that is, an economic or legal impediment that prevents other firms from entering the market. In some cases, the barrier to entry involves control of an essential factor of production. In other cases, the barriers are legal restrictions, such as patents, licenses, or other entry restrictions conferred and enforced by government.

The Aluminum Company of America (Alcoa), for example, held a near monopoly in aluminum production in the United States for almost 50 years. Its market power was the result both of control over an essential factor of production and of government patents. Alcoa received a patent in the late 1880s for a process that extracts oxygen from bauxite to produce aluminum. Shortly before the initial patent expired, it patented a more efficient process (in 1903). It also made a concerted effort to buy bauxite mines around the world. At one time Alcoa owned 90 percent of the world's deposits of bauxite, an essential factor of production in producing aluminum.

Another barrier to entry occurs when there are significant economies of scale. With economies of scale, per-unit costs decline as the amount of production increases. This is called a natural monopoly since the barrier to entry is simply the fact that a single large firm has lower costs than any potential smaller competitors would have. Natural monopolies tend to occur where there are large fixed costs, such as those of laying pipes underground throughout a city or building rail tracks over large distances. Once the pipes or tracks have been constructed, it is unlikely that another firm will enter the market to compete with the natural monopolist, since the new entrant would have higher per-unit costs.

MONOPOLY AND DEADWEIGHT LOSS

Unlike perfectly competitive firms, a monopoly is a price setter. In order for the firm to sell a greater quantity, however, it must lower the price to all consumers. As a result, the marginal revenue curve—the additional revenue the firm receives from selling one additional unit—is below the demand curve (Figure 17.1). To maximize profits, the monopolist produces at the point where marginal revenue equals marginal cost.

While this quantity (Q_M) maximizes profits for the firm, it is not a socially efficient outcome. Compared to perfect competition, the monopolist produces less output and charges a higher price for it. Since the demand curve (which represents the marginal benefit to consumers) is greater than the marginal cost between the output level of the monopolist (Q_M) and the output level under perfect competition (Q_{PC}), society would be better off if output expanded to Q_{PC}. The deadweight loss (the shaded triangle) is the reduction

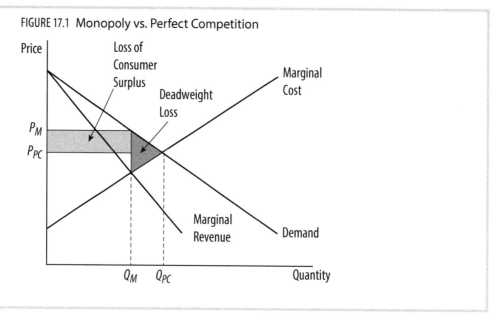

FIGURE 17.1 Monopoly vs. Perfect Competition

in economic surplus that results from the monopoly. Some of the consumer surplus under perfect competition is also transferred to the monopolist, as shown in the shaded rectangle.

OLIGOPOLY

An oligopoly describes a market structure in which there are only a few sellers of a product. With just a few firms in the market, those firms have the ability to set prices. Economists model the strategic behavior of firms under oligopoly using game theory, which demonstrates how the decisions of one firm influence, and are influenced by, the decisions of other firms. As a result, market outcomes often resemble a game like chess, where one player's moves are based in part on how she or he anticipates that the other player will respond.

Oligopolistic competition can lead to a wide range of market outcomes. In some cases, firms may collude with one another to keep prices high, as in the case of monopoly. Collusion is an agreement among firms in an industry to divide the market up and to charge the same price. A cartel is a group of firms that agrees to collude in this way: by acting as a single monopolist, they earn monopoly profits.

In other cases, there can be aggressive competition that increases production and lowers prices for consumers. This can lead to a relatively efficient outcome that approaches perfect competition. However, the prisoner's dilemma game suggests that while collusion can occur, it is unlikely to be a long-term outcome.[3] Consider Table 17.1, which shows an example of possible collusion or competition between two firms, Firm A and Firm B, with the payoffs shown.

In Table 17.1, the first element in each box shows Firm A's profits, while the second element shows Firm B's profits. If the firms collude and each charges a high

TABLE 17.1 The Prisoner's Dilemma Game		
Firm A/Firm B	**High Price**	**Low Price**
High Price	($5 billion, $5 billion)	(−$1 billion, $7 billion)
Low Price	($7 billion, −$1 billion)	($0 billion, $0 billion)

price, each earns a profit of $5 billion. However, if one firm sets the high price, acting in collusion, but the other firm reneges on the agreement and undercuts the first firm by charging a low price, the firm with the higher price loses $1 billion, while the firm with the lower price earns a profit of $7 billion. If both renege on the agreement and set the low, competitive price, then neither firm earns a positive economic profit.

Now consider the incentives that each firm faces. Note that the policy of always setting a low price yields a higher profit, regardless of what the other firm does. If Firm A sets a low price, it either earns a profit of $7 billion (if Firm B sets the higher collusion price) or gains $0 billion (if Firm B also competes and sets a low price). From Firm A's perspective, setting a low price is the dominant strategy since the competition payoff is higher than collusion payoff, regardless of what Firm B does (i.e., $7 billion is greater than $5 billion, and $0 billion is greater than –$1 billion). Firm B faces the same incentives, so to "compete" and set a low price is the dominant strategy for both firms.

In this simple example, it appears that collusion cannot occur because each firm has an incentive to undercut the price of the other firm. There are several reasons why collusion may be more robust than the simple prisoner's dilemma game suggests. First, the example above is modeled as a "one-shot" game: after the game is over, neither firm has any further contact with the other. In the one-shot case, neither firm can punish the other for breaking the agreement to collude. In the real world, however, most situations are "repeat-player" ones, where the same firms meet period after period. In the repeat-player case, cartel members may be able to punish firms that deviate from the agreement to collude, and this increases the probability and stability of collusion.

Firms have also developed institutional mechanisms that can lead to stable collusive behavior, such as trusts and holding companies (see Section 17.2). Cases of strategic cooperation among firms can also be more subtle. For example, in some industries, there is an acknowledged industry leader which sets prices: other firms then mimic the industry leader. The industry leader may be large enough to be able to undercut the prices of any competitor who does not follow the leader, thereby driving smaller rivals out of business. Because of this threat, smaller rivals in an oligopolistic industry find it more profitable to follow the industry leader than to compete. This is known as the dominant firm or price-leadership model.

Economic History in Action 17.1 provides an illustration of strategic behavior and market outcomes when there are more than two firms in an industry but where each firm is able to set the price it charges. In this example, a wide range of outcomes is possible; the greater the number of firms, however, the more likely it is that the outcome will approach the perfectly competitive and efficient equilibrium.

ECONOMIC HISTORY IN ACTION 17.1

The Oligopoly Game[4]

To better understand the benefits and difficulties of collusive behavior, consider the following "oligopoly game". You can play this game with a group of friends or as part of a classroom exercise.

In this game, each person or each small group of people represents a firm that is part of an oligopoly. The game tends to work best when there are between 3 and 10 firms. The goal of each firm is to have the highest profits, and it is best if there is a real reward so that there is a real incentive for everyone to try to maximize profits.

Each firm can make decisions independently, or it can collude with other firms in the room to decide on the quantity that each produces. Below, consider the profit-maximizing level of output (Q) if all of the firms act together, as a monopolist (cartel). The market demand function that everyone faces is a function of the market price (P):

$$Q = 70 - P$$

It is more convenient below to write this instead as an inverse demand function:

$$P = 70 - Q$$

Recall that profit maximization requires that the monopolist produce at the point where marginal revenue equals marginal cost. Total revenue (TR) is PQ, so in this case:

$$TR = PQ = (70 - Q)Q = 70Q - Q^2$$

To determine marginal revenue (MR), use the power rule to take the first derivative of total revenue with respect to Q:

$$MR = \frac{dTR}{dQ} = 70 - 2Q$$

Suppose, for simplicity, that the marginal cost (MC) is constant at $10 per unit and there are no fixed costs to production, so that marginal cost (MC) is equal to average cost (AC). To find the profit-maximizing level of output, set $MR=MC$ and solve for Q:

$$70 - 2Q = 10$$
$$Q = 30$$

Once you have solved for Q, you can plug this value into the demand function and solve for P:

$$P = 70 - Q = 70 - 30 = \$40$$

We can now compute the profit to the profit-maximizing monopolist:

$$Profit = TR - TC = P \cdot Q - AC \cdot Q = P \cdot Q - \$10Q = (P - \$10)Q = (\$40 - \$10)30 = \$900$$

That is, if all the firms collude to act as a monopolist, the total production in the industry should be 30 units and the cumulative profit will be $900 shared among all of the firms. For example, if there are 6 firms, each firm should agree to produce 5 units to maximize cumulative profits among the 6 firms, so that each firm receives $150 in profit each round ($900/6 = $150). Of course, if any firm reneges on an agreement and produces more, then their profits will go up as long as the other firms stick to the agreement; but if everyone produces too much, then everyone suffers.

Consider playing the game for at least 5 rounds. There needs to be someone to keep track of production decisions and profits for each firm in each round. In each round, each firm (which selects a name) will give the scorekeeper a folded piece of paper with that firm's production decisions on it (e.g. "U.S. oil produces 5 units" or "Standard Steel produces 8 units"). Between rounds, firms may talk amongst themselves and with other firms in the room to make agreements, etc.

If each firm colludes perfectly in each round, agreeing always to act as a monopolist would, the cumulative profits after 5 rounds will be $4,500 (5 rounds times a possible maximum profit of $900 per round). If the industry were perfectly competitive, however, then the cumulative economic profits would be zero each round and zero over the 5 rounds.

Compare the results from your game to both the monopoly outcome and the perfectly competitive outcome: which did your oligopoly end up closer to—monopoly or perfect competition? Discuss why you think things turned out the way they did. Which firm was the winner and what strategy did that firm employ?

CONTESTABLE MARKETS

Research suggests that the degree of concentration in an industry at a given time may be less important than the extent to which there is possible entry of new firms into the industry. If there is a credible threat of entry, then the market is contestable and firms, even in highly concentrated industries, will have incentives to innovate and to keep prices low.[5]

The theory of contestable markets is controversial, however, as the efficiency conclusions are sensitive to small changes in assumptions.[6] Even so, this theory "has been instrumental in causing antitrust analysts to reduce their emphasis on concentration and take proper account of potential competition."[7]

17.2 ANTITRUST POLICIES

Antitrust laws are designed to prevent businesses from making agreements or engaging in any other behavior that limits competition and harms consumers. U.S. antitrust policies focus on three main areas: agreements among competitors; monopolization of markets; and mergers. Antitrust activity attempts to prohibit firms from monopolizing or cartelizing markets, and it is pursued in the courts both by government attorneys and by individual firms that file lawsuits against other firms, accusing them of violating antitrust laws.

A variety of economic changes took place in the latter part of the nineteenth century that created a political climate supportive of antitrust legislation. Technological breakthroughs led to a more extensive use of capital and to larger optimal plant sizes in manufacturing and other industries (Chapter 10). In addition, the spread of railroads, from 9,000 miles of track in 1850 to 167,000 miles of track by 1890, lowered transportation costs and extended the geographic spread of markets (Chapter 8).

With large fixed costs and, as a result, large-scale production, economic downturns sometimes led to firms cutting prices in an attempt to stimulate sales, but this proved to be to the detriment of all firms in the market. One solution was for competing firms to create a trust: each firm transferred its voting shares of stock to a single board of trustees, and these trustees would make decisions in the interest of the entire group of firms. Trusts were formed in many industries, including oil, kerosene, meatpacking, sugar, whiskey, lead, coal, and tobacco. The organizers of these trusts were called robber barons, and trusts were viewed as making enormous profits by stifling competition, to the detriment of small businesses and consumers (Figure 17.2).

One problem with trusts was that the agreements were a matter of public record. In 1889, the New Jersey legislature changed its statutes of incorporation to allow any corporation to hold the stocks of one or more subsidiary companies. When trusts were made illegal in many states, groups of firms often just obtained corporate charters in New Jersey as "holding companies." Like trusts, holding companies provided an institutional mechanism that allowed firms to collude.

RAILROADS AND COURT CASES

After the Civil War, American farmers complained of falling prices and incomes, and they believed it was unfair for railroads to charge high rates, and frequently different rates

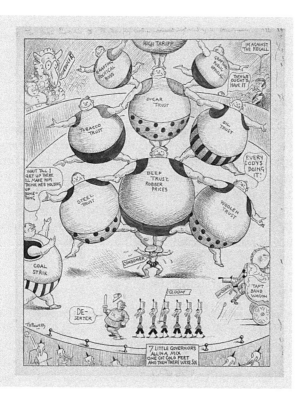

FIGURE 17.2 The Monopoly Brothers Supported by the Little Consumer, 1912
Source: Thomas E. Powers, Library of Congress, www.loc.gov/pictures/item/2009617175/ (accessed: February 7, 2016).

to different farmers, to transport grains and crops to market. (Note that in the modern world consumers have come to accept such differences as a fact of life. On any airline flight, for example, the differences in fares from passenger to passenger can be vast, depending on when the flight was booked, even though, from the airline's perspective, the costs of providing passage does not vary from customer to customer.)

During the late 1860s and early 1870s, a group of farmers, known as The National Grange of the Order of Patrons of Husbandry, successfully lobbied state governments in several Midwestern states to pass laws to make railroad rates more favorable for farmers, and particularly for small rural farmers, who often had only one way of getting their grains and crops to market. Grain storage and elevator companies were also subject to these so-called Granger laws.

In Illinois, Granger laws prohibited railroads from discriminating between long- and short-haul rates of railroads, and set the maximum prices that could be charged by grain storage facilities. In 1877, a grain storage company, Munn and Scott, was found guilty of violating the Illinois law in the case of Munn vs. Illinois. The case eventually reached the U.S. Supreme Court, which ruled that state governments could indeed regulate railroads and grain elevator rates because these companies served the public interest.

In 1886, however, in the case of Wabash, St. Louis, and Pacific Railway Company vs. Illinois, the Supreme Court overturned Munn vs. Illinois, ruling that in this case the Illinois Granger laws were unconstitutional because they attempted to regulate interstate commerce. In 1824, in Gibbons vs. Ogden, the regulation of interstate commerce had been deemed a federal responsibility. The Wabash ruling led to the creation of the Interstate Commerce Act (1887) and the formation of the Interstate Commerce Commission to regulate railroads, and it also set the stage for federal regulation of other industries through antitrust laws.

THE SHERMAN ANTITRUST ACT AND EARLY ENFORCEMENT

In the 1880s, many states passed antitrust laws, but the increasingly interstate operations of many corporations led to federal legislation. The Sherman Antitrust Act (1890) was the first federal antitrust statute, passed in response to the widespread growth of large-scale business combinations or trusts, many of which were formed in the 1880s. Cattlemen's associations may have been the impetus for the passage of the Sherman Antitrust Act.[8] They were upset with the "Chicago meatpacking monopolists" of Swift and Company, Armour, and Morris, who they believed were charging unduly high prices which reduced the profits from raising cattle.

The Sherman Antitrust Act stated that "every contract, combination in the form of trust or otherwise, or conspiracy, in restraint of trade or commerce among the several States, or with foreign nations, is declared to be illegal." The problem with the Act, however, is that it did not define precisely what types of behavior constituted such activities. Between 1890 and 1920, further legislation and court cases established the foundations of antitrust policies in the United States.

The first antitrust case was the United States vs. E.C. Knight and Company (1895). The American Sugar Refining Company had acquired the stock of E.C. Knight and Company, along with three sugar refiners in the Philadelphia area, which increased American Sugar Refining's market share from 65 percent to 98 percent. The Supreme Court did not find E.C. Knight in violation of the Sherman Act, arguing that the Act only applied to interstate commerce and not to manufacturing within a given state. This decision also implied that the Sherman Act did not preclude the growth of large firms through mergers and consolidation. As a result, from 1895 mergers were viewed as a legal and safe method of effectively eliminating price competition between firms. The "Great Merger Wave" (1898–1902) was "motivated ... by the desire to reduce price competition."[9]

STANDARD OIL AND AMERICAN TOBACCO

During the 1904 presidential campaign, Theodore Roosevelt made "trust busting" an important part of his platform. During his Administration, antitrust suits were filed against the American Tobacco Company and Standard Oil of New Jersey. In Supreme Court decisions handed down in 1911, both companies were found guilty of violating the Sherman Antitrust Act and were required to be broken up.

These court decisions were based on the so-called "rule of reason," whereby although the possession of monopoly power is not in itself illegal, the possession of monopoly power may nevertheless be illegal in practice if the way in which it was obtained involved actions whose effect was to restrain trade unreasonably. That is, guilt is primarily based on the specific *actions*, not on the possession of monopoly power itself (provided that the monopoly power has been gained in a legal manner, such as by making a superior product, by running a better business, or through luck).

Standard Oil and American Tobacco were in violation of the Sherman Antitrust Act because of their actions, not their market size. In the former case, it was asserted that Standard Oil had achieved its powerful position by unfairly obtaining rebates from railroads and by engaging in predatory pricing—Standard Oil was alleged to have deliberately set prices below average variable costs with the intention of driving rivals from the market. American Tobacco was also alleged to have engaged in predatory pricing to drive competitors out of business. Both firms were ordered to dissolve, with Standard Oil being broken up into 34 separate companies.

THE CLAYTON ACT AND THE FEDERAL TRADE COMMISSION

Because of the ambiguities in relation to what actions constituted an "unreasonable restraint of trade" under the Sherman Antitrust Act, Congress reacted by passing the

Clayton Act (1914). This Act outlawed several specific practices, including: (1) price discrimination among purchasers that lessens competition; (2) contracts ("tying contracts") that require the buyer of one good to purchase another good from the same firm as well; (3) exclusive contracts in which purchasers agree, as a condition of sale, not to buy from competitors; (4) one firm's acquisition of shares of stock in another firm in the same industry; and (5) board members serving on boards of directors of more than one firm in the same industry.

In 1914, Congress also created the Federal Trade Commission (FTC). Today, the Antitrust Division of the Department of Justice and the Federal Trade Commission share responsibility for antitrust enforcement. Either agency can charge a firm or a group of firms with breaking the law. Firms charged with wrongdoing may be able, without admitting guilt, to sign a consent decree in which they agree not to do what they have been accused of doing. If the firm or firms contest the charges, evidence is presented in court and a judge decides guilt or innocence. In certain cases, cases are appealed all the way to the U.S. Supreme Court. Private firms can also file antitrust cases against rival firms.

U.S. STEEL

The 1901 merger that created U.S. Steel was perhaps the largest in U.S. history, with a market capitalization of 6.8 percent of GDP.[10] (In 2016, this would be equivalent to a merger capitalization of over $1.2 trillion.) Between 1907 and 1911, executives of American steel companies gathered for a series of meetings organized by the Chairman of the Board of U.S. Steel, Elbert H. Gary, known as the "Gary dinners." At these meetings, the companies announced the prices they intended to charge, but there appeared to be no written agreements amongst firms that they were bound to adhere to these prices.

In the case of United States vs. United States Steel Corporation et al. (1920), U.S. Steel was found not guilty because of the rule of reason. While the government asserted that the price agreements at the Gary dinners were illegal, U.S. Steel argued that the meetings proved that U.S. Steel could not set prices on its own, and that it could therefore not monopolize the steel industry. The majority of the Court was swayed by the fact that U.S. Steel had not engaged in the predatory practices complained of in the oil and tobacco cases. The government's assertion that the sheer size and market dominance of U.S. Steel made it a threat to competition was denied, and the Court concluded that "the law does not make mere size an offense."[11]

ALCOA ALUMINUM

After World War II, the Supreme Court's composition reflected the appointments made during Franklin D. Roosevelt's tenure as U.S. President (1933–1945), and it became known with both affection and disdain as "Roosevelt's Court." One change during the Roosevelt Administration was the passage of the Robinson-Patman Act (1936), which prohibited firms from charging buyers different prices (price discrimination) if the result would reduce competition in an industry.

Another change occurred in how courts interpreted antitrust laws. The rule of reason was largely abandoned and the "per se" criterion became the basis for antitrust decisions. Per se, a Latin phrase meaning "in itself," is a judicial standard in which a firm's size within an industry is considered sufficient evidence for the court to rule against it in an antitrust suit.

In a 1945 decision against Alcoa Aluminum, the majority of the Supreme Court ruled that the Sherman Antitrust Act did not require the Court to distinguish between good and bad monopolies, but that it did outlaw monopolies per se. That is, size in itself was the criterion, and Alcoa's 90 percent market share was sufficient evidence that it was violating antitrust laws.

By the 1970s, however, the composition of the Supreme Court had changed again, and the Court now focused primarily on the behavior of firms in the marketplace, and not on just their market share and size. That is, the rule of reason criterion once again became more important than the per se criterion.

INTERNATIONAL BUSINESS MACHINES CORPORATION (IBM)

In 1969, the U.S. Department of Justice (USDOJ) sued IBM for violating antitrust laws through tying agreements and other unfair business practices. The USDOJ argued that if a customer wanted to buy a mainframe IBM computer, the customer also had to purchase IBM software and the IBM service agreement, whether the customer wanted those or not. The court case lasted for nearly 13 years, and included 950 witnesses, 726 trial days, 17,000 exhibits, 104,400 pages of trial transcript, and over $200 million in legal costs.[12]

In 1982, the government withdrew its lawsuit. Between 1969 and 1982, several things had happened that caused the government to stop its antitrust actions against IBM. First, greater competition developed in the industry, with a number of Japanese companies entering the market and greater competition from U.S. firms (including Digital Equipment Corporation and Apple in the personal computer market). Second, by 1982 President Ronald Reagan was in office, and his appointees were generally less aggressive in enforcing antitrust laws.

AMERICAN TELEPHONE AND TELEGRAPH (AT&T)

The other major antitrust case at this time was against AT&T. Before 1982, AT&T was regulated as a natural monopoly, because it was believed that economies of scale made it most efficient for a single firm to supply telephone services. Because of its monopoly, AT&T was regulated by the Federal Communications Commission (FCC) and by state utility commissions.

In the 1970s, however, technological developments began to alter the structure of the long-distance telephone industry. Fiber-optic communication and satellite transmission made telephone cable connections just one of several ways of providing long-distance telephone services, so that AT&T no longer had a natural monopoly. Entry into the long-distance telephone industry took place, and competitors complained that AT&T charged excessively high fees for access to AT&T local lines. As a result, the USDOJ filed suit against AT&T in 1978. The case dragged on until 1982, when the USDOJ announced a settlement on the same day that it settled with IBM.

Under the agreement, AT&T agreed to be broken up into 22 local operating companies (known as the Baby Bells). AT&T kept its long-distance telephone service, its manufacturing division (Western Electric), and its research laboratories (Bell Labs). AT&T was also given considerable freedom by antitrust authorities to enter other industries, such as those providing computers and data transmission.

MICROSOFT

While the case against Standard Oil was the most important at the beginning of the twentieth century, the case against Microsoft was the big case at the end of the century. Antitrust investigation of Microsoft started in 1990, but the most important case was United States vs. Microsoft (1998).[13] The USDOJ and numerous states filed suit against Microsoft, claiming that its behavior in the Internet browser market had violated the Sherman Antitrust Act.

With Windows 95 and Windows 98, Microsoft had a near monopoly in personal computer (PC) operating systems (OS). It was accused of using its OS monopoly to unseat Netscape Navigator as the preeminent Internet browser. It was argued that by tying or bundling Internet Explorer (IE), its own Internet browser, to each copy of Windows 95 and 98, Microsoft was in violation of Sections 1 and 2 of the Sherman Antitrust Act.

The trial began in October 1998 and a guilty verdict was delivered in April 2000. Judge Thomas Penfield Jackson ordered that Microsoft be broken up into two separate companies: one company for the operating system and another for software applications such as Microsoft Word and Internet Explorer.

Microsoft appealed the verdict, and the USDOJ chose to settle with Microsoft and not to pursue the breakup of Microsoft into separate companies. However, the settlement agreement did require that Microsoft share its application programming interfaces with third-party companies, which gave them more equal access to the Windows desktop. The agreement also prohibited Microsoft from retaliating against PC manufacturers for using or promoting software that competes with Microsoft products, and it required that licensing agreements with PC manufacturers be uniform (to ensure that Microsoft was not including hidden penalties or rewards in discriminatory agreements).

EXEMPTIONS FROM ANTITRUST

Congress has granted certain industries and activities exemptions from antitrust laws. Labor unions received an exemption in the Clayton Act, to permit labor to match the bargaining power of large-scale employers. In 1922, the Capper-Volstead Act allowed agricultural cooperatives of farmers, ranchers, and milk producers to market their commodities collectively.

A Supreme Court decision in 1922 granted professional baseball immunity from antitrust law, since a sports league is a group of firms that are not simply independent but must cooperate in various ways in order to produce their product: a competitive sports league. Other professional sports are also treated more leniently under U.S. antitrust laws. One example of leniency is that sports leagues do not allow their teams to bid against each other for new players graduating from college or high school. Instead, and to try to maintain "competitive balance," players are chosen through a draft that follows league rules based on the win–loss record of each team from the previous season. In recent decades, experienced players have earned the right to become "free agents" at some point in their careers: at that point there is nearly open competition for these players, subject to salary caps and other league rules.

Another important exemption from antitrust laws is that government provides monopoly protection through patents and copyrights. With a patent, an inventor receives the exclusive right to market and sell the invention for a period of 20 years. With copyright, artists, musicians, and authors can earn royalties over the life of the copyright (70 years after the death of the creator, in most cases), and they receive the government's assurance and protection that no one can sell or use the creator's work without paying the creator for the privilege of doing so.

As with any form of monopoly, the existence of patents and copyrights creates a deadweight loss to society and monopoly profits to the inventor or creator. The rationale for the protection of intellectual property rights is that innovation and creativity will be much higher over the long run as a result, and that this gain more than compensates for the static deadweight losses incurred during the life of the patent or copyright. The long-term desirability of patents and copyrights and how long patents and copyrights should last are both controversial issues (see Chapter 4).

The financial sector is also subject to regulations that fall outside common antitrust laws. The Securities and Exchange Act (1934) established the U.S. Securities and Exchange Commission to regulate securities trading and stock exchanges. The Supreme Court has ruled that in instances where securities laws and antitrust laws conflict, securities laws prevail. Many different regulatory bodies in the United States—the Federal Reserve, the Federal Deposit Insurance Corporation, the Commodity Futures Trading Commission, the Consumer Protection Financial Bureau, and many others—share supervision and regulation of the financial system. In addition, each U.S. state has its own banking regulatory body.

MEASURING MARKET POWER AND EVALUATING POTENTIAL MERGERS

There are several measures of market power and industry concentration. One is the m-firm concentration ratio, which is simply the share of sales by the largest m firms as a proportion of total industry sales. In many instances, four-firm concentration ratios are reported, which give the percentage of industry sales by the top four firms.

In 1992, the Antitrust Division of the Department of Justice and the Federal Trade Commission began measuring concentration using the Herfindahl-Hirschman Index (HHI), named after its inventors.[14] The HHI has the advantage of incorporating more information about the relative size distribution of each firm in the industry than is conveyed by simple concentration ratios. Suppose that an industry consists of five firms, where the three largest firms each have 30 percent of industry sales while the fourth and fifth firm each have 5 percent of industry sales. In this case, the HHI is computed as follows:

$$HHI = 30^2 + 30^2 + 30^2 + 5^2 + 5^2 = 2,750$$

If an industry includes only one seller, the HHI takes on the maximum value of 10,000, since $100^2 = 10,000$. Near the other extreme, consider an industry with 10,000 firms all of the same size, so that each firm has 1/10,000 of industry sales. In this case, the HHI takes on a value very close to zero ($HHI = 0.0001$). The HHI increases both as the number of firms in an industry decreases and as the disparity in sizes between those firms increases.

Suppose that two firms with industry shares of X and Y decide to merge, and nothing else in the industry changes. In this case, the change in the HHI is:

$$\Delta HHI = (X + Y)^2 - X^2 - Y^2 = 2XY$$

Consider the five-firm example above, and suppose that two of the largest firms, each with 30 percent of industry sales, decide to merge. The change in the HHI would be:

$$\Delta HHI = 2 \cdot 30 \cdot 30 = 1,800$$

Periodically, the U.S. Department of Justice and the Federal Trade Commission issue guidelines regarding potential mergers.[15] In determining whether or not to challenge mergers, the agencies look at both the size of the HHI and the change in the HHI.

Under current policies, the agencies classify markets into three types: unconcentrated markets (HHI < 1,500), moderately concentrated markets ($1,500 \le HHI \le 2,500$), and highly concentrated markets ($HHI > 2,500$). In unconcentrated markets, where mergers involve an increase in the HHI of less than 100 points, mergers "are unlikely to have adverse competitive effects and ordinarily require no further analysis."[16] Moderately concentrated markets, which involve potential mergers that would increase the HHI by more than 100 points, "often warrant scrutiny." In highly concentrated markets, with increases in the HHI of over 200 points, it is "presumed to be likely to enhance market power ... [although this] presumption may be rebutted by persuasive evidence showing that the merger is unlikely to enhance market power."[17]

The difficulty in evaluating mergers is that not all mergers are detrimental to consumers. Where economies of scale are present, mergers may lead to lower costs, greater product variety, and lower prices to consumers. However, the motivating factor may instead be the desire for market power and for monopoly profits through higher prices.

THE COSTS AND BENEFITS OF ANTITRUST POLICIES

There is disagreement among economists about the costs and benefits of antitrust policies. Many scholars argue that the mere threat of antitrust actions serves as a useful deterrent to firms from engaging in overt attempts to monopolize markets—attempts of the kind that commonly occurred during the late nineteenth century, prior to antitrust enforcement. As one scholar wrote, "the benefits of antitrust enforcement to consumers and social welfare—particularly in deterring the harms from anticompetitive conduct across the economy—seem likely to be far larger than what the government spends on antitrust enforcement and firms spend directly or indirectly on antitrust compliance."[18]

Others, however, have questioned the necessity and success of U.S. antitrust policies. This "apparent ineffectiveness," they say, is due to several factors, including: (1) the excessive duration of antitrust cases; (2) the difficulties of coming up with effective remedies; (3) the difficulties in accurately determining when mergers and other anticompetitive behavior reduce consumer welfare; (4) the difficulties of modifying policies to deal with rapid technological changes, particularly in information technology; (5) political forces that make antitrust policies inconsistent from one presidential administration to the next; and (6) the power of markets to spur competition, which "leaves antitrust policy with relatively little to do."[19]

There are certainly instances where technological changes have been more successful in eliminating market power and monopoly than antitrust enforcement. Consider the history of the Microsoft Corporation. Around the year 2000, when antitrust actions against Microsoft were at its peak, many believed that Microsoft's monopoly of the personal computer (PC) desktop would last a very long time. Microsoft controlled nearly 100 percent of the operating system market through PC sales by other firms, and Apple Computer sold just enough of its Macintosh computers to remain in business.

Since 2007, however, the explosive growth of smartphones and tablets has shifted the operating system market toward Android (which is owned by Google) and—through the sales of the iPhone and iPad—to Apple, which has its own iOS operating system. Innovation and competition eliminated Microsoft's near monopoly, whereas the remedies after the Microsoft antitrust case did relatively little. While innovation may eventually dislodge firms with substantial market power, in some cases market power can persist for decades, particularly when a firm controls a key factor of production. Persistence can also occur in instances of natural monopoly, although even natural monopolies do not always last forever.

17.3 REGULATION OF NATURAL MONOPOLIES

Natural monopolies occur when a single firm has lower costs than those faced by any potential smaller competitor. As a result, a single firm can produce a product at a lower cost than can two or more firms. Because of large capital costs (fixed costs) of laying railroad tracks, installing natural gas pipelines, installing wires to transmit electricity, or laying underground pipes for water and sewerage, natural monopolists have downward-sloping average cost curves over the entire range of consumer demand.

The market power of many natural monopolies is enhanced by the fact that the good they provide is often a necessity, such as water or electricity, so that demand for the good is very inelastic. Since consumers are physically connected to the supplier by pipes or wires, they are especially vulnerable to price gouging and to other forms of exploitation.

With natural monopolies, the government has three main options. First, it can do nothing, allowing the natural monopoly to earn monopoly profits, though with a loss of efficiency (deadweight loss). Second, the government can itself own and operate the natural monopoly, as it did with the Tennessee Valley Authority, and many electric utilities and public transit systems. Third, it can permit the privately-owned monopoly to continue, but regulate it.

Consider the local transmission of electricity. If two competing firms strung wire side-by-side throughout a community, the average cost of providing electricity would be higher than if there were a single firm providing electricity. Figure 17.3 shows the demand and cost curves for a natural monopoly. If the monopoly is unregulated, the profit-maximizing monopolist will produce the quantity where marginal cost equals marginal revenue, denoted as Q_M, and set a price equal to P_M. The price charged is the average revenue per unit, and the difference between the average revenue and the average cost is the profit per unit. The shaded area in the figure represents the monopolist's profit (the profit per unit multiplied by the number of units sold).

Following the $MB=MC$ decision rule from Chapter 1, the efficient solution is to require the firm to produce Q_{MC} units, where the marginal cost curve intersects the demand curve, which is the marginal benefit curve. The problem with requiring the firm to set the price equal to the marginal cost is that the firm would then operate at a loss, since the price (the average revenue) would be less than the average cost. In this case, therefore, the government would need to provide the firm with a subsidy for it to stay in business.

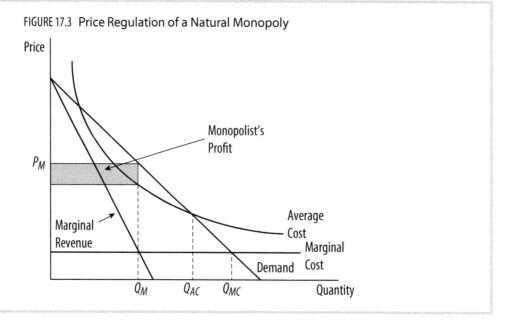

FIGURE 17.3 Price Regulation of a Natural Monopoly

Another option for regulators is to allow the firm to earn a zero economic profit (normal rate of return) by requiring the firm to produce Q_{AC} units of output and to charge a price equal to the average cost. In this case, the average revenue (the price) equals the average cost, and economic profits are zero. Recall that costs include opportunity costs, so a zero economic profit simply means that this firm is earning a normal rate of return equal to what they would be earning in their next best alternative.

The problem, however, with both marginal-cost pricing and average-cost pricing is that the regulated firm has no incentive to minimize costs. Since firms are guaranteed a price equal to their marginal or average costs, regardless of what those costs are, costs—and therefore prices—are likely to increase over time, to the detriment of consumers.

In the United States, there have been three main regulatory commissions. The Interstate Commerce Commission (1887) was created to regulate railroads and other forms of transportation. The Federal Power Commission (1920), which was later expanded to become the Federal Energy Regulatory Commission (1977), regulates natural-gas pipelines, oil pipelines, and water-power sites; while the Federal Communications Commission (1934) regulates telecommunications, including radio, television, wire, satellite, and cable. There are also numerous state and local regulatory agencies that have regulatory authority over a wide range of industries.

17.4 DEREGULATION

In the 1960s and 1970s, the federal government regulated long-distance telephone rates, cable television, trucking fees, airline ticket prices and routes, and even the interest rates banks could pay to depositors. As the result of the scholarship of economists and public policy experts who argued that consumers would benefit from new entrants and greater competition in many regulated industries, the United States began deregulating several industries in the late 1970s and 1980s. While deregulation has been mostly beneficial in transportation and communication, deregulation of the financial industry was not as successful, with many economists blaming deregulation as an important cause of the global financial crisis and Great Recession from 2007 to 2009.

DEREGULATION OF TRANSPORTATION AND COMMUNICATION

Commercial airlines were once regulated by the Civil Aeronautics Board (CAB), which was established in 1938. The CAB regulated the prices that airlines could charge and determined the routes that each airline served. If a new entrant wanted to serve an interstate route, it had to convince the CAB that the route needed another airline. During the 40 years prior to deregulation there were 150 applications for new routes, and not a single application was accepted. The CAB allowed the 10 commercial airlines to act as a price-fixing cartel, although airlines did compete on non-price factors such as the frequency of flights, the quality of meals, and the comfort of the flights.

Despite opposition from the airlines and labor unions, the Airline Deregulation Act (1978) gave airlines the freedom to set fares and allowed new entrants into the airline industry, including low-cost carriers such as Southwest Airlines. This was the start of deregulation in transportation and communication. Between 1978 and 1990, airline prices fell, passenger miles flown increased (see Chapter 8), and accident rates fell. Some of these gains have since been reversed, however, because airport capacity did not keep up with the growth of airlines. There is a lack of competition at many airports, due to a limited number of gates and the fact that gates are often controlled by only one or two airlines. For this reason, some carriers have substantial market power at certain hubs. Nevertheless, in general airline deregulation has been successful, and few are arguing for the airlines to be re-regulated.

Deregulation of the trucking industry began with the Motor Carrier Act (1980), while long-distance phone services and cable television were deregulated in 1984. In many instances, consumers have benefitted from lower prices and more choices in the marketplace, but deregulation has not worked as intended in all cases.

PROBLEMS WITH DEREGULATION

Deregulation has also led to problems. When the savings and loan industry was deregulated, the federal government insured depositors' money but allowed owners of savings and loans to make risky and reckless investments, and in the late 1980s and 1990s this resulted in a $160 billion dollar government bailout. Electricity deregulation in California led to market manipulation, corporate fraud, and widespread power shortages and blackouts, beginning in June 2000.

Deregulation of the financial industry in the 1980s and 1990s was likely one of the contributing factors of the Great Recession, which began in earnest after the failure of the investment bank Lehman Brothers in September 2008 (Chapter 18). In a series of steps, financial regulations imposed during the 1930s were reversed.

The Depository Institutions Deregulation and Monetary Control Act (1980) imposed the gradual elimination of interest-rate ceilings on loans and permitted the paying of interest on some new types of depository accounts. In 1982, the Depository Institutions Act allowed banks and other lenders to offer adjustable-rate mortgages; while in 1994, unlimited interstate branch banking was allowed, which led to a period of mergers and consolidation in the banking industry. In 1999, the Financial Services Modernization Act repealed some of the Glass-Steagall Act (1933) to allow mergers between commercial banks and insurance companies or securities firms.

These and other laws allowed for the development of many new financial instruments and the growth of the largely unregulated "shadow banking" sector. While deregulation of finance did not lead to long-run increases in economic growth, it did contribute to the return of financial crises and severe recessions.

17.5   CONCLUSIONS

Large multinational corporations are the norm in the United States today, but at the end of the Civil War the only "big business" in America was the railroads. By the early part of the twentieth century, there were large national corporations operating in many different sectors of the economy. As market power increased and became more commonplace, government reacted to the growing influence of industry with greater regulation and the establishment and enforcement of antitrust laws.

QUESTIONS

1. Why was there so little regulation of industry in the United States before the late nineteenth century?

2. Briefly describe the history of antitrust policies in the United States. What are the advantages and disadvantages of highly concentrated industries? Does market power encourage or discourage innovation? Under what circumstances should the government use its antitrust authority to limit industry concentration and market power?

3. Consider Figure 17.3. Suppose that this natural monopoly is required by a regulator to charge a price equal to the marginal cost. Is there a deadweight loss in this case? Explain. Graphically illustrate the profit or loss of the natural monopolist in this case, and explain why there *is* a profit or loss.

4. Consider an industry with 10 firms of equal size, such that each firm has 10 percent of total industry sales. What is the HHI index for this industry? Now suppose that three of these firms want to merge. What would be the industry HHI index if this merger were to occur? Would this proposed merger likely trigger regulatory action by the U.S. Department of Justice or the Federal Trade Commission? Explain.

5. What are the "rule of reason" and the "per se" rule? If you were a federal judge deciding on guilt or innocence in an antitrust case, what type of evidence would you find persuasive? Is your view more consistent with the rule of reason or the per se rule? Explain.

NOTES

[1] Edward L. Glaeser and Andrei Shleifer, "The Rise of the Regulatory State," *Journal of Economic Literature* 41, no. 2 (June 2003), 407.

[2] Glaeser and Shleifer, 407.

3 The prisoner's dilemma game was developed by Merill Flood and Melvin Dresher at the RAND corporation in 1950 to show how it is possible that two rational individuals may not cooperate, even when it is in both of their interests to do so. Albert W. Trucker presented the situation in terms of prison sentences and named it the "prisoner's dilemma game." See William Poundstone, *Prisoner's Dilemma: John Von Neumann, Game Theory, and the Puzzle of the Bomb* (New York, NY: Anchor Books, 1992).

4 I played a version of this game in class when I was an undergraduate at the University of California, Santa Cruz.

5 William J. Baumol, John C. Panzar, and Richard D. Willig, *Contestable Markets and the Theory of Industry Structure* (San Diego, CA: Harcourt Brace Jovanovich, 1982).

6 Marius Schwartz and Robert J. Reynolds, "Contestable Markets: An Uprising in the Theory of Industrial Structure: Comment," *American Economic Review* 73, no. 3 (June 1993), 488–490.

7 W. Kip Viscusi, Joseph E. Harrington, Jr., and John M. Vernon, *Economics of Regulation and Antitrust*, Fourth Edition (Cambridge, MA: MIT Press, 2005), 173.

8 Gary D. Libecap, "The Rise of Chicago Packers and the Origin of Meat Inspection and Antitrust," *Economic Inquiry* 30, no. 2 (April 1992), 242–262.

9 Anthony P. O'Brien, "Factory Size, Economies of Scale, and the Great Merger Wave of 1898–1902," *Journal of Economic History* 48, no. 3 (September 1988), 649.

10 Thomas K. McCraw and Forest Reinhardt, "Losing to Win: U.S. Steel's Pricing, Investment Decisions, and Market Share, 1901–1938," *Journal of Economic History* 49, no. 3 (September 1989), 594.

11 United States vs. United States Steel Corporation et al., www.law.cornell.edu/supremecourt/text/251/417 (accessed: September 29, 2015).

12 Franklin M. Fisher, John J. McGowan, and Joen E. Greenwood, *Folded, Spindled and Mutilated: Economic Analysis and the U.S. vs. IBM* (Cambridge, MA: MIT Press, 1985).

13 See Viscusi et al., 332–343, for a summary of the case against Microsoft.

14 The index is named after its creators, the economists Orris C. Herfindahl and Albert O. Hirschman.

15 U.S. Department of Justice and Federal Trade Commission, *Horizontal Merger Guidelines*, August 19, 2010, www.justice.gov/atr/horizontal-merger-guidelines-08192010#5c (accessed: September 14, 2015).

16 U.S. Department of Justice and Federal Trade Commission.

17 U.S. Department of Justice and Federal Trade Commission.

18 Jonathan B. Baker, "The Case for Antitrust Enforcement," *Journal of Economic Perspectives* 17, no. 4 (Fall 2003), 27.

19 The quote and the six reasons for the "apparent ineffectiveness" of antitrust policy come from Robert W. Crandall and Clifford Winston, "Does Antitrust Policy Improve Consumer Welfare? Assessing the Evidence," *Journal of Economic Perspectives* 17, no. 4 (Fall 2003), 23.

18
Recessions, Depressions, and Stabilization Policies

The growth of the American economy has gone through great fluctuations around its impressive long-run trend. In some periods, real GDP is above its long-run trend (as it was during World War II), while in other periods growth is negative and below its long-run trend. For example, during the Great Depression from 1929 to 1933, real GDP fell by over 25 percent, while the unemployment rate exceeded 20 percent. In the Great Recession, real GDP fell by more than 4 percent from the second quarter of 2008 to the second quarter of 2009.

These ups and downs in aggregate economic activity are called economic fluctuations or business cycles. The term "business cycles" is somewhat of a misnomer since they are *not* cyclical in nature, but occur at irregular intervals, and with differing degrees of severity. In recent years, "economic fluctuations" has been the preferred term, so this is what is generally used throughout the chapter, but "business cycles" and "economic fluctuations" are synonymous.

This chapter discusses how and why the economy fluctuates, and looks at some of the more dramatic episodes in U.S. history. Because of its depth and duration, there is particular emphasis on the Great Depression of the 1930s. The Great Inflation of the 1970s and the Great Recession from 2007 to 2009 are also discussed.

18.1 MEASUREMENT AND PROPERTIES OF ECONOMIC FLUCTUATIONS

The National Bureau of Economic Research (NBER) defines and determines official U.S. business cycle dates. While most would assume that the "National Bureau of Economic Research" is a government agency, it is actually a private, nonpartisan, non-profit, research institution, founded in 1920. The NBER Business Cycle Dating Committee consists of nine prominent economists who determine when the U.S. economy has entered a recession and when an expansion has begun.[1]

According to the NBER:

> A recession is a significant decline in economic activity spread across the economy, lasting more than a few months, normally visible in real GDP, real income, employment, industrial production, and wholesale-retail sales. A recession begins just after the economy reaches a peak of activity and ends as the economy reaches its trough. Between trough and peak, the economy is in an expansion. Expansion is the normal state of the economy; most recessions are brief and they have been rare in recent decades.[2]

Figure 18.1 depicts economic fluctuations. The long-run growth trend represents the long-run growth rate of the economy, which depends on the growth of the factors of production and the growth of total factor productivity (see Chapter 2). Deviations from the long-run growth trend are economic fluctuations.

The upper turning points of economic fluctuations are peaks, while the lower turning points are troughs. The length of time from a peak to a trough is a recession or contraction. Particularly severe recessions are depressions, although there is no precise definition of what specifically constitutes a depression rather than a recession. From a trough to the next peak is an expansion. Table 18.1 shows the history of U.S. expansions and contractions.

Some scholars have argued that the NBER has overestimated both the number of recessions and the length of recessions before World War I, since the methods and data used to determine these recessions differed from current practice.[3] There were, however, several severe recessions before World War I, often associated with bank failures and financial crises.

FIGURE 18.1 Economic Fluctuations

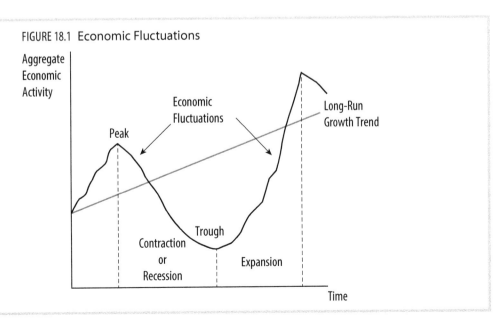

TABLE 18.1 National Bureau of Economic Research Economic Fluctuations

Trough	Expansion (months from trough to peak)	Peak	Contraction (months from peak to trough)
December 1854	30	June 1857	18
December 1858	22	October 1860	8
June 1861	46	April 1865	32
December 1867	18	June 1869	18
December 1870	34	October 1873	65
March 1879	36	March 1882	38
May 1885	22	March 1887	13
April 1888	27	July 1890	10
May 1891	20	January 1893	17
June 1894	18	December 1895	18
June 1897	24	June 1899	18
December 1900	21	September 1902	23
August 1904	33	May 1907	13
June 1908	19	January 1910	24
January 1912	12	January 1913	23
December 1914	44	August 1918	7
March 1919	10	January 1920	18
July 1921	22	May 1923	14
July 1924	27	October 1926	13
November 1927	21	August 1929	43
March 1933	50	May 1937	13
June 1938	80	February 1945	8
October 1945	37	November 1948	11
October 1949	45	July 1953	10
May 1954	39	August 1957	8
April 1958	24	April 1960	10
February 1961	106	December 1969	11
November 1970	36	November 1973	16
March 1975	58	January 1980	6
July 1980	12	July 1981	16
November 1982	92	July 1990	8
March 1991	120	March 2001	8
November 2001	73	December 2007	18
June 2009	84 (as of June 2016)	?	

Source: National Bureau of Economic Research, www.nber.org/cycles/cyclesmain.html (accessed: June 19, 2016).

18.2 THE CAUSES AND CURES OF ECONOMIC FLUCTUATIONS

Before the Great Depression, the overwhelming majority of economists believed that the aggregate economy was self-regulating. Problems of low production and high unemployment were thought to be corrected relatively rapidly through the working of the invisible hand, and government attempts to intervene were thought to be ineffective at best.

KEYNESIAN ECONOMICS

The severity and persistence of the Great Depression changed this view. In 1936, John Maynard Keynes published *The General Theory of Employment, Interest, and Money*, which established the discipline of modern macroeconomics and transformed the way most economists view economic fluctuations. At its core, Keynesian economics includes the following propositions:

- Economic fluctuations are primarily the result of fluctuations in aggregate spending or aggregate demand.
- Investor and consumer behavior is subject to "animal spirits" that can turn the economy from expansion to contraction or vice versa based on changes in optimism or pessimism.[4] That is, human proclivities and emotions influence behavior, and people are often not as rational as the model of perfect competition assumes.
- The self-regulating tendencies of the market economy are very weak and slow. One of Keynes' most famous quotes is, "In the long run, we are all dead," meaning that self-correction (i.e., the long run) sometimes takes a very long time: too long to let the economy recover on its own.[5]
- In the short run, self-correction is hampered in many markets by "sticky" wages and prices that are slow to adjust in response to changes in demand (and supply).[6] Because of this slow adjustment, decreases in demand often lead in the short run to greater changes in quantities and smaller changes in wages or prices.
- The use of fiscal and monetary policies can help to reduce the length and severity of recessions, and it can also help to rein in excessively strong expansions. That is, well-designed and timely monetary and fiscal policies can help to stabilize the macroeconomy.

Perhaps nothing in economics has generated greater disagreement than the questions of the causes and cures of economic fluctuations. For example, during the 1960s and 1970s debates over the causes of the Great Depression focused on Keynesian versus monetarist interpretations of the 1930s.[7] While Keynesians focused on shocks to consumption and investment spending, monetarists emphasized changes in the money supply as the most important reason for economic fluctuations.

Since the 1970s, new economic models and theories of economic fluctuations have developed, built upon earlier explanations of the Great Depression and other economic fluctuations, yet there is still no consensus view. While it is beyond the scope of this chapter to provide a comprehensive model of economic fluctuations, some important concepts and ideas are introduced to provide a framework for understanding the potential causes and cures of economic fluctuations.

AGGREGATE DEMAND AND AGGREGATE SUPPLY

While the long-run growth trend depends on aggregate supply, departures from the long-run growth trend are mostly due to fluctuations in aggregate demand or aggregate spending.

Consider a restaurant that serves pizza. In the long run, the amount of pizza this restaurant produces depends on the supply side: the size of the restaurant, the number of pizza ovens, the number of employees the restaurant can accommodate, and the technology and organization of the restaurant. However, in any given hour, day, or month, the amount of pizza the restaurant produces depends primarily on how many people come into the restaurant to order pizza. If very few people order pizza, then the production of pizza is low because spending on pizza is low, and production is below its long-run trend. If there is a festival in town and spending on pizza is unusually high, the restaurant is able to produce more than its long-run trend by having employees work longer and harder than is sustainable over time.

The same thing happens in the economy as a whole. In periods of recession, people are reluctant to spend, and this low spending translates into low production since firms can only sell as much as people want to buy. It is also possible for the economy to produce more than its long-run trend, as occurred during World War II.

In the economy as a whole, aggregate demand (AD) is the sum of four types of spending on final goods and services: consumption spending by households (C); investment spending by households on newly-constructed houses, investment spending by firms, and inventory investment (I); government purchases of final goods and services (G); and net exports (NX), which are exports minus imports.

This relationship is written as:

$$AD = C + I + G + NX$$

The production of real GDP depends on aggregate supply:

$$Y = AS$$

Short-run equilibrium exists when:

$$AS = AD$$

Or, equivalently, when production equals spending:

$$Y = C + I + G + NX$$

Several variables can cause AD to change. One of the most important is the real interest rate (r). Recall from Chapter 5 that the real interest rate is the nominal interest rate minus the inflation rate:

$$r = i - \pi$$

When real interest rates are high, the cost of borrowing is high, and firms and consumers will borrow less. With less borrowing, there is less spending and production, all else being equal. When real interest rates are low, borrowing will increase and, as a result, so too will investment, consumption spending, and real GDP.

The real interest rate also affects net exports. When real interest rates in the U.S. rise, all else being equal, U.S. financial assets pay a higher rate of return and there will be an inflow of foreign savings. Since U.S. assets are denominated in dollars, the increased demand for U.S. financial assets increases the demand for dollars in foreign exchange markets and causes the U.S. dollar to appreciate. As the dollar appreciates, U.S. exports become more expensive to foreigners, while imports from abroad become cheaper to Americans. That is, an exchange rate appreciation, due to an increase in U.S. real interest rates, leads to lower exports, higher imports, and lower net exports.

In summary, higher real interest rates lead to less consumption, less investment, and less net export spending, and vice versa. The inverse relationship between real interest rates and spending (and real GDP) is called the IS curve.[8]

A myriad of shocks can also affect consumption, investment, net export spending, and aggregate demand, including changes in wealth, expectations about the future, and the availability of credit. Shocks in other countries can also affect U.S. AD. For example, a recession elsewhere may cause U.S. exports to fall and lead to lower AD in the U.S. as well.

There can also be shocks that affect aggregate supply, such as crop failures and increases in oil prices, both of which temporarily reduce the productive capacity of the economy and lead to reductions in aggregate supply and real GDP.

THE PARADOX OF THRIFT AND THE SPENDING MULTIPLIER

In long-run models of economic growth, saving is a good thing. More saving leads to more investment spending and greater physical capital accumulation, which contributes positively to labor productivity and real GDP per capita (Chapter 5). In the short run, however, an increase in saving can make things worse. When households and businesses are worried about the possibility of hard times, they react by cutting their spending. That is, they save more.

While this decision is rational for each participant in the economy, it can have negative consequences for the economy as a whole. The reduction in spending depresses the economy as consumers spend less and businesses react by producing less and by laying off workers. As spending falls, so does production, which leads in turn to more layoffs, higher unemployment, and even less spending. That is, the initial decrease in spending (i.e., the increase in saving) may cause production and spending to fall more than the initial decrease through a multiplier process.

The paradox of thrift is a paradox for this reason: in the short run, seemingly responsible and virtuous behavior (preparing for hard times by saving more) can bring harm to the economy. A key part of many macroeconomic explanations of economic fluctuations is that the combined decisions of individual actors in the economy can have results that are far different from what those individuals expected or intended.

BANKING AND FINANCIAL CRISES

Many of the most severe recessions and depressions in American history were accompanied by banking and financial crises. During the nineteenth century, the United States experienced frequent banking panics, with crises in 1814, 1818–1819, 1825, 1836–1838, 1841, 1857, 1861, 1864, 1873, 1884, 1890, and 1896. Since 1900, crises occurred in 1907, 1914, the Great Depression (1929–1933), the savings and loan crisis (1986–1991), and the Great Recession (2007–2008).[9]

Bank failures and financial crises usually lead to decreases in aggregate demand and potentially in aggregate supply. Falling asset prices (like stocks, bonds, and real estate) decrease consumer wealth and increase uncertainty, which together cause AD to fall. The decrease in AD leads to falling real GDP, rising unemployment, and decreases in the rate of inflation.

There can also be adverse effects to AS. When banks and other financial intermediaries fail, "potential borrowers in the economy may not be able to secure funds to undertake worthwhile activities or investments ... [which] limit the economy's productive capacity."[10]

Financial crises are not just a common feature of U.S. recessions: many other countries, too, have experienced recurrent financial crises. Figure 18.2 shows the number of countries (out of seventeen industrialized countries) that faced financial crises in each decade from the 1870s to the 2000s.

After the 1930s, it looked as though developed economies had solved the problem of widespread financial crises, but disruptions to the world financial system from 2007 to 2009 showed that financial crises could still occur, and with detrimental ramifications.

Without institutional safeguards, banks and many other financial institutions are subject to crises because of maturity mismatch, contagion, and leverage. Banks borrow money from depositors on a short-term basis (depositors can demand to be repaid at any time by coming to the bank to withdraw their funds) and they lend on a long-term basis to households and firms (who cannot be forced to repay their loans until the end date of their loan). This is called maturity transformation: converting short-term liabilities (deposits) into long-term assets (loans that earn interest at a higher rate than the rate paid to depositors).

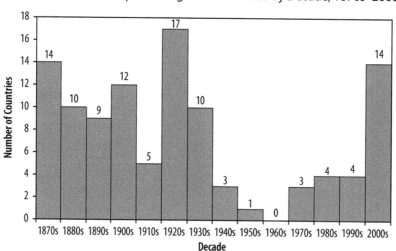

FIGURE 18.2 Countries Experiencing Financial Crises by Decade, 1870s–2000s

Source: Early Elias and Oscar Jorda, "Crises Before and After the Creation of the Fed," Economic Letter 2013-13, Federal Reserve Bank of San Francisco, www.frbsf.org/economic-research/publications/economic-letter/2013/may/crises-before-after-creation-fed/ (accessed: October 21, 2015).

ECONOMIC HISTORY IN ACTION 18.1

Balance Sheets, Leverage, and Insolvency

The fundamental identity of accounting is:

Net Worth $=$ Bank Capital $=$ Assets $-$ Liabilities

Assets are things that a financial institution owns, while liabilities are things they owe. Financial institutions own reserves, securities, and loans to consumers and firms, while they owe the money to depositors who have opened accounts at their bank. The net worth of a bank is also called the bank capital. This identity can be rearranged to yield:

Assets $=$ Liabilities $+$ Bank Capital

Double-entry bookkeeping is based on the fact that if things are to still add up, or balance, we cannot change one term in the fundamental identity without changing one (or more) of the other terms. This identity is represented using a balance sheet or T-account. Consider a simplified balance sheet for a hypothetical bank:

Assets		Liabilities	
Reserves	$15	Deposits	$150
Securities	$45		
Loans	$100	Bank Capital	$10
TOTAL	$160	TOTAL	$160

Note that in this example, the reserve ratio, the ratio of reserves (R) to deposits (D), is 0.10 or 10 percent ($R/D = \$15/\$150$); and the bank's leverage ratio, the ratio of assets to bank capital, is 16 ($\$160/\$10$).

Banks face many kinds of risks, including: (1) liquidity risk (the risk that withdrawals from a bank will exceed the bank's liquid assets); (2) default risk (the risk that loans made by the bank will not be repaid); (3) interest-rate risk (instability in bank profits caused by fluctuations in short-term interest rates and the maturity mismatch on bank balance sheets—most assets have long maturities and most liabilities have short maturities); and (4) market risk (the risk that the value of the bank's securities will decrease).

Any of these risks can lead to insolvency. An insolvent bank has liabilities greater than its assets, producing negative bank capital or negative net worth. An insolvent bank cannot stay in business, because with negative net worth it cannot pay off all of its depositors. The greater the leverage ratio of a financial institution, the more likely it is to become insolvent when there is a decrease in the asset side of the balance sheet. With a leverage ratio of 10, assets can fall by 10 percent without causing insolvency. However, with a leverage ratio of 20, assets can only fall by 5 percent without causing insolvency.

Consider a bank run, which is an extreme form of liquidity risk. Suppose a negative rumor leads to worried depositors lining up to withdraw all of their funds. The bank uses its reserves first ($15) and then sells its securities ($45). With both securities and loans, however, it may often be much more difficult to find a buyer, especially in times of crisis and urgency. Suppose that the bank must liquidate its $100 in loans for only $70. The $130 from the asset side of the balance sheet can only pay $130 of the

$150 in liabilities owed to depositors. The end result is that some depositors lose their money and the bank becomes insolvent:

Assets		Liabilities	
Reserves	$0	Deposits	$20
Securities	$0		
Loans	$0	Bank Capital	−$20

During normal times, a bank can lend out most of the funds deposited, since only a small fraction of depositors will want to withdraw their funds on any given day. However, the mismatch between short-term liabilities and long-term assets makes banks, and other financial institutions that borrow short and lend long, susceptible to runs. A bank run occurs when many of a bank's depositors, fearful of a bank failure, line up to withdraw their funds. Since banks cannot force loan recipients to pay back immediately everything they owe on a long-term loan, banks will not have sufficient reserves on hand to pay more than a small fraction of depositors. Bank failures occur when banks cannot pay off depositors and other creditors and therefore go out of business (see Economic History in Action 18.1).

Historically, bank runs have often been contagious and have often turned into widespread banking panics. When depositors start to line up at one bank, risk-averse depositors at other banks may withdraw funds as well because of imperfect and asymmetric information. That is, it is very difficult, if not impossible, for depositors to know the fiscal health of their own bank. When depositors start to see other banks fail, their rational response in the face of uncertainty is to withdraw their own funds as well.

After the banking crises of the 1930s, the United States and most other countries introduced several changes to protect depositors and to reduce the probability of banking crises in the economy. To stem the likelihood of bank runs and bank failures, regulators can now require banks to hold more reserves and to have higher bank capital requirements. The central bank can also act as a "lender of last resort" to commercial banks by providing

FIGURE 18.3 The Panic of 1884
Source: Library of Congress, http://hdl.loc.gov/loc.pnp/cph.3c27064 (accessed: March 31, 2016). Originally published in *Harper's Weekly* 28, no. 1431 (May 24, 1884), 333.

emergency loans if depositors suddenly request their funds. Finally, governments can insure deposits so that depositors do not have an incentive to withdraw their funds in the first place.

While these changes have largely protected commercial banks from bank runs and panics, the Great Recession witnessed widespread runs and panics in the "shadow banking" sector, which was not subject to deposit insurance or much regulation (see Section 18.5).

FISCAL POLICY

Fiscal policy is the use of government spending and tax policy to help stabilize the economy. In recessions, governments can engage in expansionary fiscal policy by increasing government purchases of goods and services, by cutting taxes (to increase after-tax incomes in the private sector, which in turn may encourage spending), and/or by increasing government transfer spending (such as welfare payments or unemployment insurance).

When the economy is above potential output and inflation is increasing, governments can implement contractionary fiscal policy by raising taxes (to reduce private spending) and/or by decreasing government spending to help return the economy to potential output.

MONETARY POLICY

Monetary policy refers to changes in the money supply and interest rates with the goal of changing real GDP, employment, or inflation. Expansionary monetary policy involves increasing the money supply and reducing real interest rates to increase spending and output, while contractionary monetary policy refers to policy actions that reduce the money supply and increase real interest rates to reduce spending and output.

The country's central bank, the Federal Reserve, is responsible for the conduct of monetary policy. The financial panic of 1907 and the recession that followed is credited with convincing Congress that the U.S. once again needed a central bank. The Federal Reserve Act (1913) divided the country into twelve districts, each with a regional Federal Reserve Bank. These are headquartered in the following cities: Atlanta, Boston, Chicago, Cleveland, Dallas, Kansas City, Minneapolis, New York, Philadelphia, Richmond, St. Louis, and San Francisco. At the head of the Federal Reserve System is the seven-member Board of Governors, located in Washington, DC. Each Governor is appointed by the U.S. President and approved by Congress to serve a 14-year term. The Chair of the Board of Governors serves a 4-year, renewable term.

Since 1935, monetary policy has been conducted by the Federal Open Market Committee (FOMC), which consists of the seven members of the Federal Reserve Board of Governors and five of the twelve Presidents of the Regional Federal Reserve Banks. The President of the New York Federal Reserve votes at all FOMC meetings, because New York City is the center of the U.S. financial system; and four of the remaining eleven Regional Bank Presidents vote on a rotating basis. Since 1981, the FOMC has had eight regularly scheduled meetings a year, but it can meet more often if necessary.

The Federal Reserve can change the stock of commercial bank reserves and the federal funds rate by buying or selling some asset. The primary monetary policy tool is open-market operations, in which the Federal Reserve buys and sells U.S. Treasuries (mostly short-term government bonds called T-bills) to change the amount of bank reserves in the commercial banking system.

If the Federal Reserve wants to decrease interest rates, it buys government bonds, which increases the amount of reserves in the commercial banking system. Because inflation is slow to adjust, the Fed can change real interest rates by changing nominal interest rates. When banks have more reserves, they have more funds available to make loans to households and firms, and the increase in the supply of reserves generally leads to more loans at lower interest rates, which causes spending, aggregate demand, and real GDP to increase. The interest rate that the Fed targets is the federal funds rate, the interest rate at which commercial banks make overnight loans to each other.

Another monetary policy tool is the discount rate, the interest rate that the Fed charges on any loans it makes directly to commercial banks. In times of crisis, the Fed acts as a "lender of last resort" to commercial banks that cannot borrow funds elsewhere. The third policy tool is the legal reserve requirement, the ratio of reserves to deposits that a commercial bank must hold and not loan out. During the Great Recession, the Fed also introduced several new policy tools, which are discussed in Section 18.5.

18.3 THE GREAT DEPRESSION

While the term "great" is almost certainly overused, the Great Depression of the 1930s truly deserves this moniker. It began in the summer of 1929, prior to the stock market crash in October, and the U.S. economy did not return to potential output until it entered World War II more than 12 years later. The Great Depression actually consisted of two contractions: the first one from August 1929 to March 1933, and, after a partial recovery, the second from May 1937 to June 1938.

Between 1929 and 1933, real GDP decreased by more than 26 percent and the unemployment rate increased from less than 3 percent to more than 20 percent.[11] Between 1930 and 1940, the unemployment rate averaged more than 14 percent, and it never fell below 8.9 percent.[12]

Consumer prices fell by more than 27 percent by 1933, and did not surpass July 1929 levels until April 1943.[13] The large and persistent deflation from 1929 to 1933 increased the real burden of debt, raised real interest rates, and created uncertainty that adversely affected consumption and investment spending.

The Great Depression was a worldwide event that affected virtually all countries to varying degrees. It began in the United States, however, and it was more severe and longer-lasting in the United States. Figure 18.4 shows industrial production in the United States, the United Kingdom, Germany, France, and Sweden from 1929 to 1935. In the United States, industrial production in 1932 was only 54 percent of what it had been in 1929, the sharpest drop of the five countries.

THE ONSET OF THE GREAT DEPRESSION

In January 1928, the Federal Reserve, concerned about stock market speculation and the impact of a sudden stock market collapse, began to sell government bonds and gradually increased the discount rate, in a series of steps, from 3.5 percent to 5 percent. While the recession began in August 1929, the initial year or so of the contraction was not particularly severe.

FIGURE 18.4 Real Industrial Production, 1929–1935 (Year 1929 = 100)

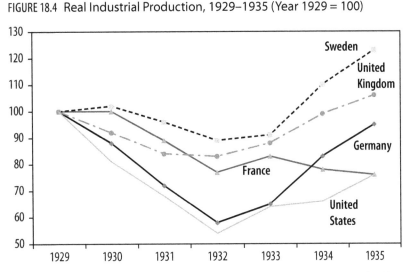

Source: League of Nations, *World Production and Prices 1938/39* (Geneva, Switzerland, 1939), Table 1, 39.

Consumption spending fell in 1930 for reasons that are still not fully understood. One explanation attributes the decrease to the heavy burden of installment debt that consumers had incurred during the 1920s.[14] The stock market crash of October 1929 also created uncertainty about future incomes and decreased wealth, and likely contributed to the decrease in spending on consumer durable goods and investment spending.[15] The stock market crash, however, is not as important as the bank failures and deflation that soon followed.

Despite the decreases in consumption and investment spending, it appeared in 1930 that the economy might soon recover, as it had done after the recession of 1920 and 1921. In December 1930, however, the first in a series of bank failures turned the recession into the Great Depression.

BANK FAILURES

Unlike Canada and the United Kingdom, where branch banking was the norm, the U.S. banking system was dominated by thousands of stand-alone unit banks. The unit-banking system was particularly susceptible to runs and panics. Unit banks were generally less diversified and more exposed to local shocks. They also had little bank capital and were unable to transfer funds from one branch to another to meet depositors' demands.

The first banking crisis began in November 1930 with the collapse of Caldwell and Company, the largest financial holding company in the South. It provided a wide range of financial services, including banking, brokerage, and insurance. It had invested heavily in the stock market, and to cover losses from these investments it began to transfer cash from the banks it controlled. On November 7, one of its banks, the Bank of Tennessee, closed its doors. Over the next ten days, other Caldwell-affiliated banks failed, and this led to the first panic. Within a few weeks, several hundred banks had suspended operations after depositors panicked and withdrew funds as contagion spread from one town to the next.

On December 11, 1930, the fourth-largest bank in New York City, the Bank of the United States, failed when a merger with another bank fell through and depositors rushed to withdraw their deposits. Some scholars have argued that the failure of this bank—a private commercial bank with no affiliation to the United States government—led to further panic since many people erroneously thought that the "Bank of the United States" was indeed connected to the U.S. government.[16]

The impact of bank failures during this first crisis varied across Federal Reserve districts due to the action (or inaction) of the Federal Reserve District Banks. In the Atlanta district, the Fed acted responsibly as a lender of last resort, providing discount lending to both member and nonmember banks. In contrast, the Federal Reserve Bank of St. Louis limited discount lending in its district and refused to help nonmember banks. As a result, there were more business failures and higher unemployment in the St. Louis district.[17]

The United States also experienced widespread banking panics in the spring of 1931, in the fall of 1931, and in the fall of 1932, the last of these continuing through the winter. One of President Franklin Roosevelt's first acts as president was to declare a national "bank holiday" on March 6, 1933: all commercial banks were closed and only those deemed solvent by government inspectors were allowed to reopen.

Between 1930 and 1933, more than 9,000 banks closed (Figure 18.5): more than a third of banks that were in operation before the crises began.[18]

One of the big questions that remains is why the Fed did not play a more active role as a lender of last resort in preventing widespread bank failures. One reason was that most banks in 1929 were not members of the Federal Reserve System because

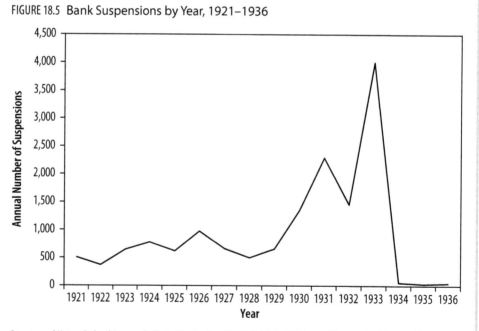

FIGURE 18.5 Bank Suspensions by Year, 1921–1936

Sources and Notes: Federal Reserve Bulletin (September 1937), Table 1, 868, https://fraser.stlouisfed.org/docs/historical/banksusp/frbull_banksus_193709.pdf (accessed: October 8, 2015). Bank suspensions include "all banks closed to the public, either temporarily or permanently by supervisory authorities or by the banks' boards of directors on account of financial difficulties."

they were too small to meet the capital requirements for membership. As a result, "most directors of the twelve Federal Reserve banks did not see the resolution of banking problems as their responsibility."[19] Instead, the overriding importance of remaining on the gold standard "still carried the day."[20]

THE MONEY SUPPLY AND THE MONEY MULTIPLIER

Large-scale bank failures led to large reductions in the money supply and the aggregate price level. The money supply (M) consists of currency held by the public (C) and demand deposits (D). Demand deposits are checking account deposits in commercial banks that are available to depositors "on demand":

$$M = C + D$$

High-powered money or the monetary base (MB) consists of currency held by the public (C) and reserves (R) held by commercial banks. Commercial bank reserves always include required reserves (RR), and may also include excess reserves (ER) if commercial banks decide to keep greater reserves than they are required to keep:

$$MB = C + RR + ER$$

Dividing the money supply by the monetary base yields:

$$\frac{M}{MB} = \frac{C + D}{C + RR + ER}$$

Next, divide the numerator and denominator on the right side of the equation above by $1/D$ and simplify:

$$\frac{M}{MB} = \frac{\frac{C}{D} + 1}{\frac{C}{D} + \frac{RR}{D} + \frac{ER}{D}}$$

Finally, multiply both sides of the equation by the monetary base:

$$M = \left(\frac{\frac{C}{D} + 1}{\frac{C}{D} + \frac{RR}{D} + \frac{ER}{D}} \right) MB$$

Or

$$M = m \cdot MB$$

The term in parenthesis above is called the money multiplier (m) because it shows how the monetary base is related to the total money supply. While the Federal Reserve has a great deal of control over the monetary base, decisions of the public and commercial banks largely determine the money multiplier.

During periods of banking panics and failures, commercial banks, fearful of bank runs, almost inevitably decide to make fewer loans and to hold more of their assets as reserves, which leads to an increase in the ratio of reserves to demand deposits (R/D), and a reduction in both the money multiplier and money supply. As households lose confidence in the banking system, they decide to hold more currency relative to demand deposits, so C/D increases as well, and this also leads to a decrease in both the money multiplier and the money supply. Between August 1929 and March 1933, the C/D ratio increased from 0.17 to 0.41 as the money multiplier fell from 3.7 to 2.3.[21]

Although the Fed thought it was being expansionary by increasing the monetary base, the collapse of the money multiplier caused the money supply to decrease by more than 28 percent between August 1929 (the peak) and March 1933 (the trough), and this led to sustained deflation.[22]

THE GOLD STANDARD

Many scholars have argued that the prevailing ideology of the importance of maintaining the gold standard, at nearly all costs, prevented the Federal Reserve from engaging in expansionary monetary policy.[23] Under the gold standard, there was a free flow of gold between countries. Fixed values of each national currency relative to gold were maintained, and as a result the relationships between national currencies were fixed also.

In the eighteenth century, the philosopher and economist David Hume explained how currencies tied to gold can maintain stable prices. Suppose there is a negative shock in one country that causes exports to fall. With fewer exports, the result is an outflow of gold, which reduces the domestic money supply and lowers prices in the exporting country. Lower domestic prices, however, encourage exports and decrease imports, leading to an inflow of gold and prices rise again until the original equilibrium is regained. This adjustment process is called the price-specie-flow mechanism.[24]

The price-specie-flow mechanism relies on perfectly competitive markets and fully flexible prices. By the 1920s, the growth of large-scale corporations and large employers meant that firms had price-setting power in both output and labor markets. As a result, prices were too "sticky" for the price-specie-flow mechanism to work. In addition, the mechanism is based on partial equilibrium analysis where only one country at a time is shocked away from equilibrium. During the 1930s, when many countries experienced negative shocks and falling exports all at once, "the process of deflation and depression chased a moving target."[25] To maintain the value of currency relative to gold, there was an incentive to encourage deflation since lower prices made a country's exports cheaper.

DEFLATION

While deflation helped maintain the gold standard, it was disastrous for the aggregate economy. At first, deflation was unexpected. Farmers and others had borrowed money with fixed loan obligations (in dollars) due each month. When prices collapsed—and the collapses were especially severe in agriculture—it was much more difficult for farmers to repay their loans. Loan defaults led to farm foreclosures; they also contributed to bank failures in agricultural areas as banks found the value of their loans decreasing, leading to insolvency.

Once market participants *expected* deflation, the expected deflation resulted in high expected real interest rates. Nominal interest rates can never fall below zero since currency also yields a zero interest rate, so deflation raised the real interest rate and the real burden of paying back loans. As a result, consumers and firms were unwilling to borrow, and this contributed to the collapse of investment and consumer spending.

RECOVERY AND RECESSION

On average, the earlier in the 1930s that a country left the gold standard, the less severe was the downturn and the more rapid was the recovery.[26] Leaving the gold standard permitted monetary expansion, price inflation, and reductions in real interest rates, all of which helped to stimulate spending.

Once the United States had left the gold standard in April 1933, recovery was quite rapid. By 1936, real GDP had increased 36 percent compared to 1933. It had also surpassed 1929 levels, although real GDP per capita was still below 1929 levels and well below the long-run growth trend.[27]

The recovery, however, was primarily the result of monetary, and not fiscal, policy.[28] New Deal spending between 1933 and 1936 was not particularly large and was financed primarily by tax increases, so that the stimulative impact of fiscal policy was very modest.

Amidst recovery, however, was another recession in 1937 and 1938. Contractionary monetary and fiscal policy were likely responsible.[29] Concern about the high level of excess reserves caused the Fed to double the legal reserve requirement. Commercial banks responded by decreasing lending so that their reserves remained higher than the new required levels, and this substantially decreased the money supply. Fiscal policy also turned from expansionary to contractionary. In 1936, a large bonus was paid early to veterans of World War I; but in 1937, there was no bonus, and instead Social Security taxes were collected for the first time.

The escalation of conflict in Europe, which led in 1939 to World War II, caused massive gold inflows into the United States. These increased the money supply by 56 percent from December 1937 to December 1942, compared to an increase of only 27 percent from December 1933 to December 1936.[30] Expansionary monetary policy, along with the expansionary fiscal policy that was the result of government spending in mobilizing for World War II, helped the U.S. economy to return to its long-run growth trend by 1942.

LESSONS FROM THE GREAT DEPRESSION

Scholars have drawn several policy lessons from the Great Depression.[31] One lesson is that the central bank's function as a lender of last resort is of primary importance to the short-run stability of the financial system. Second, a system of fixed exchange rates (like the interwar gold standard) limits expansionary monetary policy when it is needed the most. A third lesson is that severe and prolonged deflation can lead to catastrophic consequences. Falling prices, whether anticipated or not, lead to high levels of unemployment and falling real GDP. Finally, fiscal austerity during recessions contributes to and prolongs economic downturns.

18.4 THE GREAT INFLATION

The period from 1965 to 1982, known as the Great Inflation, has been described as "the greatest failure of American macroeconomic policy in the postwar period."[32] Many explanations have been proposed. Some emphasize bad luck (associated with the OPEC oil price shocks of the 1970s), but most focus blame on the decisions taken by the Federal Reserve.

The Great Inflation ended only when the Federal Reserve, under Chair Paul Volcker, committed to a strong anti-inflationary monetary policy. The federal funds rate was increased to more than 20 percent, leading to higher real interest rates and lower spending. The decrease in aggregate demand led to the so-called "Volcker recession" from July 1981 to November 1982. By pushing the economy below potential output and causing the unemployment rate to increase to more than 10 percent, the policy substantially lessened upward pressure on prices and the inflation rate decreased from over 14 percent in early 1980 to less than 3 percent by mid-1983 (see Figure 18.6).

Contractionary monetary policy eventually ended the Great Inflation, but why did the inflation rate increase in the first place? Evidence strongly suggests that the Federal Reserve did not respond aggressively enough to the increase in inflation. Recall once again the relationship between the real interest rate, the nominal interest rate, and the inflation rate:

$$r = i - \pi$$

When inflation increases by 1 percentage point, the Federal Reserve must increase nominal interest rates by *more than* 1 percentage point to increase real interest rates and thereby reduce spending and aggregate demand. The "more than one-for-one" response of nominal interest rates to inflation is called the Taylor Principle.[33]

To better understand how the monetary policymakers' failure to follow the Taylor Principle contributed to the Great Inflation, consider what happens if the Fed does not

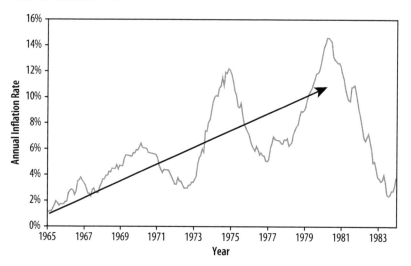

FIGURE 18.6 U.S. Inflation Rate (Consumer Price Index, All Urban Households), January 1965–December 1983

Source: U.S. Bureau of Labor Statistics, Consumer Price Index for All Urban Consumers: All Items, Index 1982–1984=100, Monthly, Seasonally Adjusted. Downloaded from Federal Reserve Economic Data (FRED), https://research.stlouisfed.org/fred2/series/CPIAUCSL (accessed: August 13, 2015). The inflation rate is the percentage change in the index over the previous 12 months.

follow the Taylor Principle and, instead, allows real interest rates to fall when inflation increases. Suppose initially that the nominal interest rate (i) is 5 percent, and the inflation rate (π) is 2 percent, so that the real interest rate (r) is 3 percent. If the inflation rate increases from 2 percent to 3 percent, and the Fed only increases the nominal interest rate from 5 percent to 5.5 percent, then the real interest rate has in fact fallen from 3 percent to 2.5 percent. Rather than discouraging spending, the lower real interest rate instead leads to *more* borrowing, *more* spending, and *more* inflation. If the Fed continues to ignore the Taylor Principle, inflation continues to increase:

$$\uparrow \pi \Rightarrow \downarrow r \Rightarrow \uparrow AD \Rightarrow \uparrow Y \Rightarrow \uparrow \pi \Rightarrow \downarrow r \Rightarrow \uparrow AD \Rightarrow \uparrow Y \Rightarrow \uparrow \pi \text{ and so on.}$$

This is what happened during the 1970s, when the FOMC did not increase nominal interest rates more than the increases in inflation: as inflation increased, real interest rates fell, which further stimulated spending, output, and inflation.

Several reasons have been offered for why the Federal Reserve did not follow the Taylor Principle. Some have argued that the Fed intended to follow the Taylor Principle but reacted to *forecasted* inflation, which turned out to be systematically below what the *actual* inflation rate ended up being. While the Fed reacted "more than one-for-one" to forecasted inflation, it ended up not raising nominal interest rates enough to increase real interest rates because actual inflation consistently outpaced expected inflation.

Other explanations focus on evidence that the Federal Reserve during the 1970s may have been more concerned with preventing recessions than with stopping inflation. In retrospect, we now know that the period from 1973 to 1995 witnessed a decrease in long-run economic growth. During the 1970s, monetary policymakers in the United States and elsewhere failed to recognize the productivity slowdown. That is, they believed that the economy was *below* its long-run trend (potential output) when it was actually *above* potential output.

Empirical evidence also suggests that the shadow of the Great Depression likely influenced the decisions of monetary policymakers during the 1970s. Countries that experienced larger and more persistent declines in output during the 1930s had central banks that responded more aggressively to deviations of real GDP from the perceived long-run trend during the 1970s.[34] While an aggressive response to output can be stabilizing when output gaps (the gap between actual GDP and the long-run trend) are accurately measured, a large monetary response to output gaps in the presence of measurement errors can make things worse.

As a result, the Federal Reserve and many other central banks consistently engaged in expansionary monetary policy when the prudent course of action would have been contractionary policy. The systematic overestimation of potential output and output gaps, coupled with the relatively large central bank responses to perceived output gaps, contributed to the length and severity of the Great Inflation—particularly in those countries, like the United States, that had experienced substantial output losses during the 1930s.

18.5 THE GREAT RECESSION

Before the housing collapse and the Great Recession, many believed that severe recessions were a thing of the past. After all, the previous recession, from March to November 2001, was brief and mild, with real GDP falling only three-tenths of 1 percent and the unemployment rate peaking at less than 6 percent.

By the mid-2000s, there was widespread praise for monetary policymakers' role in the "Great Moderation." During the twenty-five years prior to the Great Recession, the U.S. economy had only two mild recessions, which lasted sixteen months in total. Alan Greenspan, the Chair of the Fed from 1987 to 2006, was called the "maestro" for his alleged mastery and wizardry in conducting monetary policy.[35]

In retrospect, Greenspan's unwavering belief in the efficiency of financial markets resulted in little regulation of the financial system, and that helped to lay the groundwork for the Great Recession. While the Great Recession was not the Great Depression, it was the worst recession since World War II.

THE HOUSING AND BOND BUBBLES

The financial crisis and the Great Recession have been blamed on many factors. Some scholars condemn the Federal Reserve for keeping interest rates too low for too long after the recession of 2001, which encouraged excessive borrowing. Others blame regulators and "their exceedingly permissive attitudes toward subprime lending" which promoted home ownership through mortgage lending on little collateral to ever-riskier borrowers with ever-lower incomes.[36] New, dangerous loans became increasingly common, including so-called NINJA loans, which were given to people with "no income, no jobs, and no assets." Regulators did nothing to stop these practices.

The excessive proliferation of mortgage-backed securities (MBS), which bundled home mortgages into pools financed by bonds backed by these mortgages, and of credit-default swaps (CDS), which banks and others purchased as insurance against the failure of the MBS in their portfolios, are an important part of the story.

The big three credit-rating agencies (Standard and Poor's, Moody's, and Fitch) were also "essential cogs in the wheels of financial destruction."[37] These agencies routinely gave mortgage-backed securities the highest possible rating, AAA—the same rating as U.S. Treasuries. In retrospect, these securities should have received much lower ratings. If they had, they would have been far less appealing to investors.

All of these developments contributed to what most observers considered a housing bubble, where housing prices increased dramatically relative to the prices of other goods and services in the economy. A bubble is a large and persistent deviation of the price of some asset, such as a stock, bond, or house, from its fundamental value. In general, the fundamental value (price) of any financial asset should be equal to the present value of its expected income stream. The housing bubble also led to a bubble in the prices of mortgage-backed securities.

SHADOW BANKING

The "shadow banking" system is composed of a wide variety of non-bank financial firms, including hedge funds, investment banks, and money-market funds.[38] "Shadow" refers to the fact that before the Great Recession many types of financial institutions in the United States were largely unregulated and operated in the "shadows." Shadow banking refers to any financial institution that does not accept deposits but that does engage in maturity transformation, the transformation of short-term liabilities into long-term assets by borrowing over the short term but lending or investing over the longer term. At its peak, the size of the shadow-banking sector was near $20 trillion: it was as big as, if not bigger than, the traditional banking system in the United States.[39]

Because shadow banks perform the same maturity transformation as depository banks (commercial banks and savings and loans that accept deposits), shadow banks are also susceptible to bank runs. While deposit insurance and other regulations have prevented large-scale bank runs for commercial banks and other depository institutions, the 2008 financial crisis represented a classic banking panic, except that this time the banks were shadow banks instead of commercial banks.

For example, the investment bank, Lehman Brothers, borrowed funds in short-term credit markets (where their loans had to be paid back quickly, sometimes overnight) and then invested those funds in longer-term speculative assets. If a shadow bank's lenders suddenly decide that lending to that bank is no longer a safe and wise strategy, the shadow bank can no longer fund its operations—unless it can quickly sell its assets, it will fail.

When other shadow banks are also experiencing the same problems and asset prices are falling throughout the economy, buyers may not be willing to pay much for assets that are dropping in price and are considered risky. This is what happened to Lehman Brothers when it failed on September 15, 2008, which is when the Great Recession really began.

In the days and weeks after the collapse of Lehman Brothers, the U.S. and the world financial system suffered a series of setbacks. American Insurance Group (AIG), the largest insurance company in the world, had sold massive amounts of credit default swaps (CDS) to insure hundreds of billions of dollars on collateralized debt obligations (CDOs). These CDOs collapsed in value, and it then became clear that AIG had not set aside sufficient funds to honor the CDS. The Federal Reserve and the U.S. Treasury extended over $180 billion to AIG to prevent collapse, and the Fed took ownership of 79.9 percent of AIG's common stock, essentially nationalizing the world's largest insurance company.

POLICY RESPONSES

In contrast to its stance during the Great Depression, the Federal Reserve responded quickly and dramatically to the financial crisis and the Great Recession. It also cooperated internationally with other central banks. Open-market purchases decreased the federal funds rate to near zero percent, and the Federal Reserve became the lender of last resort not only for commercial banks, but also for a wide variety of other financial institutions. In addition to government bonds, with "quantitative easing" the Fed purchased massive quantities of mortgage-backed securities, commercial paper, and other assets that market participants were unwilling to purchase. For the first time, the Fed purchased private securities rather than just government-issued securities.

Prior to the Great Recession, the Fed's balance sheet contained about $750 billion in assets consisting mostly of short-term U.S. Treasuries. After the collapse of Lehman, the Fed balance sheet expanded to more than $2 trillion in a matter of weeks, and it continued to increase, reaching $4.5 trillion in 2015 (Figure 18.7).

The massive monetary policy interventions avoided sustained deflation and ensured that there were no large increases in real interest rates or the real burden of debts. Flexible exchange rates gave monetary policy authorities the freedom to use expansionary monetary policy to aid the recovery. During the contraction, the monetary base more than doubled; and although the money multiplier collapsed, the money supply still increased by 20 percent, in contrast to the 28 percent decrease in the money supply during the Great Depression (Table 18.2).

FIGURE 18.7 Assets on the Federal Reserve Balance Sheet, 2003–2015 (Trillions of Dollars)

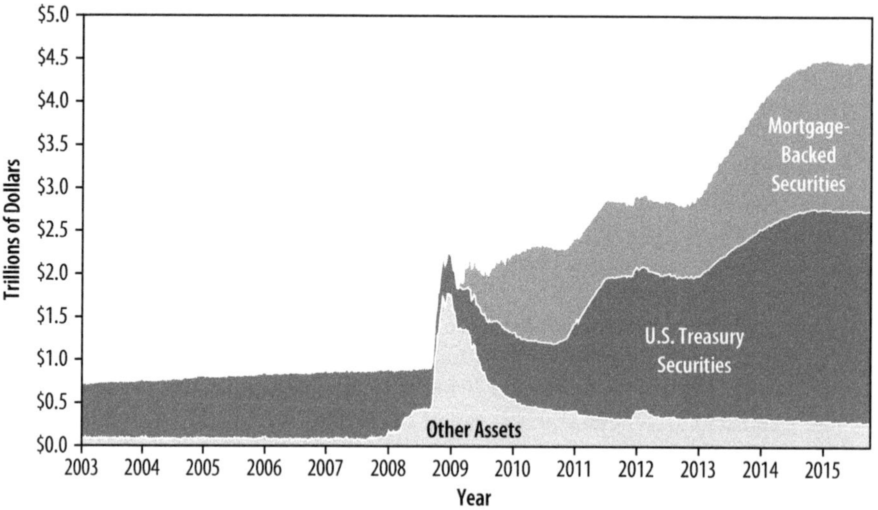

Source: Computed from Federal Reserve Economic Data (FRED), Federal Reserve Bank of St. Louis, https://fred.stlouisfed.org/ (accessed: October 15, 2015). The series shown are mortgage-backed securities (MBST) and U.S. Treasury securities, all maturities (TREAST). Other Assets are computed by subtracting MBST and TREAST from Total Assets (WALCL). All data are weekly from January 1, 2003 to October 7, 2015, and are not seasonally adjusted.

For the first time, the Fed paid commercial banks interest on their excess reserves, called the deposit rate. The Federal Reserve also committed to keep interest rates low for a sustained period in the hope of lowering long-term interest rates. This policy was called "policy duration commitment."

Through the Troubled Asset Relief Program (TARP), $700 billion was authorized to the Treasury to bail out U.S. automobile manufacturers (GM and Chrysler), and $125 billion was given to the major banks (Citibank, JP Morgan Chase, Wells Fargo, Bank of America, Goldman Sachs, Morgan Stanley, and others). The Federal Reserve purchased CDOs from Fannie Mae and Freddie Mac, and it bought large quantities of commercial paper from large private corporations. The scale and scope of this policy response was unprecedented in U.S. history.

In early 2009, the American Reinvestment and Recovery Act (ARRA) provided $800 billion dollars in direct federal spending on infrastructure, education, health, energy, federal tax incentives, expansion of unemployment benefits, and other social programs.

Most economists credit TARP, ARRA, and Federal Reserve policies for preventing the Great Recession from turning into another Great Depression. TARP proved far less costly than originally expected, since

TABLE 18.2 Changes in the Monetary Base and Money Supply: Great Depression and Great Recession

	Monetary Base (currency plus reserves)	Money Supply (currency plus demand deposits)
Great Depression (August 1929–March 1933)	18 percent	−28 percent
Great Recession (December 2007–June 2009)	101 percent	20 percent

Sources: Great Depression data computed from Milton Friedman and Anna J. Schwartz, A Monetary History of the United States, 1867–1960 (Princeton, NJ: Princeton University Press, 1963), Appendix A. Great Recession data computed from the Federal Reserve Board of Governors, H-6, www.federalreserve.gov/releases/h6/ (accessed: November 14, 2015).

the financial assets that were purchased by the Treasury during the crisis were later sold, sometimes at a profit. Although the government lost $15 billion from AIG, $14 billion from the auto bailout, and $15 billion in providing mortgage relief, it neverthe-less turned a profit of $16 billion on the sales of other assets, so that the net cost to taxpayers amounted to just $28 billion.[40]

Although many credit the Federal Reserve with reacting promptly and aggres-sively after the financial crisis and Great Recession began, there has also been wide-spread criticism that the Federal Reserve and other financial regulators did not do their jobs in adequately regulating the financial system in the years leading up to the financial crisis and Great Recession.

18.6 CONCLUSIONS

Almost all of us, including most economists, have a tendency to forget the past. The Great Recession showed that macroeconomists had learned (and remembered) some of the lessons from the Great Depression. Instead of inaction, a massive monetary policy and a modest fiscal policy response prevented the Great Recession from turn-ing into another Great Depression. Instead of allowing deflation and high real interest rates, the Federal Reserve was largely able to avoid the problems associated with deflation.

Both the Great Depression and the Great Recession, however, were preceded by periods of lax regulation and a strong belief in the efficiency of the market system. The Great Depression resulted in a regulatory transformation of the U.S. financial system, with the separation of commercial and investment banking, the introduction of deposit insurance, and greater regulation of stock markets.

In contrast, while the Dodd-Frank Act (2010) led to greater oversight in some areas and to the creation of a Consumer Financial Protection Bureau, most of the reforms were quite modest—probably too modest to prevent a recurrence of financial troubles. The modesty of the Dodd-Frank Act was likely due, in part, to the fact that the stimulative actions of the Federal Reserve and government helped to keep the Great Recession from becoming as deep as the Great Depression, causing some in Congress to decide that only minor financial repairs were needed.[41]

With the continuing proliferation of securitization and new financial assets, many fear that the underlying causes of the last financial crisis have not yet been remedied sufficiently to prevent another large-scale financial crisis and another severe recession.

QUESTIONS

1. Consider the following information for a hypothetical economy:

   Total reserves (R) = $500 billion

   Currency (C) = $400 billion

   A. If banks are holding $80 billion in required reserves, and if the required reserve ratio (RR/D) is 0.10, what is the dollar value of checkable deposits (D)?

   B. What is the dollar value of excess reserves (ER)?

   C. What is the dollar value of the money supply (M)? What is the dollar value of the monetary base (MB)? What is the value of the money multiplier (m)?

2. Why did the Federal Reserve fail to act as a lender of last resort during the Great Depression, and why did the Fed allow the money supply to contract and prices to fall by so much?

3. Why is deflation dangerous? Explain how both unanticipated and anticipated inflation can lead to lower real GDP and higher unemployment. Why was there deflation during the Great Depression, from 1929 to 1933?

4. Consider the balance sheets of two banks: Wells America and Bank of Fargo. Assume that the legal reserve requirement is 10 percent of all deposits.

   A. Suppose that Wells America has $200 billion in checkable deposits, $30 billion in reserves, $60 billion in securities, and $150 billion in loans. Draw a balance sheet (T-account) for Wells America. What is the dollar value of its bank capital?

   B. How much does Wells America hold in excess reserves? How is this related to liquidity risk? Explain.

   C. Assume that Bank of Fargo has the following balance sheet information: $240 billion in checkable deposits, $166 billion in loans, $10 billion in bank capital, and no excess reserves. Show the balance sheet for Bank of Fargo. What are the dollar values of its reserves and securities?

   D. What is the leverage ratio for each bank? Which bank is more likely to become insolvent in the event of a large decrease in the dollar value of its securities? Explain.

5. When was the Great Inflation and why did it occur?

6. What is the shadow banking system and how did it contribute to the Great Recession?

NOTES

[1] As of April 2016, the members of the NBER Business Cycles included Robert Hall (Stanford University), Martin Feldstein (Harvard University), Jeffrey Frankel (Harvard University), Robert J. Gordon (Northwestern University), James Poterba (MIT), Christina Romer (University of California, Berkeley), David Romer (University of California, Berkeley), James Stock (Harvard University), and Mark W. Watson (Princeton University). For current membership, see www.nber.org/cycles/members.html (accessed: April 2, 2016).

[2] National Bureau of Economic Research, June 7, 2008, www.nber.org/cycles/jan08bcdc_memo.pdf (accessed: October 16, 2015).

[3] See Christina D. Romer, "Remeasuring Business Cycles," *Journal of Economic History* 54, no. 3 (September 1994), 573–609; and Joseph H. Davis, "An Improved Annual Chronology of U.S. Business Cycles Since the 1790's" *National Bureau of Economic Research Working Paper*, no. 11157 (February 2005), www.nber.org/papers/w11157 (accessed: October 18, 2015).

[4] John Maynard Keynes, *The General Theory of Employment, Interest, and Money* (London, UK: Macmillan, 1936), 161–162.

[5] John Maynard Keynes, *Tract on Monetary Reform* (London, UK: Macmillan, 1924), Chapter 3.

[6] Prices may adjust slowly for several reasons, including menu costs, staggered wage and price setting, explicit and implicit contracts, and the fact that customers do not like it when prices change frequently.

[7] The most influential monetary interpretation of the Great Depression is Milton Friedman and Anna J. Schwartz, *A Monetary History of the United States, 1867–1960* (Princeton, NJ: Princeton University Press, 1963). This argues that the primary cause of economic fluctuations are changes in the money supply. In contrast, Keynesian interpretations

emphasize fluctuations in consumption and investment spending, which are argued to be largely independent of changes in the money supply and Federal Reserve policies. Peter Temin, *Did Monetary Forces Cause the Great Depression?* (New York, NY: W.W. Norton, 1976) attributes the Great Depression primarily to an exogenous fall in aggregate demand.

[8] The IS curve was introduced by John R. Hicks, "Mr. Keynes and the 'Classics': A Suggested Interpretation," *Econometrica* 5, no. 2 (April 1937), 147–159.

[9] Carmen M. Reinhart and Kenneth S. Rogoff, *This Time is Different: Eight Centuries of Financial Folly* (Princeton, NJ: Princeton University Press, 2009), Table A.4.1, 389–390.

[10] Ben Bernanke, "Nonmonetary Effects of the Financial Crisis in the Propagation of the Great Depression," *American Economic Review* 73, no. 3 (June 1983), 257–276.

[11] Estimates of real GDP from the U.S. Bureau of Economic Analysis, www.bea.gov/national/xls/gdplev.xls (accessed: October 24, 2015). U.S. unemployment rate from David R. Weir, "A Century of U.S. Unemployment, 1890–1990: Revised Estimates and Evidence for Stabilization," *Research in Economic History* 14 (1992), Table D.3, 341–343.

[12] Weir, Table D.3, 341–343.

[13] U.S. Bureau of Labor Statistics, *Consumer Price Index for All Urban Consumers, All Items, Index 1982–1984 = 100, Monthly, Not Seasonally Adjusted*. Available at https://research.stlouisfed.org/fred2/series/CPIAUCNS (accessed: October 28, 2015).

[14] Martha L. Olney, "Avoiding Default: The Role of Credit in the Consumption Collapse of 1930," *Quarterly Journal of Economics* 114, no. 1 (February 1999), 319–335.

[15] Christina D. Romer, "The Great Crash and the Onset of the Great Depression," *Quarterly Journal of Economics* 115, no. 3 (August 1990), 597–624.

[16] Friedman and Schwartz, 309–311.

[17] Gary Richardson and William Troost, "Monetary Intervention: Mitigated Banking Panics During the Great Depression: Quasi-Experimental Evidence from a Federal Reserve District Border, 1929–1933," *Journal of Political Economy* 117, no. 6 (December 2009), 1031–1073.

[18] Gary Richardson, "Banking Panics of 1930 and 1931," www.federalreservehistory.org/Events/DetailView/20 (accessed: October 30, 2015).

[19] Barry Eichengreen, *Hall of Mirrors: The Great Depression, the Great Recession, and the Uses—and Misuses—of History* (New York, NY: Oxford University Press, 2015), 155.

[20] Eichengreen (2015), 155.

[21] Friedman and Schwartz, Appendix A.

[22] Friedman and Schwartz, Appendix A.

[23] For a more in-depth discussion of the gold standard during the Great Depression, see Peter Temin, *Lessons from the Great Depression* (Cambridge, MA: MIT Press, 1989); and Barry Eichengreen, *Golden Fetters: The Gold Standard and the Great Depression, 1919–1939* (New York, NY: Oxford University Press, 1992).

[24] See Peter Temin, "The Great Depression & the Great Recession," *Daedalus* (Fall 2010), 115–124, for a discussion of the price-specie-flow mechanism and a discussion of the similarities and differences between the Great Depression and the Great Recession.

[25] Temin (2010), 117.

[26] See Barry Eichengreen and Jeffrey Sachs, "Exchange Rates and Economic Recovery in the 1930s," *Journal of Economic History* 45, no. 4 (December 1985), 925–946; and Ben Bernanke, "The Macroeconomics of the Great Depression: A Comparative Approach," *Journal of Money, Credit, and Banking* 27, no. 1 (February 1995), 1–28.

[27] U.S. Bureau of Economic Analysis, www.bea.gov/national/xls/gdplev.xls (accessed: September 5, 2015).

[28] See Christina D. Romer, "What Ended the Great Depression?" *Journal of Economic History* 52, no. 4 (December 1992), 757–784.

[29] Romer, 765.

[30] Romer, 775.

[31] Stephen G. Cecchetti, "Understanding the Great Depression: Lessons for Current Policy," *National Bureau of Economic Research Working Paper*, no. 6015 (April 1997).

[32] Thomas Mayer, *Monetary Policy and the Great Inflation in the United States: The Federal Reserve and the Failure of Macroeconomic Policy, 1965–1979* (Cheltenham, UK: Edward Elger, 1999), 1.

[33] John B. Taylor, "Discretion versus Policy Rules in Practice," *Carnegie-Rochester Conference Series on Public Policy* 39 (1993), 195–214.

[34] Mark V. Siegler and Kristin A. Van Gaasbeck, "From the Great Depression to the Great Inflation: Path Dependence and Monetary Policy," *Journal of Economics and Business* 75, no. 5 (September/October 2005), 375–387.

[35] Bob Woodward, *Maestro: Greenspan's Fed and the American Boom* (New York, NY: Touchstone, 2000).

[36] Alan S. Blinder, *After the Music Stopped: The Financial Crisis, the Response, and the Work Ahead* (New York, NY: The Penguin Press, 2013), 58.

[37] *The Financial Crisis Inquiry Report: Final Report of the National Commission on the Causes of the Financial and Economic Crisis in the United States* (Washington, DC: United States Government Printing Office, 2011), xxv, www.gpo.gov/fdsys/pkg/GPO-FCIC/pdf/GPO-FCIC.pdf (accessed: November 4, 2015).

[38] The economist Paul McCulley, who worked for the giant investment firm PIMCO, coined the term "shadow banking". See Bryan J. Noeth and Rajdeep Sengupta, "Is Shadow Banking Really Banking?" *The Regional Economist*, Federal Reserve Bank of St. Louis (October 2011), 8, www.stlouisfed.org/~/media/Files/PDFs/publications/pub_assets/pdf/re/2011/d/shadow_banking.pdf (accessed: November 4, 2015).

[39] Noeth and Sengupta, 8.

[40] Congressional Budget Office, *Report on the Troubled Asset Relief Program* (Washington, DC: Government Printing Office, March 2015).

[41] For a detailed examination of the policy differences between the Great Depression and Great Recession, see Eichengreen (2015).

19

Negative
Externalities
and Common
Resources

Economic growth has led to dramatic improvements in living standards and in life expectancies. Not all of the effects of economic growth have been positive, however, and this chapter explores the negative impact of industrialization and economic growth on the environment, and the government policy responses to mitigate these effects.

Between 1900 and the 1970s, pollution problems were particularly severe in urban areas of the United States, and many environmental protection laws were introduced. Industrial pollution affected not only air quality, but also water quality. For example, refineries and steel mills discharged so much oil into the Cuyahoga River near Cleveland that major fires broke out on the water in 1936, 1952, and 1969.

Concern about the depletion of natural capital and the preservation of forests and the natural environment extends back to the colonial period. While these concerns intensified in the nineteenth century, the modern environmental movement did not begin until the 1960s.

Environmental policies can take several forms. The "command and control" approach uses laws or other regulatory processes to *require* changes in polluters' behavior, such as requiring the use of particular pollution-abatement technologies or specifying limits on the amounts of substances emitted into the air or water.

More efficient and less costly solutions aim to achieve the same level of environmental quality by emphasizing the market mechanism and the importance of incentives. Taxes on emissions, or on products that result in emissions, allow market prices to reflect social costs. While command and control policies threaten legal penalties, taxes provide firms with better incentives to come up with ways of reducing pollution.

In recent decades, markets for emissions trading (using tradeable emissions permits) have been created: these provide incentives for firms to come up with ways of reducing pollution in the most cost-efficient manner. The U.S. Acid Rain Program, a market-based initiative created in 1995 by the U.S. Environmental Protection Agency, led to large reductions in the emissions of sulfur dioxide and nitrogen oxides, gases which then combine with atmospheric water and fall as acid rain.

Many environmental policies have been very successful in improving environmental quality. Between 1970 and 2013, real GDP in the United States increased by 234 percent, vehicle miles traveled increased by 168 percent, and population increased by 54 percent, yet aggregate emissions of the six most common pollutants decreased by 68 percent.[1] In instances where the effects of pollution are visible and (mostly) confined within the United States, policy has been relatively effective in improving environmental quality.

One big exception, however, is the emission of carbon dioxide (CO_2) and other greenhouse gases which are contributing to global warming and global climate change. Carbon dioxide is a colorless, odorless gas that accounts for over 80 percent of all greenhouse gases, and the main sources of human-caused carbon dioxide emissions are from electricity generation (37 percent), transportation (31 percent), and industry (15 percent).[2] Since 1970, carbon dioxide emissions have increased 27 percent in the United States and have more than doubled worldwide.[3] Global climate change is a potentially catastrophic problem for the United States and for all of humanity, yet the complexities of this problem make it an extremely difficult public policy challenge.

19.1   NEGATIVE EXTERNALITIES AND THE COMMON-POOL PROBLEM

Many positive and negative externalities have been examined throughout the book. Recall that a positive externality is an external benefit of an activity—a benefit received by people other than those who pursue the activity. Examples include the positive spillovers of education or basic scientific discoveries. In contrast, a negative externality occurs when a firm or individual engages in some activity that imposes a cost that is paid by society instead of by the party generating the cost. Many social problems, including nearly all environmental challenges, are the result of negative externalities.

Market prices can allocate factor endowments efficiently when property rights are well defined and easily enforceable. However, it is difficult to assign property rights to clean air, water, and soil, to fish in the ocean, or to scenic vistas; and it is difficult to enforce such rights. Indeed, pollution and other negative externalities often arise because there are no enforceable property rights to open-access goods such as the atmosphere or oceans. As a result, use of an open-access good continues unchecked until the marginal benefit of this use falls to zero.

A "tragedy of the commons" problem occurs when individuals, each following his or her self-interest, behave in a way that is contrary to the whole group's long-term interests by overusing a common-pool resource. The "commons" can include the Earth's atmosphere, oceans, rivers, forests, or animals; they can also include the office refrigerator, or any other shared resource without private property rights. In the absence of legally defined and enforceable property rights, there is a tendency for overuse or overharvesting.

OVERPRODUCTION AND DEADWEIGHT LOSS

Consider an industry that is perfectly competitive in all ways except that the production of this industry's good creates a negative externality on others in the economy, for example by emitting harmful pollution into the air or water. When firms in this industry make decisions about production, they usually only consider the marginal private costs they face and they may not internalize (i.e., take into account) the costs of pollution on others. In this case, the true marginal social costs (which include not only the marginal private costs to firms but also the marginal costs of the externality on others) are higher than the marginal private costs.

This is shown in Figure 19.1, where the marginal social costs (MSC), which are the sums of the marginal private costs plus the marginal costs of the externality, are above the firms' marginal private costs (MPC). The sums of all firms' marginal private costs (MPC) are the market supply curve. The market demand curve is equal to both the marginal private benefits (MPB) and the marginal social benefits (MSB), since there are assumed to be no externalities on the demand side.

Production occurs where supply (MPC) equals demand (MPB), but from an efficiency perspective, production is too high since at the market equilibrium (Q_M) the $MSC > MSB$. The deadweight loss of overproduction in this example is the difference between the marginal social costs and the marginal social benefits of this excess production (the shaded triangle). Only at Q_S, the social optimum, are the marginal social costs (MSC) equal to the marginal social benefits (MSB).

SOLUTIONS TO NEGATIVE EXTERNALITIES

In some situations, private actors may be able to solve negative externality problems. In 1960, Ronald Coase challenged the view that pollution problems and negative externalities necessarily require regulatory interventions by governments. Externalities will be corrected by the market if property rights are clearly defined and easily

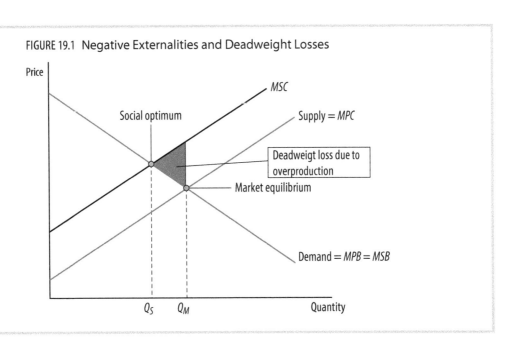

FIGURE 19.1 Negative Externalities and Deadweight Losses

enforceable, and if transaction costs are zero (or close to zero). That is, the establishment and enforcement of property rights and individual bargaining between the parties involved can lead to an efficient, socially optimal solution without the need for any further public policy interventions at all.

Consider a common resource like a lake. Suppose that as part of its production process a factory emits warm water into the lake, and that this adversely affects the profitability of a fishery on the lake. For simplicity, assume that the factory and fishery are the only two parties affected. Also assume that the value gained by the firm in emitting warm water into the lake is $1 million a year; while the value to the fishery of a cool lake, without warm water emitted into it, is $2 million a year.

The Coase Theorem states that if transaction costs are low and if property rights are clearly defined and enforceable, private bargains will ensure that the market equilibrium is efficient even when there are externalities. To see how this works, suppose that property rights to the lake are given to the fishery. In that case, the factory will be willing to pay the fishery up to $1 million to use the lake, but the fishery will not accept this offer as it gains $2 million from using the lake. In this case, the equilibrium will be that the fishery uses the lake and receives a total economic surplus of $2 million.

Now suppose that the property right to use the lake had been assigned to the factory instead. The factory would gain $1 million from using the lake, but the fishery would be willing to pay up to $2 million to use the unpolluted lake since it could derive $2 million in benefits. Suppose that, through bargaining, the fishery agrees to pay the factory $1.5 million for exclusive use of the lake. The factory gains $1.5 million from this arrangement, but the fishery gains too. The fishery's net gain is $500,000—the $2 million value of using the lake, minus the $1.5 million paid to the factory owners. In either case, therefore, whether the property right is given to the fishery or to the factory, the efficient outcome occurs where there is $2 million in total surplus with the fishery using a lake with cool water. While the assignment of the property right matters in terms of how the total surplus is allocated across the two firms, the total surplus and the end result are the same in both cases.

In the real world, there are often several problems in achieving Coasian solutions. The first is the difficulty in accurately assigning blame for the negative externality. A decline in the fish population in the lake may not just be due to warm water from the factory—there may also be natural causes, such as a disease or an increase in natural predators. Even if the blame can be assigned to a specific entity or entities, it can still be difficult to assign the damage. In the example above, it was assumed that the dollar value of the damage is known, but this is rarely the case. The Coase Theorem also assumes that the costs of the transaction and of negotiation are very low. In reality, bargaining is unpleasant, time-consuming, and difficult. This is particularly true when many parties are involved. As a result of these and other problems, some economists believe that "Coase's analysis seems much more exciting as a theoretical exercise than as a practical approach to environmental policy."[4]

Another solution to negative externalities, if they occur within a given legal jurisdiction, is to use liability laws and litigation through the court system. In common-law systems, plaintiffs and defendants make claims and counterclaims before judges and juries to decide on questions of fact, and to determine liability and just compensation in cases of guilt. To be "liable" for some behavior is to be held responsible for whatever consequences result from that behavior. In cases where liability is determined, compensation requires that those causing the damage must compensate those affected by the damage in an amount appropriate to the extent of the damage.

With environmental issues, this works by making polluters legally liable for the damage they cause. The purpose is not simply to compensate people after the damage has been done, but to encourage would-be polluters to make careful decisions. That is, if they know that they will be held responsible for environmental damages, they will, in effect, internalize the negative externality. If firms can be made to pay the full social costs, the socially optimal quantity of Q_S can occur. In reality, however, there are difficulties with this approach as well, for example in accurately assigning blame for the externality and in accurately determining the true marginal social costs.

Another way to institute a system of liability and compensation is through statutory pollution-control laws. For example, the Comprehensive Environmental Response, Compensation, and Liability Act (1980) or "Superfund" holds polluters liable for two types of costs: the costs associated with the cleanup of dump sites where companies have disposed of toxic substances in the past, and the costs of damages stemming from intentional or accidental releases of hazardous materials into the environment.

Governments can also reduce the prevalence and impact of negative externalities, particularly local externalities, through zoning laws. Extensive use of zoning laws is a twentieth-century phenomenon. By confining certain types of activities to particular lots, the government can prevent incompatible uses. For example, factories can be separated from private residences to reduce noise and other externalities.

The "command and control" approach is another solution. In this case government mandates particular limits on certain types of behavior or emissions and fines any firms that exceed these limits. Additionally, governments employ a wide array of taxes and subsidies to try to ensure that the market equilibrium occurs at or very near the socially optimal level of production. Taxes can increase the firms' incentive to internalize the negative externality by increasing their marginal private costs so that they equal the marginal social costs of their production. Subsidies can encourage firms to install pollution-abatement technologies. There are also subsidies to individuals, such as the federal tax credit for buying an electric automobile.

Finally, government can help to create markets. Under cap and trade policies, government sets a cap, or limit, on the amount of a particular pollutant, such as CO_2.[5] Businesses and individuals are issued permits to emit a certain amount of carbon into the atmosphere each year. Trading of permits is allowed, so that individuals and companies who emit less than their allowance can sell permits they do not use. By establishing property rights in emissions, cap and trade provides incentives to firms and individuals to lower emissions in the most cost-effective manner.

Cap and trade, however, can run into difficulties. First, it is often not clear how many permits should be issued. That is, what is the optimal amount of pollution from a social perspective? Second, if the pollutant extends beyond national boundaries, cap and trade requires that national governments agree on, monitor, and enforce emissions limits. There is also an incentive for governments to free ride. Without an international consensus, producers in countries that adopt and enforce cap and trade policies will experience higher production costs, and consumers in those countries will pay more for electricity and other goods that emit pollution. In contrast, individuals and firms in countries that ignore cap and trade policies will benefit in terms of lower prices and lower costs as they free ride on the sacrifices others make to reduce pollution.

THE THEORY OF SECOND BEST

Compared to the perfectly competitive outcome, negative externalities lead to over-production from the standpoint of maximizing social welfare. In the real world, how-ever, it is rarely the case that only one of the assumptions of perfect competition is not satisfied. What should governments do when more than one of the assumptions of perfect competition fails to hold in a particular market?

It is important for policymakers to recognize the theory of second best, which is "a situation in which more, but not all, of the optimum conditions are fulfilled [the assumptions of perfect competition] is not necessarily, or even likely, to be superior to a situation in which fewer are fulfilled."[6] The theory of second best means that if more than one of the assumptions of perfect competition is violated, efficiency does not nec-essarily improve if you move closer to perfect competition, unless all of the assump-tions of perfect competition are satisfied.

Consider the example of a company that has a monopoly in a particular market, but is emitting a harmful substance into the air. Recall from Chapter 17 that a monop-oly produces too little in comparison with a perfectly competitive industry. In contrast, it was shown in Figure 19.1 that the presence of a negative externality in production will cause an industry to produce too much in comparison with a perfectly competi-tive industry. Therefore, it is possible that the combined outcome of both a monopoly and a negative externality is better than having just one violation of perfect competi-tion. In this example, the underproduction of the monopoly and the overproduction due to the negative externality may "cancel each other out," so that the outcome of two violations in the assumptions of perfect competition (i.e., one seller and a negative externality) may be preferable from a social efficiency perspective.

THE ENVIRONMENTAL KUZNETS CURVE

Some believe that economic growth necessarily harms the environment—that is, they argue that there is necessarily a positive correlation between economic growth and environmental damage. However, there is evidence that environmental quality does not always worsen with economic growth.

The environmental Kuznets curve (EKC) refers to an inverted U-shaped rela-tionship between pollution levels and economic activity, with that activity usually measured as the level of real per capita income.[7] At low levels of income per capita, the level of pollution is quite low because production is low. As real income per capita increases, so does pollution in the environment, but only up to a point. Beyond that point—which differs from pollutant to pollutant—as per capita income increases, the level of pollution begins to fall. This generates an inverted U-shaped relationship between pollution and real income per capita (Figure 19.2).

There are two main explanations for this inverted U-shaped relationship. One explanation emphasizes structural changes that occur with economic growth, as the economy develops from a clean agrarian economy to a polluting industrial economy and then to a clean service economy. The second explanation stresses the tendency of people with higher incomes to have greater preferences for environmental quality. That is, at early stages of economic growth, people are willing to sacrifice the environ-ment for higher incomes, but the increase in per capita incomes changes individuals' tastes. With affluence, due to economic growth, comes both the desire for a cleaner environment and the ability to achieve it.

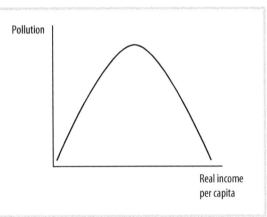

FIGURE 19.2 Environmental Kuznets Curve

Empirical support for the EKC is mixed. Only some air-quality indicators (local pollutants in particular) display evidence of an EKC.[8] In addition, there are differing estimates of the income levels at which the environment begins to improve.[9] One important exception to the EKC is carbon dioxide, the most important greenhouse gas. If there is an environmental Kuznets curve for CO_2, it is clear that the world is still on the upward-sloping part of the curve. Perhaps future economic growth worldwide might eventually cause emissions of CO_2 and other greenhouse gases to fall, but humanity may not be able to wait that long.

19.2   HISTORY OF ENVIRONMENTAL POLICIES

While many histories of U.S. environmental policy focus exclusively on the modern environmental movement, which started in the 1960s and 1970s, concern over the natural environment began even before the United States existed as a country.

THE COLONIAL PERIOD

During the colonial period, environmental policies were limited in scope, but there is evidence of some modest government involvement in seeking to prevent the depletion of forests and the extinction of animals. In 1626, only six years after the Pilgrims founded the Plymouth Colony, colonists passed laws limiting the harvesting and sale of timber.[10] There were other indications, too, that colonists recognized the possibility of overharvesting and the need for preservation. In 1681, William Penn set aside land in Pennsylvania to remain in its natural state, and Massachusetts followed suit ten years later.[11] There were also early laws to protect wildlife, including hunting restrictions to protect game animals in Massachusetts and Connecticut, and ordinances that protected coastal waterfowl in New York.[12]

THE NINETEENTH CENTURY

The Treaty of Paris was signed in 1783, ending the Revolutionary War and doubling the land mass of the original thirteen colonies. Then came the Louisiana Purchase in 1803, which again almost doubled the size of the United States. The vast western frontier must have made land and other types of natural capital seem virtually limitless. Throughout most of the nineteenth century, there was a frontier mentality in which the vast wilderness needed to be "tamed" for civilization by clearing forests for agriculture and by creating towns.

Nevertheless, the seeds of modern environmentalism extend back to the early nineteenth century. From the nineteenth century until today, environmentalism has been interpreted in two different ways: the preservationist view and the conservationist view.

Preservationists believe that land and the natural environment should be maintained in its pristine form and should not be modified by humans. There is a belief in the intrinsic value in maintaining areas of natural beauty and wonder, without the encroachment of humans and modern civilization. While humans should have access to these places, they should, in modern parlance, "take nothing but pictures, and leave nothing but footprints." During the mid-nineteenth century, preservationists such as Henry David Thoreau and Ralph Waldo Emerson emphasized an appreciation of the natural environment and the importance of preserving it. Later in the century, the naturalist John Muir co-founded the Sierra Club (1892), and he was also instrumental in helping to establish a number of national parks.[13]

In contrast, conservationists stress that the environment and its resources should be managed in a responsible and sustainable manner to ensure that present uses do not jeopardize the supply of resources or the quality of the environment for future generations. Gifford Pinchot, the first head of the U.S. Forest Service (1901–1905), was a leading conservationist. Pinchot thought of forests as a "crop" that with careful management could provide a sustainable yield, yet had multiple uses, including recreation and wildlife protection.[14]

The influence of both preservationists and conservationists is evident in nineteenth-century environmental policies. In 1832, the federal government created a public "reservation" at Hot Springs, Arkansas, to protect the mineral springs there. Yellowstone (Figure 19.3) was established as the country's first national park in 1872, to preserve its natural beauty from being degraded by access roads and billboards as had occurred with many natural wonders in the eastern U.S.

While the creation of national parks was more consistent with the preservationist view, the influence of conservationists was evident in the management of forests. Throughout much of the nineteenth century, lumber was in great abundance. Between 1790 and 1850, wood supplied more than 90 percent of all fuel-based energy in the United States (see Chapter 6). By 1910, however, wood provided only 11 percent of fuel-based energy. Population growth,

FIGURE 19.3 The Grand Falls of the Yellowstone, Yellowstone National Park, 1905

Source: Library of Congress, www.loc.gov/pictures/item/94505501/ (accessed: April 25, 2016).

westward expansion, and the railroad all contributed to deforestation. The lack of property rights to most timber created incentives to cut as much as possible as fast as possible since it was free for the taking. That is, as a common resource, it created a "tragedy of the commons" problem, with incentives for neglect and overuse.

The buildup of masses of slash (tree branches and other discarded timber) also created excessive waste and fire hazards. Massive fires occurred in the United States during the 1870s, 1880s, and 1890s, including the Peshtigo fire in 1871 which burned more than 1.28 million acres in Wisconsin and killed more than 1,000 people. Other major fires occurred in Michigan (1881), Wisconsin (1894), and Minnesota (1894).

Between 1800 and 1900, about 25 percent of forested land in the current continental United States was lost. Since then, things have improved: through conservation efforts, the number of acres of forestland has remained relatively constant, with 754 million acres of forestland in the United States in 1910 and 766 million acres in 2012.[15]

Federal forest management started in 1876 when Congress created the Office of Special Agent within the U.S. Department of Agriculture to assess the conditions and quality of U.S. forests. In 1891, Congress passed the Forest Reserve Act, which authorized the U.S. President to designate public lands in the West as "forest reserves." Between 1891 and 1900, roughly 50 million acres of timberland were set aside.

THE TWENTIETH CENTURY

Major policy changes took place under President Theodore Roosevelt (1901–1909), who took an active role in conserving timber, mineral resources, historical artifacts, and wildlife. The Bureau of Forestry was created in 1901 and became the U.S. Forest Service in 1905, under the direction of Gifford Pinchet. In 1906, the Antiquities Act gave the President the power to restrict the use of certain federal lands. It was passed to protect prehistoric lands in the western United States (called "antiquities") that were increasingly subject to looting by private collectors looking for Native American artifacts, at Chaco Canyon, New Mexico, and elsewhere. During Roosevelt's time in office, about 230 million acres of land were federally protected, and this protection included the establishment of 150 national forests, 5 national parks (including Yosemite National Park), 18 national monuments, 4 national game preserves, 21 reclamation projects, and 51 federal bird reservations.[16]

Environmental policy was also quite active during the 1930s. The Great Depression coincided with several natural disasters, including the Dust Bowl and episodes of major flooding on the Ohio and Mississippi Rivers. Recovering from these disasters and reducing the likelihood of their reoccurrence was an important part of New Deal policies.

One notable agency was the Civilian Conservation Corps (CCC). Between 1933 and 1942, over 3 million young men joined the CCC. They planted over 2 billion trees, built national park facilities, helped slow the erosion on more than 40 million acres of farmland, updated firefighting methods, created more than 800 new state parks, and built a system of service roads and public roads in remote areas.[17] While the primary purpose of the CCC was to provide employment opportunities to men aged 17–28, it also led to a greater understanding and appreciation of the importance of conserving America's natural resources.

In the decades after World War II, public recognition that economic growth could adversely affect environmental quality (Figure 19.4) eventually led to extensive public and private actions. The spread of manufacturing and automobiles led to widespread concerns about air pollution. In 1948, the town of Denora, Pennsylvania, and

FIGURE 19.4 Pollution in Dubuque, Iowa, 1940

Source: John Vachon, Library of Congress, www.loc.gov/pictures/item/fsa1997005559/PP/ (accessed: February 4, 2016).

surrounding communities were blanketed with a dense smog that led to the deaths of 20 people and made over 6,000 people sick.[18] In the 1950s, industrial cities, like Gary, Indiana, and Pittsburg, Pennsylvania, and places where the car was king, like Los Angeles, suffered from severe air pollution. In response, the National Air Pollution Control Administration was established in 1955.

After World War II there was also increased apprehension about water quality, although concerns about water quality began in the nineteenth century. In the 1840s, New York City and Boston built major aqueducts to provide uncontaminated water from far outside of the city limits. By 1870, there were more than 244 urban waterworks in the United States, and more than 3,000 by 1900.[19] In 1899, Congress passed the Rivers and Harbors Act, which limited the dumping into waterways of impediments to navigation.[20] Although the primary purpose of the law was to improve navigation, it had the added benefit of preventing further dumping in the nation's navigable waterways. The 1948 Federal Water Pollution Control Act was the first major law to address water pollution.

Events during the 1960s, however, triggered the modern environmental movement. The 1962 publication of *Silent Spring* by the biologist and naturalist Rachel Carson brought the potentially adverse effects of economic growth on the environment to the forefront of public policy discussions. Carson highlighted the dramatic impacts on the ecological environment of the aerial spraying of the pesticide dichlorodiphenyltrichloroethane (DDT), which was used to kill mosquitoes, showing that DDT led to large decreases in the populations of birds and wildlife. DDT also posed threats to human health. President Kennedy responded to the public outcry by appointing a Scientific Advisory Committee to investigate the book's claims. After the Committee had largely endorsed the claims, DDT was banned.

Other events helped spur environmental legislation. In 1969, there was a large oil spill off the coast of Santa Barbara, California, and the proximity to Los Angeles made the effects on beaches and wildlife very evident to Americans. (Later there would be even bigger spills, from the *Exxon Valdez* in 1989 in Prince William Sound, Alaska, and from BP in 2010 in the Gulf of Mexico.) Another important event was the first Earth Day (1970), which was the idea of Gaylord Nelson, a U.S. Senator from Wisconsin, after he had witnessed the devastation caused by the massive Santa Barbara oil spill. On Earth Day, more than 20 million Americans took to the streets to "demonstrate for a healthy, sustainable environment in massive coast-to-coast rallies."[21]

In 1970, Congress passed the Clean Air Act, and the Environmental Protection Agency (EPA) was created.[22] The Clean Air Act established 247 air-quality control regions across the United States, which were required to meet the National Ambient Air Quality Standards (NAAQS) set by federal guidelines established by the EPA. The 1990 Clean Air Act strengthened the policy, by adding ozone-based smog, acid rain, and chlorofluorocarbons (CFCs), along with 189 specific air toxins, to the list of substances that the Act mandated to be substantially reduced.[23]

Amendments to the Federal Water Pollution Control Act in 1972, known as the Clean Water Act, established water-quality standards and discharge limits. The Safe Drinking Water Act (1974) required the EPA to establish drinking-water standards for 26 major pollutants.[24]

Between 1970 and 1980, many other major environmental laws were passed (Table 19.1), several of which are discussed in Section 19.3. These environmental laws were partially the result of substantial lobbying and public pressure. Many major environmental groups have influenced environmental policy, including the Sierra Club, the Nature Conservancy, the National Wildlife Federation, the World Wildlife Fund USA, the National Audubon Society, and Greenpeace.

TABLE 19.1 Major Environmental Legislation Between 1970 and 1980	
National Environmental Policy Act	1970
Clean Air Act	1970
Federal Water Pollution Control Act (Clean Water Act)	1972
Coastal Zone Management Act	1972
Federal Insecticide, Fungicide, and Rodenticide Act	1972
Endangered Species Act	1973
Safe Drinking Water Act	1974
Toxic Substances Control Act	1976
Federal Land Policy and Management Act	1976
Resource Conservation and Recovery Act	1976
Fisheries Conservation and Management Act	1976
Comprehensive Environmental Response, Compensation, and Liability Act (Superfund)	1980

Sources: David Soll, "Changing Understandings of the Nature and Role of Government Policy (Early Years to Present)," in Sally K. Fairfax and Edmund Russell (eds.), *Guide to U.S. Environmental Policy* (Thousand Oaks, CA: Sage Publications, 2014), 17; and Norman J. Vig and Michael E. Crafts, *Environmental Policy*, Eighth Edition (Washington, DC: CQ Press, 2013).

19.3 RECENT ENVIRONMENTAL ISSUES

Most early environmental issues were both visible and tractable—smoke billowing out of smokestacks, forests being cleared, garbage on the side of a river, and so on—and as a result, most were relatively easy to solve. Since the early 1970s, however, the nature of environmental issues has changed. Many recent environmental challenges are not visible to the naked eye, and some concerns are based on somewhat uncertain scientific evidence. In addition, the effects often extend beyond national boundaries, so that solutions require international cooperation; and many have longer-term impacts, such that decisions made in the present will affect future generations.

Another change since the 1970s is an increasing realization that environmental issues do not affect all members of society equally. The environmental justice movement has drawn attention to widespread evidence of the unequal concentration of environmental burdens in poor and nonwhite communities. This began in 1982, when the residents of Warren County, North Carolina, protested the decision to locate a hazardous landfill in their community, arguing that the site had been chosen because it was in a community that was primarily black (65 percent). Citizens chained themselves to equipment and blocked waste trucks from entering the area. More than 500 people were arrested, including one member of Congress; and while residents were unable to stop the landfill, the protests drew national attention.[25] During the 1970s and 1980s, there was increasing evidence that hazardous treatment, disposal, and storage facilities tended to be located in predominantly poor black communities. In 1994, President Clinton signed Executive Order 12898, which directed federal agencies to collect data on low-income and minority populations that might be at risk from environmental changes and to improve methods of assessing and mitigating any health or other impacts.[26]

ACID RAIN

Acid rain is a result of sulfur dioxide and nitrogen oxide having been emitted into the air. When these chemicals combine with water, precipitation changes the acidity of the water and the land on which the acid rain falls. In the northeastern United States and in southeastern Canada, where the problem was the worst, the primary culprit appeared to be coal-burning power plants and their sulfur dioxide emissions. In the western United States, the problem was mostly due to nitrogen oxide emissions from utilities and automobiles.

The severity of the problem was due, in part, to efforts of firms to meet the requirements of the Clean Air Act. One way for manufacturers and utilities to meet local air-quality standards was to build taller smokestacks: these dispersed pollutants beyond the local air shed, and sent them into airstreams that carried them hundreds or thousands of miles away. Acid rain can have serious environmental and health consequences, from corroding metal and damaging buildings to contaminating fish in lakes and harming trees and plants.

The Acid Precipitation Act (1980) and the Clean Air Act Amendments (1990) introduced a national program of tradeable permits to reduce emissions of sulfur dioxide (SO_2). Many coal-burning utilities also installed smokestack "scrubbers," which removed more than 95 percent of SO_2 emissions. In addition, automobile vehicle emissions standards have been very successful in reducing these types of emissions. Successful regional cap and trade markets for nitrogen oxide have also been established.[27]

OZONE DEPLETION

Whereas the oxygen we breathe has two oxygen atoms (O_2), ozone has three (O_3). While breathing ozone would be very dangerous, the presence of ozone in the high levels of the atmosphere is essential to us as it blocks out much of the sun's ultraviolet radiation. Depletion of ozone means that more ultraviolet radiation reaches the Earth, increasing the rates of skin cancer and harming marine wildlife and agricultural productivity.

Ozone depletion is largely the result of the use of chlorofluorocarbons (CFCs), which were discovered in 1930, and have been used in air-conditioning, plastic foam packaging, furniture cushions, hairspray, and other aerosols, and personal computers. In 1985, British scientists documented a massive hole in the ozone layer, centered over Antarctica. The size of the ozone hole peaked in 2006; and while it grew smaller in the years after that, it has since increased in size again, reaching near historic highs in 2015.[28]

In 1987, countries met and signed a treaty known as the Montreal Protocol. In 1990, the United States phased out the production of CFCs and required safe recycling of CFC products. Since then, the use of CFCs and other ozone-depleting substances has steadily declined. Because CFCs are persistent chemicals that remain in the stratosphere for decades, however, complete recovery of the Antarctic ozone layer is not expected until the middle of the twenty-first century at the earliest.

HAZARDOUS WASTE

Another environmental issue that has come to the forefront since 1970 is the abundance of hazardous waste sites throughout the United States. The story of the Love Canal illustrates this phenomenon. In the 1890s, William T. Love partially constructed and then abandoned a canal near Niagara Falls, New York.[29] Between 1942 and 1953, Hooker Electrochemical buried 25,000 tons of hazardous wastes in the abandoned Love Canal. In 1953, Hooker sold the site to the Niagara Board of Education for one dollar, but issued a disclaimer about buried chemicals on the property. Two years later, a public school was built on the site and home construction started on and around the site.

Everything seemed fine for about 20 years, until heavy rains hit in 1976. The rains caused chemicals to surface, and residents began to complain about odors, chemical seepage, and health impacts, which were reported in the *Niagara Gazette*. That same year, the first federal laws regarding hazardous wastes, the Toxic Substances Control Act and the Resource Conservation and Recovery Act, were passed. In 1978, the EPA investigated and the New York State Health Commission declared a state of emergency at Love Canal. Soon thereafter, President Jimmy Carter declared Love Canal a national disaster area and approved emergency federal aid.

There were other newsworthy incidents near this time, as well. In 1979, the Three Mile Island nuclear power plant in Pennsylvania suffered a partial meltdown; and in 1980, a hazardous waste dump in Elizabeth, New Jersey, exploded. Because of these problems, President Carter signed into law the Comprehensive Environmental Response, Compensation, and Liability Act (1980), which established a $1.6 billion "Superfund" to help clean up hazardous waste sites throughout the country.[30]

Love Canal was added to the list of Superfund sites in 1983, and a district court in New York ruled that Hooker Electrochemical was liable for the cleanup costs at Love Canal. Six years later, the company settled with the federal government and New

York state, paying $220 million to cover cleanup and relocation costs; and in 2004, the Love Canal site was removed from the list of Superfund sites.

In May 2016 there were 1,328 Superfund sites nationwide on the National Priorities List (NPL).[31] Cleanup has already been completed at 391 sites, and 55 new sites are under consideration and may be added to this list.[32]

GLOBAL CLIMATE CHANGE

The greenhouse effect, which was first proposed by the French mathematician Jean-Baptiste Joseph Fourier in 1824, is a natural part of the Earth's climate and a necessary component for life on the planet. The Earth's atmosphere serves to warm the planet and to minimize the daily and seasonal fluctuations in temperatures. Without the atmosphere and greenhouse gases, the Earth's climate would be like that of the Moon.[33]

Since the Industrial Revolution, however, concentrations of greenhouse gases in the atmosphere have increased substantially. While there are still a few naysayers, the overwhelming majority of scientists believe that human activity is contributing to observed climate changes.[34] Atmospheric carbon dioxide, from the burning of fossil fuels like coal, oil, and natural gas, and from worldwide deforestation and other changes in land use, contributes about two-thirds of the total impact of greenhouse gas emissions.[35] There are, however, other significant greenhouse gases, including methane, nitrous oxide, and chlorofluorocarbons.[36]

Prior to the Industrial Revolution, atmospheric concentrations of carbon dioxide (CO_2) averaged about 280 parts per million (ppm): see Figure 19.5. Carbon emissions started to increase around 1850, with industrialization in the United States and in a few other countries of the world. However, large increases in atmospheric concentrations are largely a post-World War II phenomenon, and the annual emissions and atmospheric concentrations have been rising at an increasing rate. Atmospheric concentrations of CO_2 surpassed 400 ppm in 2014. This is the highest concentration in the Earth's atmosphere in at least the last 800,000 years, since well before the appearance of modern *Homo sapiens*.[37]

As concentrations of greenhouse gases in the atmosphere have increased, so too have surface and ocean temperatures. Between the late nineteenth century and today, average annual global temperatures have increased by more than one degree Fahrenheit (Figure 19.6).

Forecasting future trends regarding greenhouse gas emissions, temperature increases, and other climate changes is difficult since it requires accurate forecasts of future population and economic growth, exact estimates for the development of new energy and pollution-abatement technologies, and accurate models that capture all the ways in which higher levels of greenhouse gases will affect the climate. As a result, there is a great deal of uncertainty about what the future will bring. There is also the possibility of unforeseen catastrophic and/or irreversible events if ecosystems reach "tipping points." In addition, the impact of climate change will undoubtedly be felt unevenly across the globe. Some areas may see greater changes in temperatures and more extreme weather events than in other places. Also, the rises in sea levels will be experienced far from the melting ice sheets.

Based on current models, there is a substantial probability that in 100 years' time the average temperature could be 4°C or (over 7°F) warmer, or more, than it is now. This would lead to the disappearance of glaciers and ice caps; to more extreme weather events, such as droughts and hurricanes; to rising sea levels and flooding; to the risk of more rapid species extinction; and to the risk of the spread of infectious diseases.[38]

FIGURE 19.5 Atmospheric CO$_2$ and Worldwide Fossil Fuel Carbon Emissions, 1750–2013

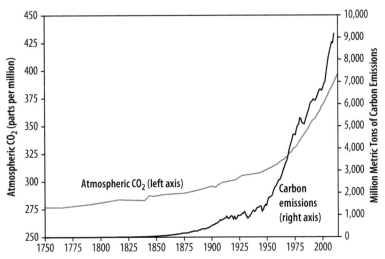

Sources and Notes: Carbon emissions computed from Tom Boden, Bob Andres, and Gregg Marland, "Global CO$_2$ Emissions from Fossil-Fuel Burning, Cement Manufacture, and Gas Flaring: 1751–2011," U.S. Department of Energy, Carbon Dioxide Information Analysis Center, http://cdiac.ornl.gov/ftp/ndp030/global.1751_2011.ems (accessed: January 24, 2016). Atmospheric concentrations of CO$_2$ for the years 1744–1953 are from Albrecht Neftel et al., *Historical CO$_2$ Record from the Siple Station Ice Core*, U.S. Department of Energy, Carbon Dioxide Information Analysis Center, http://cdiac.ornl.gov/ftp/trends/co2/siple2.013 (accessed: January 24, 2016). The estimates reported above are interpolated between benchmark years. Annual data from 1959 from U.S. Department of Commerce, National Oceanic and Atmospheric Administration, "Trends in Atmospheric Carbon Dioxide," ftp://aftp.cmdl.noaa.gov/products/trends/co2/co2_annmean_mlo.txt (accessed: January 24, 2016).

FIGURE 19.6 Global Land and Ocean Temperatures: Annual Averages, 1880–2015

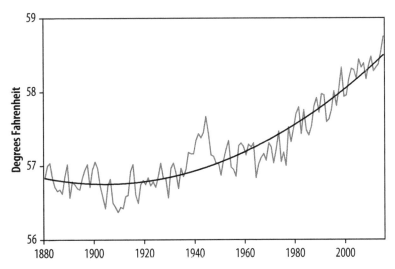

Source: National Aeronautics and Space Administration, Goddard Institute for Space Studies (NASA GISS), http://data.giss.nasa.gov/gistemp/tabledata_v3/GLB.Ts+dSST.txt (accessed: April 4, 2016). The jagged line represents the actual temperatures from NASA, while the smooth line is a fitted long-run trend.

The goal of the United Nations International Panel on Climate Change (UNIPCC) is for average annual global temperatures to increase no more than 2 degrees Celsius in excess of preindustrial levels. Thus far, global temperatures have increased about 0.85 degrees Celsius, with about two-thirds of that increase since the mid-1970s. Although projections are uncertain, to achieve this temperature goal would likely require a worldwide reduction in annual greenhouse gas emissions of between 40 percent and 70 percent by 2050.

While many scholars believe that this goal is achievable and would not substantially weaken the world economy, there are many large obstacles. First, because greenhouse gases emitted in any one country affect the global atmosphere, the damage is spread around the world. If any one country reduces emissions of greenhouse gases, it incurs the costs of doing so, but the benefits are distributed globally. In purely economic terms, it is therefore in the interest of any one country to take no action, while reaping the benefits of action taken by any other countries. That is, there is a classic free-rider problem at work. As a result, international cooperation is critically important, though difficult to achieve. There is not yet a sufficiently strong institutional framework among countries to make this happen.

Second, there is disagreement between industrialized nations (such as the United States and countries in the European Union) and currently developing countries. Emerging nations argue that they should be able to grow, just as the West did in the past, by relying on coal, petroleum, and natural gas. China, India, and Mexico, for example, are experiencing economic growth that is dependent upon burning fossil fuels. Since 1990, carbon emissions have been flat or declining in many industrialized countries, but have increased dramatically in large, emerging economies like China, which now leads the world in emissions each year (although the United States has remained the world leader in cumulative emissions since industrialization began).

Third, along with geopolitical obstacles, there are also political challenges within the United States. The partisan politics in Congress, and continuing debates about the reality, causes, and consequences of global climate change, make dramatic action unlikely.

Further contributing to the problem in the United States (and elsewhere) is the fact that global climate change is largely unobservable. While we observe day-to-day fluctuations in the weather, long-term changes in the climate are more subtle—they are not as dramatic as raw sewage dumped into rivers or black smoke spewing from smokestacks. The pressure of public opinion on politics may be more difficult to muster in the case of global climate change, but there are encouraging signs that concerted actions through international cooperation may be possible.

Finally, because carbon dioxide, in particular, remains in the atmosphere for centuries, costs incurred now in reducing the emissions of greenhouse gases will not produce a solution for a long time. With environmental issues such as global climate change, there is an inherent tradeoff between the present and the future, and the choice of the discount rate is critically important. Many of the effects of current emissions, and likewise the effect of policy decisions, will be realized only in the distant future. Assessing how to value the benefits to future generations and the appropriate sacrifices that should be made today is inherently problematic.

One of the big questions is what discount rate to choose—that is, how should we as a society (and as citizens of the world) trade off the present versus the future? Some advocate a zero discount rate, implying that all generations, present and future, should be treated identically in terms of costs and benefits. The problem with a zero discount rate, however, is that almost all of us discount the future in our everyday lives: a million dollars today is worth far more to us than a million dollars received 30 years from now. The higher the discount rate, however, the less we are willing to spend today to avoid a given amount of environmental damage in the future.

There is a natural level of "depreciation" in the stock of greenhouse gases—if we produced no further emissions at all, the present amount in the atmosphere would gradually dwindle. There are therefore two ways to reduce greenhouse gas concentrations in the atmosphere. First, emissions could be cut below the natural level of depreciation by using cleaner energy sources, driving less, and so on. This would mean a very drastic reduction in annual emissions, since the depreciation rate of carbon dioxide is very low. Second, we may still be able to reduce emissions of carbon dioxide without such drastic changes in human behavior. One potential method is carbon capture, in which the carbon dioxide is collected directly after the fossil fuel is burned, by taking it from the exhaust flue and pumping it directly into an empty geological formation underground, such as a depleted oil or gas field.[39] While this is not yet a feasible solution, there is hope that it may become possible and cost-effective in the near future.

LOSS OF BIODIVERSITY

While extinctions of plant and animal species are a normal part of the process of life on Earth, there is increasing evidence that humans are contributing to rising rates of extinction and to large losses in the populations of plants and animals.[40] Recent evidence suggests that "current rates of extinction are about 1,000 times the likely background [normal] rate of extinction."[41] Not only are rates of extinction alarmingly high, but the populations of almost all plants and animals have decreased substantially in recent decades. One study estimates that between 1970 and 2010 world populations of fish, birds, mammals, amphibians, and reptiles fell by 52 percent due to the loss of natural habitats, climate change, and hunting and fishing.[42]

GROUNDWATER SUPPLIES

Another very serious common-resource problem is groundwater depletion in the United States and in many other parts of the world. While groundwater depletion has been a serious concern in the High Plains (which includes the Ogallala aquifer) and the Southwest for a long time, increased demands on groundwater resources have overstressed groundwater basins in many parts of the country, and not just in the most arid regions.[43] Groundwater supplies about 50 percent of all drinking water in the United States, and almost all drinking water in rural areas.[44]

With climate change and increasing drought, it is likely that both surface water supplies and groundwater supplies will be under increasing stress, not only in the United States but also in many other parts of the world. According to the United Nations, already 1.2 billion people worldwide suffer from severe water shortages, and this number is expected to rise to 1.7 billion over the next decade, in part because of climate change.[45]

As ground and surface water becomes more scarce and as the price for water increases, changes in individual behavior on the part of households and farmers, together with technological innovations, may prove sufficient to remedy the problems in the United States and elsewhere.

Almost 97 percent of all the water on Earth is salt water in the oceans, and about half of the world's population lives within 65 miles of an ocean.[46] One possible solution is to convert saltwater to freshwater through a process called desalinization. While this process is still expensive, reverse osmosis, in which saltwater is forced through membranes under high pressure, has lowered costs and made the process more efficient. In 2015, a $1 billion plant near San Diego opened, and there are dozens of such plants already in operation in Israel and other parts of the Middle East.[47]

19.4   CONCLUSIONS

Industrialization and economic growth led to environmental problems, particularly prior to 1970. Although environmental regulation and conservation has improved many measures of environmental quality in recent decades, atmospheric concentrations of carbon dioxide and other greenhouse gases are continuing to increase and are almost certainly contributing to global climate change. At the time of writing, countries have not been able to agree on or enforce meaningful limitations on the emissions of greenhouse gases.

QUESTIONS

1. Describe environmental policies in the nineteenth century, and compare and contrast them with those introduced in 1970 and later in the twentieth century. Why do you suspect that government has become so much more involved in environmental issues in recent decades?

2. Suppose that you are indifferent between receiving $100,000 today and $300,000 20 years from now. What is your personal discount rate? Intuitively explain what this number means. *Hint*: Recall from Chapter 2 that. $X_0 (1 + g_x)^t = X_t$. In this case, g_x is the discount rate.

3. In 2014, there were three reported disputes between passengers on commercial airplanes over the rights to recline airplane seats, which caused these airplanes to be diverted.[48] In one instance, a passenger installed a $21.95 Knee Defender, which prevented the person in front of him from reclining his airline seat. In 2011, prior to these incidents, one journalist wrote that the economics of seat reclining "is a straightforward application of the Coase theorem."[49] What is the Coase Theorem, and why do you suspect it failed to hold in these disputes?

4. Suppose that fishing has caused a certain species of fish to be threatened with extinction. After banning fishing for many years, the fish population has rebounded. Now the government is proposing to introduce a system of tradeable fishing permits, which would entitle the holder of each permit to catch a given number of fish each year. Explain how uncontrolled fishing led to a negative externality problem and how a system of tradeable fishing permits can potentially overcome the inefficiency caused by this negative externality.

5. What is the environmental Kuznets curve (EKC) and what leads to its shape? Why is it more likely to be observed for local pollutants and less likely to be observed for global pollutants?

NOTES

[1] U.S. Environmental Protection Agency, www3.epa.gov/airtrends/images/y70_13.png (accessed: April 14, 2015). The six common pollutants are particulate matter, carbon monoxide, nitrogen oxide, sulfur dioxide, lead, and ozone.

[2] U.S. Environmental Protection Agency, www3.epa.gov/climatechange/ghgemissions/gases/co2.html (accessed: April 16, 2015).

[3] See Figure 19.5.

[4] Stephen Smith, *Environmental Economics: A Very Short Introduction* (New York, NY: Oxford University Press, 2011), 27.

[5] Lawrence H. Goulder, "Markets for Pollution Allowances: What are the (New) Lessons?" *Journal of Economic Perspectives* 27, no. 1 (Winter 2013), 87–102.

[6] Richard G. Lipsey and Kelvin Lancaster, "The General Theory of Second Best," *Review of Economic Studies* 24, no. 1 (January 1956), 12.

[7] Soumyananda Dinda, "Environmental Kuznets Curve Hypothesis: A Survey," *Ecological Economics* 49, no. 1 (August 2004), 431–455.

[8] Dinda, 431.

[9] John A. List and Craig A. Gallet, "The Environmental Kuznets Curve: Does One Size Fit All?" *Ecological Economics* 31, no. 3 (December 1999). The authors examine U.S. states from 1929 to 1994 and find evidence of an EKC, although the income levels at which emissions start to fall varies by state.

[10] Richard L. Andrews, *Managing the Environment, Managing Ourselves: A History of American Environmental Policy* (New Haven, CT: Yale University Press, 2006).

[11] Jacqueline Vaughn, *Environmental Politics: Domestic and Global Dimensions*, Fifth Edition (New York, NY: Wadsworth, 2007).

[12] Sara R. Rinfret and Michelle C. Pautz, *U.S. Environmental Policy in Action: Practice and Implementation* (New York, NY: Palgrave Macmillan, 2014), 16.

[13] See the Sierra Club website for many of John Muir's articles and books: http://vault.sierraclub.org/john_muir_exhibit/writings/ (accessed: November 16, 2015).

[14] Denise D. Fort and Christopher Vigil, "Water and Waterways," in Sally K. Fairfax and Edmund Russell (eds.), *Guide to U.S. Environmental Policy* (Thousand Oaks, CA: Sage Publications, 2014), 133.

[15] United States Department of Agriculture, *U.S. Forest Resource Facts and Historical Trends* (Washington, DC: Government Printing Office, August 2014), 7, www.fia.fs.fed.us/library/brochures/docs/2012/ForestFacts_1952-2012_English.pdf (accessed: June 22, 2016).

[16] U.S. National Park Service, "Theodore Roosevelt and Conservation," www.nps.gov/thro/learn/historyculture/theodore-roosevelt-and-conservation.htm (accessed: November 20, 2015).

[17] Neil M. Maher, *Nature's New Deal: The Civilian Conservation Corps* (New York, NY: Oxford University Press, 2008), 3–4.

[18] Marcos Luna, *The Environment Since 1945* (New York, NY: Facts on File, 2012), 1.

[19] Louise Nelson Dyble, "Urbanization and Land Use: Issues and Policies (1700s–Present)", in Sally K. Fairfax and Edmund Russell (eds.), *Guide to U.S. Environmental Policy* (Thousand Oaks, CA: Sage Publications, 2014), 106.

[20] Fort and Vigil, 121–123.

[21] Earth Day Network, "Earth Day: The History of a Movement," www.earthday.org/earth-day-history-movement (accessed: December 2, 2015).

[22] For a history of the Environmental Protection Agency, see www2.epa.gov/aboutepa/epa-history (accessed: December 2, 2015).

[23] Matthew Cahn and Rhea Mac, "The States and the Environment: History, Responsibilities, and Policies (1770s–Present)", in Sally K. Fairfax and Edmund Russell (eds.), *Guide to U.S. Environmental Policy* (Thousand Oaks, CA: Sage Publications, 2014), 168.

[24] Cahn and Mac, 168.

[25] Luna, 412.

[26] Luna, 413.

[27] See the U.S. Environmental Protection Agency (EPA) for more information on acid rain, www3.epa.gov/acidrain/reducing/index.html (accessed: December 4, 2015).

[28] The U.S. National Aeronautics and Space Administration (NASA) maintains a daily "Ozone Watch" website, http://ozonewatch.gsfc.nasa.gov/ (accessed: December 4, 2015). For annual data, see http://ozonewatch.gsfc.nasa.gov/statistics/annual_data.html (accessed December 4, 2015).

[29] Luna, 223.

[30] Luna, 219.

[31] EPA, "Superfund: National Priorities List (NPL)," www2.epa.gov/superfund/superfund-national-priorities-list-npl (accessed: June 22, 2016).

[32] EPA.

[33] Jonathan Cowie, *Climate Change: Biological and Human Aspects*, Second Edition (New York, NY: Cambridge University Press, 2013), 5–8.

[34] John Cook, Dana Nuccitelli, Sarah A. Green, Mark Richardson, Barbel Winkler, Rob Painting, Robert Way, Peter Jacobs, and Andrew Skuce, "Quantifying the Consensus on Anthropogenic Global Warning in the Scientific Literature," *Environmental Research Letters* 8, no. 2 (May 2013), 1–7.

[35] Smith, 94.

[36] See Cowie, 253–257, for a discussion of other greenhouse gases.

[37] Nicholas Stern, "The Structure of Economic Modeling of the Potential Impacts of Climate Change: Grafting Gross Underestimation of Risk onto Already Narrow Science Models," *Journal of Economic Literature* 51, no. 3 (September 2013), 840.

[38] Stern, 839–841.

[39] Smith, 472–476.

[40] See *Science* 344, no. 6187 (May 30, 2014) for several articles on the extinctions and falling populations of plant and animal life worldwide.

[41] S.L. Pimm et al., "The Biodiversity of Species and Their Rates of Extinction, Distribution, and Protection," *Science* 344, no. 6187 (May 30, 2014), 988.

[42] World Wildlife Fund, *Living Planet Report 2014*, wwf.panda.org/about_our_earth/all_publications/living_planet_report/ (accessed: December 9, 2015).

[43] United States Geological Survey (USGS), "Groundwater Depletion," http://water.usgs.gov/edu/gwdepletion.html (accessed: December 12, 2015).

[44] USGS.

[45] United Nations, www.un.org/waterforlifedecade/scarcity.shtml (accessed: December 10, 2015).

[46] USGS, http://water.usgs.gov/edu/earthhowmuch.html (accessed: December 14, 2015).

[47] Justin Gillis, "For California in Drought, California Looks Warily to Sea," *New York Times* (April 11, 2015), www.nytimes.com/2015/04/12/science/drinking-seawater-looks-ever-more-palatable-to-californians.html?_r=0 (accessed: December 14, 2015).

[48] CNN, "Seat Recline Fight Diverts Another Flight," September 3, 2014, www.cnn.com/2014/09/02/travel/airline-seat-recline-diversion/ (accessed: January 15, 2015).

[49] Josh Barro, "Coase in Flight," *National Review Online* (July 29, 2011), www.nationalreview.com/agenda/273163/coase-flight-josh-barro (accessed: January 15, 2015).

20

Social Spending and the Welfare State

People in all societies face uncertainties caused by unemployment, illness, disability, old age, and the risks of injury and death. Social spending refers to spending "with a social purpose" and it encompasses both privately provided and publicly provided benefits.[1] There are several ways of categorizing social spending. One way to organize such spending is by where it is targeted: at old age, survivors, disability, health, unemployment, housing, and early childhood education.[2]

Another way of classifying social spending is to distinguish between social assistance and social insurance. Eligibility for social assistance or "welfare" programs usually depends on income and assets. That is, only those below a certain threshold (i.e., "the poor") qualify for benefits, so social assistance is usually "means-tested." Social insurance, on the other hand, is designed to prevent people from falling into poverty, and is intended to offset income losses from specific events (such as unemployment, poor health, or old age). With social insurance, individuals contribute in the form of taxes when working (those contributions often being matched by taxes levied on employers) and benefits are received only if the triggering event occurs. With social insurance, recipients do not have to be poor to receive benefits. For example, even the very rich get a Social Security check every month after reaching retirement age, provided they are eligible (by virtue of having worked and contributed to the system for 40 quarters or 10 years).

Finally, we can distinguish between cash and in-kind programs. With in-kind programs, specific goods or services are provided to recipients, as occurs with school lunch programs, food stamps, housing subsidies, and medical care for the poor. In the United States, most social assistance is in the form of in-kind benefits. In contrast, cash benefits provide cash payments to recipients who can then do what they wish with the money received. For example, a person who receives a Social Security check can spend the money with the same freedom as money earned from work. Most social insurance programs pay cash rather than in-kind benefits, whereas a larger proportion of social assistance comes in the form of in-kind benefits.

Standard consumer choice theory shows that, from the perspective of the recipient, cash benefits will always be preferred to the equal dollar value of in-kind benefits (such as food), because cash can always be used to buy food, but the recipient will likely gain greater utility by purchasing a somewhat different basket of goods and services than the basket chosen for them by government. The reason why the majority of social assistance programs provide in-kind benefits instead of cash has to do with paternalism and the fear that recipients may not use the proceeds wisely. Since most social assistance programs are aimed at children, in-kind benefits do ensure that children are receiving food and medical care.

Social spending in the United States increased most dramatically during two episodes: the New Deal of the 1930s and the "War on Poverty" that started in 1964. The centerpiece of social spending legislation during the New Deal was the Social Security Act (1935), which was a combination of both social assistance and social insurance. It provided old-age assistance and insurance, unemployment insurance, aid to dependent children, grants for maternal health and public health, and aid to the blind. The most notable programs during the War on Poverty were in the form of health insurance for the elderly (Medicare, 1965), and for the poor (Medicaid, 1965), although the War on Poverty also encompassed a broad range of policies focused on childhood education, housing, job training, and food assistance programs.

It is widely believed that the modern "welfare state" encourages dependence and reduces productivity and economic growth. Recent scholarship, however, shows that social spending is not associated with lower levels of real GDP per capita or with lower rates of economic growth. In addition, while some programs have not had their intended effects, government programs overall have certainly reduced poverty and economic hardship. A balanced assessment of the history of social assistance and social insurance in the United States is therefore a story both of policy successes and of policy failures.

20.1 SOCIAL ASSISTANCE PROGRAMS

When the English arrived in the New World, they brought with them many customs and institutions, including the English "Poor Laws." The first colonial poor laws were modeled after the English Poor Law of 1601.[3] Following the English tradition, providing for the poor in the colonies was a local responsibility, with taxes collected to transfer to the destitute. Township officials had considerable leeway in discriminating between the "worthy" poor (typically orphans, widows, the disabled, and the elderly) and the "unworthy" poor (those considered to be drunkards, shiftless, or lazy). Officials also determined the eligibility, level, and type of support provided.

POORHOUSES AND OUTDOOR RELIEF

During most of the nineteenth century, relative land abundance, labor scarcity, and the availability of work "encouraged a harsh and suspicious view of the poor ... [where] there was little tolerance for the able-bodied pauper."[4] As a result, the amount of private and public spending on the poor was very low, and the conditions of relief were often harsh and humiliating to discourage dependence.

Prior to the New Deal of the 1930s, the most common ways of providing for the poor were poorhouses and "outdoor relief." A poorhouse or "indoor relief" was a government-run facility, usually operated by a county or a municipality, which provided housing and support for the needy in exchange for work. Outdoor relief, in contrast, provided cash and in-kind benefits to the poor and allowed them to receive aid outside the poorhouses—hence the name: "outdoor relief."

In the United States, many poorhouses were intended to be working farms that produced agricultural products. In practice, however, the bleak conditions of most poorhouses meant that it was only the most desperate and needy who sought help there, with the result that the occupants of poorhouses were often too old, too sick, or too disabled to produce much output. The "fear of the poorhouse became the key to sustaining the work ethic in nineteenth century America."[5]

Table 20.1 shows the percentages of the New York population in poorhouses and the percentages receiving outdoor relief from 1840 to 1890. It also shows the relative percentages of spending on each type of poor relief. With the exception of 1860, at least 60 percent of poor relief expenditures went to poorhouse or indoor relief. The relative prevalence of outdoor relief in 1860 stemmed from two developments. First, by the 1850s, the conditions of New York poorhouses were overcrowded and unhealthy—a state report showed that one county poorhouse, which had averaged 137 residents in the previous year, reported 36 deaths, "yet none of them from epidemic or contagious disease," but instead the culprit was "most inexcusable negligence."[6] Second, although many felt that outdoor relief made things too easy on the poor, it was relatively expensive to build and operate poorhouses, and it was far easier to dispense cash or provide in-kind benefits through outdoor relief. As a result, there was a mix during the nineteenth century of relief through poorhouses and through cash and in-kind benefits.

TABLE 20.1 Percentage of Population Receiving Relief and Percentage of Poor Relief Expenditures for Outdoor Relief and Poorhouses: New York State, 1840–1890

Year	Outdoor Relief		Poorhouses	
	Percentage of Population	Percentage of Expenditures	Percentage of Population	Percentage of Expenditures
1840	0.49%	31%	0.59%	69%
1850	2.06%	39%	1.20%	61%
1860	4.49%	60%	1.01%	40%
1870	1.27%	36%	1.46%	64%
1880	1.39%	30%	1.77%	70%
1890	0.79%	19%	1.00%	81%

Sources and Notes: Numbers of individuals receiving relief and expenditures are from Michael B. Katz, *In the Shadow of the Poorhouse: A Social History of Welfare in America*, Tenth Anniversary Edition (New York: NY, Basic Books, 1996), Table 2.1, 38. New York population is from U.S. Bureau of the Census, *2000 Census of Population and Housing: New York* (September 2003), Table 1, 1, www.census.gov/prod/cen2000/phc-3-34.pdf (accessed: September 25, 2015).

In the United States as a whole, government spent only 0.13 percent of GDP on the poor in 1850, compared to more than 4 percent today.[7] In no year prior to the Great Depression did government poor relief exceed 0.2 percent of GDP.[8] There was also very little spending by churches and private charities on the poor. During the 1920s, "government aid to the poor was still only one-sixth of one percent of national product, [and] private charity to the poor was about the same."⁹ While comprehensive figures on private spending on the poor do not exist before the 1920s, evidence suggests that private and religious philanthropy aimed at the poor "has always been negligible."¹⁰

There is a belief that the increase in government spending on the poor after the New Deal "crowded out" spending by churches and private charities, but this view is inconsistent with the evidence. The rise of government spending on the poor was not associated with a decrease in private spending. Private spending as a share of GDP actually rose slightly over the twentieth century, but it has always been well below one-half of 1 percent of GDP.¹¹ In short, there is no indication that public welfare spending crowded out private spending; and even if crowding out had occurred, it would have had little impact because there has always been very little private spending on the poor to crowd out.

AID TO FAMILIES WITH DEPENDENT CHILDREN

Although state and local governments have long provided some help for the needy, supplementing church and other voluntary programs, the federal government took the lead during the Great Depression with the New Deal. The severity of the Great Depression delivered the lesson that anyone "could lose their jobs, lose asset values, or both."¹² The widespread fear that "that could be me" increased public support for legislation to reduce the risks and uncertainties associated with events beyond an individual's control.

Many New Deal programs borrowed from preexisting programs that were already in operation in various U.S. states and expanded those programs nationwide. Perhaps the most important piece of legislation during the New Deal was the Social Security Act (1935). It consisted of many different social assistance and social insurance programs (discussed later in the chapter), but in particular Title IV of the Act established Aid to Dependent Children (ADC). Initially, the program mainly provided federal grants to help states maintain their mothers' aid laws, which 40 states had passed between 1910 and 1920.¹³ The federal government provided about one-third of the costs to offer aid to mothers caring for children without a husband.¹⁴

Federal matching grants were soon increased, and typically paid for between one-half and three-quarters of the program, depending on each state's per capita income. State governments maintained substantial control of the program, however, since it was administered mostly at the state level. States also had considerable leeway in determining benefit levels and eligibility rules.

Originally the program provided aid to needy children who lived with single mothers, but in 1962 the name was changed to Aid to Families with Dependent Children (AFDC), and the rules were changed so that states were allowed to provide aid to two-parent families in which the father was unemployed. This change in the law allowed many more poor children to become eligible for benefits. In 1961, fewer than 15 percent of poor children in the United States received ADC benefits; by 1973, almost 80 percent of poor children were receiving AFDC benefits (Figure 20.1).

As well as including two-parent families with an unemployed father, AFDC caseloads grew for other reasons too. In 1965, there were fewer than 1 million families receiving AFDC benefits; by early 1993, over 5 million families, or 15 percent of all American families with children, were receiving AFDC benefits. One cause for the increase was an effort during the Civil Rights Era to end the practice of wrongly

FIGURE 20.1 Cash Assistance to Child Recipients as a Percentage of All Poor Children, 1961–2012

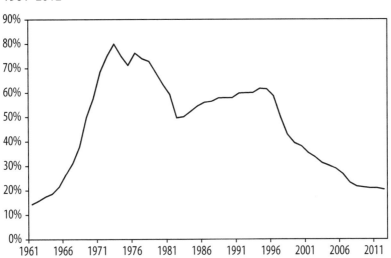

Sources and Notes: U.S. House of Representatives, Committee on Ways and Means, 2014 Greenbook, Table 7.9, http://greenbook.waysandmeans.house.gov/2014-green-book (accessed: October 2, 2015).

denying benefits to eligible black and Hispanic families. The National Welfare Rights Organization, a group led by welfare recipients and social workers, brought poor families to welfare offices to demand aid and to put pressure on program administrators to treat all applicants fairly.[15]

Another important reason for the increase in caseloads was a dramatic increase in the number of single-parent families headed by unmarried mothers.[16] In 1965, 3.1 percent of white infants and 24.1 percent of black infants were born to single mothers. By 1990, the rates had risen to 28 percent of all births, including 18 percent for whites and 64 percent for blacks.[17]

Many commentators believed that the generosity of AFDC was contributing to the rise in out-of-wedlock births, and AFDC increasingly became a target of criticism.[18] It was argued that AFDC also fostered a culture of dependency and discouraged work. Many subsequent studies, however, showed only a small effect of AFDC on single motherhood.[19]

The AFDC program, however, did discourage work. Before 1968, AFDC benefits were reduced by one dollar for every dollar in income from other sources, implying a marginal tax rate of 100 percent.[20] In 1968, the law was changed to lower the effective marginal tax rate on earnings, but in 1981, Congress again changed the rules. After four months' work in any given year, AFDC payments decreased dollar-for-dollar with earned income, except for the first $75 earned each month. There was also an allowance to exempt childcare expenses.[21] Tales of widespread fraud and of "welfare queens" living large on cash benefits also undermined public support for AFDC as many Americans came to believe that the program was a failure. By the 1990s, the War on Poverty, as one scholar put it, had become the "War on Welfare."[22]

The Secretary of Health and Human Services had long had the authority to grant states waivers from federal welfare requirements if a state proposed an experimental or pilot program, but few waivers were issued before the early 1990s.[23] By 1996, however, 27 states had received waivers.[24] Some of these waivers allowed individuals in those states to earn more money in the labor market without seeing large declines in benefits, while other state programs imposed work requirements and limited the time for which a recipient could receive benefits. Many of the features introduced at the state level became part of the federal welfare reform bill in 1996.

TEMPORARY ASSISTANCE FOR NEEDY FAMILIES

The Personal Responsibility and Work Opportunity Reconciliation Act (1996) promised to "end welfare as we know it" by replacing AFDC with Temporary Assistance for Needy Families (TANF).[25] TANF represented a significant change in welfare policy in the United States. First, it replaced federal matching grants with block grants (grants of a fixed amount of money). In fact, since 1996, the total federal block grant to U.S. states has remained fixed at $16.5 billion each year. Because of inflation, by 2015 the real value of the annual federal block grant had fallen by one-third.[26]

TANF also gave states considerably more discretion in determining both the eligibility of needy families and the benefits and services those families should receive. Perhaps the most important change, however, was the focus on moving individuals from welfare to work, with states designing and operating welfare-to-work programs.

The law also allowed states to set their own time limits on how long families can receive benefits, although it stipulated that states cannot provide cash assistance from federal TANF funds for longer than 60 months to any family that includes an adult recipient. In 2015, most states had a 60-month time limit for eligibility of TANF funds, but about one-third of states had a shorter time limit.[27] The law also allowed states to extend time limits beyond 60 months for up to 20 percent of their caseloads in hardship cases.

The discretion given to states with TANF has resulted in sizeable variations in benefits between states. In 2013, the average TANF monthly benefit for a single-parent family of three was $923 in Alaska and $789 in New York, but only $170 in Mississippi and $185 in Tennessee.[28] TANF has substantially reduced the number of people receiving cash assistance. Caseloads peaked in March 1994 with 5.1 million families receiving benefits. Although the decrease in caseloads preceded TANF, they continued to fall to only 1.7 million families by December 2013.[29]

The inflation-adjusted value of monthly benefits has also declined markedly nationwide. In 1980, the average monthly maximum benefit for a family of three was $763 (in 2012 dollars). By 2012, it had fallen to $427, a decrease of 44 percent.[30]

Figure 20.1 shows the percentage of poor children in the United States whose families received cash assistance (AFDC from 1961 to 1996, and TANF from 1997 to 2012). It is evident that changing state policies in the early 1990s, along with TANF in 1996, led to a large reduction in the percentage of children receiving assistance. In the mid-1990s, more than 60 percent of poor children received AFDC benefits; but by 2013, barely 20 percent of poor children received TANF benefits.

While TANF has been very effective at getting people off of welfare, it has done so mostly by reducing the proportion of poor families eligible for the program. After TANF was introduced, the employment rate of never-married mothers with a high school education or less increased from 63 percent to a high of 76 percent in 2000, but by 2013 it was at about the same level as in 1996.[31] In addition, the increase in the share of single mothers employed was mostly due to a strong economy (with the aggregate unemployment rate falling to below 4 percent by 2000) and the increase in the Earned Income Tax Credit (EITC), and was not primarily the result of welfare reform.[32]

SUPPLEMENTAL SECURITY INCOME

Another federal program that provides cash benefits is the Supplemental Security Income (SSI) program, which provides funds to low-income aged, blind, and permanently disabled individuals. This program was created by the 1972 Social Security Act Amendments, which combined three existing programs into SSI: Old Age Assistance (OAA), Aid to the Blind (AB), and Aid to the Permanently and Totally Disabled (APTD). Although SSI is less well known than TANF, cash expenditures for SSI exceed TANF expenditures. In 2014, SSI totaled more than $51 billion, compared to less than $32 billion for TANF (Table 20.2).

There are several reasons why SSI is now larger than TANF. In 1984, eligibility requirements for SSI were liberalized and more individuals became eligible for the program. Shifting recipients from welfare rolls to SSI is also beneficial for states, since

TABLE 20.2 Major Social Assistance Programs

Program	Year(s) Enacted	2014 Outlays (Billions of Dollars)	2014 Outlays (Percentage of GDP)
Cash Benefits			
Aid to Families with Dependent Children (AFDC)/Temporary Assistance for Needy Families (TANF)	1935/1996	$31.65 billion	0.18%
Supplemental Security Income (SSI)	1972	$51.36 billion	0.30%
Earned Income Tax Credit (EITC)	1975	$60.09 billion	0.35%
In-Kind Benefits			
Medicaid	1965	$449.40 billion	2.59%
Food Stamps/Supplemental Nutrition Assistance Program (SNAP)	1964/1998	$74.16 billion	0.43%
National School Lunch/Breakfast Program	1946/1966	$16.35 billion	0.09%
Housing Assistance	1937	$51.30 billion	0.30%
Head Start School Readiness	1965	$8.60 billion	0.05%
TOTAL		$742.91 billion	4.28%

Sources and Notes: Temporary Assistance for Needy Families (TANF) from U.S. Congressional Budget Office, www.cbo.gov/sites/default/files/114th-congress-2015-2016/reports/49887-TANF_DataUnderlyingFigures_0.xlsx. Supplemental Security Income (SSI) and Earned Income Tax Credit (EITC) from U.S. Office of Management and Budget, Historical Tables, Table 8.5, www.whitehouse.gov/sites/default/files/omb/budget/fy2016/assets/hist08z5.xls. Medicaid from U.S. Centers for Medicare and Medicaid, www.cms.gov/research-statistics-data-and-systems/statistics-trends-and-reports/nationalhealthexpenddata/nhe-fact-sheet.html. National School Lunch Program and the Supplemental Nutrition Assistance Program from U.S. Department of Agriculture, www.fns.usda.gov/sites/default/files/pd/cncost.pdf, and www.fns.usda.gov/sites/default/files/pd/SNAPsummary.xls. Housing Assistance from Congressional Budget Office, Federal Housing Assistance for Low-Income Households (Washington, DC, September 2015), data for Figure 2, 9, www.cbo.gov/publication/50782. Head Start from U.S. Department of Health and Human Services, Early Childhood Learning & Knowledge Center, "Head Start Program Facts: Fiscal Year 2014," http://eclkc.ohs.acf.hhs.gov/hslc/data/factsheets/docs/hs-program-fact-sheet-2014.pdf. Nominal GDP from U.S. Bureau of Economic Analysis, www.bea.gov/national/xls/gdplev.xls. Columns may not sum exactly due to rounding. (All data accessed: September 22, 2015.)

SSI is paid for entirely by the federal government, while TANF payments are only partially funded by the federal government through block grants. In addition, any savings under TANF can be kept by the states, which gives states an incentive to reduce the number of TANF recipients. Finally, recipients may prefer SSI because, unlike TANF, it is not subject to work requirements and time limits. There is evidence that during the 1990s, female-headed households living in U.S. states with more aggressive welfare reform were more likely to be receiving SSI benefits.[33] While TANF caseloads dropped dramatically after the mid-1990s, some of those leaving TANF moved to the SSI program.

Research also indicates that because the benefit levels are higher, SSI has had a larger effect than AFDC/TANF in reducing poverty. One study showed that SSI reduced the poverty gap 8 percent, compared to only 2.5 percent for AFDC/TANF.[34] Another study found that a child becoming eligible for SSI reduced the probability of the family being in poverty by as much as 11 percentage points.[35]

EARNED INCOME TAX CREDIT

The largest and fastest-growing cash-based social assistance program in the United States is the Earned Income Tax Credit (EITC). Introduced in 1975, it was expanded in 1993 in an effort to increase the incentives for low-skilled workers to stay off welfare. In 2015, the maximum credit was $503 for taxpayers with no children, but as much as $6,242 for taxpayers with three or more children.[36] By 2012, over 28 million families received EITC benefits, compared to 6.2 million at its inception in 1975.[37] During this time, the average tax credit increased from $200 to over $2,300.[38]

The EITC plays an important role in reducing poverty and in improving child and family outcomes. Research has shown that the EITC likely decreases child poverty, improves mental and physical health, decreases the likelihood of low birth weight, leads to higher average birth weights, and is associated with higher student test scores for children in families who receive the EITC.[39]

SUMMARY OF CASH-BASED SOCIAL ASSISTANCE PROGRAMS

As discussed above, the three major cash-benefit, social assistance programs are Temporary Assistance for Needy Families (TANF), Supplemental Security Income (SSI), and the Earned Income Tax Credit (EITC). Among those who are not eligible for these programs, some individuals without children may qualify for General Assistance or General Relief through state and county governments. However, all of these cash-based programs taken together add up to less than 1 percent of GDP. While there are strong feelings and beliefs regarding "welfare," cash benefits are not a major part of government spending or the economy. In the United States today, in-kind benefits cost much more, accounting for over 75 percent of social assistance programs (Table 20.2). In 2014, both cash and in-kind benefits totaled more than 4 percent of GDP.

IN-KIND SOCIAL ASSISTANCE PROGRAMS

In recent decades, the majority of the increases in social assistance spending have been to provide in-kind benefits rather than cash payments. In-kind programs provide health care, food, housing, job training, and early childhood education to individuals and families in need. The largest in-kind program, by far, is Medicaid, which provides medical care for the poor and disabled. It also provides nursing-home care for the elderly with insufficient assets to pay for such care. Medicaid alone accounts for well over half of all cash and in-kind social assistance in the United States.

Medicaid (1965) was part of the "Great Society" programs, established under Title XIX of the Social Security Act. It is a state–federal partnership, financed jointly by federal and state governments. The size of federal "matching" funds depends on state per capita income relative to the national average, with poorer states receiving more federal help, but with at least 50 percent of the program paid for by the federal government in all states.[40]

In 1997, the State Children's Health Insurance Program (S-CHIP) was added under Title XXI of the Social Security Act, which gave states the funding and flexibility to provide greater insurance coverage for children. S-CHIP can be part of a state's Medicaid program or it can be established independently. The federal government pays for at least 65 percent of S-CHIP costs, and a higher percentage than that in poorer states.[41]

While providing medical care is the largest in-kind benefit, nutritional assistance programs are substantial as well. The Supplemental Nutrition Assistance Program or SNAP (1998) replaced the Food Stamp program (1964). In terms of beneficiaries, it is the largest social assistance program in the United States, with over 45 million people receiving benefits in 2015—about 1 in 7 Americans.[42] The value of assistance given to families depends on family income and size. In 2015, participants received $125 per month on average in food assistance. While TANF cash assistance barely budged during or after the Great Recession, the number of Americans receiving SNAP benefits skyrocketed, from 26 million in 2007 to almost 47 million by 2013.[43]

Another nutritional program for poor children is low-cost or free lunches in schools. Providing low-cost lunches to schoolchildren began around 1900 in many American cities, including Philadelphia, Boston, Milwaukee, Cleveland, and Cincinnati.[44] By the 1920s, many municipalities were providing free and subsidized lunches. In 1946, provision of lunches became a nationwide program when President Harry Truman signed the National School Lunch Program Act. A pilot program to provide breakfast was introduced in 1966 and became a permanent program in 1975, while nutritious snacks were added in 1998. Households with incomes up to 130 percent of the federal poverty line are eligible for free meals in school, while those with incomes up to 185 percent of the poverty line are eligible for discounts.[45] In 2015, more than 31 million students received free or subsidized lunches each day in American schools.[46]

Finally, pregnant women, infants, and preschool-aged children who are at risk of inadequate nutrition can receive support under the Special Supplemental Nutrition Program for Women, Infants, and Children (WIC). This program started in 1974 with only 88,000 participants, but it peaked in 2010 at almost 9.2 million participants, before decreasing to 8.3 million by 2014.[47] In 2014, the average monthly food cost per person in this program was about $44.[48]

Substantial government involvement in subsidizing low-income housing began during the New Deal with the U.S. Housing Act (1937). By 1964, more than a quarter century after the Housing Act was passed, only 540,000 public housing units had been completed (about 25,000 a year), which served fewer than 10 percent of the poor families in the United States.[49]

The failures of many public housing projects are well documented. The worst housing projects became "a notorious symbol of failed public policy and architectural hubris."[50] One extreme example is the Pruitt-Igoe housing project in St. Louis, where

33 high-rise, crime-ridden, and vandalized apartment buildings were demolished with explosives in the mid-1970s, only 20 years after they had been built.[51]

In 1965, the Housing and Urban Development Act created the Department of Housing and Urban Development (HUD), a cabinet-level agency in charge of housing policy. This marked the start of a change in housing policy, away from building public housing projects in areas with high poverty rates to giving poor families vouchers to rent privately-owned apartments and houses in a variety of settings. By 1974, housing vouchers were the form of aid given to 17 percent of HUD-assisted households, and this increased steadily to 44 percent by 2008.[52]

The move to housing voucher programs has proved to be more successful than the building of public housing units. Although rent subsidies have not increased the labor-market earnings of recipients, rent vouchers are associated with lower levels of extreme obesity, clinical depression, and anxiety disorders, along with reported increases in subjective happiness.[53] The changes initiated in low-income housing and civil rights legislation likely "contributed to the overall reduction in residential segregation by race that has occurred in the United States since 1970."[54]

Finally, as part of the War on Poverty, Project Head Start was introduced in 1965 with the goal of providing vulnerable preschool children with early childhood education, nutrition, and health, social, and other services to help promote school readiness. Research has shown considerable short-term benefits to young children participating in Head Start programs, but many of the benefits on IQ tests and standardized tests tend to "fade out" during the early elementary school years. Recent evidence suggests that the benefits do not completely fade out, however, and that there are some long-term benefits in adult outcomes from having participated in Head Start. Overall, Head Start "can rightfully be considered a success for much of the past fifty years."[55]

THE GROWTH OF SOCIAL ASSISTANCE SPENDING

Figure 20.2 shows the growth of means-tested social assistance (both cash and in-kind benefits) over more than 50 years. During the 1960s (and before), social assistance was less than 1 percent of GDP. It did not exceed 2 percent of GDP until after the 1990–1991 recession, and it did not surpass 3 percent of GDP until the aftermath of the Great Recession in 2009. Most of the growth in social assistance spending since the 1960s was due to in-kind benefits, particularly medical care for low-income individuals and children. In 2015, cash benefit programs accounted for less than 1 percent of GDP, but more than 3 percent of GDP was devoted to providing in-kind benefits.

Although government spending on social assistance relative to GDP was nearly five times larger in 2015 than it was in 1964, the United States dedicates comparatively less to social assistance than most other advanced economies. Relative to GDP, the U.S. spends only about 30 percent of what is spent, on average, in other OECD countries on "family benefits," which include both cash and in-kind benefits targeted toward children.[56] However, a broader measure that includes total social spending on all groups (children, elderly, disabled, etc.) shows that the U.S. is much closer to the OECD average. In 2014, the United States spent 19.2 percent of GDP on social spending, compared to the OECD average of 21.6 percent.[57]

THE OVERALL EFFECTIVENESS OF SOCIAL ASSISTANCE SPENDING

Given the myriad of programs, policies, and potential effects, it may be impossible to assess all of the positives and negatives of public social assistance. Hundreds of billions

FIGURE 20.2 U.S. Expenditures on Means-Tested Entitlement Programs as a Percentage of GDP, 1962–2015

Sources and Notes: Office of Management and Budget, *Budget of the U.S. Government, Fiscal Year 2016*, Historical Tables, Table 8.4, www.whitehouse.gov/sites/default/files/omb/budget/fy2016/assets/hist08z4.xls (accessed on October 7, 2015).

of dollars are spent on social assistance each year, yet the official poverty rate has not decreased very much in the past 50 years—it was 19 percent in 1964 and in 2014 it had only gone down to 14.8 percent. Many, therefore, have argued that the War on Poverty has been largely a failure.

Others, however, have pointed out that the official poverty rate excludes the value of in-kind benefits and focuses only on pre-tax money income, thereby ignoring the effects of the EITC and other tax credits. Scholars have recently constructed a consumption-based measure of poverty that includes both in-kind benefits and after-tax income.[58] Prior to the Great Society programs, because there were few benefits for the poor and many taxes were regressive, consumption-based poverty rates were higher than the official poverty rates.

Since the War on Poverty, the consumption-based measure of poverty has fallen dramatically, from 30.8 percent in 1960 to only 4.5 percent by 2010.[59] Changes in tax policies, including the Earned Income Tax Credit, the expansion of Social Security (including Medicare and Medicaid), and increases in educational attainment are the most important reasons for the decline in the consumption-based poverty rate, but Food Stamps and the Supplemental Nutrition Assistance Program helped too. While poverty is still a persistent problem, there has likely been far more progress made in "winning the war" than is shown by the official poverty rate.

20.2 PENSIONS AND SOCIAL SECURITY

Retirement pensions for workers in the public sector have a much longer history in the United States than for private-sector workers. Pensions for retired military personnel existed prior to the signing of the U.S. Constitution.[60] Public pensions grew in scale and scope after the Civil War. The Union Army pension program expanded tremendously after the Pension Act of 1890, which provided pensions to all Union Army veterans aged 65 and over who had served for more than 90 days and who had been honorably discharged. While federal retirement pensions for military veterans increased throughout the nineteenth century, employer-provided pensions for other public-sector workers and private-sector workers were not introduced until after the Civil War.

PUBLIC-SECTOR PENSIONS

The first non-military workers to receive retirement pensions were typically teachers, firefighters, and police officers. The New York City Teachers' Retirement Plan was established in 1869, while police officers in New York City began receiving benefits in 1878.[61] Only a few other large cities, however, provided pensions for these groups prior to 1900.[62] During the Progressive Era reforms in the early twentieth century, pensions for public-sector workers became increasingly common. By 1928, pensions for police personnel and firefighters were characterized as "practically universal."[63]

Pension coverage also expanded for teachers and other state and local government employees. In 1911, Massachusetts became the first state to provide retirement for general state employees, but by 1929 only five other states had also done so.[64] Pension benefits for teachers were more widespread, with 21 states providing formal retirement plans by the late 1920s. With the passage of the Federal Employees Retirement Act (1920), pension coverage expanded to include almost all federal workers.

Pensions for other state and local workers increased as well. By 1950, over 60 percent of all state and local employees participated in pension plans (Figure 20.3) and the proportion eligible to participate was even higher. The proportion of participants increased to 85 percent of all state and local government employees by 2010, with eligibility extending to almost 100 percent of all full-time workers.

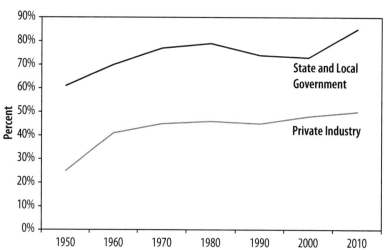

FIGURE 20.3 Retirement Plan Participants as a Percentage of the Workforce, 1950–2010

Sources and Notes: For 1950–1990 data, Employee Benefit Research Institute, "U.S. Retirement Income System," www.ebri.org/pdf/publications/facts/1298fact.pdf (accessed: November 17, 2015). For 1990–2010 data, U.S. Bureau of Labor Statistics, various tables.

PRIVATE-SECTOR PENSIONS

The growth of retirement plans for workers in the private sector, however, grew much more slowly than for public-sector workers. The American Express Company established the first private-sector retirement plan in 1875.[65] During the first three decades of the twentieth century, pension coverage in the private sector remained very low, perhaps covering only 10–12 percent of private-sector employees.[66]

Pension coverage for private-sector workers has always lagged behind coverage for public-sector workers. Figure 20.3 shows the proportion of all employees participating in pension plans for workers in state and local government compared to the proportion for workers in private industry. Private-sector workers have consistently had participation rates at least 20 percentage points lower than public-sector workers in each decade since 1950. In addition, the types of plans usually offered to private-sector workers put more of the risk on the workers themselves.

DEFINED-BENEFIT vs. DEFINED-CONTRIBUTION PLANS

There are two general types of pension plans: defined-benefit (DB) plans and defined-contribution (DC) plans. With DB plans, monthly benefits during retirement are typically calculated using a formula based on years of service and a percentage of the worker's pay while working. For example, with the California Public Employee Retirement System (CalPERS), many workers have a "2 percent at age 60" formula. For example, suppose a worker starts at the age of 23 and retires 37 years later at age 60. During retirement, this worker will receive each year 2 percent multiplied by the worker's years of service (37)—that is, 74 percent of his or her highest annual pay. With DB plans, employees and employers make contributions, and these are invested in various ways in hope that there will be sufficient funds available to make the "defined-benefit" payments. If not, the general taxpayer usually makes up the difference.

In contrast, with DC plans, both the employee and employers make "defined contributions" and the funds become the property of the employee. If the funds are invested wisely and if the employee is fortunate to retire when times are good, then she or he fully realizes these gains. However, because only the contributions are defined, and not the benefits, an employee may retire with insufficient funds for retirement—even if seemingly adequate contributions were made, investments may perform poorly. With DC plans, the money received during retirement is subject to financial market fluctuations (both good and bad), while that risk is eliminated with DB plans.

In recent decades, there has been a change from defined-benefit plans to a far greater prevalence of defined-contribution plans, particularly for private-sector workers but also increasingly common for newly-hired public-sector workers. In 1979, 28 percent of all private-sector workers had a DB plan, 7 percent had a DC plan, and 10 percent had both. By 2011, only 3 percent had a DB plan and 31 percent had a DC plan (11 percent had both available).[67]

SOCIAL SECURITY RETIREMENT BENEFITS

Social Security has long provided vital security for people in old age (Figure 20.4). The Social Security Old-Age, Survivors, and Disability Insurance (OASDI) program provides monthly benefits intended to partially replace the loss of income due to retirement, disability, or death. In 2014, over 59 million Americans (almost one in five Americans)

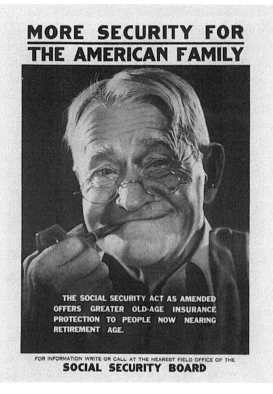

MORE SECURITY FOR THE AMERICAN FAMILY

THE SOCIAL SECURITY ACT AS AMENDED OFFERS GREATER OLD-AGE INSURANCE PROTECTION TO PEOPLE NOW NEARING RETIREMENT AGE.

FOR INFORMATION WRITE OR CALL AT THE NEAREST FIELD OFFICE OF THE
SOCIAL SECURITY BOARD

FIGURE 20.4 Social Security Poster, 1939
Source: Social Security Administration, www.ssa.gov/history/pubaffairs.html (accessed: April 28, 2016).

were receiving benefits of this kind, including almost 42 million retired workers and their families, nearly 11 million disabled workers and their families, and over 6 million survivors of deceased workers.[68] The average retired worker received $1,329 in monthly benefits, while disabled workers received $1,165.[69]

From the very beginning, the OASDI program has been financed largely as a "pay-as-you-go" system. The 1935 Act stipulated payroll tax contributions made by both employers and employees during his or her working life. Payroll tax collections began in 1937 and monthly benefits were to begin in 1942. However, because of Amendments passed in 1939, the first payments occurred in 1940 and were to retirees who had paid very little in payroll taxes.

The potential financing and equity issues with pay-as-you-go transfers are evident from the experiences of Ida May Fuller, the first American to receive Social Security benefits. Ida May worked for three years before retirement and she and her employer paid a total of $24.75 in payroll tax contributions. She received her first Social Security check in January 1940, and by the time she passed away in 1975 at the age of 100, she had received a total of $22,888.92 in Social Security benefits.[70] This was not a bad rate of return on an initial "investment" of less than $25!

With pay-as-you-go, the payroll taxes collected from current employees and employers are mostly transferred to current retirees. During the early decades of Social Security, when there were far more workers than retirees, the burdens on employees and employers were quite modest. In 1940, there were 159.4 workers contributing to Social Security relative to every person collecting old-age benefits, but this ratio fell to 5.1 to 1 by 1960 and to less than 3 to 1 by 2015.[71]

While there has been much discussion about the future of Social Security, with some Americans believing more strongly in UFOs than that Social Security will be around when they retire, the problems facing Social Security are serious, but solvable. Because of changes implemented in 1983, more payroll taxes have been collected than benefits paid out in recent decades, leading to the accumulation of U.S. Treasury securities in the Social Security trust fund. With the continued aging of the American population, however, it has been forecasted that the trust fund will be depleted by 2035. After that, Social Security benefits would not disappear, but would have to rely only on current payroll tax collections, which would only cover about 75 percent of promised benefits.

In 2015, the Social Security Administration estimated that an immediate and modest increase in payroll taxes of 2.68 percentage points (1.34 percent on employees and 1.34 percent on employers), from 12.40 percent to 15.02 percent, would solve the problem until 2089.[72] Other possibilities included an immediate and permanent reduction in benefits of 16.4 percent on all current and future beneficiaries, or a 19.6 percent reduction in benefits applied only to those who became eligible for the first time in 2015 or later.[73] A permanent increase in payroll taxes of 3.9 percentage points (or 1.3 percent of GDP) was projected to fix the problem forever.[74]

While any proposal to increase taxes or decrease benefits has serious distributional implications, the magnitude of the necessary increases in taxes (1.3 percent of GDP) to permanently fix Social Security is far from insurmountable.

20.3 HEALTH CARE

Before the twentieth century, if you got sick, one of three things could happen: you might get better on your own, you might learn to live with your health condition, or you might get worse and possibly die. Medical treatments were often worse than the ailments themselves. As a result, Americans did not spend much of their income on health care and health insurance did not exist.

MODERN HEALTH CARE AND HEALTH INSURANCE

The healthcare industry is a relatively recent phenomenon. Several developments in the late nineteenth and early twentieth centuries helped lay the groundwork for the modern healthcare industry. The acceptance of germ theory and sterile practices, together with reforms in the training of physicians in the United States, led to a change in beliefs, such that "by the 1920s … prospective patients were influenced not only by the hope of healing, but by the image of a new kind of medicine—precise, scientific, and effective."[75]

With rising incomes and increased confidence in the efficacy of medicine, demand for physician and hospital services increased. The American Medical Association was also very effective in raising standards and limiting entry, and in consequence supply failed to keep pace with demand. As a result, Americans started spending more on health care.

Initially, private insurers did not think it would be possible to make money selling health insurance, because of large adverse selection and moral hazard problems. In 1929, however, a group of Dallas school teachers contracted with Baylor University Hospital to provide services to its members for a fixed fee, a plan that later developed into Blue Cross.[76] While Blue Cross provided hospital services, Blue Shield covered visits to physicians and the care they provided.[77]

World War II provided a boost to the health insurance market. Because of wage controls combined with very low rates of unemployment, employers were forced to compete for workers by offering non-wage benefits. One popular non-wage benefit became employer-provided health insurance. The addition in 1965 of Medicare for the elderly and Medicaid for the poor dramatically increased both insurance coverage and the demand for healthcare services.

U.S. HEALTHCARE SPENDING AND HEALTH OUTCOMES

In 1960, per-capita U.S. healthcare spending was only 10 percent above that of other high-income countries.[78] The United States now spends thousands of dollars more per person per year on health care than any other country in the world, yet its life expectancy lags behind all other countries with similar levels of real GDP per capita. In 2013, U.S. life expectancy at birth was 78.8 years, compared to the OECD average of 80.5 years (Figure 20.5). While the United States lags behind the rest of the OECD by almost two years in life expectancy, it spent $8,713 per person on health care in 2013, compared to the OECD average of $3,294 (excluding the United States)—that is, over 2.5 times more than the OECD average. Why does the United States spend so much on health and why do Americans die younger, on average, than the citizens of many other countries?

Scholars have identified several reasons that largely explain why the United States spends so much. First, the U.S. system is highly fragmented, complex, and a hybrid of both private and public spending, with 28 percent of total spending being by households, 26 percent by the federal government, 21 percent by private businesses, 17 percent by state and local governments, and 7 percent from other (private) sources.[79] Compared to the U.S. system with its multitude of public and private insurance arrangements, Canada has a single-payer system where the government, rather than private insurers, pays for the vast majority of healthcare costs. Because of its complexity, the U.S. healthcare system has 44 percent more administrative staff per capita than the Canadian system, and differences in administrative spending account for 39 percent of the total healthcare spending differences between the U.S. and Canada.[80] The United States has 25 percent more healthcare administrators than the United Kingdom, 165 percent more than the Netherlands, and 215 percent more than Germany.[81]

Another component of the spending differences between the United States, Canada, and other countries is the higher salaries for physicians, nurses, and other medical staff in the United States. In 2010, the average U.S. specialist physician earned $230,000, which was 78 percent above the average in other countries.[82] In Sweden, for example, specialists earned only $71,000.[83] The high salaries of American

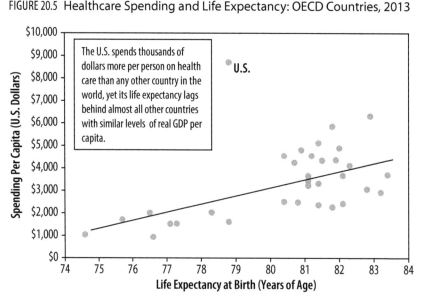

FIGURE 20.5 Healthcare Spending and Life Expectancy: OECD Countries, 2013

The U.S. spends thousands of dollars more per person on health care than any other country in the world, yet its life expectancy lags behind almost all other countries with similar levels of real GDP per capita.

Source: Office of Economic Cooperation and Development, *OECD Health Statistics 2015*, www.oecd.org/health/health-systems/OECD-Health-Statistics-2015-Frequently-Requested-Data.xls (accessed: December 4, 2015).

physicians are driven largely by "a lack of medical school openings."[84] In the U.S., there are 2.3 applicants per medical school opening, and rejected applicants are generally of very high quality. More than 20 percent of applicants who do not get into a U.S. medical school have MCAT scores higher than the mean scores of those admitted.[85] Because the supply of physicians is restricted, salaries for physicians in the United States are relatively high.

Finally, Americans receive more intensive care than do Canadians and the citizens of other countries. For example, while the population of Pennsylvania is roughly the same as the Canadian Province of Ontario, Pennsylvania has more than five times the number of heart surgery centers.[86] Together, differences in administrative costs, salaries, and the intensity of care account for 84 percent of the healthcare spending differences between the United States and Canada.[87]

20.4   SOCIAL SPENDING AND ECONOMIC GROWTH

It seems like common sense that social spending must be detrimental to economic growth. Taxing some individuals to provide benefits for others creates disincentives to work both for those paying taxes and for those receiving the benefits, which surely cannot be good for growth. The problem with this view, however, is that it is "unsupported by statistics and history."[88] How can this be?

A FREE LUNCH

Empirical evidence, examining nearly a century of data, shows that countries with more social spending have not grown more slowly and do not have lower levels of real GDP per capita today than do countries with lower levels of social spending. It looks as though social spending is a "free lunch."

While taxes and transfers undoubtedly have some adverse effects on incentives, countries with large welfare states tend to enact "a more pro-growth and regressive mix of taxes" by having low taxes on capital and higher taxes on labor and consumption.[89] Perhaps more importantly, these countries also make more investments in people through childcare and paid maternity leave, public health measures and universal health insurance, and high-quality public education. As a result, their citizens are healthier, live longer, and do better in school, on average, than does the typical American.[90] Welfare spending has its costs and its benefits, but available evidence suggests that the net benefits provided in large welfare states (as in many Scandinavian countries, for example) are likely positive, and certainly not a substantial drag on economic growth.

THE ROBIN HOOD PARADOX

Another puzzle is called the Robin Hood Paradox. Across countries, social spending is negatively correlated with both poverty and inequality. One might reasonably expect that social spending "ought" to be higher when there are more people who "need it" (when poverty rates are high) and when inequality is high. In a democracy, the poorest 51 percent could in principle be able to vote on policies to tax the rich to provide for more social spending. The Paradox is that empirical evidence shows just the opposite; social spending is higher in countries that have relatively equal distributions of income and wealth, and lower in countries with higher levels of inequality and poverty.

The Robin Hood Paradox may also be related to the Great Gatsby Curve (see Chapter 13). Since greater inequality is associated with lower social spending, low levels of social spending likely limit economic opportunity and intergenerational mobility for the poor, which leads over time to even greater inequality and even less mobility as countries move along the Great Gatsby Curve.

20.5 CONCLUSIONS

The growth of social assistance and social insurance in the United States has lessened the impacts of adverse events in people's lives and has helped to reduce consumption-based poverty rates. While fraud, corruption, and poorly designed programs have undoubtedly led to waste and inefficiencies, there is little evidence that the growth of social spending has adversely affected economic growth in the United States or elsewhere. While transfers create deadweight losses, they also contribute to better health and human capital, both of which have positive effects on productivity and growth.

QUESTIONS

1. In each case below, are the following in-kind or cash benefits? Are the following social assistance or social insurance? Briefly explain.
   A. Temporary Assistance for Needy Families
   B. Medicaid
   C. Medicare
   D. Social Security OASDI
   E. Social Security SSI
   F. Food Stamps

2. What are the advantages and disadvantages of in-kind social assistance benefits compared to cash benefits?

3. In the 50 years between 1965 and 2015, the number of families receiving AFDC and TANF benefits increased and then decreased. When and why have the number of families receiving welfare varied?

4. What is the "free lunch" puzzle? Explain.

5. What is the difference between defined-benefit and defined-contribution pension plans? Why do you suspect that defined-benefit plans are more common for public-sector workers?

6. Why did employer-provided health insurance become the norm in the United States?

7. Why is healthcare spending per capita so much higher in the United States than in other countries?

NOTES

[1] Office of Economic Cooperation and Development, *Social Expenditure Update* (November 2014), 2, www.oecd.org/els/soc/OECD2014-Social-Expenditure-Update-Nov2014-8pages.pdf (accessed: September 22, 2015).

[2] Office of Economic Cooperation and Development, 2. Primary and secondary education are also a type of social spending, but are not considered here since Chapter 11 is devoted entirely to education.

[3] John E. Hansan, "Poor Relief in Early America," The Social Welfare History Project, www.socialwelfarehistory.com/programs/poor-relief-early-amer/ (accessed: September 28, 2015).

[4] William I. Trattner, *From the Poor Law to Welfare State: A History of Social Welfare in America*, Third Edition (New York, NY: The Free Press, 1984), 53.

[5] Michael B. Katz, *In the Shadow of the Poorhouse: A Social History of Welfare in America*, Tenth Anniversary Edition (New York, NY: Basic Books, 1996), 25.

[6] Quotes from New York State Senate report, from Katz, 26.

[7] Peter H. Lindert, *Growing Public: Social Spending and Economic Growth Since the Eighteenth Century*, Volume 1 (New York, NY: Cambridge University Press, 2004), 58–65.

[8] Lindert, 58.

[9] Lindert, 61.

[10] Lindert, 61.

[11] Lindert, 60–65.

[12] Lindert, 176.

[13] Linda Gordon and Felice Batlan, *The Legal History of the Aid to Dependent Children Program*, www.socialwelfarehistory.com/programs/aid-to-dependent-children-the-legal-history/ (accessed: November 5, 2015).

[14] Gordon and Batlan.

[15] Mary E. Thiece, *Tell It Like It Is: Women in the National Welfare Rights Movement* (Columbia, SC: University of South Carolina Press, 2013).

[16] George A. Akerlof and Janet L. Yellen, "An Analysis of Out-of-Wedlock Births in the United States," *Brookings Policy Brief Series* 5 (August 1996), www.brookings.edu/research/papers/1996/08/childrenfamilies-akerlof (accessed: October 17, 2015).

[17] See Akerlof and Yellen; and Joyce A. Martin, Brady E. Hamilton, Michelle J.K. Osterman, Sally C. Curtin, and T.J. Mathews, "Births: Final Data for 2013," *National Vital Statistics Reports* 64, no. 1 (January 15, 2015), Table B, 7, www.cdc.gov/nchs/data/nvsr/nvsr64/nvsr64_01.pdf (accessed: October 18, 2015).

[18] See, for example, Charles Murray, *Losing Ground: American Social Policy, 1950–1980* (New York, NY: Basic Books, 1984).

[19] Robert Moffitt (ed.), *Welfare, the Family, and Reproductive Behavior* (Washington, DC: National Academies Press, 1998).

[20] Kevin Lang, *Discrimination and Poverty* (Princeton, NJ: Princeton University Press, 2007), 66.

[21] Lang, 66.

[22] Katz, 283.

[23] Robert Schoeni and Rebecca Blank, "What Has Welfare Reform Accomplished? Impacts on Welfare Participation, Employment, Income, Poverty, and Family Structure," *National Bureau of Economic Research Working Paper*, no. 7627 (Cambridge, MA, 2000), 7. Beginning in 1962, states were able to apply for waivers.

[24] Schoeni and Blank, 7.

[25] During the 1992 U.S. Presidential Campaign, candidate Bill Clinton promised to "end welfare as we know it." On August 22, 1996, he made good on this promise by signing the Personal Responsibility and Work Opportunity Reconciliation Act, which created TANF.

[26] "Policy Basics: An Introduction to TANF," Center on Budget and Policy Priorities, 1-7, updated

June 15, 2015, www.cbpp.org/sites/default/files/atoms/files/7-22-10tanf2.pdf (accessed: November 7, 2015).

[27] "Policy Basics," 3.

[28] Ife Floyd and Liz Schott, "TANF Cash Benefits Continued to Lose Value in 2013," Center on Budget and Policy Priorities, October 21, 2013, Appendix 1, www.cbpp.org/research/family-income-support/tanf-cash-benefits-continued-to-lose-value-in-2013 (accessed: November 8, 2015).

[29] Gene Falk, "Temporary Assistance for Needy Families (TANF): Size and Characteristics of the Cash Assistance Caseload," Congressional Research Service (August 5, 2014), Figure 1, 3, http://greenbook.waysandmeans.house.gov/sites/greenbook.waysandmeans.house.gov/files/R43187_gb_0.pdf (accessed: November 10, 2015).

[30] Gene Falk, "Temporary Assistance for Needy Families (TANF): Eligibility and Benefit Amounts in State TANF Cash Assistance Programs," Congressional Research Service (July 22, 2014), Figure 5, 11, http://greenbook.waysandmeans.house.gov/sites/greenbook.waysandmeans.house.gov/files/R43634_gb_0.pdf (accessed: November 10, 2015).

[31] "Policy Basics," 6.

[32] "Policy Basics," 6.

[33] Lucie Schmidt and Purvi Sevak, "AFDC, SSI, and Welfare Reform Aggressiveness: Caseload Reductions versus Caseload Shifting," *Journal of Human Resources* 39, no. 3 (Summer 2004), 792–812.

[34] John Karl Scholz, Robert Moffitt, and Benjamin Cowan, "Trends in Income Support," in Maria Cancian and Sheldon Danziger (eds.), *Changing Poverty, Changing Policies* (New York, NY: Russell Sage Foundation, 2009), 203–241.

[35] Mark Duggan and Melissa Schettini Kearney, "The Impact of Child SSI Enrollment on Household Outcomes: Evidence from the SIPP," *Journal of Policy Analysis and Management* 26, no. 4 (2007), 861–886.

[36] Internal Revenue Service, www.irs.gov/Credits-&-Deductions/Individuals/Earned-Income-Tax-Credit/EITC-Income-Limits-Maximum-Credit-Amounts-Next-Year (accessed: October 30, 2015).

[37] Internal Revenue Service, www.irs.gov/Individuals/Earned-Income-Tax-Credit-Statistics (accessed: October 30, 2015).

[38] Internal Revenue Service, www.irs.gov/Individuals/Earned-Income-Tax-Credit-Statistics (accessed: October 30, 2015).

[39] See Jane Waldfogel, "The Safety Net for Families with Children," in Martha J. Bailey and Sheldon Danziger (eds.), *Legacies of the War on Poverty* (New York, NY: Russell Sage Foundation, 2013), 153–178, for a discussion of the effects of safety net programs on children and families.

[40] For the federal matching percentages (FMAP) from October 1, 2015, to September 30, 2016, see http://aspe.hhs.gov/basic-report/fy2016-federal-medical-assistance-percentages (accessed: November 1, 2015).

[41] In 2015–2016, 81.92 percent of S-CHIP costs in Mississippi, the poorest state, were paid by the federal government, http://aspe.hhs.gov/basic-report/fy2016-federal-medical-assistance-percentages (accessed: November 1, 2015).

[42] For recent SNAP data on the cost and number of beneficiaries, see U.S. Department of Agriculture, Supplemental Nutrition Assistance Program, www.fns.usda.gov/pd/supplemental-nutrition-assistance-program-snap.

[43] U.S. Department of Agriculture, Supplemental Nutrition Assistance Program, www.fns.usda.gov/sites/default/files/pd/SNAPsummary.xls (accessed: November 1, 2015).

[44] Gordon W. Gunderson, "Early Programs by States," U.S. Department of Agriculture, www.fns.usda.gov/nslp/history_2 (accessed: on October 28, 2015).

45 See the *Federal Register* 80, no. 61 (March 31, 2015), www.gpo.gov/fdsys/pkg/FR-2015-03-31/pdf/2015-07358.pdf (accessed: November 1, 2015).

46 United States Department of Agriculture (USDA), *National School Lunch Program Fact Sheet*, www.fns.usda.gov/sites/default/files/NSLPFactSheet.pdf (accessed: November 12, 2015).

47 USDA, *WIC Program National Summary*, www.fns.usda.gov/sites/default/files/pd/wisummary.xls (accessed: November 2, 2015).

48 USDA, *WIC Program National Summary*.

49 Edgar O. Olsen and Jens Ludwig, "Performance and Legacy of Housing Policies," in Martha J. Bailey and Sheldon Danziger (eds.), *Legacies of the War on Poverty* (New York, NY: Russell Sage Foundation, 2013), 209.

50 "Why the Pruitt-Igoe Housing Project Failed," *The Economist* (October 15, 2011).

51 *The Economist* (October 15, 2011).

52 Olsen and Ludwig, 207.

53 Olsen and Ludwig, 223–224.

54 Olsen and Ludwig, 208.

55 Chloe Gibbs, Jens Ludwig, and Douglas L. Miller, "Head Start Origins and Impact," in Martha J. Bailey and Sheldon Danziger (eds.), *Legacies of the War on Poverty* (New York, NY: Russell Sage Foundation, 2013), 61.

56 OECD, "Family Benefits Public Spending (Indicator)" https://data.oecd.org/socialexp/family-benefits-public-spending.htm#indicator-chart (accessed: October 7, 2015).

57 OECD.

58 Bruce Meyer and James X. Sullivan, "Winning the War: Poverty from the Great Society to the Great Recession," in David H. Romer and Justin Wolfers (eds.), *Brookings Papers on Economic Activity* (Washington, DC: Brookings Institution, 2012), 133–200. Meyer and Sullivan also make corrections to account for biases in the consumer price index.

59 Meyer and Sullivan, Table 3, 163.

60 Lee A. Craig, "Public Sector Pensions in the United States," in Robert Whaples (ed.) *EH.Net Encyclopedia* (March 16, 2003), http://eh.net/encyclopedia/public-sector-pensions-in-the-united-states/ (accessed: November 2, 2015). For more information, see Robert L. Clark, Lee A. Craig, and Jack W. Wilson, *A History of Public Sector Pensions* (Philadelphia, PA: University of Pennsylvania Press, 2003).

61 For teachers' pensions, see Employee Benefit Research Institute, "U.S. Retirement Income System" (December 1998), 1, www.ebri.org/pdf/publications/facts/1298fact.pdf (accessed: November 6, 2015). For police officers, see Olivia S. Mitchell, David McCarthy, Stanley C. Wisniewski, and Paul Zorn, "Developments in State and Local Pension Plans," in Olivia S. Mitchell and Edwin C. Hustead (eds.), *Pensions in the Public Sector* (Philadelphia, PA: University of Pennsylvania Press, 2001).

62 Craig.

63 Craig. The 1928 quote comes from the U.S. Bureau of Labor Statistics, *Monthly Labor Review* (April 1928).

64 Craig.

65 Employee Benefit Research Institute, 1.

66 Craig.

67 Employee Benefit Research Institute, www.ebri.org/publications/benfaq/index.cfm?fa=retfaq14 (accessed: November 12, 2015).

68 U.S. Social Security Administration, "Fact Sheet on the Old-Age, Survivors, and Disability Insurance Program," www.ssa.gov/oact/FACTS/ (accessed: October 30, 2015).

69 U.S. Social Security Administration, "Fact Sheet."

[70] Social Security Administration, *Historical Background and Development of Social Security*, www.ssa.gov/history/briefhistory3.html (accessed: September 16, 2015).

[71] Social Security Administration, www.ssa.gov/history/ratios.html (accessed: November 12, 2015).

[72] *The 2015 Annual Report of the Board of Trustees of the Federal Old-Age and Survivors Insurance and Federal Disability Insurance Trust Funds*, 6, www.ssa.gov/oact/TR/2015/tr2015.pdf (accessed: September 20, 2015).

[73] *The 2015 Annual Report,* 6.

[74] *The 2015 Annual Report,* 196.

[75] Charles E. Rosenberg, *The Care of Strangers* (New York, NY: Basic Books, 1987), 150.

[76] Melissa Thomasson, "Health Insurance in the United States," in Robert Whaples (ed.), *EH.Net Encyclopedia* , https://eh.net/encyclopedia/health-insurance-in-the-united-states/ (accessed: September 22, 2015).

[77] Thomasson.

[78] David M. Cutler and Dan P. Ly, "The (Paper)Work of Medicine: Understanding International Medical Costs," *Journal of Economic Perspectives* 25, no. 2 (Spring 2001), 3.

[79] U.S. Centers for Medicare and Medicaid Services.

[80] Cutler and Ly, 6.

[81] Cutler and Ly, 8.

[82] Cutler and Ly, 11.

[83] Cutler and Ly, Table 2, 12.

[84] Cutler and Ly, 13.

[85] Association of American Medical Colleges, "MCAT and GPA Grid for Applicants and Acceptances to U.S. Medical Schools, 2007–2009," www.aamc.org/data/facts (accessed: September 24, 2015).

[86] Cutler and Ly, 15.

[87] Cutler and Ly, 6.

[88] Lindert, 227.

[89] Lindert, 31.

[90] Lindert, 32.

21

Connecting the Present with the Past and Future

Since the Declaration of Independence was signed in 1776, which called for "certain unalienable rights … [including] life, liberty, and the pursuit of happiness," the United States has generally been viewed as a land of opportunity where it was possible to achieve the "American Dream". While minorities and women were excluded from this grand promise for much of American history, the sense of enduring optimism that things will get better and that any obstacle can be overcome has resonated throughout American history and has shaped the country's character and development.

The term "American Dream" was popularized by the historian James Truslow Adams. During the midst of the Great Depression in 1931, he expressed this optimism when he wrote that the American Dream is:

> That dream of a land in which life should be better and richer and fuller for everyone, with opportunity for each according to ability or achievement. … It is not a dream of motor cars and high wages merely, but a dream of a social order in which each man and each woman shall be able to attain to the fullest stature of which they are innately capable, and be recognized by others for what they are, regardless of the fortuitous circumstances of birth or position.[1]

In many ways, the performance of the United States' economy from 1945 to 1973 did indeed suggest the possibility of such a world. The United States emerged from World War II as the strongest and most powerful nation on Earth. Not only was economic growth the most rapid in American history, but the fruits of this growth were widespread, with relatively small differences between rich and poor. A high school education had become the norm, and it was often the ticket to the middle class and home ownership. College education was expanding rapidly, and it was cheap and accessible. There was a greater sense of job security; there were unemployment insurance and Social Security, including disability insurance; and the economy as a whole was very stable, with only mild and infrequent recessions.

This sense of optimism reached a high point during the early 1960s, when President John F. Kennedy set the goal of "landing a man on the moon and returning him safely to the earth" by the end of the decade, and when President Lyndon Johnson promised to eliminate financial hardship in America with his "War on Poverty." Although widespread segregation and discrimination still existed in America, there was a hope of a better tomorrow, perhaps most eloquently stated in Martin Luther King's "I Have a Dream" speech in 1963. The Civil Rights Movement and the Great Migration of African Americans to northern cities increased rights and decreased wage gaps. Other problems existed, like the Cold War and Vietnam, but economic growth and opportunity were becoming increasingly widespread.

After the mid-1970s, however, much of this changed. Economic growth slowed down and inequality increased substantially, with most of the gains in income and wealth going to those in the top 1 percent of the distribution. Slower growth, rising inequality, globalization, technological changes, public policies, and recessions followed by "jobless" recoveries have resulted in real wages for the median worker barely increasing over the past 40 years.

After the Vietnam War ended, the U.S. seemed to be increasingly involved in "endless wars" in which the enemy was hard to identify and where "victory" seemed undefined and elusive. The challenges and uncertainty of global climate change suggest that future problems may be even more serious and intractable than past problems.

While iPhones, PlayStations, Facebook, Instagram, and the growing use of antidepressants may have helped people feel better, for many Americans in recent years there has been an increasing sense of diminished opportunities, even for those who have played by the rules. As one young adult stated in 2005:

> Try investigating people like me who didn't have babies in high school, who made good grades, who work hard and don't kiss a lot of ass and instead of getting promoted or paid fairly must regress to working for $7/hr., having their student loans in perpetual deferment, living at home with their parents, and generally exist in debt which they feel they may never get out of.[2]

Are these changes inevitable consequences of market forces, or do they represent a failure of public policy or the failings of individual Americans? Is broad-based, sustainable economic growth possible for current and future generations of Americans, or is the American Dream over?

How the economy of the United States performs in terms of this book's four main themes—economic growth, distributional issues, economic fluctuations, and the relationship and tensions between markets and government—will largely determine the possibilities and limitations that Americans will face in the coming decades.

21.1 ECONOMIC GROWTH

For the past century and a half, labor productivity and real GDP per capita increased at an average annual rate of nearly 2 percent, leading to a doubling of output per person roughly every 35 years. Since 2000, however, there is evidence that economic growth may have slowed. Between 2000 and 2015, real GDP per capita grew at an average annual rate of less than 1 percent. While much of this decrease may be cyclical and the result of the severe and persistent effects of the Great Recession, it may also suggest a slowdown in long-run growth rates.

The United States is lagging behind other industrialized nations in educational attainment and performance. Infrastructure—such as roads and bridges and water and sewer systems—is decaying, with little prospect that governments will have the funds to maintain our transportation system. The threats of global climate change may severely impact future growth prospects as well.

Nearly all of the issues we will face in coming decades will be made easier if long-run growth returns to rates of 2 percent or more per year. If we have entered a period of "Great Stagnation" then the choices we face will be more difficult to make.[3] Optimists point to the possibilities that robotics and information technology will improve growth and opportunities almost beyond imagination, but these changes may also lead to a more dangerous and less stable world with even greater inequalities. In 2015, a prominent group of scientists wrote an open letter warning about the dangers of artificial intelligence in creating a "third revolution in warfare, after gunpowder and nuclear arms."[4]

21.2 DISTRIBUTIONAL ISSUES

While growth rates of real GDP per capita have slowed in the past decade and a half, median household incomes have stagnated for much longer, due in large part to the increasing concentration of income. Median household incomes have barely budged in recent decades, with the overwhelming majority of income and wealth growth occurring in the top 1 percent of the distribution.

Inequality in the United States is once again near its historic 1928 highs. Not only that, but income and wealth are now distributed far more unequally in the U.S. than in nearly every other OECD country. Evidence strongly suggests that the growing disparity in income and wealth is likely to diminish opportunities for the next generation of Americans.

Segregation and discrimination also continue to limit opportunities and outcomes. In recent years, a series of widely reported police shootings of unarmed black men has sparked protests in Ferguson, Missouri, in Baltimore, Maryland, and elsewhere, and has led to the "Black Lives Matter" movement. Incarceration rates for African-American males are more than six times higher than the rates for white males, and African Americans and Latinos continue to lag behind in terms of average incomes and wealth, while experiencing higher rates of poverty and unemployment.

Persistent and large gaps between rich and poor, and wide disparities in economic opportunities because of income, wealth, or race, will almost certainly continue to remain at the forefront of public debate and policies.

21.3 ECONOMIC FLUCTUATIONS

Before the collapse of Lehman Brothers in September 2008, many economists believed that serious recessions were a thing of the past, and the decades of stability prior to the Great Recession had been called the "Great Moderation."

The Great Recession reminded us that economic fluctuations can still cause millions of people to lose their jobs and their homes. Many economists believe that the fundamental causes that led to the Great Recession have not been remedied and that financial crises and severe recessions will return, perhaps sooner rather than later.

In the aftermath of the Great Recession, monetary policy was unable to return the economy quickly to potential output, despite dramatic increases in the monetary base and keeping the federal funds rate near zero for many years. High deficits and concerns about the federal debt made fiscal policy more modest and less stimulative than it could have been.

With interest rates still near zero in 2016, nearly eight years after the collapse of Lehman Brothers, and with persistently large federal deficits, many fear that there will be little left in the monetary and fiscal policy toolkit to combat the next recession should it arrive before the Fed is able to raise interest rates.[5]

21.4   MARKETS AND GOVERNMENT

Since the ideological battles of the founding fathers, Americans have disagreed on the proper balance between markets and government. While some believe that governments need to do more, in terms of the provision of education, health care, and infrastructure, and in providing public goods and reducing negative externalities, other Americans believe that the scale and scope of government is already too expansive and too intrusive. Some feel that the government is not doing enough in some areas, while at the same time tackling too much in other spheres.

Both markets and government have the potential for great good and great harm, yet faith in the ability of government to solve problems remains low. In a recent international survey, 70 percent of Americans agreed with the statement, "Most people are better off in a free market economy, even if some people are rich and others poor."[6] But Americans are also very pessimistic about the future, with 65 percent of Americans believing that children when they grow up will be worse off financially than their parents.[7]

21.5   CONCLUSIONS

Any forecast of the future is almost certainly going to be wrong in many ways. Even so, throughout American history the United States has faced and largely overcome many challenges, as have individual Americans from all walks of life. A careful examination of those challenges, and how they have been overcome, offers hope that collective and individual decisions can still result in a bright and prosperous future.

NOTES

[1] James Truslow Adams, *The Epic of America* (Boston, MA: Little, Brown, and Co., 1931), 214–215.

[2] Barbara Ehrenreich, *Bait and Switch: The (Futile) Pursuit of the American Dream* (New York, NY: Metropolitan Books, Henry Holt, 2005), 1–2.

[3] Tyler Cowan coined the term the "Great Stagnation" in his book, *The Great Stagnation: How America Ate All the Low-Hanging Fruit of Modern History, Got Sick, and Will (Eventually) Feel Better* (New York, NY: Dutton, 2011).

[4] "Autonomous Weapons: An Open-Letter from AI & Robotics Researchers," July 28, 2015, futureoflife.org/AI/open_letter_autonomous_weapons (accessed: August 23, 2015).

[5] Mike Dolan, "Loss of Central Bank Traction Puts Mandates Under Scrutiny," September 30, 2015, www.reuters.com/article/2015/09/30/us-investment-centralbank-mandates-analy-idUSKCN0RU0E620150930 (accessed: October 10, 2015).

6 Pew Research Center, "Emerging and Developing Economies Much More Optimistic than Rich Countries about the Future: Education, Hard Work Considered Keys to Success, but Inequality Still a Challenge," October 9, 2014, www.pewglobal.org/2014/10/09/emerging-and-developing-economies-much-more-optimistic-than-rich-countries-about-the-future/ (accessed: October 14, 2015).

7 Pew Research Center.

Appendix
Chronology of Important Events

Year(s)	Event	Brief Description and Chapter References
200,000 years ago	Emergence of humans	Fossil evidence reveals the existence of modern humans, *Homo sapiens*, in Africa (Chapter 3).
16,500 years ago	Humans arrive in North America	During the last Ice Age, humans cross a land bridge connecting Siberia to Alaska (Chapter 3).
12,000 years ago	Neolithic Revolution	The Neolithic or Agricultural Revolution begins in the Middle East and North Africa (Chapter 3).
3,500 years ago	Agriculture in North America	Tribes in the American Southwest begin to cultivate corn, beans, and squash (Chapter 3).
300–1000	Hohokam and Anasazi	Both groups rely on an extensive system of irrigation for agriculture. The largest Anasazi cliff pueblo contains 800 rooms (Chapter 3).
900–1100	Cahokia	The largest and wealthiest Native American settlement is on the eastern side of the Mississippi River. At its peak, it has a population of perhaps 40,000 residents (Chapter 3).
1215	Magna Carta	This English document limits the King's powers, protects private property, and guarantees the right to trial by jury (Chapter 4).
1300	Mariner's compass	A mariner's compass, in a dry box with a pivoting needle, is invented in Europe around 1300 (Chapter 3).
1455	Printing press	Johannes Gutenberg invents a printing press with moveable type (Chapter 3).
1492	Columbian Exchange	The Columbian Exchange of diseases, plants, food crops, animals, ideas, culture, and human populations between the Old World and New World begins with Christopher Columbus' first voyage (Chapter 3).
1519	Cortés conquers the Aztecs	Hernán Cortés conquers the Aztecs at Tenochtitlan, renaming it Mexico City (Chapter 3).
1539–1540	Spanish exploration of North America	In 1539, Hernando de Soto begins a journey through the American Southeast and reaches the Mississippi River. In 1540, Francisco Vásquez de Coronado begins an expedition through the American Southwest (Chapter 3).

1565	St. Augustine	The Spanish establish the first permanent European settlement in what is to become the United States, in St. Augustine, Florida (Chapter 3).
1607	Jamestown	The first permanent British settlement in North America is established on the Chesapeake Bay of Virginia (Chapter 3).
1619	First slaves	The first group of African slaves (20) arrives aboard a Dutch ship near Jamestown (Chapter 7).
1620	Plymouth Bay Colony	Pilgrims establish a colony at Plymouth, on Cape Cod, Massachusetts (Chapter 3).
1626	New Amsterdam	The Dutch establish the colony of New Netherlands, which soon includes the town of New Amsterdam, now New York City (Chapter 3).
1626	Environmental protection law	Pilgrims pass a law restricting the harvesting and sale of timber, probably the first such law in the American colonies (Chapter 19).
1630	Massachusetts Bay Colony	A colony is established between present-day Salem and Boston, Massachusetts (Chapter 3).
1635	Boston Latin School	Boston Latin is established, the first public high school in the American colonies (Chapter 11).
1636	Harvard University	Harvard is established, the first university in the American colonies (Chapter 11).
1647	Primary education	The "Old Deluder Satan" law requires Massachusetts communities with 100 households or more to establish a formal grammar school (Chapter 11).
1754–1763	French and Indian War	The French and the British wage war on the North American continent. British military expenditures more than double compared with those before the War (Chapter 4).
1763–1775	Tax increases	A series of taxes is introduced in the American colonies to help pay for war expenses. These are modest, and far less than the taxes in England (Chapter 4).
1775–1783	Revolutionary War	War begins on April 15, 1775, in Concord, Massachusetts, and ends in American victory with the Treaty of Paris, signed on September 3, 1783 (Chapter 4).
1776	*Wealth of Nations*	Adam Smith publishes *An Inquiry into the Nature and Causes of the Wealth of Nations*. This marks the beginning of modern economics, and will later be an influence on the U.S. Constitution (Chapter 1).
1776	Declaration of Independence	The United States declares independence from Great Britain on July 4, 1776 (Chapter 4).
1781	Steam engine	After working on steam engines throughout the 1770s, James Watt invents a continuous-motion rotary steam engine in 1781 (Chapter 8).

Year(s)	Event	Brief Description and Chapter References
1782	First commercial bank	The Bank of North America, the first commercial bank, opens (Chapter 5).
1785	Land Ordinance	This ordinance establishes a system of rectangular surveys to create unambiguous property lines through the creation of square townships (Chapter 6).
1787	Northwest Land Ordinance	This ordinance establishes the principles whereby new territories can become U.S. states, with all the rights of existing states. It also prohibits slavery in the Northwest Territory (Chapter 6).
1787–1789	Constitution	A constitutional convention in Philadelphia takes place in the summer of 1787 to draft the U.S. Constitution. The Constitution takes effect in 1789, after it has been ratified by the states (Chapter 4).
1790	Cotton textiles	The first American cotton textile mill, Almy and Brown, opens in Pawtucket, Rhode Island (Chapter 10).
1791–1811	First Bank of the United States	The first central bank receives a 20-year charter as the only nationally chartered bank. As a result, it is the only bank that can operate across state lines (Chapter 5).
1792	Buttonwood Agreement	The Buttonwood Agreement is signed, marking the beginning of what will become the New York Stock Exchange (Chapter 5).
1792	Coinage Act	This Act establishes the U.S. Mint and a decimal system for currency, replacing the British system of pounds, shillings, and pence (Chapter 5).
1793	Cotton gin	The cotton gin is invented, which efficiently separates the cotton fibers from cotton seeds. Although Eli Whitney is credited with inventing it, many develop similar devices. Use of the cotton gin increases the demand for slaves and results in a rapid expansion of cotton exports (Chapter 7).
1794–1806	Unions	The Federal Society of Journeyman Cordwainers is formed to represent Philadelphia shoemakers. It will become the longest-lasting craft union (Chapter 12).
1800	Agriculture	Over 75 percent of the workforce are employed in agriculture (Chapter 9).
1800s	High fertility	Typically, a white woman who survived through her childbearing years had 7 children. By 1900, the average number of children had fallen by half (Chapter 7).
1803	Louisiana Purchase	Land is purchased from France, almost doubling the size of the United States (Chapter 6).

1804–1806	Lewis and Clark	Meriwether Lewis and William P. Clark lead an expedition to explore the Louisiana Territory. With the help of Sacajawea, a Shoshone woman, they eventually reach the Pacific Ocean (Chapter 6).
1807	Steamboat	Robert Fulton's steamboat makes the trip from New York City to Albany, New York, on the Hudson River, covering 150 miles in 32 hours. By 1865, over 1,000 boats are in operation on rivers (Chapter 8).
1808	End of U.S. slave trade	A constitutional compromise ends the legal slave trade in 1808 (Chapter 7).
1811	General incorporation law	New York introduces the first general rules for incorporation that do not require a special legislative charter (Chapter 4).
1811	National Road	Construction begins on National Road, which will eventually extend from Cumberland, Maryland to near St. Louis, Missouri (Chapter 8).
1812–1815	War of 1812	Armed conflict between the U.S. and Great Britain, some of it is fought on U.S. soil (Chapter 16).
1816–1836	Second Bank of the United States	Since the charter for the First Bank of the U.S. expired in 1811, instability has ensued. In 1816, Congress creates a second central bank: by 1830, 25 branches are operating nationwide (Chapter 5).
1817–1825	Erie Canal	Canal construction begins in 1817 and is completed in 1825. The success of the Erie Canal, from the Hudson River across the state of New York to Lake Erie, leads to a canal construction boom throughout the country (Chapter 8).
1819	End of indentured servitude	Rising wages in Europe, falling transportation costs across the Atlantic, and increasing family connections within the United States together bring the indentured servitude trade to an end around 1819 (Chapter 7)
1820	Missouri Compromise	Missouri enters the Union as a slave state, while Maine enters as a free state to keep balance in the Senate (Chapter 6). Slavery is prohibited north of latitude 36° 30'.
1825	Financial system	By 1825, the United States has over twice the bank capital per capita compared with Great Britain, and the U.S. has arguably the most developed financial system in the world (Chapter 5).
1830	First railroad	The 13-mile Baltimore & Ohio railroad opens (Chapter 8).
1830	Long hours	The average workweek in manufacturing is nearly 70 hours a week (Chapters 2 and 10).

Year(s)	Event	Brief Description and Chapter References
1830	Indian Removal Act	This Act forcibly moves Cherokee, Choctaw, Chickasaw, Creek, and Seminole tribes from their tribal lands to land west of the Mississippi River in Oklahoma. On the march in 1838 called the "Trail of Tears," over 4,000 die (Chapter 6).
1830–1890	Shrinking Americans	Average heights of native-born Americans decrease due to unhealthy conditions in an increasingly urban environment (Chapter 2).
1830–1890	Common school movement	Public primary education spreads throughout the U.S. (Chapter 11).
1833	Reaper	Obed Hussey patents and begins selling a horse-powered reaper (a mechanical device that cuts and gathers crops at harvest), but Cyrus McCormick is eventually far more successful (Chapter 9).
1836	Patent Act	This Act establishes the modern U.S. patent system by introducing an examination system (Chapter 4).
1837–1863	Free Banking Era	Without a central bank, U.S. states ease entry into banking by making legislative charters unnecessary (Chapter 5).
1837	Steel plow	John Deere produces the first steel plow (Chapter 9).
1838	Parker vs. Foote	A New York case effectively abolishes the "ancient lights" doctrine of property ownership (Chapter 4).
1842	Commonwealth vs. Hunt	A Court decision rules that labor unions are not illegal per se and provides them with some legal protection (Chapter 12).
1843	Telegraph	A telegraph line is constructed between Baltimore, Maryland, and Washington, DC. Coast-to-coast lines are completed in 1861, and lines across the Atlantic in 1866, thereby linking the world together in close to real time for the first time (Chapter 8).
1845	Texas	The U.S. annexes Texas (Chapter 6).
1846	Oregon	A treaty with Great Britain gives the U.S. possession of Oregon (Chapter 6).
1846–1848	Mexican–American War	The war ends, with the U.S. gaining possession of California and most of the western United States (Chapters 6 and 16).
1847–1854	Immigration surge	Discoveries of gold in California, the Irish Potato Famine, and political unrest in Europe together lead to a large increase in the number of immigrants to the United States (Chapter 15).
1848	Discovery of gold	Gold is discovered in the Sierra Nevada Mountains of Northern California, and soon a Gold Rush to California begins (Chapter 8).

1851	American System of Manufacturing	At the Crystal Palace Exhibition in London, English observers are impressed with what is soon called the "American system," where highly-standardized manufactured goods are made with interchangeable parts and specialized machines (Chapters 6 and 10).
1854	Kansas–Nebraska Act	This Act repeals the Missouri Compromise.
1859	Drilling for oil	Edwin L. Drake successfully uses a steam engine to drill for oil (Chapter 6).
1861–1865	Civil War	The bloodiest war in American history, with over 750,000 killed as the Union and the Confederacy fight for 4 years over slavery and other issues.
1862	Homestead Act	This Act offers 160 acres of public domain land to the head of any household who registers a claim, makes improvements within 6 months, and lives on the land for 5 years (Chapter 6).
1862	Morrill Land-Grant Act	Establishes land-grant colleges and universities to promote agricultural and industrial development (Chapter 9).
1862	U.S. Department of Agriculture	The USDA is created to serve as an information agency for farmers (Chapter 9).
1863	Emancipation Proclamation	Slaves are freed in law, but freedom in reality does not occur until the Civil War ends in 1865 (Chapter 14).
1865–1900	Farm protest movements	Grangers, Greenbacks, Alliance, and Populist movements lead to political changes as farmers complain of falling prices and the monopoly power of railroads and money lenders (Chapters 9 and 17).
1869	Transcontinental railroad	The Union Pacific and Central Pacific join at Promontory Point, Utah, allowing coast-to-coast rail travel (Chapter 8).
1869	Industrial unions	The Knights of Labor are the first industrial union to organize workers in all occupations throughout the country (Chapter 12).
1872	Yellowstone	Yellowstone becomes the nation's first national park (Chapter 19).
1874	Typewriter	Eliphalet Remington introduces the first mass-produced typewriter (Chapter 10).
1879	Electric lightbulb	Thomas Edison invents the electric lightbulb (Chapter 8).
1879	U.S. Geological Survey	The U.S. Geological Survey maps the West in search of mineral deposits, which helps the United States discover its subsurface mineral resources well before most other countries (Chapter 6).
1880s–1890s	Labor unrest and violence	The Haymarket Riot (1886), the Homestead Strike (1892), and the Pullman Strike (1894) are the most violent in a series of clashes between business and labor (Chapter 12).

Year(s)	Event	Brief Description and Chapter References
1880s	First vaccines	Vaccines become increasingly common in preventing childhood diseases and reducing childhood mortality (Chapter 7).
1882	Chinese Exclusion Act	Immigration from China is banned, except for the immediate family members of those already in the U.S. The Act is not repealed until 1943 (Chapter 15).
1883	Standard time	Railroads throughout Canada and the U.S. agree to standard time with four time zones. Standard time becomes U.S. law in 1918 (Chapter 8).
1886	Wabash, St. Louis & Pacific Railway Co. vs. Illinois	This judgment repeals the decision of Munn vs. Illinois (1877), making regulation of interstate commerce a federal, not state, responsibility (Chapter 17).
1886	American Federation of Labor	Skilled craftsmen from many different occupations form a federation of their unions (Chapter 12).
1887	Interstate Commerce Commission	A new commission regulates interstate transportation, particularly railroads. It will become the prototype for regulatory commissions. The behavior of the Commission is an example of "regulatory capture" (Chapters 1 and 17).
1887	Dawes Act	This Act is intended to reduce the power of Native American tribes by dividing remaining tribal lands into small private parcels for sale, but in reality, little of the land is sold to Native Americans (Chapter 6).
1887	Mesabi iron	Prospectors discover rich iron-ore deposits in the Mesabi Range of Minnesota (Chapter 6).
1890	Sherman Antitrust Act	This Act is the first federal attempt to regulate monopolies in industry (Chapter 17).
1890s	Industrial leadership	By the mid-1890s, the U.S. is producing more manufactured goods than any other country in the world (Chapter 10).
1890–1966	"Golden Age" of productivity	Both labor productivity and total factor productivity increase rapidly during this period, partially due to a wave of inventions, beginning in the 1870s, including electric lights and electric motors, and the internal combustion engine and automobiles (Chapter 2).
1893	Vertical filing	Vertical filing is introduced at the 1893 Chicago World's Fair (Chapter 10).
1895	United States vs. E.C. Knight & Company	The Supreme Court refuses to apply the Sherman Antitrust Act since the company is engaged in manufacture (sugar-refining) rather than interstate commerce. This decision is likely to have contributed to the Great Merger Wave, primarily from 1898 to 1902 (Chapters 10 and 17).

1896	Plessy vs. Ferguson	This judgment legalizes segregation, leading to Jim Crow laws whereby blacks and whites are legally separated in public and private facilities (Chapter 14).
1898–1902	Great Merger Wave	Mergers, mostly horizontal, reduce price competition and increase market power (Chapters 10 and 17).
1901	Forest Service	The U.S. Forest Service is established (Chapter 19).
1901	Spindletop	Oil is discovered in Spindletop, Texas, starting a decades-long oil boom in Texas (Chapter 6).
1903	Airplane	Orville and Wilbur Wright make the first flights in a heavier-than-air vehicle, near Kitty Hawk, North Carolina (Chapter 8).
1904	New York subway	Although not the first public transit system – cable cars in San Francisco (1873), electric streetcars, and the Boston T (1897) have all preceded it – the New York subway becomes the most extensive and most widely used transit system in the U.S. (Chapter 8).
1906	Meat Inspection Act	This Act is passed in response to Upton Sinclair's shocking depiction of the meatpacking industry in his book, *The Jungle* (Chapter 4).
1906	Pure Food and Drug Act	This Act creates what will later prove to have been the precursor of the modern Food and Drug Administration or FDA (Chapter 4).
1910s	Workers' compensation	42 states pass laws to establish insurance programs for workers insured on the job (Chapter 12).
1910–1940	American High School Movement	Graduation rates increase, from 9 percent in 1910 to over 50 percent nationwide by 1940, as the public high school becomes a common part of nearly every community (Chapter 11).
1911	Standard Oil and American Tobacco	The Supreme Court orders the break-up of both companies, but on rather narrow grounds that give great weight to the actions to monopolize, called the "rule of reason," and guilt is not just based on the possession of a monopoly itself (Chapter 17).
1913	Ford assembly line	The development of the automobile assembly line results in mass production of automobiles at low prices (Chapters 6 and 8).
1913	Federal Reserve	In response to the Financial Panic of 1907, the Federal Reserve Act establishes a permanent central bank (Chapter 5).
1913	Federal income tax	The first temporary income tax was imposed during the Civil War; in 1913, the income tax becomes permanent (Chapter 16).
1914	Clayton Act	This Act strengthens the Sherman Antitrust Act and exempts labor unions from antitrust law (Chapter 17).

Year(s)	Event	Brief Description and Chapter References
1914	Federal Trade Commission Act	This Act establishes an independent agency charged with maintaining a competitive economic environment by preventing monopolies and unfair trade practices (Chapter 17).
1915	Coast-to-coast telephone service	A three-minute call from New York to San Francisco costs the equivalent of about $500 in 2016 dollars (Chapter 8).
1915–1970	Great Migration	Six million African Americans leave the South for northern and western cities in pursuit of better jobs and opportunities (Chapter 14).
1917–1918	World War I	Although the War started in 1914, the United States becomes involved in 1917. Almost 120,000 Americans are killed by the end in 1918, far fewer than the 625,000 who died during the 1918–1919 Spanish flu epidemic (Chapter 16).
1919–1933	Eighteenth Amendment	The federal government intervenes with "Prohibition" to outlaw the manufacture, sale, transportation, and consumption of alcohol (Chapter 1).
1920	United States vs. U.S. Steel	The Supreme Court refuses to condemn U.S. Steel, because it was a "good trust" that did not attack its smaller rivals, although it colluded with rivals at the "Gary dinners" (Chapter 17).
1920s	Consumer revolution	Widespread advertising on the radio, the development of small electric motors in household appliances, the growth of the automobile, and consumer installment credit leads to a "consumer revolution" (Chapters 8 and 10).
1921	Emergency Immigration Act	Immigration from each country is restricted to 3 percent of the total population in the U.S. based on the 1910 Census (Chapter 15).
1924	Immigration Act	Immigration is restricted to 2 percent of the total population in the U.S., based on the 1890 Census. This reduces immigration to the U.S. and particularly shuts off immigration from eastern and southern Europe (Chapter 15).
1924	Mutual funds	The first mutual fund, a financial intermediary that holds a diversified portfolio of securities, is established (Chapter 5).
1924	Tractor	The modern general-purpose tractor is invented (Chapter 9).
1928	Penicillin	Penicillin is invented. It begins to be used for medical purposes in 1942, and thereafter the development of antibiotics shifts the focus of medicine from preventing infectious diseases to curing them (Chapter 7).

1929	Blue Cross	The first nonprofit health insurance (Blue Cross) is established in Dallas, Texas (Chapter 20).
1929–1941	Great Depression	During the Depression, the real GDP drops by more than 25 percent, unemployment rises to more than 20 percent, and falling prices lead to persistent deflation. The U.S. economy reaches the trough of the depression by 1933, although complete recovery does not come until after World War II begins (Chapter 18).
1929–1953	Great Compression	After inequality peaks in 1928, the combination of the Great Depression, New Deal policies, and World War II lead to a large reduction in income and wealth inequality in the United States (Chapter 13).
1933	Agricultural Adjustment Act	The first law in a nearly century-long process of federal legislation to help the American farmer (Chapter 9).
1933	Tennessee Valley Authority	This authority provides electricity, flood control, and economic development in the Tennessee Valley (Chapter 14).
1933	Banking Act	Also known as the Glass–Steagall Act, this Act separates commercial and investment banking and establishes the Federal Deposit Insurance Corporation (FDIC) to insure depositors' funds (Chapter 5).
1933	Gold standard abandoned	The U.S. abandons the gold standard in April 1933, allowing for expansionary monetary policy and starting the U.S. on the road to recovery (Chapter 18).
1933–1942	Civilian Conservation Corps	Over 3 million young men are employed by government to reduce unemployment and to provide public projects (Chapter 19).
1934	GDP	In 1934, economist Simon Kuznets reports his annual estimates of the national product for the years 1929 to 1932, a report that initiates modern national income and product accounting and the development of GDP (Chapter 2).
1934	Securities and Exchange Act	This Act establishes the Securities and Exchange Commission to regulate the securities markets (Chapter 18).
1934	Federal Communications Commission (FCC)	A commission is established to regulate telecommunications (Chapter 17).
1935	National Labor Relations Act	This Act allows workers to form unions, which can bargain with employers collectively. The Act also allows "closed shop" agreements, whereby union membership becomes a required condition of employment (Chapters 4 and 12).
1935	Social Security Act	This Act creates Aid to Dependent Children, unemployment insurance, Aid to the Blind, Old Age Assistance, and Old Age Benefits (Chapter 20).

Year(s)	Event	Brief Description and Chapter References
1936	General Theory	John Maynard Keynes publishes *The General Theory of Employment, Interest, and Money*. Although Keynes' policies are not very influential during the Great Depression, Keynesian macroeconomics becomes dominant in the postwar period (Chapter 18).
1936	Robinson–Patman Act	Prohibited charging buyers different prices (price discrimination) if the result would reduce competition (Chapter 17).
1938	Fair Labor Standards Act	Established national minimum wage, maximum work hours, and restrictions on child labor (Chapters 4 and 12).
1941–1945	World War II	The U.S. enters the war soon after the bombing of Pearl Harbor in Hawaii on December 7, 1941. Almost 360,000 Americans are killed, and perhaps as many as 50–80 million people worldwide (Chapter 16).
1942–1964	Bracero Program	This program permits males from Mexico to work temporarily in the United States (Chapter 15).
1944	GI Bill	The Servicemen's Readjustment Act or GI Bill of Rights provides military veterans with cash payments for college tuition, college room and board, housing assistance, and many other benefits (Chapter 11).
1945	Synthetic rubber	During World War II, rubber consumption more than doubles, due to the development of synthetic rubber as a petroleum byproduct (Chapter 6).
1946	Employment Act	This Act makes it a federal government responsibility to "promote maximum employment, production, and purchasing power," and creates the Council of Economic Advisors to advise the U.S. President (Chapter 16).
1946–1964	Baby Boom	After a long decline, fertility rates increase and remain high for almost two decades after World War II (Chapter 7).
1946	School lunches	The National School Lunch Program Act provides free or subsidized lunches to low-income children (Chapter 20).
1947	Taft-Hartley Act	This Act weakens labor unions by allowing "open-shop" agreements whereby employers can hire nonunion workers (Chapter 12).
1947	United States vs. Alcoa	Alcoa Aluminum is found guilty of violating antitrust law; the Supreme Court largely abandons the "rule of reason" and determines guilt based on the "per se" rule in which monopoly power alone is enough to constitute guilt (Chapter 17).

1947	Truman Doctrine	President Harry Truman makes an open-ended pledge that the U.S. will help any country threatened by communism. This marks the start of the Cold War, which lasts until 1991 (Chapter 16).
1947–1951	Marshall Plan	A U.S. initiative provides approximately $140 billion (in 2016 dollars) to help Europe rebuild after World War II (Chapter 16).
1950s	Television	Ownership of televisions increases from 9 percent in 1950 to 87 percent in 1960 (Chapter 8).
1950–1953	Korean War	The first limited war of the Cold War era, as the U.S.S.R. and the U.S. are involved in a Korean civil war. Almost 34,000 Americans are killed (Chapter 16).
1953–mid-1970s	Middle class America	Rapid growth and low levels of inequality lead to a large improvement in living standards for both rich and poor (Chapter 13).
1954	Brown vs. Board of Education	This judgement outlaws segregation in American schools and strikes down Plessy vs. Fergusson (Chapters 11 and 14).
1956	Interstate highways	The National Interstate and Defense Highways Act authorizes $25 billion for the construction of 40,000 miles of multi-lane, toll-free highways (Chapter 8).
1962	Aid to Families with Dependent Children	Aid to Dependent Children is changed to Aid to Families with Dependent Children, providing benefits for poor families with two parents but an unemployed father (Chapter 20).
1964	Civil Rights Act	This Act prohibits discrimination in public accommodations and gives the U.S. Attorney General authority to enforce the law (Chapter 14).
1964–1975	Vietnam War	The second limited war of the Cold War era, as the U.S.S.R. and the U.S. take different sides in the Vietnamese civil war. 58,000 Americans are killed (Chapter 16).
1964	Food Stamps	Food stamps are replaced by the Supplemental Nutritional Assistance Program (SNAP) in 1998. By 2015, 1 in 7 Americans are receiving support under this program (Chapter 20).
1965	Voting Rights Act	This Act prevents U.S. states, and local governments, from passing any laws that discriminate against racial and language minorities in voting (Chapter 14).
1965	Head Start	The beginning of a program to provide early childhood education and other programs to promote school readiness for low-income children. Later, in the 1990s, Head Start will be expanded (Chapter 20).
1965	Elementary and Secondary Education Act	This Act provides aid to schools, with the amount of aid based on the number of poor children (Chapter 11).

Year(s)	Event	Brief Description and Chapter References
1965	Immigration and Nationality Act	This Act eliminates nationality quotas in immigration, leading to an increase in immigration (Chapter 15).
1965	Medicare and Medicaid	Medicare is introduced to provide health insurance for the elderly, and Medicaid to provide health insurance for the poor (Chapter 20).
1965–1982	Great Inflation	The U.S. inflation rate rises from less than 2 percent in 1965 to more than 14 percent by early 1980 (Chapter 18).
1969	Internet	Network communication becomes possible using the Transmission Control Protocol and Internet Protocol (TCP/IP), although the Internet does not take off until interlinked hypertext documents (web pages) are invented in 1991 (Chapter 8).
1970	Mortgage-backed security	The first modern mortgage-backed security is traded (Chapter 5).
1970–1980	Environmental legislation	Between 1970 and 1980, many environmental regulations are adopted and several regulatory bodies are created (Chapter 19).
1971	Fiat money	The United States has often had fiat money during wars (such as the Continental during the Revolutionary War, and the Greenback during the Civil War). In 1971, the ties to gold are permanently severed as the U.S. moves to fiat money (Chapter 5).
1972	Title IX	Title IX, an Amendment to the Higher Education Act (1965), provides women with greater opportunities in high school athletics and in college athletics, as well as increased educational opportunities in higher education (Chapter 11).
1972	Supplemental Security Income	Part of the 1972 Social Security Act Amendments to consolidate three existing programs: Old Age Assistance, Aid to the Blind, and Aid to the Permanently and Totally Disabled (Chapter 20).
1970s–present	Great Divergence	Inequality increases markedly, to levels not seen since the early twentieth century (Chapter 13).
1975	Earned Income Tax Credit	This provides tax credits in an effort to increase the incentives for low-skilled workers to stay off welfare (Chapter 20).
1978	Airline Deregulation Act	This Act allows airlines to set prices, leading to new entrants and lower prices for consumers (Chapter 17).
1980	Motor Carrier Act	This Act deregulates the trucking industry (Chapter 17).

1980	Depository Institutions and Monetary Control Act	This Act imposes the gradual elimination of interest-rate ceilings on loans and permits banks to pay interest on some new types of depository accounts (Chapter 17).
1981	Air traffic controllers fired	President Reagan fires 11,000 federal air traffic controllers, two days after their union has declared a strike (Chapter 12).
1982	AT&T	American Telephone & Telegraph is forced to break up into regional companies (Chapter 17).
1982	IBM	A massive antitrust case against IBM, which began in 1969, is dropped since IBM's monopoly no longer exists (Chapter 17).
1986	Savings and Loan crisis	A savings and loan crisis begins, portending that deregulation does not always lead to better outcomes (Chapter 17).
1996	Temporary Assistance for Needy Families	This provision, which replaces the Aid to Families with Dependent Children (AFDC), imposes time limits, work requirements, and fixed federal block grants to states. Caseloads fall dramatically (Chapter 20).
1998	Copyright Term Extension Act	This Act increases the copyright length, from 50 years after the death of the creator to 70 years after the death of the creator. Critics term the Act the "Mickey Mouse Protection Act" (Chapter 4).
1999	Financial Services Modernization Act	This Act repeals part of the Banking Act or Glass-Steagall Act (1933), allowing mergers between commercial banks and insurance companies or securities firms (Chapter 18).
2001	Microsoft	Microsoft is found guilty of violating the Sherman Antitrust Act (because of "bundling") and is ordered to be broken up into two companies. Lesser penalties are agreed upon later (Chapter 17).
2003	Medicare Prescription Drug Improvement and Modernization Act	This Act provides prescription drug benefits for Medicare recipients (Chapter 16).
2005	Kelo et al. vs. City of New London	Expands the use of eminent domain, allowing several (non-blighted) private homes to be taken and ownership transferred to another private party, for redevelopment in the hopes of higher tax revenues for the City of New London, Connecticut (Chapter 4).
2007–2009	Great Recession	The recession begins in December 2007 and ends in June 2009, although recovery is very slow. The first major financial crisis in the U.S. since the Great Depression, it is triggered by the failure of Lehman Brothers on September 15, 2008 (Chapter 18).

Year(s)	Event	Brief Description and Chapter References
2010	Affordable Care Act	This Act expands private and public health insurance. The law requires insurance companies to cover all applicants for the same costs, regardless of pre-existing conditions (Chapters 16 and 19).
2012	U.S. student performance	U.S. 15-year-old students are ranked 24th worldwide in reading, 29th in science, and 36th in math on the OECD International Student Assessment Tests (Chapter 11).
2015	Atmospheric Carbon	Atmospheric concentrations of CO_2 surpass 400 ppm in 2014, the highest concentration in the Earth's atmosphere in at least the last 800,000 years – that is, since well before the appearance of modern *Homo sapiens* (Chapter 19). 2015 proves to be the warmest year in recorded history.

Index

References to figures, tables, boxes, and photographs are in **bold** type.